D0081245

THE PROSODY
OF GREEK SPEECH

THE PROSODY
OF GREEK SPEECH

A.M. Devine
Laurence D. Stephens

New York   Oxford
OXFORD UNIVERSITY PRESS
1994

Oxford University Press

Oxford   New York
Athens   Auckland   Bangkok   Bombay
Calcutta   Cape Town   Dar es Salaam   Delhi
Florence   Hong Kong   Istanbul   Karachi
Kuala Lumpur   Madras   Madrid   Melbourne
Mexico City   Nairobi   Paris   Singapore
Taipei   Tokyo   Toronto

and associated companies in
Berlin   Ibadan

Copyright © 1994 by A. M. Devine and Laurence D. Stephens

Published by Oxford University Press, Inc.,
200 Madison Avenue, New York, New York 10016

Oxford is a registered trademark of Oxford University Press

Library of Congress Cataloging-in-Publication Data
Devine, A. M. (Andrew M.)
The prosody of Greek speech / A. M. Devine and Laurence D. Stephens.
p.   cm.
Includes bibliographical references and index.
ISBN 0-19-508546-9
1. Greek language—Metrics and rhythmics.   2. Greek language—Spoken Greek.
3. Oral communication—Greece.   I. Stephens, Laurence D.   II. Title.
PA411.D446   1994
481'.6—dc20   94-4104

1 3 5 7 9 8 6 4 2

Printed in the United States of America
on acid-free paper

| Preface

The aim of this book is to answer the question WHAT DID GREEK PROSODY SOUND LIKE? The study of prosody stands at the intersection of a number of quite disparate disciplines, as illustrated in the diagram overleaf. From the point of view of speech production, as opposed to perception, neurology relates to the various neural mechanisms and capacities used by the speaker to encode his thoughts as a programme of neural impulses for the production of prosody. The anatomy and physiology of the vocal tract relate to how the speaker executes the intricately coordinated sequences of muscle movements that generate prosodic output. Acoustics provides physical measures of the resulting disturbances in the air surrounding the speaker. Experimental psychology relates to the behavioural study of how prosody is organized and processed in the brain and to the processing structures and devices that are theoretically postulated to account for the observed behaviour. One of the functions of prosody is to encode meaning and syntactic structure; prosody is also one of the linguistic devices commonly used to convey attitudinal and informational aspects of discourse; hence the central relevance of semantics, syntax and pragmatics to the study of prosody. Poetics is an important source of evidence for prosody in living languages as well as dead languages, since most verse involves the constrained patterning of prosodic categories and domains. Finally, musicology is a source of evidence both for the general psychological organization of rhythm and melody and for the correlation of speech prosody with musical rhythm and melody in song.

The study of Greek prosody in particular further involves a range of philological activities, which are also represented in the diagram. Data must be collected from epigraphical documents, from verse and prose texts, from the remains of Greek music and from the reports of ancient grammarians and scholiasts. Where appropriate these data must be quantified, so that we can avoid making impressionistic inferences, and subjected to appropriate statistical evaluation, so that random and chance

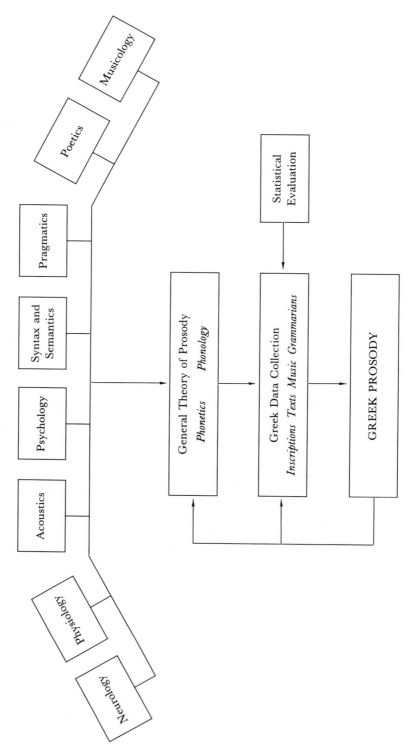

effects can be discriminated from significant and theoretically meaningful observations. The diagram has a feedback loop between reconstruction of Greek, data collection and general prosodic theory, because existing theory is used to interpret new data and new data are used to test and refine existing theory, which in turn may indicate the need to collect further data.

The reconstruction of the prosody of a dead language, particularly those aspects for which the orthography provides no evidence, is prima facie an almost impossible undertaking. In the words of one of the most popular handbooks on Greek metre,

> Even an approximately correct pronunciation of [Greek] is impossible, particularly in respect of the musical accent... the same applies to rhythm. (Maas 1962)

In light of this rather gloomy prognostication, we decided to try a rather different methodology—a sort of archaeological laboratory phonology—which is specifically articulated into the two components represented in the diagram. The premise of the method is that, although different languages have different prosodic systems, prosodic structure does not by and large vary crosslinguistically in a random, unlimited and unpredictable fashion.

We started by assembling the general background information that is potentially relevant to the task of reconstructing the (surface) prosody of Greek. This seemed to be a useful thing to do any way at this particular juncture in Classical studies, when there is increasing recognition of the importance of a general theoretical perspective, even if formalized abstract theory construction is arguably inappropriate in an areally focused subject like Classics. Just like philological data, experimental and typological data have to be collected, documented and interpreted. We hoped that a concise yet fairly comprehensive account of this material with its associated bibliography might serve as a convenient sourcebook for future students and researchers. It is important for the reader to be aware that as nonspecialists we do not have the deep knowledge and understanding that would enable us to evaluate the experimental design and data manipulation used in the individual studies we cite, and that the value of the results we report depends on the general appropriateness and methodological adequacy of the study in question. Furthermore, some experimental results are very robust and widely replicated in later studies, others are more tenuous and speculative; the investigators may not have tested all the implications of their interpretations or they may not have factored out confounding effects. Also, since we are not experts in these rather technical fields, the information we provide may not be as accurately reported, as knowledgeably filtered or as perceptively presented as it would be by a specialist. Similar qualifications apply to the linguistic typology: language descriptions vary widely according to the time spent by any particular investigator on a language, his or her general experience and sophistication, and the availability of other analyses of the same or related dialects. These qualifications are actually no greater than those that routinely apply to the philological side of prosodic investigations, where as nonspecialists we are dependent on the accuracy, judgement and experience of epigraphers, palaeographers, papyrologists and textual critics for the validity of our data.

In the second stage, we proceeded to devise ways of testing the Greek texts, inscriptions and musical remains for specific prosodic properties in the general context of the background material we had assembled, taking care to ensure the statistical significance of the results obtained. The account of Greek prosody that emerged from this in vitro source of evidence was in some respects almost as complete as available accounts of the prosody of many languages that can be investigated in vivo in the laboratory. "Study carefully the phonetic system of a language... and you can tell what kind of verse it has developed" wrote Edward Sapir, one of the founders of American linguistics, in 1921. The converse is equally true.

The method just outlined gives equal weight to general theoretical contextualization and to philological data collection, rather than de-emphasizing one relative to the other. This sort of balance might seem in principle uncontroversial, but since it departs from familiar mono-disciplinary approaches, it probably needs some explicit justification. There may be considerable disagreement — in fact, there is (Ohala 1992; Clements 1992) — as to what sort of theory is appropriate, but some sort of theory is essential, even if it is only the very minimalist, descriptive and empirically anchored theory adopted in this book: philological data are not intrinsically selfexplanatory nor do they selfevidently organize themselves into theoretically significant categories. A purely philological account of Greek prosody without any theoretical context would have been a largely meaningless and uninterpretable catalogue of text distributional classes bearing no overt relationship to the physical and cognitive realities of language and speech. Conversely a theoretical account of Greek prosody not based on a sufficient range of philological data would have been largely vacuous and gratuitous. Theory is built upon data, and if the data are deficient, there can hardly be any worthwhile theory. Theory in its turn leads to understanding, and if there is no theory, there will hardly be any understanding.

Our reconstruction of the prosody of Greek speech proceeds according to the following hierarchy of domains: syllable, word, appositive group, minor phrase, major phrase and utterance. Chapter 1 presents a brief general introduction to the physiology of prosody, covering the functions of the brain, the lungs, the larynx and the upper vocal tract in the production of tone and rhythm. Chapter 2 starts with a discussion of Greek syllable structure and syllable division, suggesting a solution to the prima facie conflict between the system of syllable division indicated by the metre and by the rules of Greek phonology and the system prescribed by the grammarians, presupposed by the conventions of the syllabic scripts and actually used in alphabetic inscriptions. It then turns to the question of the duration of syllable constituents and presents a series of tests designed to discover to what degree the rhythm of Greek speech, as revealed by Greek metre, is sensitive to a complex of experimentally and typologically established durational differences. The results of this empirical analysis serve to correct the generally intuitive conclusions of earlier approaches to the topic. After a discussion of the psychology and phonology of rhythm, Chapter 3 presents a corpus of philological evidence for rhythm in Greek and uses it to develop a theory of the rhythm of Greek speech in the domain of the word. Chapter 4 begins with a theoretical discussion of the production and perception of tone and how vocal music can be used as evidence for the melody of speech in tone and pitch accent languages. By combining typological evidence from a variety of languages with an analysis of the remains of Greek music, it was possible to reconstruct the phonetics of the Greek word accent in greater detail than has been done heretofore. Chapter 5 is devoted to the controversial topic of "stress" in Greek, which is analyzed in the framework of a crosslinguistic survey of the role of tone and stress in different word prosodic systems. The chapter concludes with a discussion of the restructuring of the Greek word prosodic system associated with the development of the Classical Greek pitch accent into the Modern Greek stress accent. In Chapter 6 we leave the domain of the word and turn to connected speech. After some preliminary remarks on variation in rate and style of speech, this chapter covers topics such as resyllabification, elision, crasis and the degree to which word rhythm can be modified in its phrasal context. Chapter 7, which begins that part of the book in which the interface between syntax and phonology becomes a central consideration, is devoted to an analysis of the constituents of the appositive group and its prosodic properties, and includes a review of the literature relating to the separate processing of function words. Musical evidence is exploited to support a re-evaluation of the traditional concept of clisis. The appositive group is the prosodic domain that occasions many of the exceptions to metrical bridges which played so important a role in nineteenth-century philology. Chapter 8 contains a reconstruction of the Greek minor phonological phrase and its prosodic properties, based on a combination of metrical, inscriptional and musical evidence. Chapter 9 confronts the problem of the phrasing of larger prosodic domains — major phrase, parentheticals, sentence, paragraph. The discussion then turns to phrasal downtrends in pitch, and a theory of the intonation of Greek speech is elaborated on the basis of evidence from the Delphic hymns. The tenth and last chapter is devoted to topic and focus and the interaction of their phonetic and syntactic actuations in Greek.

Like many subjects, prosody comes with its own array of technical terminology, which, while it tends to strike the uninitiated as just so much jargon, actually serves the theoretically useful purpose of organizing phenomena into denotationally discrete entities, properties and processes, and consequently also the practical purpose of adding precision and reducing circumlocution. Some of these terms are clarified as the discussion in the text proceeds, and they are listed in the index with the appropriate page references. Others can readily be tracked down in the dictionaries of Crystal (1991) and Trask (1993). Metrical terms are explained in West (1982) and musical terms in West (1992). For a general introduction to the subject, the reader is referred to the relevant sections of Sidney Allen's *Vox Graeca* (third edition: 1987) and *Accent and Rhythm* (1973), which have been cornerstones in the study of Greek prosody for a generation.

The task of assembling and evaluating the diverse items of evidence needed for our reconstruction of Greek prosody turned into an enjoyable and rewarding period of detective work, during the course of which we were lucky enough to receive generous help and advice from many colleagues and friends; they are not responsible for errors (which are especially difficult to avoid in a work that inevitably dispersed the authors' time and effort over a number of traditionally demarcated disciplines). We should like to mention in particular Mark Baker, David Blank, Joan Bresnan, Clara Bush, Eve Clark, Edward Courtney, Amy Dahlstrom, Kenneth Dover, Mark Edwards, Charles Ferguson, John Freccero, Chris Golston, Joseph Greenberg, Thomas Hare, Bruce Hayes, Thomas Hixon, P. Hohepa, R.A. Hudson, †Dorothy Huntington, Michael Jameson, A.W. Johnston, Ken de Jong, Paul Kiparsky, Wilbur Knorr, William Leben, Marsh McCall, John McCarthy, Armin Mester, Yasuko Nagano-Madsen, Donca Steriade, Helmer Strik, Thomas Wasow, Michael Wigodsky. Sonia Moss and John Rawlings of Stanford Library cheerfully handled an endless series of requests. A special word of thanks to Sheila Embleton, Bruce Hedin, Henry Hoenigswald, John Ohala and William Poser.

Stanford   A.M.D.
Chapel Hill   L.D.S.

ACKNOWLEDGEMENTS

We are most grateful for permission to reproduce figures from the following works:

F. Grosjean. A study of timing in a manual and spoken language: American Sign Language and English. *Journal of Psycholinguistic Research* 8:379. © 1979 Plenum Publishing Corporation. (Figure 1.1)

W. Sidney Allen. *Vox Graeca.* Third edition. © 1987 Cambridge University Press. (Figure 1.3)

K.R. Scherer. Methods of research on vocal communication. *Handbook of Methods in Nonverbal Behavior Research,* ed. K.R. Scherer and P. Ekman: 136. © 1982 Maison des Sciences de l'Homme and Cambridge University Press. (Figure 1.4)

W.V. Summers. Effects of stress and final-consonant voicing on vowel production. *Journal of the Acoustical Society of America* 82:847. © 1987 Acoustical Society of America. (Figure 2.1)

Y. Nagano-Madsen. Phonetic reality of the mora in Eskimo. *Working Papers in General Linguistics and Phonetics, Lund University* 34 (1988): 79. (Figure 2.2)

E. Pöhlmann. *Denkmäler altgriechischer Musik.* © 1970 Verlag Hans Carl. (Musical Examples)

M. Liberman. *The Intonational System of English.* © 1979 Mark Liberman. Garland Publishing. (Figure 4.2)

A.M. Jones. *Studies in African Music I.* © 1959 A.M. Jones. Oxford University Press. (Figure 4.3)

Y. Nagano-Madsen. Effects of tempo and tonal context on fundamental frequency contours in Japanese. *Working Papers in General Linguistics and Phonetics, Lund University* 31 (1987): 103. (Figure 6.1)

E. Gårding and J. Zhang. Tempo and prosodic pattern in Chinese and Swedish. *Working Papers in General Linguistics and Phonetics, Lund University* 34 (1987): 116. (Figure 6.2)

S.R. Anderson. Kwakwala syntax and government-binding theory. *Syntax and Semantics* 16:21. © 1984 Academic Press. (Figure 7.1)

N. Willems. *English Intonation from a Dutch Point of View.* © 1982 Foris Publications. Kluwer Academic Publishers. (Figure 9.1)

M.E. Beckman and J.B. Pierrehumbert. Intonational structure in Japanese and English. *Phonology Yearbook* 3:255. © 1986 Cambridge University Press.

A. Iivonen. On explaining the initial fundamental frequency in Finnish utterances. *Nordic Prosody III,* ed. C.-C. Elert, I. Johansson and E. Strangert: 107. © 1984 Antti Iivonen. (Figure 9.3)

F. Grosjean and M. Collins. Breathing, pausing and reading. *Phonetica* 36:98. © 1979 S. Karger AG, Basel. (Figure 9.4)

N. Grønnum. Schema for downtrend in Danish terminal declarations. (Figure 9.5)

I. Lehiste and P. Ivić. *Word and Sentence Prosody in Serbocroatian.* © 1986 Massachusetts Institute of Technology. (Figure 9.6)

W.J. Poser. *The Phonetics and Phonology of Tone and Intonation in Japanese.* © 1985 William J. Poser. (Figure 9.7)

S. Inkelas and W.R. Leben. Where phonology and phonetics intersect. *Papers in Laboratory Phonology I,* ed. J. Kingston and M.E. Beckman: 17. © 1990 Cambridge University Press. (Figures 9.8, 9.11 and 10.2)

J. Pierrehumbert and M.E. Beckman. *Japanese Tone Structure.* © 1988 Massachusetts Institute of Technology. (Figure 9.12)

D. O'Shaughnessy. Linguistic features in fundamental frequency patterns. *Journal of Phonetics* 7:119. © 1979 Academic Press. (Figure 10.1)

C.E. Williams and K.N. Stevens. Emotions and speech: Some acoustical correlations. *Journal of the Acoustical Society of America* 51:1238. © 1972 Acoustical Society of America. (Figure 10.3)

A. Fernald, T. Taescher, J. Dunn, M. Papousek, B. de Boysson-Bardies and I. Fukui. A crosslanguage study of prosodic modifications in mother's and father's speech to preverbal infants. *Journal of Child Language* 16:477. © 1989 Cambridge University Press. (Figure 10.4)

We are also most grateful to the American Philological Association, *Classical Philology* (University of Chicago Press) and *Greek, Roman, and Byzantine Studies* for permission to reproduce materials of our own that originally appeared under their imprint (see p. 561).

| Contents

ABBREVIATIONS

ABV	Beazley 1956	*IGA*	Roehl 1882
Arg.	*SEG* 11.314	*I.T.*	*Iphigenia Taurica*
ARV	Beazley 1963	*JHS*	*Journal of Hellenic*
Ath.	*DAM* 19		*Studies*
Call.	I³.1.45	KA	Kassel-Austin
CEG	Hansen 1983	*Lim.*	*DAM* 20
CIG	*Corpus Inscriptionum*	*LSAG*	Jeffery 1990
	Graecarum	*MDAII*	*Mitteilungen des Deut-*
DAA	Raubitschek et al.		*schen Archäologischen*
	1949		*Instituts, Istanbul*
DAM	Pöhlmann 1970	ME	Musical Example
DGE	Schwyzer 1923	*Milet.*	*LSAG* 64.33
EG	Guarducci 1967	*Naup.*	IX².1.718
Eleus.	I³.1.5	*O.C.*	*Oedipus Coloneus*
Eph. Aug.	*IGA* 499	*Oeanth.*	*LSAG* 15.4
Eph. Art.	*LSAG* 66.53	*O.T.*	*Oedipus Tyrannus*
Eph. Frag.	Sokolowski	*Psamm.*	Masson et al. 1988
	1955:n.30B	*P.V.*	*Prometheus Vinctus*
Eur.	Euripides	*REG*	*Revue des Etudes*
GD	Buck 1955		*Grecques*
GDK	Heitsch 1961	*SEG*	*Supplementum Epi-*
Hal.	Jameson 1974		*graphicum Graecum*
Her.	*LSAG* 42.6	Soph.	Sophocles
H.F.	*Hercules Furens*	*T.D.*	*IGA* 497, *SEG*
I.A.	*Iphigenia Aulidensis*		31.984–85
ICS	Masson 1983	UR	Usener-Radermacher
Id.	*ICS* 217	WI	Winnington-Ingram

THE PROSODY
OF GREEK SPEECH

1 | The Physiology of Prosody

Overview

In addition to deciding the semantic content of a message, establishing its syntactic structure and specifying its lexical content, the brain must devise a programme for its pronunciation. On the basis of that programme, a set of instructions issues from the brain in the shape of nerve impulses which produce contractions of muscles in the area of the chest, the throat and the mouth. As a result of these muscular contractions, the air in the vocal tract is disturbed and sound waves are generated, variably filtered according to the shape of the vocal tract, just as in many musical instruments. If these sound waves reach the ear of a listener, they cause his eardrum to vibrate, much like a loudspeaker; the motions of the eardrum are transferred via the inner ear to the cochlea and there transduced to nerve impulses in the auditory nerve; when the latter reach the brain, the auditory signal is decoded and the semantic content of the message apprehended. At the same time, the speaker will be monitoring his utterance by auditory, tactile and kinesthetic feedback. Language is a code, or more precisely an encoding and decoding system, for transferring ideas from one human brain to another, and speech is the mechanism for the acoustic implementation of the code. The message of the speaker is successively represented in three different sub-codes — as neural impulses, as coordinated muscular movements (myomotor phase) and as soundwaves, i.e. vibrations of air molecules adjacent to the speaker (acoustic phase).

The prosodic, or suprasegmental, features of sound, namely duration, frequency and intensity, are all manifestations in the medium of sound of general physical dimensions applicable to many of the events of the world in which we live. Duration is simply a measure of the time taken up by an event. Frequency expresses the rate of repetition of a regularly recurring event. The concept of intensity relates to the amount of force, power or energy of an event, for instance the force of an explosion or the brightness of a light.

The prosodic features of sound can be investigated from all of the various perspectives of phonetic science and linguistic theory. The sound wave can be recorded and analyzed: this is the acoustic record. The perception of the sound wave by the listener can be studied: this is the auditory aspect of sound. Finally, the various physiological activities that produce the sound wave can be investigated by a whole variety of techniques (Baken 1987), ranging from the analysis of the electrical activity associated with muscle contraction by means of electrodes to the measurement of air pressure at various points along the vocal tract to the making of high speed X-ray motion pictures of articulators. Once phonetic measurements have been made, the investigator is faced with the problem of the linguistic interpretation of those measurements, and, specifically, with their significance for the definition and substantiation of theoretical concepts such as the syllable, the foot, the word accent, the phonological phrase, the sentence accent, the intonation contour.

NEUROLOGY

The idea that linguistic ability is not a widely diffused cerebral function but, except for some lefthanded people, predominantly localized in the left hemisphere of the brain has been traced back to the observations of Marc Dax, a French military surgeon during and after the Napoleonic wars (Joanette et al. 1990). This insight became widely recognized with the work of Paul Broca (Joynt 1964), who found that speech production was seriously impaired by damage to the posterior inferior part of the left frontal lobe, and of Carl Wernicke, who discovered that comprehension of spoken and written language is affected by damage in the posterior superior area of the left temporal lobe. Broca's area is situated close to the area of the brain that controls the muscles of the face, and Wernicke's area close to the primary auditory area of the brain. Practically all righthanded aphasics, and about 60% of lefthanded aphasics, have left hemisphere lesions. A study using intracarotid injection of the anaesthetic amobarbital found that, under the conditions of the test, language was represented in the left hemisphere for 77% of the subjects, in the right hemisphere for 2%, and bilaterally, mostly with left dominance, for 21% (Loring et al. 1990). Evoked potentials recorded directly from the left cortical surface were stronger than from the right (Mateer et al. 1989). Both agrammatic and paragrammatic signing has been found in left lesioned patients who use American Sign Language to communicate, which indicates left hemisphere specialization for visuospatially implemented language as well as acoustically implemented language, even though visuospatial relations are otherwise associated more with the right hemisphere (Poizner et al. 1989). A left hemisphere advantage for speech syllables as opposed to a right hemisphere advantage for musical notes has been found already in three and four month old children (Best et al. 1982). However, prosody is one of the areas in which the situation seems to be more complex. Evidence from aphasia and from dichotic listening, an experimental technique whereby different auditory stimuli are presented simultaneously one to each ear, suggests a significant role for the right hemisphere in the processing of certain linguistic and paralinguistic features of speech — including personal voice recognition (Van Lancker et al. 1986), formulaic language such as serial counting, expletives and social interaction formulae (Van Lancker et al. 1986b), and some aspects of prosody, particularly those relating to emotional expression (Ross 1981; Weniger 1978; Kent 1984; Heilman et al. 1984; Tompkins et al. 1985; Bowers et al. 1987; Shipley-Brown et al. 1988).

A number of studies have sought to draw distinctions of lateralization among the various general faculties related to prosody. A left hemisphere superiority has been claimed for processing durations of less than 50 msec (Mills et al. 1979) and for the perception of rhythm (Robinson et al. 1974; Benowitz et al. 1984) and temporal serial order (Carmon et al. 1971; Brookshire 1972). In one interesting case, a Bulgarian violinist became unable either to perceive or to produce rhythm and differential duration following a left hemisphere stroke, while tonal perception and production remained intact (Mavlov 1980). However, left and right brain damaged subjects performed comparably on the Seashore Rhythm Test, which requires recognition of similarities and differences in pairs of rhythmic beats (Reitan et al. 1989), and rhythm was relatively well preserved after left or right carotid anaesthesia (which causes unilateral depression of hemispheric functions for three to five minutes) (Gordon et al. 1974). The right hemisphere is apparently more important for pitch, particularly among musically untrained subjects (Blumstein et al. 1974; Sidtis et al. 1988). Surgical removal of the left (dominant) hemisphere markedly impaired speech but not singing, whereas after right carotid anaesthesia singing was monotone or off key (Gordon et al. 1974). In a task requiring recognition of rising and falling (nonlinguistic) pitch contours, male subjects performed more accurately than females with binaural, but not with dichotic presentation, suggesting a sex difference in the coordination of the hemispheres (McRoberts et al. 1992). Affective (and, to some extent, linguistic) fundamental frequency was impaired in a patient whose corpus callosum (the major connection between the hemispheres) suffered damage consequent on a haemorrhage, whereas duration was relatively intact, suggesting a right hemisphere role for pitch mediated by the corpus callosum (Klouda et al. 1988). When patients were asked to read sentences expressing particular affective states such as sadness or anger or happiness, the versions of patients with right hemisphere lesions were prosodically flatter than those of patients with left hemisphere lesions; right hemisphere patients also have difficulty with the perception of affect (Tucker et al. 1977). However, the more linguistic or grammatical the function of a prosodic property, the greater the left hemisphere dominance (Van Lancker 1980; Gandour et al. 1983). The lexical tone of tone languages is associated more with the left hemisphere; however, left hemispheric dominance is not evidenced when the tones are presented to subjects without their linguistic context as hums (Van Lancker et al. 1973), which indicates that it is the linguistic function of tone rather than its acoustic properties that influences lateralization (Ross et al. 1986). In a study of lexical tone and affective intonation in Mandarin speakers suffering from right hemisphere strokes, it was found that affective prosody was impaired but the tones were not disrupted (Hughes et al. 1983). However, left hemisphere damaged speakers in the acute stage of recovery experienced a tonal production deficit (Packard 1986). Left hemisphere advantage has been found for pitch differentiated stress in Norwegian (Ryalls et al. 1986) and for stress in English (Behrens 1985; Emmorey 1987), but when English test materials were lowpass filtered at 200 Hz to eliminate segmental information while retaining the stress patterns, the advantage shifted to the right hemisphere (Behrens 1985). Right hemisphere anaesthesia resulted in lost control of musical pitch in singing but not of linguistic tonality or rhythm for speakers of Norwegian (Borchgrevink 1982). Left hemisphere superiority is likewise indicated for pitch and duration as exponents of syntactic structure through intonation and phonological phrasing (Zurif et al. 1972; Cooper et al. 1984); nevertheless, while the left hemisphere may be more involved in the processing of relatively local and transient prosodic information, the right hemisphere may play a more significant role in the global processing of longterm events (Behrens 1989; Grant et al. in Joanette et al. 1990). Abnormality in the production of intonation by patients with right hemisphere damage is less severe than that of patients with left hemisphere damage, and consists in hypermelodic or monotonic production according as the lesion is posterior or anterior (Shapiro et al. 1985). The famous case of the Norwegian woman who developed what was perceived as a German accent due to defective word accent and intonation while maintaining musical melody unimpaired involved a left hemisphere lesion suffered during an air raid (Monrad-Krohn 1947; Moen 1991). Distinctions of phonological vowel length were well preserved in two Thai Broca aphasics; however, their rhythm was severely impaired (Gandour et al. 1984); and a study of three Finnish Broca aphasics revealed that the phonological distinction between short and long vowels and consonants was relatively well preserved, although Broca aphasics tend to have slow and disturbed timing (Niemi et al. 1985). One interpretation of these data is that Broca aphasics have a narrower than normal temporal unit of speech planning.

Two subcortical structures have been found to be particularly associated with the motor control of prosody. Basal ganglia disease (Parkinson's disease) is associated with an impairment of the motor control of fundamental frequency and timing (Darkins et al. 1988). The cerebellum regulates and coordinates muscular activity including that associated with prosody. Lesions to the cerebellum result in problems with equilibrium, posture and smooth motor activity. In prosody, cerebellar damage is associated with unnatural fluctuations in pitch and intensity and abnormalities in the timing of articulatory gestures (Kent et al. 1975; Kent et al. 1979; Kent et al. 1982; Gentil 1990); the syllables of speech tend to be produced as uniform prosodically autonomous units often dissociated by pauses. Tasks such as finger tapping and repetition of CV-syllables were performed much less rhythmically by subjects having cerebellar lesions than by normal subjects (Keller 1990); one study also found impairment in the perception of timing (Keele et al. 1987; Ivry et al. 1989; Keller 1990).

RESPIRATION

The function of the respiratory system in speech is to produce compressed air, the energy of which is used to create the acoustic vibrations that comprise the sounds of speech. The respiratory cycle consists of inhalation and exhalation; a pause commonly occurs between each cycle. Inhalation is effected by activity of the muscles of the chest and abdomen. The rib cage is pushed upward and outward by the external intercostal muscles, and the floor of the thoracic cavity is lowered by contraction of the diaphragm, thereby expanding the chest and consequently the volume of the lungs. This causes lung pressure to fall below atmospheric pressure so that air flows into the lungs. In exhalation the inspiratory muscles are relaxed, the chest recoils downward and inward towards its position of rest, and air is consequently forced out of the lungs. This elastic recoil process may be reinforced by the action of the expiratory muscles, particularly when physical exercise increases the need for oxygen, which is met by more rapid and deeper breathing. In normal vegetative breathing, the respiratory cycle is repeated roughly fifteen times a minute, and the inhalation phase lasts about as long as the exhalation phase.

Breathing in speech differs from normal breathing most obviously in the relative duration of inhalation and exhalation. If their respective durations were about the same, as is the case in normal breathing, speech would be very choppy and incoherent, due to the overly frequent and extended pauses for inhalation. Consequently, in speech inspiration is rapid and the duration of the expiratory phase is spun out according to the length of the utterance. In speech it generally lasts from two to ten seconds, but in singing it can reach twenty seconds or more. It was found that one speaker reading aloud a Hungarian story varied the intervals between inhalations from 1.7 sec to 7.16 sec (Fónagy et al. 1960). The different breathing patterns occurring when the same passage was read aloud and communicated by American Sign Language are illustrated in Figure 1.1. In part, the prolongation of the expiratory phase is the automatic result of the impedance to airflow caused by the obstructions involved in phonation and consonant articulation; in part it is due to additional muscle activity. Particularly after a deep breath, the inspiratory muscles may be used to check the recoil force of the lungs, thereby regulating the air pressure and prolonging deflation. This braking effect is not significant in normal conversational speech. As lung pressure decreases with recoil, the expiratory muscles are progressively exerted to maintain a constant air pressure and so eliminate major differences of loudness in the resulting acoustic signal. Consequently the activity of the expiratory muscles increases towards the end of an utterance. However, at the very end of an utterance, air pressure and therefore loudness decrease as the speaker prepares for the next inhalation.

The amount of air inhaled and exhaled in vegetative breathing is around half a litre. For speech, the average inhalation is half to three

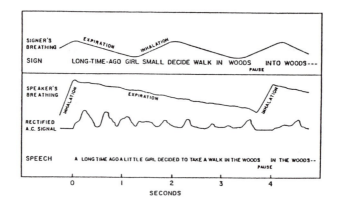

FIGURE 1.1

Breathing patterns in American Sign Language
and reading at normal rate (from Grosjean 1979)

quarters of a litre of air. This means that, in normal speech, speakers use only about a fifth of the total volume of air that they can inhale and fully exhale. For speech in an upright posture, speakers generally start an utterance with about 60% of that total inhaled and end with about 37% remaining, which is the same as the volume remaining in the rest position of the vegetative breathing cycle. Restriction of normal speech to these lung volumes minimizes the muscular effort required to meet the air pressure demands of normal speech in the face of varying recoil forces. Louder speech requires higher air pressure to drive the speech production apparatus. The speaker meets this need in two ways. Prior to the initiation of speech, inspiratory muscle activity is increased resulting in greater lung inflation and higher recoil forces; during the production of speech, expiratory muscle activity is increased, and any inspiratory muscle activity used to check recoil at the beginning of an utterance is decreased. Higher lung volumes were used in the delivery of Shakespearean monologues and in the singing of dramatic opera arias by trained performers (Hixon et al. 1987).

There is potentially independent expiratory muscle activity during an utterance in both the chest and the abdomen (Hixon et al. 1973, 1976). One function of the abdominal muscles may be to prevent some of the rib cage movement being absorbed by downward movement of the diaphragm and outward movement of the abdomen. Another function may be to keep the diaphragm in an optimal configuration for inspiration (Weismer 1985). During the inspiration preceding an utterance, some expiratory activity of the chest muscles often continues, but this is completely overcome by the major inspiratory contraction of the diaphragm.

Chest pulses

The central role played by the syllable in the rhythm of speech and consequently in many types of verse has encouraged a search for physiological correlates of the syllable. According to one view (Stetson 1951), syllable production is correlated with respiratory activity: each syllable is supposed to be accompanied by an individual burst of action on the part of the expiratory muscles (more precisely, the internal intercostal muscles at midrange lung volumes), so that each syllable involves a separate puff of air. These chest pulses are comparatively minor expiratory pressure fluctuations superimposed on the relatively smooth subglottal pressure curve resulting from the overall respiratory strategy adopted for speech production. The validity of the chest pulse theory of the syllable has been the subject of much discussion (Draper et al. 1959; Ladefoged 1962; Ladefoged 1968). The methodology used to support the chest pulse theory has been criticized as inadequate (Ladefoged 1962), as has the methodology of its opponents (Weismer 1985). It appears that syllables can, but do not have to be produced by a chest pulse. A number of variables govern the strategy actually adopted by the speaker for syllable production. On the one hand, early studies found evidence for respiratory adjustment to compensate for subsyllabic units with high airflow requirements such as voiceless fricatives (Ladefoged 1968), which would lead to syllables having more than one chest pulse. Reiterant speech has a greater airflow rate with the syllable *fa* than with *ma*, but since this difference is not reflected in the overall subglottal pressure contour for the utterance (Gelfer 1987), there must be some form of active or passive compensatory adjustment. On the other hand, there is as yet no clear evidence that in a sequence of syllables such as *pa-pa-pa-pa* pronounced at a normal speech rate of four or five syllables per second, each syllable is associated with a separate minor chest pulse, and even the correlation between stressed syllables and chest pulses was not replicated in one study of connected speech (Adams 1979). Some short term variations in subglottal pressure can be explained as a reflex of resistance to the airflow associated with consonant closure (Ohala 1990); these segmental effects result in a sort of ripple on an overall smooth subglottal pressure contour; larger subglottal pressure peaks are associated with focus stress (Gelfer 1987). Major pulsatile movements often involving abdominal wall contraction and correlating with individual syllables were found in a series of discrete emphatic *ha*-syllables, and in emphatically stressed syllables in poetry reading, but not in ordinary syllable production except in the unnatural speech of a speaker with serious hearing impairment (Hixon et al. 1987).

Arrested syllables

Respiration has also been invoked to explain another question of major concern in prosody, namely why in many languages syllables having the structure (C)V̆C (such as the first syllable of πέμ-πω) are classed together with syllables having the structure (C)V̄ (such as the first syllable of πῆ-μα) for the purposes of speech rhythm and quantitative metre. According to the theory of thoracic arrest (Stetson 1951; Allen 1973), in the production of long open syllables [(C)V̄] airflow is not merely arrested by the articulatory constriction of the onset consonant of the following syllable (or by a potential glottal closure for identical vowels in hiatus), nor does it merely trail off until reinforced by a chest pulse associated with the next syllable, but it is positively arrested by a burst of activity on the part of certain of the inspiratory muscles (the external intercostal muscles); this arrest is seen as parallel in function to the articulatory closure that arrests the closed syllable (C)V̆C. This result was not replicated in a study using Stetson's methodology (Hoshiko 1960), and the theory remains in need of further experimental corroboration.

PHONATION

The airflow used in speech passes from the lungs up the trachea and through the larynx into the oral cavity. The larynx is a structure consisting mainly of muscle and cartilage that functions as a valve to prevent food from entering the trachea and to trap air in the lungs when a rigid thorax, and thus inflated lungs, are required for certain types of strenuous physical exertion, such as weight-lifting. In the larynx there are three sets of muscular folds that can be moved closer to each other to constrict the laryngeal airway or brought into firm contact with each other to close it off entirely. The lowest of the three sets, the "true" vocal cords, is the one used for phonation. The vocal cords stretch from the thyroid cartilage at the front of the larynx, a little below the Adam's apple, to the arytenoid cartilages at the back. At the front the two folds merge, at the back they are separate, so that there is a triangular opening between them called the glottis.

Glottal aperture

During quiet respiration, the vocal cords are open and the glottal aperture is somewhat under a half the diameter of the trachea; for deep breathing the vocal cords are spread wider apart to allow more air to pass. For the production of voiceless sounds, the glottis is open, but the degree of aperture depends on the airflow demands of the consonant in question. Voiceless unaspirated stops (π, τ, κ) are pronounced with a narrower glottal opening than voiceless aspirated stops (φ, θ, χ), while for voiceless fricatives such as σ the glottal opening is deliberately made wider than for both types of voiceless stops and wider too than in quiet respiration: greater glottal abduction reduces resistance to the passage of air through the glottis and thereby caters to the relatively high oral airflow demands of fricatives. For the aspiration of the voiceless aspirated stops, not only is the glottis much more open than for unaspirated voiceless stops, it also reaches its maximum aperture later in the production of the stop, that is nearer the time of oral release (Sawashima et al. 1983; Dixit 1989); the adduction of the vocal cords for the onset of voicing in the following vowel is delayed. Experiments on a number of languages having phonologically distinctive aspiration, as does Greek, show that the delay after the release of the stop consonant before the onset of voicing is on the average about 60 milliseconds greater for the aspirated than for the unaspirated stop consonants (Lisker et al. 1964). The duration of aspiration varies according to the nature of both the stop and the following vowel. Aspiration, which is the glottal frication occurring during this delay, is characterised in spectrographic display by noise in the second and third formants, whereas a whispered vowel has a more strongly defined first formant (Delattre 1964). After release of a voiceless aspirated stop, there is a rapid outflow of air and consequently subglottal air pressure drops significantly, so that vowels after voiceless aspirated stops tend to have less intensity than vowels after voiced stops (Ohala 1978). Whispered sounds (Tartter 1989) are produced with a relatively narrow glottal aperture and little or no vocal fold vibration; the difference between quiet whisper and forced whisper depends on glottal configuration and degree of supraglottal constriction (Monoson et al. 1984; Solomon et al. 1989). The glottal stop, as its name implies, can be produced with complete closure of the glottis; in this case the vocal cords may be considered to function as articulators rather than as phonators.

Fundamental frequency

For the production of voiced sounds, such as the vowels and the voiced stops (β, δ, γ), the vocal cords vibrate, that is they cycle between open and closed position, with the result that air is released into the oral cavity in a series of puffs or bursts. This vibration is not, according to the normally accepted opinion (von Leden 1961), effected by separate muscle contractions in each closing cycle. Rather the vocal cords are drawn together in preparation for a voiced sound, whereupon, in the first phase of the cycle, air from the lungs blows them apart, and, in the second phase, they are drawn together again by a combination of elastic recoil and the aerodynamic factor known as the Bernoulli effect.

Vibration of the vocal cords produces a complex periodic sound wave sometimes called laryngeal tone. Laryngeal tone varies along three major parameters. Its amplitude relates to the auditory property of loudness; its fundamental frequency relates to that of pitch; and its spectral slope, which correlates with the proportion of the overall cycle during which the vocal cords are closed and the rapidity of the closing action, relates to voice quality. Greater amplitude of laryngeal tone is largely determined by increased subglottal air pressure, which in turn requires increased compression of the vocal cords to maintain voicing. Fundamental frequency is largely controlled, both in singing and in speech, through deliberate manipulation by the laryngeal muscles of the mass, the length and the tension of the vocal cords. These three factors—mass, length, tension—likewise affect the pitch of string instruments such as the violin. The vocal cords are tensed, like a violin string, to produce higher pitch. The exact mechanisms used in the tensing and relaxation of the vocal

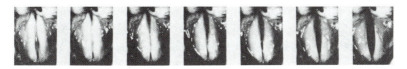

FIGURE 1.2
Stroboscopic views of the vocal cords at different stages
of aperture in the vibratory cycle (from Lecluse in Baken 1987)

cords have been the subject of detailed investigation. Raised pitch correlates particularly with increased activity of the cricothyroid muscle (Rubin
1963; Hirano et al. 1969). Singers' vibrato is associated inter alia with
quasiperiodic bursts and attenuations of cricothyroid activity (Shipp et
al. 1988). The cricothyroid muscle applies longitudinal tension to the
vocal cords by causing a rocking movement of the cricoid cartilage around
its pivotlike attachment to the thyroid cartilage: since the vocal cords
are attached anteriorly to the inside front of the thyroid cartilage and
posteriorly to the arytenoids and the arytenoids to the posterior part of
the cricoid, a backward tilting movement of the posterior part of the
cricoid elongates the vocal cords. The vocal cords can also be stiffened
or tensed by contraction of the vocalis muscles, which likewise contributes to raised frequency. Electromyographically measured cricothyroid
activity correlates very well with the accent in Japanese (Simada et al.
1970; Yoshioka et al. 1981), and in Swedish (Gårding et al. 1970, 1975);
peak cricothyroid activity occurs roughly 70–100 msec before peak
fundamental frequency (Dyhr 1990). Finnish sentence stress is characterized by increased subglottal pressure and laryngeal muscle activity;
in whisper, the role of the cricothyroid muscle is negligible and subglottal pressure is the major factor (Vilkman et al. 1987). Conversely, for
a continuation rise at the end of a major phrase in Dutch, raised pitch
results from laryngeal muscle activity since subglottal pressure falls in
this context (Collier 1987); similarly for a final interrogative rise in
English, the activity of the cricothyroid and vocalis muscles increased
markedly, while intensity decreased presumably due to falling subglottal
pressure (Hirano et al. 1969). The height of the larynx can also vary
with pitch (Ewan et al. 1974). In the production of the Japanese accent,
which is a pure pitch accent and mutatis mutandis an instructive typological model for the Greek accent, an upward displacement of the larynx
was found to accompany a rise in pitch and a downward displacement
a fall in pitch (Kakita et al. 1976). Systematic activity of the sternohyoid
muscle was not correlated with accentual pitch fall in Swedish (Gårding
et al. 1975), but did appear in a study of Japanese (Sawashima et al.
1973) and has been found in certain Low toned morae for some speak-

ers of Osaka Japanese (Sugito et al. 1978; Kori 1987; Pierrehumbert et al. 1988).

Although, as just noted, it is generally assumed that fundamental frequency is mainly controlled by the action of the laryngeal muscles, it is frequently the case that when subglottal pressure is increased fundamental frequency also rises. Subglottal pressure is assumed to influence frequency partly through aerodynamic effects and partly through the relationship between the amplitude of vibration and the stiffness of the vocal cords. In view of this frequency-amplitude correlation, it was proposed that in a stress accent language the pitch rise occasioned by the stress was not caused by the laryngeal muscles but by increased subglottal pressure, that is mainly by a chest pulse associated with the stress (Lieberman 1967). Such a view would have a number of potential implications for Greek prosody. If Greek is assumed to have a nonaccentual stress (Allen 1973), then speakers would have to make laryngeal adjustments to counteract this effect on syllables that were stressed but unaccented. Secondly, if pulmonary activity was largely responsible for the accentual pitch peak, then increased amplitude would also have characterized the pitch accent, a feature that would complicate a phonetic definition of the nonaccentual stress. However, the pulmonary theory of accentual pitch control is not widely held. Air pressure in speech is measured in terms of the height of a column of water in a U-shaped tube; a minimum subglottal pressure of 2–3 cmH_2O is necessary for phonation, and conversational speech is produced in the range of 5–10 cmH_2O, although shouting or loud singing can involve much higher pressures, even up to 60 cmH_2O for very loud sung notes. The ratio of fundamental frequency to subglottal pressure has been estimated on the basis of two types of experiments. In one type, air is blown through a freshly excised larynx, a technique that is 250 years old (Ferrein 1741; van den Berg 1968). In the other, a subject, instructed to phonate at a constant pitch and intensity, is pushed in the stomach at random intervals. This has the effect of a sudden and rapid increase in subglottal pressure accompanied by a correlated increase in fundamental frequency. During normal speech, subglottal pressure changes at rates in the range of 3–8 cmH_2O per second: the push in the stomach can produce an average rate of change of 25 cmH_2O/s. A reflex adjustment of the laryngeal muscles to the push occurs at least 30–40 msec after the push; prior to this, during the first 30 msec after the push, fundamental frequency changes at the rate of about 3–4 Hz/cmH_2O in the chest voice (Baer 1979; Strik et al. 1989). Consequently, only a small proportion of the rise in pitch associated with stress in English can be accounted for by increased subglottal pressure (Ohala 1978; Gelfer 1987). Furthermore, increased subglottal pressure can arise not only from a chest pulse but also indirectly from changes in glottal resistance owing to increased vocal fold tension (Isshiki 1964; Hirano et al. 1969; Aaltonen et al. 1988); therefore, some portion of the observed correlations between subglottal pressure and fundamental frequency may be due to the effects of the latter on the former rather than vice versa (Ohala 1978). Musical instruments in general are relatively free from the frequency-amplitude dependence just described for the vocal cords: they have a much smaller ratio of vibrational amplitude to length of the string — 0.001 for a piano string versus 0.1 for the vocal cords (Titze 1989). The Greek pitch accent apparently does not significantly affect word rhythm, although its location is governed by temporal factors; therefore, it is important to know that the physiological mechanisms involved in its production are largely separate from any that could potentially be involved with speech rhythm.

Pitch range

The average speaker has a pitch range of over 2 octaves and tends to phonate within an octave in the lower part of this range. (A famous phrase for the bass voice in Verdi's *Don Carlo* spans two octaves.) Average pitch for men is about 125 Hz, for women about 225 Hz, and for children a little higher still, because men generally have longer and larger vocal cords than women and children. In shouting, average fundamental frequency increases two to three octaves (Rostolland 1982). Average pitch can also vary according to age and physical condition. In male speakers pitch declines from age 20 to 40 but increases from age 60 to 80, probably due to differences in vocal cord thickness and elasticity at different times of life. Pitch differences arising from sex and age variables among speakers are discounted by the listener for the purpose of extracting the linguistic information contained in a pitch contour. Movements from one register to another, falsetto versus chest voice for instance, are achieved by resetting the overall posture of the laryngeal muscles. In the falsetto register, the vocal cords are highly tensed and elongated; the activity of the vocalis muscle is decreased relative to the chest register, thereby reducing the effective mass of the vocal cords and confining vibration chiefly to the thin glottal edge of the cord (Hirano et al. 1970; Sawashima et al. 1983).

ARTICULATION

Whereas respiration and phonation are in one sense or another directly related to suprasegmental parameters, articulation is definitionally segmental in nature. However, some knowledge of articulation is essential for an understanding of many aspects of prosody, such as intrinsic and contextual duration and fundamental frequency, rules of syllabification, and so on; and, conversely, prosody can have a profound effect on the extent, velocity and timing of articulatory gestures.

Vowels

The preceding section described the production of tone in the larynx by vibration of the vocal cords resulting in a complex periodic sound wave, that is a sound wave having a fundamental frequency and a range of higher frequency harmonics. The higher the frequency, the lower the amplitude of these harmonics, the difference being roughly 12 dB per octave for regular voice and about 20 dB for falsetto up to 1200 Hz (Monsen et al. 1977). But we never actually hear this laryngeal tone, because to reach us it must first pass through the vocal tract where it is crucially modified. If the glottis were connected directly to the lips, it would radiate about 10–15 dB less power (Titze et al. 1992). The vocal tract consists of three tubular cavities stretching from the vocal cords to the lips, namely the pharyngeal cavity, the oral cavity and the nasal cavity. By virtue of its resonant pattern, the vocal tract acts as a filter on laryngeal tone. The energy of the sound source at or close to the resonant frequencies of the vocal tract is privileged whereas energy in other frequencies is significantly attenuated. The resonant frequencies of the vocal tract depend on its length and the nature and degree of any constrictions along its course. The articulation of the different vowels is achieved by varying these two factors. The tongue is moved backwards/forwards and up/down, creating constrictions of varying shapes, according as the tongue is humped forward towards the alveolar region for front vowels, backwards toward the velar region for high back vowels, and downwards and backwards toward the pharyngeal region for low back vowels. Furthermore, the height of the larynx can be adjusted, and the lips can be variously protruded and constricted. Different speakers can adopt different strategies for producing the acoustic signals associated with the different vowels. Nevertheless, the vowel descriptions of traditional articulatory phonetics still afford a fairly serviceable scheme, particularly for major distinctions of tongue height and front-back position, although there are some complications with the back vowels, and vowels in connected speech are much less stable than vowels pronounced in isolation. For the vowel $\bar{\imath}$, as in Lat. $l\bar{\imath}ber$, the front of the tongue is high in the mouth, for the vowel $\bar{u}$, as in Lat. $\bar{u}ber$, the rear of the tongue is raised, and for the vowel $\bar{a}$, as in Lat. $\bar{a}ter$, the tongue (and jaw) are lowered. (The doctor who told his patients to "say $\bar{\imath}$" would be unable to conduct his examination.) Each configuration produces a different pattern of vocal tract resonances, therefore a different filtering of laryngeal tone, and therefore a different vowel quality. Since the length and shape of the vocal tract differ from person to person and particularly between male and female and between adult and child, vowel resonance patterns differ accordingly, but these linguistically nonsignificant differences are disregarded in normal speech perception. According to the analysis of Allen (1987), the classical Greek vowel system may be represented as in the vowel triangles in Figure 1.3. If the vowel triangle is conceived of as located in the mouth of the speaker with the *i*-corner facing forwards, it provides a very rough and schematic indication of the tongue positions for each vowel. The internal vowel triangle diagrams the short vowel system, the external triangle the long vowel system. The bottom corner of the vowel triangle represents the low central vowel *a*, the top left hand corner the high front vowels and the top right hand corner the high back vowel.

The brilliance and sonority of vowels sung by male opera singers has been analyzed (Sundberg 1974, 1987; Tatsumi et al. 1976). Prominent spectral components have been found around 3000 Hz. This enhancement of spectral components results from a crowding of the third, fourth and possibly also the fifth formant frequencies, which is achieved physiologically mainly by lowering the larynx and widening the pharynx. The sung vowels of female singers also differ from their spoken vowels in that they increase the power of their singing by raising the frequency of the first formant as fundamental frequency rises, mainly by adjusting the opening of the jaw (Sundberg 1975, 1987).

Whispered vowels occur when turbulent noise rather than tone is produced in the larynx. Turbulence is a type of aperiodic noise characteristic of fricative sounds (*s*, *f*, etc.). Like laryngeal tone, this turbulence is filtered by the vocal tract, so that the quality of a whispered vowel likewise depends on the configuration of the vocal tract.

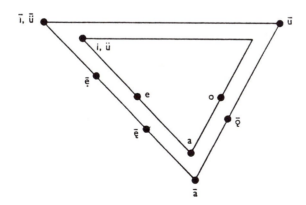

FIGURE 1.3
Classical Attic vowel system
(from Allen 1987)

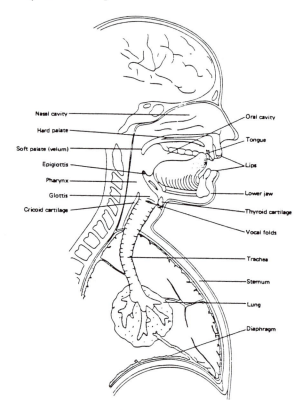

FIGURE 1.4
Schematic diagram of the human vocal mechanism
(from Scherer 1982)

Consonants

Although the degree of constriction of the vocal tract varies according
to vowel quality, even the closest vowels (*i* and *u*) are articulated with
the vocal tract relatively open in comparison with the degree of constriction typical in the articulation of consonants. Consonants are classified
according to their place of articulation (location in the vocal tract of the
major constriction) and their manner of articulation (a cover term for
a number of variable features relating to the nature of the airflow path
and the type of constriction).

The following are the most important locations of major constrictions
in the articulation of consonants:

1. *Labial.* The constriction is at the lip. When both lips are involved,
the constriction is termed "bilabial," as in π, β, μ. When the constriction
involves one lip and the teeth, it is termed "labiodental," as in English *f, v.*

2. *Dental.* The constriction is made by the tongue at the teeth, as in
τ, δ, ν (Allen 1987:16). If the constriction is made by the tongue at the

alveolar ridge behind the teeth, it may be termed "alveolar" as in English *t, d, n*.

3. *Palatal.* The constriction is made by the blade of the tongue against the hard palate, as in English ʃ (*sh*).

4. *Velar.* The constriction is made by the back of the tongue against the velum, as in English ŋ (*ng* as in *bang*), Greek ἄγμα (Allen 1987).

5. *Uvular.* The constriction is made by the uvula or the rear margin of the soft palate against the back of the tongue; in French and German, *r* is often produced as a uvular fricative or trill.

6. *Glottal.* The constriction is made by the vocal cords, often with adduction of the false vocal cords also, as in the cockney pronunciation of intervocalic and word final *t*.

Two features define the nature of the airflow path:

1. *Oral vs. nasal.* If the velum is raised to seal off the nasal cavity, the airflow passes through the oral cavity only, as in consonants such as π, τ, σ, which are termed "oral." If the velum is lowered, the airflow passes through the nasal cavity even though the oral cavity is occluded, as in consonants such as μ, ν.

2. *Central vs. lateral.* If the airflow passes through the centre of the vocal tract, as in most cases, then the consonant is termed "central." If the centre of the vocal tract is constricted in such a way that the airflow continues to pass on either or both sides of the constriction, then the consonant is termed "lateral." λ is a lateral consonant.

The following are the most important types of articulatory constriction:

1. *Occlusive.* Occlusives (also known as stop consonants or plosives) are produced with complete closure of the vocal tract, held long enough for the air pressure to rise behind the occlusion, and then rapidly released in most variants. The Greek occlusives are π, φ, β, τ, θ, δ, κ, χ, γ.

2. *Flap and tap.* The constriction involves a single momentary touching of one articulator against the other, and as such is distinct from the occlusive on the one hand and from the trill on the other. The area of contact between the articulators may be significantly smaller for flaps than for stops. Many varieties of English *r* fall into this category. In American English, dental stops are commonly pronounced as flaps in certain environments, for instance in words like *pity*.

3. *Trill.* Rapid vibration of one articulator against the other, comparable to phonation. Greek ρ is a trill (μάλιστα σειομένην Plato *Cratylus* 426e; Allen 1987).

4. *Fricative.* In the production of fricatives, the vocal tract is obstructed but not occluded entirely: the constriction is great enough to generate turbulent noise as the airflow passes through it. Greek σ is a fricative. Greek *h* (rough breathing) may be considered a glottal fricative, although

the source of turbulence for *h* can also be supraglottal. Pronunciations of *h* lacking sufficient energy in the high frequencies will approximate to voiceless vowels; the rate of airflow for initial *h* was found to be more than twice that of a following whispered vowel (Lehiste 1962). In Japanese, intervocalic *h* is produced with some form of vocal fold vibration, even though the glottis maintains the high degree of aperture associated with voiceless fricatives (Yoshioka 1981). In general, the shape and narrowness of the laryngeal constriction and the characteristics of the airflow together determine the intensity and frequency of the fricative noise generated. Greek *h* does not block elision as other consonants do; similarly in English, dental flapping occurs before vowels and before (undeleted) *h*: flapping applies to *it a* and *at home* but not to *at work* (Shockey 1973). *h* need have little duration of its own, and can be actuated mainly as a modification to the beginning of the following sound or to the transition between the preceding and following sounds (Clements et al. 1991).

5. *Affricate.* The constriction starts as a complete vocal tract closure which is then modified to a fricative slit as the consonant is released. When the category of affricate is invoked, care should be taken to specify whether the term is chosen on purely phonetic grounds or on phonological (distributional-systematic) grounds or on both.

6. *Approximant.*

6.1. *Glides.* The constriction of the vocal tract is marginally greater than for the high vowels, but the combination of airflow rate and degree of constriction are not normally such as to create audible turbulence. In Greek, a palatal glide occurs when *ι* appears in synizesis (Allen 1987); the *w*-glide is digamma.

6.2. *Certain liquids.* In the pronunciation of λ there is an occlusion but not a complete closure of the vocal tract, since the airflow continues to escape laterally. Certain types of *r* (that are neither trills nor flaps) are also approximants.

6.3. *Nasals.* In the pronunciation of the nasal consonants (μ, ν), there is an occlusion involving complete closure of the oral cavity (which is why nasals can also be classified as obstruents), but the airflow continues to escape through the nasal cavity.

In addition to the above distinctions in place and manner of articulation, consonants also differ according to the type of phonation with which they are produced. π, τ, κ, σ and *p̌* are pronounced with little or no vocal cord vibration in their basic actuations, β, δ, γ, μ, ν, λ, ρ have a significant degree of voicing, while the aspirated stops φ, θ, χ are produced with delayed onset of voicing.

2 | The Syllable

The child's earliest vocalizations consist of vowel-like sounds; consonant-like sounds appear from about two months of age. Consonants and vowels begin to combine into appropriately timed syllable-like sequences around seven months (Oller 1980); it has been suggested that in the earliest stage there is no neuromuscular activity specifically associated with individual segments but merely opening and closing jaw movements representing a segmentally neutral CV-frame, labial consonants cooccurring with central vowels and tongue front consonants with front vowels in both monosyllabic and reduplicated babbling (MacNeilage et al. 1990, 1991). CV-syllables continue to dominate at the next stage of development: single consonants outnumber clusters and initial consonants outnumber final consonants. In a study of one child's speech, the percentage of CV-syllables at the age of one year and three months was 89% in monosyllabic words and 87% in disyllabic words; these percentages fell progressively over the period of a year to 8% and 14% respectively (Ingram 1978). When words were interrupted in the spontaneous speech of 2–3 year old children, if the interruption coincided with a syllable boundary the child tended to resume articulation at the point of the interruption, but if the interruption occurred within a syllable, the child tended to go back to the beginning of the word or to the beginning of the preceding syllable (Wijnen 1988).

Crosslinguistic evidence likewise suggests a privileged status for the alternation of consonant and vowel in the sequencing of segments. Contiguous vowels in hiatus within the word are not permitted in about half the languages of the world, and a sequence of two or more consonants is not permitted within the word in about 10–15% of languages. In some languages CV is almost the only syllable type permitted, that is only one consonant is allowed in the onset and none in the coda (Bell et al. 1978). Other languages severely restrict the range of permissible coda consonants. Languages differ significantly in the degree to which they favour open syllables. About two thirds of all unstressed syllables have CV-structure in Italian, as compared with only about one third in Dutch (den Os 1988). CV-syllables are favoured in Greek too. In a sample of trisyllabic and longer words from the beginning of Lysias' *Against Eratosthenes*, the ratio of open to closed nonfinal syllables, counting light muta cum liquida clusters as tautosyllabic, was found to be three to one. Word internal hiatus is rare in statistical terms: the ratio of V.V to VC̥V in the same sample was one to twelve and a quarter. The overwhelming majority of instances of word internal hiatus involves the high, front, unrounded vowel *ι* as the first vowel, as in *τριάκοντα*, and most of these are predesinential, as *ἀφθονίας, κατηγορίας, δημοσίων*. Nonlexical words and high frequency lexical words contribute a number of cases of the diphthong *οι* before a vowel, such as *τοιαύτας, ποιοῦμαι*. Hiatus after *ι* may have been mitigated, or for diphthongs actually eliminated, by gliding. In word initial position, however, syllables lacking an onset are more common: the ratio V- to C̥V- to hV- word initially was 5.37:8:1. The ease of production of CV̆-syllables and its consequences for phrasing are emphasized by Dionysius of Halicarnassus

> οὐ δὴ γίνεται διάστασις αἰσθητὴ μὴ διηρτημένων τῶν λέξεων, ἀλλὰ συνολισ-
> θαίνουσιν ἀλλήλαις καὶ συγκαταφέρονται καὶ τρόπον τινὰ μία ἐξ ἁπασῶν
> γίνεται διὰ τὴν τῶν ἁρμονιῶν ἀκρίβειαν. *De Compositione Verborum* 20.92UR

Sonority

In general articulatory and acoustic terms, the consonant–vowel alternation involves cycling between a more and a less open vocal tract with the vowel phase being more consistently associated with voiced phonation, higher intensity and stable rather than transient formant patterns over a certain duration. When syllabic liquids are followed by identical nonsyllabic liquids in Czech, as in *Petr raportuje* 'Peter reports,' the syllabic liquid has greater duration and intensity than its following nonsyllabic counterpart (Lehiste 1965). Similarly, in pairs such as *plight* versus *polite*, *prayed* versus *parade*, duration (particularly related to the surrounding context: Taub 1990) and intensity were both found to be important differentiating cues (Price 1980). It is convenient to use the term sonority, which in a narrow interpretation refers to the perceptual correlate of intrinsic intensity or acoustic energy, to indicate some form of combination of some or all of the properties of acoustic prominence commonly associated with the syllable nucleus — amplitude, periodicity, spectral composition, relatively greater duration. Sonority cannot simply be equated with intensity, since fricatives tend to have greater intensity but lower sonority than nasals (Fujimura et al. 1982). Attempts at the automatic segmentation of speech into syllables on the basis of an intensity measure require a correction for fricatives (Mermelstein 1975).

Sonority sequencing

It was noted long ago that segments are arranged in the words of the lexicon in such a way that certain classes of segments are preferred in particular positions in the syllable and that, as a very general rule, the sonority of segments increases from the margins of the syllable to its nucleus, that is sonority increases through the onset to the nucleus and decreases from the nucleus through the coda; consequently, the order of segments in the coda tends to be a mirror image of their order in the onset (Sievers 1893; Jespersen 1904; de Saussure 1916; Ohala 1990b). Physiologically, this arrangement tends to obviate backtracking in opening or closing jaw movements (Lindblom 1983). Acoustically, consonant-vowel sonority sequencing prototypically favours larger and more easily perceptible modulations of the acoustic parameters in speech, for instance rating *bash* more highly than *wool* (Ohala 1990b). Furthermore, if a consonant cluster is divided between coda and onset, the more sonorous consonant is preferred in the coda and the less sonorous consonant in the onset, as illustrated by metathesis in Sidamo (Ethiopia: Vennemann 1988b): *hab-nemmo* → *hambemmo* 'we forget.' The degree of change in sonority from one consonant to another is called the sonority slope of the consonant cluster. Syllable division rules prototypically generate syllables that start with the sonority valley and have a consistently rising sonority slope up to the nucleus, which is the sonority peak. Rules for permitted segment sequences at the beginning and end of the word have been used as a hermeneutic for internal syllable division, but distribution in the syllable is one of the factors explaining distribution in the word and not vice versa. Segments can be broadly classified in the following hierarchy of decreasing sonority: vowels > glides > liquids > nasals > fricatives > stops (Hooper 1976), but hypotheses vary as to which features are admitted into the hierarchy and with what ranking (Zec 1988; Cho 1991), and in the degree to which a posited distributionally based ranking can be supported in acoustic terms. Voiced fricatives and stops have greater sonority than voiceless fricatives and stops respectively. Central liquids (type *r*) are more sonorous than lateral liquids (type *l*), and open vowels are more sonorous than close vowels. Glides have a close affinity with vowels, but they have more transient formant patterns and weaker voice amplitude. Although syllabic nasals are more common than syllabic liquids, liquids have a greater tendency than nasals to vocalize in the coda, and when a liquid and a nasal occur in sequence, the preferred order is nasal + liquid word initially and liquid + nasal word finally. When an obstruent and a liquid occur in sequence, the preferred order is obstruent + liquid initially and liquid + obstruent finally (Bell et al. 1978). Fricatives are more sonorous than stops and more likely to be syllabic, as in *Pst!*, yet they constitute a systematic exception to the postulated sonority slope: *s* + stop occurs initially and stop + *s* finally. The special status of such consonant clusters manifests itself in special rules for reduplication (Steriade 1988c) and for alliteration in Germanic verse (Sievers 1893b), and in their greater propensity to develop prothetic vowels as in Spanish *escuela* 'school.' In phonological analyses, the *s* is commonly treated as an extrasyllabic segment adjoined to the edge of the syllable. Acoustically, fricatives tend to be rather loosely bound to the syllables with which they are associated (Mermelstein 1975). When subjects were asked to repeat V̆CCC-syllables as fast as possible, a faster rate was achieved with syllables ending in *s*, type *elps*, than with those not ending in *s*, type *ilsk* (Mackay 1974). Apart from these clusters, it is generally the case that the more common a cluster, the steeper its sonority slope, particularly if it is tautosyllabic. Voiced obstruents tend to occur closer to the nucleus than voiceless obstruents, and in general clusters with reversed sonority as in Polish *krwi* 'of blood' are disfavoured (Greenberg 1965). When vowels are deleted in fast speech, one of the factors conditioning deletion is the sonority slope of the resulting cluster (Zwicky 1972b; Dalby 1986). However, many factors other than sonority can influence the acceptability of a consonant cluster. Languages can differ in the details of the classification of their segments into the sonority hierarchy, and, to avoid circularity, care should be taken to establish that postulated differences correlate with phonetically observable differences in the production of the segments in question. Languages can also differ in the way they syllabify identical sequences, notably according to which segments they allow to be syllabic and in what environments — to Polish monosyllabic *krwi* corresponds Serbocroatian disyllabic *krvi* 'of blood' — and which clusters they permit in the onset and coda. Differences in syllabification bring with them differences in phonetic implementation, and this can result in a phonetic mitigation of the reversed sonority (Bell 1970).

Syllabification

Syllabification can be interpreted as the lowest level in a hierarchy of prosodic prominence assignment. Just as stress seeks out long and sonorous syllables and renders them even longer and more sonorous, so syllable nucleus identification seeks out sonorous segments and makes them more sonorous than they would be as syllable margins. Both processes are relative, in that they choose entities relative to other potential candidates in the environment rather than on strictly absolute criteria (Goldsmith et al. 1990). This is a corollary of the fact that syllables must be formed even in the absence of maximally sonorous segments, and as a general principle in most stress languages each word has to have a stress even if it consists entirely of light syllables. In this sense, the syllable is at the low end of a hierarchy of prosodic prominence which increases with the extent of the prosodic domain through the foot and the word to the minor phrase, the major phrase and the utterance. The phonological representation of syllable structure and syllabification has been the subject of various hypotheses (Halle et al. 1980; Steriade 1982; Clements et al. 1983; Levin 1985; Hyman 1985; McCarthy et al. 1986; Itô 1988; Clements 1990; Goldsmith et al. 1990).

In Greek, the phonotactic effects of the preference for a steep sonority slope in consonant clusters are illustrated by the structure of permissible internal triconsonantal clusters (excluding those at the prefix seam). In such clusters, the central segment is always a stop and at least one of the peripheral elements is always a sonorant; there are reasons to believe (p. 43) that in triconsonantal clusters the syllable boundary falls in such a way that a coda cluster always has the structure sonorant or σ + stop and an onset cluster the structure muta cum liquida. This is just the structure of the occurring quadriconsonantal clusters, which consist of muta cum liquida preceded by its mirror image: $-\lambda\kappa\tau\rho$-, $-\mu\pi\tau\rho$-.

Indeterminacy

A verse system that counts syllables, a writing system based on syllables and orthographic conventions of hyphenation demand forced binary choices: in any one instance, a sequence of segments either is or is not treated as a separate syllable, a consonant is treated as belonging either to the preceding or to the following syllable. Phonetic evidence suggests that such binary organization is not always selfevident. Ambisyllabicity is not merely a convenient trick of phonological formalism, it has phonetic reality (Läufer 1985), although one articulatory study found more evidence for oscillation between onset and coda assignment than for a combination of both (Krakow 1989). Ambisyllabicity may also be indicated by the patterning of speech errors (Stemberger 1983). Hypershort vowels occur when the first consonant of stop + stop clusters is released, and in positions of particular reduction such as utterance initial position in West Greenlandic Eskimo where they have a duration of less than 20 msec (Nagano-Madsen 1992). A slight lengthening of the sibilants in *insists* has an evident effect on the rhythm of the word, a fact that has been related to the transposition of sibilants in word initial consonant clusters in child language (Allen et al. 1978). Transitional stages between pairs such as *lightening–lightning, pedaling–peddling* appear indeterminate as to the number of syllables; they can be evaluated acoustically according to their intensity and duration and from an articulatory perspective according to the degree to which they involve a separate vowel gesture (Browman et al. 1990). The cues used by listeners to discriminate pairs like *s'port* 'support' versus *sport*, when they are differentiated in production, were complex and variable (Fokes et al. 1993). That the pronunciations noted above can have some sort of systematic rhythmic status is suggested by the double beat found in some African gong and drum surrogates (p. 48), which consists of either two quick submoraic beats or a hypershort beat followed by a longer one; the double beat is particularly associated with reduced syllables and stop plus sonorant (muta cum liquida) sequences (Sebeok et al. 1976).

The syllable as a perceptual unit

A series of experiments over the past dozen years have sought to establish the role of the syllable as a unit of perceptual organization intervening between reception of the acoustic speech signal and access to the mentally stored representations of words. The experimental technique generally used is to have subjects listen to lists of unrelated words and press a response key as fast as possible after hearing a specified word initial sound sequence. It emerged that, in French, syllable division is perceived by the listener and exploited in speech comprehension: subject response time was shorter for French *balance* than for *balcon* when the target was *ba-* but longer when the target was *bal-* (Mehler et al. 1981). These results were not replicated in English, presumably because in English some intervocalic consonants are ambisyllabic (Cutler 1986), nor in Japanese (Otake et al. 1993); evidence for Spanish was conflicting (Sebastian-Gallès et al. 1992; Bradley et al. 1993). It was suggested that the syllable could be bypassed if sufficient information was available in the onset and nucleus. Japanese subjects may have been using the mora rather than the syllable as their unit of perceptual organization.

Other perceptual evidence suggested different representations for onset versus coda consonants (Ades 1974; Samuel 1989) and for single consonant onsets versus cluster onsets (Cutler et al. 1987).

Syllable demarcation

When a string of open syllables is produced at an abnormally slow rate of speech, as in syllable by syllable dictation, a short period of silence will separate the syllables. Consequently, each syllable will be uniquely correlated with discrete glottal and/or subglottal activity. Intensity and articulatory energy will be rising at the beginning of the syllable and falling at the end. The association of a vowel with the onset consonant of the following syllable will be limited because the closing of the articulators takes place mainly during the silence intervening between syllables. Transconsonantal coarticulation will be reduced. In Swedish nonsense *VpV*-disyllables with sentence stress in slow speech, the tongue position for the first vowel was relaxed prior to the consonant gesture, even when the vowels were identical; this relaxation was weak or absent in faster speech (Engstrand 1988). Likewise, in a string of closed syllables, there will be less coarticulation between coda and onset consonants at slow dictation speed than in more fluent speech. As the speech rate increases, these characteristics of syllable demarcation are progressively reduced, but not to the point of being consistently and entirely eliminated at normal speech rates. Most obviously, a long vowel with a smooth intensity curve is likely to be perceived as a single nucleus, but the same vowel with a medial fall in intensity due to a period of creaky voice or a glottal stop is likely to be perceived as two syllables: such a difference can be found in pairs like *beater* versus *bea-eater*.

Acoustic evidence

Syllable division at normal speech rates is most directly studied by comparing alternate syllabifications of the same segmental sequence — for instance, when a consonant cluster is heterosyllabic in slow speech and homosyllabic in fast speech; when the variable location of a morpheme boundary in the same segmental sequence results in different syllabification; and when resyllabification in sandhi applies in fluent speech but not in deliberate speech. However, it is often difficult to factor out the phonetically similar effects of potentially interfering influences such as demarcation of prosodic units greater than the syllable, differences in stress in contiguous syllables, or different degrees of coarticulation unrelated to syllable division. Most applications involve comparing open to closed syllables, that is comparing the onset allophones of a consonant to its coda allophones, and comparing vowel allophones in syllables with and without a coda and with and without an onset. While the acoustic differences are fairly well established, perceptual studies and slips of the ear suggest some difficulty with their recognition (O'Connor et al. 1964; Lee 1970; Bond et al. 1980). Some major allophonic differences depending on position in the syllable are apparent even without instrumental analysis, for instance the aspiration in English voiceless stops in some onsets, particularly those of stressed syllables, and its absence in codas: *play taught* versus *plate ought*, *grey tie* versus *great eye*. Another instance is the difference in some types of English between onset clear *l* in *holy* 'sacred' and coda dark *l* in *holey* 'full of holes' (Maddieson 1985; Fujimura 1990). Major allophonic differences provide comparatively strong cues for the perception of syllable division (Nakatani et al. 1977). Comparable tendencies are present in lower level allophonic rules too: consonants tend to be stronger and more consonant-like in the onset and weaker and more vowel-like in the coda. The variably syllabified prevocalic nasal in the pairs *a nice man–an ice man, see Mabel– seem able, hoe-maker–home-acre* has rising intensity and greater duration in the onset and falling intensity and less duration in the coda (Lehiste

1960). The difference appears equally in the voiced fricative of the French pair *il doit v(e)nir–ils doivent nier* (Rialland 1986). It is not entirely due to independent factors like word demarcation and stress; the motivating articulatory differences remained even after these independent effects had been factored out (Krakow 1989).

Articulatory evidence

The physiological correlate of these effects is a differential degree of innervation of the vocal tract, which emerges when the spatial and temporal properties of articulatory gestures are studied in relation to syllable structure. Syllable onset *m* may involve more extreme gestures of the lower lip and greater compression of the lower lip against the upper lip than coda *m*; for onset *m* the end of velar lowering coincided with the end of the lip raising gesture, but for coda *m* the end of velar lowering coincided with the beginning of the lip raising gesture (Krakow 1989). The velum may also be higher for onset nasals than for coda nasals (Fujimura et al. 1978; Fujimura 1990); the higher velum position results in less nasalization. The difference in timing and extent of the velar gesture is related to the phonological observation that vowels are more likely to become nasalized by a coda nasal than by an onset nasal. The velar nasal is more vowel-like than the other nasal consonants, reflecting the relative reduction of the oral resonating cavity when there is a velar constriction (Ohala 1992); there are also evident distributional restrictions on the velar nasal, which is more likely to develop from *n* in the coda than in the onset. Differences in jaw height have been found to correlate with syllable structure for intervocalic labial stops (Macchi 1988). At the phonological level, sound changes whereby consonants are reduced to a glottal stop or entirely lost affect coda consonants far more than onset consonants. In Hausa, labial and velar obstruents are weakened to *w* and dentals to *r* in the coda but not in the onset (Klingenheben's law).

Glottal gestures

During the voiceless portions of an utterance, the glottis does not maintain a single and static open position, but the degree of opening is continually adjusted according to the airflow requirements of the individual segments. The glottal gestures for contiguous consonants can be merged into a single gesture, but this is more likely to occur for homosyllabic consonants than for heterosyllabic consonants, at least when the latter span a word boundary. Electromyographic and fiber optic studies of the larynx have revealed that for the heterosyllabic voiceless consonant sequence *sk* with intervening word boundary, as in "My ace caves," there are two gestures of glottal abduction, but for the homosyllabic cluster *sk*, both in the onset as in "I may scale" and in the coda as in "I mask aid," there is only a single glottal abduction (Yoshioka et al. 1981b). For "Kiss Ted" two separate abduction gestures were found in slow speech, a single smooth gesture in fast speech and partially overlapping gestures at intermediate tempi (Munhall et al. 1988). Similar rate dependent variation was found for *s # p* in Danish (Frøkjaer-Jensen et al. 1973). In the case of geminates, a single articulatory gesture and a single glottal gesture (Sawashima et al. 1974; Yoshioka et al. 1981b) span the syllable boundary.

Vowel length and transitions

There is a well established tendency for the vowels of closed syllables to be shorter than the vowels of open syllables. In Italian, long vowels occur in stressed open syllables, short vowels in stressed closed syllables and in unstressed syllables; similar restrictions are found in Swedish. In the Italian nonsense words *mipa* and *mippa*, the timing of the tongue gestures for the two vowels was almost identical; the difference was that the lip gesture for the geminate consonant occurred earlier than for the single consonant, with the result that the vowel is acoustically but not gesturally shorter (C.L. Smith 1991). The most controlled test for the difference is to compare vowel length before single consonants with that before geminates: in this environment a difference was found in a large number of languages ranging from Hausa (Nigeria) and Amharic (Ethiopia) to Dogri (Pakistan) and Telugu (S.E. India) (Maddieson 1985). In comparing the stressed syllables of German *Biete–bitte, Sehne–Senne*, where in the first word the stressed syllable is open but in the second it is closed by the ambisyllabic consonant, the auditory impression is that in the former the vowel trails off before the consonant articulation, while in the latter it is interrupted in full swing by the closing consonant, which is stronger because it belongs, in part, to the stressed syllable. The difference is sometimes referred to as open and close contact. In addition to the vowel length and consonant strength, experimental evidence indicates that the distance from the intensity peak to the end of the vowel is important: in close contact, the vowel intensity falls more rapidly and more steeply; airflow measured at the point of transition from the vowel to the consonant was weaker in open contact (Fischer-Jørgensen et al. 1970). The auditory effect of close contact in American English *bop* versus open contact in *bob* may reflect not only the shorter vowel duration before the voiceless coda consonant but also the more rapid jaw closure and correspondingly shorter first formant transition (Summers 1987). The length and strength of the arresting and releasing formant transitions, reflecting articulator movement to and from the consonant, have also been exploited in the comparison of homosyllabic

and heterosyllabic consonants. The perceptual consequences of varying these parameters were first tested with synthesized speech (Malmberg 1955; Delattre 1963). By progressively adjusting the formant
transitions from stronger on the left to stronger on the right, the pronunciation of "An old Arab ate an apple" was made to sound more and
more French, because resyllabification across word boundary is far
stronger in French than it is in English (Delattre 1963). Formant pattern
differences are frequently reported in spectrographic studies of variable
syllabification in natural speech (Lehiste 1960; Gårding 1967; Läufer
1985; Rialland 1986).

Fundamental frequency turning points

There is some evidence for a correlation of syllable or mora division
and fundamental frequency. Provided there is sufficient duration, a
monosyllabic long vowel will be perceived as disyllabic by speakers of
English if the fundamental frequency is manipulated so that it falls and
then rises during the production of the vowel (Ainsworth 1986). For
certain languages, reports link the turning point of fundamental frequency
curves to some consistent point in the syllable or mora. In modern Greek,
the fundamental frequency peak associated with the word accent is located
at the boundary between the stressed and the poststress syllable (Arvaniti
1992). For the Slovene circumflex accent in nonfinal syllables, the turning
point was at or somewhat before the end of the accented syllable (Srebot-
Rejec 1988). In the lexical tone language Hausa (Nigeria: Lindau 1985),
the peak fundamental frequency for the High tone and the minimum
fundamental frequency for the Low tone are located at the syllable boundary. This contrasts with tentative reports for Bambara (W. Africa:
Mountford 1983; Hertz 1990), which locate the tone targets halfway
through the vowel for both long and short vowels. Certain disyllabic
words in Danish have the turning point located between an onset resonant and the following stressed nucleus (Thorsen 1982). According to
a study of Chinese, the generalization is that tonal turning points tended to occur at the boundary between consonant and vowel (Gårding
1987). In Japanese bimoraic nonsense words with the structure VmV,
lip closure for the nasal consonant beginning the second syllable was
fairly well synchronized with the onset of the pitch shift both for Low
High and for High Low patterns (Sawashima et al. 1982). Another study
of Japanese found that the High-Low turning point was particularly
strongly fixed to the syllable or mora boundary: if the turning point was
moved to the central part of the nucleus—under experimental conditions or in utterances by nonnative speakers—listeners tended to hear
the vowel as having two moras; since the duration of the vowel in the
synthesized version had not been changed, the High-Low turning point

was evidently interpreted as a cue for a mora boundary (Nagano-Madsen 1987, 1989; Nagano-Madsen et al. 1989). Conversely, when *béeru* 'veil' was synthesized with the pitch fall postponed, it was perceived as *béru* 'bell' even when the duration of the accentual vowel was very long (Nagano-Madsen 1990); this effect was not found for speakers of Japanese dialects lacking the pitch accent (Nagano-Madsen 1990b). This sort of evidence may be related to phonological evidence from accent location rules which point to the syllable and the mora as the units of timing for tonal events, and also to perceptual properties of tone movement: it has been suggested that a High-Low sequence is perceived in a VCV-structure when the turning point is located at some point between just before the beginning of the consonant and just after the beginning of the vowel (House 1990).

Muta cum liquida

The potentially tautosyllabic status of medial muta cum liquida is well established in a number of languages. It is claimed that no language has tautosyllabic medial consonant clusters without also having initial clusters, and muta cum liquida clusters are the most common type of initial cluster. In a sample of 32 languages with recently formed or restricted initial clusters, more than half the languages had only muta cum liquida clusters (Bell 1971). When a language has both heterosyllabic and tautosyllabic medial consonant clusters, as opposed to merely the former, it is usually some or all sibilant plus consonant or muta cum liquida clusters that are tautosyllabic. This is the case in Eastern Armenian (Allen 1950), Cham (Vietnam: Blood 1967) and Yakur (Nigeria: Bendor-Samuel 1969). In Icelandic, *p, t, k, s* plus *j, r, v* are tautosyllabic but other clusters are heterosyllabic (Einarsson 1949). In Gujarati (W. India: Cardona 1965) one and the same muta cum liquida cluster can vary between tautosyllabic and heterosyllabic status. As a general rule, rapid speech favours open syllables and consequently tautosyllabic status for medial clusters (Läufer 1985). The maximum rate at which syllables can be repeated is greater for syllables having muta cum liquida onsets than for syllables having *s* + stop onsets (Sigurd 1973). Muta cum liquida sequences are more likely to be homosyllabic than *s* + stop sequences in scribal divisions at line end in Old English manuscripts (Lutz 1986) and in an experiment in which words were repeated with reduplication of one syllable (Treiman 1992).

Although heterosyllabic clusters are often produced with a single tongue gesture, homosyllabic consonant clusters generally have a greater overall degree of integration and coarticulation than heterosyllabic clusters. In the slow speech pronunciation of French *technique*, the nasal begins after the stop has been released, whereas in fast speech the stop is released into the nasal and the formant transitions leading to the preceding vowel are much weaker. In a possible slow speech pronunciation of French *athlétisme* 'athletics,' the liquid has relatively great duration and voicing and sharply rising intensity, the stop release is brief and weak, and there are long and well marked formant transitions from the vowel to the stop; by contrast, in fast speech, the liquid is completely devoiced and more strongly coarticulated with the stop, which is laterally released, and formant transitions to the stop are weak. In both these words, the acoustic evidence is reliably interpreted as reflecting variable syllabification of muta cum liquida clusters, especially as similar properties can differentiate *coupe-les* 'cut them' from *couplets* 'couplets' (Läufer 1985). Coarticulatory lip rounding in French *a.ku, ar.ku, a.kru* was found to start in the last segment of the rime of the first syllable, reflecting the homosyllabic status of the muta cum liquida cluster (Giannini 1987). However, the correlation of syllable division and coarticulation can be disturbed by interfering factors: in English *kl* coarticulation is often greater when the cluster is heterosyllabic than when it is homosyllabic depending on the nature of the stop release (Hardcastle 1985).

GREEK SYLLABLE DIVISION

Metrical evidence

It is a well established crosslinguistic generalization that CV̆C-syllables can behave like CV̄-syllables for the purposes of phonological rules such as accent assignment, and that they can be distributed like CV̄-syllables in quantitative metrical systems. When this combination of phonological and metrical facts is found in a dead language, it represents a primary source of evidence for syllable division. If the first syllable of a string V̆CCV is phonologically and metrically heavy, the implication is that the syllabification is V̆C.CV; if it is phonologically and metrically light, the implied syllabification is V̆.CCV. The metrical practice of the tragic trimeter indicates that, with the exception of certain muta cum liquida clusters which vary (Rumpel 1865; Kopp 1886; Naylor 1907; Schade 1908), word medial biconsonantal clusters are heterosyllabic, as in the following examples:

> *long consonants*
> > ἵπ.πον *Helen* 1258
> > ἐβάκ.χευσεν *H.F.* 966
> > γραμ.μάτων *Hippolytus* 954
> > τυράν.νου *Helen* 35
> > ἄλ.λος *Phoenissae* 417
> > λίσ.σομαι *Hecuba* 1127

stop + stop

    ἐπ.τά Phoenissae 1093

    ἠχ.θόμην Alcestis 815

    ἐτρέφ.θην Eur. *Electra* 1046

    ἐβ.δόμαις Phoenissae 1134

sibilant + stop

        ἀσ.πίδων Heraclidae 823

        πάσ.χομεν Alcestis 258

        ὀσ.τέων Orestes 404

        φάσ.γανον Hecuba 543

stop + sibilant

        ἔκ.σομεν Orestes 1125

        ὄπ.σεται Medea 352

sibilant/nasal + nasal

        ἐσ.μούς Bacchae 710

        δεμ.νίων Alcestis 186

muta cum liquida

	V̆.CCV	V̆C.CV
πρ	*Κύ.πρις Hippolytus* 101	*Κύπ.ρις Hippolytus* 2
τρ	*πα.τρός O.C.* 442	*πατ.ρί O.C.* 442
κρ	*νε.κρῶ Antigone* 1240	*νεκ.ρός Antigone* 1240
φρ	*τά.φρου Phoenissae* 1188	*ἀφ.ρόν Bacchae* 1122
θρ	*μέλα.θρα I.T.* 69	*μέλαθ.ρον Troades* 746
χρ	*πολυ.χρύσους Helen* 928	*πολυχ.ρύσους Bacchae* 13
πλ	*ὅ.πλω H.F.* 570	*ὅπ.λον H.F.* 161
τλ	*ὅ.τλον Septem* 18	*σχέτ.λι' Alcestis* 824
κλ	*κύ.κλος I.A.* 717	*κύκ.λον Hecuba* 412
φλ	*τυ.φλῶ Hecuba* 1050	*τυφ.λόν Hecuba* 1117
θλ	*γενέ.θλ' Ion* 653	*γενέθ.λια Ion* 805
χλ	*ὅ.χλον Hecuba* 605	*ὅχ.λος Hecuba* 607
πν	*ὕ.πνου H.F.* 1011	*ὕπ.νον H.F.* 1013
τν	*πό.τνι' Eur. Electra* 487	*πότ.νι' I.T.* 1082
κν	*ὄ.κνω Soph. Electra* 321	*ὀκ.νεῖν Soph. Electra* 320
φν	*ἄ.φνω Alcestis* 420	*ἀφ.νεωτέραις Soph. Electra* 457
θν	*ὀ.θνείου Alcestis* 810	*ἀποθ.νήσκοντα Eur. Frag.* 578.6
χν	*ἴ.χνος I.T.* 266	*ἰχ.νεύω Ajax* 20
τμ	*δυσπό.τμου Orestes* 1078	*ἐρετ.μά I.T.* 1485
κμ	*τέ.κμαρ Hecuba* 1273	*ἀκ.μῆς Helen* 897

θμ	στα.θμῶν *I.T.* 49	ἀριθ.μός *Troades* 620	
χμ	ὀ.χμάζεις *Orestes* 265	ὀχ.μάσαι *P.V.* 5	
βρ	ὕ.βρις *O.C.* 883	ὕβ.ρις *O.C.* 883	
δρ	ἔ.δρας *H.F.* 51	συνέδ.ρου *Ajax* 749	
γρ	ἀ.γρῶν *O.T.* 1051	ἀγ.ρῶν *O.T.* 1049	
βλ	βύ.βλου Aesch. *Supplices* 761	ἔβ.λαψεν *Helen* 868	
γλ	—	ἀγ.λάϊσμα *Helen* 282	
δν	—	ἔδ.νοις *Andromache* 153	
[γν	—	ἀγ.νός *Heraclidae* 1011]	
δμ	—	ἀδ.μήτης *O.C.* 1321	
[γμ	—	ἀγ.μός *I.T.* 263]	

γ in γν and γμ was probably not a stop but a velar nasal (Allen 1987:35), so that at least in their surface phonetic form these clusters belong with μν above.

Sonority

Phonological conditioning emerges clearly for the sonorant hierarchy when the stop is voiced: voiced stop + ρ is allowed as a word internal onset, voiced stop + λ is rare as an onset, voiced stop + nasal is always heterosyllabic. This ordering reflects the postulated sonority hierarchy. As already noted, in Icelandic, only r is allowed in onset muta cum liquida clusters: *vī.trir* 'wise,' but *vĭt.ni* 'witness,' *ĕp.li* 'apple'. Spanish has words in which liquids have been metathesized so that the onset cluster has r rather than l, as in *peligro* < *periclu*, *palabra* < *parabla* (Vennemann 1988b). The hierarchical relationship of voiceless and voiced stops emerges in Greek from the greater constraint on voiced stops in the onset; even when the sonorant is ρ, if the muta is voiced, the cluster is heterosyllabic about twice as often as if the muta is voiceless. The relative frequency of the two syllabifications in different lexical items is in part a reflex of the ease with which different word shapes can be fitted into the trimeter and in part reflects phonological and morphological factors (the latter are noted in the next section). However, when these differences are factored out, it is likely that some variation will remain correlating with the text frequency of individual words and the degree to which they occurred in colloquial speech. Excluding anceps, the internal cluster is heterosyllabic in 13% of the instances of ὕβρις and 0.05% of μακρός and πικρός combined as compared with 75% for ἁβρός and 55% for ἄκρος (Naylor 1907). Internal onset muta cum liquida is overall more common than heterosyllabic muta cum liquida in tragedy, and overwhelmingly so in comedy (Schade 1908). Heterosyllabic muta cum liquida in comic dialogue metres is mainly associated with a formal style, as when the style of tragedy is being parodied. This indicates that onset muta cum liquida was the norm in colloquial Attic, and that the variation in tragedy is due to the influence of non-Attic verse; in Homer, for instance, internal muta cum liquida is usually heterosyllabic, with exceptions involving liquids rather than nasals. This is not meant to preclude the possibility of some degree of variation among speakers of colloquial Attic or indeed among the styles or tokens of a single speaker.

Morphology

Morphological constituency can also be a conditioning factor (Porson on *Orestes* 64; von Mess 1903; Naylor 1907; Ancher 1978). Where syllable division is metrically unambiguous, that is excluding occurrences in anceps, it stands at the morpheme boundary overwhelmingly in reduplicated verb forms

> κε.κλῆσθαι *Ion* 75
> κέ.κρυπται *Helen* 62;

exceptions are rare

> κεκ.λῆσθαι Soph. *Electra* 366
> κικ.λήσκειν *Troades* 470.

Syllabification of augmented verb forms and of verbs prefixed by ἐκ- is likewise morphologically conditioned

> ἐκ.λείπει *Ion* 1435
> ἐκ.λύει *Phoenissae* 695
> ἔ.κλυον *Phoenissae* 919
> ἐκ.ραίνει *Trachiniae* 781
> ἔ.κραινε *Helen* 1318.

However, onset to coda resyllabification of muta cum liquida at the prefix seam occurs occasionally in tragedy

> ἀπότ.ροποι *Phoenissae* 586
> κατακ.λύσειν *Troades* 995.

Prefixes are in general more autonomous than suffixes in the Indo-European languages; for instance, in Polish syllabification inflectional boundaries are ignored but prefix boundaries are respected (Rubach et al. 1990). Resistance to resyllabification at the prefix boundary is illustrated by English *dis.pair* 'undo the pairing of' with no resyllabification except in rapid speech, as contrasted with *de.spair* 'lose hope' (Davidsen-Nielsen 1974); Plautine Latin *ab.rumpit* but *tene.brae*; Spanish *sub.rayar* 'to underline' but *a.brigo* 'shelter' (Bell 1970); Catalan *sub.ratllar* 'to underline' but *ca.bra* 'goat' (Wheeler 1986).

Orthographic evidence

There is a partial conflict between the metrically evidenced syllable divisions just documented and those actually used in alphabetic inscriptions, those presupposed by the conventions of the syllabic scripts and those explicitly formulated in the Greek grammatical tradition (Meister 1894; Hermann 1923; Beekes 1971; Viredaz 1983; Ruijgh 1985; Davies 1987b). The main points of difference emerge clearly from Herodian's cover rules

> τὰ σύμφωνα τὰ ἐν ἀρχῇ λέξεως εὑρισκόμενα, καὶ ἐν τῷ μέσῳ ἐὰν εὑρεθῶ-
> σιν, ἐν συλλήψει εὑρίσκονται, οἷον ἐν τῷ κτῆμα τὸ κτ ἐν ἀρχῇ λέξεως ἐστίν,
> ἀλλὰ καὶ ἐν τῷ ἔτικτον εὑρεθέντα ἐν τῷ μέσῳ τὸ κ καὶ τὸ τ ὁμοῦ ἐστιν.
> II.393.33 Lentz

> ὅσα σύμφωνα μὴ δύναται ἐν ἀρχῇ λέξεων ἐκφωνεῖσθαι, ταῦτα καὶ ἐν μέσῃ
> λέξει εὑρεθέντα χωρισθήσεται ἀλλήλων· οἷον ἄνθος, ἔργον· οὐ δύναται δὲ
> εὑρεθῆναι ἀπὸ τοῦ νθ ἀρχομένη οὐδὲ ἀπὸ τοῦ ργ· πλὴν τούτων ἤγουν θμ, φν,
> γδ, χμ, κμ, σγ, σδ· ταῦτα γὰρ οὐδέποτε ἐν συμπλοκῇ ἐν ἀρχῇ εὑρισκόμενα,
> ἐν μέσῳ ἀλλήλων οὐ χωρίζονται οἷον ἴθμα, ἀφνειός, ὄγδοος, αἰχμή, ἀκμή,
> φάσγανον, θεόσδοτος. II.396.2 Lentz

The basic principle is that any consonant cluster which can occur at the beginning of a word is an onset word medially; the second passage, which is less transparent, apparently extends this principle to medial clusters which fill structural gaps in the list of attested initial clusters, differing from them in a single feature such as voice (γδ, σγ, σδ) or aspiration (θμ, φν). Herodian excludes the prefix seam from the application of these rules (393.39). A passage in Sextus Empiricus (*Adversus Grammaticos* 174) reports πολλὴ καὶ ματαία παρὰ τοῖς γραμματικοῖς μωρολογία on the subject of syllable division and *st* is one of the clusters explicitly mentioned; similarly a passage attributed to Theodosius (Hilgard 1894:lxxxi) reports

> ὅταν ζητῶμεν ποίᾳ συλλαβῇ συντάξωμεν τὰ στοιχεῖα, οἷον ἐν τῷ ἀσθενής
> τὸ σ πότερον ληκτικόν ἐστι τῆς προτέρας συλλαβῆς ἢ ἀρκτικὸν τῆς δευτέρας.
> Bekker, *Anecdota Graeca* 3:1127

These passages suggest some indeterminacy in the grammatical tradition regarding clusters of sibilant + stop.

Many Attic inscriptions starting with the Hellenistic period follow a consistent set of principles for dividing consonant clusters at the end of the inscriptional line; these principles correspond by and large to Herodian's rules (Threatte 1980); similarly at Delphi (Rüsch 1914). In particular, line end precedes stop + stop clusters

$$\varepsilon.\kappa\tau\varepsilon\iota \quad \text{II}^2.949.2$$
$$\varepsilon.\beta\delta o\mu\eta\varsigma \quad \text{II}^2.1012.2$$

and orthographic voiced stop + liquid or nasal

$$\delta o.\gamma\mu\alpha \quad \text{II}^2.1343.38.$$

The division of σ + stop and to some extent σμ is variable

> πλει.στην II².1008.55
> καλλισ.τον II².1028.17;

variation with σ + stop was also found in a crossdialectal survey (Hermann 1923). Adherence to consistent principles of syllable division in earlier Attic texts is less well established, partly because such division is generally not used in boustrophedon writing and is not compatible with strict stoichedon writing. In a few cases the stoichedon arrangement has been slightly altered to achieve the preferred syllabification (Threatte 1980:70), while in a couple of non-Attic inscriptions the preferred syllabic divisions have been achieved by making corrections to a text previously written without regard for syllable division at line end (Hermann 1923:138).

The syllable division of internal clusters implied by the Cyprian syllabic script conforms to the practice found in the alphabetic inscriptions rather than to the metrically evidenced syllable division.

> *ti-mo-wa-na-ko-to-se* Τιμοϝανα.κτος *ICS* 150
> *ti-pe-te-ra-lo-i-po-ne* δι.φθεραλοιφων *ICS* 143
> *a-pi-ti-mi-li-ko-ne* ’Α.βδιμιλκων *ICS* 220.

Again there is variation with σ + stop

> *e-pe-se-ta-se* ἐπεσ.τασε *ICS* 103
> *e-pe-sa-ta-se* ἐπε.στασε *ICS* 92, 93.

The syllable divisions implied by the Linear B writing system are similar to those of the Cyprian script and likewise partially in conflict with the later metrical evidence

> *e-ko-to* Ἑ.κτωρ
> *wa-na-ke-te* Ϝανα.κτει, also *wa-na-ka-te* Ϝανακ.τει
> *re-po-to* λε.πτος
> *de-so-mo* δε.σμος
> *a-mi-ni-so* ’Α.μνισός.

It is not possible to reconcile the evidence of the syllabic scripts with the metrical evidence by assuming that Cyprian and Mycenaean had different syllabification rules from other types of Greek. This approach fails to account for the agreement of the alphabetic inscriptions with the syllabic inscriptions. Some of the syllable divisions indicated by the script also would inflict further damage on the apparently rather shaky versification of the Cyprian metrical inscriptions (*ICS* 261, 264).

To the extent that the orthographic evidence for syllable division conflicts with the metrical evidence, it has to be decided which of the two has deviated from the syllable divisions of normal speech and what might be the motives for such a deviation. The metrical evidence cannot be discounted because it conflicts with an a priori theory of syllabification (Pulgram 1975, 1981) or explained with a principle that metrical variation implies metrically relevant intermediate syllable durations (Snell 1962; West 1970; cp. DS 1977b, 1980b); earlier theories positing a metrical syllable distinct from the linguistic syllable are now discredited (Zirin 1970; Allen 1973:59). It is probably easier to motivate the alternative assumption, namely that the orthographic evidence partially fails to reproduce the syllable divisions of normal speech. The difference is not between phonetic syllabification and (morpho)phonological syllabification, as apparently in some other languages, notably Malayalam (Wiltshire 1991), but may rather pertain to speech rate. The orthographic syllable divisions may represent not those of normal speech but those of an artificially slow rate of speech (Ephron 1961) associated with the teaching and probably also the practice of writing. Writing is a slower activity than speaking, and the writer needs to adopt certain specific strategies to slow down his speech to align it with what is being written. These strategies have the side effect of disturbing syllable rhythm and the mapping of consonants onto onset and coda slots. It is a common intuition that slow speech has different syllable divisions from normal speech and normal speech from rapid speech (Kahn 1976). The variable degree of aspiration in prestress clusters of s + stop in English words like *asparagus, historic, posterity* suggests that these clusters are heterosyllabic in careful speech and homosyllabic in rapid speech (Bailey 1978). Most experimental observations relate to differences at comparatively natural speech rates (Stetson 1951; Läufer 1985); even the field technique of inserting a 500 msec pause to test for the perception of natural syllable boundaries (Derwing 1992) does not involve deliberate segmental lengthening. So the following account is merely introspective. There are some remarks on the effect on syllable division of a prolonged note in singing in an old article by Stetson (1931:155). In artificially slow speech, vowels are greatly lengthened and syllables may be separated by pauses; coda consonants are in open rather than in close contact with the preceding lengthened vocalic nucleus; to the extent that they are unreleased, syllable final stops will be hard to perceive unless geminated or simply resyllabified into the onset of the next syllable. A coda resonant or fricative can be lengthened, as an alternative strategy to lengthening the preceding vowel, in which case it would remain in close contact with the syllable nucleus. The choice between these two strategies may be influenced by the phonotactic structure of word initial onsets, so that resonants remain coda consonants, but fricatives allow either lengthening of the vowel or lengthening of the fricative. So the syllable divisions of the orthography are just those to be expected when the utterance of syllables is synchronized with the act of writing them. It is not strictly correct to say that the metrical syllabification is linguistic and the orthographic syllabification is nonlinguistic. Rather the metrical syllable divisions are those of normal speech, the orthographic syllable divisions are those of an artificially slow rate of speech. The fact that more sonorous segments are easier to lengthen explains why orthographic syllable division can be stated in terms of a sonority hierarchy (Viredaz 1983). These specula- tions are supported by a certain amount of direct evidence. The open syllable is basic in the Linear B and Cyprian syllabic scripts, and its importance in the teaching of alphabetic writing is demonstrated by the alphabet chorus in the *Grammatical Tragedy* Edmonds 1.176

βῆτα ἄλφα βα... βῆτα ἰῶτα βι... βῆτα ὦ βω

and by one type of writing exercise on papyri (Wachter 1991). There are a considerable number of inscriptional spellings in which coda consonants are geminated (Hermann 1923; Threatte 1980), suggesting just the sort of lengthening postulated on theoretical grounds

μετεσστιν I².26.8
μαλισστα I².924.4
μισσθος II².1672.11
’Ασσκληπιο II².4966
δεσσμων IV.1484.218; δεσμων ibid. 223.

Stops too are sometimes written geminate in muta cum liquida clusters

Καλλικκρατου II².5487; Threatte 1980:531

and in stop + stop clusters

Εκκτορ *CIG* IV.xviii

suggesting an alternative strategy of lengthening the silence between implosion and explosion of a coda stop and releasing the stop into the next syllable. This strategy was less favoured than the vowel lengthen- ing with resyllabification posited above; but such spellings are quite common with ἐκ before a word beginning with a stop consonant

εκ κτων ιδιων II².657.40;

either coda consonant gemination was a favoured strategy across a prepositive boundary or these spellings are a compromise between main- taining the orthographic integrity of the word and representing the re- syllabification that underlies the homosyllabic status of κτ in the orthography.

Linguistic evidence

There is also a complex of linguistic data almost all of which indicates unequivocally that the syllable divisions of normal speech are just those found in the metrical evidence. For the morphophonemic rhythm rule of the thematic comparative and superlative (p. 104), V̆CCV-sequences behave like V̄.CV-sequences, which implies the syllable division V̆C.CV

> λεπτότερος
> σεμνότερος
> πιστότερος

like ὠμότερος, not like σοφώτερος. Muta cum liquida is mostly heterosyllabic for the application of this rule to the core vocabulary

> μακρότερος
> πυκνότερος,

but some marginal forms show variation across the corpus of Greek literary records

> βαρυποτμώτατος *Phoenissae* 1345
> βαρυποτμότατος Plutarch *Tiberius Gracchus* 5
> ἐρυθρώτερος Plato *Timaeus* 83b
> ἐρυθρότερος Anaxandrides 22 Edmonds
> εὐτεκνώτατος *Hecuba* 581
> εὐτεκνότερος Diodorus Siculus 4.74.

The accentual rules that are sensitive to the weight of nonfinal syllables (p. 102) indicate with varying degrees of certainty a syllable division V̆C.CV for biconsonantal clusters; onset muta cum liquida is evidenced by the Attic rule known as Vendryes's law, but not by the neuter diminutive nouns law (Ruijgh 1985)

> *Wheeler's law*
> > αἰγοβοσκός
> > πατροκτόνος
> *Neuter nouns law*
> > πυκτίον
> > τεκνίον
> *Vendryes's law*
> > ἀστεῖος
> > ἄγροικος
> > ἄχρειος.

Further evidence comes from the morphology of reduplication (Kühner et al. 1890:307, 1892:22; Ruijgh 1972; Steriade 1982, 1988). The present reduplication of verbs beginning with a consonant cluster is of the form Ci-

> γιγνώσκω
> τίκτω < *τι-τκω
> ἵστημι.

But for perfect reduplication the synchronic rule is that it takes the form
Ce- when the resulting reduplicated form starts with an open syllable
and *e-* when the resulting form starts with a closed syllable

παίω	πέπαικα
πταίω	ἔπταικα
πυνθάνομαι	πέπυσμαι
ψύχω	ἔψυγμαι
χέζω	κέχεσμαι
κτίζω	ἔκτισμαι.

For the purposes of the reduplication rule, the "lighter" muta cum liquida clusters are not resyllabified across the reduplication seam

κλέπτω	κέκλοφα
τρέφω	τέτροφα
γράφω	γέγραμμαι, dialect ἔγραμμαι,

and, as already noted (p. 35), resyllabification of such clusters across
the reduplication seam is rare in tragedy. The "heavier" muta cum liquida clusters are more variable

βλάπτω	βέβλαφα, κατεβλαφοτες VII.303.51
βλαστάνω	βεβλάστηκα, ἐβλάστηκα
γλύφω	γέγλυμμαι, ἐξέγλυμμαι
γιγνώσκω	ἔγνωκα.

Even a few other clusters appear originally to have resisted resyllabification, since the reduplication rule has a few exceptions, such as

κτάομαι	κέκτημαι, Ionic ἔκτημαι
μιμνήσκω	μέμνημαι
πτήσσω	πεπτηώς Homer, ἔπτηχα Attic.

Such forms are evidence that resyllabification failed across the reduplication seam, not that these clusters were regularly assigned to the onset
word medially in prehistoric Greek. In this sense they are more comparable to

θυγατρὶ μνηστήρων *I.A.* 68

than to

εὔ.μνος Epicharmus 91 Kaibel
? βα.κτηρίη Hipponax 20 West, cp. Herodas 8.60
(Cunningham 1971:200)

V̄CCV

Metrical evidence cannot provide a direct indication of the syllable division of biconsonantal clusters after long vowels. Clusters that are onsets after short vowels in Attic may be supposed to be onsets after long
vowels also

μη.τρῶος
σώ.φρων.

It is normally assumed that other biconsonantal clusters were syllabified as after short vowels, which will create superheavy syllables. This view receives some confirmation from a test performed below (p. 78), which indicates that superheavy syllables so formed were constrained in certain metrical environments. On the other hand, it is known from Osthoff's law that Greek has a tendency to eliminate superheavy syllables ending in a resonant; so it is conceivable that some other superheavy syllables could have been avoided by weakening the constraints otherwise applying to word medial onsets. A sensitivity of syllable division to the length of a preceding vowel (Pulgram 1970; Treiman et al. 1988) is found in Old English, where stress attracts consonants into the coda more strongly after short vowels than after long vowels on the evidence of scribal practice at line end (Lutz 1986); similarly in Gothic, unlike the Codex Argenteus, the Codex Ambrosianus B has heterosyllabic division of muta cum liquida after short vowels and variation between heterosyllabic and onset treatment after long vowels (Vennemann 1987).

VCCCV, VCCCCV

For clusters of three and four consonants, evidence for syllable division is likewise indirect. It is clear that for such clusters too the orthographic syllable is not a reliable guide to syllable division in normal speech

ai-ka-sa-ma Linear B αἰκσμανς
re-u-ko-to-ro Linear B Λευκτρον
Καλλι.στρατου II².850.12
Λαμ.πτρεα II².1322.22.

Metrical evidence indicates that all triconsonantal clusters are divided so as to give a heavy first syllable

ἄστρον S̄S̆ *Phoenissae* 835
νίπτρα S̄S̆ *Ion* 1174.

While the metrical evidence excludes the possibility of all three consonants being assigned to the onset, it does not directly indicate whether the syllable division is after the first or the second consonant. It is reasonable to assume that biconsonantal clusters that are onsets in Attic postvocalically will also be onsets postconsonantally

σκῆπ.τρον
ἐχ.θρός.

For more ambiguous clusters, the division which gives the steeper sonority slope within the cluster has the greater chance of being correct (Allen 1973)

θέλκ.τρον

κάμπ.τρα.

This direct appeal to the sonority slope is supported by phonotactic evidence. All triconsonantal clusters beginning with σ have muta cum liquida as their second and third elements, which suggests that in these clusters the division was after the first element, and that other onsets having a less steep sonority slope, such as κτ, πτ, πσ, were not possible in triconsonantal clusters. Conversely, all triconsonantal clusters ending in σ have the mirror image of muta cum liquida as their first two elements, which suggests that in these clusters the division was after the second element. These purely distributional considerations for coda and for onset both point to syllable divisions of the type

ἄρκ.τος

πέμπ.τος

ἄελπ.τος

κομπ.σός.

That stop + σ was not an acceptable coda is also indicated morphophonemically by the deletion of σ in triconsonantal clusters in which neither division would result in a sufficiently steep sonority slope (Kühner et al. 1890:283; Steriade 1982)

γεγράφσ-θαι > γεγράφθαι

λελέγ-σθαι > λελέχθαι

ἐψ-τός > ἐφθός.

SYLLABLE DURATION AND WEIGHT

In its physical nature and, to a large extent, in its physiological implementation, duration is the simplest and most easily understood of the three prosodic features of speech; it is also the most important component of rhythm. In gross terms, speech segments are produced and perceived serially in time; they involve a number of rapid articulatory and phonatory gestures overlaying a set of mainly slower respiratory gestures. The combination of the former, or at least their targets, is symbolized by the segments of a traditional linear phonetic or phonological representation of an utterance. The difficulty is that duration as measured from the acoustic record or from a record of motor events is not always easy to correlate with a phonologically based segmentation of speech. Individual articulators begin their movements at different times and with different velocities according to their individual mobility, the distance they must travel and the degree of coarticulation. Different studies are not necessarily consistent in their segmentation of the acoustic record. For instance, it is important to know whether the duration between the release of a voiceless stop and the beginning of voicing for a following vowel has been assigned to the consonant or to the vowel, and whether the voiced formant transitions following the release of a voiced stop are viewed as part of the consonant or part of the vowel. It is disputed to what extent the duration of segments is the automatic result of the interacting activity of the muscles involved in the articulatory gestures (Fowler 1983) and to what extent it is under neurocognitive control (Keller 1990), a distinction related to that between universal and language specific durational properties (Fourakis 1986). Another complication is that there are dramatic differences in the actual durations of the same segment. Vowel duration can vary as much as 10 to 1 in connected discourse in English (Umeda et al. 1975). On the other hand, comparatively minor durational differences are used to signal, and interpreted as signalling, a wide variety of phonological and morphosyntactic distinctions. Listeners are able to "hear through" the surface durations to the more abstract durational system. Children learn both relative and absolute durations of unreduced vowels by about three years of age, while adult norms for consonants are achieved at a later stage (Allen et al. 1980). The disturbance of the natural durations of speech makes a significant contribution to the "machine accent" of computer-generated synthetic speech. Likewise, badly disturbed timing, as occurs, for instance, in the speech of the deaf, can lead to serious loss of intelligibility, even though all the segments of the utterance are correctly articulated (Huggins 1979).

The general perception of stimulus duration varies according to a number of conditioning psychoacoustic factors. Stimuli having greater intensity are perceived as having greater duration (Zelkind 1973). Durations filled by sound are perceived as longer than demarcated periods of silence having the same objective duration (Thomas et al. 1974). Complex stimuli and stimuli composed of many elements are perceived as having greater duration than objectively equal stimuli that are simpler or have fewer elements (Schiffman et al. 1974, 1977). Some studies of speech sounds have found that stimuli with changing fundamental frequency are perceived as having greater duration than equally long stimuli with level fundamental frequency (Lehiste 1976); this result was replicated for vowels in German monosyllables but not for disyllabic words (van Dommelen 1991).

The study of duration in a dead language on the basis of metrical evidence is complicated by the fact that absolutely identical speech durations can be metrically distinctive and very substantially disparate speech durations may be treated as identical for the purposes of the metre. When a line of verse is recited, feet containing the same number of syllables can have quite different durations and feet containing different numbers of syllables can have quite similar durations (Eriksson 1991). This problem of variation in the durational implementation of phonological categories is just one manifestation of the overall problem of variation in the phonological production of language and needs to be understood in that overall context: one of the central challenges of phonetic analysis in general is the potential prima facie lack of correlation between measurable differences and linguistic function.

Nonce durations

It is clear that the poet and his audience do not assess metricality on the basis of the actual durations they hear in each utterance, for the relatively trivial reason that every utterance, like every snowflake, is in fact unique: humans are in general unable to replicate any behaviour exactly, and if a person were asked to repeat a phrase or even a sound a dozen times, each occurrence would be somewhat different from the others. The categories of language to which metre is sensitive must clearly be more general and more abstract than the precisely quantified phonetic measurements of nonce utterances, if metre is to be able to function as a system shared by an entire speech community. At the same time, speakers can, if asked to do so, repeat words with almost no variation in duration, so that clearly the rather large durational variations occurring in actual speech must have some other origin.

Idiolect and tempo

The poet and his audience also do not assess metricality on the basis of the durations they hear in each utterance but abstracting away from differences caused by the performance limitation factor discussed in the preceding paragraph. There are a number of factors outside the phonetic substance of the utterance itself that can cause variation from one speaker to another within the speech community (Crystal et al. 1982) and also from utterance to utterance of the same speaker. Such factors include the anatomy, age, sex and health of the speaker and the discourse situation as it affects dialect, sociolect and speech tempo. The discourse situation, including its correlation with different registers of literary style, can have significant effects on metricality. Not only the domains within which the rules of rhythm apply but also the rhythm of speech itself can change as the speaker shifts from slow to fast tempo, and both of these effects have potential significance for metre. On the other hand, it is a basic principle of metre that durational categories are defined relative to each other and not in terms of actual durations at any given tempo. For instance, in Japanese a light (one mora) syllable in slow speech can have almost the same duration as a heavy (two mora) syllable in rapid speech (Hiki et al. in Nishinuma 1979; Fujisaki et al. 1971), but this fact is not relevant to the metre of Japanese verse. Similarly, it is clear that metricality for a Greek poet and his audience did not depend on the physical durations of syllables as they heard them, but on their relative duration, abstracted from variability due to the factors just mentioned. The very fact that speech is intelligible across a wide range of tempi suggests that the perception of duration involves relative rather than absolute intervals. A number of studies have shown that whether a vowel or consonant of a given duration is perceived as short or long depends on the speech rate (Summerfield 1981; Miller 1981; Miller et al. 1986). The rate of speech of the context influenced the perception of short and long vowels in English (Ainsworth 1972; Verbrugge et al. 1977), and of short and long consonants in English *topic* versus *top pick* (Pickett et al. 1960) and in Japanese *ise* [a place name] versus *isse* [a unit of area] (Fujisaki et al. 1975). Listeners judge the speaking rate on the basis both of the immediately contiguous segments and of the broader phonetic environment. The degree to which attributes of the preceding context influence the determination of speech rate depends on proximity to the target syllable and unit of prosodic domain (Summerfield 1981).

Subcategorical differences

One further level of abstraction remains. The poet and his audience do not assess metricality on the basis of the durations they hear in each utterance and abstracting away only from the effects of the factors discussed in the two preceding paragraphs. Even after discounting all the factors already mentioned, as well as the fact that each vowel and each consonant has its own intrinsic duration, there remains an enormous amount of variability in the actual duration of what, at a more abstract level, would be considered the same phonological unit; models of speech timing that directly specify the duration of each articulatory event are quite unwieldy (Fowler 1983). This variability arises from the influence of the context in which the phonological unit is embedded. Large portions of the rest of this book are devoted to eliciting the complex of factors that make up that context. They include: the segmental environment, stress hierarchy, foot structure and environment, prosodic domain hierarchy, demarcation hierarchy, length of the prosodic domain, tonal movement, informational and pragmatic content, grammatical category. So, for instance, a vowel could be lengthened because it is stressed, or because it stands before a voiced consonant, or because it occupies a monosyllabic foot, or because it stands at the end of a phrase, or because it carries a large tonal excursion, or because it stands in the accented syllable of an emphatic word. Figure 2.1 illustrates how a syllable with contrastive stress ending in a voiceless consonant can be durationally comparable

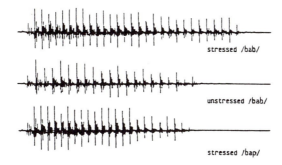

FIGURE 2.1
Waveforms from three syllables differing in stress
and voicing of the final consonant (from Summers 1987)

to a syllable without contrastive stress ending in a voiced consonant in English. In fact, short vowels at the end of a sentence can be lengthened so much in some languages that their durational range more or less overlaps that of long vowels sentence internally. Although the result of all these lengthening processes is an acoustically longer segment, different processes may involve different articulatory mechanisms affecting different phases of the lengthened segment (p. 147).

The mora

The Greek syllable can have any one of over a thousand different possible segmental structures. Each consonant and each vowel has its own intrinsic duration, and each consonant and each vowel has different durations in different segmental environments. It follows that the syllables of the Greek language had a very large number of different durations. Although speakers do make some compensatory adjustments for durational differences of segmental origin within units of speech rhythm such as the syllable and the foot (Campbell 1989), such compensation comes nowhere near to neutralizing the effects of all these differences, although it is particularly successful in mora-timed Japanese (Port et al. 1987). On the other hand, in most languages phonological and morphophonological rules of rhythm, especially rules governing the location of word and phrase accent, disregard these multiple durations; insofar as they are sensitive to quantity at all, they classify syllables into at most two, or rarely three, categories of syllable weight, according as they contain one, two or, less commonly, three units of rhythmic measurement called morae. If syllables having different structures are assigned to the same class by the phonology in rules relating to rhythm, that must be because they share some intrinsic property relating to rhythm, namely their mora count. Diachronic changes can also occur in moraically determined environments (Auer 1989).

The most tangible evidence for the mora comes from some surrogate languages which use gongs or drums to transmit messages over distances too great for ordinary vocal communication. Gong and drum beats are physically rather staccato events; two strategies are used for communicating vowel length. One strategy is to allow a greater interval before the next stroke after a stroke representing a long vowel, as in Luba (Zaire), Balanta (Guinea Bissau), and the Ewe drumming of Twi. The other strategy is for one drum stroke to represent a short vowel and two drum strokes a long vowel, thereby effectively drumming the mora count, as in Manjaco (Guinea Bissau) and Zanniat Chin (Burma); both strategies are reported for Jabo (Liberia) (Sebeok et al. 1976).

The status of the mora is not the same in all languages. In socalled syllable weight languages, light syllables have one mora and heavy syllables have two morae overall. In socalled mora timed languages, heavy syllables also have two morae, but there is a greater tendency for each mora to be timed independently, so that particularly in slow speech vocalic morae and consonantal morae tend to make roughly equal contributions to bimoraic weight (p. 73). This difference is not grounds for dispensing with the mora in syllable weight languages. Conversely, it is not possible to dispense with the syllable in the description of a mora language like Tokyo Japanese, where the accent can occur on the first but not the second mora of the syllable and the moraic nasal can occur in the second but not the first mora of the syllable. Mora-timed Japanese is characterized by a pattern of bidirectional temporal adjustments designed not so much to equalize the durations of all morae as to produce identical average mora durations within a domain (Port et al. 1987). The foot in Japanese is bimoraic, but the boundaries of feet need not coincide with syllable boundaries (Poser 1990). Similarly in the mora counting verse of Japanese, Ponapean (Micronesia: Fischer 1959), Kinyarwanda pastoral poetry (Rwanda: Coupez et al. 1970; Mbonimana 1983; Jouannet 1985) and generally in the mora counting lyrics of African song (Jones 1964), a heavy syllable may straddle an assumed foot boundary. In Winnebago (Wisconsin: Halle 1990), the two morae of a heavy syllable may belong to different stress feet.

Languages in which pitch movement is assigned to strings of morae irrespective of syllable boundaries provide a further demonstration of the potential independence of the mora. Such is the case with the phrase final High-Low-High contour of West Greenlandic Eskimo, which is a combination of a lexical High Low pitch accent with a phrase final High tone; it is assigned to the last three morae of the sequences ...CV̄CV̆ and ...CV̆CV̄, as illustrated in Figure 2.2. In both syllable sequences the peaks are, as far as one can tell, asssociated with the first and third morae respectively, and the valley is associated with the second mora (Mase

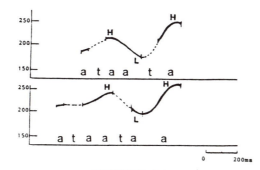

FIGURE 2.2
Moraic alignment of phrase final High Low High
tonal contour in West Greenlandic Eskimo
(from Nagano-Madsen 1988)

1973; Nagano-Madsen 1988, 1993). In Chonnam Korean, the High-Low fall of the pitch accent occurs from the second to the third mora counting from the beginning of the word, irrespective of syllable structure (Jun 1990).

Submoraic distinctions

The organization of syllable weight into moraically defined categories, while it characterizes the basic application of rhythm rules, is often insufficient for more finegrained analyses along diachronic or particularly phonostylistic parameters. It is clearly the case that speakers can hear submoraic durational distinctions. Deviations as low as 10 msec can be perceived by the listener as abnormal (Huggins 1972); typical noticeable differences for vowels ran about 14% and for consonants about 50%. (Just noticeable differences with nonspeech sounds can be even lower: Ruhm et al. 1966; Abel 1972.) In Japanese, which has phonological length, a difference of 10 msec was likewise found to be just noticeable (Fujisaki et al. 1975). In Dutch, differences in vowel duration due to foot and word rhythm were perceived by listeners with great accuracy (Nooteboom 1973) and were taken into account in distinguishing between short and long vowel categories. Under typical discourse conditions, as opposed to ideal experimental conditions, larger just noticeable differences were found in English (Klatt et al. 1975). These figures should be interpreted relevant to the range of durations of speech sounds which is from about 30 msec to about 300 msec. In English, the average duration of a stressed vowel in connected discourse is about 130 msec, while consonants average about 70 msec (Klatt 1976). Not only can allophonic differences in vowel duration be heard, they can be a factor in the choice of preferable alternative word order by speakers of English (Bolinger

1962). Differences in the intrinsic duration of short vowels may be a factor governing the order of elements in expressions like *chit-chat*, *zigzag*, *tit for tat* (Cooper et al. 1975).There is no reason to believe that poets are not consciously or intuitively aware of such differences and able to exploit them for stylistic purposes. To what extent infracategoric differences in syllable duration are also systematically relevant for the rules of Greek metre, and consequently for the rules of the rhythm of Greek speech, is a question that needs to be answered empirically rather than in a priori theoretical terms. The danger of omitting this step and relying on intuition or preconceptions is illustrated by the fact that in American English the disyllable *steady* can actually have shorter duration than the monosyllable *stead*, due mainly to trochaic shortening and flapping of the intervocalic dental (Lehiste 1971).

Whereas there has been a tendency in the phonologically influenced tradition to assume that submoraic duration is uninteresting and definitionally irrelevant (DS 1977b), in the philological tradition there has been a tendency to make just the opposite assumption, namely that submoraic duration is automatically relevant. In antiquity, the diversity of syllable durations within the categories of heavy and light syllables arising from differences in segmental structure (subcategorical syllable duration) was widely recognized. Dionysius of Halicarnassus has a full discussion in the fifteenth chapter of *De Compositione Verborum*:

αἰτία δὲ τίς ἐστι τοῦ μήτε τὰς μακρὰς ἐκβαίνειν τὴν αὐτῶν φύσιν μέχρι γραμμάτων πέντε μηκυνομένας μήτε τὰς βραχείας εἰς ἓν ἀπὸ πολλῶν γραμμάτων συστελλομένας ἐκπίπτειν τῆς βραχύτητος, ἀλλὰ κἀκείνας ἐν διπλασίῳ λόγῳ θεωρεῖσθαι τῶν βραχειῶν καὶ ταύτας ἐν ἡμίσει τῶν μακρῶν, οὐκ ἀναγκαῖον ἐν τῷ παρόντι σκοπεῖν. ἀρκεῖ γὰρ ὅσον εἰς τὴν παροῦσαν ὑπόθεσιν ἥρμοττεν εἰρῆσθαι, ὅτι διαλλάττει καὶ βραχεῖα συλλαβὴ βραχείας καὶ μακρὰ μακρᾶς καὶ οὐ τὴν αὐτὴν ἔχει δύναμιν οὔτ᾿ ἐν λόγοις ψιλοῖς οὔτ᾿ ἐν ποιήμασιν ἢ μέλεσιν διὰ μέτρων ἢ ῥυθμῶν κατασκευαζομένοις πᾶσα βραχεῖα καὶ πᾶσα μακρά.

In this passage, Dionysius explicitly recognizes the systematic metrical relevance of the two categories of syllable weight and the phonetic reality of multiple durations arising from different segmentally structured syllables. Compare the similar comments of Quintilian 9.4.84. Herodian II.709 Lentz indicates that $C\bar{V}(C)$-syllables are longer than $C\breve{V}C$-syllables. Marius Victorinus 39 Keil reports that the syllable ημ is longer than the syllable ἄμ and seems to include the durational contribution of onset consonants to infracategoric durational differences, at least in the case of light syllables. Aristides Quintilianus 41f.WI tries to reconcile the binary categories of syllable weight with the multiplicity of segmentally motivated durations by a system based on summing up the durational contributions of differently weighted segments: short vowels count as one unit, long vowels as two, and consonants as half a unit. Choeroboscus in his commentary on Hephaistion 180 Consbruch likewise states that πᾶν σύμφωνον λέγεται ἔχειν ἡμιχρόνιον, and that οἱ ῥυθμικοί measure the syllable ω as δύο χρόνων and the syllable ως as δύο ἡμίσεος χρόνων, although the γραμματικοί and the μετρικοί count both as two units. Pompeius 113 Keil comments: "esse aliquas syllabas plurimas quae et plura habent tempora quam oportet, ut est *lex*... invenitur ista sylla-ba habere tria tempora." Nevertheless, "omnis syllaba, quae naturaliter brevis est, unum habet tempus; quae longa est, sive natura sive posi-tione, duo habet tempora. Cetera tempora ex superfluo sunt, nihil prae-stant." Priscian I.52–53 Keil, after giving examples of heavy syllables in Latin that have *duo, duo semis*, and *tria tempora*, states "tamen in metro necesse est unamquamque syllabam vel unius vel duorum accipi tempo-rum." The ancient distinction between rhythmics and metrics correlates to a certain extent with the modern distinction between phonetics and phonology. Modern metrists, by contrast, have increasingly come to claim that Greek metre is immediately sensitive to segmentally motivated infra-categoric differences in syllable duration. A number of scholars have sought to return to a system of computing syllable weight similar to that of Aristides Quintilianus, counting the vowel and all following consonants in their durational computations (Verrier 1914; Sturtevant 1922; Schmitt 1935; Dale 1969). Others moved in the same direction, but on the basis of detailed philological work, which, beginning in the early nineteenth century, brought to light an increasing number of real or apparent restric-tions on the metrical distribution of segmental structures. For example, it was thought that muta cum liquida clusters are avoided in resolution, because "such syllables are too long for the shorts produced by resolu-tions" (Parker 1972). Most intervocalic consonants were thought to be avoided in resolutions made by the final two syllables of a word, because they added too much duration to an already overloaded sequence (Seidler 1812; Wunder 1823; Fix 1843; Mueller 1866; Witkowski 1893; Zieliń-ski 1925). However, ρ was considered permissible because of some special articulatory property: "quo loco [Euripides *Medea* 505] pronun-tiatione liquidae excusatur solutio" (Mueller 1866). Differences in the intrinsic duration of short vowels were invoked: it was claimed that Babrius admitted -ᾱ at the end of the choliamb but excluded other short vowels, because ᾰ is the longest of all short vowels and therefore a better substitute for a long vowel (Crusius 1897). A recent theory distinguish-es about twenty types of heavy syllable reflecting gradations in dura-tion, grouping these into the durational hierarchy CV̄C > CV̄ > CV̆C and claiming that the longer types of heavy syllable gravitate to the biceps of the hexameter and the shorter types to the longum; such a distribu-tion is taken as establishing the metrical significance of Dionysius' ἄλογος μακρά (Irigoin 1965). The situation is further complicated by the durational interpretation of responsion in dactylic and iambotrochaic (Maas 1962) and of the nonresolution of the longum in the hexameter (Wifstrand 1933). Elaborating a theoretical framework already developed in the nineteenth century to account for restrictions on the positional lengthening of short final vowels (Hilberg 1879), one modern account integrates all these currents into an explicit theory, positing seven different syllable quantities in an attempt to define metre in terms of slots of varying durational capacity (West 1970). The concrete phoneticism of such approaches was best and most clearly expressed in the following words: "it will not be enough to classify an element as long or short or anceps: it will have to be more precisely defined in relation to the phonetic durational range of its occupying syllables" (Haslam 1974). These twentieth century durational approaches to Greek metre mostly shared the following basic premises: biceps has greater duration than longum and anceps has a duration somewhere between that of longum and that of breve. According to these definitions of the metrical elements, it was either explicitly claimed or implicit in their assumptions that the segmentally longer types of heavy syllable are preferred in the biceps and the shorter types in anceps, while the shorter types of light syllable are preferred in resolution and the longer types in anceps. It would follow that metrical distribution could be exploited as a valuable source of evidence not merely for moraic but also for submoraic and segmental duration in Greek: the extent to which these claims are valid is an important theoretical question which, as already noted, needs careful empirical investigation.

Method of investigation

On the basis of experimental and typological evidence, it is possible to establish durational differences likely to be valid for most languages and consequently also for Greek. Segment and allophone durations are certainly not identically ranked in all languages for which measurements are currently available, but many clearly recurring regularities make it an easy task to choose test types having widely disparate durations. Statistical samples of the texts can then be taken to see if the differences so established are metrically relevant. This is best done by testing the end points (maximum and minimum values) of the linguistic parameter as they are distributed at the end points of the metrical parameter (highly constrained versus relatively unconstrained locations). In other words, the test should be directed to the largest possible phonetic difference of any given type at the most and least metrically sensitive locations. If no statistical difference is found between the end points of the parameter of duration tested, then it can be assumed a fortiori that the metre is not sensitive to the differences tested in less sensitive locations nor to smaller differences of the same type in any location. If, however, a statistically significant difference in distribution is found, then that is prima facie evidence for a metrically relevant durational distinction. However, there are often a number of extraneous factors that could produce the difference without any metrical sensitivity to duration. In particular, controlling for word shape or position within the word greatly reduces the danger of mistaking automatic, reflex phenomena for evidence of metrical sensitivity to durational differences. As an additional control, it is desirable to establish a well defined trend correlating with the stylistic development of the trimeter. Distributional differences correlating with the degree of strictness of versification are less likely to arise from random or nondurational factors such as vocabulary differences.

The choice of metrically sensitive locations and mappings to test the significance of durational distinctions is relatively uncontroversial. For heavy syllables, third anceps in the trimeter is widely recognized as such a location: Callimachus (p. 105) goes so far as to eliminate long third anceps in his noncholiambic trimeter, with the exception of a single proper name (Pfeiffer 1934). For light syllables, resolution is the obviously sensitive context, as indicated by the numerous constraints both on the location of resolution in the line and on the rhythmic organization of the word shapes in which it occurs. An even higher degree of constraint is found on long anceps and on resolution when these mappings involve a departure from the basic rhythmical organization of a word shape, as in the case of words of the shape ionic a minore. Any sensitivity on the part of the mapping rules of Greek rhythm to the segmental structure of light and heavy syllables is likely to surface in these metrically sensitive contexts.

Syllable onset

Syllable structure

The canonical form of the syllable comprises a nucleus (usually, but not necessarily vocalic) optionally preceded and followed by one or more consonants, the onset and the coda consonants respectively. As already noted, it is the absence of the preceding consonant and the presence of the following consonant that are the marked situations: CV is less marked than both V and CVC. In a number of languages all syllables must begin with a consonant and in a number of others no syllable can end with a consonant. Speech errors rarely involve movement of complete syllables, unless they are also morphemes; movement of nucleus plus coda is comparatively rare, and movement of onset plus nucleus in a closed syllable even rarer (Stemberger 1983; Shattuck-Hufnagel 1983; Fudge 1987). Both in English and in Japanese (Kubozono 1989b), speech errors characteristically involve identical syllabic positions — onset, nucleus, coda; this indicates that these positions are real constituents of syllabic structure whose occupants are liable to misselection in speech errors (Laubstein 1988). However, exchanges between onset and coda of the same syllable and metathesis between coda of one syllable and onset of the next were well represented in a corpus of Arabic speech errors and typically involved liquids (Abd-El-Jawad et al. 1987). Since assimilation errors can occur across word boundary, as in *breen beret* or *roaf beef*, syllable structure must be simultaneously available over a phrasal domain (Blumstein 1988; Dell 1988). The onset of the first syllable of many words is the most likely position for speech errors, so it is possible that it is encoded separately from the rest of the word (Shattuck-Hufnagel 1987). In segment monitoring tasks, French and Spanish subjects were able to focus their attention preferentially on coda or onset positions rather than simply on serial position in the word as a strategy for faster detection of the target segment (Pallier et al. 1993).

The consonantal and vocalic constituents of syllables are not discrete items of a serial string; rather they interrelate with each other to various degrees and in ways that have been differently represented in different phonological theories. Some data suggest, or can be interpreted as suggesting, a close relationship between onset and nucleus, giving support to a hierarchical left branching representation of the syllable [onset nucleus][coda]; other data suggest a right branching representation [onset][nucleus coda] (Vennemann 1988). The constituent consisting of nucleus plus coda is often called the rime. It is useful to make a distinction between the rime of a syllable and the rhyme, the latter being the unit that rhymes in verse. Rime and rhyme correlate in the case of monosyllabic words such as *sin* – *pin*, but not in polysyllabic words, where rhyme involves repetition of everything from the stressed vowel to the end of the word, as in *sinister* – *minister*. The nonrhyming section of the word, that is everything from the beginning of the word up to but excluding the stressed vowel, was found to be transposed as a unit in a type of Pig Latin used by a six year old boy (Cowan 1989). Word games that divide syllables into onset and rime or words into onset and rhyme are easier to learn than games involving other divisions (Treiman 1983; Davis 1989b); this does not apply to mora timed Japanese, where the functional unit of word games is the mora and not the rime (Kubozono 1989b; Katada 1990). Young children find it easier to categorize monosyllabic words on the basis of a shared nucleus + coda than on the basis of a shared onset + nucleus (Kirtley et al. 1989). In a consonant exchanging task, subjects made onset exchanges more rapidly than coda exchanges, even when the interfering factors of frequency and sonority were factored out (Fowler 1987).

Reduplication, alliteration, cooccurrence

In reduplication rules, the coda consonant is often omitted, but consonant clusters in the onset are also reduced (Moravcsik 1978; Marantz 1982, Steriade 1988c); both phenomena recur in child language, but in reduplication segmental dissimilation is also a potential factor. Although alliteration in verse normally involves just the first consonant or the onset, CV-alliteration is found in the Finnish *Kalevala*; Finnish also has a word game that involves interchanging the first consonant and vowel of pairs of words whether there is a coda consonant or not (Anttila 1989). Cooccurrence constraints in general are far stronger between nucleus and coda than between onset and nucleus; in Shanghaiese fourteen vowels may occur in open syllables but only six in closed syllables (Cairns et al. 1982). In Chinese, a central vowel assimilates to a glide in the coda, or to a glide in the onset provided the syllable is open, suggesting that the nucleus attaches more closely to the coda if there is one, otherwise it attaches to the onset (Steriade 1988b).

Stress, tone

Although both onset and coda consonants contribute duration to the acoustic signal, the contribution of the onset is interpreted by the prosody as insignificant compared to that of the coda: prosodic processes requiring extra time for their implementation, such as stress or distinctive tone, interpret coda consonants, but not onset consonants, as providing the requisite additional duration. In terms of morae, coda consonants are moraic and onset consonants are not moraic. Rules for the location of stress are almost always (Everett et al. 1984) sensitive only to the rime, the nature of the onset being irrelevant. Some Australian languages have a situation in which, as a result of weakening of a previously stressed initial syllable, stress falls on the first syllable in the word having an onset (Davis 1985, 1988). In Spanish, antepenultimate stress is excluded if the onset of the final syllable is diachronically derived from a consonant cluster (Clements et al. 1983). The reverse situation, in which rime sensitive stress is explained as having arisen by sound change from an earlier onset sensitive stress rule rather than from the inherent stress attracting properties of heavy rimes, is not recorded. There is some phonological evidence that complex onsets are less acceptable in unstressed syllables than in stressed syllables: Italian *pioppo* < *pōplus*, *fiaba* < *fábla* with metathesis (Vennemann 1988b). Once a syllable is chosen as a location for stress, its onset can receive increased intensity and duration: in English the closure or constriction of onset consonants has greater duration in stressed than in unstressed syllables (Löfqvist et al. 1984), and in Italian word initial consonants have greater duration in stressed syllables

(Farnetani et al. 1986). The difference is that in the onset the increase tends to be less significant, while in the rime it can even lead to phonologically relevant vowel lengthening or consonant gemination. Similarly in tone languages and pitch accent languages, pitch movement in a sonorant consonant may be contrastive in the coda but not in the onset; in fact, when tone bearing coda consonants are resyllabified into the onset of the following syllable, their tones are delinked (Hyman 1984). The diachronic correlate of the irrelevance of the onset to the rhythmic weight of the syllable is that vowels are never or hardly ever phonologically lengthened to compensate for the deletion of a preceding consonant, even though word medial consonants often actually have greater duration in the onset than in the coda. Apparent counterexamples involve intermediate rules such as metathesis of the deleted consonant from the onset to the coda.

Duration, rhythmic alignment, gestural overlap

When subjects were asked to produce syllables as fast as possible, they were able to produce a CCV-syllable like *sku* faster than a VCC-syllable like *usk*, and even a CCCV-syllable like *sklu* faster than a VCC-syllable like *ulk* (Mackay 1974). In some languages, such as Tamil (S.E. India: Balasubramanian 1980), vowels in syllables without a consonant onset are longer than their counterparts in syllables with a consonant onset, but not by nearly enough to compensate entirely for the absence of the onset: syllables of the structure V̆ averaged 64 msec, those of the structure CV̆ 96 msec; similarly V̄ 119 msec, CV̄ 159 msec. The same was true of Slovene (Srebot-Rejec 1988). In Italian, vowels in syllables lacking an onset tended to have slightly greater duration than vowels in syllables having a single consonant onset, but this effect was not found consistently for all consonants: a trilled *r* onset had the effect of lengthening the following vowel (Farnetani et al. 1986). The presence of an onset contributes to the overall duration of the syllable even when there is some compensation or durational coarticulation (Fowler 1981). Not only the presence of an onset but also its nature can affect the duration of the nucleus: in general, the more consonants in the onset, the shorter the vowel (Fowler 1983); the second vowel of the nonsense word *astrád* was found to be shorter than than of *asád* and *atád* (Rapp 1971). In Italian, vowel duration was found to correlate with onset complexity for the series *rana – grana – sgrana* (Farnetani et al. 1986). However in general, coda consonants have a greater shortening effect than onset consonants (Fowler 1983). When speakers were asked to produce identical stressed syllables in time with a metronome, both onset and nucleus were isochronous, but when they were asked to produce rhyming syllables with alternating single consonant and cluster onsets, such as *sad strad sad strad*, the onsets did not remain isochronous, but the syllables starting with clusters were abutted more closely to their predecessors than were those starting with a single consonant (Fowler et al. 1981). This suggests that the reference point used to align the syllables was not the acoustic beginning of the onset (p. 95), but it was not the beginning of the vowel either: the nature of the onset contributed significantly to the location of the reference point. In word initial onset clusters of the type *s* + stop the gesture for the vowel starts at the achievement of the target of the first consonant and almost completely overlaps the cluster, whereas in word final coda clusters of the type stop + *s* the vowel gesture is completed as the target of the first consonant is reached, so that the second consonant is independent of the vowel gesture (Browman et al. 1988). The fact that onset consonant clusters are almost completely overlapped by the vowel gesture while coda consonants are more independent could be interpreted as an explanation for, or a correlate of, the nonmoraic status of the onset and the moraic status of the coda. In Japanese, although temporal compensation within the mora is rather weakly attested (Beckman 1982), the duration of the onset is liable to be stretched or compressed as necessary to improve the regularity of timing between morae and probably between feet, but again the intrinsic duration of the onset does not contribute to the mora count (Port et al. 1987); formalisms which either exclude the onset from the mora, or include it on equal terms with the nucleus, fail to represent this relative situation. In English words of the structure CR_1VR_2C, where R_1 is a liquid and R_2 a liquid or nasal, the final obstruent is shorter than in words of the structure CVRC without a prevocalic liquid, which may suggest some degree of temporal compensation in the coda for the structure of the onset (Lehiste 1974). The weight of the onset is also one of the factors potentially affecting the order of elements in frozen expressions like *sea and ski*, *fair and square*, *helter-skelter*, *harum-scarum*, where the element with the lighter onset is placed first (Cooper et al. 1975).

The simplest and most direct way to test for the metrical relevance of the syllable onset, while holding other factors constant, is to compare the frequencies of the onset types Ø, C, CC, and CCC in two different metrical contexts, one which would be most sensitive to the added duration effected by C, CC, and CCC respectively, and the other less sensitive or completely insensitive to it. Resolved and unresolved third longa in the trimeter provide such contexts. So that initial clusters will be free to occur in this position, only dactylic and spondaic feet will be examined. The structure of the word initial onset of tribrach-shaped words, type

> ἄνοσος *Ion* 1201
> θύγατερ *Ion* 970
> πτέρυγα *Ion* 1143
> στροφίδας *Andromache* 718

is compared to that of the word initial onset of trochee or extended trochee-shaped words, type

> ἄνδρας *Ion* 832
> δοῦλος *Ion* 856
> πτηνὸς *Ion* 1196
> σκληρὰ Eur. *Supplices* 884.

If the onset is metrically relevant, then CC and CCC, at least, should be constrained in resolved as compared to unresolved third longum, and insofar as there is any chronological development, the constraint should be relaxed in later Euripides. Table 2.1 presents the data for resolved third longum in each of the four style groups of Zieliński and for unresolved third longum in the *Medea*.

The data of Table 2.1 offer no support for the metrical relevance of the duration of the syllable onset. The ex hypothesi more constrained position, resolution, in the strictest style, the Severior, has fewer zero onsets than the unresolved longum, and also fewer than in the Liber and Liberrimus; furthermore it has a higher frequency of CC onsets than the unresolved longum.

Another test of the relevance of the syllable onset is to compare the ratio of cluster onsets to single consonant onsets at the beginning of tribrach-shaped words located line initially, type πεδία *Heraclidae* 393, with the same ratio in tribrach-shaped words located after a word ending in a consonant in the resolved third longum, type ὅπλοις σφάγια *Heraclidae* 399. In the former class, the word initial onset would affect the duration of a short anceps, in the latter class the duration of the more sensitive resolution. In the two stricter styles of Euripides, the ratio of cluster to

TABLE 2.1
Test of syllable onsets

	#V %	#C %	#CC %	#CCC %
Unresolved	29.17	56.55	13.67	0.60
Resolution				
Severior	16.18	63.24	20.44	1.47
Semiseverus	12.90	72.04	13.98	1.06
Liber	22.26	53.17	24.20	0.00
Liberrimus	25.00	56.25	18.75	0.00

single consonant onsets is one to thirty-six in line initial tribrach-shaped words and one to five and a third (11:59) in tribrach-shaped words in resolved third longum. The ex hypothesi more constrained location has fewer of the supposedly favoured onset types than the less constrained position.

Muta cum liquida

An analysis of the metrical relevance of syllable onsets should include some discussion of syllables beginning with a sequence of consonants consisting of plosive plus liquid or nasal. It is widely held that such sequences are avoided after either vowel of a resolution (Zieliński 1925), because they confer additional duration (Irigoin 1959; Snell 1962; West 1970; Parker 1972; Ancher 1978).

It is clear from the typological evidence cited above (p. 31) that the prosodic variation associated with muta cum liquida in Greek is best explained in terms of varying syllable division. It follows that in a sequence of two light syllables, the onset of the second syllable may be either a single consonant or a tautosyllabic muta cum liquida cluster. The question arises whether the complexity and potentially greater duration of the cluster onset might be metrically relevant in a highly constrained metrical environment such as resolution. The simplest test for this is to compare the incidence of muta cum liquida as the onset of the light syllables of resolution with its incidence as the onset of heavy syllables following ordinary brevia. A more complex test would take account of confounding effects arising from the different frequencies of muta cum liquida clusters in different word shapes and from the relative facility with which each word shape can be located with the variant heterosyllabic division of the cluster. The results of the simpler test are presented in Table 2.2, in which column 1 gives the percentage of light syllables implementing the second syllable of a resolution that have muta

TABLE 2.2

Test of muta cum liquida onsets
in the second syllable of resolutions

	Resolution V̆.TRV̆ %	Even-numbered longa V̆.TRV̄/V̆C %
Severior	0.36	2.53
Semiseverus	2.93	2.89
Liber	4.15	3.35
Liberrimus	2.13	2.51

cum liquida onsets, type δάκρυα Hecuba 518, and column 2 gives the percentage of heavy syllables implementing even-numbered longa that have muta cum liquida onsets, type δυσπότμῳ Bacchae 1144. The data of Table 2.2 show that for all styles except the Severior, the rate of muta cum liquida onsets in the second syllable of resolutions is nearly identical to the rate in even numbered longa. The difference between the rate of 0.36% and 2.53% in the Severior is significant, but it does not follow that muta cum liquida onsets are metrically relevant because they add duration either to the second syllable of a resolution or to the whole resolution matrix. Rather, the difference is a reflex of a combination of factors: the compositional strategy used to avoid resolution in general in the strictest styles of the trimeter, the effect of morpheme boundaries on the syllabification of muta cum liquida clusters, and statistical tendencies in the phonological structure of Greek words. Most words with V̆.TRV̆ have no morpheme boundary before the muta cum liquida cluster, such as πατρίδος, μέτρια, δάκρυα, πότνια. In such words, the muta cum liquida can more readily be treated as heterosyllabic than in words in which it is preceded by a morpheme boundary (p. 35), and this option, which yields a cretic- or dactyl-shaped word, is preferred in styles in which resolution in general is avoided. This principle is confirmed by the fact that the only resolution with V̆.TRV̆ in the Severior has a morpheme boundary before the muta cum liquida cluster, namely ἄ-κριτον Hippolytus 1056, whereas uncompounded forms like ἄγριον Hippolytus 1214 occur as cretics in the Severior and with resolution only in later styles, as ἄγριον Eur. Electra 1116.

The traditional hypothesis of the metrical relevance of muta cum liquida is formulated in terms of muta cum liquida following either vowel of a resolution. This formulation seems to imply either some form of suprasyllabic computation or a degree of ambisyllabicity, the plosive element being thought of as belonging to some extent to the rime of the preceding syllable, whence the metrically relevant durational effects. Ambisyllabicity is favoured after a stressed vowel, and, if resolution is interpreted as a stress matrix (Allen 1973), such an effect might be postulated at least for the first syllable of a resolution. Ambisyllabicity before muta cum liquida has been suggested in English *likely* (Higginbottom 1964). The traditional hypothesis may be tested most simply by comparing the incidence of muta cum liquida following the short vowels of resolutions with its incidence following the short vowels of brevia. The results of this test are presented in Table 2.3. The first two columns of Table 2.3 give the percentages of vowels preceding muta cum liquida out of all vowels in each of the two syllables of resolutions, types δάκρυα Hecuba 518 and νεοχμόν I.T. 1162. Column three gives the average for both the first and the second vowels of resolutions, and column four gives

TABLE 2.3
Test of traditional hypothesis of muta cum liquida

	First vowel of resolution V̆.TRV̆ %	Second vowel of resolution V̆CV̆.TR %	Average in resolution V̆.TRV̆ + V̆CV̆.TR %	Breve V̆.TRV̄/V̆C %
Severior	0.36	3.62	1.99	2.53
Semiseverus	2.93	2.39	2.65	2.89
Liber	4.15	2.67	3.41	3.35
Liberrimus	2.13	3.06	2.60	2.51

the rate for brevia, which is simply the rate for the onsets of even-numbered longa repeated from Table 2.2. It is clear from the table that the average rates of muta cum liquida after either vowel of resolutions do not differ significantly from style to style, and that in any one style it does not differ significantly from the rate after brevia. The same holds true for muta cum liquida after the second vowel of resolutions. The data of Table 2.3 offer no support for the traditional hypothesis of the metrical relevance of muta cum liquida. The low rate of muta cum liquida after the first vowel of resolutions in the Severior has already been explained as a reflex of the fact that most eligible words are uncompounded trisyllables that could also appear as cretics. By contrast, the rate of muta cum liquida after the second vowel of resolutions in the Severior is much higher. This is because a high proportion of eligible words in this category are lexical or prefixal compounds in which the base begins with a muta cum liquida cluster

πολυ-πλόκοις *Medea* 481
δια-πρεπεῖς Eur. *Supplices* 841
περι-δρόμοις *Troades* 1197
μονο-τράπεζα *I.T.* 949.

It is less natural in Attic to treat the muta cum liquida clusters in these words as heterosyllabic; the necessity to avoid too strong a departure from Attic syllabification in dialogue exerts added pressure for these words to be used in resolution. This explains the observation that the average rates of muta cum liquida after either vowel of resolutions in the Severior is lower in tribrach-shaped words than in longer words (DS 1980).

Intrinsic vowel duration

Different vowels in identical contexts can have different durations, and these differences are generally correlated with tongue height. Lower vowels tend to have greater duration than high vowels. Low vowels typically show about 115% the duration of high vowels, with mid vowels tending to form an intermediate category. Languages in which vowel durations are more or less correlated with tongue height include English, German, Danish, Swedish, Finnish (Lehiste 1970), Slovene (Srebot-Rejec 1988), Tamil (Balasubramanian 1981b), Yoruba (Nagano-Madsen 1992), Japanese (Homma 1973; Nagano-Madsen 1992). The greater jaw movement associated with low vowels is normally assumed to be the physiological motive for their greater duration: the longer durations are due to longer travel times, not to longer steady states (Peterson et al. 1960; Lisker 1974; Westbury et al. 1980). This should not be taken to suggest that it would be physically impossible to perform the greater articulatory movements characteristic of *a* in the time allotted to the comparatively minor articulatory movements characteristic of *i*, but rather that greater movement requires greater time and that speakers do not completely correct vowel durations to make up for this discrepancy, even though the velocity of jaw closure for any consonant tends to increase with the distance the jaw has to travel to attain closure (Fowler 1977), and in labial consonants the lip gestures partially compensate for differences in vowel duration between open and close vowels (Lindblom 1990). Electromyographic study of a jaw lowering muscle revealed that the muscle fired not only more strongly but also for a longer duration for low vowels than for high vowels, indicating that intrinsic vowel duration was not a purely mechanical effect but under some form of neural control (Westbury et al. 1980; Keating 1985). When the jaw is fixed by use of a bite block or by having subjects clench their teeth, intrinsic vowel duration differences are reduced but not completely eliminated; this result might indicate that intrinsic vowel duration is partially due to nonmandibular factors such as mechanical effects of tongue movement or alternatively that speakers seek to maintain intrinsic vowel duration despite the artificial constraint of the fixed jaw (Smith 1987). Perception experiments indicate that speakers of Danish automatically compensate for intrinsic vowel length in evaluating the distinction between phonologically long and short vowels and between stressed and unstressed vowels (Petersen 1974; Rosenvold 1981). There is also some evidence for apparent compensation in production: in mora-timed Japanese, as already noted (p. 57), at least for the reading of words in repeated carrier sentences, the duration of the onset (and of the nucleus of the following syllable) can be adjusted to compensate for differences in the intrinsic duration of the nucleus, thereby regularizing mora timing. In English stressed monosyllables, two out of three subjects in one study showed a decrease in the duration of a coda consonant when it followed an intrinsically longer vowel (Munhall et al. 1992).

The metrical relevance of intrinsic vowel duration can be tested by comparing the intrinsically shortest vowel *i* with the intrinsically longest vowel *a*: a fortiori, if the difference between *a* and *i* is not relevant, the smaller differences between other pairs of vowels will not be. The test compares the frequencies of short *a* and *i*, with the other short vowels treated together, in a hierarchy of metrical locations: resolved third longum, third breve, and short first anceps. For resolution the first two vowels of the tribrach-shaped word are considered (type μιγάδες *Andromache* 1142, σφάγιον *Hecuba* 305, προδότιν *Andromache* 630), for breve and anceps the first syllable of iamb-shaped words (type φίλαι *Medea* 765, κάλων *Medea* 770, λόγους *Medea* 773). In Table 2.4 the resolution data are reported according to the four Zielinskian style groups; for breve and anceps the frequencies are given from the iambographers (Archilochus, Semonides, Solon) and the *Medea*. If intrinsic vowel duration is metrically relevant, one would expect *a* to be more constrained in resolution than in anceps or breve, and *i* to be more frequent in resolution than in anceps or breve.

The data of Table 2.4 offer no support for the metrical relevance of intrinsic vowel duration. There is no statistically significant difference between anceps and breve in the direction required for metrical relevance; on the contrary, the iambographers have a higher frequency of *a* in breve than in anceps and the *Medea* has a lower rate of *i* in breve than in anceps. This is the reverse of what would be predicted on the basis of metrically relevant intrinsic vowel duration. Furthermore, in all periods the frequency of *a* is greater in resolution (in tribrach-shaped

TABLE 2.4
Test of intrinsic vowel duration

	$\breve{a}$ %	$\breve{\iota}$ %	other $\breve{V}$ %	$\breve{a}:\breve{\iota}$ ratio
Anceps				
Iambographers	15.63	6.25	78.13	2.50
Medea	23.58	11.32	65.09	2.08
Breve				
Iambographers	28.80	11.20	60.00	2.57
Medea	19.50	8.67	71.83	2.25
Resolution				
Severior	35.53	17.67	46.71	2.00
Semiseverus	27.57	17.19	57.01	1.50
Liber	29.53	17.11	53.36	1.73
Liberrimus	33.64	10.91	55.45	3.08

words) than in anceps. These results indicate that the durational difference between *a* and *i* is not metrically relevant. It follows that it is not
a major factor in Greek speech rhythm, either because it is simply not
substantial enough or because it is at least partially compensated for by
the inversely correlated durations of neighbouring segments, thereby
minimizing its influence on syllable and foot duration. In the choliambs
of Babrius, which belong to the imperial period, there is a clear preference for -ă over other vowels in lines ending in a final short vowel. Intrinsic duration differences can be exaggerated when vowels are lengthened
under stress or by final lengthening; for instance, the ratio of finally
lengthened *a* to *i* can be greater than the ratio of medial *a* to *i*. It may
be that, in the particular context of line end, intrinsic vowel length differences became substantial enough to be metrically relevant in Babrius.

Contextual vowel duration

In English, Danish, Spanish and Tamil, vowels before labial stops were
found to be shorter than vowels before dental and velar stops; in English
vowels before *f* are shorter than vowels before *s* and *ʃ*. This phenomenon is plausibly interpreted as reflecting the extent to which an articulator has to move: labials, which do not use the same articulators as
vowels, can follow a vowel with minimum delay, whereas dentals and
velars require the mobile tongue tip and the comparatively less mobile
blade of the tongue respectively to move from the various vowel positions to the consonant closure posture. The fact that vowels are longest
before retroflex consonants in Tamil suggests that this interpretation is
well founded, since the curling back of the tongue tip is a relatively
complicated and time consuming articulatory gesture. The voicing of
a following homosyllabic or heterosyllabic consonant affects the duration of a vowel in English: for instance vowels (as well as postvocalic
liquids and nasals) are significantly longer before *d* than before *t* and
before *z* than before *s* (Peterson et al. 1960; Klatt 1976). The phenomenon is replicated to some degree in a number of other languages: Swedish, Dutch, Arabic (Port et al. 1980; Fant et al. 1989), Russian, Japanese
(10% Chen 1970; 20% Port et al. 1987). The average duration of a
medial Cv̆-syllable before a voiceless consonant was 129 msec in Yoruba and 148 msec in West Greenlandic Eskimo, as compared with 146
msec and 160 msec respectively before a voiced consonant (Nagano-
Madsen 1992). Various articulatory and perceptual explanations have
been offered for this effect (Kluender et al. 1988; Fowler 1992). However,
since it is not found in all languages and varies in strength from one
language to another, presumably with no correlated variation in the
nature of the triggering consonant, and since in Russian it applies before

voiced consonants that are subject to final devoicing, it cannot simply be an uncontrolled and biomechanically automatic event (Keating 1985). Listeners can use it as a cue, though not necessarily the only one (Parker 1974), to postvocalic voicing: in perception tests, it was found that judgements as to whether a postvocalic consonant was voiced or voiceless could often be changed simply by manipulating the duration of the preceding vowel (Raphael 1972). Vowels also tend to be shorter before coda clusters than before single consonant codas: one study found a shortening effect on the vowel of 13 msec, but this came nowhere near to compensating for the 97 msec increment due to the additional consonant; the shortening was mainly effected by anticipating the raising movement of the jaw (Munhall et al. 1992).

The metrical relevance of the influence of a following consonant on vowel duration can be tested by examining intervocalic consonant frequencies after short third anceps (type δοκῶν *Medea* 67, ἄγαν *Medea* 305, φόβος *Medea* 356), third breve (type πατήρ *Medea* 342, ὀδούς *Medea* 376, σοφός *Medea* 320), and after the second vowel of tribrach-shaped words in resolved third longum (type θάνατον *Andromache* 428, δρομάδα *Troades* 42, ἔλαβεν *Orestes* 502). The resolution sample is restricted to the second vowel of the resolution, so that the inherent duration of the consonants themselves will not contribute to the overall duration of the resolution matrix. The results are presented in Table 2.5 for third anceps and breve in the *Medea* and *Orestes* and for resolution in the four Zieliń-skian style groups; + vce indicates a voiced stop, – vce a voiceless stop, T/K a dental or velar stop and P a labial stop.

TABLE 2.5
Test of contextual vowel duration

	– vce %	+ vce %	ratio	T/K %	P %	ratio
Anceps						
Medea	38.76	10.08	3.85	79.41	20.95	3.86
Orestes	32.12	7.25	4.43	77.36	22.64	3.41
Breve						
Medea	33.20	9.31	3.57	82.58	17.42	4.74
Orestes	33.44	9.00	3.72	78.50	21.50	3.65
Resolution						
Severior	33.77	3.90	8.66	82.35	17.14	4.80
Semiseverus	27.97	13.51	2.07	85.39	14.61	5.84
Liber	24.41	15.05	1.62	83.26	16.74	4.97
Liberrimus	38.24	8.82	4.34	82.95	17.05	4.86

The data of Table 2.5 offer no support for the metrical relevance of differences in contextual vowel duration depending on the place of articulation of the following consonant. The rates for (abbreviating) labial consonants appear to be higher in the ex hypothesi longer anceps position than in resolution. In the case of the effect of stop voicing, however, the Severior does show a statistically significant rarity of voiced stops after the second short vowel of tribrach-shaped words in resolved third longum: a test of the difference between 3.90% in the Severior and 15.05% in the Liber yields a chi-square of 6.83. This difference, however, may be connected with the restricted vocabulary of Severior resolutions rather than motivated by any durational sensitivity of the metre (p. 142). It may be concluded that contextually motivated differences in vowel duration may have been at least partially compensated for in neighbouring segments and were in any case not substantial enough to make a significant impact on the rhythmic system of Greek speech.

Intrinsic consonant duration

There is a tendency in the languages for which experimental data are available for labial stops to be intrinsically longer than dentals and velars (and *m* longer than *n*); perhaps this is because labials, unlike dentals and velars, involve jaw movement, the jaw being more massive and less easily moved; and, as already noted, labials have more freedom to coarticulate with vowels. Voiceless stops tend to have longer closure duration than voiced stops, perhaps because it is difficult to maintain voicing over time during a period of oral closure; this latter difficulty is overcome by passive or active expansion of the oral cavity (Ohala 1983b). In Japanese intervocalic *p* was found to have 125% the closure duration of intervocalic *b* (Homma 1981). Voiceless fricatives tend to be among the longest sounds and single flap consonants such as one type of *r* among the shortest. Some of the distinctions in this section may be at least partially neutralized by the distinctions tested in the preceding section. In one study on Japanese, intervocalic voiced obstruents were 30% shorter than voiceless ones, but preceding vowels were 20% longer (Port et al. 1987); similarly for Swedish (Fant et al. 1989). Such prima facie compensation is not universal: in Polish, changing the voicing of an intervocalic stop changes the duration of the stop but not that of a preceding vowel (Keating 1985). Conversely, in Arabic changing the voicing of a medial stop affects the duration of the preceding vowel but not the duration of the stop itself (Port et al. 1980). Even in Japanese, there was no compensation in the preceding vowel for the greater length of fricatives as compared with stops (Port et al. 1987). Any compensatory effect in Greek would not be relevant to the particular test used

TABLE 2.6
Test of intrinsic duration of coda consonant

	(C)V̆P %	(C)V̆T/K %	ratio	(C)V̆m %	(C)V̆n %	ratio	CV̆s %
Iambographers	0.00	33.33	0.00	33.33	0.00	—	33.33
Severior	2.33	27.90	0.08	4.67	6.97	0.67	30.23
Semiseverus	5.26	36.85	0.14	10.52	10.52	1.00	31.56
Liber	3.58	17.85	0.20	10.73	21.88	0.49	32.15
Liberrimus	2.78	30.55	0.09	8.33	8.33	1.00	30.55
Aristophanes	5.00	29.99	0.17	5.00	20.01	0.25	22.51
Homer	2.94	23.53	0.12	5.87	32.34	0.19	14.72

in this section unless the postvocalic consonant belonged to the rime of the syllable tested.

The metrical relevance of the intrinsic duration of the coda consonant can be tested in the first syllable of the constrained shape s̄s̄s̄s̆̆ beginning in third anceps in the trimeter (types ἑπτάστομον *Bacchae* 919, κεκτήμεθα *Orestes* 267; ἐνδύσεται *Bacchae* 853, συμπλεύσομαι *Helen* 1067; δυσπραξία *H.F.* 57), and in words beginning s̄s̄... in the third biceps of the hexameter. Since it is only the differences in intrinsic duration between the various coda consonants that are being tested, the frequencies of those consonants must be calculated relative to the class of CV̆C-syllables, and not heavy syllables of all types. This procedure automatically controls for any potential differences in the rates of CV̄- and/or CV̆C-syllables which will be investigated below. The results are presented in Table 2.6 for the iambographers, the four Zielińskian style groups of Euripides, and Aristophanes, and for the third biceps in Homer. P indicates a labial stop, T/K a dental or velar stop.

The data of Table 2.6 offer no support for the metrical relevance of the intrinsic duration of the coda consonant. The various styles of the trimeter tend to have higher rates of the typologically longer CV̆s and CV̆m-syllables in anceps than the Homeric hexameter in biceps. Furthermore, the distribution of CV̆P- and CV̆T/K-syllables in the biceps of the hexameter is quite close to that in the anceps of the Severior style.

Contextual consonant duration

In general, consonants are also shorter when in clusters than when single next to vowels, although the degree of abbreviation, which can be as much as 30%, depends on the nature of the consonants comprising the cluster according to as yet rather unclear principles (Haggard 1973; Walsh et al. 1982). In English *the spy* the duration of both *s* and the closure

of *p* were less than in *the sigh* and *the pie* respectively (Klatt 1976); *s* in
the cluster *sp* was also comparatively short in French (O'Shaughnessy
1984) and in Italian (Farnetani et al. 1986). However, there is also the
potential for compensatory adjustment, since in postvocalic clusters the
duration of the *s* is inversely correlated with the duration of the following stop consonant (Schwartz 1970). In Estonian, stops were found to
be particularly short after nasals in intervocalic clusters (Lehiste 1966).
In Swedish, consonant durations are progressively abbreviated as the
length of the cluster increases (Lindblom et al. 1981). Coarticulation
of adjacent consonants can also lead to single gesture articulations, as
in the case of the affricate pronunciation of English *tr*. Durational reduction is possible in consonant clusters because, by comparison with a
consonant + vowel sequence, the vocal tract is relatively closed for a
consonant cluster and the articulators have shorter distances to travel;
moreover different consonants often involve different articulators, the
movements of which are to some degree independent of each other, so
that they can partially overlap in time. Such a temporal overlap, apart
from yielding more fluent and coherent articulatory movements, can
also have the effect of evening out part of the durational differences between equivalent units of rhythm. The temporal integration of consonant
cluster production tends to be less marked in child language than in adult
speech (Hawkins 1979). Notwithstanding the phenomenon of temporal
integration, it remains true that by and large the longer the consonant
cluster, the greater its duration. The duration of the intervocalic
consonant(s) including aspiration where present was found to be 100
msec for *a peach*, 180 msec for *a preach*, 235 msec for *a speech* and 300
msec for *a spree* (Gay 1979). The metrical relevance of consonant cluster duration in the syllable onset is tested in Table 2.1.

Rime structure

So far, the analysis of the syllable rhyme has been directed towards testing
for the metrical relevance of differences in the intrinsic or contextual
duration of individual segments. The next step in the analysis is to
proceed from segmental differences to major differences in syllable structure, such as those relating to phonologically distinctive vowel length
(CV̆ – CV̄, CV̆C – CV̄C) or to the presence versus the absence of a coda
consonant (CV̆ – CV̆C, CV̄ – CV̄C). The different syllable structures first
need to be arranged into a hierarchy of syllable weight on the basis of
typological evidence. The relevance to Greek metre of the various typologically established distinctions can then be tested. For syllable structure, experimental measurements are no longer the major source of
typological evidence. The categories involved are now important enough
to play a large role in the operation of phonological rules, particularly

those for the location of a stress accent. Furthermore, as will emerge from the ensuing discussion, there is reason to believe that the categories of syllable weight are not uniquely determined by the factor of duration. It is important to bear in mind that syllable weight hierarchies need to be interpreted with reference to the nature of the rule on the basis of which they are evinced. Lengthening rules privilege structures that are already long and those that are easier to lengthen, that is more vocalic. Shortening rules privilege structures that are easier to shorten, again those that are more vocalic. And rules mapping tonal excursions to structures privilege those that are suitable carriers of tone, again those that are more vocalic, and those that are long enough for the excursion to be comfortably accommodated.

The typological study of stress location is very revealing, but, unfortunately, not itself entirely unambiguous. It is likely that stress, in addition to being sensitive to the weight a syllable intrinsically possesses, is also sensitive to the phonetic and phonological ease or difficulty with which that syllable can be rendered even more heavy or prominent, and it is not necessarily the case that this latter factor need be a component of the definition of syllable weight, particularly with respect to quantitative metre. Of the various prosodic properties to which stress is attracted, inherent duration and the ability to carry incremental duration are the most important factors. Pitch also plays a role, as for example in Ayutla Mixtec (Pankratz et al. 1967), but the suggestion that $C\bar{V}$ is a preferable location for stress as against $C\bar{V}C$ because $C\bar{V}$ can more easily carry the pitch movements often associated with stress than can $C\bar{V}C$ is at best only part of the explanation. In Karok (California: Bright 1957), stress is located preferentially on a long vowel in words in which all vowels have low tone. In Djuka (a Surinam creole: Huttar 1972), stress goes preferentially on a long vowel of whatever tone; if the word has no $C\bar{V}$-syllable, it goes on the first High-toned $C\check{V}$-syllable, and in the absence of any High tone, it goes on the penultimate $C\check{V}$-syllable. The hierarchy of syllable types is therefore: $C\bar{V}$ > High-toned $C\check{V}$ > Low-toned $C\check{V}$: durational prominence takes precedence over pitch prominence in this language.

Light syllables

In a survey of over four hundred languages (Hyman 1977), syllable weight was found to influence stress location in two dozen languages. In all instances, stress was preferentially located elsewhere than on $C\check{V}$-syllables. $C\check{V}$-syllables are clearly established as a category distinct from other syllables and occupying a lower rank on the hierarchy of syllable weight. Whereas the large differences of duration associated with phonological vowel length can affect stress location, the mostly, but not always, comparatively small differences of intrinsic and contextual vowel duration do not seem to affect the basic rules of a stress system. However, in some languages, stress seeks out full vowels as opposed to reduced, centralized vowels: such is the case in E. Cheremis (Russia: Greenberg et al. 1976; Hayes 1981); stress is sensitive to a similar binary categorization of vowels in some dialects of Komi (Russia: Kiparsky 1973). In Gujarati (Greenberg et al. 1976) there may be a three point hierarchy of stressability: a, other full vowels, $ə$; the distinction between open and closed syllable is a secondary factor. It is not known if differences in intrinsic duration alone are responsible for such rules, or if they also reflect differences of sonority (intrinsic acoustic intensity or some integrated measure of intensity and duration) or different degrees of physiological effort required for different articulatory gestures. Open vowels have greater sonority than closed vowels, the difference in acoustic intensity being about 5 dB (p. 197). The open oral cavity associated with a provides less acoustic impedance than the comparatively closed oral cavity associated with i. That such differences are not metrically relevant in Greek is established by the data in Table 2.4.

Heavy syllables

The next question to be addressed is the position of CV̆C-syllables in the hierarchy of syllable weight. There is evidence from a number of languages that CV̆C-syllables can occupy the mid-section of a three point hierarchy of stressability. In Maltese Arabic, stress is preferentially located on the last (or only) CV̄(C)-syllable; if there is no CV̄(C)-syllable, then on the last (or only) CV̆C-syllable; if there is no CV̄(C)- or CV̆C-syllable, then on the penultimate CV̆-syllable (Borg 1973). In Klamath (Oregon: Barker 1964), stress is preferentially located on CV̄-syllables; in the absence of CV̄-syllables in the word, it is placed on penultimate or antepenultimate CV̆C-syllables. In Luiseño (California: Bright 1965), the rule holds that, morphological conditioning apart, a word is obligatorily stressed on the first syllable if that syllable occupies a higher point on the ternary syllable weight hierarchy CV̄ > CV̆C > CV̆ than the second syllable; a similar sort of rule applies in S.E. Tepehuan (Mexico: Willett 1982). Axininca Campa (Peru: Black 1991) has a hierarchy CV̄ > CV̆N > CV̆. Counterevidence is not very strong: one analysis of Dutch posits CV̆C > CV̄, and Seneca (New York) is cited as a language which has long vowels but assigns stress on the basis of whether a syllable is open or closed irrespective of vowel length (Stowell 1979; Lahiri et al. 1988). Phonologists have in the past tended to think of syllable weight as relevant only in languages having phonologically distinctive vowel length. But in a number of languages from the Pacific area which do not have phonologically long vowels, primary or secondary stress is preferentially located on closed rather than open syllables (CVC > CV): Kunimai-pa (New Guinea: Pence 1966), Maung (N. Australia: Capell et al. 1970), Aklan (Philippines: Hayes 1981). In Sentani (New Guinea: Cowan 1965), stress is retracted from a penultimate open syllable to the antepenultimate syllable if and only if the vowel of the penultimate syllable is centralized and the antepenultimate syllable is closed. In other languages, CV̆C is classed with light syllables, that is stress seeks out vowel length and ignores coda consonants: some stress location rules in Karok (Bright 1957), Huasteco (S.E. Mexico: Larsen et al. 1949), Selkup (Siberia: Tranel 1991), Nunggubuyu (N. Australia: Hughes et al. 1971) and Polabian (Trubetzkoy 1969) work this way. CV̆C-syllables also differ from CV̆-syllables distributionally in relation to stress, in that in some languages such as Italian and Yupik (Siberia, Alaska: Miyaoka 1971; Krauss 1985; Goldsmith 1990) CV̄-syllables are always stressed, whereas CV̆C-syllables may be stressed or unstressed. In Yupik, noninitial CV̆C-syllables are light, that is like CV̆-syllables they do not inherently attract stress; if stress is assigned to a CV̆-syllable, the short vowel is lengthened, but if stress is assigned to a CV̆C-syllable the vowel is not lengthened. In Carib (Guiana: Peasgood 1972), for the purposes of the accent, CV̆C-syllables are heavy like CV̄-syllables, but for the purposes of the rhythmic system they may be either strong (like CV̄-syllables) or weak (like CV̆-syllables). Such distributions could be explained as resulting diachronically from an earlier stage in the languages concerned at which CV̆-syllables were lengthened under stress and/or CV̄-syllables shortened when unstressed. However, the converse situation also exists. In the Slovak rhythm rule, CV̄-syllables are heavy enough to trigger the vowel shortening rule, but CV̆C-syllables are not. The Slovak rule is not a historical relic: in children's play language in both Slovak and Czech V̄ is copied as V̆ (Trubetzkoy 1969; Kenstowicz 1972; Birnbaum 1981). The above facts when taken together suggest that CV̄-syllables attract stress more than CV̆C-svllables and do so not merely because they are easier to lengthen further under stress, but also because they are inherently heavier. In light of this evidence, theories that assume radical reductions to explain Latin brevis brevians in closed syllables (Corssen 1870; DS 1980b) may be unnecessary.

For stressing, the static and the dynamic factors work in the same direction. For the reduction of unstressed syllables, however, the static and the dynamic factors work in opposite directions. From a static point of view, CV̆C is lighter than CV̄, but from a dynamic point of view CV̄ is easier to shorten than CV̆C. There is ample diachronic evidence that V̄ > V̆ is more readily admitted than V̆C > V̆. In Vulgar Latin all unstressed long vowels are shortened, but coda consonants in unstressed syllables are not subject to overall elimination, although there is a long standing tendency to shorten prestress geminates, the so-called *mamilla*-rule. The complete deletion of a segment results in a greater loss of information than the reduction of a segment from long to short status, and the omission of an articulatory gesture represents a more significant departure from the speech production goal than the mapping of a segment onto a shorter timing unit.

The durational difference between short and long vowel in languages which, like Greek, have phonologically distinctive vowel length is quite significant. The relative durations of short and long vowels have been measured in a number of languages, and it emerges that, other things being equal, short vowels have roughly 50% the duration of long vowels or less. Such is the case for Danish with 50.5%, Finnish with 44.1% in the first syllable (Lehiste 1970), and Tamil with 49–55% in the first syllable (Balasubramanian 1981b) and Yakut (Siberia: Krueger 1962) with 33–50%. These ratios are likely to vary according to speech tempo (p. 227): the figures for *a* in West Greenlandic Eskimo were 41% in slow speech and 36% in normal speech (Nagano-Madsen 1990c). The equation $\bar{V} = 1.9\breve{V} - 45$ msec was suggested as covering a range of different speech rates for stressed vowels in Swedish (Fant et al. 1989). A difference in vowel quality often accompanies the quantity distinction.

While the distinction between $C\breve{V}$ and $C\bar{V}$ correlates with a major and consistent difference in duration, such measurements as are available do not suggest any significant durational difference between $C\breve{V}C$ and $C\bar{V}$; if anything, $C\breve{V}C$ tends to be marginally longer. Evidence has already been cited (p. 29) that in a language like Italian the timing of the vowel gestures is almost the same whether the structure is $C\bar{V}.CV$ or $C\breve{V}C.CV$. Data on the duration of various syllable types in Tamil and Colloquial Meccan Arabic (unstressed syllables; Ohsiek 1978) are cited in Table 2.7. In Japanese, the duration of $C\breve{V}C\breve{V}$ up to the burst of the onset consonant of the second syllable was marginally less than that of $C\breve{V}CC\breve{V}$ (Port et al. 1987), and $C\breve{V}C$-syllables in which the coda con-

TABLE 2.7
Durations of syllable structures

Syllable type	Average duration (msec)	
	Tamil	Meccan Arabic
$C\breve{V}$	96	74
$C\breve{V}C$	167	150
$C\bar{V}$	159	149
$C\bar{V}C$	227	—

sonant is the nasal have been reported as having greater duration than CV̆-syllables (Hoequist 1985); no significant difference in overall duration was found between a proceleusmatic-shaped word and a spondee-shaped word with moraic nasals (Nagano-Madsen 1991). In Southeastern Finnish dialects, disyllabic words of the shape CV̆C.CV̆(C) had 3–9% greater duration than disyllabic words of the shape CV̄.CV̆(C) (Leskinen et al. 1985). In Swedish, V̄C was found to be on the average about ten percent longer than V̆CC (Fant et al. 1989). For West Greenlandic Eskimo, in slow speech, which is mora timed, the durations of consonant mora and vowel mora were very comparable, clustering around 130 msec; this relationship did not apply at normal speech rates (Nagano-Madsen 1990c). If duration cannot explain why CV̆C-syllables are ranked lower than CV̄-syllables in the hierarchy of syllable weight, then one possibility is that the overall sonority of the rime is also involved, since consonants have less sonority than vowels. Another possibility is that stress location is sensitive not only to the weight of the complete rime but also to the weight of the segment that is rendered more prominent by stress. For CV̄-syllables, this is the long vowel; for CV̆C-syllables the durational increment often falls predominantly on either the short vowel or the following consonant rather than equally on both. It may be that the rules for stress assignment in Maori support this approach (Hohepa 1967). In Maori, both primary and secondary stress are located according to the following order of preference: long vowels or long diphthongs > short diphthongs > short vowels. There is no significant durational difference between long vowels and short diphthongs, but long vowels are heavier; diphthongs cannot be interpreted as vowel plus glide, and there are no closed syllables in Maori (Hohepa pers. comm. 1983).

For the motor theory of syllable weight (Allen 1973), duration is not an independent factor in the determination of syllable weight, the crucial factor being rather syllabic arrest. On this theory, light syllables are unarrested; CV̆C-syllables are orally arrested by the coda consonant; CV̄-syllables are described as thoracically arrested (p. 10); the fact that both types of heavy syllable are arrested explains their functional equivalence in the rhythm of the language. Hierarchies of light syllables, like the three types of light syllable in Gujarati, cannot be explained in terms of arrest except by assuming different degrees of arrest correlating with different degrees of vowel strength. Unless it is assumed that articulatory arrest is weaker than thoracic arrest, arrest is a binary feature which can be either present or absent; it cannot by itself account for ternary hierarchies of the type CV̆ > CV̆C > CV̄. Another difficulty is the possible existence of light arrested syllables. The structure CVʔ (ʔ is a glottal stop) seems to be light in Cayapa (Ecuador: Lindskog et al. 1962; Hyman

1977, 1985), Capanahua (Peru: Loos 1969; Safir 1979) and Zoque (Mexico: Goldsmith 1990). In the Thai chăn metres, which are quantitative,
CV̆C and CV̄ are heavy and CV̆ʔ and CV̆ are light (Hudak 1986). Provided the laryngeal feature cannot be treated as suprasegmental (Yip 1982)
or as part of the nucleus, one simple explanation would be that these
glottal stop syllables are light because they have insufficient duration
to be heavy: a glottal stop tends to shorten a preceding vowel, as in Karen
(Burma: Jones 1961), Burmese (Okell 1969) and Copala Trique (Mexico: Hollenbach 1988). In Chitimacha (Louisiana: Hyman 1985) closed
syllables with full vowels (CVC) are heavy but closed syllables with
reduced vowels (CəC) are light. One way of interpreting this situation
is again to assume that very short closed syllables can be light. The
evidence just collected is difficult to integrate into the theory of thoracic
arrest.

The metrical relevance of the heavy syllable weight hierarchy can be
subjected to an initial test by examining the relatively unconstrained
medial syllable of the molossus-shaped word in third anceps across a
range of styles of the trimeter (type ἐκπηδᾷ *Bacchae* 705, ἐξάπτειν *H.F.*
1342) and also in the first biceps of the Homeric hexameter. The results
of this test are presented in Table 2.8, which gives the percentages of
CV̄ and CV̆C types out of all syllable types in this word shape in the
positions tested.

The data of Table 2.8 offer no support for the widely held view that
anceps is a position of smaller durational capacity than biceps and that
CV̆C had less duration than CV̄ in Greek. The biceps of the hexameter
has a lower rate of the CV̄ type than the strictest style of the trimeter
and a higher rate of the CV̆C type. The less strict styles of the trimeter
also stand in a relation to the strictest that is the opposite of the requirement for metrical relevance. Rather, the data in Table 2.8 suggest a
hierarchy CV̆C > CV̄, which as noted above, is a hierarchy of resistance

TABLE 2.8
Medial syllable of the molossus-shaped word

	(C)V̄ %	(C)V̆C %	ratio
Iambographers	85.71	11.43	7.50
Severior	67.37	22.45	3.00
Semiseverus	65.48	26.19	2.50
Liber	72.45	19.39	3.74
Liberrimus	59.15	28.17	2.10
Homer	63.38	24.79	2.56

to shortening and reduction. This interpretation is strengthened by the following considerations. The iambographers avoid CV̆C also in the penultimate syllable of the left extended molossus-shaped word (type φιλοκτήμων Solon 36.21, ἐκτελευτήσει Semonides 1.5). The rate of CV̆C in this word shape in third anceps in the iambographers is 6.25%, but in the *Medea* it is 44.00%; this difference is highly significant statistically, and it does not seem to be a side effect of other differences such as word order or vocabulary. The only substantial difference between the *Medea* and the iambographers in the composition of their sets of left extended molossus-shaped words is the absence in the iambographers of infinitives, particularly middle infinitives—which always give CV̆C or CV̄C in third anceps. However, since active infinitives occur among the molossus shapes in this position in the iambographers, their non-occurrence cannot be attributed to an exclusion of infinitives per se in this portion of the line. Furthermore, the avoidance of CV̆C in the iambographers declines steadily as one moves to less sensitive ancipitia. The ratio of CV̆C:CV̄ in the *Medea* to that in the iambographers is 4.44 for molossus and extended molossus shapes in third anceps; for palimbacchiac and left extended palimbacchiac shapes (type λείπουσιν Semonides 1.19, ὁρμαίνοντας Semonides 1.7) in second anceps the ratio of the ratios is 1.43; for palimbacchiac shapes in first anceps it is only 0.90, meaning that here the iambographers have a higher rate of CV̆C with 43.48% than the *Medea* with 39.43%. This phenomenon cannot be ascribed to a general avoidance of CV̆C in all metrical positions. For the same word shapes, mutatis mutandis, the ratios of the CV̆C:CV̄ ratios of the *Medea* to the iambographers are as follows: fourth longum 1.25, third longum 1.25, second longum 0.93 (all nearly equal), and first longum 0.67. The strong avoidance of CV̆C in third anceps is not replicated in the longum. This conclusion is theoretically instructive: it supports the hypothesis that the permissibility of heavy syllables in anceps is related to the reduction of heavy syllables in rhythmically weak positions, termed subordination in chapter 3, rather than to the stressing of syllables in rhythmically strong positions (Allen 1973), although neither process excludes the other. The metre is sensitive not only to the categorical distinction between heavy and light syllables but also to strength or heaviness relations that are introduced by lower level rhythmic rules.

The next step is to test for this difference in a word shape which is known on other evidence to be rhythmically difficult and subject to prosodic constraint in some styles of the trimeter: a suitable candidate is the word shape s̄s̄s̄s̆ˣ when the first syllable stands in third anceps (Knox 1932). Accordingly, it might be thought that, insofar as a heavy syllable was permitted in third anceps in such a word shape (type κεκτήμεθα *Orestes* 267, κηδευμάτων *Medea* 76), CV̆C would be preferred to

TABLE 2.9
Structure of the first syllable of $\bar{s}\bar{s}\bar{s}\overset{x}{\bar{s}}$-shapes

	(C)V̆C %	(C)V̄ %	ratio
Iambographers	25.00	75.00	0.33
Severior	32.50	56.14	0.58
Semiseverus	35.24	58.64	0.60
Liber	42.49	46.08	0.92
Liberrimus	39.05	54.02	0.72
Aristophanes	47.22	48.78	0.97
Homer	25.56	67.19	0.40
Plato	36.36	63.64	0.57

CV̄ in the strictest styles. The data are presented in Table 2.9 for the iambographers, the four Zielińskian style groups of Euripides, Aristophanes, a sample of Plato's *Laws*, and word initial syllables in contracted third biceps in Homer.

The data of Table 2.9 offer no support for a traditional durational interpretation of the syllable weight hierarchy in the constrained word shape $\bar{s}\bar{s}\bar{s}\overset{x}{\bar{s}}$. The rate in the iambographers is almost exactly the same as that in the supposedly longer biceps of the hexameter, and there is a trend from the iambographers to Euripides Liberrimus and Aristophanes in the opposite direction of that required for a durational interpretation. This trend again suggests a preference for CV̄-syllables as easier to reduce in rhythmically weak positions.

Superheavy syllables

In almost all languages, phonologically distinctive duration is limited to two categories, short and long. The best documented instance of a phonologically distinctive hyperbinary difference is in Estonian, where there are superheavy syllables that involve either overlong vowels or overlong consonants or both, as evidenced by the following minimal triads (Vihman 1974): *veri* 'blood' – *veeri* – 'spell' 2nd sg. impv. – *veeeri* 'edge' part. pl; *kalas* 'fish' iness. sg. – *kallas* 'bank, shore' – *kalllas* 'pour' third sg. pret. The ratios of the durations of the three degrees of vowel length in Estonian are 1.00 : 1.72 : 2.02 (Liiv in Lehiste 1970). In most cases, the overlong segments are the result of the loss of a short vowel from what was originally a disyllabic sequence (Lehiste 1978), as is the case for some overlong vowels in two North German dialect areas (Hock 1986); the number of syllables has been reduced but the underlying rhythmic pattern stays the same. It may be that the real synchronic organization is in terms of two binary distinctions rather than a single ternary distinction of duration (Prince 1980; Fox et al. 1987, 1989). Qualitative differences are associated with vowels of all three degrees of length. In Estonian folk songs the distinction between long and overlong is not metrically relevant. Another language that is reported to have three degrees of vowel length is Yavapai (Arizona: Thomas 1990). For languages that do not have overlong segments, superheavy syllables can arise when a coda consonant follows a long nucleus.

In terms of pure duration, it is evident from the Tamil measurements in Table 2.7 that CV̄C can be longer than CV̄/CV̆C by the same amount that CV̄/CV̆C is longer than CV̆. The additional duration of a CV̄C-syllable need not be realized entirely in the vowel: in Japanese, both the vowel and the coda consonant are longer in (trimoraic) CV̄C-syllables than in (bimoraic) CV̆C-syllables (Poser 1988, 1990); this suggests that syllable weight is controlled by a rhythm generator or internal clock and is not merely the fortuitous result of the stringing together of different segmental durations. Vowels in closed syllables tend to be somewhat shorter than vowels in open syllables (p. 29), so that in Greek the duration of the long vowel may have been less in CV̄C-syllables than in CV̄-syllables, just as it was probably less in CV̆C-syllables than in CV̆-syllables.

The preferential stressing of superheavy syllables is well established in both Arabic and Hindi (Allen 1983) in final syllables. Superheavy syllables occur also word medially in Hindi, but both linguists and native informants disagree over the stressing of crucial instances (M. Ohala 1977; Gupta 1987; Pandey 1989; Davis 1989); according to one discussion (Pandey 1984), word internally superheavy syllables always have primary or secondary stress in Hindi, whereas heavy syllables are sometimes unstressed. In Finnish tetrasyllabic words, if the third syllable is CV̆C, it has secondary stress, except that a final superheavy syllable sometimes attracts the secondary stress from the third to the final syllable (Hanson 1992). Superheavy syllables are avoided in Rigvedic cadences (Hoenigswald 1989). In Classical Persian verse, superheavy syllables implement a metrical trochee line internally, unless reduced to regular heavy syllables by sandhi resyllabification (Elwell-Sutton 1976; Hayes 1979; Heny 1981). An additional reduced vowel is pronounced at the ends of these syllables in the recitation of Persian verse by Turkish and Indian readers, but not by native speakers. In Urdu verse, very similarly, CV̄C scans as a trochee within the hemistich except before a pronounced caesura (Russell 1960); the Urdu convention may be an imitation of Persian. In some languages, final superheavy syllables have been phonologically analyzed as disyllabic (Repetti 1993).

Since languages generally organize durational differences into two categories only, overlong segments and superheavy syllables tend to be treated in one of two ways: either they can be shortened to ordinary long or heavy units, or they can be kept and classified as one type of long or heavy unit. In the case of vowels, almost all languages adopt the former strategy. For instance, in Greek, as in Luganda (Uganda: Tucker 1962), two short vowels can give a long vowel by contraction, but the contraction of a long vowel with a short vowel results not in an overlong vowel but in a long vowel. Homeric "distractions" like ὁρόω, ὁράασθαι are artificial creations to restore the necessary precontraction scansion, not evidence for an overlong contraction product. Superheavy syllables too tend either to be eliminated or to be categorized with heavy syllables. Languages in which CV̄C is nontrivially absent include Hausa and Bolanci (Nigeria: Newman 1972), Alabama (Texas: Rand 1968), Tewa (New Mexico: Hoijer et al. 1949) and Kaliai (New Britain: Counts 1969). CV̄C is eliminated diachronically and morphophonemically by vowel shortening, deletion of the coda consonant or vowel epenthesis. In Yokuts (California: Goldsmith 1990), epenthesis is favoured when there is no long vowel or long consonant available for shortening, thereby preserving the segmental material.

In Homer, final superheavy syllables arising by position are thought to be less frequent than they would be by chance, particularly at the end of the line (Drewitt 1908; Platt 1921; Parry 1928; Pipping 1937), although the effect of compositional strategies unrelated to the specific property of superheaviness has not been assessed; word internal -CV̄C- may also be rarer in the last two longa than elsewhere (Hoenigswald 1990).

The frequencies of CV̄C-syllables in long third anceps in the central syllable of the molossus-shaped word (type ἐξώστης Rhesus 322) and in the first syllable of the tetrasyllable of the shape S̄S̄S̄S̆ (type οἰμώγμασιν Bacchae 1112) are presented in Table 2.10 as percentages of all heavy syllables counted in Tables 2.8 and 2.9 respectively.

TABLE 2.10
Test of the metrical relevance
of CV̄C-syllables

	Molossus	Tetrasyllable
Iambographers	2.86	0.00
Severior	10.20	11.36
Semiseverus	8.33	6.12
Liber	8.16	11.43
Liberrimus	12.86	6.93
Homer	6.84	6.25

Although the data of Table 2.10 offer no statistically significant support for the metrical relevance of the distinction between superheavy and heavy syllables overall, the number of molossus and, particularly, tetrasyllable shapes available from the iambographers is quite small, and if the observed percentages were to hold in even slightly larger samples, the iambographers would indeed show a statistically significant tendency to avoid CV̄C syllables in third anceps. When tetrasyllables, molossus- and left extended molossus-shaped words are combined, the rate of CV̄C in the iambographers is 3.13% as compared with 11.42% in the Medea; this difference is statistically significant ($\chi^2 = 3.94$). Any such sensitivity has been effaced in the tragic trimeter. The fact that tragedy tends to have a higher rate of CV̄C in third anceps in both word shapes than does the purportedly longer biceps of the hexameter does not support a traditional durational account of these data. Superheavy syllables apparently resist reduction in anceps position both because they have an additional degree of intrinsic duration and because they are closed. However, there is no metrical evidence that they are systematically differentiated from heavy syllables in being assigned three rather than two units of rhythmical measurement (morae).

Prepausal location

It is clear from a number of languages that the rules determining syllable weight categorization in verse are not necessarily the same at the end of the line as they are line internally. In Hausa verse (Greenberg 1960), the last vowel of the line may be brevis in longo; most words in Hausa end in open syllables. Final brevis in longo may, like the quantitative metre itself, be based on the Arabic model, but it is supported by the prosodic properties of the Hausa language. In Hausa, the quantitative and qualitative distinctions between short and long vowels are not neutralized at the end of words, but before a pause short vowels are significantly lengthened and the associated qualitative differences are eliminated; in horn signalling, a final short vowel is represented by a long note of the horn (Greenberg 1941). In Classical Persian verse CV̆C is heavy prepausally, and CV̆ is not permitted at the end of the line; superheavy syllables scan as trochees within the line, as just noted, but as simple heavy syllables at various metrically or syntactically determined caesural positions (Elwell-Sutton 1976). In such cases, it is worth considering whether the metre could reflect an earlier stage of the language at which word final vowels had been lost prepausally but not within the phrase.

For word final position in general, that is not restricted to prepausal contexts, there are also various reports of syllable weight categorizations that differ from those for the rest of the word; many of these cases could likewise be explained as reflecting earlier loss of a word final vowel or consonant. In Malayalam (S.W. India: Mohanan 1982), CVC-syllables in which the last segment is a liquid are light morpheme finally but heavy morpheme internally for metrical purposes; in the colloquial language, word final liquids are pronounced with a following reduced vowel. Vowel lengthening in monosyllabic words with a rime structure V̆C in Icelandic and Ponapean points to word final V̆C being light (Itô 1988). In a number of Arabic dialects, CV̆C is light word finally but heavy word medially: this is the case for the stressing of Classical Arabic words by speakers of Cairene Arabic (McCarthy 1982). For the Moroccan Arabic stress rule, final CV and Cə are light, final CVC and CəCC are heavy. For the Estonian stress rule, CV̆C is light word finally but heavy elsewhere (Prince 1980). In Nez Perce (Idaho: Aoki 1970; Crothers 1979), there is a tendency for stress to be attracted from a light penultimate to a heavy final syllable: final CV̆C is light. In Menomini (Wisconsin: Pesetsky 1979), for the purpose of rules governing vowel length, CV̆C is heavy nonfinally and light finally; final CV̆C may be derived from CV̆CV̆. In all these cases, the final consonant is discounted in the computation of syllable weight. This phenomenon is often called "extrametricality," a term that is also used to describe cases when a larger constituent such as a whole syllable is invisible to the rhythmic computation underlying accent location. On the other hand, in other languages CV̆C is heavier than CV̄ word finally but lighter than CV̄ elsewhere. In Goroa (Tanzania: Hayes 1981), in words not having a long vowel stress falls on the final syllable if it is CV̆C, otherwise on the penultimate syllable. A similar rule is reported for Bhojpuri (N.E. India: Hyman 1977). Although such rules probably often reflect earlier stages of the language, the diachronic developments involved are themselves the consequence of the synchronic properties of final position. The final syllables of utterances, phonological phrases, and, to a lesser extent, words tend to be weaker than the central syllables in both suprasegmental and articulatory parameters. Final vowels, for instance, can have lower pitch, less intensity, reduced voicing, and more centralized articulation; if final lengthening falls on a stronger syllable earlier in the word or phrase, a final vowel can also have reduced duration. In Nyangumata (W. Australia: O'Grady 1964), the final vowel of an utterance is often voiceless; in Tarascan (Mexico: Foster 1969), most unstressed vowels are devoiced phrase finally. In Goajiro (Colombia: Holmer 1949), word final vowels are usually voiceless and final long vowels are shortened in some word shapes; in Zuni (New Mexico: Newman 1965), word final vowels may be devoiced. In Dakota final vowels have reduced duration (Boas et al. 1939). In quite a number of languages, Itonama for instance

(Bolivia: Liccardi et al. 1968), closed syllables occur word medially but not word finally.

The following analysis of brevis in longo in Greek provides evidence for a syllable weight hierarchy in prepausal position. It is important to note that the evidence for this hierarchy is based on the way it interacts with other factors such as phrase final lengthening and the rhythmic organization of certain tetrasyllabic word shapes in line final position. It is not the case that any phrase internal hierarchy would necessarily be identical to the prepausal hierarchy or metrically relevant for the mapping of syllables onto thesis and arsis line internally. In some word shapes there is no stylistic-diachronic evidence for any constraint on the application of brevis in longo to different syllable structures. Table 2.11 presents the proportions of different rime structures in the final syllable of iambic and pyrrhic disyllables at the end of the trimeter (types δόμους *Medea* 969, ἔχει *Medea* 778, φόνον *Medea* 795, χθόνα *Medea* 880) in three different styles of the trimeter; there is no discernible evidence for any greater constraint in the stricter styles.

However, in other more difficult word shapes the application of brevis in longo is clearly constrained. One instance involves proceleusmatic-shaped words at the end of the trimeter. If fifth longum is resolved in Euripides, the resolution is implemented on the first two syllables of a fourth paeon-shaped word, or in four late instances of a syntagmatic fourth paeon-shaped word (*Bacchae* 1260, *I.A.* 844, 1247, 1414), ending in -V̄(C) or -V̆C

βασιλέων *H.F.* 182

ἀναμένει *Andromache* 444

λεγόμενος *Ion* 1541.

Line final proceleusmatic-shaped words ending in -V̆ are excluded, as they are also in Aeschylus and Sophocles, although they occur rarely in Aristophanes

πολεμικὰ *Peace* 674.

TABLE 2.11

Rime structures in disyllabic words
at the end of the trimeter

	-V̄(C) %	-V̆C %	-V̆ %
Iambographers	58.34	27.27	14.39
Medea	58.62	25.52	15.86
I.A.	54.70	28.19	17.11

TABLE 2.12

Rime structures at the end of the pentameter

	-V̄(C) %	-V̆C %	-V̆ %
Archaic	68.17	23.87	7.96
Callimachus	59.67	27.62	12.71
Asclepiades	52.88	28.48	18.62
Antipater of Sidon	44.44	37.18	18.37
Antipater of Thessalonica	64.29	23.70	12.01
Philip of Thessalonica	44.39	42.86	12.63

Proceleusmatic-shaped words have an alternative nonfinal location with resolution implementing the two central syllables

ἀγόμεθα *Troades* 614;

this location is highly constrained too, but not as much as line final position. This is demonstrated by a comparison with words of the shape ŠŠŠ(C)V̆C. 20 words of this latter shape are located with resolution implementing the two central syllables as opposed to 5 line finally, whereas for the proceleusmatic shape (ending in -V̆) there are 19 instances none of which are located line finally; if the distribution of the type ending in -V̆C is taken as reflecting the relative preference for the two locations and if there were no constraint against the occurrence of the type ending in -V̆ line finally, then there would be less than a one in twenty chance that none of the type ending in -V̆ would be located line finally ($p = 0.0489$). So it may be concluded that the difference in rime structure between -V̆ and -V̆C is a significant factor in the mapping of tetrasyllabic words with resolution at the end of the trimeter: in these word shapes the rime structure V̆ is lighter than the rime structure V̆C prepausally. But there is no evidence for any constraint on V̆C in the same environ-

TABLE 2.13

Rime structures in paroxytones at the end of the pentameter

	-V̄(C) %	-V̆C %	-V̆ %
Archaic	84.97	10.88	4.15
Callimachus	79.57	13.98	6.45
Asclepiades	76.00	22.00	2.00
Antipater of Sidon	62.66	26.58	10.76
Antipater of Thessalonica	79.66	15.68	4.66
Philip of Thessalonica	73.08	19.23	7.69

ment. Out of all fourth paeon-shaped words ending in -V̆C beginning in third, fourth and fifth longum, 4.42% are located beginning in resolved fifth longum as compared with 6.26% for fourth paeon-shaped words ending in -V̄(C), a small difference which is not statistically significant; inclusion of the cases with resolution on the two central syllables of the word shape does not change the results of this test.

However, evidence is available from the pentameter that -V̆C is lighter than -V̄(C) prepausally. Table 2.12 gives the proportions of the rime structures -V̄(C), -V̆C and -V̆ in all word shapes for the archaic elegists Tyrtaeus, Mimnermus, Solon and genuine Theognis, and for Callimachus, Asclepiades, Antipater of Sidon, Antipater of Thessalonica and Philip of Thessalonica. The rate of final -V̆ is lower in the archaic pentameter than in each of the later poets, and the rate of final -V̆C is lower in the archaic pentameter than in all the later poets except Antipater of Thessalonica; correspondingly, the rate of final -V̄(C) is the greatest in the archaic pentameter. These differences are not merely side effects of the trend towards elimination of oxytone and perispomenon accentuation at the end of the pentameter and increasing preference for paroxytones (Hanssen 1883; Stephens 1985b). Table 2.13 reports rime structure rates for the final syllables of pentameters ending in paroxytones only: even with a control for accent type, it is clear that -V̆C is avoided at the end of the pentameter. So combining the evidence of the trimeter and the pentameter, it may be concluded that insofar as there is evidence for a hierarchy of rime structures prepausally, the order is -V̄(C) > -V̆C > -V̆.

The evidence of the trimeter and the pentameter for the syllable weight hierarchy in prepausal position is confirmed by the choliamb, which shows a strong trend towards the exclusion of both -V̆C and -V̆ at the end of the line (as well as a trend towards the exclusion of V̆C in the penultimate syllable). The data for these trends are presented in Table 2.14. In Hipponax, Callimachus and Herodas there is no tendency

TABLE 2.14
V̄(C)-rimes in the last two syllables
of the choliamb

	Penultimate syllable %	Final syllable %
Hipponax	58.33	59.58
Callimachus	65.51	61.79
Herodas	74.57	64.36
Babrius	92.55	97.33

TABLE 2.15
Rime structures in the last syllable of the choliamb
in disyllabic paroxytones with first syllable
long by position

	V̄(C) %	V̆C %	V̆ %
Herodas	72.45	19.39	8.16
Babrius	92.29	5.71	0.00

towards increasing paroxytonesis (Stephens 1985b), so that the increasing preference for V̄(C) cannot be the reflex of an accentual trend. Even in Babrius, where paroxytonesis is nearly exceptionless, the additional propensity for V̄(C) as compared with Herodas is not totally a side effect of paroxytonesis, as shown by the data in Table 2.15 for the rime structure of the final syllable of disyllabic paroxytones with V̆C-rimes in the first syllable, types βόσκω, φόρτον, πάντα.

Conclusion

As was anticipated on theoretical grounds, neither the syllable onset, including muta cum liquida, nor intrinsic or contextual segmental duration turned out to be relevant to those aspects of the rhythmic organization of speech that correspond to the mapping of syllables onto thesis and arsis in verse, with the exception of one instance of intrinsic duration under phrase final lengthening in the late choliamb. However, evidence was found for the metrical relevance of the difference between CV̄ and CV̆C, although these two syllable structures may well have had almost identical duration. The metrical relevance of this difference was not a general rule applying to any longum or long anceps, but was mainly restricted to long third anceps (in the word shapes tested). The difference between superheavy and heavy syllables was also metrically relevant under certain conditions. Consequently, it is not possible to sustain either the idea that segmentally based submoraic distinctions in duration are metrically relevant or the overly restrictive position according to which the metre gives evidence for no durational distinctions other than the binary distinction between heavy and light syllable. An explanation of these results in terms of traditional durationalist theory is not possible, since, in those word shapes in which there is a difference, the data indicate a preference in long anceps for CV̄ rather than for CV̆C. What these data suggest is a theory in which syllable sequences are phonologically processed into rhythmic structures for speech production. The nature of such a component of Greek prosody and the evidence for it will be investigated in the next chapter.

3 | Rhythm

THE PSYCHOLOGY OF RHYTHM

Rhythm is a central property of the natural world around us and of our perception of it. Any measurement in physics involving a frequency is a manifestation of rhythm. Rhythm is everpresent both in our daily experience of life, whether it be the succession of night to day and of winter to summer or the lapping of waves on the beach, and in our daily behaviour. Animals as well as humans exhibit rhythmic behaviour, which is basic to forms of locomotion such as flying and swimming, in addition to characterizing vegetative functions such as the heartbeat and respiration. At least some animals can also perceive auditory rhythm: frogs and crickets are apparently able to produce rhythmic calling songs in synchrony with artificial calling song models (Vos 1977), and starlings have been taught to discriminate between rhythmic and arrhythmic strings of 2000 Hz tones (Hulse et al. 1984). The earliest rhythmic behaviour of the newborn baby is sucking; infant babbling is syllabic and rhythmic, and one study found that as early as seven months of age a child can distinguish iambic rhythm from isochronous rhythm (Allen et al. 1977). Rhythmic behaviour learned by the child later on includes walking and, as will be seen, speech.

The Greeks themselves were pioneers in the theoretical investigation of rhythm. In modern times, rhythmic patterns have been studied experimentally for at least a century, sometimes from the perspective of verse rhythm, more usually in relation to the organization of memory or the perception and production of music. Although these psychological experiments test very basic human perceptual and psychophysical properties, with the exception of a few Japanese studies they have almost universally been conducted with subjects from the modern Western European cultural tradition, and where some doubt arises as to the cross-cultural validity of the results, they could perhaps be integrated with the available ethnomusicological evidence.

In a broad, general sense, any regular recurrence implies rhythm, but in a narrow sense rhythm implies a patterned temporal sequence in which the stimuli occur with a frequency within the range of about 8 to 0.5 events per second, or with durations in the range of 120 to 1800 msec. Slower stimuli tend to be perceived as discrete events not joined to each other in a rhythmic pattern, and faster recurrence leads to various other perceptions such as vibration or tone. Rhythm implies regularly occurring events, although accelerating and decelerating patterns can be learned and reproduced by synchronized tapping with some degree of accuracy (Ehrlich 1958). Although in principle rhythm is not restricted to any one modality, it is particularly associated with the auditory modality. Coding and reproduction are more accurate for (nonlinguistic) temporal patterns presented auditorily than for similar patterns presented visually (Glenberg et al. 1989); more generally, memory for both content and order was better when a list of items was presented auditorily than when it was presented visually (Drewnowski et al. 1980). Arrhythmia can be supramodal, discrimination and reproduction being impaired when rhythm is presented via hearing, sight, or touch (Mavlov 1980).

If someone is asked to tap his finger at a tempo of his own choice, the tempo chosen will vary greatly from one person to the next, unless they are identical twins, but one and the same person will be surprisingly consistent from one tapping session to another. An interval of about 600 msec between taps is fairly typical. Maximum tapping speed varies according to the part of the body doing the tapping and is in the range of 160–205 msec per tap (Keele et al. 1987). The phenomenon of spontaneous tapping tempo reveals a number of important properties of rhythm. First, rhythm is preferred to arrhythmia. In fact, when subjects were asked specifically to tap as irregularly as possible, they found it difficult to do so (Fraisse 1946). Secondly, as just noted, humans are predisposed to perform repetitive motor actions at a specific frequency falling within the range of frequencies perceived as rhythmic. Thirdly, and even more fundamentally, they have the ability to compute that frequency; in other words, spontaneous tapping implies some sort of internal clock.

Not only do people tap with spontaneous rhythm, they can also tap in time to a metronome or march and dance in time to music or work in time to a worksong: in general, this computational ability permits the synchronization of social activity (Shaffer 1982). What is interesting is that when a subject taps to a completely random and unpatterned temporal sequence, the tap follows the signal; just as in most human behaviour, the reaction follows the stimulus. But when one taps to a regular series of sounds, the tap is synchronized with the sound: in fact, the tap occurs about 30 msec prior to the stimulus, suggesting that what is synchronized is the auditory and the tactile perception. Tapping after the sound is actually more difficult, particularly when the interval between stimuli is less than 1000 msec (Fraisse 1966; Fraisse et al. 1971). If the experimenter delays one of the stimuli, the tap will occur at its rhythmically predictable point in time. The subject anticipates the stimulus in order to synchronize his tap with the stimulus. He has learned the pattern and is using it to perform the task of synchronization.

There is considerable evidence that humans can efficiently perform only one rhythmic motor task at a time. When subjects pressed one telegraph key with the left hand and another with the right hand in response to two different rhythms, the respective tapping rhythms interfered with one another unless they were harmonically related (Klapp 1979). A similar interference was found when tapping and repeating the syllable *la* to different rhythms (Klapp 1981), or when tapping and reciting a nursery rhyme (Peters 1977). A related difficulty was found with the perceptual monitoring of two temporal sequences (Klapp et al. 1985).

The linguistic evidence presented in chapter 2 indicated that syllables can be classified as having one or two, or more rarely three, morae, and that bimoraic rimes tended to have very approximately twice the duration of monomoraic rimes. This situation is not peculiar to language but reflects general properties of the psychology of rhythm. When subjects are asked to produce patterns of five or six taps having an interval structure of their choice, the durations of the intervals used fell into two categories only, one in the range of 200–300 msec and the other in the range of 450–900 msec (Fraisse 1946, 1956). A similar result was obtained when subjects were asked to reproduce patterns having unequal feet, for instance a group of three taps followed by two groups of two taps: each pattern produced used two intervals, a short interval averaging 320 msec for foot internal taps and a long interval averaging 645 msec for foot final taps; sometimes a dummy tap movement was inserted in the middle of the long interval (Essens et al. 1985). In another study, subjects were asked to imitate iambic and anapaestic auditory patterns by tapping: ratios of intervals between the onset of adjacent nonidentical tones were .25, .33, .40, .50, .60, .66, .75, .80. Only patterns in which the intervals stood in the relation .50 were correctly imitated; errors in reproduction of the other ratios were not random, but there was a systematic tendency for responses to move closer to a 1:2 ratio (Povel 1981). The subject is evidently aware that the ratio is not .50, but he underestimates or overestimates it in the direction of .50, striving to represent complex temporal relationships in terms of a simple 1:2 metrical structure. This and other perceptual studies of this type (Essens et al. 1985; Essens 1986;

Deutsch 1986) indicate that subjects code pattern intervals not in terms of absolute durations but relationally, and that relations other than 1:2 are disfavoured. This tendency toward a .50 ratio is not directly related to pure discriminability: the just noticeable delay in a pattern of otherwise isochronous tones was about 6% for intertone intervals of 200 msec and about 12% for intervals of 100 msec (Hirsch et al. 1990). When the experimental design forces subjects to compute ratios of duration, these just noticeable differences are not found. Subjects were able to distinguish iambic sequences consisting of noise bursts with the ratios of 1:2 and 2:3 from trochaic sequences with the ratios of 3:2 and 2:1, but were not able to distinguish one type of iambic or trochaic sequence from the other; this was true whether the native language of the subjects was English or Estonian (Fox et al. 1987). When the experiment was repeated with synthesized disyllabic speech stimuli in place of noise bursts, subjects were equally unable to perform the task successfully (Fox et al. 1989). The definitional 1:2 ratio is subject to modification in performance reflecting higher level hierarchical structure of the pattern, specifically grouping of the pattern elements into rising or falling rhythms and the demarcation and prominence relations of higher level structures. Similar factors condition the performance of music (Gabrielsson 1974; Bengtsson et al. 1983; Clarke 1985).

One of the best known and most fundamental characteristics of the human mind is its drive to relate and organize the information it is processing. The categories used to organize serial information are serial segments, or chunks as they are usually called: the most familiar everyday example of this process is the chunking of telephone numbers. Interest in chunking was stimulated by the observation that, while the capacity of short term memory was notoriously limited, it could be significantly increased if sequences of items were recoded into informationally richer chunks (Miller 1956). When asked if a pair of letters was part of a previously memorized letter sequence, subjects answered more rapidly if both letters belonged to the same chunk than if they straddled a chunk boundary (Johnson 1978). Error patterns in recall are quite different for a chunked sequence and an unstructured serially associated sequence. In the latter, errors tend to cluster in the middle of a sequence; in the former, they cluster at the beginning of chunks. Recall of the first item of a chunk implies recall of the following item in the same chunk more than recall of the last item in a chunk implies recall of the first item of the following chunk (Johnson 1970). Chunk organization is an intrinsic part of the learned sequence: learning the letter sequence SBJ FQLZ was no faster for subjects who had previously learned SB JFQ LZ than it was for subjects who had previously learned an entirely different sequence (Johnson et al. 1971). A second presentation of a string of digits with different chunking was not recognized as a repetition of its earlier occurrence (Bower et al. 1969), and the same effect was found with nonverbal material, namely minimelodies of five tones each not in key (Dowling 1973). When subjects were presented with a list of digits and instructed to rehearse them in groups of varying sizes, recall improved as group size grew from 1 to 2 to 3 and deteriorated as it further increased to 4 and 5 (Wickelgren 1964, 1967). Four-item sequences were treated as single chunks by half the subjects and as two chunks by the other half, and five-item sequences were almost invariably analyzed as either 2 + 3 or 3 + 2 (Johnson 1970). Pattern induction is such a basic cognitive activity that we have a propensity to look for and "find" patterns even when they are objectively not there. When presented with randomly sequenced binary events, subjects behave as though the stimuli were patterned and predict grouped subsequences of events (Simon et al. 1968). In particular, our perception of isochronous auditory events having a frequency within the range of rhythmical perception tends not to be a string of equipollent elements; rather, we have the impression that the sequence is grouped into subsequences of two or three, the most familiar instance being the tick-tock of a clock.

Many temporal patterns are made up not of identical repeating events but of objectively differentiated repeating events. The relative contribution of the prosodic properties intensity, duration and frequency to grouping has been studied experimentally since the turn of the century. In one famous early experiment (Woodrow 1909), when subjects were presented with a regular series of sounds lasting 135 msec followed by a silent interval of 615 msec of which every alternate sound had greater intensity, they uniformly perceived trochaic rhythm; that is, the less intense sound was grouped with the more intense sound in such a way that the less intense sound ended the foot. The next step in the experiment was to increase gradually the duration of the silent interval following the more intense sound and correspondingly decrease the duration of the silent interval preceding the intense sound, thereby maintaining a constant clock measure for the foot. As this was done, the perception of trochaic rhythm became progressively weaker until, passing through a neutral stage of ambivalent grouping, it began to change into iambic rhythm. The effect of varying the durations of the sounds and their following silent intervals in the absence of any difference in intensity was also studied both in this early experiment and in more recent ones. In general, the longer the relative duration of the period from the onset of one tone to the onset of the next, the more likely that longer element is to sound accented and to end the group, that is, the greater the likelihood of iambic grouping (Povel et al. 1981). If the tones are identical in duration and intensity, any change in frequency can be interpreted as an accent; frequency rises have a slightly stronger effect than frequency falls (Thomassen 1982).

Another study varied both tone duration and silent interval (Vos 1977). The first two tones and the first two following silent intervals were assigned durations of either 80 msec (short) or 320 msec (long), and the resulting pattern was repeated throughout the string. Subjects made a forced choice judgement as to whether the string was trochaic or iambic. When one of the tones was long and the other short, the long tone was judged prominent. When one tone was long and the other short and their intervals were identical (320_{80} 80_{80}), the string was judged iambic, that is the long tone was judged to end the foot. But when the long tone was followed by the short interval and the short tone by the long interval (320_{80} 80_{320}), the string was judged trochaic: the longer tone was prominent, but the longer interval demarcated the feet. When both tones were short but one interval was long and the other short (80_{320} 80_{80}), the tone followed by the longer interval was perceived as foot final and so the string was judged iambic. The staccato nature of many of these experimental stimuli — as compared to the relatively legato prosody of speech in which nondemarcative periods of silence are associated only with the closure portions of stop consonants — is very useful, since by uncoupling tone duration from silent interval duration, it tends to confirm the idea that whereas the strength of the signal cues the accent, the duration of the silent interval cues the end of the group. When subjects were instructed to produce patterns described to them in terms of the number of taps per foot, they spontaneously used short intervals for foot internal taps and long intervals for foot final taps (Essens et al. 1985).

It is pointed out in a number of experimental studies (Woodrow 1909; Fraisse et al. 1954; Handel et al. 1975; Povel et al. 1981) that the pattern structure initially presented to subjects can determine the outcome of the analysis, and various strategies have been adopted to circumvent this socalled orientation effect (Preusser et al. 1970). The orientation effect was also critical when subjects were asked to classify Dutch recited verses as iambic or trochaic (Loots 1980). One factor that can counteract the orientation principle is that subjects rarely if ever analyzed a pattern as beginning in the middle of a run of identical sounds (Royer et al. 1970). When taken together, run unity and orientation effect suggest that pattern perception is a hypothesis testing activity that starts at the beginning of the stimulus and privileges hypotheses that do not require the pattern to start in the middle of a foot. One study took a repeating eight element sequence of alternating tones such as HH LL HL HL; when pauses were inserted after even numbered tones, i.e. at run induced foot boundaries, subjects almost always recognized the tonal pattern, but when pauses were inserted after every third element, thereby splitting the feet, the tonal pattern was only correctly recognized about half the time (Handel 1973).

The grouping of tones into feet has been observed to depend on tempo in a number of different studies (Bolton 1894; Fraisse 1956; Handel et al. 1981; Povel 1984); the faster the tempo, the more tones are grouped into a foot. Tempo likewise affects the identification of the beat in music perception (Madsen et al. 1986). When asked to tap to the perceived beat, musically trained subjects reacted to faster stimuli by tapping at half the presented rate and to slower stimuli by tapping at double the presented rate (Duke in Radocy et al. 1988). The processing of relatively rapid tempi having intertap intervals of about 250 msec may involve different mechanisms from the processing of slower tempi having intertap intervals of 500 or 1000 msec, since children younger than four years and a brain damaged subject synchronized well with the former but not with the latter (Kohno et al. 1991); speech syllables at ordinary speech rates fall mostly into the former category.

Some letter chunking studies have produced evidence for superordinate grouping into metra (Johnson 1970; Keeney 1969). Subjects presented with continuous sequences of evenly spaced identical sounds grouped them not only into feet but also into metra, and judged not only one sound in the foot to be stronger than the other but also one foot in the metron to be stronger than the other (Woodrow 1951). The psychological reality of more complex hierarichical foot organization, involving correlates of linguistic phrases and verse hemistich and stichos, was studied in a number of investigations of pattern organization (Restle et al. 1970; Restle 1970; Restle 1972): the error rate in recall at the metron boundary was less than at the hemistich boundary and the error rate foot internally was the lowest of all; the distribution of error rates (lower within any domain than across the boundary between two such domains) indicated that subjects were using a hierarchical analysis and not sequential association or random chunking. In finger tapping an eight element sequence using the index and middle fingers with alternating hands, subjects organized the sequence as a binarily branching tree, since intertap intervals were greater between metra than between feet and greater between feet than foot internally (Rosenbaum et al. 1983); similar results were obtained with other tree structures and other finger combinations (Collard et al. 1982).

RHYTHM IN SPEECH

Phonological evidence

To both ordinary speakers and trained phoneticians, speech sounds rhythmical (Fowler 1983). Even young infants are able to discriminate a sequence of trisyllabic words from a sequence of disyllabic words (Bijeljac-Babic et al. 1992) and a disyllabic word with trochaic stress from one with iambic stress (Jusczyk et al. 1978). The essentially rhythmic nature of speech is attested by a considerable amount of evidence, both phonological and experimental. In the former category one thinks immediately of the many languages from all over the world having stress on alternating syllables: in such languages, stressed and unstressed syllable constitute a linguistic foot. Systematic ternary stressing yielding dactylic or anapaestic feet is rare: it is the rule in Cayuvava (Bolivia: Key 1961); in Island Carib (Honduras: Taylor 1955), stress tends to occur on the second syllable and every third succeeding syllable. In Auca (Ecuador: Pike 1964), stress is alternating, but a pentasyllabic suffix sequence is organized into dactyl plus trochee; some instances of optional trisyllabic feet are cited below (p. 125). The rhythm of stress languages is founded on the system of word accent, and, under certain conditions, the location of the accent can be varied to achieve optimum rhythm (see p. 276). Conversely, rhythm that is difficult in some way can increase the likelihood of speech errors that remedy the rhythm: the need for regular rhythm can override the need to enunciate correctly (Cutler 1980). English child language favours a rhythm in which accented and unaccented syllables alternate (Allen et al. 1980). At the same time, accent location rules tend to enhance the rhythm already inherent in a word or phrase as a result of its segmental properties: for instance stress is attracted to vowels that are long by nature and away from short vowels and onto heavy syllables and away from light syllables. However, rhythm is theoretically independent of word accent; that is, although rhythm in speech implies a tendency towards the synchronization of certain events, the synchronized event need not be the accent. The rhythm of Japanese speech is largely unrelated to the accent, which significantly is not a stress but a pure pitch accent. Languages can also have rules constraining the segmental structure of syllables independently of any accent. For instance, in some languages, such as Hausa, superheavy syllables are eliminated as rhythmically unsatisfactory (p. 78); this presupposes a conflict between the segmental durations in superheavy syllables and an internal clock assigning one or two units of rhythmic measurement or morae to a syllable. The structure of the Estonian stress foot is constrained in the direction of eliminating major durational differences between feet: if the foot contains only one syllable, then that syllable is superheavy; if it contains three syllables, then the third syllable must be light.

Many languages require words, and also stems and affixes, to have some minimal prosodic weight; for instance in Choctaw (Oklahoma: Lombardi et al. 1991), monosyllabic nouns have the canonical shape CV̄C. English disallows monosyllables ending in a short vowel: *see, sea, sit,* *si: this seems to be a requirement that lexical words consist minimally of a monosyllabic foot. Nonlexicals do not have to satisfy the requirement (p. 304), since they are naturally joined to their host words to make feet. In much the same way, affixes can be exempt from the prosodic requirements of canonical root structure, since they are not autonomous but only occur joined to roots: for instance, in Indo-European affixes can be nonmoraic but roots have a canonical CV̄C-structure. In Greek, the minimal word weight rule, for which final consonants are "extrametrical," requires that all lexical words be at least bimoraic: the only exceptions are a few monosyllabic imperatives and participles like δός and στάν (Golston 1991). Words that satisfy the minimality constraint may nevertheless be phonetically manipulated in the direction of optimal or unmarked foot structure. In abnormally slow and rhythmic speech, such as the deliberate recitation of telephone numbers, monosyllabic words can be phonetically stretched to fit a trochaic template: *fi-ive, si-ix*. Similarly in Japanese telephone number recitation, monomoraic numbers are lengthened to make bimoraic feet (Itô 1990). In connected speech, too, monosyllabic feet may be liable to some degree of lengthening, as is posited for Greek in the heavy syllable prolongation rule (p. 135).

There is also some phonological evidence for the existence of a metronsized unit, intermediate between the linguistic foot and the phonological word/minor phrase, functioning as a domain of rhythmic organization. For instance, in Passamaquoddy (Maine: Stowell 1979) alternate feet are stressed, the main stress being the last. In Hungarian, which has trochaic stress feet, stressed syllables after the primary stress alternate between tertiary and secondary stress, effectively organizing stress feet into metra in long words (Hammond 1987). Many aspects of prosody seem to have a hierarchical organization (p. 411) in which every level of structure has its own head, and phonological theories aimed at formalizing hierarchical stress relations have enjoyed considerable success (Hogg et al. 1987).

Syllable

The reality of both the syllable and the foot as units of linguistic rhythm is increasingly being confirmed by experimental evidence. The average rate at which syllables are uttered in speech falls within the range of rhythmic perception — approximately 5 syllables per second in English and 7 morae per second in Japanese (Klatt 1976; Fujisaki et al. 1971); similar rates are recorded for Yoruba and West Greenlandic Eskimo (Nagano-Madsen 1992). It is difficult to say the English syllable *tə* at a rate greater than 8 syllables per second, and syllables that require less mobile articulators or that are structurally more complex have correspondingly lower maximum rates of production (Hudgins et al. 1937; Lehiste 1971; Sigurd 1973); such a task is repetitive and so cannot be coarticulated. It has been suggested that the average rate of syllable production reflects a natural opening and closing frequency of the jaw (Lindblom 1983). There is a widespread intuition that the rhythm of languages like English is more stress timed and the rhythm of other languages like Italian and Spanish is more syllable timed (Pike 1945); native speakers of English commonly give the impression of hurrying over unstressed syllables when they are learning to speak Italian; similarly Danish learners of West Greenlandic Eskimo, which is a mora timed language, tend to make one syllable in a word more prominent and reduce the other morae (Nagano-Madsen 1990c). These impressions have been the object of considerable experimental study, the results of which are partially inconclusive (Roach 1982; Wenk et al. 1982; Dauer 1983; Miller 1984; den Os 1988; Bertinetto 1989; Bertinetto et al. 1989; Fletcher 1991). It may be that the more strongly marked stress of languages like English is a more efficient cue to foot structure (Eriksson 1987): the lengthening induced by the accent in nonprepausal feet is significantly less in French than in English, and French is more resistant than English to the tendency for articulatory reduction of unaccented syllables (Fant et al. 1991).

When speakers are asked to produce a string of identical stressed monosyllables at a slow rhythmic rate, they can do so with nearly isochronous rhythm, if demarcation effects are factored out. However, if the syllables have identical rimes but different onset consonants, the start of acoustic energy for each syllable, that is the first visible evidence of the syllable onset in a spectrographic or oscillographic display, is not so nearly isochronous, and the degree of deviation from isochrony is positively correlated with the duration of the onset consonant(s) (p. 57). These anisochronous syllables sound more rhythmic to listeners than versions with artificial electronically introduced isochrony (Fowler 1979). When asked to adjust the intervals between syllables so that they sound isochronous, or to tap on the beat of a designated syllable in a sentence, listeners introduce the same systematic departures from acoustic isochrony as those just noted in production experiments (Allen 1972; Morton et al. 1976). Unstressed syllables are less regular, since what is actually being aligned in these experiments is the stress of the linguistic foot. The reference point used to align stressed syllables, commonly called the P-centre which stands for perceptual centre, is none of the anticipated locations, such as the beginning of acoustic energy in the syllable, the beginning of periodic energy in the vowel, or the peak intensity of the vowel: for instance, if the onset of a syllable is an aspirated stop, the reference point is not the release of the stop nor the beginning of voicing in the vowel, but falls during the aspiration. The greater the duration of the syllabic onset, the more the reference point tends to be distant from both the beginning of the syllable and the beginning of vocalic voicing, although different subjects used different reference points (Rapp 1971); the greater the duration of the vocalic nucleus, the later in the syllable the reference point occurs (Fox et al. 1987b). Even the duration of the coda consonant is relevant, at least in English, though its contribution is less important than that of the onset (Marcus 1981; Cooper et al. 1988). Such rhythmic reference points or syllable beat loci have also been reported for Spanish and Japanese (Hoequist 1985; Fox 1987). According to one view, the phenomenon is mainly articulatory in origin: speakers produce isochronous articulatory gestures timed to coincide with some point in the articulatory cycle of the vowel, but these do not translate into isochronous acoustic events because they are blurred by coarticulation (Fowler 1983, 1986; Fowler et al. 1988). When the gestures of individual articulators of onset consonants and onset consonant clusters were studied, their timing seemed to reflect a mechanism similar to that involved in the perceptual reference points (Browman et al. 1988). An alternative explanation is that the syllable beat is located on the basis of some sort of weighted average of the acoustic modulations occurring at the beginning (Ohala et al. 1984) and throughout the syllable (Fox et al. 1987b). There is some evidence that factors other than simple duration can cause shifts in the syllable beat (Pompino-Marschall 1989, 1990). So it is reasonable to assume that in Greek the onset, while not relevant for the phonological distinction between light and heavy syllables, as confirmed by the evidence presented in Chapter 2, may have been relevant for the location of the point in the syllable used in the computation of rhythm in speech and verse performance.

Foot

When subjects are asked to perform finger tapping and syllable pronunciation tasks simultaneously, they have a strong tendency to produce stronger taps with stressed syllables and vice versa, despite instructions to the contrary, which indicates both the status of the syllable and the foot as components of rhythm, and the unity of the motor commands for rhythmic prominence in speech and other physical activity (Kelso et al. 1983). The average interstress interval, excluding prepausal locations, in reading aloud was 550 msec for Swedish and 565 msec for English (Fant et al. 1989, 1991): this coincides with the interval between beats in a typical march tempo in music and is practically identical to the typical intertap interval in spontaneous tapping (600 msec). It has been suggested that the timing of entire syntactic units is precomputed and stored before they are uttered (Allen 1972), and that in this computation stress feet play a more central role than syllables or words (Sternberg et al. 1978). Experiments in which the speech of subjects was impeded by the presence of a bite block suggest that word rhythm is a temporal target at least in part independent of the processes of motor execution (Lindblom et al. 1987).

The duration of syllables in the Estonian stress foot has been the subject of extensive experimental investigation (Lehiste 1965b, 1966; Ojamaa 1976; Prince 1980). In this language there exists a complex of rules affecting the duration of the various syllable types, the net effect of which is drastically to reduce the overall durational differences between the variously structured feet. For instance, in disyllabic feet the duration of the vowel of the second syllable is inversely correlated with the weight of the first syllable, so that for example phonologically pyrrhic feet become phonetically iambic, although the stress pattern remains trochaic. Similar rules affect the length of unstressed light syllables in many Finnish dialects (Leskinen et al. 1985). One study of Southwestern Finnish found that in proceleusmatic-shaped words the vowels of even-numbered syllables are on the average 141% longer than those of odd-numbered syllables, but after a heavy odd-numbered syllable no lengthening occurs (Lehiste 1965b). The situation in Finnish is complicated by the fact that Finnish can have phonologically long vowels in even numbered syllables, and these get lengthened after an initial light syllable too (Välimaa-Blum 1987). One possible explanation would involve demarcative lengthening of feet that begin with quantitatively weak elements. At all events, durational adjustment rules like those of Estonian and Finnish evidently presuppose the existence of feet as a domain of rhythmic organization in spoken language as well as in verse. Such rules are the phonetic counterparts of rules at the phonological level which constrain the type and number of syllables that can form a legitimate foot. The phonological rules accept or reject syllable types for mapping, the phonetic rules manipulate the duration of those syllables that have been accepted and mapped onto foot structures. The phonetic rules serve both to optimize the rhythm and to permit mappings that otherwise would not be possible.

The reality of the stress foot as a unit of temporal organization in English speech has been a subject of dispute (Lehiste 1973, 1977, 1979b; Huggins 1975; Donovan et al. 1979). It was found that in the sentence "Davis signed the paper," the duration of the first stressed vowel was significantly greater than in the sentence "Davis assigned the paper" (Fowler 1977); although an increase in the number of syllables can affect duration in domains larger than the foot, this difference is most simply explained by assuming that the first foot of the former sentence has two syllables and that of the latter sentence has three. This experimental finding supports the phonologically based hypothesis of an English stress foot as a basic structure of speech rhythm. It follows that, in principle, the rhythms of English verse are based on pre-existing speech rhythms.

Although, as just noted, the average duration of stress feet is comparable to the typical intervals in spontaneous tapping, the feet of speech rhythm are not isochronous: they mostly fall into the range of about 200–1000 msec (Nakatani et al. 1981; Dauer 1983; Fant et al. 1991; Eriksson 1991). When the verse text of a Swedish song was sung in a scanned manner, it was forced into a very regular pattern with almost isochronous feet; but when the same text was read as prose, the duration of the feet was much more variable, reflecting differences not only of segmental structure but also of phrasing and stress prominence (Nord et al. 1989). However, experiments involving synchronized tapping appeared to indicate that speakers of English have a perception that objectively anisochronous feet are isochronous, although they would not judge a sequence of simple mechanical noise bursts timed to coincide with linguistic feet to be isochronous (Darwin et al. 1979; Donovan et al. 1979), and even though the anisochrony considerably exceeds the precision with which listeners can discriminate pairwise presentations of interstress intervals (Eriksson 1991). This suggested that what the listener is reacting to is a change in duration in the direction of isochrony (Lehiste 1977). But this conclusion was not confirmed by later experiments. It was also established that the important factor was the complexity of the acoustic signal rather than the straight distinction between speech and mechanical noise; subjects may simply tend to tap regularly when the stimulus is difficult to follow (Scott et al. 1985). In Swedish poetry reading, feet were actually less isochronous than in prose, although the stresses were more elaborately implemented and the feet were separated from one another by a micropause in the order of 10–40 msec (Eriksson 1987).

There is some evidence that the duration of an English stress foot is sensitive to the duration of contiguous feet: for instance, the stressed syllable of a foot tends to be shorter if the following foot is an anapaest rather than an iamb; this would indicate compensation in the planning of the timing of domains larger than the foot (Fourakis et al. 1988). In a study of the oral production of verse in various languages, one case was found, namely Faroese ballads, in which disyllabic and trisyllabic feet differed in duration by little over 10% (Lehiste 1990b).

Word length effect

It is fairly well established, subject to potential qualifications about experimental design (p. 271), that the greater the number of unstressed syllables in the word, the lower the duration of the stressed syllable. This phenomenon can reflect temporal organization at the level of the foot, the metron and the word. In English, the trochaic shortening of *speed* in *speedy* is weaker than the dactylic shortening in *speedily* (Lehiste 1972); similarly German [*lang*], *langsam*, *langsamer*; Estonian *pádu*, *pádustamàtu* (Lindblom et al. 1981); trisyllabic words were found to have a slightly shorter stressed vowel than disyllabic words in Danish (Fischer-Jørgensen 1982) and in Italian (Farnetani et al. 1986). In Hungarian (Lehiste 1970), Icelandic (Pind 1986) and Tamil (Balasubramanian 1981b), the duration of the first vowel of a polysyllabic word tended to be inversely proportional to the number of syllables in the word, with differences of as much as 50 msec or more. This effect was already noted for the first vowel of French *pâté* (200 msec) versus *pâtisserie* (120 msec) in a turn of the century experiment (Grégoire 1899). In Swedish nonsense words, shortening was found both in falling rhythm (*dádad* vs. *dádadadad*) and in rising rhythm (*dadád* vs. *dadadadád*) (Lindblom et al. 1981), with a greater shortening in falling rhythm. There may also be a weak tendency for the average duration of the mora to decrease as word length increases in Japanese (Port et al. 1987). However, little or no evidence for this word length effect was found for Spanish or Finnish (Strangert 1985). Not only the number of syllables in the foot or the word, but also the segmental composition of the syllables can be a factor affecting the duration allotted to each syllable. This accounts for the fact that within the category of trochaically shortened words, the stressed vowel was longer in *speedy* than in *speeder* and longer in *speeder* than in *speeding*; and within the category of dactylically shortened words, the stressed vowel of *speedily* was longer than that of *speediness* (Lehiste 1972).

Iambic vs. trochaic

It has already been noted that iambic rhythm and trochaic rhythm do not have the same timing relationship between strong and weak elements of the foot, the strong element being more nearly equal in duration to the weak element in trochaic than in iambic rhythm. This general rhythmic principle is manifested in the rhythm of language. Iambic shortening is a minor effect compared with trochaic shortening (Lindblom et al. 1981). Iambic stress is associated with longer duration (Kawasaki

et al. 1988). It has been suggested that in languages having a phonological distinction between long and short vowels or heavy and light syllables, stress feet tend to be iambic, while in languages lacking such
distinctions stress feet tend to be trochaic since trochees have more nearly
equal elements than iambs (Hayes 1985; Prince 1990). Rising and falling rhythm are correlated with different moods and attitudes of the
speaker or the discourse context (p. 471). Various measurements of
recited poetry over the years have found that trochaic verse feet tend
to have less overall duration and a more equal ratio of strong to weak
elements than iambic verse feet (Chatman 1965; Newton 1975). In Swedish poetry reading, the weak syllable in iambs averaged 150 msec and
that in trochees had an increment of 35 msec attributable to the rhythmic difference (Nord et al. 1989; Kruckenberg et al. 1991).

EVIDENCE FOR GREEK SPEECH RHYTHM

There are three main sources of evidence for the rhythm of Greek speech:
the phonology of the language, the verse texts and the surviving musical settings. With regard to the last of these, it is a reasonable assumption that the rhythms of Greek vocal music to some degree reflect, or
at least do not reverse, the rhythms of Greek speech, just as it is known
that the melodies of nonstrophic Greek vocal music reflect the tonal relationships associated with the Greek pitch accent. The remarks of
Dionysius of Halicarnassus *De Compositione Verborum* 11.42UR reflect a
situation not evidenced by most of the musical documents, and the negative position of Wilamowitz (1895) is unwarranted: two aspects of the
rhythmic notation of sung verse, namely absence of a sign for the short
note and inconsistent use of the diseme, presuppose a correlation of the
units of musical rhythm with the units of linguistic rhythm, that is the
heavy (bimoraic) and light syllables of the language, which is confirmed
by the association of melisms with heavy syllables. While the musical
fragments are of postclassical date, most of them provide little evidence
for the later stage of the language when the syllable quantity based rhythm
of classical Greek gave way to the stress based rhythm of late Greek.

Language and metre

The exploitation of metrics as a source of evidence for the rhythm of
Greek speech raises two fundamental metatheoretical problems, namely
the relationship of metrics to rhythmics and the relationship of verse
to language. In ancient writers, metrics and rhythmics are mostly treated
as well-defined and separate topics, although at least one tradition explicitly recognizes that metre is based on rhythm (Longinus *Prolegomena*

to Hephaestion's Enchiridion 81.10 Consbruch; Choeroboscus *On Hephaestion* 177.12 Consbruch), and their general relationship to each other is acknowledged (Aristides Quintilianus 38.15, 45.20WI). Modern scholarship has also maintained a fairly strict distinction, based largely on a positivist preference for the empirically controllable data of philological texts to the exclusion of the more hypothetical, but at the same time more explanatory, field of rhythmics. The position taken in this work is that metrics is a subdivision of rhythmics in the broad sense of that term. Metrics can be viewed as the central segment of a hierarchy. Above metrics in the hierarchy lies the highly abstract rhythmics that is the ontogenetic basis of metre, and below it lies the surface phonetic rhythmics that are generated in the performance of verse. Metrics is assumed to share a common property with rhythmics: the rules of metrics and the rules of rhythmics belong to one and the same system because they work together towards a single final objective, namely a degree of rhythmic regularity that neither could achieve alone.

The relationship of Greek metre to the Greek language is also a topic of considerable disagreement. The view implicit in some modern work is that the rhythms of Greek verse are of primarily nonlinguistic origin and that versification involves searching through language for phonetic categories that can appropriately be mapped onto these extraneous rhythmic patterns and categories. It is tacitly assumed that while verse has rhythm, language — or at least pitch accent languages — have only intrinsic durations: segments and syllables just have the durations that they have, and those sequences that coincidentally fit the verse pattern are metrical. According to this conception of metre, the durational categories of language do not necessarily correlate with those of verse and are not organized into rhythmical patterns at all (or, if they are, it is into rhythms different from and unrelated in any direct way to the rhythms of verse). This view is not well supported by evidence from other languages. If English were a dead language, it would be reasonable to assume that it was a stress language on the basis of English verse. In fact, many of the details of English stress patterns can be deduced from the careful analysis of English metre. For instance, the rhythm rule responsible for the context sensitive initial stressing of words like *Tennessée* is recoverable from the limerick composed specifically by two linguists to illustrate this point: "A Ténnessee drummer named Bette..." (Kaisse 1987, 1990). Quite subtle effects like the stronger stressing of focused modifiers and the reduction of stress on semantically general nouns like *thing* and *man* and on vocatives have been identified in quantitative studies of English metrical practice (Tarlinskaja 1989). According to one diachronic analysis, Chinese verse became additionally tonal when the language developed lexical tone (Yip 1984). So the position taken in this work is that verse is "merely the language itself, running in its natural grooves" (Sapir 1921). "If one wants to study rhythm, one will do well to look where rhythm can be expected to be found — in the metric structure of poetry developed in a given language over the years" (Lehiste 1990). Due to its high degree of patterning and its association with unaccelerated speech styles, "Poetry is like speech, only more so." (Allen 1972). The rhythms of Greek verse are simply more highly constrained versions of rhythms already existing in Greek speech: the ῥυθμιζόμενα of verse are a selection of the most amenable ῥυθμιζόμενα of prose. The basic principles of the two rhythmic systems are the same, as are their basic units of organization. Whatever the importance of literary convention, in principle Greek verse rhythm is born of the rhythm of Greek speech, and the former is consequently a valuable source of information about the latter. Just as an analysis of the distribution of words like *Tennessee* in English verse will show that in English speech they have primary stress on their final syllable or, under certain conditions, on their initial syllable but never on their medial syllable, so, for instance, a study of the distribution of fourth paeon-shaped words in the trimeter will indicate which rhythmic organizations of that word shape were possible in Greek speech and which were not, and which were usual at a certain speech rate and which less so.

Finally, it is our position that however abstract the phonological terms in which metrical rules are stated and interpreted, most metrical rules reflect some form of measurable acoustic correlate at some rate of (prose) speech, not excluding artificially slow rates and styles. Whereas metrical rules can, and often do, abstract away from physically existing distinctions, it is reasonable to ask for empirical confirmation of the converse assumption, namely that some nonconventionalized metrical rule reflects a distinction that has no measurable surface correlate in any type of speech. The extent to which this position can be defended depends critically on the appropriate formulation of metrical rules. For instance, if a metrical rule of English verse regulating the relative strength of contiguous stresses were misinterpreted as a rule regulating the location of stressed and unstressed syllables, it would lead to quite misleading conclusions about English stress.

Many previous studies, particularly during the nineteenth and early twentieth centuries, have used the evidence of the musical fragments as a basis for conclusions about the rhythms of Greek song and the evidence of metrics as a basis for conclusions about the rhythms of Greek verse recitation and performance. If the positions adopted above are correct, then it follows that both types of evidence can further serve as a basis for conclusions about the rhythms of everyday Greek speech.

1. Recession of the Greek acute accent is constrained by the weight of the final syllable of the word: the accent cannot stand farther back than the penult if the final syllable is heavy. The only exceptions result from quantitative metathesis: πόλεως < πόληος, whence by analogy πόλεων, words of the Attic declension such as ἵλεως and by analogy in compounds such as δύσερως, φιλόγελως (Allen 1973:237). For the computation of syllable weight in the last syllable, the final consonant is "extrametrical," so that V̆C counts as light and -V̄(C)CC as heavy just like -V̄(C)(C); this also applies to the bimoraic minimal word constraint (p. 93). The same formula for computing syllable weight is used prepausally (p. 80), which suggests that accent location is based on the citation form of the word, in which the final syllable is prepausal. Conditioning by syllable weight, as opposed to length of the nucleus, is seen most readily in categorially recessive words such as *bahuvrihi* compounds, type πολύβοτρυς, ποικιλόνωτος, and compounds whose first element is semantically the head of the word, type ἀρχέκακος, φυγόμαχος (Goodwin et al. 1930; Steriade 1988): πολυάνθραξ, ποικιλοφόρμιγξ, φιλοκόλαξ are accented on the penult like πολυπύργων, ποικιλομόρφων, φιλοξένων and unlike πολύπυργος, ποικιλόμορφος, φιλόξενος.

2. In Attic, properispomena retract the accent to the antepenultimate syllable if it is a light syllable (Vendryes' Law: Vendryes 1945:262; Lejeune 1972:298; Allen 1973:237; Collinge 1985:199): ἕτοιμος < ἑτοῖμος, ἔρημος < ἐρῆμος. Vendryes' Law does not apply to properispomena arising by vowel contraction in Attic: φιλοῦμεν, ἐμοῦγε contrast ἔγωγε. The effect of the law is disrupted by columnarization of the accent in paradigms: δοτῆρα beside δοτήρ, ἀγῶνα beside ἀγών. The law is also blocked by the rule that in verbs the accent cannot stand farther leftward than the augment: παρεῖχε. Furthermore, the law does not apply to properispomena ending in -V̆(C)CC, type καλαῦροψ, πολυπῖδαξ; consequently it was subject to the constraint on the weight of final syllables computed as in (1) above. The law is most regular in originally properispomenon words in -αιος, -ειος, -οιος: βέβαιος, τέλειος, γέλοιος contrast σπουδαῖος, ἠθεῖος, αἰδοῖος. Although the chronology of Attic contractions is problematic (Bartoněk 1966:71), it appears that Vendryes' Law is recent in Attic:

τροπαῖον ἡ παλαιὰ Ἀτθίς... τρόπαιον ἡ νέα Ἀτθίς Scholiast on Thucydides 1.30

τροπαῖον προπερισπωμένως ἀναγνωστέον παρὰ Ἀριστοφάνει καὶ παρὰ Θουκυδίδῃ, τρόπαιον δὲ προπαροξυτόνως παρὰ τοῖς νεωτέροις ποιηταῖς Scholiast on *Thesmophoriazusae* 697.

The weight of the antepenultimate syllable correlates with accent location also in the case of the neuter diminutives in -ιον. These are generally paroxytone if the antepenult is heavy and proparoxytone if it is light

(Vendryes 1945:166): βωλίον, θηρίον, καρφίον but θρόνιον, θύριον, ἱμάτιον. Maximum regularity of this rule is obtained by counting muta cum liquida as heterosyllabic — λυχνίον, τεκνίον — and having it apply before diphthongization of vowel + ι: γῄδιον, ζῴδιον. Exceptions are then limited mainly to proparoxytones with heavy antepenults: κλίσιον, ἀνθρώπιον. This rule is definitely restricted to the category of diminutives, since other neuters in -ιον are mostly fully recessive regardless of the weight of the antepenult.

3. Original oxytones become paroxytones if they are or end in a dactyl-shaped syllable sequence (Wheeler's Law: Wheeler 1885; Lejeune 1972:297; Allen 1973:239; Collinge 1985:221): ἀγκύλος, ποικίλος but Vedic aṅkurás, peśalás. Wheeler's retraction is regular for words in -ιλος and -υλος, in nearly all of which a heavy syllable precedes: ἡδύλος, ἀρκτύλος, αἱμύλος, ναυτίλος. The retraction did not take place in the one word in -υλος in which a light syllable precedes; *παχυλός is presupposed by the perispomenon adverb παχυλῶς, Vedic bahulás. Retraction also failed in words with a heavy penult: ῥιγηλός, ἁμαρτωλός. The effect of Wheeler's Law was greatly disrupted by analogy (Vendryes 1945:148), and there are many synchronic exceptions: ὀμφαλός, ὀρφανός, μυελός and all adjectives in -ικος such as ἀστικός. Instances of retraction in words ending in V̆(C)CC with a preceding trochee-shaped shaped sequence all involve otherwise recessive compounds, so that crucial cases are lacking to decide whether originally Wheeler's Law required reference to the quantity of the nucleus of the final syllable or to its weight as computed in (1) above.

Wheeler's Law has been invoked as the starting point for the paroxytone accentuation of perfect middle participles (Brugmann 1930:963; Vendryes 1945:149; Lejeune 1972:298) and as an explanation for the paroxytonesis of datives in -ασι, which are regularly preceded by a heavy syllable (Vendryes 1945:149; Lejeune 1972:298). But it has also been claimed that a general Indo-European zero-grade retraction rule (Kiparsky 1973b) was the starting point for Wheeler's Law (Miller 1976). Wheeler's Law has also been taken as the diachronic basis for a partial synchronic regularity in the accentuation of compounds with active meanings, the second element of which is semantically the head of the word. Such compounds are generally claimed to be basically oxytones, whereas passive compounds are fully recessive, but when they end in a dactyl sequence they are paroxytone: αἰγοβοσκός but θυοσκόπος; however there are numerous examples of paroxytone active compounds that end in a tribrach sequence such as λιθοβόλος, and paroxytone accentuation is so frequent among active compounds in general that Herodian I.234.29 Lentz erroneously states it to be the rule. Diachronically, these paroxytone tribrach-ending active compounds are often taken as analogical extensions from those ending in a dactyl sequence, but the highest level of synchronic regularity for the accentuation of active compounds is obtained by a rule stating that active compounds are oxytone only if the penult is heavy and paroxytone only if it is light (Vendryes 1945:194).

Another, synchronically less regular, retraction conditioned by syllable weight is Bartoli's Law (Bartoli 1930; Collinge 1985:229), according to which oxytone words ending in an iambic sequence, probably those which are trisyllabic or longer (Miller 1976), become paroxytone. The retraction is regular for words ending in -σύνη, Vedic -tvaná-; other examples are θυγάτηρ, Vedic duhitā́, νεφέλη, ἐργάτης. However, there are numerous exceptions and Bartoli's Law has little synchronic validity.

The laws associated with the names of Bartoli, Wheeler and Vendryes share syllable weight conditioning and have the common effect of accent retraction, but there are difficulties with the various attempts to integrate them into a long term conspiracy of accent retraction rules (Kiparsky 1967; Voyles 1974; Miller 1976; Collinge 1985).

4. In the formation of comparatives and superlatives, the short stem vowel -o- is lengthened after a light syllable but not after a heavy syllable: compare σοφώτερος with ὠμότερος, λεπτότερος (de Saussure 1884 [1922:464]; Wackernagel 1889; Hirt 1902; Moorhouse 1949). This rhythmic tendency may have its roots in pre-Greek, since it is possibly manifested also in Sanskrit forms with lengthening of the stem vowel. The phonological lengthening was no longer operative at the time of the loss of digamma: κενότερος, στενότερος; but this does not mean that such forms did not have some phonetic lengthening of the stem vowel; forms like στενώτερος are later analogical reformations. Comparatives in -τερος and superlatives in -τατος from u-stem adjectives were resistant to phonological lengthening, probably because u is intrinsically shorter than o: βαθύτερος, γλυκύτερος.

A number of other forms quite possibly show a related rhythmic lengthening or a rhythmically based preference for alternate forms with ŠŠ̄ as against those with ŠŠŠ: ἑτέρωθεν, στρατιώτης, ἱερωσύνη but πόθεν, ἱππότης, δουλοσύνη.

5. Strings of more than two light syllables are avoided in much of the rhetorical prose of Demosthenes (Blass's Law: Blass 1893; Adams 1917; Vogel 1923; McCabe 1981). The reality of Blass's Law is easy to demonstrate, since it does not apply in many other prose writers (Bodendorff 1880; Vogel 1923). Less than 1 % of all heavy syllables were followed by more than two unambiguously light syllables in a sample from Demosthenes, as compared with over 5 % in a sample from Isaeus; only about 7.5 % of all unambiguously light syllables appeared in strings of more than two in a sample from Demosthenes as compared with over

30% in Isaeus (McCabe 1981). It has been suggested that a disproportionate number of exceptions to Blass's Law occur in single words or appositive groups (Blass 1893). If this apparent tendency is real and not merely an automatic reflex of the text frequency of the words in question, it could be phonologically motivated like the parallel constraints against split and divided resolution in verse, or it could reflect the relative ease with which a string of light syllables can be avoided. The latter factor is clearly relevant when the string occurs in proper names, as with Φιλοκράτης in Demosthenes 19, which accounts for a large proportion of muta cum liquida onsets in strings of two or more light syllables.

6. In the (noncholiambic) trimeter the central syllable of a molossus-shaped word (s̄s̄s̄) may stand in third anceps in all styles except in Callimachus (DS 1984:53, 122): type αἰτήσει Andromache 1002. In the noncholiambic trimeters of Callimachus, third anceps is always short with the exception of a single instance involving a proper name (Pfeiffer 1934). By comparison, in a sample of 846 trimeters from the Antigone, 42.67% of all third ancipitia not involving a proper name were filled by the central syllable of a molossus-shaped word. By the binomial distribution ($p = 0.4267$) it can be calculated that there is only a one in two million chance of the absence of molossus-shaped words in this position in Callimachus being due to chance. Like some other cases of Hellenistic metrical strictness, this may be interpreted as aiming for the highest degree of rhythmic regularity rather than as a mere formal artificiality.

7. A lexical word final heavy syllable (...s̄#) may not stand in third anceps in the trimeter except in comedy (Porson 1802; Allen 1973:304; DS 1984:1–56). A line end such as ἐραστὴν πραγμάτων Clouds 1459 is therefore forbidden in Archilochus, Semonides, Solon and the tragedians. A parallel rule constrains first and third anceps in the tetrameter (Havet 1896).

8. Dispondee-shaped words (s̄s̄s̄s̄: type μυθήσασθαι) are overwhelmingly located in the hexameter of all styles at the end of the verse, so that their odd-numbered syllables are mapped onto the last two theses (Ludwich 1866:8, 1885:250; Allen 1973:285). Out of 1445 instances of dispondee-shaped words in the Iliad and the Odyssey, over 95% occur at the end of the hexameter. Of the 71 occurrences ending in internal positions, over 97% have their odd-numbered syllables mapped onto arses. Only two instances, one each line initially in the Iliad and the Odyssey, have their odd-numbered syllables mapped onto theses (O'Neill 1942:177)

ἠπείλησεν μῦθον Iliad 1.388.

The distribution of dispondee-shaped words is nearly identical in Hesiod, Aratus, Callimachus, Apollonius and Theocritus, with the additional constraint that the preference for verse-final position becomes even stronger in the four later poets: in one thousand line samples from each no instance was found in other than line final position (O'Neill 1942:147).

9. In the trimeter of the iambographers, the first syllable of tetrasyllabic words of the shape S̄S̄S̄S̆ (type μωμήσεται Semonides 7.113) is avoided in third anceps (DS 1984:43–48). Table 3.1 compares the distribution of light and heavy syllables in third anceps for tetrasyllabic and trisyllabic word shapes in Archilochus, Semonides and Solon with their distribution in representative samples from Sophocles and Euripides. In the case of the central syllable of the trisyllabic word shapes (molossus and cretic) the rate of long third anceps is almost identical in the two styles, but the odds of getting a short third anceps in a line final tetrasyllabic word are over three and a half times as great in the iambographers as in tragedy, with a χ^2 of 17.489, corresponding to a better than one in thirty-four thousand chance of being random.

10. Palimbacchiac- and molossus-shaped words (S̄S̆S̄: type θνητοῖσι, and S̄S̄S̄: type ἀνθρώπους) are strongly avoided at the end of the hexameter (DS 1984:48–51). Table 3.2 compares the distribution in Callimachus of the palimbacchiac word shape with that of its uncontracted counterpart, the extended anapaest-shaped word (S̆S̆S̄S̆), and the distribution of the extended molossus-shaped word (S̄S̄S̄S̆) with that of its uncontracted counterpart, the extended choriamb-shaped word (S̄S̆S̆S̄). The ratio of the odds ratios indicates that in contracted fifth biceps the heavy initial syllable of palimbacchiac-shaped words is avoided seventeen times as strongly as the heavy second syllable of extended molossus-shaped words. The constraint varies through time: the ratio of the odds ratios ranges from 4.17 in Homer and 5.99 in Hesiod to over 40 in Theocritus and Apollonius.

TABLE 3.1

Tetrasyllables in the iambographers and in tragedy

	Medial in molossus/cretic-s.w.			Initial in tetrasyllable		
	S̄ %	S̆ %	Ratio	S̄ %	S̆ %	Ratio
Iambographers	57.81	42.19	0.73	13.19	86.81	6.58
Tragedy	54.75	45.26	0.83	36.76	63.24	1.72
	Odds ratio: ω_{med} = 0.88			Odds ratio: ω_{init} = 3.82		
	χ^2 = 0.214			χ^2 = 17.489		

TABLE 3.2
Relative frequencies of contracted and uncontracted
bicipitia in line final and non-line final locations

	$\bar{s}\bar{s}\bar{s}$	$\bar{s}\check{s}\check{s}\check{s}$	Ratio	$\bar{s}\bar{s}\bar{s}\bar{s}$	$\bar{s}\check{s}\check{s}\check{s}\check{s}$	Ratio
	%	%		%	%	
end of line	2.95	97.05	0.03	63.38	36.62	1.73
elsewhere	46.31	53.69	0.86	74.25	25.75	2.88

Odds ratio: $\omega_a = 28.47$ $\omega_b = 1.66$

Ratio of the odds ratios: $\omega_a/\omega_b = 17.15$

11. Two light syllables may be mapped onto the thesis in the trimeter subject to a number of different constraints, but such mapping, known as resolution, is relatively rare in the strictest styles of the trimeter (Allen 1973:316–33; DS 1984:59–99). Table 3.3 gives the rate of occurrence of resolution per thousand nonlyric trimeters for its seven major word shapes in the various styles of tragedy: the pyrrhic-shaped word (type πόδα *I.T.* 32), the tribrach-shaped word (type λογάσι *Hecuba* 544), the dactyl-shaped word (type μητέρα *I.T.* 79), the anapaest-shaped word (type γονάτων *Andromache* 573), the fourth paeon-shaped word (type θανασίμους *Medea* 376), the ionic a minore-shaped word (type ἀποδώσεις *Helen* 965), and the first paeon-shaped word (type δεινότερα *Bacchae* 674). The overall growth of resolution is exponential. Each word shape grows in frequency, but some word shapes grow faster than others.

12. In nonmelic anapaests, a sequence of four light syllables, whether in a proceleusmatic foot or when a dactylic foot is followed by an anapaestic foot, is strongly avoided. Melic proceleusmatics such as

TABLE 3.3
Rate of occurrence per thousand trimeters
of different word shapes in resolution

	Total	Pyrrh.	Tribr.	Dact.	Anap.	4 P.	Ion.	1 P.
Aeschylus	51.01	9.10	21.10	0.23	4.21	14.50	0.47	1.40
Sophocles	45.24	5.60	24.40	0.27	5.30	8.62	0.40	0.66
Severior	55.81	2.90	25.00	0.00	7.42	19.57	0.68	0.24
Semiseverus	106.92	18.10	51.90	0.36	15.99	18.84	0.71	1.42
Liber	193.90	47.80	64.78	5.69	27.24	38.63	6.24	3.52
Liberrimus	279.68	83.30	68.34	10.89	35.56	62.06	14.30	5.23

αἰνῶς αἰνῶς ἐπὶ γόνυ κέκλιται *Persae* 930
κακὸν ἄρ' ἐγενόμαν *Persae* 933

and melic sequences of dactyl plus anapaest

τὰν παρὰ προθύροις *Troades* 194
παιδὸς δαίσομεν ὑμεναίους *I.A.* 123

are highly constrained. In the comic trimeter, contiguous resolution and substitution is highly constrained: an anapaest following resolved longum is avoided under most conditions, and there are no secure cases in Aristophanes of anapaestic substitution preceding resolved longum, which would give a proceleusmatic foot. About forty potential cases of contiguous resolution and substitution have come under discussion in Aristophanes, and perhaps another ten in the fragments of other Attic comic poets (Dawes 1745; Porson 1812; Reisig 1816; Hermann 1816; Dobree 1820; Rumpel 1869; Wilamowitz 1911; Holzinger 1940; Coulon 1953; Newiger 1961; Stephens 1988b). Some are corrupt on nonmetrical grounds, others are introduced by conjecture, and yet others involve split resolutions or substitutions. About half a dozen secure instances remain, mostly involving resolved second longum followed by anapaestic substitution with intervening major syntactic boundary (p. 280). (Proceleusmatic feet are likewise rare in Finnish iamboanapaestic verse: Hanson 1992).

13. Proceleusmatic-shaped words (šššš: type ὀνόματα *Helen* 498) are strongly avoided in resolution in all styles of the tragic trimeter except for the latest style of Euripides (DS 1984:88). The rates of occurrence for the various styles of tragedy are given in Table 3.4.

14. When two light syllables implement a resolution, a lexical word boundary should occur neither between them (split resolution) nor, with a few exceptions, after them (divided resolution) (Seidler 1812:385; Wunder 1823:31; Fix 1843:lxvii; Mueller 1866; Christ 1879; Zieliński 1925; Descroix 1931:155; Irigoin 1959). In the manuscripts of tragedy

TABLE 3.4
Rate of occurrence per thousand trimeters
of proceleusmatic-shaped words in resolution

Aeschylus	0.23
Sophocles	0.67
Severior	0.00
Semiseverus	0.71
Liber	1.71
Liberrimus	9.07

and comedy may be found a number of violations of the rule against split resolution, some involving a split between two lexical words and others an appositive that coheres in the wrong direction. Modern editors usually emend both types of split. For instance

αἰνῶ σε, Μενέλαος, ὅτι I.A. 506

was emended already in 1694 by Barnes to Μενέλεως ὅτι and by Markland in 1771 to Μενέλα’ ὅτι, the usual modern text. The split initial tribrach

βαρὺ τὸ φόρημ’ Eur. Frag. 643 Nauck

was emended to βαρύ τι φόρημ’ by Wagner. The resolution split between two lexical words

τὰ χοιρίδι’ ἀπέδου Acharnians 830

was emended despite the mitigating elision by Elmsley to ἀπέδου τὰ χοιρία. Emendations which remove a divided resolution in tragedy are less readily accepted: Dindorf's transposition of

λευκῆς χιόνος ἀνεῖσαν Bacchae 662

to λευκῆς ἀνεῖσαν χιόνος with the more usual location for the tribrach-shaped word is not widely accepted.

The constraint against divided resolution is greatly relaxed line initially, even in tragedy. In fact, the location ending in first longum is the next most favoured position for tribrach-shaped words after the postpenthemimeral position. The proportions of tribrach-shaped words located line initially out of all tribrach-shaped words in the trimeter is very roughly 15% for Aeschylus and Euripides Severior, Liber and Liberrimus and 25% for Sophocles. Yet line initial location of the tribrach-shaped word in the trimeter is still constrained relative to its incidence in the tetrameter: in tetrameters, averaged over all three tragedians, 40.32% of all tribrach-shaped words are line initial and 43.55% occur after the diaeresis. The ratio of the two locations is nearly equal in the tetrameter (1.08:1), whereas in the trimeter the ratio of postpenthemimeral to line initial location is 4.97:1. The tribrach-shaped word is less favoured line initially in the trimeter because word end follows the resolution, whereas in the tetrameter line initial tribrach-shaped words have the resolution on the first two syllables of the word. The constraint against divided resolution is somewhat relaxed in comedy, yet even there divided resolutions generally involve longer words such as first paeon-shaped words or syntagmatic first paeon-shaped words

ἀργύριον ἤν τις διδῷ Clouds 98
τὰ σκόροδα πορθούμενος Acharnians 164.

There is still a significant constraint against resolutions of the form

τὴν κεφαλὴν κόρακος ἔχων Wasps 43, cp. 45.

The constraint against divided resolution operates more strongly when the preceding arsis is implemented by a heavy syllable, that is with preceding long anceps. In tragedy, dactyl-shaped words, type μητέρα, are highly constrained in line initial position until Euripides Liber. They never occur ending in third or fifth longum. In Aristophanes, they are rare ending in third longum and almost excluded ending in fifth longum; in Menander, a dactyl may end in fifth longum if followed by a postpositive

κοιτίδα τινά Epitrepontes 381

or in a fixed phrase

μὰ τοὺς δώδεκα θεούς Samia 306, Colax 127.

Dactyl- and left-extended dactyl-shaped words in Aristophanes (δικαστήριον Ecclesiazusae 460, Φιλοκτήμονος Wasps 1250) account for only 2.47% of resolution after long third anceps, 1.06% after long second anceps and 7.19% after long first anceps; in contrast, tribrach- and left extended tribrach-shaped words account for 21.13% of the cases of resolution after short third anceps, 3.57% after short second anceps and 24.04% after short first anceps (White 1912:40, 43). These data illustrate the interaction between the weight of the arsis syllable and the strength of the constraint against divided resolution.

In lyric, split resolution is less constrained, particularly in the first longum of iambic and trochaic metra and in dochmiacs (Parker 1968).

15. In the trimeter, fourth paeon-shaped words in precaesural position (type ὁμογενὴς Orestes 244) are not permitted in Aeschylus and the earlier styles of Euripides (DS 1984:81); the proportion located in precaesural position in the various styles of tragedy is given in Table 3.5. At Lysistrata 132 Aristophanes locates a fourth paeon-shaped word so that the second and third syllables implement resolved fourth longum.

16. Lexical pyrrhic-shaped words are avoided in resolution in Aeschylus, Sophocles and the earlier styles of Euripides (DS 1984:73). Elided

TABLE 3.5

Precaesural fourth paeon-shaped words as a percentage
of all fourth paeon-shaped words

Aeschylus	0.00
Sophocles	7.81
Severior	0.00
Semiseverus	0.00
Liber	5.62
Liberrimus	20.83

TABLE 3.6
Lexical pyrrhic-shaped words filling resolved longum

	Lexical as % of all pyrrhic-s.w. in resol.	Lexical rate/1000	Elided as % of lexical + elided
Aeschylus	8.57	0.7	70.00
Sophocles	13.89	0.7	50.00
Severior	30.00	0.7	60.00
Semiseverus	23.26	3.6	38.46
Liber	39.33	16.00	25.19
Liberrimus	31.31	21.60	13.51

tribrach-shaped words remain avoided in all styles, while lexical pyrrhic-shaped words filling resolved longum grow from a minimum of less than 10% of all pyrrhic-shaped words in resolution in Aeschylus to a maximum proportion of almost 40% in Euripides Liber. The data are given in Table 3.6.

17. In Aeschylus the final two syllables of a first paeon-shaped word (˘˘˘˘) implement the resolution (type τυμβοχόα Septem 1022), whereas in Euripides it is more often the second and third syllables (type ψευδόμεθα I.A. 846) (DS 1984:85). The overall rate of occurrence of this word shape and the percentage of all first paeon-shaped words in which the final two syllables implement the resolution are given in Table 3.7.

18. In the trimeter, words of the shape ionic a minore (˘˘˘˘: type ἀποδείξω Orestes 1062) are strongly avoided in Aeschylus, Sophocles and the earlier styles of Euripides (DS 1984:84). The rate of occurrence of words of this shape in the various styles of tragedy is given in Table 3.3. Resolution before long anceps is also avoided in dochmiacs (Parker 1968).

TABLE 3.7
First paeon-shaped words

	Rate/1000 trimeters	% with last two syllables in resolution
Aeschylus	1.40	100.00
Sophocles	0.66	40.00
Severior	0.22	0.00
Semiseverus	1.42	25.00
Liber	3.52	19.24
Liberrimus	5.23	26.67

19. In lyric iambic, if an arsis is syncopated, a following thesis may be resolved but a preceding thesis is never or hardly ever resolved (Diggle 1981; Cole 1988). If resolution does follow a syncopated arsis, the two light syllables of the resolution are preferentially word initial (Blass 1899). This preference for a word initial resolution appears to be significantly stronger than in unsyncopated iambics and stronger than any tendency to word boundary before a monosyllabic thesis following a syncopated arsis. When in unsyncopated structures a sequence of three heavy syllables implements the metrical structure thesis – arsis – thesis, the second syllable may not be the final syllable of a word: see (7) above. When in syncopated structures a sequence of three heavy syllables implements thesis – thesis – thesis, the second syllable is not infrequently the final syllable of a word, type

πνεόντων μεῖζον ἢ δικαίως,
φλεόντων δωμάτων ὑπέρφευ *Agamemnon* 375–76.

20. In the trimeter, when fifth longum is resolved, line final proceleus-matic-shaped words in which the rime of the final syllable is V̆ are strongly avoided (p. 81); and in the archaic pentameter the rime structures V̆ and V̆C are avoided in the final syllable of the line in all word shapes (p. 83).

21. In the Berlin Paean *DAM* 30, the diseme mark is used to indicate prolongation on line final syllables before the leimma (ME 3.1) and on the second and fifth syllables of the line (ME 3.2). This rhythmical

ME 3.1   ΚΡΑΝΑ Ż Ċ Ṅ Ϲ   *DAM* 30.6

ME 3.2   Ȧ⅃ :ῙΖ Ξ̇ :Ι̇Ζ Ī   *DAM* 30.11
        ΤΩ ΓΑ   ϹΕΝ ΒΩ ΛΟΙϹ

notation correlates with a strong metrical rule favouring word boundary after all prolonged syllables: the first caesura is usual but optional, the second caesura is obligatory.

22. In the Michigan papyrus *DAM* 39–40, the meagre available evidence produces the diseme on probably long first anceps and the triseme on probably long second anceps (ME 3.3–4), but there is no available instance of third anceps with a diseme mark, which may or may not be coincidental (Pearl et al. 1965).

ME 3.3   ΠΑΝ ΤΗ Θ̇̄ Ẏ̄ *DAM* 39.4

ME 3.4   Ṳ̈ ⊖υ υ̣Α ῠ̤Ζ̄   Α Ζ̄Ι̣   *DAM* 39.11
ΟΥΚΕC   ΤᾹ ΕΛ   ΠΤΟΥ

Ῠ̄Ζ Pᴇᴀʀʟ, Ῠ̄Ζ dub. Wɪɴɴɪɴɢᴛᴏɴ-Iɴɢʀᴀᴍ, Ῠ̄Ζ Pap.
ΑΖ̄Ι̣ Pᴇᴀʀʟ, ΑΖ̄Ι̣ dub. Wɪɴɴɪɴɢᴛᴏɴ-Iɴɢʀᴀᴍ, fort. ΑΖ̄Ι̣ i.e. ΑΖ̄Ι̣ Pap.

23. In the Delphic hymns, the assignment of melisms correlates not only with the word accent but also with position within the cretic structure. In *Ath.* and *Lim.*, 25% of the heavy syllables not bearing the circumflex are assigned melisms in the first position of the cretic structure, but only 10.4% of the uncircumflexed heavy syllables in the last position are assigned melisms. As a result nearly 70% of all melisms on uncircumflexed heavy syllables occur in the first position of the cretic structure, whereas only 45% of uncircumflexed heavy syllables without melisms occur in that position. This distribution is not merely an automatic result of a preference for two short notes (whether from resolution or melism) in the first position: only 58% of the total of resolutions plus melisms in the two hymns occur in the first position (West 1992:142). Consequently settings such as ME 3.5 are preferred to settings such as ME 3.6-7.

ME 3.5   *Ath.* 7
ε - οὐ - ὑ-δρου

ME 3.6   *Ath.* 12
μῆ - ρα τα-οὐ- ρων·

ME 3.7   *Ath.* 6
Δε-ελ - φί - σι-ιν

24. In the anapaests of the Oslo papyrus *DAM* 36, when the biceps is contracted, melisms may be assigned either to the biceps or to the longum or to both, unless a spondee-shaped word (s̄s̄) fills the foot, in which case only the second syllable can bear a melism (ME 3.8-12).

ME 3.8   Κ̄̇ ΟΛ   *DAM* 36.7
θάρσει

ME 3.9   Ξ̄ Ξ̄Ο̄   *DAM* 36.9
βαίνει

ME 3.10   C̄ Ξ̄Ο̄   *DAM* 36.9
φωνή

ME 3.11   Φ̇C̄ Ξ̄ Ξ̣̇Φ C̄Φ[ ]   *DAM* 36.4
Ι̇ - - - ἐειω [ν]

ME 3.12　　ΙΟ ΟΦ Χ　*DAM* 36.10
και πασα

25. In the Orestes fragment *DAM* 21, wherever the text is clearly legible, the diseme mark is used over the antepenultimate element of the dochmiac, except when it is set to two notes (ME 3.13–15). The absence

ME 3.13　　] Π P C　　*DAM* 21.1
ʟκατολο]φύρομαι

ME 3.14　　] Π P　C　　*DAM* 21.3
ʟμόνιμο]ς ἐμ βροτοῖς

ME 3.15　　] CP Π　C P　　*DAM* 21.4
ʟτι]ς ἀκάτου θοᾶς

of the diseme in this latter case is probably associated with the use of the older notational convention, whereby the vowel letter is doubled in the spelling (ωως and εεν) to mark the syllable as bearing a melism. The diseme is not used over heavy syllables in other positions. This suggests that the diseme mark has the function of the triseme here: alongside the notational system ⁻ ⌐ there existed the variant ∅ ⁻. The dochmiac is termed ὀκτάσημος by a scholiast on Aeschylus *Septem* 101 and 128; this could be based on a purely metrical count, or possibly the dochmiac could have either a disemic or a trisemic antepenultimate element (Rossbach et al. 1889:761; Lieger 1914; Král 1925).

26. In the Seikilos inscription *DAM* 18, syncopation consistently results either in a triseme over one or two notes or in three notes assigned to a single syllable. This occurs not only line finally but also between the first and second metron and, in the case of φαίνου, also word medially, so that it is clearly causally related to the syncopation of a breve (ME 3.16). Further evidence is provided by the κῶλον ἑξάσημον of the Anonymus de Musica of Bellermann *DAM* 7, which has catalectic syncopation in the final metron and a trisemic final element.

ME 3.16　　C Z̄ Z̄ ΚΙΖ Ῑ　　*DAM* 18.6
·Οσον ζῆς, φαίνου

27. The cretic is generally classified as πεντάσημος (Rossbach et al. 1889), but according to another tradition ascribed to Heliodorus it was ἑξάσημος: ἡ ἀνάπαυσις ⟨ἐπι⟩διδοῦσα χρόνον ἐξασήμους ποιῇ τὰς βάσεις Choeroboscus *On Hephaestion* 247.11 Consbruch: there may have been some variation. In a number of passages in Aristophanes, e.g. *Wasps* 1062 = 1093, 1064 = 1095, *Lysistrata* 785 = 809, a first paeon sequence

responds strophically with a trochaic metron (Christ 1879:388; Rossbach et al. 1889:743; Wilamowitz 1896:265; Schmid 1908; Schroeder 1909; White 1912; Lieger 1930). A cretic sequence is also found responding with a trochaic metron, as at *Peace* 349 = 388.

28. According to *POxy* 2687, Col. ii.2–14, when a cretic structure is embedded in iambic rhythm, its first syllable is prolonged, as in

$$...\overline{ἄ}μβροτοι\ λεῖμακες\ βαθύσκιον.$$

This is confirmed by the location of the leimma, indicating prolongation, not pause, following the note assigned to the first syllable of cretic structures, mainly cretic-shaped words, in the syncopated iambics of *DAM* 38. In the case of the spondaic metron, both notes are followed by leimmata. In one case (ME 3.17) a leimma follows the note set to

ME 3.17 $\overline{ΤΛ}$ ʊ z ἰ $\overline{ΞΛ}$ o:$\overset{\cdots}{ΦC}$ *DAM* 38.6
π υ ρ σ ὸ ς ἔ τ ι λ ε ί π ε τ αι

λεί- as well as the note set to πυρ-: this constitutes an indisputable case of resolution preceding a syncopated arsis and prolonged thesis, contrary to the classical rule (19). At line 8 three notes are set to a (disemic) heavy syllable preceding a prolonged thesis.

29. That in trochaic rhythm a cretic structure had its final syllable prolonged, as opposed to the initial prolongation in iambic rhythm, is clear from *POxy* 2687, Col. ii.2–14 and Col. v.9–20; both passages probably suggest that a trochaic context results in a durational hierarchy between the two heavy syllables of the cretic opposite to that resulting from an iambic context. This distinction may be confirmed by *DAM* 39, if the metre is trochaic in the relevant sections. In this text, the leimma is used to indicate pause or prolongation of a word final syllable (ME 3.18), and in at least one case (ME 3.19) the syntax and metre suggest prolongation.

ME 3.18   ʊ $\overset{\cdots}{ʊ}$ ἡ   *DAM* 39.4
Π Ε Λ Α C

ME 3.19   Α Ζ ἡ   ʊ [ ] $\overline{\overline{Ξ}}$ *DAM* 39.1
Ω   Φ Ι Λ Τ Α Τ Ε [ ]

30. According to *POxy* 2687, Col. ii.21–31, when a cretic structure is embedded in choriambic rhythm, its first long syllable is prolonged, as in

ῥιπτείσθω ποδὸς ἱερὰ̄ βάσις
Διόνυσο̄ν τὸν ἐκ πυρός.

31. In Mesomedes' Hymns to the Sun and to Nemesis *DAM* 4–5, when the final cretic is syncopated to a spondee by a form of catalexis, a leimma is often but not consistently written at the point of syncopation, mostly over the final syllable, after the note of the preceding syllable and before the note of the final syllable (ME 3.20–21). In other

ME 3.20   M I Λ M
           π ώ λ ω ν   *DAM* 4.8

ME 3.21   I Z Λ Z
           δ ι ώ κ ε ι ς   *DAM* 4.9

musical texts the leimma is located at the point of a pause or at the point of a prolongation, such that note note → note leimma. In the latter case, it is the note preceding the leimma that is prolonged, consequently too the syllable to which that note is assigned. Therefore, the prima facie interpretation of the practice of Mesomedes' Hymns is that the penultimate syllable, rather than the final syllable, is prolonged, but the question has been the subject of intricate discussion (Pickel 1880; Westphal et al. 1887; Rossbach et al. 1889; White 1912; Wagner 1921; Král 1925; Winnington-Ingram 1955).

32. Phrase final lengthening is indicated by a number of instances in the musical records in which a length mark (triseme or diseme functioning as a triseme) is used at the end of trimeters or lecythia.

33. There is a well established ancient tradition that trochaic is a faster rhythm than iambic: iambus... ἀπὸ τοῦ ἰέναι βάδην... huic contrarius trochaeus, dictus a cursu et celeritate, Marius Victorinus 44 Keil; ἔστι γὰρ τροχερὸς ῥυθμὸς τὰ τετράμετρα Aristotle *Rhetoric* 1409a1; διχόρειοι τέλεον εἰς ὀρχηστικὸν συνεκπίπτοντες [Longinus] *De Sublimitate* 41; ἐκ μεταφορᾶς τῶν τρεχόντων B Scholiast on Hephaestion 300.7 Consbruch; ὁ τροχαῖος τροχαλὸν ποιεῖ τὸν λόγον Scholiast on Hermogenes *Rhetores Graeci* 7.2:982. The tradition is confirmed by the contexts in which trochaic is used in drama, where it is often associated with lively situations. It is likely that a similar difference characterized dactylic versus anapaestic. Anapaests have certain metrical rules not shared by dactyls, but the ancient tradition is less clear: some passages, for instance Aristides Quintilianus 82.4WI, seem to suggest the opposite, and the interpretation of Dionysius of Halicarnassus *De Compositione Verborum* 17.70UR is disputed. A further passage of Dionysius, 20.92UR, suggests that a heavy syllable had less duration in amphibrachic word shapes than in dactylic word shapes. There must also be some rhythmical basis for the fact that in comedy, whereas the anapaest is readily admitted in place of the iamb

in iambics, the dactyl is rarely admitted in place of the trochee in trochaics.

34. *τὸ δὲ σχῆμα τῆς λέξεως δεῖ μήτε ἔμμετρον εἶναι μήτε ἄρρυθμον... διὸ ῥυθμὸν δεῖ ἔχειν τὸν λόγον, μέτρον δὲ μή· ποίημα γὰρ ἔσται. ῥυθμὸν δὲ μὴ ἀκριβῶς· τοῦτο δὲ ἔσται, ἐὰν μέχρι του ᾖ... ὁ δ' ἴαμβος αὐτή ἐστιν ἡ λέξις ἡ τῶν πολλῶν· διὸ μάλιστα πάντων τῶν μέτρων ἰαμβεῖα φθέγγονται λέγοντες* Aristotle *Rhetoric* 1408b21; cp. [Isocrates] *Techne* 6, Cicero *Orator* 168–203, Marius Victorinus VI.113 Keil.

35. The ancient doctrine of the "irrational" proportion of arsis to thesis has often been cited as evidence for the durational adjustment of heavy syllables in anceps positions (Westphal 1867; Brambach 1871; Jusatz 1893). The originator of this theory is Boeckh (1811), who himself posited a durational adjustment of both arsis and thesis. Hermann (1815) immediately pointed out the absence of ancient evidence for the latter assumption. Evidence for the former is rather indirect too. No ancient discussion of *ἀλογία* explicitly relates it to anceps or gives an example involving anceps. Bacchius *De Musica* 315 Jan cites the spondee *ὀργή* as an example of a foot having an irrational arsis, but no context is given and the irrationality may have been attributed according to a theory that computed syllable weight on the basis of time values assigned to vowels and consonants; note that Bacchius cites next *σπένδω* as an example of the spondee with a long arsis. In Aristoxenus the term *ἄλογος* is applied to the arsis of a *χορεῖος* having a ratio of arsis to thesis midway between 1:1 and 2:1: *τὴν δὲ ἄρσιν μέσον μέγεθος ἔχουσαν... καλεῖται δ' οὗτος χορεῖος ἄλογος* Aristoxenus *Elementa Rhythmica* 20 Pearson. The *ἄλογοι χορεῖοι* of Aristides Quintilianus 37.24WI seem to be different structures. The passage is difficult to interpret and emendations have been suggested: one reasonable interpretation is that these *ἄλογοι χορεῖοι* correspond to long anceps plus resolution in iambic and trochaic.

A THEORY OF GREEK SPEECH RHYTHM

Whereas the most familiar use of foot structure is as a mechanism to account for the phonological patterning of accent or syllable weight, the objective of the following analysis is to reconstruct the system of submoraic duration in Greek as it reflects foot structure in the domain of the word. Numbers in parentheses refer to the various items of evidence presented in the preceding section.

The basic contrastive elements of the rhythmic patterns of Greek speech are heavy and light syllables, or, more precisely, their rimes. The distinction of syllable weight underlies certain phonological rules of an evidently rhythmic nature, namely the comparative rule and the ἑτέρωθεν rule (4). Syllable weight also plays an important role in determining the location of the pitch accent through the recession rule (1) and various other regularities such as Vendryes' law (2) and Wheeler's law (3), in contrast to the trochee rule (1) which counts only the morae contributed by tone bearing units, that is vowels. The importance of such phonological rules lies in the fact that they establish heavy and light syllables as basic structural components of the rhythm of the language and consequently of everyday speech, and not merely intrinsic phonetic durations that play no systematic part in the rhythm of speech but are simply measured off for the purpose of fitting language into verse patterns.

The next step in the analysis is to determine the higher ranked structures into which syllables are arranged in the system of Greek rhythm. Any sequence of syllables bounded by pauses is obviously a higher ranked rhythmic structure, and there is very clear evidence of lengthening of prepausal syllables and perhaps also evidence for the neutralization of syllable weight in prepausal position (20). Below the level of the pause-bounded structure, evidence is available for lengthening of syllables at the end of clauses (32) and at the end of words (7, 14). The fact that syllable durations are regulated or manipulated within a certain phono-syntactic structure means that the structure in question functions as a domain for the rhythmic organization of syllables.

The most difficult question in this area — and at the same time the most crucial one for an understanding of the rhythm of Greek speech — is whether there exists a rhythmic structure ranked between the syllable and the word: does the foot belong exclusively to Greek verse, or is it a property of the rhythm of everyday Greek speech? There are some strong indications that feet, along with their definitional constituents thesis and arsis, are the basic structures into which syllables are organized in the rhythm of the Greek language (as in many other languages).

Feet must exist in some everyday prose utterances, or verse would not have feet either, since verse lines are special instances of prose lines. Cicero recognized this: versus saepe in oratione per imprudentiam dicimus (*Orator* 189). Dionysius of Halicarnassus gives some examples from the stylized rhetoric of Demosthenes, arguing that they are intentional rather than coincidental (*De Compositione Verborum* 25); modern studies have found similar lines in Herodotus and Thucydides (Kaibel 1893). So the question is really whether feet are an inherent property of all prose utterances or merely a coincidental property of some, namely of those that happen to scan. A similar question could be asked about rhyme and alliteration, but the answer would be different, for there is no reason to suppose that, except in special situations, speakers deliberately organize their utterances to produce a greater degree of rhyme or alliteration than is automatically present in the phonological structure of the lexicon. Aristotle remarks that iambic rhythm is typical of conversational speech (34). Iambic rhythm presupposes iambic feet. Similarly, the quantitative iambic foot not only plays a major role in the metrical structures of Arabic verse but is also an important feature of the rules for plural formation in the Arabic language (McCarthy et al. 1990). The clearest evidence that iambic rhythm in Greek involved not only the alternation of light and heavy syllables in the phonological structure of the lexicon but also the rhythmical manipulation by the speaker of nonalternating lexical structures comes from two metrical rules governing the admissibility of certain word shapes at the end of the trimeter and the hexameter.

The fact that heavy syllables are permissible at all in anceps positions could, taken by itself, be explained in purely metrical terms: internal arses in the metron allowed only one of two prosodic categories, while external arses allowed a choice. Whatever the merits of such an approach, it cannot account for (9): if heavy syllables are permitted or avoided in anceps according to the word shapes in which they occur, then the metre must be sensitive to some additional property that is distributed over one subclass of heavy syllables only. According to (9) and (10), the prose pronunciation of the first syllables of the word shapes s̄s̄s̄s̄ and s̄s̄s̄ was unsuitable for mapping onto the metrical arsis of the trimeter and the hexameter respectively in the positions and styles noted. A prosodic pattern that is unsuitable for mapping onto a target metrical pattern is logically simply some other pattern which does not conform to the target pattern and would consequently disrupt it. There are various ways in which an iambic or a dactylic pattern can be disrupted, but in this particular case there is only one reasonable reconstruction of the disrupted pattern. The heavy syllable in question did not implement an arsis because it could only implement a thesis in this particular linguistic context. Such a state of affairs cannot have arisen without a substantive reason: there must be something about the pronunciation of these word shapes that occasioned it. In the framework of a stress theory (Allen 1973), the conclusion would be that the first syllable of these word shapes was stressed. In the framework of a durational theory of Greek metre, the natural assumption would be that it had extra duration, as is assumed for word final heavy syllables which are also not allowed to stand in the verse arsis in third anceps in many styles of the trimeter (Porson's bridge) (7) and in fifth biceps in the hexameter. Additional duration was apparently assigned to a heavy syllable standing before another heavy syllable in certain contexts including the word shapes in question, in such a way that the second heavy syllable could be mapped onto a verse thesis (there is no evidence against that), but the initial heavy syllable could not be mapped onto a verse arsis: it suggested another verse thesis.

Such an assumption about the phonetics of Greek implies a rule in the phonology of Greek rhythm to generate the additional duration. The rule will be called the heavy syllable prolongation rule. Phonological rules are natural rules, which means inter alia that they reflect the physiology of human speech and hearing and the structural system of the particular language to which they apply. In this sense, it is possible to "explain" phonological rules. The facts relevant for the explanation of the Greek heavy syllable prolongation rule are as follows: (i) no additional duration is assigned to heavy syllables that are not word final in regularly alternating light – heavy syllable sequences such as those found in iambic and trochaic rhythms; (ii) additional duration is assigned to the first of two contiguous heavy syllables in the word shapes in question. The phonological prolongation rule generating (ii) finds a natural explanation in the assumption that the rhythm of Greek speech was based on the alternation of long and short rhythmic units. The heavy and light syllables of the Greek language are mapped onto these long and short rhythmic units. In some word shapes, this mapping would break down because there is no light syllable separating two heavy syllables and none of the other mapping strategies allowed at the rate of speech in question can be called upon to generate an alternating rhythmic pattern. In such cases, the rhythm is preserved by a rule adding some of the duration of the "lost" short rhythmic unit to the pronunciation of one of the heavy syllables, thereby ensuring a less uneven temporal succession of rhythmic units. In formal terms, heavy syllables mapped onto long rhythmic units have regular long duration, light syllables mapped onto short rhythmic units have regular short duration, and heavy syllables mapped onto a combination of a long and a short rhythmic units have prolonged duration. In the context of such a hypothesis, the heavy syllable prolongation rule ceases to be an isolated and incidental philological fact and becomes the natural consequence of the underlying principles of the rhythm of Greek speech. The timing of speech gestures in Greek, as in other languages, is not adequately accounted for by atomistic rules that lengthen the final syllables of words and shorten medial syllables. Rather, there is an underlying and regularly patterned structure which controls the timing of the segments and the syllables of Greek speech. Such assumptions about the rhythm of Greek (prose) speech do not conflict with the remarks of Dionysius of Halicarnassus *De Compositione Verborum* 11.42UR: *ἡ μὲν γὰρ πεζὴ λέξις οὐδενὸς οὔτε ὀνόματος οὔτε ῥήματος βιάζεται τοὺς χρόνους οὐδὲ μετατίθησιν*; Dionysius means moraic (phonological) shifts rather than submoraic (phonetic) adaptation.

The long and short units of the rhythmic system of Greek speech will be called thesis and arsis respectively. Since they alternate in the basic rhythmic pattern, their alternation generates a higher level rhythmic structure consisting of thesis plus arsis in either sequential order: this structure will be called a foot. Monosyllabic feet lack an arsis syllable. Although monosyllabic and bimoraic feet are permissible word shapes, they are not primary feet but marked mappings. This is one reason why the traditional distinction between foot and thesis needs to be maintained. There is even some ground for assuming the existence in the rhythm of Greek speech of a metron-sized unit in which the metron level thesis heads the whole higher level structure as well as its own foot. It has already been pointed out that such units can occur in rhythmic patterns in general and in the rhythm of some languages. In a Greek diiambic word, the last syllable probably had greater duration than the second syllable; consequently there existed a relationship of prominence or of degree of demarcation between the two feet, which may have characterized the iambic metron also when it was not followed by a word boundary.

The units of rhythmic structure that have emerged from this discussion of the rhythm of Greek speech are in principle identical to the units of verse structure that are normally referred to by those same terms. It is therefore reasonable to assume that the rhythmic structures of Greek verse reflect, arise from and already exist in the rhythms of Greek speech and are not in principle the result of mapping the rhythms of Greek speech onto extraneous patterns, that is onto temporal patterns of non-linguistic origin. This interpretation is supported by the fact that the avoidance of strings of more than two light syllables in the prose of Demosthenes (5) obviously reflects the same difficulty in mapping such strings that underlies the avoidance of resolution in the stricter styles of verse (11). Both in their structures and in the durational patterns of their performance, verse rhythms are much more regular than speech rhythms. This regularization is largely achieved by metrical rules which constrain the choice of linguistic structures. It is not clear to what extent linguistically unnatural mappings are acceptable in verse: particularly in some types of lyric, a greater degree of deviation from the natural speech rhythm is allowed than in dialogue verse.

Mapping

The rhythm of Greek speech is based on a pattern in which the constituent elements thesis and arsis are prototypically arranged into a binary alternation. In a sample of six thousand nonfinal syllables in polysyllabic words in Plato and Xenophon, the ratio of light to heavy syllables was one to one (O'Neill 1939). However, the lexicon of Greek is not structured in such a way that heavy and light syllables alternate in all word shapes. In fact, a perfectly alternating structure such as ἐπισκοπουμένην is comparatively uncommon, and complete absence of alternation, as in δουλευόντων or προσεθέμεθα, can easily occur. Consequently, the syllable sequences in the different word shapes have to be organized into a rhythmical structure. This organization is achieved by a set of rules which map heavy and light syllables onto thesis and arsis according to their prosodic context and by a second set of rules which adjust the phonetic duration of the syllables to generate surface temporal relations that reflect their underlying assigned status as thesis or arsis. One convenient descriptive formalism for schematizing mapping and durational adjustment is illustrated in Figure 3.1, which is a diagrammatic representation of the rhythmic processing of the citation form of a left-extended molossus-shaped word such as κασιγνήτῳ. The penultimate syllable of this word shape is mapped onto arsis by the heavy syllable subordination rule (45), and its relative duration is adjusted accordingly. The suprascript symbol x is used to represent any duration less than that indicated by the macron and greater than that indicated by the breve; the word final durational increment is not represented. S represents 'syllable,' T 'thesis' and A 'arsis.' In the particular formalism chosen here, the segments of the word are represented separately from the prosodic units of rhythm and these in turn are represented separately from the rhythmical pattern itself, much as the words and the music of a song are separable.

That such a separation of segments and rhythm is psychologically real is indicated by data from word games in a number of different languages. In Bakwiri (Cameroon: Hombert 1973, 1986), there is a word game

Segments	κα	σιγ	νή	τῳ
Syllable duration	Š	S̄	S̄ˣ	S̄
Syllable weight	Š	S̄	S̄	S̄
Foot structure	[A	T]	[A	T]

FIGURE 3.1
Extended molossus-shaped word

that changes the order of syllables in the word: the vowels and consonants of syllables are exchanged, but phonological vowel length and lexical tone do not change. A trochee-shaped word remains trochaic under syllable inversion and does not become iambic: *zéyà* 'burn' → *yázè*, not **yàzé*. A similar separation of the rhythm of a word from its segments is evidenced in word games in Hanunóo (Philippines: Conklin 1959), Sanga (Zaire: Hombert 1986), Luganda (Clements 1986), Finnish (Vago 1985; Anttila 1989), and in Tagalog (Philippines: Conklin 1956) where vowel length depends on stress. The autonomy of rhythm is also indicated by production speech errors involving semantically unrelated words, such as *cinema* for *cylinder* or *apartment* for *appointment*, which not only share many segments with the target word but also nearly always have the same number of syllables and the same stress pattern. Stress pattern was also one of the factors conditioning error intrusion in a short term memory study requiring the recall of disyllabic words (Drewnowski et al. 1980). Japanese speech errors and neologisms generally have the same number of morae as the underlying target and model words respectively (Kubozono 1989). Errors in perception likewise tend not to involve misperceived prosody (Garnes et al. 1975). Similarly, when words are on the tip of the tongue, it is often the case that we can recall the number of syllables and the stress pattern without being able to supply all the segments correctly (Brown et al. 1966; Fay et al. 1977; Browman 1978; Cutler 1986). Sometimes, the rhythm of an underlying syllable sequence is preserved in an altered surface representation, as in Turkish where surface long vowels derived by contraction following the deletion of *g* were found to be about 13% longer than underlying long vowels because they preserved the duration of the underlying VCV sequence (Rudin in Dalby 1986). In Swedish, when a nasal consonant is realized by nasalization of the preceding vowel, as often occurs before an unvoiced sibilant, the duration of the vowel is comparable to what would have been allotted to a vowel plus nasal sequence (Fant et al. 1989). This situation can represent an intermediate stage in the diachronic process known as compensatory lengthening.

It was stated above that the complex of rules by which Greek speech is processed into rhythmic structures can be analyzed as a set of mapping rules and a set of duration adjustment rules. Among the former, it is useful to distinguish the mapping rules proper from the various principles of pattern structure and directionality with which they interact.

Principles of pattern structure

36. According to the principle of alternation, thesis and arsis follow each other sequentially within the rhythmic domain in the basic representation of the pattern. Amphibrach stress feet have been posited in one

analysis of stress in Cayuvava and in the Chugach dialect of Yupik Eskimo (Halle 1990), but other analyses are possible (Haraguchi 1991); there is little reason to suppose that in Greek an arsis can ever be adjacent to another arsis within the same domain, which precludes analysis of the choriamb into trochee plus iamb (Aristides Quintilianus 38.6WI, Caesius Bassus 263.25, 264.5 Keil). However, it often happens that an underlying arsis is deleted, with the result that a less abstract representation of the thesis-arsis level can contain contiguous theses. The slow speech pronunciation of the tetrasyllabic word shape s̄s̄s̄s̄ (type σωθή-σομαι) in its citation form is an example: it is diagrammed in Figure 3.2 on the assumption of trochaic footing.

37. According to the principle of final syllable prominence, when there are contiguous syllables of the same weight, if one of them is the final syllable of a word, then that syllable has greater rhythmic prominence, except under certain conditions prepausally, and resists durational reduction. As a consequence of this principle, if a word ends in two heavy syllables, they may be mapped onto the sequences TT or AT but never onto TA except in rapid connected speech (7). Likewise, if a word ends in three light syllables, the penultimate and the antepenultimate syllables can be reduced to a matrix (Allen 1973) and mapped onto a thesis (14), but a word final light syllable is generally autonomous and only rarely allowed to be processed as part of a matrix.

38. It is not infrequently the case that a syllable sequence could be processed into two alternative structures, according as the mapping rules (45) and (46) are or are not applied. In such cases, according to the principle of preference for the basic mapping rules, the less complex processing is preferred except in rapid speech. In general, the basic mapping

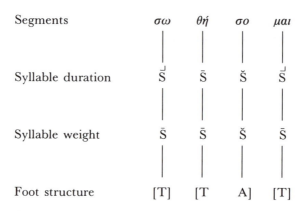

FIGURE 3.2
Extended cretic-shaped word

rules (41, 42, 43) have a low cost attached to them, whereas subordination (45) and matrix formation (46), and particularly a combination of both of them, are viewed as more complex and costly, also because relative to slow speech mapping they usually involve defooting. Thus words of the shape ionic a minore presumably have the structure ATT in their citation forms, and there is considerable resistance to mapping them onto TAT within the phrase (18), even though this would achieve two of the rhythmical objectives of fluent speech, namely to extend the scope of the rhythmical domain and to eliminate monosyllabic feet. The availability of more than one option for the rhythmic organization of speech is reported for various languages. In Mantjiltjara and Walmatjari (W. Australia: Odden 1979), stress may fall on every other syllable or on every third syllable. In Swedish unstressed syllable sequences, a subsidiary stress, implemented by increased duration, was found to be introduced variably by different subjects, so that a pentasyllabic stress foot was structured either as trochee plus dactyl or as dactyl plus trochee (Strangert 1984). This variability also appeared in a psychological study of letter grouping, where a five letter sequence was variably chunked 2 + 3 or 3 + 2 (p. 89).

39. The first principle of directionality requires that the assignment of syllables to thesis and arsis proceed from right to left, that is from the end of the word to the beginning. More specifically, the rightmost syllable or light syllable sequence that can be mapped onto thesis is sought out as a pivot, and the mapping proceeds from that syllable back towards the beginning of the word (Allen 1973). The clearest evidence for this principle comes from a conjunction of the dispondee and the molossus word shapes, provided that these words have the rhythm ATAT and TAT respectively in their citation forms at normal speech rates; at artificially slow speech rates, no heavy syllable was mapped onto arsis. There are two variables and consequently four theoretically possible systems.

(i) Map trochaically from left to right: this would give correct results for the molossus but not for the dispondee, which would appear as TATT.

(ii) Map iambically from left to right: this would give correct results for the dispondee but not for the molossus, which would appear as ATT.

(iii) Map trochaically from right to left: this is precluded by the principle of final prominence (37) and would give wrong results for both shapes (TATA and ATA respectively).

(iv) Map iambically from right to left: this gives correct results with both shapes.

The first principle of directionality does not imply a locally bound and mechanistic progress from right to left; alternative computations may be tried out and a choice made among them so that rhythm may be optimized according to the mappings that are appropriate to the speech rate in question and other potentially conditioning factors. This elasticity of rhythmic organization is further increased when citation form rhythm is manipulated by remapping in connected speech (Chapter 6). Principle (39) is formulated here as a useful heuristic and an empirical generalization. It is possible to construct a more economical theoretical system in which (39) is a predictable consequence of (36) and (37).

40. The second principle of directionality states that the assignment of foot structure proceeds from left to right within the word. This extrapolates from foot assignment in the phrasal context of the verse line and replicates the socalled orientation effect already noted (p. 90). The trimeter and the tetrameter end with the same structures: their rhythmical difference arises from the additional cretic sequence at the beginning of the latter. The implication is that the distinction between rising (iambic, anapaestic) and falling (trochaic, dactylic) rhythm depends on whether the rhythmic domain begins with thesis or arsis. The claim is that in Greek the initial sequence determines the analysis: the words of the language are not uniformly rising or falling, but one or the other depending on word shape; however, words are uniformly rising or falling within the domain of the word, that is words cannot have a combination of rising and falling rhythm. In Yidin (Australia: Hayes 1982) disyllabic stress feet are assigned left to right, and words are iambic if the second syllable of any foot has a long vowel, otherwise they are trochaic. The claim also implies that stray syllables, that is syllables left over after feet have been constructed according to (39) and (40) and the mapping rules, are adjoined at the end rather than at the beginning of words. Consequently the citation form of the amphibrach will not have been a trochee with anacrusis but an iamb with adjoined stray syllable; the distinction may have had implications for the durational ratio of light to heavy syllable in this word shape. The opposite claim, that all words had rising rhythm (or all words had falling rhythm) entails more marked mappings for many word shapes. For instance, universal rising rhythm would imply that the citation form of the ditrochee-shaped word šŠšŠ had a monosyllabic foot followed by an iambic foot with adjoined stray syllable *[š][ŠšŠ]. Such a theory would also make trochaic verse very unnatural in Greek. There seems to be no reason for analyzing a trochee as a monosyllabic iamb with adjoined final stray syllable or an iamb as a monosyllabic trochee with adjoined initial stray syllable other than the probably spurious one of replicating the rhythmic uniformity of refooted connected speech at the level of citation forms.

There is a prima facie contradiction between the directionality of the assignment of thesis-arsis (right to left) and the directionality of the assignment of foot structure (left to right). At least in very general terms, such contradictions are not untypical of rhythm rules. In Huasteco (S.E. Mexico: Larsen et al. 1949), stress assignment involves two counting operations with contradictory directionality: first a search is made for the last (rightmost) long vowel syllable, which receives stress, and then, if there are no long vowels, the first (leftmost) syllable is chosen for stress. A similar rule is found in certain Komi dialects (Russia) and its mirror image in E. Cheremis (Russia) (Kiparsky 1973). In languages with a lexically defined stress, the stressed syllable is the rhythmical pivot and any secondary stresses are likely to be assigned counting right to left back from the pivot syllable for pretonic stress and left to right forward from the pivot syllable for posttonic stress, as in Cahuilla (California: Seiler 1965). Auca (Ecuador: Pike 1964) has a different system: here stress is assigned trochaically from left to right in the stem section of the word and from right to left in the suffix section of the word.

Mapping rules

Of the seven rules for the mapping of syllables onto thesis and arsis, three are basic, in the sense that they are applied preferentially and consist of natural and straightforward correspondences involving little modification of intrinsic duration. The remaining four are subsidiary, in the sense that they are less frequently invoked and less transparent strategies designed to disambiguate the rhythm of overtly nonalternating syllable sequences. The rules comprise the list of all possible mappings: they therefore serve to exclude impossible mappings such as ŠŠ → A or ŠŠŠ → T. But, although specification of the contexts in which the rules apply reduces overlap between them significantly, they are not mutually exclusive. Observance of the principle of word final prominence (37) and of the principle of preference for the basic mapping rules (38) is less rigorous in fluent speech and this results in alternative mappings, as for instance in the case of the first paeon word shape (17). Furthermore, two of the subsidiary mapping rules (44, 47) are applied more readily in slow, deliberate speech, while the other two (45, 46) are more typical of fluent speech.

The basic mapping rules are:

41. T ← Š. A heavy syllable may be mapped onto thesis.

42. A ← Š. A light syllable may be mapped onto arsis.

43. A ← ŠŠ. A sequence of two light syllables may be mapped onto arsis.

The basic mapping rules always apply except when a subsidiary mapping rule is invoked. Therefore, a heavy syllable is always mapped onto thesis except when rules (45) or (47) are applied; and so on. As a consequence of rules (42) and (43), in a prose utterance monosyllabic and disyllabic arses can alternate freely, whereas in podic verse with its stricter requirements for podic regularity this is not permitted except in the case of substitution in comedy. There would have been a range of different rhythms for disyllabic arses; the general relationship between tempo and foot structure has already been noted (p. 91). For very slow and deliberate speech, one could posit a bimoraic "subfoot" for the anapaest with the external mora stronger than the internal mora. This would gradually accelerate through the range of speech rates until in rapid conversational speech the disyllabic arsis had lost its rhythmic autonomy and had changed from a differentiated subfoot having a stronger and weaker mora to a simple unstructured bimoraic arsis. A more radical interpretation would be that this arsis also lost its properly bimoraic status in rapid speech and was temporally compressed in a manner often assumed for unstressed syllables in stress timed languages. A final question is to what extent the timing of prima facie ternary feet in prose major phrases that happen to consist predominantly of binary feet differs from the timing of ternary feet in a predominantly ternary context and vice versa. It has already been noted (p. 97) that feet can be temporally adjusted under the influence of the structure of contiguous feet (Fourakis et al. 1988).

Another implication of the mapping rules as stated is that in Greek rhythm the trochee is trimoraic, not bimoraic. The monosyllabic trochee (and the monosyllabic iamb) are interpreted as contractions of the unmarked trimoraic foot types; it is not the case that trimoraic trochees are expansions of an unmarked bimoraic trochee. There is a difference in the ratio of thesis to arsis in the trochee and the iamb, but this difference is submoraic, not moraic (p. 98). The mapping of heavy syllable onto thesis is consistent across different foot structures. Although the disyllabic arsis is a permissible subconstituent of the foot, the bimoraic trochee, that is the heavy syllable or the pyrrhic, is an illicit underlying verse foot, as already pointed out by Aristoxenus

τῶν δὲ ποδῶν ἐλάχιστοι μέν εἰσιν οἱ ἐν τῷ τρισήμῳ μεγέθει· τὸ γὰρ δίσημον μέγεθος παντελῶς ἂν ἔχοι πυκνὴν τὴν ποδικὴν σημασίαν. Aristoxenus *Elementa Rhythmica* 31 Pearson.

Also, as noted below (p. 138), the disyllabic bimoraic trochee, that is the pyrrhic, is an illicit surface foot in syncopated trochaic. It is unlikely that a language would structure its verse system in such a way that the basic variant of the foot was illicit in its disyllabic actuation while the expanded variant had unmarked distribution.

The following is a brief preliminary statement of the subsidiary mapping rules without full specification of the environments of their application, which depend partly on the domain within which rhythmic structure is assigned and partly on the degree of flexibility allowed in the observance of principles (37) and (38).

44. Light syllable prolongation. T ← Š. A light syllable may be mapped onto thesis.

45. Subordination. A ← S̄. A heavy syllable may be mapped onto arsis.

46. Matrix formation. T ← ŠŠ. A sequence of two light syllables may be mapped onto thesis.

47. Heavy syllable prolongation. AT and TA ← S̄. When a heavy syllable is mapped onto thesis, zero may be mapped onto arsis in the same foot, that is an arsis preceding or following within the same foot may be deleted.

Light syllable prolongation

The light syllable prolongation rule is a natural and common approach to the rhythmic disambiguation of sequences of quantitatively undifferentiated syllables in languages all over the world. In Swedish, in strings of unstressed syllables, every second or every third syllable tends to be lengthened by 10–20%, resulting in a low level stress that organizes unstressed syllables into rhythmic groups (Strangert 1984, 1985; Bruce 1984, 1986); similar data are available for Dutch (Nooteboom 1972, 1973; Slootweg 1988), but Italian allows sequences of equally short unstressed vowels (Farnetani et al. 1990). Rules generating rhythmic alternation are not confined to stress languages: in Japanese, which has a pitch accent, alternate light syllables are lengthened in deliberate speech, and there is a similar lengthening rule in Choctaw, which also has a type of pitch accent (p. 214). As a result of such rules, longer words are split into shorter word-like rhythmic components. The application of the light syllable prolongation rule in Greek is represented schematically in Figure 3.3 for a proceleusmatic-shaped word in its citation form. The light syllable prolongation rule posits that a light syllable can be mapped onto thesis between two single light syllable arses, and that when a light syllable is mapped onto thesis its duration is augmented. The rule rests on a conjunction of linguistic and metrical evidence. Vowel lengthening in comparatives (4) indicates that a sequence of light syllables could be pronounced with this sort of rhythm in very early Greek, while other apparent rhythmic lengthenings suggest an alternative rhythm ŠŠŠŠ → ŠŠŠ̌Š

Segments	ἐ	κό	μι	σα
Syllable duration	$\breve{S}$	$\overset{x}{\breve{S}}$	$\breve{S}$	$\overset{x}{\breve{S}}$
Syllable weight	$\breve{S}$	$\breve{S}$	$\breve{S}$	$\breve{S}$
Foot structure	[A	T]	[A	T]

FIGURE 3.3
Proceleusmatic-shaped word

with disyllabic arsis. Although this sort of rhythmic processing was presumably quite general, it was submoraic, that is it did not lead to an actual phonological change in vowel quantity, except in a few morphological categories mostly involving a stem vowel. The rhythm rule is a general phonetic rule, but in its manifestation as the phonological quantity shift it is a restricted morphophonemic rule (4). In its citation form a proceleusmatic-shaped word ($\breve{S}\breve{S}\breve{S}\breve{S}$) is pronounced with iambic rhythm and consequently with lengthening not only at the end of the word ($\breve{S}\breve{S}\breve{S}\overset{x}{\breve{S}}$) but also at the end of the foot ($\breve{S}\overset{x}{\breve{S}}\breve{S}\overset{x}{\breve{S}}$). That this sort of rhythmic mapping persisted in deliberate speech in classical times is suggested by the metrical evidence in (13), which indicates a considerable reluctance to map the second and third syllables of a proceleusmatic-shaped word onto thesis as a matrix. If dactylic, anapaestic and amphibrachic rhythm were disfavoured for this shape phrase internally (12, 13), and if cretic rhythm was probably disfavoured phrase finally (13), some other rhythm must have been normal, and it is hard to see what that could have been other than diiambic, perhaps with a ditrochaic alternate in certain phrasal contexts in connected speech. It is reasonable to think that fourth paeon-shaped words too could be pronounced with diiambic rhythm ($\breve{S}\overset{x}{\breve{S}}\breve{S}\bar{S}$) in deliberate speech; this supposition follows automatically from the view that matrix formation is rare in deliberate speech (11). The data concerning the first paeon-shaped word (17) and paeonic-trochaic responsion (27) are consistent with a tendency to ditrochaic rhythm in $\bar{S}\breve{S}\breve{S}\breve{S}$ structures. The responsion of ‒ ᴗ ‒ ᴗ with ‒ ᴗ ᴗ ᴗ is probably motivated both by light syllable prolongation and by the greater durational ratio of $\breve{S}$ to $\bar{S}$ in trochaic (33). If the heavy syllable in thesis had less duration in trochaic than in iambic rhythm, then some degree of prolongation, even if less than in iambic rhythm, could motivate the responsion.

Subordination

While light syllable prolongation introduces rhythmic alternation into a series of three light syllables by lengthening the medial syllable, subordination does the same for a series of three heavy syllables by shortening the medial syllable. Subordination and similar related processes are natural rules of speech rhythm found in a number of different languages. These processes remedy the rhythmic difficulty arising from contiguous strong elements. In English, the stress of a syllable may be reduced in nondeliberate speech if it stands between two other stressed syllables within a phonological phrase; this is particularly well established in fixed phrases such as *bíg bàd wólf* and *thrée blìnd míce*. According to one interpretation, the central stress foot has become defooted, and the three contiguous theses have been replaced by the alternating two foot structure [TA][T] (Giegerich 1985). Correspondingly, in the English iambic pentameter a stressed monosyllabic word may stand in the arsis (weak) position. In Italian, stress clash can be resolved by destressing or remapping; in other cases the duration of the first stressed vowel is incremented (Nespor 1990). In Yidin, long vowels in the weak position of iambic feet are shortened (Hayes 1982). The application of the subordination rule (45) has already been represented schematically in Figure 3.1, and the metrical evidence on which the rule is based is given in (6). The environment of the rule is as follows: it applies to a heavy syllable preceded and followed by a thesis. In very slow speech, such a heavy syllable would be mapped onto thesis and constitute a monosyllabic foot. At more normal speech rates, this foot is defooted and the heavy syllable in question is mapped onto arsis. The contiguous thesis on the left should preferentially be a heavy syllable rather than a disyllabic matrix (18); data were cited in Chapter 2 indicating that subordination applies more easily to CV̄-syllables than to CVC-syllables. For its basic application, the subordination rule requires that all three heavy syllables of the molossus structure be in the same word. #(...)s̄s̄s̄(...)#. Implicit in the hypothesis of subordination is the assumption that, when a heavy syllable is mapped onto arsis, it is pronounced with less duration than a heavy syllable mapped onto thesis. The law of the tetrasyllables (9) indicates that subordination fails to apply in a deliberate speech style when the second syllable of the molossus begins a word: (...)s̄ # s̄s̄(...)#. Porson's bridge (7) indicates that subordination fails to apply when the second syllable of the molossus ends a word: (...)s̄s̄ # s̄(...). This is the case also for monosyllabic lexical words, which constitute a minimal foot in the domain of the word and consequently can be mapped only onto thesis, not onto arsis. The constraint on word boundary preceding a subordinated syllable is relaxed in the nondeliberate speech styles on which the dialogue of tragedy is based, and it is probable that the constraint against full word boundary following a subordinated syllable is relaxed in the conversational speech styles on which the dialogue of comedy is based (p. 280). Finally, in artificially slow and deliberate speech, subordination was probably not permitted at all: this follows from the theoretically motivated claim just made that subordination is a defooting process, and it is also one reasonable interpretation of the practice of Callimachus (6).

The above account of the application of subordination, based on the metrical evidence, is consistent with the musical evidence, as far as the latter goes. The evidence of the Michigan Papyrus (22), although hardly sufficient to prove anything, fits with the assumption that subordination applied in the complete molossus environment (long third anceps) but not, in the speech style in question, to a postpausal spondee-shaped word; that is, pause cannot replace the first syllable of the molossus in the formulation of the rule in this speech style. Subordination also did not apply to a prepausal spondee-shaped word; more precisely, the sort of phonological boundary associated with the caesura effectively blocked subordination. This latter point suggests that a word final heavy syllable, which was metrically permitted in second anceps in the trimeter, was pronounced without subordination. However, in third anceps a heavy syllable was not metrically permitted unless it could be pronounced with subordination. There is also some evidence (24) that melisms, at least in spondee-shaped words, were avoided on syllables most subject to subordination. The existence of a subordination rule does not, of course, imply the nonexistence of other durational differences, both those arising from the different segmental composition of syllables and those arising from lengthening before syntactic boundaries.

Matrix formation

The equivalence of šš to š is a well attested feature of language rhythm for which evidence has already been cited (p. 48). The rules for reduplication in Manam (New Guinea: Lichtenberk 1983; McCarthy et al. 1986) provide a clear illustration of this prosodic equation in a language that does not have long vowels or diphthongs: in this language, heavy syllables are syllables closed by a nasal consonant, all other syllables are open and light. Reduplication in Manam involves suffixing a bimoraic prosodic unit, perhaps a foot. If the word ends in a pyrrhic syllable sequence, the last two syllables are copied, as in *salaga* → *salagalaga* 'long.' If the word ends in a heavy syllable, the last syllable only is copied: *malaboŋ*

→ *malabomboŋ* 'flying fox.' Verb reduplication in Warlpiri (Australia: Tranel 1991) also involves a bimoraic template if closed syllables are classified as light. In Japanese speech errors, a heavy syllable is more readily replaced by two light syllables than by a single light syllable (Kubozono 1985). When Luganda poems and songs are accompanied on the drums, a single drumbeat is assigned to a light syllable and two drum beats are assigned to a heavy syllable (Tucker 1962). In Japanese verse, the mora count of the line is fixed: in satisfying the mora count, light syllables are valued as one mora and heavy syllables as two moras; similarly in Tongan verse (de Chene 1985) and Kinyarwanda pastoral poetry (Coupez et al. 1970). Among the various Arabic metres, the kāmil and the wāfir metres allow šš to respond with š (Wright 1955). In Hausa Islamic verse, this responsion occurs in locations in which it is not found in the corresponding Classical Arabic metres (Hiskett 1975). In Middle Indian metres such as those of Pali (Warder 1967) and in the traditional Hindi metres (Fairbanks 1981), the equivalence of a heavy syllable to two light syllables is a basic feature. In Classical Persian verse, the two light syllables may be replaced by a heavy syllable except at the beginning of a line (Elwell-Sutton 1976). In Urdu verse, šš is frequently substituted for š, but probably not under the metrical ictus or in precaesural position (Russell 1960). The equivalence of a sequence of two syllables with short vowels to one syllable with a long vowel is found in the palimbacchiacs of the classical Somali gabay verse genre (Johnson 1979). Two light syllables respond with one heavy syllable in the praise poems of the Bahima (Uganda: Morris 1964). In Germanic, the equivalence of šš to š interacts with stress and morpheme structure (Campbell 1959; Allen 1973), as perhaps also in Tamil verse (de Chene 1985). Even allowing for the widespread borrowing of quantitative verse systems, particularly from Arabic (Greenberg 1960), the cumulative evidence for this prosodic equivalence substantiates it as a natural phenomenon of rhythm in language.

The application of the matrix formation rule is represented schematically in Figure 3.4, where š denotes a syllable pronounced with less duration than regular Š. Relative to slow speech mapping with light syllable prolongation, matrix formation vacates an arsis position and can involve defooting. The metrical evidence on which the rule is based is given in (11). Implicit in the hypothesis of a matrix formation rule — as opposed to a simple T ← šš mapping rule — is the assumption that the sum of the durations of the light syllables in a matrix is less, other things being equal, than the sum of the durations of two independent single light syllable arses. Although it has not been possible to substantiate the philological evidence that has been cited over the years in support of this assumption (DS 1980, 1981), intervocalic consonant reduction

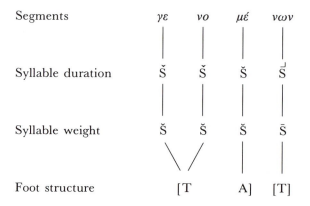

FIGURE 3.4

Fourth paeon-shaped word

seems to be associated with a matrix, as in English and Efik (Hyman 1990). In the framework of stress theory (Allen 1973), matrix formation is occasioned by stress. In that case, it is possible that the intervocalic consonant of the matrix was ambisyllabic: both in English and in German, stress seems to encourage ambisyllabicity. However, stress is not a precondition for matrix formation, since Efik does not have a Germanic type stress. The phonological environment for the rule is as follows: it applies to a pyrrhic structure preceded by an arsis or a pause and followed by an arsis. The surrounding arses should preferentially consist of a single light syllable rather than of two light syllables (12) or a subordinated heavy syllable (18). The rareness of resolution in strict versification (11) suggests that matrix formation was not widely invoked in deliberate speech, and this in turn supports the idea that matrix formation in Greek is a subtractive mapping rule rather than a simple moraic equivalence rule. In mora-timed Japanese, the duration of the *b* and *k* onsets in *baaku* was somewhat longer than in *bakudo* as read in frame sentences, suggesting some compensation for bimoraic *baa-* having slightly shorter duration than bimoraic *baku-* (Port et al. 1987). The avoidance of sequences of more than two light syllables in some Greek oratorical prose (5) can be interpreted as an analogous preference for basic mapping as opposed to matrix formation and light syllable prolongation. Unlike subordination, which is well established as a word-level process by its application to molossus-shaped words, in matrix formation the preceding arsis is often in a different word from the matrix, which suggests that matrix formation is more characteristic of the fluent phrasing of connected speech than it is of citation forms: the proceleusmatic-shaped word itself probably had a basic diiambic rhythm (44). However, two light syllables belonging to different words cannot be mapped onto a thesis as a matrix (14): in this sense, the integrity of the word as the underlying domain of rhythmic organization is preserved. Idiomatic phrases that appear to violate the split resolution rule actually have reduced demarcation (p. 349). The second syllable of a matrix should also not be the last syllable in a word (14): it is not clear whether the permissibility of line initial tribrach-shaped words in the tragic trimeter has some linguistic basis or is merely a relaxation in postpausal position of the metrical requirement for strictly iambic rhythm. In more rapid and conversational speech, the matrix can be shifted from its position in the citation form of a word shape to permit extension of the domain of rhythmic alternation (15), and the constraint against the matrix consisting of the last two syllables of a word is relaxed in lexical pyrrhic- and first paeon-shaped words (16, 17).

Heavy syllable prolongation

The heavy syllable prolongation rule (47), which applies when a heavy syllable constitutes a monosyllabic foot, has already been represented schematically in Figure 3.2. The rule is based partly on metrical evidence (9, 19), partly on the statements of *POxy* 2687 (= *POxy* 9 with additional fragments) and partly on the evidence of the musical documents. The effect of the application of this rule on the duration of heavy syllables is not only implicit in its formulation but also explicitly documented by the last two categories of evidence just mentioned. Since the rhythm of Greek song was so closely tied to the rhythm of speech, one interpretation of the musical evidence is that prolongation in song reflects some degree of prolongation in speech. It could also be assumed that prolongation in song had a purely musical basis; in that case, one would still expect the prolonged syllable to be the same syllable that would undergo any independent linguistically motivated lengthening in speech.

The phonological environments of the rule are not exhaustively known. The location of prolongation resulting from syncopation of an arsis in lyric has been greatly disputed since the time of Bergk, who believed that the thesis in the same foot was prolonged (Goldmann 1867; Pickel 1880). Before the publication of the Seikilos inscription and of *POxy* 9, the standard nineteenth-century view held that it was the thesis preceding the syncopation that was prolonged in all cases, i.e. in rising as well as in falling rhythm (Brambach 1869; Christ 1879; Rossbach et al. 1887, 1889). There was some initial surprise at finding ⌣ ‒ ⌐ rather than ⌣⌐‒ in the Seikilos inscription (Crusius 1894), and it was even suggested that the metre of the inscription was trochaic (Brandt 1902). The iambic prolongation of the cretic λέξις (⌐ ⌣ ‒) indicated by *POxy* 9 (28) likewise met with initial disbelief (Reinach 1898; Succo 1906). But Blass (1899) clearly recognized that *POxy* 9 required a modification of the standard theory of Rossbach and Westphal to permit prolongation of the first longum parallel to that of the second already attested in the Seikilos inscription. For a while there appeared to be developing a consensus in favour of Bergk's foot-based prolongation (Weil 1902; Petr 1912; White 1912; Lieger 1914; Král 1925), but soon it became apparent that there were difficulties in the uniform application of prolongation in the same foot under all circumstances (Schroeder 1908; Wilamowitz 1909).

The major problem is to reconcile the statements of *POxy* 2687 and the evidence of ancient musical notation (21)–(32) with the distribution of resolution in iambo-trochaic (19). The rules in Attic drama are: resolution never or hardly ever occurs before a syncopated arsis, but it can occur after a syncopated arsis (19). As Rossbach and Westphal recognized, the classical rules receive a unitary explanation given the two hypothetical premises (a) that the two light syllables cannot be prolonged to trisemic value, and (b) that syncopation results in the prolongation of the preceding thesis in both iambic and trochaic. In its usual formulation, premise (a) states that prolonged syllables may not be resolved, or that a resolved triseme could only yield three light syllables (Koster 1953). The premise has traditionally been defended on the grounds that two syllables of 1.5 durational units each are either impossible or very suspect. Resolution is a mapping rule, prolongation is a duration adjustment rule. Since mapping logically precedes duration adjustment, it is tautological that resolution cannot apply to a prolonged thesis. It is an empirical question whether, and if so precisely how, two light syllables mapped onto a thesis can be prolonged.

Premise (a) has been rejected by some scholars (Vogelmann 1877; Lieger 1914, 1930, 1933), and there is reason to question at least the generality of its application. From the Seikilos inscription, it is clear that the two note melism, which is the musical counterpart of resolution, also occurs on trisemically prolonged syllables. In the Hymns of Mesomedes, there are apparently cases of two notes set to a trisemically prolonged syllable, whether the penultimate or the final is assumed to be prolonged, for instance *DAM* 4.13 with the leimma separating two pairs of notes and *DAM* 5.9 without leimma. Similar cases may occur in *PMich* 2958. In cretic-paeonic, as distinguished from syncopated iambo-trochaic, and in dochmiac, prolongation of any longum would conflict, on premise (a), with the relative freedom of resolution. In genuinely cretic passages, e.g. Aeschylus *Supplices* 418–422 = 423–427 and *Ath.* and *Lim.* (*DAM* 19–20), either of the longa of a cretic may be resolved: however, in clear contrast to its exclusion before ‾ ˘ ‾ in syncopated iambics, the first paeon type of resolution (‒ ˘ ˘ ˘) is preferred to the fourth paeon type (˘ ˘ ˘ ‒), particularly in Aristophanes. In the dochmiac, all three longa can be resolved. Resolution of the first is by far the most frequent, and simultaneous resolution of the first and the second is not uncommon. According to premise (a), prolongation and resolution are incompatible. Consequently, if premise (a) could be assumed to apply with equal strictness to all rhythms, the straightforward conclusion would be that neither true cretic nor dochmiac metra underwent syncopation and heavy syllable prolongation, but rather permitted contiguous theses, neither of which was prolonged. This conclusion would accord with the respective classifications of the cretic and the dochmiac as πεντάσημος (27) and ὀκτάσημος (25). However, the Orestes fragment is fairly strong evidence for prolongation of the antepenultimate element of the dochmiac. The permissibility of resolution in the dochmiac and in cretic-paeonic could simply reflect the fact that these metres are in general less constrained than iambo-trochaic. Split resolution, for instance, is more common in true cretic-paeonic and dochmiac than in iambo-trochaic.

Premise (b) is consistent with the well-known fact that, on a number of counts, such as Knox's, Porson's and Havet's bridges and the constraints on resolution, the iambic rhythm of the trimeter and the trochaic rhythm of the tetrameter behave in a parallel fashion, and foot structure is not relevant. However, even without the musical evidence, it would be reasonable to expect that the prolongation should be in the same foot as the syncopation. This is in fact the case in trochaic, but if it were the case in iambic, then it would be necessary to find an explanation for why resolution was forbidden in the unprolonged thesis and permitted in the prolonged thesis. One rather improbable solution to this dilemma lies in resuscitation of the old doctrine of anacrusis, first introduced by Bentley and Hermann. Anacrusis would find its linguistic basis in a posited permissibility of adjoined syllables, and consequently amphibrachic feet, at the beginning as well as at the end of rhythmical units, at least in certain as yet undefined environments. This would be an argument in favour of uniformly left dominant foot structure, a hypothesis that was rejected above (p. 126). Another possible solution would be to accept a basic rule of prolongation in the same foot and assume that it applied in trochaic, but that in iambic there was a secondary readjustment producing prolongation of the preceding thesis: ˘ ‒ | . ‒ | ˘ ‒ → ˘ ‒ | ♩ | ˘ ‒ → ˘ ♩ | ‒ | ˘ ‒ . Such a readjustment rule could be supposed to apply in general, or only when the thesis following syncopation was resolved (Schroeder 1908). It was suggested, on the basis of the tendency for resolution to be word initial following syncopation (19), that in the case of resolution following a syncopated arsis there was a pause rather than prolongation (Blass 1899). Apart from various other possible objections, such devices go no way towards meeting the crucial difficulty that the evidence of *POxy* 2687 and the musical documents indicates fairly clearly that prolongation *was* in the same foot as syncopation. In the syncopated iambics of *POxy* 2436, not only is the prolongation marked on the thesis following the syncopated arsis, but there is also a violation of the classical rule prohibiting resolution before a syncopation (28). Although some of the musical evidence may reflect postclassical developments, there are hardly sufficient grounds for maintaining premise (b). It follows that the rule restricting resolution in syncopated iambics and trochaics must have some other motivation. This rule simply states that an anapaestic syllable sequence may not be mapped onto T T in these rhythms: ‾ ˘ | ˘ ˘ | ‾ ˘ and ˘ ‾ | ˘ ˘ ˘ | ‾ | are forbidden in syncopated trochaic and iambic respectively. It is well known that even in unsyncopated iambic and trochaic, resolution is constrained before long anceps, i.e. the mapping of an anapaestic syllable sequence onto TA is avoided in stricter styles (18), which is to be expected since the natural mapping of an anapaestic sequence is obviously AT, and that of a fourth paeon sequence ATAT or TAT. Even in the comparatively unconstrained dochmiac, resolution before long second anceps is very rare. It is reasonable to assume that mapping onto TT was difficult and therefore avoided. Both resolution and syncopation are complications of the basic mapping strategy, and it is known from metrical evidence that the difficulty of applying two nonbasic mapping rules together is greater than the simple sum of each applying in the absence of the other (DS 1984:118). Consequently, it is to be expected that the preference for the easier types of resolution should be more marked in syncopated

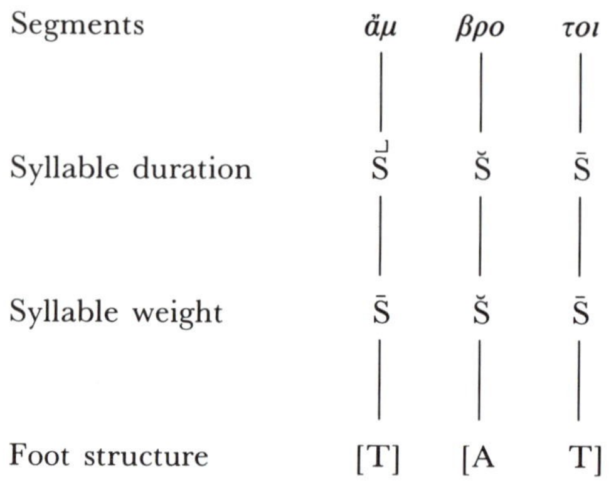

Segments	ἄμ	βρο	τοι
	|	|	|
Syllable duration	S̩	Š	S̄
	|	|	|
Syllable weight	S̄	Š	S̄
	|	|	|
Foot structure	[T]	[A	T]

FIGURE 3.5
Iambically organized cretic-shaped word

iambic than in unsyncopated lyric iambic, and this turns out to be so for the rule favouring word initial resolution (19).

It is clear from the preceding discussion that there is an outright conflict between the natural interpretation of the musical evidence and the straightforward and traditionally accepted explanation of the distribution of resolution in syncopated iambo-trochaic. If the conflicting evidence can be reconciled along the lines just suggested, then it can reasonably be supposed that in some, and possibly in all, cases of contiguous monosyllabic theses, the rhythmic organization involves arsis deletion with consequent prolongation of the thesis that stood in the same foot as the deleted arsis. The location of the deleted arsis is determined regularly by rule (39) and foot structure is assigned regularly by rule (40). Therefore, when a cretic structure, and particularly a cretic-shaped word, is embedded in iambic rhythm, the first syllable constitutes the monosyllabic foot (28), as in Figure 3.5. However, when the same word or structure is embedded in trochaic rhythm, the last syllable constitutes the monosyllabic foot (29), as in Figure 3.6.

In addition to the above, *POxy* 2687 may give some further evidence pointing to a hierarchization between the two mappings of Figures 3.5 and 3.6 that might, in turn, go some way toward answering the question whether cretics have rising or falling rhythm in their citation form. At the very end of column 1 and the beginning of column 2, where, apparently, the rhythmicization of the λέξις S̄S̆S̄ in the context of trochaic rhythm was discussed, the papyrus states: *οἰκειότατοι μὲν οὖν εἰσιν οἱ ῥυθμοὶ οὗτοι τῆς τοιαύτης λέξεως*. But in the discussion of the same λέξις embedded in iambic rhythm, it is stated: *ἐπὶ πολὺ δὲ τῇ τοιαύτῃ ῥυθμοποιίᾳ οὐ πάνυ χρῆται ὁ ῥυθμὸς οὗτος*. The straightforward inference would be that S̄S̆S̄

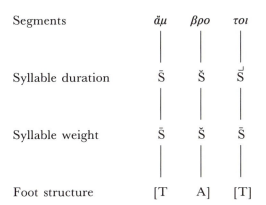

FIGURE 3.6
Trochaically organized cretic-shaped word

is an easier and more natural organization of the cretic than S̄S̆S̄. If this inference is correct, then, insofar as an arsis is assumed to be deleted in the citation form, it would be after the second thesis and the principles of foot structure assignment (40) would yield falling rhythm, as in Figure 3.6. A preference for trochaic organization of the cretic would accord with the principle of final syllable prominence (37) and could provide a linguistic motive for the strong tendency to metron diaeresis that characterizes true cretic rhythm in contradistinction to syncopated iambo-trochaic.

Heavy syllable prolongation is also apparently possible in the dochmiac structure on the evidence of the Orestes fragment (25). In the dochmiac, the central heavy syllable would be the monosyllabic foot, as in Figure 3.7. Such an interpretation of the dochmiac rests on a long tradition (Hermann 1816; Pickel 1880; Lieger 1914). To the extent that there was prolongation in speech, it was presumably located on the same syllable. That the rhythm posited by this interpretation is not unnatural is indicated by the Chinese five- and seven-syllable Gǔ Shī verse, which developed about two thousand years ago in the Han dynasty and in which dochmiac rhythm alternates with regular iambics, as often in Greek. In the dochmiac type, the antepenultimate syllable, which is not lengthened but preceded by a caesural pause, constitutes the monosyllabic foot (Yip 1984).

Of considerable theoretical significance is the problem of the rhythmic organization of the citation form of the antispastic syllable sequence (S̆S̄S̄S̆, type ἀκούουσι). If this structure simply consisted of an iambic foot followed by a trochaic foot, then it would violate the principle that rhythm is uniformly rising or falling in the domain of the word. It is also possi-

Segments	ἐ	πεσ	τη	σά	μην
Syllable duration	S̆	S̄	S̄	S̆	S̄
Syllable weight	S̆	S̄	S̄	S̆	S̄
Foot structure	[A	T]	[T]	[A	T]

FIGURE 3.7
Iambically organized dochmiac-shaped word

ble that one of the heavy syllables was prolonged, as is generally pre-
sumed to have been the case in the performance of syncopated lyric.
The second heavy syllable of the bacchiac structure is prolonged in the
Seikilos inscription and in the dochmiac, but neither is fully parallel.
If prepausal final syllables can be adjoined to a preceding foot to give
an amphibrach foot, then the antispast must have had rising rhythm
with prolongation of the second heavy syllable in the citation form:
[šš̄][s̄́]š. But if postpausal initial syllables can be adjoined, a possibility excluded in the above analysis, then the antispast could also have
had falling rhythm with prolongation of the first heavy syllable:
š[s̄́][šš̄].

Ratio of light to heavy syllable

The ratio of the phonetic duration of š to that of s̄ is not constant but
is sensitive inter alia to foot structure. The principle that the surface
duration of a syllable depends on its mapping is exemplified by the subordination (45) and prolongation (44, 47) rules, and it is possible that a
disyllabic arsis did not have a duration twice that of a monosyllabic arsis
nor equal to that of a disyllabic thesis. Furthermore, a well established
ancient tradition (33) indicates that the ratio of š to s̄ was greater in
trochaic rhythm than in iambic rhythm, reflecting very general properties of rhythmic structure. As already noted, the greater ratio of š to
s̄ in trochaic, that is the relative reduction of the duration of s̄, would
combine quite concordantly with the principle of light syllable prolongation (44) to provide a strong linguistic motive for the association and
responsion of ‾ ˇ ‾ ˇ with ‾ ˇ ˇ ˇ found in comedy (27). While the Greek
trochee was phonologically trimoraic, it was phonetically closer to being
bimoraic than was the iamb. The durational ratio of short to long vowel
has also been found to vary significantly according to the rate of speech
(p. 227).

Text Frequency

There is a well established relationship between the frequency of lexical
items and their fluency in speech production. For instance, frequency
is one of the factors affecting the centralization of vowels in lexical words
in English. If the frequency of a word is different in one particular variety of the language, this can affect the application of the rule. The word
trombone is pronounced by many speakers with unreduced first vowel,
but in the speech of trombonists it tends to be pronounced with reduction; place names reduce more readily in the speech of the locality itself,
as in the local pronunciations of *South Africa, Australia* (Fidelholtz 1975).
This suggests that phonological reduction is conditioned by lexical

frequency because it is inversely correlated with information load; in lexical decision experiments, frequency is negatively correlated with latency (Glanzer et al. 1979). In the reading of lists of pairs of words that were homophones without being homographs, like *through* and *threw*, the less frequent items were longer in duration by about 3% (Whalen 1991). Words that are predictable and have a very general semantic reference take on less exaggerated acoustic attributes than words that are unpredictable and have a very specific semantic reference. Such an interpretation is corroborated by the observation that discourse frequency and absence of focus have the same effect as text frequency (p. 467). Discourse shortening decreases the intelligibility of words when they are excised from their context and presented in isolation to listeners for identification (Fowler et al. 1987; Fowler 1988). So presumably discourse and text frequency compensate for the reduction of information in the acoustic signal. Consequently, frequency might exert some conditioning effect on the application of the subtractive mapping rules in Greek speech rhythm; it is apparently one of the factors conditioning the application of the English rhythm rule (p. 276). On the basis of statistical procedures developed specifically for the study of text frequency (Yule 1944; Herdan 1960), a test was designed to discover what restrictions, if any, affected Euripides' use of vocabulary in resolution (DS 1984). The results of this test are presented in Table 3.8. These results indicate that in the Severior style of Euripides tribrach-shaped words with a comparatively low text frequency are used less than predicted by the test, whereas the more common tribrach-shaped words are used more or less at their predicted rate. One interpretation of this evidence is in terms of compositional strategy. In the Severior style, Euripides allowed items central in the lexicon to occur with resolution but sacrificed more marginal items, since there is a constant and basic semantic need for the former while the latter represent an avoidable luxury. However, it

TABLE 3.8

Tribrach-shaped words with 5 or fewer occurrences
in Euripides Severior

Frequency of occurrence	Expected number of different words	Observed number of different words
1	47	30
2	10	8
3	4	5
4	2	2
5	1	1

is also possible to interpret the higher incidence of resolution in more common words as a direct reflex of a phonological correlation between text frequency and matrix formation. The more common the word, the more liable it would be to a subtractive mapping rule such as matrix formation.

Category

Evidence is presented in Chapter 7 (p. 352) that lexical words are somehow categorially hierarchized, with the result that nouns can have greater phonological prominence than verbs and can be more resistant to phonological reduction. There is some tentative evidence for such a hierarchy in the rhythmic processing of Greek from the iambographers. Insofar as tetrasyllabic words with heavy first syllable are allowed to stand at the end of the trimeter in Archilochus and Semonides (9), they are all verbal forms, with the exception of one proper name at Archilochus 24.2; nonverbal forms of this shape do occur at the end of the line in tragedy. This difference could be due to chance or to some factor of vocabulary or compositional practice, or it could indicate that verbs were prosodically less salient and therefore less resistant than nouns to subordination of the first syllable in this word shape.

Prepausal location

Although no new mapping rules are required to account for syllable rhythm in prepausal position (20), the absence of a linguistically specified right hand environment obviously entails a modified set of contexts of application for each rule. Since final light syllables were presumably lengthened at the end of clauses and sentences (p. 79), those rules that map a sequence of two light syllables onto arsis (43) or thesis (46) are not permitted to apply prepausally. The exclusion of these two rules in prepausal position is indicated by metrical evidence, namely the non-clausulaic character of the acatalectic dactyl and the constraints against resolution of a line final longum. On the other hand, both the remaining subsidiary mapping rules, by which a light syllable can be mapped onto thesis and a heavy syllable can be mapped onto arsis, are permitted to apply prepausally. It seems that the requirement for a phonologically based alternation, which underlies the basic mapping rules, is relaxed in the absence of a phonologically specified right hand environment. At the same time, application of the subsidiary mapping rules to a prepausal syllable did not necessarily result in the preferential rhythm for all word shapes.

A prepausal light syllable could be mapped onto thesis both when a monosyllabic arsis preceded in the same foot, as in the case of line final pyrrhic-shaped words in iambic, and when it was the only syllable in the foot, as in the case of a line final light syllable in the catalectic iambic and trochaic tetrameters and in clausulaic paroemiacs. However, after a disyllabic arsis, mapping of a prepausal light syllable onto thesis was avoided, as is clear from the avoidance of light syllables at the end of the pentameter (20) and from the judgement of Aristotle *Rhetoric* 1409a12 that a prepausal first paeon was rhythmically difficult. For this syllable sequence, and perhaps also for the prepausal proceleusmatic-shaped word (20), ditrochaic rhythm was presumably preferable (27). These prepausal constraints on the rhythmic organization of words ending in light syllables confirm that the brevis in longo lengthening rule is ordered after mapping has been completed: if phonetic lengthening of final light syllables applied before mapping, it would tend to eliminate the differences presupposed by the prepausal mapping constraints.

The mapping of a prepausal heavy syllable onto arsis in the syllable sequence ŠŠS̄ is sensitive to foot structure. Such mapping applies in falling rhythm, where, as in the hexameter and in acatalectic trochaic, the final heavy syllable is preceded by a thesis in the same foot, but not in rising rhythm, as in the paroemiac, where the preceding thesis does not belong to the same foot. This constraint follows automatically from three basic properties of the foot: no foot may have more than one thesis, monosyllabic feet consist of a thesis only, and, if the arsis is disyllabic, the two arsis syllables must be contiguous. It is possible that the mapping of prepausal heavy syllables onto arsis just described is not obligatory. The rhythm of prepausal ŠŠS̄ in syncopated trochaic (Raven 1968) suggests a slow speech variant ending in two monosyllabic feet, resulting from application of the basic rule (41) mapping a heavy syllable onto thesis prepausally in falling rhythm. A prepausal reversal in the rhythmic organization of dispondee words is implied by their acceptability at the end of the hexameter (Allen 1973); this sort of reversal can occur in stress languages, as in the Nunivak dialects of Yupik Eskimo (Alaska: Halle 1990), where iambic stress is replaced by trochaic stress at the end of the major phrase.

It is fairly clear from metrical evidence that a prepausal heavy syllable in the sequence ŠŠS̄ cannot be mapped onto arsis in rising rhythm. A prepausal light syllable in the sequence ŠŠS̄ could be mapped onto thesis and constitute a monosyllabic foot, as indicated by the catalectic iambic tetrameter. However, it is possible that, as an alternative, such a light syllable could simply be adjoined to the preceding foot. In that case, it would not be true that amphibrachic feet do not occur in speech rhythm, as claimed above. It would be true that amphibrachic feet do not occur except at the end of domains. Such an assumption might help to explain the constraints against amphibrachic division of the hexameter

(p. 274). However, the particular association of catalexis with trochaic rhythm in verse suggests that prepausal lengthening disturbed the mapping of Š to arsis.

Postpausal location

Once information has been organized and represented in memory, deviations that do not match the memory representation of the original constitute easily recognizable contradictions of the expected stimulus. When subjects were presented with two melodies in succession, one completely diatonic and the other identical except that one tone was replaced by a nondiatonic tone, the melodies were more accurately discriminated when the nondiatonic tone occurred in the second melody. Similarly, discrimination between an isochronous rhythmic sequence and its disrupted variant was better when the rhythmic sequence was presented before the disrupted sequence rather than following it (Bharucha et al. 1986). The discrimination of durationally equal and unequal mechanical noises is less precise at the beginning of a sequence of four stimuli (Lehiste 1979b), and synthetically increased and reduced durations in simple French two-phrase sentences were more acceptable in initial than in other syllables (Nishinuma et al. 1989). In the verse systems of many languages, major departures from the metrical pattern cluster at line initial and postpausal locations. In the Plautine senarius, a dactyl-shaped word may not coincide with the foot except at the beginning of the line, presumably because in this latter position the clash of ictus and accent was less disruptive to the iambic pattern due to the absence of a left-hand evironment. In the Kalevala (Leino 1986) and in the related metre of the Estonian folk song (Teras 1965), the trochee may be replaced by a dactyl or first paeon in the first foot only; temporal variability in a corpus of Estonian trochaic poems was greatest line initially and decreased progressively through the line (Lehiste 1990). In the English iambic pentameter, trochaic inversion is generally only allowed postpausally, although here pause is defined both in metrical terms (end of line) and in linguistic terms (syntactic boundary): the percentage of all inversions located in the first foot varies according to the metrical strictness of the author, with 87% of all inversions in a polysyllabic word occurring in the first foot in Kyd's *The Spanish Tragedy* but only 48% in Webster's *The Duchess of Malfi*. By contrast, the strictest actuations of bridges and other metrical constraints cluster in penultimate position in the verse, which was just the position of greatest sensitivity in the mechanical noise discrimination task noted above (Lehiste 1979b).

The postpausal clustering of metrical anomalies suggests that some caution is needed in drawing conclusions about the rhythm of speech on the basis of postpausal mappings in verse. Choriambic inversion, which is restricted to the first metron of the trimeter, does not require the assumption of postpausal remapping in Greek speech. However, it is not only metrical anomalies that cluster line initially: more complex and less transparent mappings that are linguistically based also tend towards line initial and postpausal locations, as for instance monosyllabic biceps in Stesichorus' *Geryoneis* and *Iliou Persis* (West 1969) and resolution in the trimeter and the tetrameter. The tendency to postpausal location is stronger the more difficult the word shape in resolution. In the strictest styles of the tragic trimeter 95 % of all anapaest-shaped words are located postpausally. Lexical pyrrhic-shaped words are excluded from all line internal locations except first and third longum, and proceleusmatic-shaped words are most common line initially. Such evidence does not indicate that there is no basis for resolution in the rhythm of ordinary Greek speech, nor that resolution involved a type of mapping confined to a postpausal environment in speech. Rather, it reflects the fact that, since resolution involves a relatively complex and opaque mapping, the danger of misperception is greater than with the basic mapping rules; and if misperception occurs, the damage inflicted on the metre will be minimized if it is located before the anticipated rhythm is reinforced by the perseveration of the metrical pattern during the actuation of the verse line.

Nevertheless, languages can have specifically postpausal rhythmic organization rules. In Modern Hebrew, pentasyllabic words with penultimate stress mostly have secondary stress on the second syllable, except that it tends to be shifted to the first syllable utterance initially and postpausally (Bolozky 1982). So it would be unwise to preclude a linguistic basis for certain specifically line initial verse mappings, such as the line initial iambic organization of the tribrach-shaped words in the trimeter (14), which might have been a variant in iambic context of the usual trochaic organization.

Demarcation

One further factor that affects the temporal relations of syllables to each other is demarcation. The timing of speech is programmed within domains, and these domains are commonly demarcated by a lengthening of terminal elements (Delattre 1966; Klatt 1976; Lindblom et al. 1981). It is a general perceptual principle that longer intervals tend to demarcate (Garner 1974). Later segments are lengthened more than earlier segments, and the vowel closing gesture is lengthened more than the vowel opening gesture, which suggests that final lengthening works inward from the end of the domain (Edwards et al. 1988). Final lengthening affects both vowels and consonants, and, particularly in larger domains, can spread back from the final syllable, especially to a stressed penultimate syllable (Flege et al. 1982). In a study of disyllabic personal names with stress on the second syllable in Hebrew, the following amounts of final lengthening were found in sentence final position as compared with sentence internally: first syllable 13%, second syllable 88%; onset of the second syllable 24%, nucleus 50%, coda fricative 196% (Berkovits 1993). Although purely in terms of measured duration both final lengthening and lengthening under stress have results tending in the same direction, they are predominantly produced by quite different mechanisms. At normal rates of speech, in a stressed syllable like *pop* the closing gesture begins later than in unstressed syllables and the jaw may also open further. The additional duration of stressed syllables in slow speech was achieved by slowing down the opening and closing gestures. By contrast, final lengthening (of stressed syllables) at normal rates of speech was achieved by slowing down the jaw closing gesture; in slow speech some subjects apparently supplemented this basic strategy by delaying the closing gesture as in nonfinal stressed syllables (Edwards et al. 1991; Beckman et al. 1992). This evidence suggests that final lengthening is a localized change of tempo; however, it is not an automatic and mechanical effect of the velocity of the articulators, since speakers can where appropriate use other strategies to achieve it. So, informally, final lengthening is a sort of drawling at the end of a group of articulatory events, while stress is an actuation of the rhythmic beat. Final lengthening is a feature of the temporal organization of the prosodic domain and not merely a correlate of pause, since it often occurs in the absence of pause. However, the lengthening may be greater before a pause than otherwise, as in Dutch (Nooteboom 1972) and English (Umeda 1975). The duration of the pause is perceptually equivalent to the same duration of final lengthening of a stressed syllable and an accompanying pause combined (Scott 1982). It may be the case that final lengthening provides extra time for the planning of the phonological production of the next constituent or for checking that the constituent just uttered was properly executed; and it is clear that particularly in questions final lengthening can provide the extra time necessary for the pitch movements often associated with the end of a constituent, although it cannot be entirely accounted for on this basis (Edwards et al. 1988; O'Shaughnessy 1979; Bannert 1982). More generally, the relationship between duration and pitch is one of independence and interdependence and not one in which either is consistently primary (Bannert 1986). The primary motivation of final lengthening is presumably related to the overall pattern of acceleration followed by deceleration that is typical of various types of human motor activity, such as running or eye movements (Fowler

1977). When subjects were instructed to pronounce syllable strings as fast as they possibly could, the final section of the string tended to include a retardation phase (Sigurd 1973). Schwa in word final syllables in English is comparatively resistant to deletion in fast speech (Dalby 1986), and words having sentence final lengthening are relatively less affected by durational reduction at faster speech rates than other words in the sentence, which again can be interpreted as reflecting more general properties of decelerating movement (Weismer et al. 1979). In addition to deceleration, final lengthening may perhaps reflect a partial temporal allowance for a "deleted" pause or for a "gapped" constituent.

Final lengthening has a counterpart in the ritardando of Western music, which occurs mainly at the end of musical constituents, and perhaps also in some types of birdsong and insect chirps (Cooper et al. 1980). When a final interval had the same duration as a penultimate and antepenultimate interval, it was perceived as being shorter not only for speech stimuli but also for nonspeech stimuli, which suggests that listeners factor out final lengthening (Lehiste 1973). However, it still seems to constitute learned behaviour, since it varies from one language to another and can be absent from the speech of deaf speakers (Lindblom 1978). Evidence on the existence of final lengthening in the premeaningful vocalizations of young children is contradictory (Oller et al. 1977; Robb et al. 1990); either final lengthening is a natural property of speech that is liable to be exaggerated or inhibited following the adult model, or it is a property of adult speech that has to be learned (Hallé et al. 1991). Unlike terminal pitch fall it is, for whatever reason, impaired in the speech of Broca's aphasics (Danly et al. 1982) and alexic dysarthrics; final lengthening is absent in the very slow speech of normal speakers, presumably because the sentence is no longer a domain of temporal organization or execution, and this might explain the absence of final lengthening with aphasics whose speech is slow (Bell-Berti et al. 1991). Like other prosodic properties of speech (Garnica 1977; Fernald et al. 1989), final lengthening is exaggerated in the speech of mothers to very young children (Ratner 1986). In general, the larger or higher ranked the domain, the greater the final lengthening (Ladd et al. 1991; Wightman et al. 1992). Lengthening at the end of an utterance is often greater than at the end of a major phrase; lengthening at the end of a major phrase tends to be greater than at the end of a minor phrase (English: Cooper et al. 1980; Danish: Fischer-Jørgensen 1982); and lengthening at the end of a minor phrase is greater than lengthening at the end of a word (Klatt 1975; Klatt et al. 1975; Hayes 1988).

When a word is uttered in isolation, its last syllable is not only word final, but also phrase final, sentence final and prepausal, and consequently undergoes very significant final lengthening. In lower ranked constituents, the durational increment assigned to the final syllable is progressively reduced. Final lengthening in minor phrase internal words is a relatively small effect, particularly in fluent connected discourse, but it has been found in Swedish (Lindblom et al. 1973), English (Klatt 1975), Dutch (Nooteboom 1973) and variably in Italian (Farnetani et al. 1990). The effects of demarcation are apparent before certain suffixes in English: for instance, trochee shortening is greater in simplex words than in words containing the suffix -ness: minus < slyness < sly Nestorian, monomorphemic Highness < bimorphemic highness < high (Harris 1951). Compound phrases like Itálian teacher have greater temporal cohesion than noncompound phrases like Italian téacher (Farnetani et al. 1988). The degree of coarticulation and integration of articulatory movements tends to covary with the degree of demarcation: for instance, in Dutch the duration of consonant clusters was found to be greater across word boundary than across syllable boundary in compound words (Slis 1986); and nasal coarticulation is impeded by word boundary (Umeda et al. 1975).

There is some Greek evidence that may indicate a minor degree of demarcation of certain prefixes and of the stem before certain suffixes, but other interpretations are also possible. Specifically, although resolution in fourth paeon-shaped words increases at a rate just over the average rate for the major word shapes (see Table 3.3), not all morphological categories comprising this word shape increase at the same rate. The following classification reflects the major distinctions

> middle participles, type γενόμενος
> monosyllabic prepositional prefix, type ἐν-όδιος
> disyllabic prepositional prefix, type ἀπο-λαβών
> lexical compound, type νεόγαμος, κεροφόρος
> simplex, type πολέμιος, θανάσιμος.

The data are presented in Table 3.9. Compounds and simplices increase at less than the general rate of increase for fourth paeon-shaped words; they go up approximately one and a half and two times respectively between Euripides Severior and Euripides Liberrimus, as compared with almost four times for the general rate. By contrast, the remaining categories all increase at a notably faster rate than the general rate; the category of fourth paeon-shaped word with disyllabic prepositional prefix increases tenfold, that of middle participles thirteen and a half times. These trends could be explained on the basis of changes in the lexicon of different styles (Prato 1975) or of compositional strategy: prepositional compounds are in general less central in the lexicon than simplices, and

TABLE 3.9

Percentage of fourth paeon- and ionic a minore-shaped words
in various morphological categories

	Middle participle	Monosyllabic prefix	Disyllabic prefix	Compound	Simplex
Aeschylus	4.69	10.94	25.00	21.88	37.50
Sophocles	1.52	7.58	27.27	9.09	54.55
Severior	2.22	1.11	14.44	15.56	66.67
Semiseverus	5.66	7.55	32.08	9.43	45.28
Liber	7.31	8.23	31.40	11.89	41.16
Liberrimus	7.88	13.79	39.41	6.40	36.96

therefore easier to avoid, given a stronger preference for the basic mapping rules and consequently avoidance of resolution in the stricter styles. However, a prosodic interpretation is also feasible. The data would in that case suggest a degree of rhythmic autonomy for stem and affix in the fast growing structures: a slight lengthening at the end of preposi- tional prefixes and at the end of the stem before the participial ending -μενος would have the rhythmic effect of blocking the application of the matrix formation rule. The rhythmic autonomy of prepositional prefixes is also attested by the failure of resyllabification of muta cum liquida across the prefix seam (p. 35).

There are also various indications of a degree of rhythmical auton- omy for lexical compounds, at least in very deliberate speech. In Linear B, compounds are in a few instances written with a word divider between the two elements (Davies 1987)

> e-ne-wo|pe-za beside e-ne-wo-pe-za 'nine-footed'
> ke-re-si-jo|we-ke 'of Cretan workmanship.'

There are a few possible instances of compounds bridging the caesura in verse

> κρυσταλλοπῆγα διὰ πόρον Persae 501
> τῆς οἰστροδινήτου κόρης P. V. 589,

and the proper names Ἀριστογείτων and Ἀπολλόδωρος are divided between two lines metri gratia (Allen 1973:121). It is intuitively obvi- ous that caesura or line end within the noncompound word would seri- ously disrupt the natural rhythm; in fact, if pauses of 200 msec are mechanically inserted into an utterance, without regard for segment, syllable or word end, intelligibility is significantly degraded, even though none of the message has been discarded (Huggins 1975b).

Greek verse notoriously abounds with a variety of constraints on word end, commonly termed bridges. The central role of the word as the basic domain of rhythmical organization, presupposed by the discussion of rhythm in Dionysius of Halicarnassus (Ruijgh 1987), is confirmed by the evidence of the metrical bridges. Some bridges involve constraints on mapping: the major factor in Porson's bridge, for instance, is a constraint against subordination of word final syllables; the righthand environment for this mapping rule must lie within the domain of the word in the style of speech to which tragedy has access. Other bridges do not involve a mapping constraint, but it is often difficult to establish which prosodic property or combination of prosodic properties they are designed to block. Some bridges, like Bulloch's bridge (p. 427), are constraints against potential phrase demarcation; but others seem to relate primarily to word demarcation. One probable instance of the latter class of bridge is Knox's iamb bridge in the trimeter. According to Knox's iamb bridge, in the trimeter of the iambographers a lexical iamb-shaped word may not end in fifth longum preceded and followed by lexical words. A line ending such as

φαρμάκων στυγεῖ πόσις *Andromache* 205

is permitted in tragedy but not in Archilochus, Semonides or Solon. Knox's iamb bridge rests on a sound statistical foundation. Trimeters ending in two lexical iamb-shaped words or in iamb- plus pyrrhic-shaped word were found to occur at a rate of 62.5 per thousand in a sample of 400 trimeters from the *Phoenissae* and *Bacchae*. If Semonides and Solon had no constraint, fourteen such line endings would be expected in the extant 225 trimeters: the actually occurring number is zero. We would have to have two million samples of the size of the extant corpus of Semonides and Solon before we could expect to find one sample with zero instances due purely to random fluctuations. If the word ending in fifth longum is longer than an iamb, the constraint does not apply: line endings such as

ἐκτελευτήσει θεός Semonides 1.5
ἵξεσθαι φίλος Semonides 1.10

are perfectly acceptable. Knox's trochee bridge in the trimeter, and the tetrameter counterparts of both bridges, are related constraints. The additional evidence relating to nonlexicals at Knox's bridges is discussed later (p. 283). What is required by Knox's bridges is that a disyllabic word ending in the last metron be located in such as way as not to replicate the preceding word end in terms of the coincidence or noncoincidence of word end with foot end. Iteration of word end coinciding with metron end or trochaically dividing the metron is also avoided in the hexameter, and the requirement that the medial division be a caesura rather than diaeresis helps to reduce word boundary patterning. Patterned iteration of word boundary replicating caesura or diaeresis is even more strongly avoided. Such rules presuppose that word final syllables are prosodically differentiated from word medial syllables, and demarcation typically has just this function.

Accent calculus

The Greek word is a prosodic domain not only for rhythmic organization but also for tonal organization: each nonclitic word has one and only one tonal prominence in its citation form. Furthermore, the location of the accent is prosodically constrained and, in the case of recessive words, prosodically determined. If the final syllable of a word having three or more syllables is light according to the citation form mora calculus (1), the recessive accent falls on the rightmost or only tone bearing unit of the antepenultimate syllable: πήματα, ἄνθρωπος. If the final syllable is heavy according to the citation form calculus, the recessive accent falls on the rightmost or only tone bearing unit of the penultimate syllable: πημάτων, ἀνθρώπου, φιλοκόλαξ. (If the final heavy syllable contains only one tone bearing unit, the trochee rule secondarily retracts the accent to the leftmost mora of the penultimate syllable, as in πολυπίδαξ.) Consequently, in recessively accented words of three or more syllables, the fall from the accentual peak is distributed over a prosodic span defined as -s̄(s̆)/-s̆s̆. This raises a number of questions. How is this span measured? Does it represent some type of prosodic constituent? If it does, what, if any, is the relationship between this accentual constituent and the constituents of word rhythm that have been called feet above?

The accentual fall span may be either monosyllabic or disyllabic, and the first syllable of the disyllabic type may be either heavy or light if syllable weight is the measure, or it may have a long or short vowel if tone bearing units are the measure. These structural properties of the fall span are reflected in the various formal mechanisms that have been suggested to account for the recessive accent. The variation in syllable count leads to the idea that final syllables that are light according to the citation form calculus are "extrametrical" in some environments or overall, or otherwise unfooted. The variation in syllable weight or vowel length in the first syllable of the span has suggested that accentual feet are insensitive to quantity. Finally, if both the preceding assumptions are adopted, then the fall span becomes a single syllable whose weight is irrelevant: consequently, if an accentual foot is to be constructed, the accentual peak as well as the relevant segment of the fall span will have to be included in the foot in order to create a disyllabic foot. By contrast, theories that leave at least two morae in the fall span can construct a foot over the fall span alone without including the preceding peak.

Here are some concrete examples. According to one analysis (Steriade 1988), final light syllables are "extrametrical" and the accentual foot consists of the (remaining) two final syllables in the word irrespective of their quantity; the foot has trochaic prominence, that is the left syllable is the thesis, and the accentual peak is aligned with the thesis. The resulting accentual feet are unrelated to the rhythmical feet which were posited above mainly on the basis of the metrical evidence. The thesis of this accentual foot may be light and its arsis may be heavy, giving accentually trochaic rhythmic iambs like [τίθη]μι. More generally, there is little correlation of the location of all accents, recessive or otherwise, with the rhythmic thesis (p. 210). Another analysis (Sauzet 1989) dispenses with "extrametricality" and posits that heavy syllables are prominent in their foot; left dominant, trochaic, feet are constructed from right to left, with the result that only s̄s̆, s̆s̆ and s̄ may be feet; the accentual fall occurs on the resultant final foot, and the accentual peak is linked to the syllable immediately preceding the foot. The correlation of the strong element of this accentual foot with rhythmic prominence is greater in this analysis than in the preceding one, since there is a better general correlation between the theses of rhythmic feet and postaccentual syllables (p. 210). However, the prominence correlation breaks down in the case of word final pyrrhic feet, which appear to have been rhythmically iambic rather than trochaic in citation form. The assignment of syllables to feet is also potentially different: for instance, in diiambic-shaped words (s̆s̄s̆s̄), the light syllable in penultimate position is footed with the final heavy syllable in the rules for the construction of rhythmic feet but with the preceding heavy syllable for accentual feet on this approach. Finally, the assumption of moraic trochees (Golston 1993), that is binary left prominent feet consisting of two light syllables or one heavy syllable, allows a final light syllable after a heavy syllable to remain unfooted, at least on the first pass, yielding [s̆s̆] and [s̄]s̆ as the feet for the accentual span, again with the peak assigned immediately to the left of the foot. The trochee rule (see below) still has to be treated separately, since to account for the type φιλοκόλαξ final syllables closed by a consonant cluster must be heavy for recessive accentuation (but not for the trochee rule). Given that the accentual fall span is bimoraic plus or minus a final light syllable after a heavy syllable, this analysis is the simplest and most direct account of the data. It too does not correlate with rhythmic structure since, as already noted (p. 126), there are good arguments for believing that Greek rhythmic feet are minimally trimoraic in their underlying structure: what is bimoraic is the thesis, and potentially also the arsis, not the foot.

The discrepancies that have emerged between the computation of the accentual fall span and the rhythmic structure of the word are problematic to the extent that, without excluding the possibility of some degree of differential stratification, one expects languages to be in principle rhythmically coherent (Dresher et al. 1991). So the question arises to what extent it is actually appropriate to call the accentual fall span a foot at all. If the recession rule exists merely to delimit a suitable span for the accentual fall (which, as suggested by the data presented in Table 4.11, may actually consist of two components, the accentual fall proper and a boundary tone), it does not automatically follow that this span should have the same prominence relations as a rhythmic foot or be aligned with one in any way. At the cost of simultaneous reference to morae and syllables, recessive accentuation can be accounted for by the following simple algorithm: go to the syllable containing the penultimate mora in the word and place the accentual peak on the rightmost or only tone bearing unit of the preceding syllable. The effect of the syllable requirement is that, when an antepenultimate syllable is available, the recession rule does not create circumflexes: the accent does not stand on the third mora from the end if that mora is the first mora of a long vowel but docks on the preceding mora. A recent study suggests that tonal movement through spectral change favours perception in terms of level High and Low tones, whereas tonal movement through a steady state vowel favours perception in terms of a falling or rising glide (House 1990); this might mean that recession to the antepenult afforded a more positive accentual cue. At all events, recession to the antepenult means that the first mora of the postaccentual fall, which is the steepest part of the overall fall, crosses the syllable boundary, and prototypically (as in τίθημι rather than ἵημι) travels through the additional phonological substance provided by the onset consonant(s) and coda consonant(s) if any, assuming that the turning point in fundamental frequency is located at or near the end of the accented syllable. There is a rule in Japanese for the accentuation of foreign words that is in some respects similar: go to the syllable containing the antepenultimate mora and place the accent on the first or only mora of the syllable (Kubozono 1989b). In Japanese, the bimoraic span assigned to the accentual fall in these words by this rule is structurally equivalent to a rhythmic foot; whether it is also aligned with a rhythmic foot depends on whether rhythmic feet in Japanese are assigned from right to left or, as in one study of phrasal footing cited later (p. 213), from left to right, which is not entirely clear (Poser 1990). The reason for simultaneous reference to the syllable and the mora is that in Japanese the accent can only stand on the first mora of a bimoraic syllable and so must be retracted from the third to the fourth mora from the end where necessary to meet this requirement.

The trochee rule has no inherent connection to recessive accentuation. Although it applies, often but not always vacuously, to recessively accented disyllabic words, it also applies to nonrecessively accented words such as ἀγῶνα, σωτῆρος. The trochee rule, which is diachronically later than the recession rule and does not apply in Doric, requires that if the accent falls on a long vowel in the penultimate syllable, it must be a circumflex if the final syllable has a short vowel or -αι/-οι not in the optative or the locative: hence the alternations δῶρον – δώρων, λῦσαι – λύσαι. The only exceptions arise when the final syllable was originally an enclitic as in ὥστε or as the result of crasis. The trochee rule can be seen as an intranuclear retraction of the accentual peak which increases the span of the overall accentual fall from one mora to two without crossing a syllable boundary. The main problem raised by the trochaic rule is that, unlike the recession rule, it is sensitive not to the weight of the final syllable but to its vowel length; not only the location of the accent but also its environment is computed in terms of tone bearing units: hence κῆρυξ, ἤνοψ like δῶρον. Although it is prima facie surprising that different accent rules should presuppose different mora measures, it does appear that disparate weight rules can apply to different weight sensitive processes (Hyman 1992), particularly if they reflect different diachronic or synchronic strata (Wiltshire 1991). But establishing the formal possibility of contradictory mora measures is not the same thing as explaining their different applications in substantive terms, which would entail finding some difference either in the strength of the final consonants or in the way in which tonal excursions are mapped onto vowels and consonants. The problem is a sort of language internal correlate of explaining why CV̆C is classed with heavy syllables in some languages and with light syllables in others. One might speculate that the older recession rule reflects a period (before the loss of several intervocalic consonants and subsequent widespread vowel contraction) when Greek was more mora timed, in the sense of Japanese, so that a coda consonant was timed as an autonomous mora, whereas the later trochee rule reflects the situation as it was in Classical Greek when timing was based on simple syllable weight (after vowel contraction and the intranuclear High Low movement it produced on penultimate heavy syllables). (Just the opposite historical development has been posited in Japanese to account for syllable weight dialects in peripheral northern and southern areas of the country [Shibatani 1990]). In concrete terms, the relative durational contribution of the consonant to the weight of the final syllable would have been greater, at least in deliberate speech, for the stratum of the recession rule than for the stratum of the trochee rule. Another possibility is that the difference in timing pertained to final consonant clusters only: between the time of the recession rule and the time of the trochee rule, according to this more localized hypothesis, there was some degree of reduction of final consonant clusters. Finally, it is possible to speculate that there was, for whatever reason, a differential acceptability of tonal interpolation through obstruents. In Swedish, there is an idiolectal and dialectal variation in the mapping of accentual excursions onto short, as compared to long, vowels; in most cases, speakers just let the earlier consonant following the short vowel cut into the tonal movement, but in some cases an effort is made to execute more or all of the tonal movement on the vowel by increasing the rate of fundamental frequency change (Bannert et al. 1975). Discrepancies involving morphological status, like the bimoraic weight of -*ai* and -*oi* in the optative, point to a diachronic explanation specific to the morphemes in question, in these instances loss of a final consonant.

Conclusion

It is a reasonable procedure to look to verse as a source of information about the rhythm of ordinary speech. Greek verse is sensitive not only to the intrinsic weight or mora count of a syllable but also to its syllabic context. The distribution of heavy and light syllables in the metres of Greek verse cannot be accounted for without the additional principle that syllables are systematically different according to the positions they occupy in the various word shapes in which they are embedded. Greek verse does not treat the syllables of Greek words as sequences of monomoraic and bimoraic units following one another according to an equipollent mora or syllable timing scheme within the domain of the word; rather, there must be some sort of temporal organization below the level of the word domain that is reflected in the metre. Some of the uneven metrical distributions — particularly the rule governing the tetrasyllabic word shapes in the last metron of the trimeter in its strictest style — are immediately recognizable as typical examples of footing effects. Foot based analyses of the rhythm of speech have produced successful results especially in a wide range of stress languages but also in other languages. By collecting and analyzing a variety of mainly metrical data it is possible to tease out some of the likely properties characterizing the podic structure of the rhythm of Greek speech and make a first attempt to account for them, however tentatively, in terms of a coherent system.

4 | Pitch

Pitch and F_0

Our sensation of pitch is a function of the fundamental frequency of a periodic sound, that is the number of cycles per second of sound pressure variation generated in the fundamental mode of vibration. Frequency is therefore a property of the sound stimulus, pitch a property of auditory sensation; in this and many other works, the term pitch is often used informally to refer to fundamental frequency. There are various measures of frequency and pitch, each of which has its own appropriate application. The Hertz (Hz), a linear scale, is used for the physical properties of sound; semitones, a logarithmic scale, are used for music; psychoacoustics uses various subjective measures: the Mel scale, the Bark scale, and more recently the socalled ERB scale which is derived from the frequency selectivity of the auditory system and which, for frequencies below 500 Hz, is neither linear nor logarithmic. For accentual excursions in speech, the ERB scale has been found to be most appropriate: excursions that are equal in Hertz or equal in semitones are not perceived as having the same prominence when presented in different registers. Furthermore, speakers of Dutch found it difficult to analyze accentual excursions in terms of musical intervals, which suggests that the perception of linguistic tone at least in a stress language and the perception of musical pitch are in principle different tasks for the human perceptual mechanism (Hermes et al. 1991). Given the musical nature of the Greek evidence, the ensuing analysis of accent and intonation in Greek will operate mainly in terms of semitones.

The relationship between fundamental frequency and pitch in music is that equal increases in pitch are the result of doubling the frequency. For instance, if middle C has a frequency of 261.6 cycles per second or Hertz, C one octave above middle C has a frequency of 523.3 Hz, and C one octave below middle C a frequency of 130.8 Hz. The distance in semitones between two frequencies is calculated by the formula

$$\frac{12}{\log_{10} 2} . \log_{10} \frac{\text{frequency}'}{\text{frequency}''} .$$

More or less the entire audible frequency range can be represented by ten octaves ranging very roughly from 16 to 16,000 Hz. In the socalled equal temperament of Western music, the chromatic scale divides the octave into twelve equal pitch intervals called semitones. The ratio of a semitone step is 1.059:1, so that if C is 261.6 Hz, C♯ is 277.2 Hz, and so on. (There are inclusively eight notes rather than seven in an octave because two pairs of notes, B/C and E/F, are separated by a semitone instead of a full tone.) The approximate fundamental frequencies of the notes of this musical scale (A = 440 Hz) in the three octaves covering the fundamental frequency of most human speech are given in Table 4.1. Other types of music divide the octave into a different number of equal steps, such as the seven steps of traditional Siamese music, or into unequal steps, such as the Pythagorean scale. A survey of over one hundred African peoples revealed that forty percent employed seven-interval scales, forty percent five-interval scales and the remaining twenty percent six-interval scales (Tracey 1958, 1963).

Production and perception

In speech, pitch reflects the fundamental frequency of laryngeal tone, and consequently the rate at which the vocal cords are cycling from their closed to their open positions. Our perception of pitch, however, depends on the overall waveform including the harmonics and not merely on the fundamental frequency; the third through the fifth harmonics are the most important for pitch perception (Ritsma 1976). Pitch can still be perceived when the fundamental frequency is absent from the acoustic signal, as it is particularly for the male voice in telephone conversation;

TABLE 4.1

Fundamental frequencies of notes of the chromatic scale
in the speech range

C	65.4	130.8	261.6
C♯/D♭	69.3	138.6	277.2
D	73.4	146.8	293.7
D♯/E♭	77.8	155.6	311.1
E	82.4	164.8	329.6
F	87.3	174.6	349.2
F♯/G♭	92.5	185.0	370.0
G♯/A♭	103.8	207.7	415.3
A	110.0	220.0	440.0
A♯/B♭	116.5	233.1	466.2
B	123.5	247.0	493.9

the telephone does not transmit frequencies below 300 Hz. The fundamental frequency of speech sounds does not generally remain stationary but changes through time. Although it is physically possible for pitch rises to be made at a rate of 120 semitones per second (Sundberg 1979), it was found that in Dutch even the most rapid pitch changes do not exceed a rate of about 50 semitones per second; the preferred rate of change for an accentual fall in German was about 40 semitones per second; rates for English have been calculated as ranging from 8.4 to 13.3 Hz per centisecond sentence internally and from 10.2 to 14.5 Hz per centisecond sentence finally where terminal fall is added to accentual fall (Hata et al. 1991). More rapid changes are more likely to be confined to a single syllable and slower changes to be spread over a number of syllables (Collier 1991). The rate of change necessary for a tonal glide to be perceptibly different from a stationary tone and the degree to which the rates of change of two tonal glides must differ in order to be perceptibly distinguished depend among other things on the duration of the stimulus ('t Hart et al. 1990). Provided that the magnitude of a frequency change and the duration of the transition are not too large, the perception in vowels will be that of unchanged pitch rather than of changing pitch; the actual pitch perceived corresponds to the fundamental frequency at a point about two thirds of the way into such an unperceived frequency glide (Rossi 1971; 1978). As already noted (p. 154), in fundamental frequency movement through V̌CV̌-sequences, it is possible that the consonant release inhibits the perception of continuous pitch movement, with the result that the vowels are perceived as having High or Low level tones (House 1990). It would follow that when a single note is assigned to a syllable in vocal music, the note reflects the perceived level tone: the reinterpretation of the physically changing acoustic signal as a level tone occurs at the stage of speech perception rather than at the stage of the musical representation of speech melody. Although the perceived pitch of a pure tone can be affected considerably by the intensity of the tone, this effect is much weaker for complex tones like vowels (Terhardt 1975). However, increasing or decreasing amplitude can have an effect on the perceived pitch of a fundamental frequency excursion (Rossi 1978b).

People who can tell the pitch of a single pure tone to within a semitone are comparatively rare. But many people who do not have absolute pitch can tell whether two sequentially presented tones have identical fundamental frequencies or not: for tones in the region of 1000 Hz, just noticeable differences can be below 1 Hz. With synthetic vowels having constant fundamental frequency throughout their duration, listeners were likewise able to perceive differences of less than 1 Hz (Flanagan et al. 1958), but when frequency is changing, as it usually is in real speech situations at normal speech rates, just noticeable differences of 2–2.5 Hz were found (Klatt 1973). In another study, adjacent syllables were found to differ perceptually in pitch if their fundamental frequencies were 5% apart (Isačenko et al. 1970). Experiments with singing indicate that pitch changes are never completely abrupt; they always require time for their execution: in the case of rising changes, the minimum time required depended on the size of the interval, while the time required for falling changes was relatively constant (Sundberg 1979). These production phenomena have perceptual correlates, in that it is easier to perceive pitch changes when pitch is rising than when it is falling (Klatt 1973), and the amount of change is perceived as greater for a rising fundamental frequency excursion than for a falling excursion of the same magnitude (Black 1970).

A change in frequency between two successive tones of identical duration and intensity can be interpreted as an accent; that is, accents can be perceived even if their actuation is purely melodic with no durational or intensity component (Thomassen 1982). However, if a melody consisting of different tones having identical duration and intensity is reproduced by tapping, the melodic accent is rendered by heavier (more intense) taps (Ehrlich et al. 1956). The accuracy with which people can differentiate two consecutively presented pitch intervals is relevant to any description of word accents: subjects showed considerable variation in their capabilities and in their strategies in this task, with the most successful performers able to discriminate differences as low as 1.5 semitones ('t Hart 1981). A peak height difference of 1.5 semitones was also sufficient to create a perceptible difference in the prominence of a Dutch focus accent (Rietveld et al. 1985).

SPEECH TONE AND SONG MELODY

The evidence for the reconstruction of the surface pitch patterns of the Greek word derives mainly from the musical settings of what remains of Greek vocal music. For such evidence to be used with confidence, it is necessary to establish the general likelihood of two propositions: first that the tonal properties of words and of larger domains are melodies in some sense independent and separable from the articulatory events to which they are linked in speech, and second that the greater the functional role of pitch in the prosody of speech, the more likely it is that the melodies of speech will be reflected in song.

Word melody

There are various indications that speakers have a representation of the melody of a word separate from their representation of its articulatory segments. When speakers of the Kagoshima dialect of Japanese use standard Japanese words, they generally accentuate them according to the accentuation of the related dialect form, with the result that the accent can easily fall on a different syllable, e.g. dialect form *kanásin* 'grieve,' Kagoshima pronunciation of the standard form *kanasímu*. A word or minor phrase is accentuated according to one of two accent rules, and the resulting word melody is associated with the lexical item and not with its individual syllables (McCawley 1978). In restricted tone languages too, the tonal patterns seem to be autonomous and represented over the word independently of the segments and syllables. For instance, in Luganda (Uganda: Cole 1967; Kalema 1977) the syllables of a noun are mapped onto the configuration Low High Low, or a two unit subsequence thereof: the syllable sequence *mukazi mukulu* with the tones Low High Low Low High Low is two words meaning 'the woman is elderly,' but the same sequence of syllables with the tones Low High High High High Low is one word meaning 'elderly woman.' In Iraqw (Tanzania: Tucker et al. 1966), verbs can be said to have the tonal configuration Low High, variously mapped onto different verbs according to their syllable structure (Figure 4.1). Further evidence for independent word melodies in some types of tone language comes from the word game in Bakwiri (Cameroon: Hombert 1986), in which the serial order of the syllables of a word is changed in such a way that the last syllable of the word becomes the first, but neither the rhythm (p. 123) nor the tonal melody is affected: *kʷéli* 'falling' → *líkʷè*, not *líkʷé*. However, in Asian tone languages, such as Cantonese and particularly Thai, tone can be exchanged along with the segments, a difference that is probably related at least in part to basic differences in word structure between African and Asian tone languages. Despite the fact that the functional yield of pitch differences tends to be greater in tone languages than in pitch accent languages, it is clear that even lexical tone has an autonomous representation. When a vowel is elided or deleted in a tone language, it often happens that its tone is preserved and secondarily associated with an adjacent syllable. Tone plays a central role in many of the drum and whistle languages that are used to signal messages across distance in various cultures of the world. In these speech surrogates, the lexical tones

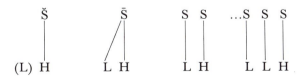

FIGURE 4.1
Verb tones in Iraqw

of the utterance are signalled, either in full or by an abridged system, by whistling or by playing a wind instrument such as a flute or horn, or a percussive instrument such as a drum or gong (Stern 1957; Umiker 1974; Sebeok et al. 1976). The message is often in the form of a stereo-typed poetic phrase, which helps to reduce ambiguity, and it may be transmitted a number of times instead of just once. The interval between the two notes of the gong or drums is often in the range of a third to a fifth. Multitonal systems may be abridged by neutralizing one or more of the tonal contrasts, or they may be reproduced on multiple instru-ments. These surrogate languages are feasible because the melody of speech can be abstracted from its segmental constituents. In the majority of cases, it is speech rather than song that is transmitted by the tones of the surrogate message.

Speech tone in song

In tone languages, notably in Africa and Asia, the correlation of song melody with speech tone is so high that it can generally be expressed in terms of rules, although for a few tone languages, such as Mixtec (S. Mexico: Pike 1948), little if any correlation has been found. This characteristic of the vocal music of tone languages is obviously related to the important functional role played by pitch in those languages. For example, in Igbo (Nigeria: Ekwueme 1974), a song might contain the following line: *Akwa adigh n'elu igwe.* This line has a number of different meanings, depending on the tones of both syllables of the first and last word. If a song composer arbitrarily composed a melody for this line, he would be arbitrarily assigning one of the following meanings to the line: 'There is no sorrow in heaven,' 'There are no tears on the bicycle,' 'There are no eggs in the sky,' 'There is no clothing among the crowd,' 'There is no egg on the iron,' etc. In order for the composer to convey the correct meaning of the text, he must compose a melody that reflects the speech tones of the two words in question. Since nearly all Igbo music is based on song, linguistic tone (and intonation) have a formative influence on the melody of Igbo music. Similarly, it is reported that when schoolchildren in Africa sang in their own (tone) language to European music, the results were hardly intelligible (Rattray 1922). However, it is not the case that the melody of song in tone languages is faithful to the linguistic tones only when ambiguity would otherwise arise. The correlation of speech and song melody is an overall rule and so more probably related to the general high functional yield of pitch differences in these languages. In fact, because of the inbuilt redundancy of language, Chinese without tones, as often spoken by foreigners, is fairly intelligi-ble provided that the pronunciation and syntax are otherwise free of distorting errors (Chao 1956). In the songs of the Lushai (N. India: Bright 1957b), the melody can override the tones of the language not only in modern songs but also in traditional songs, but the Lushai claim that they can still understand the meaning of songs in which this happens. On the other hand, in the central section of Navaho ritualistic songs, the disregard of speech tones combines with poetic and obsolete diction to make the texts hard to understand for the Navaho layman (Herzog 1934). For avoidance of speech-song tonal mismatches in a pitch accent language, there is a passage from Zeami (1363–1443), the foremost writer and theoretician of the Japanese sung noh theatre, which probably indicates that such mismatches are undesirable in major lexical categories (Omote et al. 1978).

That absolute pitch levels are not without significance is indicated by some evidence from Lahu speech surrogates (Thailand: Bradley 1979), which use a gourd reed-organ of various sizes as their signalling instrument. The smallest reed-organs, which produce notes of the highest pitch, are used by speakers of the dialect having a lexical preponderance of high tones, while the largest reed-organs, which have the lowest pitch, are used by speakers of the dialect having a lexical preponderance of low tones. However, in general, it is much more important for song melody to preserve, or at least not to reverse, the direction of pitch movement of an utterance than it is for it to maintain the true pitch of an utterance or to replicate the pitch intervals precisely. (Conversely, if a text is composed to a pre-existing melody, as in traditional Thai songs, then the words must be chosen so that the direction of their tonal movement does not conflict with that of the melody.) For instance, a rising tonal configuration in speech will be matched by a musical pitch rise, but the latter could be anything from a second to a fifth depending on the environment. In some languages, all the tone distinctions are respected in song, in others the tone system as reflected in song is an abridged version of the speech system. For example, in one type of Yoruba music (Nigeria: Wolff 1962), namely the *rárà* chant, the contour (rising and falling) tones of the language are replaced by level tones. Another aspect of the language-music correlation is the preponderance of one note for each syllable: melisms and other types of ornamentation are avoided on one syllable.

The actual peak to valley excursions occurring in speech do not necessarily correspond to pure musical intervals; that is they often cannot be accurately expressed by a simple numerical ratio, although attempts have been made to find some linkage (Hirst 1981). However, the frequency of pure intervals could conceivably have been higher in Greek than it is in English, since one study found about twice as many pure intervals in Norwegian, which has a tonal accent, as in English (Lehiste 1970). The tones of song also differ from the tones of speech in that they tend to be more sustained and stable than those of speech, as pointed out by Aristoxenus

δύο τινές εἰσιν ἰδέαι κινήσεως, ἥ τε συνεχὴς καὶ ἡ διαστηματική... τὴν μὲν οὖν συνεχῆ, λογικὴν εἶναί φαμεν. διαλεγομένων γὰρ ἡμῶν, οὕτως ἡ φωνὴ κινεῖται κατὰ τόπον, ὥστε μηδαμοῦ δοκεῖν ἵστασθαι. κατὰ δὲ τὴν ἑτέραν, ἥν ὀνομάζομεν διαστηματικήν, ἐναντίως πέφυκε γίγνεσθαι. ἀλλὰ γὰρ ἵστασθαί τε δοκεῖ, καὶ πάντες τὸν τοῦτο φαινόμενον ποιεῖν οὐκέτι λέγειν φασίν, ἀλλ᾿ ᾄδειν. *Harmonica* 1.8, 1.9 Macran

These characteristics are also found in speech prosodies akin to chant, as illustrated by the vocative chant in Figure 4.2, which differs from the spoken exclamation by having more level pitch, greater overall duration and different foot structure (Liberman 1979). Aristides Quintilianus mentions a type of chant used in reciting poetry: μέση [κίνησις], ᾗ τὰς τῶν ποιημάτων ἀναγνώσεις ποιούμεθα *De Musica* 6.4WI. However, there are cases of the transference of tonal glides from speech into particular song styles, as in one type of Igbo singing (Ekwueme 1974) and in the recitative of traditional Chinese drama (Chao 1956). Another difference is that the pitch range of song may be less than that of speech, as for instance in Thai songs (List 1961). The general effect of the need to coordinate speech and song melody is to limit the range of musical possibilities with a resulting tendency towards rather stereotyped melodies. The degree to which tone and melody can be correlated in a tone language is illustrated in Figure 4.3, which maps the tones of an Ewe song.

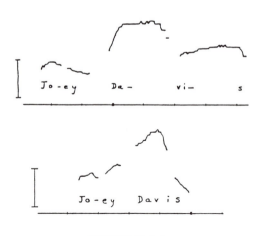

FIGURE 4.2
Vocative chant (from Liberman 1979)

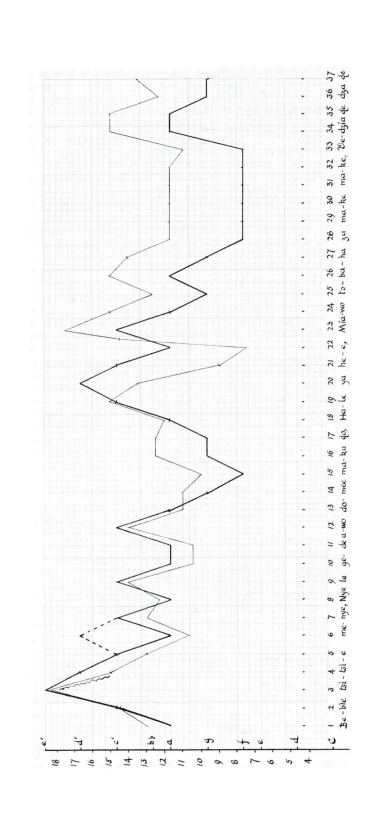

FIGURE 4.3

Coordination of melody and speech tone in an Ewe Song. Thick line: melody.
Thin line: speech tone. Dotted line: alternative version of the melody.
Wavy line: gliding tone (from Jones 1959)

Mismatches

Speech-song tonal mismatches are often not simply random, but tend to occur under certain conditions. In Ewe (Ghana: Jones 1959), mismatch can occur at the beginning and end of the song line, which are typical points of relaxation of constraint in any pattern, and the intended musical note can be replaced by a "harmony note." In Ewe and Yoruba, the melody is sometimes out of step with the speech tone in that it antici- pates a tonal movement or smooths a rising or falling tonal excursion by substituting a level melody, thereby eliminating an excursion but not reversing its direction. Before any particular case of mismatch is attributed to melodic smoothing, it is necessary to be sure that it is not actually linguistically based, in that it reflects an optional or obligatory rule of tonal smoothing in sandhi (connected speech). In the Hausa tonal sequence High Low High, the Low tone can sometimes be realized by the same note as the preceding High; this is not a (nonreversing) mismatch, but a feature of phrase intonation in fluent speech (Leben 1985). This observation about Hausa is important in that it indicates that the tonal relations reflected in the music are those of the surface phonetic output, after the lexical tones have been adjusted by factors like sandhi and intonation. It follows that, conversely, the evidence of Greek vocal music may be expected in principle to reflect similar surface tonal relations rather than merely the abstract tonal patterns of lexical representation. Nonsense words, exclamations and perhaps proper names tend to be exempt from the requirement of matching speech tone, as in Igbo (Ekwueme 1974) and Navaho (Herzog 1934). Overall mismatch is a deliberate feature of many Igbo funeral songs.

In the Greek settings that show any respect for the accent, mismatches between melody and accentuation are rare. Among those suggested (Duysinx 1981; Bélis 1992), two musical circumstances certainly license violation of the basic rule that the accented syllable is not set lower than any unaccented syllable of the same word. At the beginning of a melody or melodic section, pitch may rise after an accent (Winnington-Ingram 1955) but not fall to the accent. Such rise is observed only with the acute, and may be more common with nonlexical words than with lexicals. The first word of the Seikilos epitaph ὅσον *DAM* 18 is set to a-e¹. Simi- larly, the first word of the Hymn to the Muse ἄειδε *DAM* 1.1 is set to the rising sequence a-e¹-e¹. In ὅδ᾽ ἐστ᾽ *DAM* 37.18 set to e-e¹c¹g, ἐστ᾽ may be orthotone. A second possible licence concerns the octave inter- val. τρίποδα, βαῖν᾽ *DAM* 20.22 violates the regular reset of pitch in clause initial position by falling an octave from peak to peak rather than rising (p. 450). If ἐφο]βήθησαν *DAM* 37.19 is the correct supplement, the accented syllable is set to e, which is an octave below the note that would give a regular pitch pattern to the word (e¹).

Aside from these licences, which are similar to the mismatches noted above in other languages, and from cases which can be explained as due to accentual recomposition of compounds (p. 350; Crusius 1894b: 116), variable domains of anastrophe (p. 364), and paroxytonesis of εἰμί (p. 355), mismatches in lexical words violating the basic rule that the accented syllable is never lower than any unaccented syllable number only about fifteen, and several of these are probably errors of the composer or manuscript corruptions. Apart from these licences and linguistically motivated types, lexical mismatches are extremely rare in the Delphic hymns, the Seikilos epitaph, the Berlin paean, the Michigan papyrus or either of the probably two poems of the hymn to the Muse attributed to Mesomedes. In the A portion of the Oslo papyrus *DAM* 36, three of the four lexical mismatches seem to have been corrected or cancelled; the only unchanged mismatch is σαφῶς *DAM* 36.10 set to g♯-f♯. In *DAM* 38 μνημονεύσατ] 5 and μαινάδες 8 are mismatches. Lexical mismatches are more frequent in Mesomedes' Hymn to the Sun and Hymn to Nemesis *DAM* 4-5, but they cluster from 4.13 to the end of 5, which is the portion preserved in only one manuscript; so they may reflect errors in the transmission of the notation rather than original mismatches (Pöhlmann 1970)

> παγὰν c¹b♭-b♭a 4.13
> τίκτουσιν b¹-c¹-d¹ 4.16
> χαλινῷ d¹-c¹-c¹ 5.4
> γαυρούμενον e-g-b♭-b♭ 5.10.

Relative to the extent of the preserved setting and text, lexical mismatches are most frequent in the very melismatic Christian hymn *DAM* 34. Secure mismatches on nonlexical words involve prepositions not in anastrophe. The grave of disyllabic prepositions has lower pitch than the preceding syllable in ἐπὶ *DAM* 36.5, 36.8 and probably κατὰ 36.6 (Winnington-Ingram 1955:72). ἡμῶν *DAM* 34.3 set to bc¹-f could be the unemphatic form ἤμων. των in the second line of *POxy* 3162 set to c¹d¹ could be either nonlexical τῶν or the end of a lexical word: in the former case it violates the rule assigning a falling melism to circumflexes, in the latter case it either violates this rule or constitutes a basic mismatch since the preceding note is b.

Strophic verse, genre

African song in general is characterized by improvisation. When a soloist sings several verses of a song, he adapts the melody to accommodate the different words of each verse. Soloists are actually chosen for their ability to make quick and appropriate adaptations of the tune to fit the words (Ekwueme 1974). Conversely, when word changes occur in successive cycles of a Tsonga song (Mozambique: Johnston 1973), the new words tend to be chosen so that their tone pattern replicates that of earlier verses, with the result that a melody change is not obligatory. This is hardly possible when each verse has a completely new text but is required to have the same tune, as when a European-style hymn is composed in a tone language: a successful Yoruba example has been described as a "tour de force" (Carrol 1956). The construction of tonally matching sentences is a common classroom exercise in China (Pike 1948). In the curing songs of the Navaho medicine man, all lines of the main body of the song are sung to practically the same melody imposed irrespective of the varying speech tones of the different lines.

It is often the case that different genres of chant and song show different degrees of correlation between tone and tune. In Thai, for instance, there is a greater correlation in folk songs than in classical song. In China, contemporary song writers pay no attention to tone. The spread of Western music has tended to reduce or eliminate traditional tone-melody coordination in many areas. In Thailand, contemporary popular songs show reduced sensitivity to level speech tones but still tend to reflect the contour tones of the language. A Lingala song (Zaire: Carrington 1966) celebrating the accession to power of President Mobutu in 1965 is an interesting hybrid. This song was composed in a European idiom and accompanied by European instruments tuned to European scales; nevertheless, the melody respects the tones of the Lingala text.

In Greek, different genres of vocal music show different correlations between musical settings and speech tones. There is no certain exception to the generalization that those pieces that show little or no respect for the accent come from compositions that either are known to be or could be strophic (Winnington-Ingram 1958; Pöhlmann 1970; West 1992). Conversely, those pieces which show the strictest regard for speech tones are surely or probably nonstrophic. In the first category are the *Orestes* fragment *DAM* 21, the Berlin *Ajax DAM* 32, *DAM* 35, *DAM* 22 (threnodic anapaests), and *DAM* 23 (possible iambics). In the second category are the Delphic Hymns *DAM* 19–20, the Seikilos epitaph *DAM* 18, *DAM* 38, *DAM* 39–40 (iambo-trochaic), the Berlin paean *DAM* 30, *DAM* 36 (nonthrenodic anapaests), *DAM* 37 (iambic trimeters), the Hymn to the Muse *DAM* 1–2, the Hymn to the Sun and the Hymn to Nemesis of Mesomedes *DAM* 4–5 and even to some extent the later Christian Hymn *DAM* 34. The validity of the principle that nonstrophic music respects the accents while strophic music does not, is confirmed by the fact that it continues to hold true for material published subsequently to *DAM*. Surely or possibly from strophic compositions and not respecting the accent are *I.A.* 784–92 (Jourdan-Hemmerdinger 1973) and *POxy* 3161. In the latter there are at least three lexical words that violate the basic rule: τέκνον, ἐλθέ, φωνήν. Four words are set to level pitch, so that while they do not violate the rule they also do not follow the accentual excursions. There are four words that show a rise to the accent, all oxytone. This is a far higher rate of nonconformity with linguistic pitch patterns than found in the Delphic hymns. Furthermore, the preposition σύν is set higher than both syllables of its object ἐμοί in contravention of the rule in the Delphic hymns, the Seikilos epitaph and *DAM* 38 (p. 360). In contrast, *POxy* 3162 (Haslam 1976) is like *DAM* 36–37 and *DAM* 39–40 in that it sets a nonlyric metre and strictly respects the accent. *POxy* 3704–05 seem not to respect the accent, but they are too fragmentary for reliable inferences to be drawn about their genres. The disregard of the accent in the settings of the first category involves a generalization of this feature throughout the genre; it cannot be entirely accounted for as a direct mechanical result of the exigencies of strophic responsion (Mountford 1929), since *I.A.* 784–92 belong to an epode.

This genre based difference in regard for the accent cannot automatically be extrapolated back to the music of the pre-Hellenistic period. Dionysius of Halicarnassus *De Compositione Verborum* 11.42UR states that at *Orestes* 140–42, the beginning of the parodos, the musical setting did not respect the accents, but it has been argued that Dionysius did not possess Euripides' original music, but rather a Hellenistic setting, and that no music from the fifth century B.C. survives at all (Henderson 1957). It is generally assumed, although there is no compelling external evidence (Winnington-Ingram 1958; Dale 1968; Pöhlmann 1960), that the same melody was employed for strophe and antistrophe. It is also apparent that there is no strict responsion of word accents between the text of the strophe and that of the antistrophe, at any rate not so strict as the responsion of syllable weights and rhythmic equivalence classes in rhythmic structures. This evidence seems to confirm Dionysius' report. Nevertheless, it has been claimed that a significant degree of accentual responsion can be detected in certain strophe-antistrophe pairs (Wahlström 1970), in particular *Orestes* 316–31 – 332–47 (Feaver 1960; the subsidiary claim that the setting in *DAM* 21 respects the accents involves a number of phonological misinterpretations). Certainly a higher degree of accentual matching in corresponding pairs of syllables is observed from strophe to antistrophe than in pairs of corresponding syllables from one iambic trimeter to the next (not in stichomythia). To provide a baseline for the comparisons, it may be assumed as a first approximation that the probability of a match in accent type (or absence of accent) between corresponding syllables from responding metrical structures a and β is simply the product of the probability of the respective accent types in a times the probability in β. Then the total proportion of matches expected, $E(m)$, will simply be the sum over all the types of the probability of a match on each type. In a sample of nonstichomythic iambic trimeters from the *Orestes*, the observed proportion of matches, $O(m)$, was found to be nearly identical to the expected: $O(m) = 36\%$, $E(m) = 37\%$. By contrast, in the dochmiac chorus of *Orestes* 316–31 – 332–47, with nonresponding resolutions and the uncertainly paired 322–23 – 338–40 excluded, the observed matches exceeded the expected: $O(m) = 57\% > E(m) = 44\%$. Similar results were found for aeolic (*Ion* 184–93 – 194–204: $O(m) = 54\% > E(m) = 38\%$; Eur. *Electra* 167–78 – 179–90: $O(m) = 67\% > E(m) = 48\%$) and for other lyric metres as well. For the presence or absence of accents of any kind in ionics the figures were 60.32% in *Persae* 65ff. and 52.90% in *Bacchae* 370ff., and in dactylo-epitrite 56.45% in *Trachiniae* 94ff. (Comotti 1989). On the assumption of melodic identity of strophe and antistrophe, the figures of observed matches, even if nonrandom in respect to the simplest models, would represent a far weaker correlation of musical setting and speech tone than found in nearly all of the surviving nonstrophic musical settings. Furthermore, before it can be concluded that these observed proportions of accentual matches reflect a real tendency toward accentual respon-sion governing strophic composition, it must be shown that they are not merely side effects of independently motivated stylistic tendencies that would automatically increase the rate of accent matching. For exam-ple, certain metres (even dochmiacs) show a very high rate of metron diaeresis, and between strophe and antistrophe there are frequently observed correspondences of word boundary patterns in general and parallelisms at the levels of morphology, lexicon, grammar, and rhetor-ical figure, all of which will automatically increase the probability of a match in accentual type between corresponding syllables, since they all increase the correspondence of the linguistic factors that constrain and determine the location of the accent.

Stress and song

Any correlation of stress with higher notes in European vocal music is likely to be less significant than the correlation of stress with musical duration and downbeat. However, the socalled accentual cadence is well established in Gregorian psalmody (Bailey 1976). Two cases can be found of the melody of song coordinating with the pitch patterns of a word stress. In Swahili (E. Africa: Allen 1971; Jones 1975), which is not a tone language and which has penultimate word stress, the melody of the epic songs tends to assign higher notes to stressed syllables. The songs of the Havasupai (Arizona: Hinton 1977) have verse texts in a stress-based metre. The first hemistich of the verse has two strong positions of which the second is always implemented by a syllable with primary stress and the first may have secondary stress or be unstressed. A strong-weak metrical sequence usually exhibits a downward melodic movement, less often level melody and only very rarely upward movement. The highest note of a line usually falls on a strong position, and, at least in some songs, the lowest note can only fall in a weak position. In both Swahili and Havasupai, stress has a pitch component in its implementation. However, the evidence of these two languages does not seriously weaken the view that the laxity of the later Greek musical fragments is related to the spread of the new stress accent. For both Swahili and Havasupai are geographically close to musical traditions in which melody reflects tone in tone languages, and in both cases the characteristic could be a foreign import into the stress language rather than an endogenous development.

PITCH IN ACCENTED AND UNACCENTED SYLLABLES

Given the validity of the two premises discussed in the preceding section, it is methodologically reasonable to look for evidence of the melody of Greek speech in the melodies of Greek vocal music. What emerges from such an analysis of Greek vocal music is an array of statistically non-random correlations between the musical melodies and linguistic structure. Furthermore, the physical substance of these correlations is not random or accidental either, but replicates demonstrable correlations between linguistic structure and the tonal melodies of speech in living languages.

Dionysius

The main direct evidence for the tonal patterns of the Greek word comes from Dionysius of Halicarnassus

> διαλέκτου μὲν οὖν μέλος ἑνὶ μετρεῖται διαστήματι τῷ λεγομένῳ διὰ πέντε ὡς ἔγγιστα, καὶ οὔτ᾽ ἐπιτείνεται πέρα τῶν τριῶν τόνων καὶ ἡμιτονίου ἐπὶ τὸ ὀξὺ οὔτ᾽ ἀνίεται τοῦ χωρίου τούτου πλέον ἐπὶ τὸ βαρύ... καὶ ταῖς μὲν δισυλλάβοις οὐδὲν τὸ διὰ μέσου χωρίον βαρύτητός τε καὶ ὀξύτητος· ταῖς δὲ πολυσυλλάβοις, ἡλίκαι ποτ᾽ἂν ὦσιν, ἡ τὸν ὀξὺν τόνον ἔχουσα μία ἐν πολλαῖς ταῖς ἄλλαις βαρείαις ἔνεστιν. De Compositione Verborum 11.40UR

The interpretation of the first sentence of this passage is not absolutely certain (Corssen 1870; Roberts 1910; Postgate 1924; Sturtevant 1940; Carson 1969; Aujac et al. 1981; Usher 1985; Allen 1987; DS 1991), but its prima facie meaning is that the interval between High and Low tone in speech does not exceed three tones and a semitone. The interval of a fifth fits quite well with the intervals reported for excursions involving word accents in living languages. The fundamental frequency contour for a Japanese sentence reproduced in Figure 9.7 (p. 437) has peak to valley ratios starting at 150% (a fifth) and falling about 10% per pitch accent to approximately 125% (a major third), factoring out the additional terminal fall. In Dutch, which is a stress language, accentual prominence rarely involves excursions of more than half an octave in normal, nonemphatic speech ('t Hart 1981); similar typical values for accentual obtrusions were found for Italian (6 semitones) and for German (7.5 semitones) (Collier 1991). One speaker of Slovene used the range of very approximately 100–125 Hz for accentual excursions in words accented on a nonfinal syllable, equal to 4 semitones (Srebot-Rejec 1988). Average fall in the stressed syllable of accent II words for Swedish male speakers was 5 semitones (Fant et al. 1989). Interestingly, in Thai words uttered in isolation, the pitch excursions involved in the falling and rising lexical tones were also typically just under a fifth (Abramson 1978; Gandour et al. 1988). Emphatic speech is quite another matter: High-Low movements of 300 Hz were found on expressively exaggerated focus accents in sorority speech (McLemore 1991). So, while the reported interval of a fifth conforms quite well to the upper end of the range of intervals associated with ordinary, unemphatic accentual prominence, it does not conform at all with the overall frequency range of an utterance measured from the peak of the highest prominence to the lowpoint of the terminal fall, a measurement which can easily exceed an octave. In a study of simple Chinese sentences, one speaker used an overall range of less than an octave, but another, who spoke in a declamatory style, used a range of more than two octaves (Gårding 1987). This confirms the simplest interpretation of the passage, according to which Dionysius is referring to the domain of the word rather than to the domain of the utterance; the latter would be appropriate on the less likely interpretation that Dionysius is measuring a fifth up and a fifth down from a midline (Carson 1969).

The second sentence just cited from Dionysius is valuable for a preliminary understanding of the tones of unaccented syllables. Dionysius says that in Greek there is only one High toned syllable (more precisely mora) per accented word; the other syllable in the case of a disyllabic word, and the other syllables in the case of polysyllabic words, are Low toned; the same tradition appears in Pseudo-Sergius 532.14 Keil: graves numero sunt plures. That polysyllables do have Mid tones follows logically and is clearly suggested by the antithesis ταῖς μὲν δισυλλάβοις... ταῖς δὲ πολυσυλλάβοις. βαρύς means 'unaccented' phonologically and 'Low toned,' as opposed to Mid toned, phonetically. Dionysius' report provides clear confirmation that in Greek none of the unaccented syllables is High toned: Greek is not like Tokyo Japanese, in which all morae between the first and the accentual fall are phonetically High toned.

The Delphic hymns

Of all the remains of Greek vocal music, the Delphic hymns show the strictest rules of correspondence between the pitch accent of speech and the musical setting; they are, therefore, the best potential source of the data that will be needed to amplify Dionysius' skeletal account. It has been established that in the Delphic hymns the accented syllable is not set lower than any other syllable of the word: specifically, the acute accent in trisyllables and longer words is preceded by a rise and followed by a fall in pitch; the circumflex is most frequently set to a melism, the second note of which is generally lower than the first; the grave is not set lower than any other syllable of the word — it cannot be higher than the next following acute or circumflex, and is often not higher than following unaccented syllables (Winnington-Ingram 1955; Pöhlmann 1970). The strictness with which these rules are observed establishes for the Delphic hymns a high level of respect for the pitch relations and movements of Greek speech.

The Delphic hymns (Pöhlmann 1970; Chailley 1979; West 1992; Bélis 1992) are composed in the diatonic and chromatic genera. Theoretical small differences between intervals in the tetrachord such as tones of 9/8 and 8/7 for Archytas' diatonic genus are ignored in the ensuing analysis. *DAM* 19, whose author's name (Bélis 1988, 1992) or less probably ethnic is Athenaeus, and *DAM* 20, whose author is Limenius, are referred to as *Ath.* and *Lim.* respectively; transcriptions of the vocalic and instrumental notations into staff representation are reproduced from *DAM*.

Intrinsic F_0

Although the production of laryngeal tone is in principle quite distinct from articulation, there are a number of situations in which articulation can influence fundamental frequency. High vowels (i, u) have been found to have higher intrinsic fundamental frequency than low vowels (a) in a variety of languages — English, Danish, French, Itsekiri (West Africa), Japanese, Korean, Serbocroatian. In English a difference of 12–16 Hz was found in one study (Peterson et al. 1952); a range of 10–35 Hz was found in Danish (Petersen 1978). The reason for the phenomenon has been the subject of intense investigation (Hombert 1978; Silverman 1984; Steele 1985). One possibility is that when the tongue and jaw are raised for the articulation of high vowels, extra tension is exerted which is, in one way or another, transmitted to the vocal cords and consequently induces higher fundamental frequency (Ewan 1979; Rossi et al. 1981; Ohala et al. 1987; Vilkman et al. 1989; Zawadzki et al. 1989). However, there are a number of problems with this theory (Fischer-Jørgensen 1990). The short lax vowels i and e have more or less the same intrinsic fundamental frequency as the long tense vowels $\bar{i}$ and $\bar{e}$ respectively; but, although they also have more or less the same amount of jaw opening, they have considerably lower tongue height (and correspondingly higher first formants). Furthermore, cricothyroid activity starts earlier and is stronger for high vowels, which raises the possibility that intrinsic fundamental frequency is actively controlled (Dyhr 1990). Finally, intrinsic fundamental frequency is also found in the oesophageal speech of laryngectomized patients (Gandour et al. 1980). Despite their rather different vocal tract configuration, an intrinsic fundamental frequency effect associated with front rather than high vowels was found for one-year old children (Bauer 1988). For eight- and nine-year old children, intrinsic fundamental frequency was weaker and more variable, particularly after labial consonants, than for adults (Ohde 1985).

Intrinsic fundamental frequency differences are smaller in connected discourse than in sentences read under experimental conditions (Ladd et al. 1984); they are greatest sentence initially and in strongly stressed syllables (Steele 1985); they are amplified by emphatic focus and attenuated in fast speech (Hata 1986) and in accentually and intonationally weaker positions (Shadle 1985). A comparatively large difference of almost 10 Hz in the intrinsic fundamental frequency effect between High toned and Low toned words was found in the tone language Kammu (Laos: Svantesson 1988). The magnitude of the difference seems to vary from language to language. In a comparison of three different languages, the differences were smallest in the tone language Itsekiri, intermediate in the pitch accent language Serbocroatian, and largest in the stress language English (Lehiste 1970), suggesting a sensitivity to interference with other functions of tone in the language and perhaps a correlation with the physiological effort associated with stress.

Intrinsic fundamental frequency differences mostly fall within the range of 1–2 semitones (di Cristo et al. 1986), which is above the normally assumed differential threshold; even the smaller differences between high and mid vowels can be used as cues to segmental identification under experimental conditions (Petersen 1986). However, there also exists an intrinsic pitch effect which is inversely correlated with but weaker than intrinsic fundamental frequency (Chuang et al. 1978; Stoll 1984). When speakers of English were presented with low and high vowels having the same fundamental frequency and instructed to judge which one has the higher pitch, they chose the low vowel two and a half times as often as the high vowel (Hombert 1978). Similar results were obtained with vowels in locations of intonational prominence (Silverman 1985). An intrinsic pitch effect was also found in the perception of poststress syllables in Danish (Rosenvold 1981), and it was too large to be accounted for by the perceptual phenomenon known as "pitch bias" (Petersen 1986). The intrinsic fundamental frequency of vowels can be exploited in whistle languages, as at Kusköy (Turkey: Leroy 1970) where *a* is whistled at a frequency of 1750 Hz, *e* at 2100 Hz and *i* at 2600 Hz. In the drum language of the island of San Cristoval (Solomon Islands: Snyders 1969), a low-toned drum is used to represent the low vowel *a* and a high-toned drum is used to represent the mid and high vowels *e, o, i, u*. The effect of vowel height on fundamental frequency is reduced in singing as compared to speech: Swedish choir singers have been found to compensate fairly successfully for intrinsic fundamental frequency differences by auditory monitoring of their performance (Ternström et al. 1988). However, the intrinsic fundamental frequency effect that remains in singing is still well above the threshold of detection; in unaccompanied solo singing, listeners, including the singers themselves, seem to compensate perceptually for this effect (Petersen 1988).

Some studies, but not all, have also found that rounded vowels (which tend to be pronounced with a lower larynx than unrounded vowels: Ohala et al. 1987) can have higher intrinsic fundamental frequency than their unrounded counterparts and even than unrounded vowels which have higher tongue positions, as is indicated by some data from Estonian (Vende 1972); *u* normally has higher intrinsic fundamental frequency than *i* in Slovene (Srebot-Rejec 1988). Short vowels tend to have not only greater intensity than their corresponding long vowels but also higher fundamental frequency (Fischer-Jørgensen 1990), and the same interaction appears in various tone languages in which High toned vowels are shorter than Low toned vowels (Gandour 1977); tonogenesis in Hu (China: Svantesson 1989) involves short vowels becoming High toned and long vowels Low toned.

One way of discovering whether the musical setting of the Delphic hymns is sensitive to intrinsic fundamental frequency is to test the interval between the pitch peak of a nonfinal accented syllable and the pitch valley of the final (unaccented) syllable of the same word. Any sensitivity would lead to results in which the interval between an accentual peak on a high vowel and the valley on a final vowel was greatest when the final vowel was low, intermediate when it was mid, and smallest when it was high,

TABLE 4.2

Mean intervals in tones between accentual peak and valley of the unaccented final syllable in words bearing the acute in *Lim.* classified according to vowel height combinations

ĹL	ĹM	ĹH	ḾL	ḾM	ḾH	H́L	H́M	H́H
0.93	1.19	1.00	1.39	1.64	1.56	1.57	1.86	2.67

and so on through all combinations of vowel height. The mean intervals were calculated for each of the resulting nine combinations of vowel height in words bearing the acute accent in *Lim.*, with vowels and diphthongs classified simply as high, mid and low, ignoring the difference between high-mid and low-mid. The results are presented in Table 4.2. They do not indicate any sensitivity to intrinsic fundamental frequency; an analysis of variance confirmed that the differences among the mean intervals are merely random.

Contextual F_0

Voice of a preceding consonant

The fundamental frequency of a vowel is liable to be influenced by the presence or absence of voice in a preceding stop consonant (Lehiste et al. 1961; Lea 1973; Meyers 1976; Umeda 1981; Ohde 1984, 1985). Fundamental frequency tends to be falling from an absolute higher value after voiceless stops except immediately following the stop release, and level or rising from an absolute lower value after voiced stops; some reports of rising fundamental frequency after voiced stops may be due to a failure to factor out the intonational context (Silverman 1986). In Swedish, peak fundamental frequency was about 15 Hz lower and occurred 25 msec later after voiced than after voiceless consonants (Löfqvist 1975). In Japanese, it was found that the pitch peak in accented syllables occurred later after voiced stops than after voiceless stops (Kawasaki 1983). Contextual fundamental frequency can serve as a perceptual cue to consonant voicing (Haggard et al. 1970; Kohler 1982; Whalen et al. 1990). The net effect of the preceding consonant lasts longer into the vowel in English than in tone languages such as Thai (Gandour 1974), Yoruba (Hombert 1978; Connell et al. 1990) and Hausa (Meyers 1976), probably because speakers of tone languages make an effort to limit segmental frequency effects that could interfere with the perception of the tones, much as the duration of nasal coarticulation may be expected to be more limited in languages with distinctively nasalized vowels. On the other hand, in a number of African tone languages certain voiced obstruents have the phonological effect of lowering the tones of contiguous vowels and in such cases they are called "depressor" consonants (Goldsmith 1990). Consonant voice can also affect the pitch of whistled vowels in whistle languages (Pike 1970). The reasons for the conditioning effect of preceding consonants is again poorly understood (Hombert 1978; Kingston 1984). One interpretation supposes a difference in tension of the vocal cords associated with consonant voicing: the arrest of glottal vibration for the voiceless consonant may be effected not only by opening the glottis but also by a change in the tension of the vocal cords, which has a temporary effect on the fundamental frequency of the following vowel (Löfqvist et al. 1989). Contextual fundamental frequency explains why tones or additional tones can easily develop in languages that lose a distinction of voicing in prevocalic consonants, as in Chinese, Vietnamese and Hottentot languages. Given the magnitude and the duration of the frequency perturbations arising from the influence of prevocalic consonants, although a small pitch difference can be perceived (Hombert 1978; Hombert et al. 1979), it is less likely to be reflected in the melody of vocal music than the generally less transient and more substantial pitch differences associated with pitch accents and stress. Perceptual evidence from experiments using synthesized intonation suggest that listeners discount such consonantal effects in judging intonation (Beckman 1986); as in the case of intrinsic fundamental frequency, the perceptual system seems to be elastic enough to "hear" the differences for the purposes of segmental identification and factor them out for prosodic purposes (Petersen 1986; Silverman 1990). However, in the Zulu praise poems, which are chanted in the upper pitch range of the performer's voice, syllables with a low speech tone are often assigned a lower note if their onset is a nonimplosive voiced consonant than if it is a voiceless or implosive consonant; and syllables with a high speech tone are often assigned a high note with rising on-glide after a nonimplosive voiced onset consonant as opposed to a nongliding high note after other consonants (Rycroft 1960, 1962). (Voiced implosives have fundamental frequency effects similar to those of voiceless stops [Greenberg 1970], while voiceless labial-velar stops have effects similar to those of voiced stops [Connell et al. 1990]).

One way of testing for contextual fundamental frequency effects in the Delphic hymns is to calculate the average pitches of syllables of different types. Since the Greek musical notation does not provide absolute pitches, as implied by the staff transcription, the pitch measurement must be made in terms of intervals above or below an arbitrary reference. A contextual fundamental frequency effect would be implied if, on the average, the pitch of syllables with a voiced consonant onset such as the -δύ- of ἀδύθρους *Ath.* 15 stood lower in relation to the reference pitch than syllables with a voiceless stop onset such as the -θύ- of θύγατρες *Ath.* 2. Since accented syllables have a higher mean pitch than unaccented syllables, the two classes must be treated separately. Accented syllables were limited to those bearing the acute, and their mean calculated for *Ath.* and *Lim.*; unaccented syllables were taken from *Ath.* only. The arbitrary reference chosen was c^1. The results of the test are presented in Table 4.3, where TV represents a syllable with an unaspirated or aspirated voiceless stop onset and DV a syllable with a voiced stop onset; m indicates the sample mean in tones and s the sample standard deviation.

TABLE 4.3
Test of contextual fundamental frequency

	Acute	No accent
TV	$m = 1.86$	$m = 1.03$
	$s = 1.58$	$s = 1.47$
DV	$m = 2.31$	$m = 1.45$
	$s = 1.69$	$s = 1.80$

For both accented and unaccented syllables the mean intervals above the reference pitch are actually slightly greater for syllables with voiced onsets; the differences are not statistically significant.

Although intrinsic and contextual fundamental frequency have different characteristics — intrinsic fundamental frequency is not localized to the first part of the vowel and involves level rather than rising or falling tone (Hombert et al. 1979) — their effects tend to neutralize each other or to compound (di Cristo et al. 1986). The cumulative impact in Greek of the intrinsic and contextual fundamental frequency effects discussed so far, as in πίθος versus βάθος or sequentially in ἐπίβασις, may reasonably be assumed to have been quite substantial: in English, a difference of 30 Hz was found between the peak fundamental frequencies of [pi] and [bæ] (Lehiste et al. 1961). However, the results presented in Tables 4.2–3 indicate that the effects of intrinsic fundamental frequency and contextual fundamental frequency arising from the voice of the preceding stop onset were not of such perceptual salience that the Greek musical settings would be constrained to reflect them; they do not indicate that these effects, which are presumably universal, were absent in Greek. These negative results are methodologically important, in that it follows that these stop onset and intrinsic fundamental frequency effects can be ignored in other tests of the musical settings, which greatly simplifies test design and permits the use of larger sample sizes.

Voice of a following consonant

A consistent contextual difference in fundamental frequency has also been found in the transition from a vowel into a following obstruent: during the last about 60 milliseconds of the vowel, fundamental frequency was lowered about 10 Hz before a voiced obstruent but only about 6 Hz before a voiceless obstruent, and listeners can use this difference as a cue to the voicing of the consonant (Bannert et al. 1975; Kohler 1990; Silverman 1990). This rather small contextual difference is discounted in the following tests of the musical settings.

Aspirated stops

Evidence from tonogenesis indicates that when a language develops two tones from the merging of two series of a voiceless aspirated, voiceless unaspirated and voiced stop system, the aspirated series usually patterns with the unaspirated series, but when a language develops three contrastive tones from the same stop series, the higher tones usually develop from the aspirated series. A number of reports indicate higher fundamental frequency at the beginning of a vowel following an aspirated voiceless stop as compared to one following an unaspirated voiceless stop, but the evidence is not uniform; no difference was found between vowels after the aspirated allophone of English stops and after the unaspirated French stops (Hombert 1978). Nevertheless, in the Chonnam dialect of Korean, when aspirated stops and *s* (which, like the aspirated stops, is characterized by wide glottal aperture) appear as the onset consonant of the first syllable of the accentual phrase, the basic Low High Low pattern is realized as High High Low: the raising effect of aspiration at the onset of the vowel is extended throughout the vowel resulting in a level High tone (Jun 1990). The higher tone after voiceless aspirated stops and *s* was striking enough in Carrier (British Columbia), which is a pitch accent language, to be carefully recorded in a noninstrumental study (Pike 1986).

The Delphic hymns evidence a clear effect of a preceding aspirated stop (T^h) on the fundamental frequency of a following vowel in Greek, as shown by the following test. In words (excluding proper names) bearing the circumflex or (nonfinal) acute, the intervals from the (lowest) pitch of the immediately preaccentual syllable to the peak of the accented syllable, denoted SŚ, were assigned to one of three classes, according to the magnitude of the pitch rise: 1) level pitch (and the rare cases of fall), 2) rise of a semitone, and 3) rise of a whole tone or more. The relative frequency of aspirated stops in the onset of the preaccentual syllable, T^h(R)VŚ, was calculated for each class. (There was insufficient data to test for *s*.) The results are presented in Table 4.4. If there is a rise in pitch of a whole tone or more from the preaccentual syllable to the accentual peak, then aspirated stops are entirely excluded from the onset of the preaccentual syllable; if the rise in pitch is no more than a semitone, the structure T^h(R)VŚ is permitted, as in φιλόμαχον *Ath.* 28, although there are only two instances; if there is no rise in pitch at all, the structure T^h(R)VŚ is freely admitted, type θιγοῦσ' *Lim.* 6, νιφοβόλους *Lim.* 3, φιλένθεον *Lim.* 23, χρυσέα *Ath.* 15. These results may be summarized more revealingly in converse form: if the onset of the preaccentual syllable contains an aspirated stop, its musical setting must not be more than a semitone lower than that of the peak of the accent, and generally

TABLE 4.4

Aspirated onset in the preaccentual syllable

Interval in tones	$T^h(R)V\acute{S}$ %	N
$S\acute{S} \leq 0$	25.93	27
$S\acute{S} = 0.5$	10.00	20
$S\acute{S} \geq 1$	0.00	29

$$\bar{\chi}^2 = 0.0919, \ c = 0.5851$$
$$p = 0.005$$

it should be at the same pitch as the accentual peak. The results presented in Table 4.4 are highly significant statistically according to Bartholomew's test for a gradient in qualitatively ordered proportions (Fleiss 1973); there is a chance of less than one in two hundred that the gradient could have arisen purely at random. The tendency for level pitch in the musical settings of $T^h(R)V\acute{S}$, as opposed to rising pitch in the settings of other $S\acute{S}$ structures, evidently reflects a contextual frequency effect of the aspirate on a following vowel in Greek speech. However, no attempt has been made to introduce a correction for this effect in other tests of the musical settings; aspirated stops are not that frequent, and if some correction were applied to compensate for uneven distribution, it would be unlikely to reverse any of the trends established in the other tests.

Grave accent

In order to be clearly actuated, an accentual fall needs to be distributed over an adequate phonological span; light final syllables in particular afford a rather restricted span to carry both the accentual High tone and the subsequent fall. This is probably one reason why some languages have distributional constraints on accents in final syllables or morae as well as peak retraction phenomena. In the pitch accent language Carrier, certain accented word final syllables have falling rather than high pitch (Pike 1986); if this effect is not simply demarcative, it could be a reflex of the accentual pitch fall realized in the narrow phonological space resulting from the absence of a postaccentual syllable. In Greek, the turning point between falling and rising tone coincides with the word boundary; the word boundary is demarcative (Allen 1973:246). Some data presented in Table 4.11 suggest that this could be formalized by positing a boundary Low tone at the end of the word. The accentual fall cannot cross this demarcation and spill over onto the beginning of the following word (unless that word is a clitic, in which case the demarcation is reduced). If the last mora of a Greek word carries the accent, little or no phonological substance remains to carry the fall. So the Greek grave can be viewed as a sort of compromise between the accentual High and the postaccentual Low or between the accentual High and the word final Low. The grave is not found at the end of major phrases; this indicates that the grave is basically a phrasal phenomenon, perhaps also reflecting the need for the following word to have some form of preaccentual rise. For some speakers of Osaka Japanese, Low beginning words with accented final mora are pronounced with an accentual fall and lengthening of the final mora in citation forms; however, when such words are followed by a Low-toned enclitic particle, the word final mora is High throughout, there is no lengthening, and the accentual fall is from the final syllable onto the enclitic; other speakers have no fall even in citation forms (Kori 1987). This illustrates the conflicting strategies speakers can adopt to accent a final mora, where the segmental substance available to carry the accentual fall is constricted. Not all languages necessarily require the turning point to be located at the end of the word: in Russian rising stress accents, the valley is located at or just before the beginning of the accented syllable and the peak at or near the end of the stressed syllable; the fall from peak to valley can be distributed over posttonic syllables of the first word and pretonic syllables of the following word (Yokoyama 1986).

The evidence of the musical documents indicates that the grave accent is a lowered High tone, not an unaccented syllable; this is confirmed by statistical analysis of the Delphic hymns. Table 4.5 presents the results of a test of the mean rise to the grave in *Ath.* and *Lim.* in polysyllabic nonlexical and lexical words (including proper names), type λωτὸς *Ath.* 14, ἑσμὸς *Ath.* 17, κλυτὰν *Lim.* 14, ἐπὶ *Lim.* 14, compared with the mean rise to the acute in *Lim.* in the same class of words, type 'Ατθίδ' *Lim.* 14, ἐκείνας *Lim.* 19; word initial acutes are excluded. The test is restricted to words occurring after the first acute or circumflex in the clause. The results show that, on the average, the rise to the grave is about a third of a tone. This mean rise is significantly greater than zero ($t = 4.89$,

TABLE 4.5
Mean rise in tones to grave and acute

To grave	To acute
$m_g = 0.31$	$m_a = 0.92$
$s_g = 0.53$	$s_a = 1.43$
$t = 2.01$, $df = 68$ $m_g < m_a$: $p < 0.025$	

$df = 23$), so that it may be concluded that the grave has a higher pitch than the syllable preceding it in the same word. In comparison, the mean rise to the acute is nearly a tone; the difference between the rise to the grave and the rise to the acute is statistically significant. It follows that syllables bearing the grave accent are neither unaccented nor fully accented.

The status of the grave as a lowered High tone may also be established by comparing its pitch to that of the nongrave accent of an immediately following word. Table 4.6 gives the mean rise from the grave to the following nongrave accent ($_gA$), excluding proper names, nonlexical words and accents on the first lexical word of a clause or participial phrase. Despite the fact that there are only nine cases preserved which meet the criteria defined for the test, the mean rise of little more than a tone is statistically significant. This result is quite striking, since within major phrases there is a mean FALL in pitch from one nongrave accent to the next.

The magnitude of the excursion to the grave varies according to the status of the grave word as proclitic or lexical and according to the number of morae over which the rise is distributed. The rise to the grave triples as one moves from proclitics having one or two pregrave morae with 0.07 tones through lexicals having exactly two pregrave morae (iamb- and trochee-shaped words) with 0.21 tones to lexicals having three or more pregrave morae (spondee-shaped and longer words) with 0.63 tones. These data are presented in Table 4.7 along with the results of the Jonckheere-Tempstra test, which shows that there is only about a one in twenty chance of these differences being random.

It is also useful to analyze the relationship of the grave to the first unaccented syllable of the following word. When a word initial unaccented syllable is preceded by a word final unaccented syllable within the same major phrase in *Ath.*, there is a mean rise of 0.85 tones ($s = 1.35$) from the unaccented final to the unaccented initial syllable. By contrast,

TABLE 4.6
Mean rise in tones from grave
to immediately following nongrave

$$-\grave{S}\#(\ldots)\acute{S}S(\ldots)\#$$
$$_gA = 1.22$$
$$s = 0.57$$

$$_gA > 0 : t = 6.12, \; df = 8$$
$$p < 0.0025$$

when a word initial unaccented syllable is preceded by a word final grave syllable in the same major phrase, the mean rise from the grave to the unaccented initial syllable in *Ath.* and *Lim.* is only 0.24 tones ($s = 0.56$); there is less than one chance in twenty that a difference as great or greater would arise at random ($t = 1.88$, $df = 47$). However, the difference between 0.24 tones and zero is not statistically significant ($t = 1.84$, $df = 17$); so although the pitch of the grave may generally have been slightly lower than that of a following unaccented syllable, it was not possible to provide statistical confirmation of this assumption.

Mid-High-Low contour

In the pitch accent language Japanese, in tetrasyllables having the accent on the second syllable, the initial syllable has higher pitch than the final syllable (Poser 1985). In the stress language Diegueño (S. California: Langdon 1970), in which the main exponents of stress are intensity and pitch, pretonic syllables have higher pitch than any posttonic syllables there may be. This relationship is predictable from the fact that low tones as well as high tones fall as the utterance progresses due to the effects of catathesis and declination (p. 435). Mid-High-Low contours can also appear in citation forms. In Kinyarwanda, the tonal sequence High High High uttered in isolation is modified to Mid High Low, rather than to Low High Low or Low High Mid (Furere et al. 1985).

A number of settings in the Delphic hymns exemplify a Mid-High-Low contour for medially accented Greek polysyllabic words (ME 4.1–3).

ME 4.1   *Ath.* 15

ά - δύ-θρου[ς]

TABLE 4.7

Mean rise in tones to grave according to lexical status
and number of pregrave morae

Grave class, pregrave morae	Mean total rise
$MG(p, x \le 2)$	0.07
$MG(l, 2)$	0.21
$MG(l, x \ge 3)$	0.63

$$MG(p, x \le 2) \le MG(l, 2) \le MG(l, x \ge 3) :$$
$$J = 116, \; z = 1.61$$
$$p \approx 0.054$$

TABLE 4.8

Preacute rise and postacute fall

	Ath.		Lim.	
	Ś>S %	Ś≤S %	Ś>S %	Ś≤S %
#(...)SŚ(...)#	62.75	37.25	63.51	36.49
#(...)ŚS(...)#	87.04	12.96	87.65	12.35
	$\omega = 0.25$		$\omega = 0.24$	
	$\chi^2 = 8.31$		$\chi^2 = 12.40$	

ME 4.2   *Ath.* 18

με-γά - λου

ME 4.3   *Lim.* 23

δει - ρά - δα

One implication of such a contour is that the proportion of preaccentual syllables set to the same note as or a higher note than the immediately following accentual peak should be greater than the proportion of post-accentual syllables set to the same note as or a higher note than the immediately preceding accentual peak, since a mismatch between speech tone and musical setting involving the postaccentual syllable would be more serious than one involving the preaccentual syllable. The proportions found in trisyllabic and longer words bearing the acute accent including proper names are presented in Table 4.8. The odds for a preacute syllable to be set lower than the acute are approximately 5:3 as opposed to 7:1 for a postacute syllable; the odds ratios mean that the odds for the former event are only a quarter those for the latter.

TABLE 4.9

Mean rise to and mean fall from the acute in tones

#(...)SŚ(...)#	#(...)ŚS(...)#
$m_r = 0.80$	$m_f = 1.33$
$s_r = 0.21$	$s_f = 1.12$
$m_r < m_f : t = 2.03,\ df = 65$	
$p < 0.025$	

Another implication of the postulated Mid-High-Low contour is that, in those cases which do in fact show preaccentual rises and postaccentual falls in the musical settings, the mean fall should be greater than the mean rise. The results of a test of this implication on the same class of words are presented in Table 4.9: the average pitch fall from the acute is greater than the average rise to the acute by a little more than a semitone. This difference is statistically significant, and there is less than two and a half chances in a hundred that a difference greater than or equal to that observed could have arisen at random.

Intramoraic peak location

Data pertaining to the location of the peak within the mora have already been presented (p. 30). The situation in Japanese, a language in which turning points are quite well synchronized with mora boundaries, is illustrated in Figure 6.1 for different rates of speech in the Osaka dialect. At slow rates of speech, the accentual mora consisted of a rise to the peak followed by a plateau at the peak, and the fall to the valley was located at the beginning of the postaccentual mora; at normal and fast rates of speech, the plateau was eliminated, and the peak was located at the end of the accented mora and the valley at the end of the post-accentual mora. If the rate of fall from the peak is comparatively great and the location of the peak is anticipated, it can result that the accent is perceived as located on the prepeak syllable (Hata et al. 1991; Hasegawa et al. 1992).

Number of morae in rise and fall

Another factor that potentially affects the magnitude of an accentual excursion is the number of pre- and postaccentual morae or syllables in the word. Theoretically, three situations can be envisaged. Either the target peak or the target valley or both are fixed and the slope from one to the other varies according to the number of unaccented syllables, or the slope is fixed and the targets vary, or both the targets and the slope vary. In a study of Swedish (Alstermark et al. 1971), it was found that the target peaks and valleys tended not to vary with syllable number, but that under certain conditions the addition of postaccentual unstressed syllables could displace the peak towards the right and change the rate of decline; peak height was quite stable and the addition of preaccentual unstressed syllables did not have comparable effects. In Japanese, the valley, and, to a smaller degree, the following and preceding peaks are sensitive to the number of postaccentual morae; the greater the number of postaccentual morae, the lower the valley and the higher the preceding peak. Moreover, the peak of the following minor phrase is somewhat lower after a deep valley than after a shallow valley. None of these effects generally exceeded 15 Hz for a male speaker, and there may be an absolute limit beyond which a valley cannot be depressed to accommodate additional postaccentual morae (Kubozono 1987). In Danish, fundamental frequency did not always rise as high when there was only a single posttonic syllable as when more than one unstressed syllable followed the accent (Thorsen 1982).

In Greek, the magnitude of accentual excursions to and from the acute and circumflex varies according to the number of syllables covered (as well as the lexical status of the word). Table 4.10 presents the results of a test for this effect in paroxytone and proparoxytone words; in order to control for potentially interacting factors, words which have a secondary pitch rise or are likely to be particularly focused and words in initial or final position in a major phrase are excluded. In this table, n means 'nonlexical,' l means 'lexical,' P, V, and M mean 'peak,' 'valley' and 'Mid tone' respectively. These results show that the peak to valley interval increases from nonlexical to lexical words and from paroxytone to proparoxytone lexicals; there is only one chance in a thousand that this trend could arise at random. There is no meaningful correlation between the peak to valley interval and the presence of a preaccentual syllable.

Maintaining the same controls as in Table 4.10 but averaging over paroxytones, proparoxytones, perispomena and properispomena, it was found that the mean rise over one syllable to the peak is 0.70 and the mean rise over two or more syllables to the peak is 1.00. Although this difference cannot be demonstrated to be statistically significant in the small data set available, it is in the same direction as the peak to valley increase and suggests that the rise to the peak may also be an increasing function of the number of syllables it covers.

TABLE 4.10
Correlation of peak to valley interval in tones
with lexical status and number of syllables

#Ś...	#SŚ...
$PV(n,1) = 0.70$	$MPV(n,1) = 1.00$ (ἐκείνας)
$s = 0.84$	————
$PV(l,1) = 0.92$	$MPV(l,1) = 1.18$
$s = 0.69$	$s = 0.82$
$PV(l,2) = 2.20$	$MPV(l,2) = 1.58$
$s = 0.98$	$s = 1.28$

$$PV(n,1) \leq PV(l,1) \leq PV(l,2):$$
$$J = 377.5, \ z = 3.50, \ p < 0.001$$

When all other variables are factored out, it appears that the accentual peaks of words are relatively independent of word length, although they show a small tendency to be higher with increasing intervals of preceding rise. It is the final Low and initial Mid tones that fall substantially as additional syllables are added on their respective sides of the peak. So the peaks represent a fairly stable phonetic target, whereas the valleys are variable and contextually determined. This reconstruction, along with the small correlation of peak level with prepeak morae, is represented schematically in Figure 4.4, where the length of the vertical lines indicates the magnitude of the rise to the peak, P, from one preaccentual syllable, $M(1)$, over two, $M(2)$, or three, $M(3)$, and the fall from the peak to the word's pitch valley over one, $V(1)$ or two, $V(2)$ postaccentual syllables.

Slope

It cannot be automatically assumed that the slope of the rise from the first syllable of the word to the accentual peak and the slope of the fall from the peak to the final syllable of the word can be represented by straight lines. It is also theoretically possible for the line to have a "kink" in it, that is for the slope to be steeper at some point than at other points. This occurs when one or more syllables in a rise or fall account for more than their proportional share of the pitch movement. For instance, most of the fall may be localized on the postaccentual syllable, or, as in "plateau" languages, most of the rise may occur at the beginning of the word. Table 4.11 gives the results of a test on proparoxytones of all lengths of the intervals from the peak to the first postaccentual Low (HL_1) and from the first to the second postaccentual Low (L_1L_2), maintaining the same controls on position, secondary rise and focus as for Table 4.10. The interval of fall from the peak to the first Low is over two and a half times as great as the interval of fall from the first to the second Low; the difference is statistically significant. The same pattern holds for the few

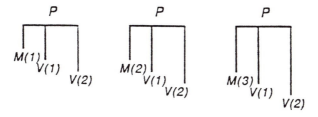

FIGURE 4.4
Correlation of intervals of rise and fall
with the number of pre- and postpeak syllables

TABLE 4.11

The interval in tones from peak to first Low
compared with the interval
from first Low to second Low

#...ŚSS#	
$HL_1 = 1.29$	$L_1L_2 = 0.50$
$s = 1.16$	$s = 0.50$
$HL_1 > L_1L_2$: $t = 2.33$, $df = 32$, $p < 0.025$	

words having bimoraic fall spans and one postpeak syllable whose pitch relations are fully preserved. So pitch does not fall at a constant rate from peak to valley, but there is a discrete change in the rate of fall after the first Low, and the immediate postpeak fall is the major component of the total peak to valley excursion. The fall from High to the first Low can therefore be assumed to have been the most salient cue of a full accent. The much smaller interval of the fall from the first to the second Low probably did not play a central role in signalling the accent.

Data for trajectory of the rise to the accentual peak covering two or more syllables are quite restricted. Table 4.12 gives the mean rise from the third to the second preaccentual syllable (M_3M_2), from the second to the first (M_2M_1) and from the first to the peak (M_1H), using the same controls as above but including words bearing the circumflex. The variation over the syllables in these data is probably random and not indicative of any significant deviation from a basic straight line slope for the rise to the accent.

The results of these tests are represented schematically in Figure 4.5, which shows a steady rise to the peak followed by an abrupt drop over

TABLE 4.12

Mean rise in tones syllable by syllable
to the accentual peak

$M_3M_2 = 0.13$
$s = 0.25$
$M_2M_1 = 0.59$
$s = 0.49$
$M_1H = 0.36$
$s = 0.32$

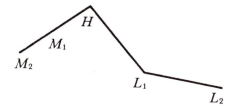

FIGURE 4.5
Mid-High-Low contour of the accentual excursion

the first postpeak mora and a slower, flatter fall over subsequent post-peak morae. This suggests the following possible phonological interpretation of the overall accentual fall: the accentual peak and fall sensu stricto is a High Low tone combination, and the flatter ensuing fall is a movement from the accentual Low tone to a boundary Low tone linked to the final syllable of the word; as already noted, the fundamental frequency turning point demarcates the word.

Secondary rise

When connected speech having tonal coarticulation is compared with citation form pronunciations, and when rapid speech is compared with slow speech (p. 230), substantial differences are found in the execution of the movements between target tones. The pitch range can be compressed, that is peaks can be lowered and valleys raised; complex movements can be replaced by simpler movements; and the association of target tones with segments can be subject to modification. These effects have been investigated in Swedish (Gårding et al. 1987), Japanese (Nagano-Madsen 1987) and Chinese (Shih 1988; Shen 1990). In Swedish, the accentual peaks were relatively fixed, but the relationship between fundamental frequency and segments was otherwise more variable (Bruce 1983). In English, the peak of a focus accent occurs comparatively early in the syllable if the syllable has final lengthening or is the first syllable of a stress clash; one interpretation of the latter finding is that the peak is moved to the left to minimize tonal crowding (Silverman et al. 1990). In Yoruba, High tone is realized as rising after Low tone, and Low tone is realized as falling after High tone, so that for instance in a High Low Low sequence the central syllable has a tonal transition (Hombert 1976; Connell et al. 1990). The general conclusion is that tonal events are not necessarily related in a stable manner to articulatory events but can vary to accommodate the surrounding environment or the rate of speech.

There are a number of cases in the Delphic hymns which are exceptions to the tendency observed above for pitch to continue to fall after the first postpeak Low, so that there is a rise in pitch following the accentual fall. Since pitch never rises and then falls back after the accentual fall, the maximum secondary rise is simply the interval from the beginning of the secondary rise to the end of the word; an example is given in ME 4.4. Secondary rise can definitionally be observed only in properispomena, in proparoxytones, and in paroxytones with melisms set

ME 4.4 *Ath.* 11

βω - μοι-οῖ-σιν ῞Α - φαι - στος

to their final heavy syllables. The analysis in Table 4.13, which excludes properispomena whose circumflexes are not set to falling melisms, is designed to test the proposition that secondary rise is restricted to contexts in which the following word initial syllable is set at least three semitones higher than the first postpeak pitch of the preceding word; Δ means the intervallic magnitude. The odds ratios show that the odds are overwhelming for secondary rises to occur only if the threshold condition on the interval to the next word is met.

The interpretation of secondary rise is ambiguous. One possibility is that secondary rise had no linguistic basis but was partly or entirely motivated by a stylistic preference for smaller intervallic jumps within musical phrases. This assumption implies that in this one case there was a complete reversal of a linguistic pitch pattern, turning pitch falls into rises, in a text which otherwise shows a very high level of strictness in its respect for the pitch movements of the language. According to this interpretation, secondary rise is a type of melodic smoothing (p. 166); it occurs under conditions in which the language creates a tonal excursion that is too steep to be conveniently accommodated by the melody. A large majority of the word initial syllables set above the threshold interval and occasioning a secondary rise occur either in proper names, which generally have abnormal pitch obtrusion in the Delphic hymns, or in situations of nonbasic word order associated with emphasis, such as

TABLE 4.13

Threshold interval for secondary rise

	#(...)ŚSS# and #(...)S̃S#		#(...)ŚS̄#	
	$\Delta \geq 1.5$ %	$\Delta < 1.5$ %	$\Delta \geq 1.5$ %	$\Delta < 1.5$ %
Secondary rise	92.31	7.69	100.00	0.00
No secondary rise	16.67	83.33	7.50	92.50
	$\omega = 60$		$\omega = \infty$	
	$\chi^2 = 21.71$		$p = 0.0003$	

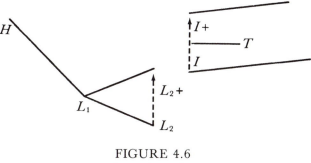

FIGURE 4.6
Secondary rise

prolepsis or adjective fronting. Secondary rise is also largely or entirely confined to positions within the major phrase; it does not occur before a major syntactic boundary. Since secondary rise is linguistically conditioned, it is also possible to interpret it as a properly linguistic feature occurring in connected speech. Under normal circumstances, that is in the absence of focus or emphasis, the pitch of the initial syllable of the following word would not be so much higher than the pitch of the first postpeak Low that a continued shallow fall to the second postpeak Low would occasion an extremely abrupt jump from the second Low to the following word initial syllable. If however the latter were abnormally raised due to focus, the turning point between falling and rising pitch could be moved leftwards, thereby creating a shallower valley and spreading the steep rise over more syllables. The movement from the first to the second postpeak Low would then change from falling to rising, smoothing the pitch movement within the phrase. The change from a falling to a rising slope is naturally interpreted as an assimilatory process, a type of pitch sandhi (as distinct from the phonological tone sandhi of tone languages): it is represented schematically in Figure 4.6. Since secondary rise is phrasal, it properly belongs in Chapter 8; it has been presented here so that all the data on slope can be analyzed together. Secondary rise can be interpreted either as deletion of the posited boundary tone, or as linking of the boundary tone to the same syllable that is linked to the postaccentual Low, as is presumably the case in perispomena.

Resonants

Tonal movements commonly continue through both voiced and voiceless consonants, although the latter cause gaps in the acoustic record and some consonants give rise to small perturbations in the overall direction of movement. Both the rise from Low to an accentual High, and the accentual High-Low movement itself may be largely implemented on an onset consonant. In Osaka Japanese a moraic voiceless obstruent can even be accented, as in the word *sankaƙkei* 'triangle': in this word the preaccentual vocalic mora is High and the High Low fall, which is steep, begins with the voice onset of the postaccentual syllable; by contrast, if the accent had been on the vowel (*sankákkei*), the postaccentual syllable would have had a Mid Low fall (Sugito 1986); the type with accent retracted onto the vowel is an optional variant (Kori 1987). The less sonorous and often comparatively brief and transient character of (voiced) consonants make them in principle less suitable carriers of tonal information than vowels. As might be expected, resonants are more likely than other voiced consonants to be distinctive tone bearing units; in Lithuanian, resonants in the rime are tone bearing units just like the second elements of diphthongs. Osaka Japanese has a near minimal pair *káNbaN* 'signboard,' *koŃbaN* 'tonight': the tonal contour of the latter was very similar to that of the tetrasyllabic word *komádori* 'kind of bird,' although the turning point was during and not at the end of the vowel preceding the moraic nasal; either the tonal boundary or the mora boundary or both were not synchronized with the segmental boundary (Nagano-Madsen 1991, 1992). By contrast, in English a terminal fall on a word such as *feel* is implemented on the vowel; if it is distributed over both the vowel and the following resonant, as it was in the speech of one deaf subject, it sounds unnatural (Lehiste 1970). There is some evidence for tonal movement on resonants in Greek: the Homeric enclitic accentuations of the type *Λάμπέ τε* can be explained if the first postaccentual Low was on the resonant rather than on the following syllable (Postgate 1924; Allen 1973).

There is also evidence for tonal movement on resonants in the settings of the Delphic Hymns. In the Hymns, melisms may be assigned not only to circumflexed syllables but also to heavy syllables that are unaccented or bear the acute or grave accents. The convention, which is also found in papyri such as *DAM* 21, is for vowels in syllables bearing a melism to be written double and diphthongs to receive an extended spelling

ιιεὶς Ath. 24

εοὐύδρου Ath. 7.

Melisms can occur on syllables having a V̆C-rime structure

Δεελφίσιιν Ath. 6

ἀάμπέχει Lim. 12,

but in such cases the coda consonant is overwhelmingly a resonant rather than an obstruent. 9 of the 19 immediately preaccentual syllables of this type with resonant coda consonants bear melisms as compared with only one of the 10 with obstruent coda consonants, a significant difference ($p = 0.0461$). The same constraint applies to V̆C-rimes in acute sylla-bles, although statistical significance cannot be demonstrated in this small data set: of the 12 acute syllables of this type with resonant coda consonants two have melisms, but none of the 16 with obstruent coda consonants have melisms ($p = 0.1746$). Similarly only two of the post-accentual and grave syllables with melisms have rimes consisting of short vowel plus obstruent, although such rimes are proportionally much more frequent among the nonmelismatic postaccentual and grave heavy syl-lables.

When a rising melism is assigned to a syllable bearing the acute on a long vowel or diphthong, the melism is a direct musical reflection of the rise on the second nuclear mora, in contrast to the fall on the second mora of circumflex vowels and diphthongs. But in two certain cases in the Hymns (ME 4.5–6), and perhaps in a third (ME 4.7) which is phrase

ME 4.5   Λ M O
         τ α ο ύ ρ ω ν   *Ath.* 12

ME 4.6   ⊏   <
         τ η λ έ σ κ ο π ο ν τ α ά ν [δ] ε   *Lim.* 1

ME 4.7   ⊔ <
         θ̣ η η̣ ή ρ   *Lim.* 29

final (p. 432), a falling melism is assigned to the acute. In these cases, if the High-Low sequence were distributed over the nuclear morae, the resulting pattern would be the same as that of the circumflex. However, since in all three cases a resonant follows the vowel either as coda or, more surprisingly, as onset, the pitch fall may have occurred on the reso-nant, with the result that the tonal movement would remain distinct from that of the circumflex. In fact, the nuclei of melismatic acute syllables of all types are overwhelmingly followed immediately by resonants, whether in the rime or in the following onset: of the 25 cases in which a resonant follows a nucleus with the acute, 6 bear melisms, whereas of the 32 cases in which a consonant other than a resonant follows a nucleus with the acute only one (ME 4.8) bears a melism ($p = 0.0232$).

ME 4.8   Λ K Λ
         α ι ε ί θ ε ⟨ι⟩   *Ath.* 12

Since song tends to reflect a much slower rate of production than ordi-nary speech, the perception of tonal movement on resonants as reflect-ing a separate musical note may be more indicative of the situation in very slow speech (as in Figure 6.2) than in ordinary conversational speech. In particular, in ordinary speech the accentual fall may have been more evenly divided between a postaccentual resonant and the following syllabic nucleus than is suggested by the evidence of melisms in the Delphic Hymns. The tone-bearing status of an onset resonant in song is easier to accept for a rate of delivery in which the onset has become more independent, in terms of timing and coarticulation, from the following vowel.

5 | Word Prosody

The analysis of Greek rhythm outlined in Chapter 3 still has to be integrated with the analysis of pitch properties developed in Chapter 4 into an overall theory of Greek word prosody. It needs to be determined what were the phonetic properties of rhythmically prominent syllables, in particular whether they were stressed; whether the system of rhythm correlates or interacts with that of the word accent, and if not, how the two systems could coexist without tending to neutralize each other; and what were the consequences for the Greek word prosodic system of the emergence of a stress accent in later Greek. The problem of how to reconcile accentually patterned pitch with increasingly strong metrical evidence for an accentually patterned system of rhythm has become a serious obstacle to an overall understanding of Greek word prosody, even to the extent of undermining confidence in the value of metrical data that are established beyond any reasonable doubt. The problem cannot be confronted solely on the basis of the linguistic intuitions we all derive from a knowledge of the more familiar modern European languages; it needs to be studied in the perspective of a typological survey of pitch and stress in word prosodic systems.

Intensity

Before embarking on this survey of word prosodic systems, it is necessary to introduce a further, hitherto neglected, prosodic property, namely intensity. The loudness of a sound refers to the auditory sensation by our nervous system of the acoustic property called intensity. Intensity is most closely related to the power or energy of a sound, which is a function of the amplitude of the sound wave (the maximum displacement of air particles from their position of rest by the vibration) and of the distance between the source of the sound and the point at which its intensity is being measured. The linguistic investigation of intensity often focuses on the amplitude component on the assumption that other factors are or can be held relatively constant.

There are various ways to measure the intensity of a vowel. An acoustic study of stress (Beckman 1986) used the following three measures: one measure was simply the point at which amplitude peaks; another involved taking measurements of the amplitude at 10 msec intervals during the duration of the vowel, adding them up and dividing the total by the duration to give the average amplitude; the total, by itself, not divided by the duration, is a measure that integrates the factors of intensity and duration; this last measure was found to be a good correlate of stress in English. When the fundamental frequency and the vocal tract configuration are held constant, variations in intensity correlate directly with variations in the amplitude of the acoustic signal, which in turn primarily reflects different degrees of respiratory effort and glottal resistance. Greater subglottal pressure results in a faster moving glottal air burst, which has a stronger impact on the air in the vocal tract, thus producing a more intense acoustic signal. Doubling subglottal pressure increases intensity by very roughly 10 dB. At lower fundamental frequencies, increased subglottal pressure does not necessarily result in a correspondingly increased airflow. A 10 dB increase in intensity correlated with a mean increase of 5% in airflow at a fundamental frequency of 98 Hz, 30% at 196 Hz and 80% at 392 Hz. As subglottal pressure increases, the open quotient of the glottal vibratory cycle is reduced and the closing phase becomes sharper, thereby modifying the glottal pulse and increasing its high frequency energy (Isshiki 1964, 1965; Hirano et al. 1970; Strik et al. 1987). Consequently, a vowel uttered at one and the same fundamental frequency will have a different voice quality according as it is a High tone produced with low vocal effort in quiet speech or a Low tone produced with high vocal effort in loud speech (Pierrehumbert 1989). Professional singers produce greater intensity than nonsingers from the same subglottal pressure (Titze et al. 1992). Intensity can also be increased by a more open vocal tract due to greater muscular effort in the articulators. Vowels bearing the main sentence stress tend to be pronounced with more open jaw positions than unstressed vowels, and the speed at which the jaw opens in the transition between stop consonant and vowel in a CV-syllable likewise tends to be greater if the syllable is stressed than if it is unstressed (p. 206). The location, as well as the degree, of peak amplitude can vary in a vowel of a given duration and this difference can affect the perception of syllable rhythm (Edwards et al. 1988).

In the typical discourse situation, a speaker chooses the general level of intensity most suited to his environment. The level chosen for discourse in a church will be different from that for discourse in close proximity to a pneumatic drill. Variations in intensity also reflect the attitudes and emotions of the speaker. Increased intensity is one of the characteristics of the impatient as opposed to the neutral pronunciations of sentences in a number of different languages such as English, French, Polish and Ukrainian (Léon et al. 1980). In loud shouting, the increase in intensity found in the frequencies above 500 Hz was approximately 32 dB as opposed to only 6 dB below 500 Hz; consequently the spectrum of normal spoken voice is deformed in shouting (Rostolland 1982); vowel length also tends to be increased and the duration of stop consonants to be decreased (Schulman 1989). The choice of an absolute level of intensity is, unlike intrinsic intensity, under the control of the speaker, but it is of pragmatic rather than grammatical significance. The relative intensity assigned by the speaker to different components of an utterance is what is often linguistically significant.

Frequency and duration can both affect the perceived loudness of sounds having identical measured intensities. The ear hears low frequencies and very high frequencies less efficiently than the broad mid range of frequencies from 300–8000 Hz, so that pure tones below and above the mid range need to have greater physical intensity to be perceived as equally loud. The effect of frequency on the loudness of a complex tone is more complicated, since it depends on the distribution of energy among its components and on the degree of masking resulting from their frequency separation. At least up to a certain level of duration, shorter sounds need to have greater intensity than longer sounds if they are to be perceived as equally loud (Scharf 1978): such an effect was found for vowels having durations of less than 200 msec (Nishinuma et al. 1983).

The sounds of a language do not all have the same intensity, even if the utterance is produced with stable input energy and unchanging fundamental frequency. For instance, in English there is about a 5 dB difference in intrinsic intensity between the close vowels *i* and *u* and the open vowel *a* (Lehiste et al. 1959). Differences in the same direction have been recorded for various unrelated languages such as Kiowa (Oklahoma: Sivertsen 1956) and Japanese (Homma 1973). The more constricted the vocal tract, the greater the impedance it provides to acoustic vibrations. This is why in loud speech vowels tend to be produced with much greater jaw openings (Schulman 1989). Similarly, lip rounding and, in most cases, nasalization have the effect of reducing intensity. Short front vowels in Danish had higher intensity than long front vowels, and short lax vowels in German often had higher initial intensity and lower final intensity than long tense vowels (Fischer-Jørgensen 1990). Other intrinsic intensity differences between segments are due to the varying efficiency with which individual sounds are generated: *s* and *ʃ*, as in *sip* and *ship*, have greater intensity than the stop consonants, but *f* and *θ*, as in *fish* and *think*, have lower intrinsic intensity than both the former and the latter. As a rule, vowel sounds have greater intrinsic intensity than consonants, since the latter are produced with greater articulatory constriction. Conversely, intensity differences arise for the same vowel, if the pitch at which it is pronounced is varied. In this situation, the articulatory configuration of the vocal tract, and hence its filtering properties, remain constant, but the fundamental frequency and thus the harmonic frequencies of the sound are changed. The degree to which the harmonics coincide with the resonant frequencies of the vocal tract as configured for the articulation of the sound in question will affect the intensity of that sound.

Intrinsic differences among sounds can easily be heard by speakers, but they are regularly discounted, since they have no linguistic significance. Close vowels that have a measurable intensity of 5 dB less than open vowels seem to the listener to be as loud as the open vowels. Conversely, when the two types of vowels are pronounced with identical measured intensities, the close vowels are judged by listeners to be louder than the open vowels, presumably because the listener corrects for the intrinsic differences, although the different spectral distributions of energy have also been cited as a possible factor (Rossi 1971b). In the light of the above facts relating to perception, intrinsic intensity differences are a priori unlikely to have any metrical relevance. The data cited in Table 2.4 offer no evidence to suggest the metrical relevance of the intensity difference between open and close vowels.

Some intensity differences are related to the position of segments within a phonological domain such as the syllable, word or phrase. The intensity of a voiceless fricative such as *s* in English is greatest before stressed vowels in word initial syllables, lower in intervocalic and word final position, and even lower in prepausal position. Such intensity differences may serve as one of the cues disambiguating segmentally identical phrases of the type *a nice man* versus *an iceman*. Intensity is more likely to be increasing in the onset of the stressed syllable *ni-* and decreasing in the coda of the unstressed syllable *an* (Lehiste 1960) (p. 27). The most important function of intensity is to convey prosodic prominence. The stressed syllable of a word often has greater intensity than its unstressed syllables, just as the syllable bearing the sentence stress often has greater intensity than other stressed syllables.

Pitch in word prosody

There is presumably no language in the world in which the system of word prosody is such that every syllable of the word is pronounced with identical pitch (or with identical duration or intensity). However, the

Morpholexical tone	Restricted tone	Pitch accent	Pitch differentiated stress	Stress
non-accentual		accentual	reinforced accentual	

FIGURE 5.1

Functions of pitch in the word

function of pitch differences within the word and the rules for generating them vary from one language to another. In some languages, functional pitch differences are in principle associated with every syllable and serve to differentiate lexical and grammatical items almost like articulatory segments. Such languages are called tone languages. In other languages, pitch melodies within the word are less varied, and pitch is used principally to implement the word or minor phrase accent, by itself or in conjunction with other prosodic features. Such languages are called pitch accent languages and stress languages respectively. These differences in function and autonomy can be viewed along a parameter ranging from nonaccentual through accentual to accentual reinforced by duration and/or intensity. This parameter is represented in Figure 5.1; the categorical distinctions represented by the vertical lines are not intended to indicate watertight compartments — the structures of some languages may be indeterminate in this regard or insufficiently analyzed or they may be at a diachronically transitional stage.

Tone languages

The role of tone in Asian languages is mainly lexical, since they lack a developed morphology. An example of such a language is Modern Standard Chinese (Kratochvíl 1968). In this language, tonic syllables may bear one of four distinctive tones in monosyllabic words uttered in isolation (tones are modified in sandhi). The word *ba* means 'eight' with Level High tone, 'to uproot' with Rising tone, 'to hold' with Low tone, and 'a harrow' with Falling tone. Chinese has a stress accent, which can be distinctive: *junshi* means 'military affairs' with stress on the first syllable and 'balance of power' with stress on the second syllable; in both words the first syllable has High tone and the second syllable Falling tone.

African languages, on the other hand, often have complex morphological systems in which tone can play an important role, resulting in a rich variety of tonal patterns in the word. In Hausa (Nigeria: Abraham 1941), each syllable of the word has High, Low or Falling tone, and tone can be distinctive: *mātā* means 'wife' with Low tone on the first syllable and High tone on the second, and 'wives' with High tone on both syllables. Hausa is widely thought to have a word stress, but this is not certain since what is reported as stress could be merely the fall from High to Low tone (Greenberg pers. comm.; Hunter 1980). However, in general the possibility of word stress in tone languages is well established. Golin (New Guinea), Marinahua (Peru), Eastern Popoloca (Mexico) are examples (Pike 1979). Word stress in tone languages is generally implemented by duration and/or intensity. Stress can also raise a tone above its normal height, as is reported for stress on Low tone syllables in Awiya (Ethiopia: Palmer 1959; Hetzron 1969) and on all three tones in Tiwa (New Mexico: Trager 1971), but it does not necessarily do so. Rather, stress can have the effect of emphasizing the tonal characteristics of the stressed syllable. In Tenango Otomi (Mexico: Blight et al. 1976), a Low tone in a stressed syllable is slightly lower than in an unstressed syllable. In Chinese, stress tends to exaggerate the pitch contour as well as affecting the duration, intensity and vowel formants of the stressed syllable; conversely, in the Northern Wu dialects, in unstressed syllables preceding a stressed syllable contour tones are simplified to level tones (Rose 1990); the same simplification occurs in Isthmus Zapotec (Mexico: Mock 1985) when syllables bearing contour tones are destressed. The durational increments occasioned by stress in many languages should be distinguished from the very minor additional duration that can be intrinsically associated with High tones, such as the 1.05% increment found on High tones in Yoruba (Nagano-Madsen 1992).

Tone languages such as those just mentioned provide a useful typological perspective on one of the ways in which pitch and stress can coexist in the word prosody of a language. But they should not be cited, as they sometimes are, as a parallel in the analysis of Greek word prosody. In a fully developed tone language, the number of different pitch contours or word melodies is much larger and more varied than in a pitch accent language; the tone system has the function of implementing lexical and morphological distinctions and not of making a single syllable of the word prominent by virtue of its bearing the highest tone or being the point at which tone falls from high to low.

Restricted tone languages

In a completely unrestricted tone language, any syllable in the word can bear any tone, so that, for instance, trisyllabic words in a language with two tones have eight (2^3) different tonal patterns; in an unrestricted accent language, accented trisyllabic words have three different tonal patterns, depending upon which syllable bears the accent (Odden 1985). A number of tone languages, many of which are Bantu or Cushitic, have tonal systems in which the distributional freedom of the tones becomes restricted to a point at which the tones begin to show two common characteristics of accentual systems, namely predictability and culminativity. Predictability refers to the existence of one or more fixed tonal melodies and also to the possibility of formulating a rule specifying which syllable gets which tone, and culminativity refers to there being one syllable, or one series of contiguous syllables, that functions as the tonally prominent section of the word; a more detailed typology will be presented below.

Many restricted tone languages are African. In Maasai (Kenya: Tucker et al. 1955), the syllables of a word are, with the exception of certain polymorphemic words, mapped onto the fixed tonal patterns Low-High-Low or Low-High-Downstepped. In Bambara (W. Africa: Courtenay 1974), the vast majority of native lexical items have either a level tone configuration with all High-toned vowels or a rising configuration with one or more Low-toned vowels followed by one or more High-toned vowels (apart from sandhi variants). Consequently, the tonal configuration can be predicted if it is known which is the first High-toned syllable in a word. Bambara is also reported to have a stress falling on the last High-toned syllable, the exponents of which are extra-high tone, increased intensity and increased duration (Bird in Woo 1972), but the domain of the stress has not been fully determined (Mountford 1983). Kinyarwanda (Rwanda: Furere et al. 1985) has a pitch accent system in which a (Low)High(Low) contour is variably assigned to the syllables of accented words; some words are unaccented; in accented words the spread of High tone from the accented syllable is sensitive to foot structure. In Luganda, there is no more than one fall from high to low pitch in any word; however, it is necessary to specify both the beginning and the end of the High tone sequence and to distinguish tonic Low tone morae from atonic morae (Hyman et al. 1993). A stress has also been reported for Luganda, falling on the first syllable of the stem, rather than on the penultimate syllable as in Southern Bantu languages such as Zulu (South Africa) and Shona (Zimbabwe). Other languages show roughly parallel restrictions. In Mahas Nubian (Sudan: Bell 1968), a word may have all High or all Low tones; otherwise it may contain no more than one tone shift, and it is always rising. In Korku (Central India: Zide 1966), only one tone shift per word is allowed, and it is always downward. Tone is even further restricted in the Bantu language Safwa (Tanzania: Voorhoeve 1973). In Safwa, one and only one syllable in each word has High tone, the location of which is not predictable but has to be given in the lexicon and the morphology. It is reported that the High-toned vowel also has greater intensity. Tone patterns are also highly restricted in a number of Cushitic languages. In Iraqw (Whiteley

1958; Tucker et al. 1966), verbs are mostly mapped onto a rising contour with High tone on the final syllable (p. 161), and nouns mostly onto a falling contour with tone fall on the penultimate syllable; there is only one tone shift in the word in both cases. In Bilin (Eritrea: Palmer 1957, 1958), a word may lack any High-toned syllables or have one or more contiguous High-toned syllables; it may have a tone rise or tone fall or both, but not more than one of each. In Beja (Sudan: Hudson 1973), Saho (Eritrea: Welmers 1952) and Somali (Hyman 1981), basic word forms may have only one High-toned syllable.

Some languages of New Guinea also have restricted tone or pitch accent systems, for instance Fore (Pike et al. 1963; Scott 1978). In Fasu (May et al. 1965), there is a distinction between High- and Low-toned vowels, but it occurs only in stressed syllables. Conversely, the exponents of stress vary according to the tone of the stressed vowel: on High-toned vowels stress is implemented by increased intensity, on Low-toned vowels by increased duration. In Nimboran (Anceaux 1965), High tone can occur only once in the word, but its location is not predictable.

The Otomanguean languages, which are tone languages from Mexico, offer some restricted tone systems. In Isthmus Zapotec, lexically specified tonal information is underlyingly required for the first syllable of the root of lexical words, which is also the syllable that bears the stress (implemented by increased duration and exaggerated pitch movement). Clitics and destressed lexicals are also tonally marked and affixes have tonal marking independent of that of the roots to which they are attached (Mock 1985, 1988). In Copala Trique, lexically specified tones are assigned to the final syllable of noncomplex words, which also bears the stress; the rest of the word is tonally predictable on the basis of the assigned tone; destressing leaves the tone in place (Hollenbach 1988).

Restricted tone languages are typologically important in that they illustrate the ambiguous transitional area in Figure 5.1 that lies between tone languages and pitch accent languages. Restricted tone languages are located at various points along a continuum that leads from fully tonal systems to fully accentual systems. The following are some of the interrelated parameters along which these systems can vary with different stages cited by way of examples.

1. Inventory of tonal melodies
    1.1. No restriction
    1.2. The number of permitted melodies is less than the logically possible maximum
    1.3. Only one melody occurs

2. Paradigmatic distribution of tonal contrasts
   2.1. Full tonal contrasts on all syllables
   2.2. Full tonal contrasts on some syllables; other syllables are predictable
   2.3. Tonal contrast on one syllable only

3. Melody mapping
   3.1. No restriction
   3.2. The melody is aligned by lexical or morphological stipulation
   3.3. The melody is aligned by rule on the basis of phonological (prosodic) structure
   3.4. Combination of 3.2 and 3.3

4. Domain of melody assignment
   4.1. Morpheme
   4.2. Word

5. Level of tonal regularity
   5.1. The regularity characterizes some underlying level, but is disturbed by potential complex derivational manipulation
   5.2. The regularity characterizes the surface level

6. Categorial domain of regularity
   6.1. Regularity characterizes only certain categories of words; for instance, the verbal system is largely accentual, whereas the nominal system is basically tonal
   6.2. Regularity characterizes all words

7. Structure of the melody or melodies
   7.1. There are no patterned restrictions on the sequence of tones
   7.2. All High tones are contiguous
   7.3. Some words have a single rising or falling tone shift, other words have all High or all Low tones
   7.4. No word has more than one High tone
   7.5. All words have one and only one High tone

Restricted tone languages are best understood in a diachronic perspective: they represent a transitional stage between a tone language and an accent language. The sequence of development is tone language > restricted tone language > pitch accent language > stress language. While tone languages having a stress are quite common, it is probably significant that those Bantu languages in which tonal patterns are more accentual are also those that tend not to have the typical surface penultimate stress accent, for instance Haya, Kimatuumbi and Tonga (Odden

1985). Insofar as the tonal melody is implemented without significant correlated changes in duration or intensity, the accent is not a stress but a pitch accent: the question has been explicitly investigated in the case of Tonga (Zambia: Goldsmith 1984). Interestingly enough, these languages also illustrate the development of pitch accent into stress, suggesting that the comparative rarity of pure pitch accent systems in the languages of the world may be related to the fact that at least under certain conditions pitch accent systems do not seem to be very stable, giving way fairly easily to stress. For instance, one dialect of Runyankore (Uganda: Johnson 1976) has accentual tone: some words are unaccented or Low-toned, others contain a High or Falling tone; in about seventy percent of the latter class, the High or Falling tone occurs on the penultimate syllable. The other dialect of Runyankore has the typical penultimate stress accent on all words, including those that are Low-toned in the pitch accent dialect. It is not clear what antecedent states other than restricted tone there might be for pitch accent languages, nor how Greek fits into such a diachronic typology.

Stress languages

At the other end of the parameter from the tone languages in Figure 5.1 are the stress languages, or, more precisely, those stress languages in which pitch is a significant exponent of stress. Stressed vowels in English are generally longer and more intense than unstressed vowels; pitch is also often higher, but varies according to intonational context, so that the stressed syllable may actually fall to a Low tone rather than rise to a High tone (p. 464), and either raising or lowering the pitch of a syllable can result in its being perceived as stressed (Morton et al. 1965); unstressed syllables are not necessarily Low toned but are contextually variable. Likewise in Hungarian, the stressed syllable has High tone in unmarked contexts, but the last word of a yes-no question can have a Low-toned stressed syllable and a High-toned unstressed syllable (Kornai et al. 1988). The direction of pitch movement onto and within the stressed syllable is variable (O'Shaughnessy 1979; Pierrehumbert 1980); this is also the case in Russian, where nonfocus and nonfinal stress have rising pitch within the accented syllable, while focus and final stress are mostly falling except in questions and exclamations (Yokoyama 1986). In many languages, pitch excursions on stressed syllables are reduced in the neighbourhood of a focus accent (p. 466); for instance, in modern Greek, stress is implemented by increased duration, intensity and pitch before the focus accent, and by duration and intensity alone after the focus accent (Botinis 1989). One interpretation of these data would be that words have both rhythmic and tonal prominence patterns which are aligned in stress languages, and that these patterns are overlaid by higher level (phrasal) rhythmic and intonational patterns, whose events are often aligned with word level prominences and have the potential to exaggerate or neutralize them.

The relative importance of pitch and duration as cues to English stress depends on this interaction of word stress with intonation, and the additional duration associated with stress is not merely an automatic consequence of the additional time required to execute a pitch movement (Huss 1978; O'Shaughnessy et al. 1983); intensity by itself tends to be the weakest cue (Fry 1955, 1958; Beckman 1986). Duration is said to be the leading cue to stress in Russian, pitch in Estonian (Eek 1987). If a digitized utterance is manipulated in such a way that the fundamental frequency component of a focus accent is moved to another word, the formerly focused syllable still tends to sound prominent since it retains the other components of a focus accent (Silverman 1990).

The strength of stress in English is evidenced by the abbreviation and centralization of the unstressed vowel system. Descriptions of stress in some other languages, for instance Georgian (Vogt 1938) and Kota (S. India: Emeneau 1944), specifically note that stress is less strong than in English. There is a potential indeterminacy between weakly marked final stress and pitch accent with demarcation: the phrase final syllable bearing the accent in French can have greater duration and higher pitch, but the intensity of this accented syllable tends to be lower than that of unaccented syllables (Delattre 1966).

The role of duration in stress marking can reflect its segmental status. In colloquial Meccan Arabic, stressed vowels have both higher pitch and greater duration than unstressed vowels; in the case of long vowels durational differences between stressed and unstressed vowels are relatively great and pitch differences less significant, whereas for short vowels duration is exploited less and pitch more, presumably so as to prevent stress-related durational increments from interfering with phonological vowel length (Ohsiek 1978). Likewise, in the Mayan language K'ekchi (Guatemala: Berinstein 1979), which has phonologically distinctive vowel length, duration is less important than pitch and intensity as a cue to stress, whereas in the related language Cakchiquel, which does not have distinctive vowel length, duration is a significant cue to stress.

Physiologically, many types of stress seem to involve a quantum of additional energy (Öhman 1967) applied to most or all of the speech musculature, resulting in larger gestures having longer durations (Munhall et al. 1985; Krakow 1989; Goldstein 1992), which, on the evidence of reaction times in segment monitoring tasks, are more easily perceived (Cutler et al. 1977). This is particularly clear for emphatic focus accent:

there is some evidence for additional expiratory muscle activity (Ladefoged 1968) and greater than normal decrease in lung volume (Ohala 1990); the higher pitch commonly associated with stress is reliably attributed to laryngeal muscle activity (p. 14); articulatory properties include higher rates of articulator movement and closer approximation of articulators to vowel target positions (Engstrand 1988; Fujimura 1990); some of these effects may be weaker or absent in word stress. Occasional reduced airflow on stressed syllables is explained as due to increased glottal resistance (Ohala 1990). The gesture opening the glottis for the pronunciation of unvoiced stop consonants can be stronger in stressed syllables (Löfqvist et al. 1987; Dixit 1989). In English and Swedish, voiceless stops are aspirated before stressed vowels, but less so or not at all before unstressed vowels; in Georgian, where aspiration is distinctive, it is stronger in stressed syllables (Robins et al. 1952). Aspiration under sentence stress is stronger than aspiration under word stress (Engstrand 1988). Electromyographic measurements of the lip muscles in the production of labial consonants and of the genioglossus muscle in the articulation of *i* can be greater in stressed syllables (Tuller et al. 1982); the velum is lower for nasal consonants and higher for oral consonants in stressed than in unstressed CVN-syllables (Vaissière 1988); and jaw movements in the articulation of vowels can be more rapid and more extensive if the vowel is stressed (Kent et al. 1972; Stone 1981; Summers 1987).

The rhythmically prominent syllables in Greek are those syllables that are mapped onto thesis according to the analysis in Chapter 3. If such syllables are interpreted as stressed, the implication is that they were pronounced with the additional energy often associated with stress and consequently with its physiological and acoustic correlates, such as those just detailed. The difficulty with this assumption is that, in most or all other languages, the prominence associated with stress is accentual, whereas in Greek the accentual function is traditionally associated with pitch and not with rhythm. The question is discussed later (p. 214).

Pitch differentiated stress

A number of languages, such as Serbocroatian, Lithuanian and Swedish, which are commonly said to have a pitch accent, differ from ordinary stress languages in that the pitch component of the stress is differentiated into two distinctive accents. Such languages can be more accurately termed pitch differentiated stress languages.

In Serbocroatian, accented vowels have approximately 50% greater duration than their unaccented counterparts as well as higher pitch; intensity seems to depend more on position in the word than on accent (Lehiste et al. 1986). There are two types of accent; their distribution is restricted, but both can occur on the first syllable of polysyllabic words (Inkelas et al. 1988). In one type of long vowel accent, the pitch peak occurs early in the vowel, and the vowel of the following syllable has lower pitch. In the other type of long vowel accent, the pitch peak occurs late in the vowel, and the vowel of the following syllable has equally high or higher peak pitch. This dislocation of pitch from the other exponents of stress results from a historical change whereby, when the word accent was moved one syllable to the left, high pitch remained on the old accented syllable as well as being placed on the new accented syllable. Variation in the location of the pitch peak within the accented syllable also occurs in simple stress languages like English and German, but there it is merely an effect of intonation.

In Swedish, accented vowels have greater duration and intensity than unaccented vowels, as well as higher pitch. The timing of the pitch peak relative to the accented syllable differentiates the two types of accent. Since the intensity peak tends to occur in the middle of the vowel, at the point of maximum oral aperture, the pitch peak is dislocated therefrom when it occurs early or late in the vowel. On the other hand, in whispered speech periodic voice is replaced by aperiodic noise and there is no fundamental frequency; consequently, a different strategy has to be adopted by the speaker, and the location of the intensity peak is the primary cue to distinguishing the two accents. There is considerable dialectal variation: in some dialects (Eastern Swedish) the pitch peak of the socalled accent 1 occurs so early that it can appear in the syllable preceding the accented syllable.

In Lithuanian, stressed syllables have greater duration and intensity and higher pitch than unstressed syllables; the duration of short *i/u* in the first syllable of disyllabic words of the structure CV-TVC (where T is a stop consonant, either voiced or voiceless) was found to be approximately 80 msec when the vowel was unaccented, as in *sukaĩs* 'you turned,' and approximately 140 msec when accented, as in *sùkes* 'having turned' (Ekblom 1925; Jernudd 1968; Pakerys 1982; Anusiene 1991). In Latvian, which in fact may be a type of tone language, accented vowels are on the average nearly a third longer than unaccented vowels (Ekblom 1933). Another type of pitch differentiated stress accent is found in Karok (California: Bright 1957). One syllable of each word is stressed; additionally there are three types of tone on stressed syllables: Level High, Falling High and Low (cp. Fasu). The last occurs preferentially and the second only on long vowels. The tonal contours of pretonic and posttonic syllable sequences are predictable.

The pitch differentiated stress languages just surveyed are commonly cited as providing parallels for the Greek pitch accent (Sealey 1963). They clearly do provide parallels for a rising/falling accentual opposition, but the comparison cannot be carried any further without the assumption of a significant element of stress in the Greek pitch accent. The descriptions of the Greek pitch accent by the ancient grammarians do not explicitly support the assumption of prosodic properties other than pitch as exponents of the accent. The terms they apply to the accent, τόνος, τάσις, προσῳδία, are taken from the realm of pitch and melody. Whereas ancient descriptions such as Plato *Phaedrus* 268d and Aristotle *Rhetoric* 1403b always specify the melodic character of the accent, they never refer to any feature of loudness or added duration. Some increase in intensity can arise automatically as a correlate of higher pitch and vice versa. Increased subglottal pressure results in an increased rate of vibration of the vocal cords and thus higher frequency, unless the vocal cords are adjusted to compensate for the increase in driving force; electro-myographically measured cricothyroid activity can be negatively correlated with intensity (Hirano et al. 1969; Strik et al. 1989). Conversely, higher subglottal pressure is required to maintain voicing at higher frequencies; it is more difficult to sing ascending tones with decreasing intensity than with increasing intensity — the former may require some training and seems to involve greater neurological effort (Hirano et al. 1969). Increased subglottal pressure has been found to correlate with higher pitch both in declarative sentence intonation and in the tones of tone languages: in Mandarin Chinese oral pressure is often higher for an initial consonant followed by a High tone, and in Taiwanese the High tone has an overall greater intensity than the Mid tone, and the Mid tone than the Low tone (Ladefoged 1968; Zee 1978). Such intensity variations commonly associated with frequency need to be distinguished from the additional intensity increments associated with stress in some languages; similarly, as already noted (p. 200), for any durational correlates of tone. The various arguments that have over the years been proposed in favour of a stress component in the Greek accent have not found general acceptance (Ehrlich 1912; Schmitt 1953; Szemerenyi 1964), and there is no metrical evidence to support such an assumption.

Low-toned stress and dislocation

There are also some simple (not pitch differentiated) stress languages, in which the syllable bearing the highest pitch in the word is systematically not the stressed syllable but some other syllable. This dislocation of pitch and stress was the subject of a footnote in the article in which Verner presented the law which bears his name (Verner 1877). In Chamorro (Guam: Topping 1973), the stressed syllable, usually the penultimate, is accompanied by low pitch, so that pitch rises on the final syllable. Similarly in Welsh, the penultimate syllable of the word is

stressed, whereas the highest pitch is often on the unstressed final syllable; this situation would be explained by the assumption that in the
eleventh-century Old Welsh accent shift pitch prominence tended to
remain on the final syllable while the other properties of stress were
retracted to the penultimate syllable (Williams 1986); it is also the final
syllable rather than the stressed penultimate that carries the intonational
rise-fall movement which is so characteristic of Welsh and of Welsh
English (Williams 1985). A similar historical development has been
suggested for Onondaga (Ontario: Chafe 1977), where the pitch peak
can be dislocated one syllable back from the syllable which has the intensity peak. In Danish, the stressed syllable has lower pitch than the first
of a string of following unaccented syllables (Thorsen 1980), and in
certain types of Scottish English stressed syllables have lower pitch (Brown
et al. 1980). In Malayalam (S.W. India: Mohanan 1986), stressed syllables, which have increased duration, have low pitch: in the rest of the
word, from stressed syllable to the end of the word, pitch rises to high
on the next long vowel, or, if there is none, on the last syllable; intensity is not a major factor in word prosody in this language. This pattern,
which is the converse of the more familiar situation in which the stressed
syllable has higher pitch than the unstressed syllables, is also found in
other Dravidian languages.

These languages cannot be viewed as providing a very close parallel
for the coexistence of stress and a pitch accent in Greek. Whether the
stress is Low-toned or the pitch peak is simply dislocated from the stress,
stress and pitch prominence evidently pattern as two exponents of a single
accentual system, and stress does not constitute an autonomous system
patterned independently from pitch. Dislocation mostly arises from the
fact that pitch movement associated with the word accent is not precisely
aligned with the stress, although the link is predictable by rule. On the
other hand, in Greek rhythmic prominence is in principle distributionally independent of the pitch accent. Rhythmically prominent syllables
are neither systematically Low-toned nor systematically High-toned nor
systematically dislocated from a High tone. Every legal pattern of pitch
accentuation can co-occur with each rhythmic pattern. For example,
the spondee-shaped word is rhythmically organized as Arsis-Thesis, but
it can have any one of the four possible pitch accentuations: κῆρυξ,
φεύγειν, ψευδεῖς, πλευράς. Similarly the tribrach-shaped word has three
possible accent patterns: ἔλαβε, φυγάδα, ὑγιές; but there is no difference
in rhythmic organization correlating with the accentual differences.
Nevertheless, there are statistical tendencies in the location of rhythmic
prominence relative to the different types of accent (including the grave).
These tendencies are redundant, arising inter alia from the fact that

circumflex syllables are always heavy and therefore preferentially theses, whereas the acute occurs frequently on light syllables which are preferentially arses; the exclusion of the acute from final syllables which are frequently heavy and therefore theses; and the fact that if the acute stands on a penultimate long vowel the final syllable will always be heavy and therefore a thesis, whereas if the circumflex stands on the penult, the final syllable may be light so that the penult will be the thesis. The first column of Table 5.1 lists six locations relative to the various types of pitch accent, while the second column gives the rate at which syllables in the specified locations would be rhythmically prominent. For the purposes of this test, rhythmic prominence is defined according to the rules for primary and secondary stress in the stress theory of Greek metre (Allen 1973) rather than according to the rules presented in Chapter 3. These results replicate and confirm the results of a slightly different earlier test (Allen 1967). The data are from samples of Plato's *Republic*; prepausal words have been omitted, as have the comparatively rare disyllabic matrices. The circumflex and postacute syllables more often than not coincide with rhythmic prominence, while acute syllables more often than not coincide with the absence of rhythmic prominence. The rate of prominence for postcircumflex and postpostacute syllables is explained by the fact that they are final, final syllables are frequently heavy, and final heavy syllables are prominent.

Word prosodic systems in which the pitch peak is dislocated from the syllable that is rhythmically most prominent are more complex and less natural than aligned systems; consequently, they are not very common in the languages of the world and tend to be unstable. There can be stylistic or dialectal variation between dislocation and alignment, and historical change tends to eliminate the dislocation. In Onondaga, there is a tendency to eliminate the dislocation by shifting the pitch peak to

TABLE 5.1
Location of rhythmic prominence
relative to the pitch accent

Location relative to pitch accent	% of syllables in prominent position
Preceding any accent	33
Postcircumflex or postpostacute	81
Acute	23
Postacute	65
Circumflex	87
Grave	65

the stressed syllable (Chafe 1977). The same applies to pitch differentiated stress. Some Norwegian dialects have discarded the distinction between what is usually analyzed as aligned and dislocated accent by changing the latter into the former; the same direction of change has been found in aphasia (Lorentz 1984). In Slovene, the dislocated acute accent is giving way to the aligned circumflex (Srebot-Rejec 1988). In the instances just cited, pitch prominence is aligned with rhythmic prominence and not vice versa. In the late Greek shift from pitch to stress accent, on the other hand, rhythmic prominence was aligned with accentual pitch prominence; this presumably reflects the fact that the Greek rhythmic prominence was nonaccentual and may also indicate that it was phonetically rather weak. It is known that High tone attracts stress, but, on the evidence of Djuka (p. 69), it is more likely to do so in the absence of intrinsic rhythmic prominence such as vowel length.

Pitch accent languages

In the present work, the term "pitch accent" is used to denote a word or phrase accent implemented by pitch without the additional exponents of duration and/or intensity that characterize stress. It is not used for intonational pitch obtrusions whether they are independently located or aligned to lexical stress accents, like English focus accents.

Of the languages having a pitch accent, the one that has been investigated experimentally in the greatest detail is Japanese. In the standard Tokyo dialect of Japanese, a minor accentual phrase may have at most one point at or immediately after which pitch falls from High to Low. In the traditional analysis, this point is specified diacritically by the accent mark; there have also been analyses of Japanese in terms of a restricted tone system. Phrases that do not have the pitch fall are therefore unaccented. Both accented and unaccented phrases have High tone syllables, although the high region of accented phrases is about 5 Hz higher than that of unaccented phrases, and the class of unaccented words is not restricted to grammar function words as the class of clitics largely is in Greek. The remainder of the tonal pattern of the phrase is predictable. The first mora of the minor phrase is Low, but when it is either itself accented or constitutes the first mora of a bimoraic sonorant sequence (long vowel, diphthong, etc.), the Low tone is shallower and temporally restricted to the very beginning of the mora (Poser 1985; Pierrehumbert et al. 1988). The initial Low has been interpreted as a demarcative Low tone postponed from the preceding phrase (Pierrehumbert et al. 1988). If an accented syllable is polymoraic, the pitch fall is always located from the first to the second mora: this means that standard Japanese, unlike Osaka Japanese, cannot have a rising/falling or acute/circumflex type of accentual distinction. Morae standing between the first mora and the accented syllable are all High in the Tokyo dialect. In other dialects of Japanese, this is not the case. In the dialect of Nagoya, tone rises gradually to the High tone level of the accented syllable, as it does in Greek. Some Japanese dialects also have rules for the location of high pitch that are typically culminative. In the dialect of Kagoshima, for instance, high pitch occurs once in each word, on either the penultimate or the final syllable. There is evidence of an emerging pitch accent in the speech of Japanese children at about 18 months (Hallé et al. 1991).

Accented vowels are not audibly longer than unaccented vowels in Japanese. Some experimental studies have found small increases in duration in the accented syllable (Mitsuya et al. 1978; Nishinuma 1979; Hoequist 1983; Kuriyagawa et al. 1984). Disyllabic minimal pairs in a carrier frame sentence showed greater duration for the accented vowel than the unaccented vowel in the first syllable in slow speech and in both syllables in fast speech (Kuriyagawa et al. 1987); since the main durational difference between slow and fast speech lies in the shortening of the second syllable, this result could suggest that the time required for accentual pitch movement impedes the full reduction of vowel duration aimed at in fast speech. Between voiceless consonants, accented vowels tend to be more sonorous than unaccented vowels, because the need to produce an abrupt drop in fundamental frequency at the end of the accented mora counteracts the tendency found in unaccented syllables for vowels to undergo assimilatory devoicing between segments requiring a wide glottal aperture (Yoshioka 1981; Sugito et al. 1988; Kuriyagawa et al. 1989; Simada et al. 1991). Devoicing of close vowels between voiceless consonants is actually a useful criterion for a typological analysis of word prosodic systems: the more accentual Japanese dialects favour this devoicing and the more tonal ones disfavour it (Nagano-Madsen 1992). The role of duration and intensity as exponents of the Japanese accent is marginal compared with their role as exponents of the English stress accent (Beckman 1986). The Japanese accent should therefore be distinguished typologically from stress and from pitch differentiated stress: it is a pure pitch accent. Japanese does have a stress, but it is a discourse stress associated with focus and emphasis (p. 468). The durational exponent of emphatic stress has been phonologized in the long consonants of the emphatic varieties of some Japanese adverbs (Beckman et al. 1986).

In Seoul Korean, there is a phrase final pitch accent and, in longer phrases, a secondary pitch obtrusion towards the beginning of the phrase. Added duration is found on the first syllable of the word, with the durational increment falling on the onset consonant rather than on the vocalic nucleus (de Jong 1989). Chonnam Korean has a phrasal pitch accent fixed on the second mora of the phrase (Jun 1990).

The Central Algonquian language Kickapoo (Oklahoma/Mexico: Voorhis 1971) is described as having a plateau type phrasal pitch accent, with some intonational and segmental conditioning; the accented vowel does not appear to have greater intensity than many unaccented vowels. The Athapaskan language Carrier is a fairly clear case of a language with a surface pitch accent which also has word final stress (Pike 1986; Story 1989). The patterning of the pitch accent in Carrier is reminiscent of that in Japanese: preaccentual tones are High, postaccentual tones are Low and in unaccented words all tones are High. However, the verbal morphophonology of Carrier is described in terms of a tone language. The stress gives the impression of having an intensity component, and Carrier speech appears to be stress timed (Story 1989). The Muskogean languages, Creek, Seminole, Chickasaw, Choctaw, are described as having a type of pitch accent; some accounts also refer to an independent stress (Munro 1985). West Greenlandic Eskimo has a pitch accent manifested as a High Low tone sequence on the last two morae of phrase internal words; this accent is shifted back one mora to the left in phrase final position to accommodate the phrase final High tone (Nagano-Madsen 1993).

The rhythm of Japanese speech turns out to be quite independent of the pitch accent. The subjective impressions of speakers suggest that, in deliberate speech, Japanese has a system of bimoraic feet with greater intensity or related features on the odd-numbered mora and greater duration on the even-numbered mora. At the level of the word/minor phrase, intensity is likewise reported to be greatest on the first syllable and there is added duration on the final syllable. The internal durational relations of the bimoraic foot have been investigated (Teranishi 1980, 1990; Nagano-Madsen 1991). According to these studies, in very slow and deliberate speech, in a sequence of monomoraic syllables every second mora, i.e. the final mora of each foot, is lengthened. Consequently, an iambic durational pattern is imposed on pyrrhic and proceleusmatic structures. In this analysis, feet are mapped counting from the beginning of the phrase; if this leaves a single syllable at the end of the phrase, this syllable constitutes a foot by itself and receives extra prolongation. Moraic nasals too may be lengthened foot finally. As speech tempo increases, the amount of lengthening applied to even-numbered morae decreases, so that foot structure is evanescent and speech rhythm becomes mora timed rather than foot timed. The phonological significance of the bimoraic foot in Japanese is evidenced by a variety of data including verbal reduplication and rules for the formation of hypocoristics (Poser 1985, 1990; Itô 1990). When the hypocoristic suffix -tšaN is added to a personal name, the name often appears as a modified stem. This stem typically consists of one or two bimoraic feet. Polysyllabic names may be truncated, and monomoraic names, which are rare, may have their vowels lengthened. The product of these morphological processes is always a complete bimoraic foot, never a partial foot. Phonological lengthening of the thesis of disyllabic bimoraic feet in verbs, adjectives and shorter nouns is found in the Okinawa dialect Nakizin (Haraguchi 1991). There is no reason to think that the combination of iambic rhythm with some sort of pitch accent is idiosyncratic: it resurfaces in Choctaw (Oklahoma: Lombardi et al. 1991), which has lengthening of alternate light syllables.

In Japanese verse, the different metres are defined by the number of morae in conjunctions of lines. The *haiku*, for instance, consists of a five mora line, a seven mora line, and a five mora line. The pitch accent is not relevant in Japanese verse. One style of verse recitation involves an iambic rhythm. The line is divided into bimoraic feet with lengthening of the second mora of the foot, as long recognized in literary research. Each line is treated as composed of four bimoraic feet. The missing one or three morae in each line are filled in by pauses (Haraguchi 1987). It is evident that the foot of verse recitation is the same unit as the foot postulated for slow speech and, at least in its structure, as the one suggested by morphological evidence.

The prosodic system of Japanese illustrates how a system of durational rhythm can coexist with an independently patterned pure pitch accent. Such a system provides a closer typological parallel to Greek than the other systems discussed in this chapter. There are also a number of further parallels between the two systems. In both languages the existence of the foot is indicated by rules of a morphological or morphophonemic order: in Japanese the rules for the formation of hypocoristics and other rules, in Greek the rule for the formation of comparatives (p. 104). In Japanese, the degree of durational modification and probably the domain in which it is applied vary significantly according to the rate of speech. In Greek it is hardly possible to explain the differing degrees of metrical strictness among genres without the assumption that the rules for achieving rhythm varied according to phonostyle and rate of speech.

Whether rhythmic prominence in Greek can aptly be called "stress" depends in part on the theoretical adequacy of the term for describing the phenomenon and in part on what would be implied by the term "stress," given current usage. The theoretical need to distinguish intensity prominence, durational prominence, pitch prominence and accentual function has been recognized for over a century (Ellis 1873: "I consider force, pitch and length to be mutually independent"). The exponents of prominence are all potentially independently patterned in the word and any one of them or any combination of them can have accentual function. In current usage, the term "stress" normally implies (1) accentual function and (2) one or more of the exponents of prosodic prominence, except that accentual pitch prominence by itself is termed pitch accent; a functionally based distinction has been made above between "pitch accent" and "focus accent." For many people, "stress" also has the physiological implication of a degree of additional energization of the speech musculature. As such, "stress" is not a very suitable term for nonaccentual durational prominence. Nevertheless, there are signs that it is beginning to be used in this latter sense in the typological literature, and should this sense of the term become current, there would be little reason not to speak of "stress" in Greek. A terminological question also arises from the first component of the label "nonaccentual stress," since rhythmic prominence in Greek patterns rather like an accent. An accent is a prosodic prominence that helps to keep count of prosodic domains such as feet, words and clitic groups; accents may additionally help to demarcate domains, but not all accents unambiguously demarcate domains and not all demarcative properties are accents. Rhythmic prominence in Greek is probably termed "nonaccentual" because it is presumably less salient than the pitch accent; it also differs from the pitch accent in extending down to the level of the foot. Consequently a Greek word may have more than one rhythmically prominent element but it may not have more than one pitch accent in its citation form.

DEVELOPMENT OF THE STRESS ACCENT

The development of stress accentuation in Greek was part of a more general process of restructuring the entire prosodic system which also involved the loss of distinctions of vowel quantity and syllable weight (Kretschmer 1890; Schwyzer 1959; Allen 1987b). This process began in less educated sociolinguistic strata, perhaps as early as the fourth century B.C. in vulgar Attic (Ehrlich 1912; Schmitt 1924; Drerup 1929). It was probably promoted by bilingual interference from languages lacking quantity distinctions and having stress accentuation, for instance by Coptic in Egypt (Knight 1919; Gignac 1976). The erosion of the old prosodic system did not penetrate extensively into the literary register until quite late, and then first among Christian writers of the early fourth century A.D. such as Methodius, Areius and Gregory of Nazianzus, a large portion of whose audience probably spoke varieties of Greek devoid of the old prosodic system (Maas 1962), while learned writers continue to imitate the old system in their often successful attempts to write quantitative verse.

There are two natural ways in which the restructuring of the Greek word prosodic system could have developed, depending on how the loss of quantity distinctions related to the transition to stress accentuation. If vowel quantity ceased to be phonologically relevant before changes in the old melodic character of the accent began the transition to stress accentuation (Schwyzer 1959; Teodorsson 1974), the restructuring probably proceeded as follows. The disappearance of vowel quantity contrasts removed the primary phonological basis of the old rhythmical patterning, namely syllable weight. While it would have been perfectly possible for the old durational and rhythmical patterns to survive implemented by lower level phonetic adjustments, it would also now be possible for duration to be used to reinforce the prominence of the accented syllable. When pitch prominence is reinforced by duration, it becomes stress. On the other hand, if changes in the nature of the accent arose before the loss of quantity distinctions (Kretschmer 1890, 1932; Drerup 1929; Allen 1973), the restructuring would probably have been a case of the phonologically culminative high pitch syllable attracting additional accentual exponents, such as increased duration, thereby also producing a stress accent. The old rhythmical patterning would have been in conflict with the tendency to lengthen accented syllables and shorten unaccented ones.

Segmental evidence

Spelling errors in inscriptions and papyri have often been used as evidence to decide between the two possible courses of development just described, but qualifications have also been expressed about the value of such orthographic data for prosodic, as opposed to segmental, phonetic change (Sturtevant 1911; Allen 1987). Yet to the extent that a speaker possesses a phonological distinction and is literate, he will tend to represent that distinction insofar as his alphabet permits, and this is in fact true in the case of ει and ι. The qualitative change from close mid to high front vowel resulted in a phonological merger which motivated the replacement of the digraph ει by the letter ι. Since the digraph had always represented a long vowel, whether $\bar{e}$ or $\bar{\imath}$, the inverse use of the digraph ει for the letter ι would adequately represent the phonological distinction of vowel length only if it were used for $\bar{\imath}$ and not $\breve{\imath}$. In fact, the use of ει to represent short i remained very restricted down to the end of the first century B.C. The ratio of the frequency of the spelling ει for long i to that of ει for short i in Attic inscriptions is 7 in the second century and 23.5 in the first, whereas in the Greek language the ratio of long to short i is considerably less than one. Given the value of such spellings as evidence for vowel length distinctions, it becomes possible to exploit them to resolve problems of relative chronology in the development of the prosodic system. The hypothesis that stress developed before and conditioned the loss of vowel quantity leads to the prediction of several correlations between misspellings and accentuation that would not be expected on the converse hypothesis that quantity distinctions were lost before the development of stress. If there was a tendency to lengthen accented vowels, spellings such as $ει$ for $ῐ$, $ω$ for $ŏ$ reflecting the qualitative change from open to close mid round vowel, and $η$ for $ĕ$ reflecting the qualitative change from open to close mid front vowel, would be more likely in accented syllables, so long as the process was still in progress and had not produced a complete neutralization of quantity contrasts. Conversely, if there was a tendency to shorten unaccented vowels, the inverse of the last two misspellings, namely o for $ō$ and $ε$ for $ē$, would be more likely in unaccented syllables. Also, since unaccented vowels are less salient in a stress language than in a pitch accent language, if vowel letters are omitted in unaccented syllables at a higher rate than in accented syllables, this effect will be stronger in a stress language than in a pitch accent language.

To test these predictions, it is not possible, as has sometimes been done, simply to compare the rates of accentuation of the various classes of misspellings, for this procedure would leave the test subject to spurious correlations arising from processually irrelevant distributional restrictions and tendencies linking the old pitch accent with phonological and morphological factors. The ideal procedure would be to compare the rate of accentuation in misspellings of a vowel with the rate in correct spellings in the same corpus. Since the evidence for the correct spellings is not available, random samples were taken from Plato and Xenophon in order to obtain estimates of the rates at which $ῐ$, $ō$, $ŏ$, $ē$, $ĕ$ and all vowels in interconsonantal environment, C(#)...(#)C, bear an accent (including the grave). In Table 5.2, these control rates, given in the second column, are compared with the rates at which the six types of spelling errors listed in the first column correspond to accented vowels. Asterisks mark differences that are statistically significant at the 5% or more stringent confidence levels. The accentuation rates of misspellings are calculated for Attic to 200 B.C. (Teodorsson 1974), Attic 199–1 B.C. (Teodorsson 1978) and Ptolemaic koine 325–1 B.C. (Teodorsson 1977). As a control, rates are also given for some misspellings that do not reflect loss of quantity distinctions in vowels, namely $η$ for $ει$, $ι$ for $υ$, and their inverses. The analysis presented in Table 5.2 is provisional, since differences in vocabulary, redundancy of content, use of particles and so on could account for some of the differences observed, and no account is taken of possible tendencies for misspellings to cluster in specific words

TABLE 5.2
Rate of accentuation in misspellings of vowels

Type of error	Etymological %	Attic −200 %	Attic 199–1 %	Ptolemaic %
V >Ø/C...C	42.55	*30.00	*20.69	n.a.
εɩ for ῐ	31.19	*53.13	*100.00	30.38
o for ō	43.86	42.62	*15.63	*28.96
ω for ŏ	38.22	49.18	57.14	34.68
ε for ē	50.95	52.31	37.50	44.48
η for ĕ	37.74	36.11	35.71	43.54
η for εɩ	42.31	20.00	76.47	59.38
εɩ for η	50.95	0.00	50.00	72.57
ɩ for υ	20.00	32.30	14.29	29.41
υ for ɩ	31.19	8.82	14.29	23.81

or documents. Table 5.3 lists the type of spelling error, the frequency relations (greater than or less than) between the rate of accentuation of the misspelled vowel (M) and the average rate for the corresponding etymological vowel (E) that would be expected if the misspellings reflected phonological developments conditioned by accentual change, and whether the observed relation agrees (+) or disagrees (–) with the prediction in each corpus of texts. It turns out that of the 17 observations, 12 (70.6%) agree with the predictions and, more importantly, 100% of the 6 statistically significant differences agree with the predictions. By contrast, no statistically significant correlations with accentuation were found in the control group of misspellings. These results lend some support to the hypothesis that changes in the nature of the accent developed before and in such a way as to condition the loss of quantity distinctions via processes of tonic lengthening and atonic shortening.

Metrical evidence

The orthographic evidence is corroborated by early instances of false quantities in verse, which provide some evidence for a stage at which poets retained a quantitative nonaccentual target pattern, at least stichos internally, but interpreted accented light syllables as heavy and unaccented syllables as light. *GDK* 3 (second to third century A.D.) and the first five verses of *GDK* 4 (on a papyrus datable to 250–280 A.D.: Dihle 1954) are miuric paroemiacs, that is the thesis of the last anapaest is replaced by a light syllable. *GDK* 3 is completely paroxytonetic, and

TABLE 5.3
Agreement of prediction with observation
for rate of accentuation in misspellings

Type of error	Prediction	Attic −200	Attic 199–1	Ptolemaic
V > Ø/C...C	M < E	* +	* +	n.a.
ει for ῑ	M > E	* +	* +	−
o for ō	M < E	+	* +	* +
ω for ŏ	M > E	+	+	−
ε for ē	M < E	−	+	+
η for ĕ	M > E	−	−	+

$R(+) = 70.67\%$, $R(*+) = 100.00\%$

there is some tendency to paroxytonesis in *GDK* 4. Aside from paroxy-tonesis, the verses show no tendency to regulate the accent; specifically, there is no tendency for heavy syllables in the first two theses to be accented: 36.84% of heavy syllables in the thesis bear some kind of accent, which compares with 42.5% in a sample of the first two theses in the normal paroemiacs of Mesomedes (first half of the second century A.D.) and 66.3% of the heavy syllables in the first two theses of the definitely accentual miuric paroxytonetic paroemiacs of *GDK* 45.4 (fourth century A.D.). The difference from Mesomedes is not statistically signif-icant, but the difference from *GDK* 45.4 is significant ($\chi^2 = 5.67$). In *GDK* 3–4 there are three false quantities, all involving an accented light syllable implementing the thesis

μέρεσι 4.2
πλέειν 4.3
μένειν 4.4.

In comparison to the rate of 21.3% at which correctly scanning light syllables in arsis are accented in *GDK* 3–4, the total exclusion of un-accented light syllables among these three is statistically significant ($p = 0.0146$ by the hypergeometric distribution). There is only one instance of a false quantity involving a heavy syllable implementing a breve of the arsis in *GDK* 3–4

Νείλου 3.6;

the nonaccentuation of this type of false quantity could be coincidental, but that is not very likely as all six of the heavy syllables correctly implementing the contracted arsis in *GDK* 3 are accented.

The Christian hymn *GDK* 45.4 probably represents a later stage at which the metrical rules associate accentuation with the thesis and require avoidance of accentuation in the arsis, particularly when contracted. As just noted, the 66.3% rate of accentuation of heavy syllables correctly implementing the thesis in this hymn is significantly higher than the rate in the same metre in *GDK* 3–4. Similarly, the rate of 50% accentuation of heavy syllable correctly implementing contracted first and second arses is significantly less than the 88.9% rate in *GDK* 3–4 ($p < 0.05$ by the hypergeometric distribution). Accordingly, the rate of approximately 71% for accentuation of false quantities involving a light syllable implementing the first two theses probably does not indicate that an accented light syllable was assessed as the quantitative equivalent of a heavy syllable but simply that the accent could implement the thesis. Similarly, two of the four certain light syllables implementing contracted arses are accented, a rate that is the same as that for heavy syllables correctly implementing monosyllabic arses. This stage also seems to be reflected in *GDK* 45.3 (fourth century A.D.) and in the Partheneion of Methodius (obiit 311 A.D.): the poets reinterpret the quantitative patterns of classical verse as additionally accentually reinforced, but their knowledge of the prosody of the literary register is imperfect and in their own speech all accented (stressed) vowels are probably long and all unaccented vowels short.

Musical evidence

It is generally supposed that the overall level of strictness with which the accent is respected in nonstrophic musical settings decreases through time (Pöhlmann 1960). As part of this development, it has been suggested that the subordination of the grave to a following acute or circumflex was the first feature of the pitch system to be lost (Pearl et al. 1965), probably accompanied by a loss of pitch movement on circumflex syllables (Winnington-Ingram 1955). Two major difficulties confront any diachronic analysis of this material: (1) only a terminus ante quem can be assigned to most of the settings preserved on papyrus, and (2) many of the documents are very scanty, so that chance cannot always be ruled out when differences are observed. The relatively securely dated compositions are the Delphic Hymns (*Ath.* and *Lim.*, 127 B.C.), the Seikilos epitaph (first century A.D.), the hymns attributed to Mesomedes (circa 150 A.D.), and the Christian hymn *DAM* 34 the false quantities of which, for instance

> πατέρᾱ 4
> πνεῦμᾱ 4,

make it likely that it was not composed long before the papyrus was written (third to fourth century A.D.).

The survey of mismatches already presented (p. 166), particularly the evidence of lexical words with unaccented syllables set higher than the accent, conforms to the general hypothesis of increasing laxity in the musical setting of the accent as stress replaces pitch. As for the subordination of the grave, in *Ath.* and *Lim.* there is only one grave which is set higher than the full accent of an immediately following word, a rate of violation of 2.5%

δὲ βαρύβρομον Lim. 10,

and in light of the steep fall on the last two syllables this could be an instance of the music imitating the sense of the word. Out of five graves followed by full accents in the next word in the Seikilos epitaph, none violates the grave subordination rule (paroxytone ἔστι is to be read in line 9). In *DAM* 1–2, one of three grave–full accent pairs violates the rule

ἐμὰς φρένας 1.4,

and in *DAM* 4–5 there is one certain exception

μετὰ χεῖρα 5.13,

for an overall rate of violation in the Mesomedes material of 10%. In *DAM* 34, in each of its occurrences the liturgical formula

ἀμὴν ἀμήν 4, 5

is set with the grave higher than the acute; if the restoration

καὶ δόξα 5 Pighi

is correct, the pitch of the grave and the peak of the melism set to the acute would be the same. *DAM* 30, from a papyrus of the second to third century A.D., has one violation

ὃς Μούσαις 5

out of six grave–full accent sequences. *DAM* 36, from a papyrus of the first to second century A.D., has three violations out of eight grave–full accent sequences

γυμνὰ προλιποῦσαι 9
καὶ πᾶσα 10
κατὰ γῆς 6 almost certainly.

DAM 37, also first to second century A.D., has one violation out of five

δὲ ὁμοῦ 16;

the restoration

ὃν ἐφοβήθησαν 19

may be not a violation but a licence of the octave interval. *DAM* 38, from a papyrus of the first to second century A.D., has one violation out of three. Finally, *DAM* 39–40, from a second century A.D. papyrus, has no violation in three certain grave–full accent sequences; in line 18 the first note of the melism probably set to the grave of φοβηθεὶς is lost (the second note of the melism is f¹), but it was probably not higher than the g¹ set to the circumflex of the following word δεῖμα. Although no simple trend emerges, it is a reasonable conclusion that there was some erosion of the subordination of the grave. This loss of grave subordination is expected, since the grave develops into a stress accent just like the acute and the circumflex, and certainly by the fourth century A.D. the grave is equipollent with the acute and circumflex in accentual cola in prose (Serruys 1904; Meyer 1905; Hansen 1962).

The loss of pitch movement distinctions within the syllable is a necessary condition for the complete merger of the circumflex with the acute in a single undifferentiated stress accent. It is also the phonological basis for the loss of the rule that accents the final syllable of properispomena before enclitics, type μισοῦσά σε, since if the High-Low turning point did not occur early in the syllable as with the classical circumflex but was delayed to the center or the end of the syllable, the result would be contiguous accentual peaks with insufficient phonological space for an intervening valley. In later Greek accentual prose cola, properispomena plus enclitic are treated as proparoxytones (Maas 1901, 1903, 1908), and this treatment may already occur in the fourth century A.D. if instances such as

> ἐπιβοᾶσθαί μοι λείπεται Himerius 46.1
> ἐκκαλυφθῆναί σοι Themistius 7.93a

are clausular. The same development is also responsible for the loss of enclitic accentuation on the final syllable of proparoxytones, type ἄνθρωπός τις, with the development of stress on the enclitic. In Byzantine stress-based verse and accentual prose cola, proparoxytone plus enclitic is most frequently treated as ś́SS#Ś

> γίνεταί μοι Romanus 18ζ′7
> λέξατέ μοι Romanus 18ιθ′7;

retention of the old enclitic accent and apparent neglect of the original word accent, giving SSŚ#S, is rarer

> ἔβαλέ με Romanus 18ιη′7
> μνήσθητί μου Romanus 18κ′7.

Accordingly, it might be expected that traces of the process leading to the loss of differentiated pitch movement within the syllable might be found in the musical settings of the circumflex. The musical settings are difficult to assess in this regard, since the acceptability of melisms seems to be an independent stylistic-dialectal factor. In the Delphic hymns, excluding the Aeolic section at the end of *Lim.*, which has no melisms either on circumflex syllables or on other heavy syllables, 61.54% of the circumflexes are set to melisms, but one of these

θνατοῖς *Ath.* 20 d♭¹-f¹

is rising. In the Seikilos epitaph, three out of four circumflexes are set to melisms, all falling. In *DAM* 1-2, three of the six circumflexes are set to melisms, all falling, but in *DAM* 4-5 the rate decreases to four out of eighteen (22%), all falling. In the very melismatic Christian hymn, six of seven circumflexes are set to melisms, as are many noncircumflex and unaccented syllables, but three are rising (including the restoration θεῷ 5). In the florid *DAM* 30, all eight circumflexes are set to melisms, but only three are falling, one is rising, two are definitely and two more probably rising-falling. In *DAM* 36, only one of five circumflexes has a melism; in *DAM* 38 one of the probable six circumflexes has a melism, but it is rising; in *DAM* 39-40 eight of the seventeen circumflexes have melisms, none definitely rising. In all this material, there is no tendency for the circumflex on diphthongs to have a higher rate of melisms than the circumflex on simple vowels, nor is any feature such as vowel rounding associated with melisms. The picture that emerges from the musical settings, particularly when rising melisms are counted as violations, is consistent with a gradual loss of the old pattern of differentiated pitch movement within the syllable.

Conclusion

The question raised at the beginning of this chapter was whether the coexistence in a single language of the rhythmic system reconstructed in Chapter 3 and the accentual system analyzed in Chapter 4 is typologically suspect. A native speaker of English might be apt to think that rhythmically prominent syllables should be accented and liable to carry some degree of pitch obtrusion, and that accented syllables should be rhythmically prominent and carry some degree of durational increment. No really relevant typological support for the situation envisaged for Greek was afforded by pitch differentiated stress languages nor by the fact that tone languages can have a stress accent. However, when the function of pitch in word prosodic systems was systematically studied in a crosslinguistic perspective, it emerged that a foot based system of rhythm can coexist with an independently patterned pure pitch accent. Whether the former can appropriately be called a stress system depends partly on what are assumed to be the phonetic exponents of rhythmic prominence in Greek (which is a substantive matter), and partly on what are assumed to be the general phonetic and phonological implications of calling a syllable stressed (which is largely a matter of terminology).

6 | Connected Speech

RATE AND STYLE OF SPEECH

As everyday experience suggests, speakers can differ from one another in their normal speech tempo (Gaitenby in Port 1977). The difference can be idiolectal, dialectal or sociolectal; in Swedish, women tend to speak marginally more rapidly than men (Elert 1964). Conversely, one and the same speaker can vary his rate of speech according to the time required for planning the content of an utterance, according to his emotional attitude, or according to the stylistic demands of the discourse context. Actors and singers are known to regulate their speech tempo to simulate various emotional attitudes (p. 472). Slow speech rates are associated with sorrow, for instance, and faster rates with impatience (Léon et al. 1980).

Average rates of speech have been calculated for English as approximately 5 syllables per second (Klatt 1976), with a range of from 4.4 to 5.9 syllables per second (Goldman-Eisler 1961); the range of conversation is greater than that of reading (Shockey 1973). English was not found to differ significantly in speech rate from a number of other European languages (Kowal et al. 1983). Rates for Spanish were 4.8 syllables per second for slow speech, 5.4 for normal speech and 6.8 for fast speech (Carrio i Font et al. 1991). In Japanese, the rate at which a news broadcast was read was found to be 7.1 morae per second; a fast rate of reading in Japanese would have approximately 8.1 morae per second and a slow rate approximately 5 morae per second (Fujisaki et al. 1971). The rate of production of phonological segments is about the same in English and Japanese (Osser et al. 1964). Perception of relative speech rates by listeners and particularly speakers tends to exaggerate actual differences into much larger subjective differences: when a speaker doubles his reading rate, he perceives a sixfold increase and a listener approximately a threefold increase (Lane et al. 1973). Various facts are relevant to the interpretation of these data. First of all, since pause (p. 432) takes up a significant proportion of the overall time used for speech, gross rate figures are not a direct indication of how fast the articulators are producing sounds or syllables (Clevenger et al. 1963). Secondly, many different factors combine to cause variability. Although one and the same speaker is fairly constant in his rate at different sessions, variations in rate between speakers are fairly great, and one and the same speaker can vary his rate from one section to another of a session. When typical syllable rates for different languages are compared, one factor potentially contributing to variability is the fact that different languages have different preferential syllable structures; more complex syllables have more segments and therefore take longer to produce ceteris paribus.

Domains

The range of variation between slow and fast speech in the duration of pauses is far greater than that in the duration of speech-filled periods, and differences in pause time account for most of the overall durational difference between slow and fast speech (Goldman-Eisler 1968): slow talkers use longer and more frequent pauses than fast talkers (Crystal et al. 1982). In fast speech, pauses within the sentence are largely eliminated and pausing tends to be restricted to when it is physiologically required for respiration (Grosjean et al. 1979). Further data on pause and speech rate are presented in Chapter 9. The suppression of pause in fast speech is accompanied by the reduction or elimination of demarcation and the progressive extension of the domains of word internal phonology, sandhi, coarticulation (Hardcastle 1985) and syllable structure optimization. This is presumably universal in language. For example, in Arapaho (Wyoming: Salzmann 1956), in formal speech such as is used in ceremonies or in the deliberate storytelling of an old Arapaho to his grandchildren, in the sentence "Néhéʔ hinén nonoohówoot núhuʔ hísein" 'This man sees this woman' the nonlexicals are separate prosodic units; but in informal discourse or spontaneous narration they are joined into a single prosodic unit with their following lexicals and sandhi rules apply at the seam to give "Néhéʔinén nonoohówoot núhúʔúsein."

The extension in fast and casual speech of the domains of rules such as resyllabification and refooting is a fundamental feature of prosodic processing; static models of prosody do not reflect the variability of discourse. For instance, in slow speech the syllable boundary coincides with the word boundary in German *Tag.und Nacht* 'day and night' and in French *toutes.les nuits* [tut.le] 'every night,' but in more rapid and casual speech resyllabification produces *Ta.gund Nacht* and *tou.teles nuits* [tu.tle]

(Läufer 1985). In Slave (British Columbia: Rice 1987), resyllabification of final -*h* is more frequent in fast speech. In Ecuadorian Spanish,
hiatus across word boundary is progressively eliminated as speech rate
increases (Cloward 1984); identical vowel coalescence in Modern Greek
and in Italian increases with speech tempo (Nespor 1987). Elision in
Zulu (S. Africa: Doke 1926; Laughren 1984) and in Maasai (Kenya:
Tucker et al. 1955) is more common at normal speech rates than in slow,
deliberate speech. Elision in Swedish and Norwegian is more common
in fast and casual speech (Eliasson 1986). In slow speech, the foot bound-
ary coincides with the word boundary in English "Jan | is running," in
fast speech refooting produces "Jan is | running" with timing compara-
ble to "Janice | running" (Fowler 1977). The remapping of Italian *metà*
torta to *méta torta* 'half a cake' (p. 277) is blocked in slow, deliberate speech
when the two words are not phrased together. Variable phrasing depending on speech rate is illustrated by the data on Southern Italian diphthongization under phrase stress (p. 287). The domain of tone sandhi can
be extended in less deliberate speech, as in Ewe (Clements 1978) and
in Mandarin Chinese (Shih 1985). Major phrase boundary involving
final lengthening and separate pitch accents can be eliminated in fast
speech in Dutch (Rietveld et al. 1987); another study found that 40%
of boundary marking pitch movements were eliminated in fast speech
(Caspers et al. 1991). In Japanese, the syntagm *takonado tabeta* 'ate octo-
pus etc.' can be pronounced as two major phrases in unnaturally slow
speech, as a single major phrase containing two minor phrases, or in
more rapid speech as a single minor phrase (Vance 1987). French liaison is exceptional in having more extensive domains in more deliberate
speech, but this is related to its artificiality and obsolescence (Hayes 1990).

Prosodic readjustment

An increase in the rate of speech implies an increase in the number of
syllables produced in a given time period. Simply speeding up the rate
of syllable production is not the only strategy available to the speaker.
It is common also to find some degree of readjustment of the way
segments are mapped onto syllables and the way syllables are organized
into feet and mapped onto thesis and arsis; this has already been illustrated by a number of examples in the preceding paragraph. Open
syllables are favoured in fast speech (Läufer 1985). Refooting and remapping are processes that characterize the transition from the additive strategies of slow speech to the subtractive strategies of fast speech. According
to one study, in Japanese there is a progressive reduction of the thesis
in the direction of temporal equality with the arsis as speech rate increases,
to the point that the rhythm of fast speech is quite different from the

rhythm of slow to very slow speech, the latter being foot timed and the former mora timed (p. 213). The direction of the adjustment is the opposite from that found in stress languages, where duration in the thesis, which is accentual, is more resistant to reduction than in the arsis. In syllable timed languages, unaccented vowels are more resistant to durational compression (Fletcher 1987) and to centralization (Delattre 1968) than in stress timed languages. In English, stressed closed syllables were found to be shortened less than unstressed syllables in fast speech (Peterson et al. 1960); both stressed vowels and stops immediately following stressed vowels shortened less than other parts of a sentence in fast speech, thereby increasing the proportion of the overall sentence duration allotted to them (Port 1977). Conversely, in the English of young children syllables have greater absolute duration and the rhythm is more syllable timed (Allen et al. 1980). Likewise, syllable timing and a tendency to produce temporally isolated or separated syllables is reported for certain types of aphasic speech in English and Thai (Kent et al. 1982; Gandour et al. 1984) and is also characteristic of artificially slow syllable by syllable dictation.

Durational ratios

The effects of change in tempo on segmental duration in different languages have been studied in some detail. In an experiment on Arabic in which sentence durations in slow speech were 130 %, and in fast speech 80 %, of those in neutral tempo, stressed initial vowels had in slow speech 150 % and in fast speech 75 % of their neutral tempo duration (Port et al. 1980). Whereas vowels show greater than average lengthening and shortening, consonants show less: in Arabic medial consonant duration in slow speech was 112 %, and in fast speech 88 %, of its neutral tempo duration. It follows that the durational ratio of vowel to consonant can vary according to rate of speech. It has been claimed that the timing of syllable onset intervocalic consonants relative to the timing of articulatory gestures for the contiguous vowels is quite stable across different speech rates (Tuller et al. 1984; Weismer et al. 1985), but this claim has been disputed on methodological grounds (Gentner 1987; Keller 1987; Löfqvist 1990). Consonants which are intrinsically very short, such as flaps, are subject to a proportionally smaller reduction than intrinsically longer consonants. Readjustment of the neutral tempo ratios is more farreaching when speech is speeded up than when it is slowed down (Port 1977). In absolute terms, depending on conditioning factors, the durational difference between a slow speech vowel and a fast speech vowel can be comparable to that between a stressed vowel and an unstressed vowel at the same rate of speech (Fourakis 1986).

The ratio of short to long vowel likewise varies according to rate of speech. In Arabic short vowels were found to have 43.5% the duration of long vowels in neutral tempo, as compared with 55.6% in fast speech and 35.7% in slow speech. In English, the durational distinction between long and short *i* in *bead* versus *bid* is reduced from 35% in slow speech to 28% in fast speech (Port 1977); this effect may vary according to the nature of the coda consonant (Gopal 1990). In Swedish, short vowels were found to have 65% the duration of long vowels in neutral tempo, as compared with 80% in fast speech (Elert 1964). In Tamil (S.E. India: Balasubramanian 1980), $C\check{V}$ and $C\bar{V}$ syllables both had approximately 84% of their neutral tempo duration in fast speech and 113% in slow speech; in this language, the ratio of the duration of the syllable type $C\check{V}$ to that of $C\bar{V}$ remained fairly stable at a little over 50% at all speech tempi. The reduction of duration in fast speech when it is a cue to another segmental distinction is illustrated by an analysis of the distinction of voicing in English medial stops, for instance *rapid* versus *rabid* (Port 1977). The voicing distinction is cued inter alia by the duration of the stop closure itself, the duration of the preceding vowel (longer before the voiced consonant), the duration of the voiceless portion of the stop, if any, and its timing relative to the following vowel (the presence of aspiration). In fast speech, the purely durational cues are reduced: the stop closure contrast decreases from 32% in slow speech to 14% in fast speech, the vowel duration contrast from 14% to 8% (Port 1977).

Articulatory strategy

The temporal restructuring of fast speech is achieved by various strategies affecting the extent and the velocity of articulatory gestures, among which the speaker seems to choose so as best to fulfil the dual requirements of articulating at the faster speech rate and preserving acoustic cues to segmental distinctions. A similar choice of strategies apparently applies to reduction in prosodically weak positions, for instance unstressed syllables, at one and the same speech rate (Vaissière 1988). Rapid speech can entail more forceful muscular contractions and consequently an increase in articulatory velocity, but this effect is not consistent (Tuller et al. 1982; Nelson et al. 1984; Ostry et al. 1985; Flege 1988). Increased activity of the orbicularis oris muscle in fast speech was found not only in the production of labial stops but also in the lip protrusion gesture that accompanies a rounded vowel (Gay 1978). On the other hand, consonant closures can be replaced by less time consuming articulatory gestures, as when an oral stop is replaced by a glottal stop or eliminated entirely by complete failure to reach the articulatory target; and vowel articulation in fast speech is often, but not always (Kuehn 1973), characterized by some degree of destressing and centralization, with consequent changes to the amplitude and spectral energy distribution as well as to the duration of the vowel (Lindblom 1963; Shockey 1973). Centralization can be viewed as a tendency to undershoot the target of the vowel by reducing the extent of the articulatory gesture, and it may actually correlate with decreased muscular activity revealed by electromyography (Gay 1978) and reduced velocity revealed by glossometry (Flege 1988). Vowel centralization can also have the reflex effect of reducing the distance travelled by articulators in the production of a following consonant; this potentially affects also their velocity, since peak velocity may depend on the distance the articulator has to travel (Kent et al. 1972b). In Japanese, vowels in fast speech can be characterized by more rapid jaw movement and in some cases by undershoot (Masaki et al. 1986; Sonoda 1987; Imaizumi et al. 1987), which establishes that undershoot can occur in languages that do not have a stress accent; consequently, undershoot cannot be excluded for rapid speech in Greek. An electropalatographic study of intervocalic dental consonants in Italian found that the degree of linguopalatal contact was strongly correlated both with stress and with rate of speech (Farnetani 1990); it is reasonable to assume some degree of consonant reduction in fast speech also for Greek. The degree of overlap in the articulatory and laryngeal gestures associated with contiguous consonants also increases with speech rate (Hardcastle 1985; Marchal 1988; Munhall et al. 1988; Browman et al. 1990). Conversely, in slow speech articulatory movement becomes slower; however a study of jaw movement in slow speech found that the increase in movement duration was less than a third of the increase expected on the basis of a proportional relationship with sentence duration (Wieneke et al. 1987).

Segmental reduction

Phonological reduction is typical of fast speech, particularly in stress timed languages. In English, schwa deletion, apical flap deletion and consonant cluster simplification are all more common in fast speech. The following are some of the processes involved, with examples of languages in which they occur (Dressler 1973): phonological vowel shortening [Breton]; vowel centralization [Breton]; vowel devoicing [first vowel of English *potato, potential* (Ueda 1978)]; syncope and apocope, often giving rise to consonant clusters not found in slow speech [German *geschnitten* → *kšnitn̩* 'cut,' Russian *bljúdečko* → *bl'úḍčʺkə* 'plate']; synizesis, even of stressed vowels [Breton *gúā* → *gwā̃* 'winter']; development of syllabic consonants with loss of a contiguous vowel, which involves reducing the segmental composition of a syllable while maintaining the syllable pattern of the word rhythm [Dutch clitic schwa deletion (Berendsen 1987); Russian *nóvəvə* → *nóvvə* 'new,' gen. sg. masc.]; denasalization; consonant cluster simplification and loss of word final consonants in anteconsonantal environment; loss of weak approximants and continuants [ʔ, *h*, *w* in Persian].

Tone

Just as the temporal requirements of pitch movement can affect duration (a large fundamental frequency excursion in a narrow segmental slot tends to lengthen the segments onto which it is mapped), so, conversely, duration and particularly rate of speech can affect the degree to which target tones are reached and how segments are associated with tonal movements. In very general terms, as tempo increases, the register tends to get higher and the range compressed (Kohler 1983; Yokoyama 1986); a higher level of activity is found in the laryngeal muscles controlling pitch (Gårding et al. 1975). Compression of the range implies that as duration decreases, the slope of the frequency excursion is not simply adjusted so as to meet the target in the reduced time, but that the excursion is to some degree truncated as a consequence of the reduced time available for its completion. In Osaka Japanese (Figure 6.1), certain syllables which have a stretch of level fundamental frequency in slow speech, have continuously moving fundamental frequency at normal and fast rates of speech; High tones tend to become lower and Low tones higher as the speech rate is increased, but the turning points remain fairly securely synchronized with the beginning of the mora across the different rates of speech (Nagano-Madsen 1987, 1992). In Southern Swedish *en mànli(g) nùnna* 'a masculine nun' (Figure 6.2), in slow speech

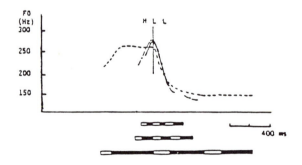

FIGURE 6.1
High Low Low tone sequence at different speech rates
in Osaka Japanese (from Nagano-Madsen 1987)

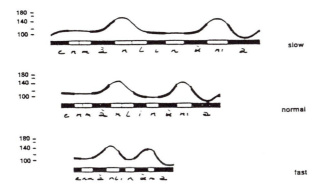

FIGURE 6.2
Synchronization of tonal and segmental events
at different speech rates in Southern Swedish
(from Gårding et al. 1987)

the High-Low movement associated with the first accent takes place largely on the *l* of *mànli*, the following *i* having Low level tone; but in fast speech, the High-Low movement is executed not only on the *l* but also on the following *i*; the Low level interval between the two accentual movements has been eliminated to allow more phonological space for the execution of the accentual movements in the reduced time frame associated with rapid speech (Gårding et al. 1987).

Style of speech

Although rate of speech is probably the most important source of prosodic variability, a number of other linguistic and paralinguistic factors can also be relevant, many of them interacting with rate of speech and with each other (Labov 1972; Bailey et al. 1973; Cedergren 1973; Cedergren et al. 1974; Dressler 1976; Berdan 1983). Closely related to rate of speech, but distinct from it, is style of speech. Clear speech, which is characterized by increased duration and intensity and closer approximation to targets, is used for maximum intelligibility (Lindblom 1990). Casual speech (Hasegawa 1979) is typical of informal conversation in relaxed surroundings with a well known interlocutor, careful speech of a serious discussion of important issues with one's superiors. Casual speech is generally faster than careful speech, but given two utterances spoken at the same rate, the more casual of the two will show more reduction (Shockey 1973). The speech of a drunk person combines slow tempo (Lester et al. 1974) with casual style. Regional and socioeconomic dialect differences, and those relating to the age and sex of the speaker, can also be stylistic differences: for instance, working class pronunciations may be used in casual speech and middle class pronunciations in careful speech, as in *Pygmalion*. In American English, women tend to use more advanced forms of casual speech than men and to correct more sharply to the other extreme in formal speech (Labov 1972). Discourse factors, which have already been mentioned in relation to rate of speech, can equally affect speech style; they include the emotional state of the interlocutors, the relative importance and novelty of a topic in the discourse, or the impact of any factor tending to lower the attention of the speaker to careful enunciation, such as the occurrence of a tongue twister in a different part of the utterance (Dressler 1974).

Variation in verse

An appreciation of the range of possible variation in speech is central to a proper understanding of variation in metrical texts and consequently to the exploitation of the latter as evidence for the prosody of a dead language. The philological evidence for bridges, caesurae, resolution and the like more often than not lacks uniformity. Some styles or genres of verse permit linguistic structures to map in a way that other styles of verse do not permit or only rarely permit. In other cases, a mapping is rare in earlier styles of verse and becomes progressively more acceptable through time. In such instances, it is usual to characterize the less strict or the later styles as being "metrically lax." This term tends to obscure the important question whether the poet is using a variant mapping that actually occurs in some style of speech, or a mapping that is never actually used in ordinary speech but which deviates from normal speech to a degree that the author finds metrically acceptable. In the former case, metrical laxity means accessing linguistic variants that other styles of verse are not allowed to access. In the latter case, access is to a metrically acceptable distortion or abstraction, to a potential rather than to a real pronunciation. A variety of evidence, such as the rules for resolution in lyric, suggest that in Greek, as in Finnish (Leino 1986), sung verse could depart more from ordinary speech rhythm than spoken verse. An intermediate case is represented by a pronunciation that is real but whose occurrence is restricted to artificially slow and deliberate speech. There are fairly reliable indications that most of the Greek metrical data relating to variable prosodic domains represent real linguistic variants. The linguistic structures involved contain either nonlexical words or certain types of phrasal structures or both. The extension of the domains of prosodic rules in such structures from lexical to progressively broader postlexical application is one of the best established aspects of linguistic variation. It is entirely reasonable to assume that ὁ γάμος with resolution in the first two syllables was not a poetic artificiality but was actually pronounced with a matrix like the first two syllables of πεδία; and that the final syllable of ἄρχειν standing before γάρ at Porson's bridge was not a metrical artificiality but was actually pronounced with subordination like the medial syllable of προσβῆναι. Conversely, it is reasonable to assume that such pronunciations were not usual in all styles of speech, since there are certain metrical styles in which appositives in split resolution and at Porson's bridge are avoided. However, this assumption may need qualification, since it is possible that the stricter metrical styles are allowing themselves to access only an artificially deliberate style of speech in which rules which normally have postlexical as well as lexical application are restricted to lexical application only. It has been found that when the same text is read both as poetry and as prose, the speech rate chosen for the poetry reading is somewhat slower than that chosen for the prose reading (English: Lehiste 1985; Swedish: Eriksson 1987); pauses are more frequent and have greater duration (Kowal et al. 1975). In Hungarian, it was found that poetry was recited at a rate of 9.40 segments per second as compared with 12.89 segments per second for conversation (Fónagy et al. 1960). Intraphrasal rates of 3–4 syllables per second for verse and 5–6 syllables per second for prose were reported for German (Meinhold 1972). This does not mean that different metrical styles cannot access different speech rates, but only that the prosody of verse at any particular register may be a step behind what would be normal for a comparable discourse situation. It is instructive that the postlexical rules of connected speech can be applied in surrogate whistle and drum languages: elision is found in Kickapoo whistle speech (Voorhis 1971), a "liaison" vowel in Manjaco (Guinea Bissau: Wilson 1963), and sandhi vowel shortening implemented by a double drum beat in Akan (Nketia 1974).

In principle, the more extensive the domain of a subtractive prosodic rule like matrix formation or subordination, the less slow, deliberate and formal the style of speech is likely to be. As a general rule, the styles of verse whose mapping rules suggest less formal and deliberate speech are just those whose subject matter and vocabulary are also less elevated and formal and more familiar and colloquial. For instance, the domain of subordination as evidenced by Porson's bridge is more extensive in satyric than in tragedy and more extensive in comedy than in satyric. This correlation tends to corroborate the interpretation of metrical laxity in terms of access to speech variants, but it should not be interpreted in a simplistic manner. Access to the prosody of informal speech does not preclude access to the prosody of formal speech in the same genre of verse; and access to the prosody of informal speech can be constrained by a variety of factors other than genre and subject matter. However,

TABLE 6.1
Incidence of appositives per thousand trimeters
at Porson's bridge

Medea	0.96
Hippolytus	5.06
Heraclidae	11.26
Alcestis	29.92
Cyclops	61.50

the correlation can still manifest itself in quite finegrained distinctions. For instance, the incidence of appositives at Porson's bridge in the *Alcestis* is greater than in any other work in the Severior, Semiseverus and Liber styles with the exception of the *Ion*; this discrepancy is evidently due to the status of the *Alcestis* as a prosatyr play, standing midway between tragedy, which in the Severior style has a very low incidence of appositives at Porson's bridge, and satyric, which on the evidence of the *Cyclops* has a very high incidence of appositives at Porson's bridge. The data are presented in Table 6.1.

Not only rhythm rules like matrix formation and subordination, but also segmental sandhi rules like elision evidence the progressively greater access to fluent phrasing in the stylistic development of Euripides. This can be demonstrated by studying elision across the orthographic comma: this is relatively constrained when the elided word is not a nonlexical such as γε, δέ, με, σε, τε and when the elision is not before or after a vocative phrase

$$\text{ἀλλ᾽, ὦ τέκν᾽, εἰσελθόντε Medea 969.}$$

The growth of elision across comma in structures other than the latter, termed constrained elision, is compared with the growth in resolution and in appositives at Porson's bridge for the eight securely dated plays of Euripides in Table 6.2. The date (d) is expressed in terms of years from the production of the *Alcestis*. A regression analysis confirms the statistical significance of the growth in the percentage of constrained elisions; there is almost only one chance in a hundred that the regression equation should be the result of random fluctuations: the domain of elision is less syntactically constrained in the later plays.

THE SYLLABLE IN CONNECTED SPEECH

When words are spoken in isolation, the segments of the word are mapped onto syllables according to rules which, whatever their language particular characteristics, nevertheless reflect universal principles of optimal

TABLE 6.2

Growth of constrained elision across comma
as a percentage of all elisions across comma, compared to
growth of resolution and of appositives at Porson's bridge

	Date	Constrained elision over comma %	Resolution rate per 1000 trimeters	Appositives at Porson's br. rate per 1000 trimeters
Alcestis	0	49.06	62.34	29.92
Medea	7	55.24	65.57	0.96
Hippolytus	10	58.73	42.55	5.06
Troades	23	59.32	211.58	20.15
Helen	26	58.54	275.33	23.94
Orestes	30	64.89	394.18	37.03
Bacchae	33	59.57	375.81	33.76
I.A.	33	56.00	383.04	51.47

$$arcsin \sqrt{E} = 0.1751\, d + 46.2549$$
$$t = 3.6286$$

syllable structure. As remarked in Chapter 2, syllables having an onset are preferred to syllables without an onset, homosyllabic consonant clusters in which sonority decreases towards the syllable nucleus are disfavoured, and, particularly in rapid speech, open syllables are favoured over closed syllables. Some languages also have canonical rules that exclude certain less favoured syllable types from word initial or final position, requiring that all words begin with a single consonant or end in a vowel: in Moroccan Arabic, a word cannot begin with a vowel (Harrell 1962); in Kota (S. India: Emeneau 1944), native words do not begin with consonant clusters; in Itonama (Bolivia: Liccardi et al. 1968), words do not end in a closed syllable; in Spanish, words do not end in a consonant cluster. In the absence of such rules, syllable structure cannot be optimized word initially and finally in citation forms: there is no choice of mapping when the words are uttered in isolation. Obviously, if a word does not start with a consonant, it cannot be syllabified so that its first syllable has an onset, although a nondistinctive onset can be supplied in the form of a glottal stop.

Resyllabification

In connected speech, languages tend to improve syllable structure by resyllabifying across word boundaries within certain prosodic domains. This tendency, which varies from language to language, becomes stronger as one proceeds from careful, monitored speech to rapid, casual speech.

Resyllabification can lead to a domino effect with extensive differences in syllabification throughout the word between citation and sandhi forms, as in Kabyle Berber (Algeria: Kenstowicz et al. 1985). It is clear that postlexical resyllabification is in principle distinct from the original lexical process of syllabic mapping. In the first place, resyllabification rules do not necessarily replicate exactly the rules of lexical syllabification: for instance, consonant sequences often resist resyllabification. Furthermore, in a number of instances resyllabification can be shown to be ordered after a lexical rule in which the resyllabified consonant functions as a constituent of a syllable of the word to which it lexically belongs. For instance, the vowel in the final syllable of French masc. *premier* 'first' is a close *e*, while in the fem. *première* it is open *e*, because in French mid vowels are open when followed by a coda consonant: when the coda consonant of the feminine form is resyllabified, the vowel remains open, as in *la première étagère* 'the first shelf' as opposed to *le premier étage* 'the first floor' (Tranel 1981). A resyllabified consonant can itself have undergone a phonological rule affecting coda consonants. In many dialects of Spanish syllable final *s* becomes *h*, and the aspirate can be resyllabified by a later rule, as in *tienes espacio → tiene.hespacio* 'you have space' (Harris 1983). The *d* of German *Süditalien* 'Southern Italy' is first subject to final devoicing and then resyllabified in fast speech (*zü.ti*); similarly in Dutch (Booij et al. 1987). On the other hand in Turkish, final stop devoicing and vowel shortening in closed syllables apply after resyllabification (Rice 1989). Resyllabified consonants can undergo the allophony applicable in the host syllable, as with the palatalization and depalatalization of resyllabified consonants in Turkish (Kaisse 1990). Nevertheless, a resyllabified coda consonant need not be identical to the syllable initial allophone, but, even in the absence of major phonological rules, may be characterized by various finegrained phonetic properties that are a reflex of its optional coda consonant status. In other terms, the phonetic processes associated with resyllabification need not all apply completely (Läufer 1985): a consonant is said to be resyllabified when host syllable structure features predominate over underlying syllable structure features. The phonological property of resyllabification involves a binary classification of a parameter of phonetic data, just as the phonological property of assimilation requires the classification of various transitional types with double articulations, intermediate articulations and residual articulations (Barry 1985; Wright et al. 1989) as either assimilated or not assimilated.

Perception of resyllabification

Resyllabified consonants tend to be perceptually indistinguishable from onset consonants in fluent discourse. In French, although potentially ambiguous phrases can be disambiguated by the suspension of resyllabification of nonlatent consonants in explicit speech, in normal speech subjects were unable to distinguish phrases with resyllabification like *les aulnes* 'the alder trees' from *les zones* 'the areas' with underlying onset (Wenk et al. 1982). By contrast, in English, where resyllabification is not as systematic as in French, subjects were much more successful but still had a 33% error rate in discriminating pairs of phrases like *an ice man – a nice man*, presented at a fluent conversational rate of speech with the speakers unaware of the intended contrasts (O'Connor et al. 1964); the success rate was significantly improved when similar phrases were read as contrasting pairs (Lehiste 1960). Although errors in English word boundary assignment are comparatively rare in speech production, they are fairly common in speech perception, as would be predicted on the basis of the former study; for instance *new dimensions* may be misunderstood as *nude mentions* or *a loose crew* as *a loose screw* (Garnes et al. 1975).

Domains of resyllabification

The domains of the various rules of resyllabification vary from one rule to another and from one language to another: within a given language the different rules of resyllabification do not necessarily all have the same domains, nor do all languages have all types of resyllabification. In Spanish, resyllabification applies to the major phrase in casual speech (Harris 1983), in French mainly to the minor phrase (Läufer 1985). In Chonnam Korean, the domain of resyllabification is the accentual phrase (Jun 1990). Resyllabification domains are more restricted in Germanic languages such as English, German and Dutch, where failure of resyllabification distinguishes lexical pairs like *holy* 'sacred' and *holey* 'full of holes' (Maddieson 1985) as well as phrasal sequences like *see the meat* and *see them eat, its wings* and *it swings* (Lehiste 1960); Dutch *lood.spet* 'drop of lead' and *loods.pet* 'sea captain's cap' (Nespor et al. 1986). In Choctaw, prefixes can remain unresyllabified under certain conditions (Lombardi et al. 1991). In Berber verse, resyllabification applies within the line, which reflects the situation in speech where the maximum domain of resyllabification is a string bounded by pauses (Dell et al. 1988). In Classical Persian verse, resyllabification within the line can be blocked by major syntactic boundaries and by metron diaeresis (Heny 1981).

That clitic boundaries can be weaker than compound boundaries is shown by Turkish, for instance, where, in addition to the accentual difference, the clitic group is a single domain for vowel harmony but the compound is two domains (Nespor et al. 1986). This hierarchy is reflected in the German rules for resyllabification: in slow, but not artificially slow, speech resyllabification applies to sequences such as *schon im, sag' es, bald ist*, but not to the compound *Süditalien*; resyllabification in the compound applies only in more rapid and casual speech (Läufer 1985). There may also be evidence for a hierarchy of cohesion within the class of clitics and within the class of affixes, although some of the differences in syllabi- fication may be a reflex of relatively greater stress on the proclitic and the prefix. In Serbocroatian, proclitics are not resyllabified, whereas enclitics are resyllabified by most speakers: *nad ovcu* 'above the sheep' → *nad.ov.cu*, *od sad se* 'from now on itself' → *ot.sa.ce*; both examples have a single word accent on the proclitic, so that the domain of accentual prominence and that of resyllabification do not coincide (Gvozdanović 1986).

From coda to onset

The most common resyllabification rule applies when the first word ends in a consonant and the second word begins with a vowel: VC.V → V.CV. For example, in very careful monitored pronunciation, Spanish *tienes alas* 'you have wings' is distinguished from *tiene salas* 'it has rooms' by the syllable division, but in ordinary speech the prevocalic word final *s* becomes the onset of the first syllable of the next word, so that the syllable division is the same in both phrases: *tie.ne.sa.las* (Harris 1983); similarly in Hungarian (Hall 1944). In English and German, when there is no resyllabification, the word initial vowel can start with a glottal stop or a period of laryngealization, that is slow and irregular vocal fold activity, as in German *Südafrika, im Urlaub* 'on leave' (Läufer 1985), English *seem able* as opposed to *see Mable*, *grade A* as opposed to *grey day* (Lehiste 1960). Something similar characterizes initial vowels when resyl- labification is deliberately suspended in hypercareful speech in French, in order to distinguish e.g. *petite amie* 'small friend' from *petit tamis* 'small sieve' or *mauvaises eaux* 'bad waters' from *mauvais zoo* 'bad zoo' or when the second word has emphatic stress. Absence of resyllabification in English does not necessarily imply absence of coarticulation, provided no major syntactic boundary intervenes (Su et al. 1975). As already noted, a resyllabified consonant is phonetically similar to but not neces- sarily identical to a word initial consonant; it may, fully or partially, retain some of the properties of final position while adopting the other properties of onset consonants. For instance, in slow and careful speech in French, resyllabified stops can show a weaker release spike and no frication noise, and resyllabified fricatives and nasals can have some- what less duration than if they had been lexical onsets; the same holds for the resyllabified muta cum liquida cluster in *votre acte* 'your act' as opposed to *vos tracts* 'your tracts.' However, such differences tend to be small and are apparently obliterated in fluent speech. Some styles of colloquial French differentiate resyllabified consonants from originally initial consonants by lengthening the latter, as in *qui l'aime* 'who loves him' with long *l* as opposed to *qu'il aime* 'that he loves' with short *l* (Läufer 1985).

In Greek, coda to onset resyllabification is involved in the potential ambiguity of pairs like ἔστι νοῦς – ἔστιν οὖς, ἔστι Νάξιος – ἔστιν ἄξιος Eustathius 1170.33, scholiast on Dionysius Thrax 156 Hilgard. The latter indicates that it is possible to differentiate such pairs, but that if the words are linked in pronunciation (συνημμένως, κατὰ συνάφειαν), there is a danger of ambiguity. It is reasonable to assume that in Greek the ambiguity resulting from resyllabification can be resolved by a word for word pronunciation in which resyllabification is blocked. Resyllabification after elision is presumably a component in puns like ἀπ' ὄνου–ἀπὸ νοῦ scholiast on *Clouds* 1273, τήνδ' ἐμοῦσαν–τήνδε μοῦσαν Athenaeus 14.616 (Stanford 1939). Whether elision involved complete deletion of the vowel or not, failure of resyllabification is probably a component in the notorious speech error of the actor Hegelochus γαλῆν ὁρῶ for γαλήν' ὁρῶ scholiast on *Orestes* 279 (Strattis 1 and 60, Sannyrion 8), scholiast on *Frogs* 303, scholiast on Dionysius Thrax 163.22 Hilgard. Hegelochus is reported to have failed to produce the elision due to shortness of breath (further symptoms in Tzetzes on *Frogs* 303). The implication is that elision automatically triggers resyllabification: at normal speech rates both phrases are resyllabified, at deliberate speech rates γαλῆν ὁρῶ is distinct from γαληνά ὁρῶ without elision. Herodian II.408 Lentz has a rule specifying that a consonant is orthographically syllabified with a following vowel if they are in the same word, but not if they belong to different words unless the first word is elided; the same rule appears in the B scholiast on Iliad 8.207: τὸ πρὸ τῆς ἀποστρόφου σύμφωνον τῷ ἐπιφερομένῳ συνάπτεται φωνήεντι. The phonetic basis of this rule may be that elision implies resyllabification. Finally, unresyllabified slow speech γαλῆν.ὁρῶ is distinct from resyllabified normal speech γαλή.ν' ὁρῶ in having the syllable final allophone of *n*, which is likely to have been shorter and more vowel like (Läufer 1985). The accentual component is discussed later (p. 265). It is less likely that γαληνά and γαλῆν were segmentally distinct after resyllabification. Any allophonic modifications of the segments in the syllable *-nho-*, such as voicing of *h*, or partial nasalization of the vowel passing through the *h* (Ohala 1975), would probably apply equally to both words. If there had been some regressive nasalization and height change in the vowel before the homosyllabic nasal in γαλῆν but not before the heterosyllabic nasal in γαληνά (Kawasaki 1986; Beddor et al. 1986), it is conceivable that this difference continued to apply after resyllabification, but such an explanation is more speculative and involves a less substantive phonetic cue than the assumption of a difference in syllabification.

Domain of coda to onset resyllabification

For the analysis of the domain of coda to onset resyllabification, two classes of word shapes are analyzed separately: (a) amphibrach- and palimbacchiac-shaped words ending in -V̆C at the beginning of the trimeter followed by words beginning with a vowel (-V̆C # V-)

$$καθεῖλον\ ἡμᾶς\ Orestes\ 862$$
$$ἡδεῖαν\ ὄψιν\ Orestes\ 727$$

and (b) extended anapaest-shaped words also at the beginning of the trimeter ending in -V̆C followed by words beginning with a vowel (-V̆C # V-)

$$ἐπίσημον\ ἔτεκε\ Orestes\ 249.$$

The sample for class (a) consists of all occurrences in the *Medea* and the *Orestes*, the sample for class (b) of all occurrences in the extant tragedies of Euripides. Four domain types are distinguished:

1. Appositive groups, and potentially appositive groups involving at least one nonprepositive nonlexical

$$κατάρατός\ εἰμι\ Helen\ 54$$
$$δαπανηρὸς\ ἆρ᾽\ Phoenissae\ 566;$$

2. Vocative plus following word

$$βασίλεια,\ βακχεύουσαν\ Troades\ 341$$

and simple phrasal structures of lexical words such that both words belong to the same syntactic phrase XP and neither belongs to a branching

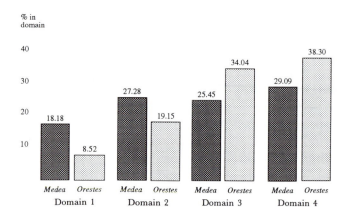

FIGURE 6.3
Amphibrach- and palimbacchiac-shaped words
with coda to onset resyllabification according to domain type
in the earlier and later styles of Euripides

phrase YP to which the other does not—this subtype generally corresponds to the structures [XY]$_{XP}$ or [YX]$_{XP}$

> μητρῷον αἷμα *Orestes* 285 [Adj N]$_{NP}$;

3. Complex phrasal structures of two lexical words (or lexical plus nonpostpositive nonlexical) such that one is the head of the phrase and the other belongs to a branching phrase subconstituent, whether or not that subconstituent is continuous or discontinuous

> κάλλιστον εἶπας μῦθον *Medea* 1127 [Adj V N]$_{VP}$
> ἐπίσημον εἰς Ἕλληνας *Orestes* 21 [A [PP]]$_{AP}$
> πρήσαντες οἴκους τούσδε *Orestes* 1150 [V [N Det]]$_{VP}$;

4. Nonphrasal sequences of two lexical words such that neither belongs to the phrase headed by the other, whether a clause boundary intervenes

> μανίαισιν· ὀνομάζειν *Orestes* 37

or not

> ἔβλαψε δόξα *Medea* 293 Verb Subject;

type 4 also includes cases in which a still larger phrase of which neither word in question is the head contains them

> πρόσωπον εἰς γῆν *Orestes* 958

where both the NP and the PP are contained in the VP. These four domain types constitute a hierarchy of cohesion 1 > 2 > 3 > 4. To ensure that any change observed not be a side effect of other changes not directly motivated by changes in domain constraint on coda to onset resyllabification, the same word shapes in the same metrical locations

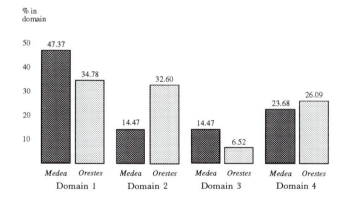

FIGURE 6.4

Amphibrach- and palimbacchiac-shaped words
without coda to onset resyllabification according to domain type
in the earlier and later styles of Euripides

but ending in -v̆ will be analyzed as an additional control. The results of the test are presented as bar graphs in Figures 6.3–6.6.

It can be seen from these bar graphs that for both the class of amphibrach-/palimbacchiac-shaped words ending in -v̆C and the class of extended anapaest-shaped words ending in -v̆C, there is a decrease in relative frequency from the earlier to the later styles of Euripides in the two more cohesive domain types 1 and 2, and a corresponding increase in the two less cohesive domain types 3 and 4: coda to onset resyllabification is more readily permitted in the less cohesive domains in the later styles. The statistical significance of the change was established by a ridit analysis, with values of $\bar{r}$ indicating odds of about three to two for amphibrach- and palimbacchiac-shaped words ($\bar{r} = 0.5940$), and better than two to one for anapaest-shaped words ($\bar{r} = 0.6867$), that a case of coda to onset resyllabification in the Liberrimus will occur in a less cohesive domain than a case in the earlier styles. The change through time is not merely a reflex of any tendency to increasing enjambement, since the changes seen in the classes of resyllabified words are not paralleled by changes in the classes of unresyllabified words. The frequency changes observed and tested reflect a tendency to extend the domain of coda to onset resyllabification in later styles of Euripides, which may be interpreted as evidence that resyllabification of this type is constrained in less cohesive structures in deliberate Greek speech, and that its domain is extended in less deliberate and more fluently phrased speech.

In another type of coda to onset resyllabification, the first word ends in a consonant and the second word begins with a consonant, but the resulting consonant sequence would be homosyllabic according to the rules of lexical syllabification. In such cases, the consonant sequence can be resyllabified to conform with the lexical rule: VC.CV → V.CCV. The

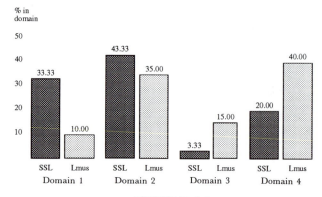

FIGURE 6.5

Extended anapaest-shaped words with coda to onset resyllabification according to domain type in the earlier and later styles of Euripides

phonological factors governing such resyllabification are the occurrence of the resulting cluster as an onset in the lexicon and its sonority slope. For instance, in fluent French *tr* and *pl* are homosyllabic not only in *petit trou* 'small hole' and *couplet* 'couplet' but also in *petite roue* 'small wheel' and *coupe-les* 'cut them'; clusters of stop plus nasal and stop plus stop, as in *avec nous* 'with us' and *attrape tout* 'catch everything,' require a more rapid rate of speech to resyllabify (Läufer 1985). This type of resyllabification is less favoured than the first type. In German, it only occurs in rapid speech (Läufer 1985); in Spanish, it is normally *club. lindo*, not *clu. blindo* 'nice club.' This type of resyllabification does not occur in Greek (Snell 1958).

From onset to coda

Resyllabification can also involve right to left movement of a consonant. The first word ends in a vowel and the second word begins with a consonant cluster, the first segment of which becomes the coda consonant of the preceding syllable: V.CC → VC.C. Resyllabification occurs where the cluster would be heterosyllabic by the rules of lexical syllabification. Such resyllabification should be particularly likely with words ending in a final stressed vowel. In some varieties of Italian, after a final stressed vowel an initial *s* plus stop cluster is resyllabified: *metà scatola* → *metàs. catola* 'half the box' (Vogel 1982; Saltarelli 1983; Chierchia 1986); for clusters that are homosyllabic word medially, resyllabification entails gemination: *metàt. treno* 'half the train.'

In Greek, right to left resyllabification is the cause of what is known traditionally as "lengthening by position," as in ἔσχε.σχῆμα → ἔσχεσ.χῆμα,

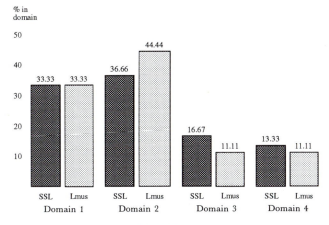

FIGURE 6.6
Extended anapaest-shaped words without coda to onset resyllabification according to domain type in the earlier and later styles of Euripides

φίλτατε.ξένων → *φίλτατεκ.σένων*. The propensity of any particular cluster to resyllabify is in general determined by the slope of the sonority gradient between the consonants involved. In comedy, voiceless stop plus liquid or nasal and voiced stop plus *ρ* are never resyllabified in metrical synaphea. In tragedy, possible cases are rare and disputed (Descroix 1931:18; Denniston on Eur. *Electra* 1058); however, since almost all involve right-linking nonlexicals, they seem to have a linguistic basis and probably should not be emended unless otherwise suspect

> *παρὰ κλαίουσι* Alcestis 542
> *παρὰ κρατῆρα* Euripides Frag. 642.1 Nauck
> *διὰ χρόνου* I.A. 636; see app. crit.
> *ὁ χρόνος* Sophocles Frag. 832 Nauck
> *ἵνα πλήξειεν* I.A. 1579; see app. crit.
> *ἃ κρύπτειν χρεών* Euripides Frag. 411.4 Nauck;

for the one case with a lexical first word, *ἥλικα τραπείς Medea* 246, the *Hauniensis* has *ἥλικας* confirming Porson's conjecture. Resyllabification of potentially homosyllabic muta cum liquida clusters across lexical word boundary is well documented in Hellenistic verse (Lesky 1953). By contrast, for voiced stop plus *λ* it is failure of resyllabification that is exceedingly rare, and, in the few cases when it does fail, right-linking nonlexicals are not involved

> *δὲ γλῶσσαν Agamemnon* 1629.

Resyllabification never fails with voiced stop plus nasal, even with lexical words

> *αἰθέρα γνάθοις Cyclops* 629.

For word initial clusters of stop + stop, stop + *σ* and *σ* + stop, metrical evidence provides a censored distribution, since resyllabification is not allowed to fail for any of these clusters in verse. Investigation of the effect of the sonority slope on resyllabification must therefore proceed through intermediate and inferential steps. One approach is to test for a correlation between the steepness of the sonority slope and some other linguistic factor that promotes resyllabification, for instance phrasal environment. The relative frequency of onset to coda resyllabification in more cohesive and less cohesive phrasal environments is calculated for each segment of the sonority slope hierarchy starting with voiced stop + *l*. Those segments are represented by the following samples:

1. Clusters of stop + stop: all instances of *κτ-* and *πτ-* following a short word final vowel in the extant plays of Euripides, in both dialogue and lyric, wherever the weight of the resulting syllable is unambiguously heavy

2. Stop + *s*: all instances of ξ- and ψ- in Euripides under the same conditions

3. *s* + stop: all instances of σκ- and σπ- under the same conditions

4. Voiced stop + *l* or *N* (which must be classed together given their rarity): all instances of βλ-, γλ-, and γν- under the same conditions.

The object of this test was to determine the percentage of all clusters of each type, following a short vowel and resyllabified to result in an unambiguously heavy syllable, that occur in articular or prepositional phrases, such as

> ὁ κτείνας *Rhesus* 893
> κατὰ πτυχὰς I.T. 1082.

Such phrases are known to show a high degree of rhythmic cohesion (p. 341) and therefore may be expected to promote resyllabification. The sample was reanalyzed to include only cases before which the article or preposition could occur, so that finite verbs and nonsubstantival infinitives were excluded. It is evident from the results presented in Figure 6.7 that the steeper the sonority slope of a cluster type, the higher the proportion of articular or prepositional phrases. This result may be interpreted as follows: the steeper the sonority slope of a consonant cluster, the more it needs the additional inducement of cohesive phrasing to resyllabify. The following overall hierarchy of propensity to resyllabify emerges: stop + stop > stop + σ > σ + stop > voiced stop + nasal > voiced stop + λ > voiced stop + ρ, voiceless stop + sonorant. Since this hierarchy replicates the sonority slope of the clusters arranged from flatter

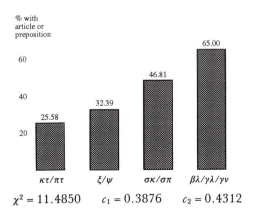

$$\chi^2 = 11.4850 \qquad c_1 = 0.3876 \qquad c_2 = 0.4312$$

FIGURE 6.7

Correlation of sonority slope with phrasal environment
in onset to coda resyllabification

to steeper, it may be concluded that in Greek the sonority slope between the consonants of a word initial cluster is a prime determinant of that cluster's ability to resyllabify from onset to coda.

A similar type of test can be used to discover the relative propensity to resyllabification of word initial triconsonantal and biconsonantal clusters starting with σ. In this test, triconsonantal clusters were represented by a sample consisting of all instances of στρ- following a verb ending in a short vowel in Euripides such that the weight of the resulting syllable is metrically unambiguous; biconsonantal clusters were represented by a sample consisting of all instances of σκ-, σπ- and στ- in Euripides under the same conditions. The phrasal criterion used for this test was whether the word starting with the cluster belongs to the verb phrase of which the preceding verb is the head, type

> ἐσήμηνε στρατῷ Helen 749
> πολλοὺς ὤλεσε στρατηλάτας Eur. Supplices 162

or to the following subject noun phrase, type

> ἐπηύξατο στρατός Hecuba 542.

The results of this test are presented in Table 6.3. It is apparent that onset to coda resyllabification is not permitted across the boundary between verb phrase and subject noun phrase when it involves the biconsonantal cluster but, when it involves the triconsonantal cluster, it is nearly as frequent across that phrase boundary as it is within the verb phrase. Despite the rather small sample size, there are only about three chances in a hundred that the exclusion of biconsonantal clusters from the interphrasal structures is the result of random fluctuations. The cluster type σ + stop needs the additional inducement of a more cohesive phrasal environment to resyllabify as compared with the cluster type σ + stop + liquid.

Domain of onset to coda resyllabification

That onset to coda resyllabification is constrained across minor phrase boundary is indicated by its relative avoidance across masculine caesura in the hexameter (Drewitt 1908). For a syntactically based test of the domain of onset to coda resyllabification, the factors of lexicality and syntactic structure were classified into a five-level hierarchy as follows:

1. Article or preposition

> ὁ κτείνας Rhesus 893
> κατὰ πτυχὰς I. T. 1082;

2. Other prepositive nonlexical or nonlexical syntagm

> τόνδε κτενῶ Andromache 382;

TABLE 6.3
Interaction of cluster length
and syntactic structure

	Interphrasal %	Intraphrasal %	N
σΤ-	0.00	100.00	13
σΤL-	42.86	57.14	7

$$p = 0.0307$$

3. Postpositive nonlexical monosyllable

    τε πτανοί *Ion* 154

and simple phrases with nonbranching constituents

    ὄρνιθι πταμένῳ *I.A.* 795
    ἐνάλια κτερίσματα *Helen* 1391
    ματέρα κτανόντος Eur. *Electra* 1197;

4. Complex phrases involving head and branching constituent

    σχήσετε στερρὸν δόρυ Eur. *Suppl.* 711
    ἱεροὺς ἀνέσχε πτόρθους *Hecuba* 459;

5. Nonphrasal sequences

    λοχίαις ἀνάγκαισι πταμένας *Bacchae* 89
    ὤλλυτο πτόλις *Hecuba* 767.

The word initial clusters πτ- and κτ- were chosen for the test both as a control on potential spurious correlations involving associations of cluster type with syntactic category, and because the flat sonority slope of stop + stop clusters makes them phonologically the most likely to be resyllabified and therefore the type in which any relaxation of constraint would be most readily observable.

The results of this test on metrically unambiguous onset to coda resyllabification in the extant plays of Euripides, excluding the satyr play *Cyclops*, are presented in Figure 6.8. It is clear that the relative frequencies of each of the two most cohesive domains 1 and 2 decrease from the earlier to the later tragedies, whereas the relative frequencies of each of the progressively less cohesive domains 3, 4 and 5 increase from the earlier to the later tragedies. The mean ridit ($\bar{r} = 0.6146$) indicates odds of slightly better than three to two that onset to coda resyllabification will take place in a less cohesive structure in the later tragedies as compared to the earlier ones; there is less than one chance in eighty that the observed excess of the mean ridit over 0.50 could have arisen from

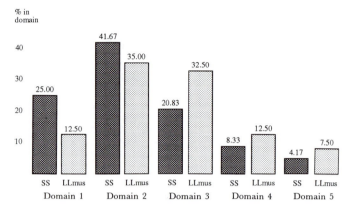

FIGURE 6.8

Comparison of the distribution of onset to coda resyllabification of κτ/πτ-
according to lexical status and syntactic configuration
in earlier and later styles of Euripides

random variation. So it may safely be concluded that onset to coda resyllabification is constrained in less cohesive structures in deliberate Greek speech and its domain is extended in less deliberate and more fluently phrased speech.

Segmental modification

In the cases of resyllabification discussed above, the mapping of the sequence of segments at the boundary onto syllables is modified; the remapping is achieved by the application of allophonic rules that change coda allophones into onset allophones or vice versa, and the sequence of segments is unchanged. In other cases, however, resyllabification is associated with some modification to the segments. Since changing a segment sequence is a more complex process than merely rearranging its syllable divisions, a greater degree of grammaticalization is often encountered in such cases.

Gemination

One type of modification is for a segment to be added by gemination, as in the "raddoppiamento sintattico" of central and southern Italy, Sardinia and Corsica: *tre cani* → *trec.cani* 'three dogs.' From a diachronic point of view, gemination can reflect an earlier situation in which the first word ended in a consonant that was lost in variants generalized from prepausal and other positions: *amav(i)t Carolum* > *amòc.carlo*. Gemination can then be analogically extended, as in dialect *tuc.canti* 'you sing.' In Sanskrit sandhi *ch*-gemination (*na chidyate* → *nacchidyate* 'it is not cut

TABLE 6.4
$\dot{\rho}$-gemination in tragic dialogue and lyric

	Dialogue %	Lyric %	N
$-\breve{V}\#\dot{\rho}\text{-}\to\breve{S}$	40.00	60.00	20
$-\breve{V}\#\dot{\rho}\text{-}\to\bar{S}$	95.45	4.55	22
	$\chi^2 = 15.0742$		

off"), a consonant cluster has been simplified to a single consonant word initially but remains word medially and in sandhi after a short vowel (Allen 1962).

It is clear from metrical evidence and some inscriptional spellings

αρτεματα ρρυμοις I².314.40

that Greek had a similar gemination of word initial $\dot{\rho}$ after a short vowel as in τὰ ρρήματα (Rumpel 1867; Stephens 1990); this gemination reflects the fact that word initial ρ is mostly derived from a consonant cluster (Allen 1987). An analysis of the distribution of $\dot{\rho}$-gemination in the dialogue and lyric metres of tragedy shows that $\dot{\rho}$-gemination is almost excluded from tragic lyric; the data are presented in Table 6.4. There is considerably less than one chance in a thousand that a difference as great or greater would arise at random. By contrast, in the nondialogue metres of comedy $\dot{\rho}$-gemination is preferred; the data are presented in Table 6.5. The odds for failure of $\dot{\rho}$-gemination in the nondialogue metres of tragedy are fifty-two times as great as in comedy. The language of dialogue verse is closer to standard spoken Attic than the language of lyric on various criteria such as alpha impurum and use of Homeric forms; and the language of comedy is on the whole closer to standard colloquial Attic than that of tragedy on many criteria such as correptio Attica. So the distribution of $\dot{\rho}$-gemination indicates that it was a feature

TABLE 6.5
$\dot{\rho}$-gemination in nondialogue meters
in tragedy and comedy

	$-\breve{V}\#\dot{\rho}\text{-}\to\breve{S}$ %	$-\breve{V}\#\dot{\rho}\text{-}\to\bar{S}$ %	N
Tragedy	92.31	7.69	13
Comedy	18.75	81.25	16
	$\omega = 52.0000$, $\chi^2 = 15.5416$		

associated with Attic speech: $\acute{p}$-gemination was perceived as particularly inappropriate in tragic lyric and as more appropriate in comedy than in tragedy.

Domain of $\acute{p}$-gemination

Unlike other types of resyllabification—which, with very few exceptions primarily involving proper names in the hexameter, are obligatory within the stichos—$\acute{p}$-gemination does not have hundred percent application wherever its phonological environment is met within the stichos. Consequently, the sensitivity of $\acute{p}$-gemination to syntactic factors can be tested directly without reference to stylistic or diachronic changes. The incidence of metrically unambiguous $\acute{p}$-gemination in the same five classes of syntactic structure as those just used for the test of onset to coda resyllabification is presented in Table 6.6 for the dialogue and lyric of tragedy and comedy including the fragments. As one proceeds down the hierarchy of progressively less cohesive structures, the rate of failure of $\acute{p}$-gemination increases. This gradient is statistically significant, as shown by the $\bar{\chi}^2$ of Bartholomew's test (Fleiss 1973). The mean ridit $\bar{r}$ indicates that odds are slightly better than three to one that a case of nongemination will occur in a less cohesive structure than a case of gemination. There are less than three chances in a hundred thousand that a mean ridit this great or greater would have been obtained due to random effects.

When $\acute{p}$-gemination is compared to onset to coda resyllabification in the same five classes, $\acute{p}$-gemination is seen to require closer lexico-syntactic connection between the words involved than resyllabification. Table 6.7 compares the proportions of each of the five classes of structure for metrically unambiguous $\acute{p}$-gemination with their respective

TABLE 6.6
Relative frequency of $\acute{p}$-gemination
in different syntactic contexts

Syntactic structure	$-\breve{V}\#\acute{p}\text{-}\rightarrow\check{S}$ %	$-\breve{V}\#\acute{p}\text{-}\rightarrow\bar{S}$ %
1	9.52	90.48
2	46.15	53.85
3	52.63	47.37
4	75.00	25.00
5	80.00	20.00

$$\bar{\chi}^2 = 14.9317, \quad \bar{r} = 0.7692$$
$$z = 4.6655$$

TABLE 6.7
Relative frequencies of different syntactic structures
for $\acute{p}$-gemination and onset to coda resyllabification

	1 %	2 %	3 %	4 %	5 %	N
-V̆#$\acute{p}$- → S̄	51.35	18.92	24.32	2.70	2.70	37
-V̆#κτ-/πτ- → S̄	33.03	20.18	32.11	10.09	4.59	109
			$\bar{r} = 0.3856$			

proportions for metrically unambiguous resyllabification of κτ-/πτ- in the same sample. It is clear that context 1, the most cohesive structure, accounts for a greater proportion of all $\acute{p}$-geminations than of all resyllabifications and that this relationship is reversed for the less cohesive structures 3–5. The mean ridit $\bar{r}$ indicates that the odds are about three to two that a case of $\acute{p}$-gemination chosen at random will occur in a more cohesive structure than a randomly selected case of onset to coda resyllabification. So $\acute{p}$-gemination is more strongly associated with closer lexicosyntactic structures and occurs less easily in the less cohesive phrasal structures.

Latent segments

Another common development is the insertion of a latent segment, as in French liaison, where, according to one interpretation, a lexically determined consonant is inserted as the onset of the first syllable of the following word: *petit ami* (*pti.ta.mi*) 'little friend' vs. *petit garçon* (*pti.gar.sõ*) 'little boy.' *n* and *r* are favoured epenthetic consonants in European languages. For instance, Swiss German has both: *mitt əmə vuəss* 'mit einem Fuss,' *mitt əmən ārm* 'mit einem Arm'; *də mā* 'der Mann,' *dər ezəl* 'der Esel' (Moulton 1986). Such cases represent prevocalic preservation of consonants that are lost preconsonantally and prepausally. There can also be analogical extension to cases where there is no historical justification for a consonant (as in English *Indiar and China*): *wiən ēr* 'wie er,' *mər iž nümə juŋ* 'man ist nicht mehr jung.' A preconsonantal linking *r* is found by historical accident in Walloon (Francard et al. 1986), and it too can be analogically extended to forms without etymological justification. Suffix alternation provides a lexical parallel (Bopp 1856), both from derivational morphology, as English *tobacconist*, French *cafetière* 'coffee-pot,' *bijoutier* 'jeweller' (Brugmann 1930), *numéroter* 'to number' (Marchand 1951), and from inflectional morphology, as Greek τίνος, Ζηνός (Meyer 1896). In Axininca Campa (Peru: Payne 1981), word internal syllable structure is improved both by the epenthesis of a consonant in hiatus and by the epenthesis of a vowel in consonant clusters. Paez (Colombia: Gerdel 1973), by contrast, seems to have a morphology that encourages hiatus.

Movable nu is the most important antihiatic consonant in Greek (Kuryłowicz 1972). It is restricted to certain morphological categories and lexical items, namely nominal and verbal inflections in -σι, third person singular -ε, ἐστί, the numeral εἴκοσι and a few other forms. Apart from the nominal dative plural, for instance

ανδρασιν *GD* 59,

its use is mainly associated with the Attic and Ionic dialects (Sommer 1907; Rüsch 1914)

ανεθεκεν *DAA* passim
εγραφσεν *ABV* passim.

The conventions for the use of movable nu in manuscripts are not equally applicable to the orthography of inscriptions, as can be seen by comparing the restoration of the stoichedon inscription of the Hundred Years Alliance I².86 with the version of the same treaty in the manuscript tradition of Thucydides 5.47 (Tod 1933). In Attic inscriptions, movable nu is frequently written before consonants and prepausally as well as before vowels. However its use before consonants is less consistent than its use before vowels; this difference in distribution is evidence of an antihiatic function. Movable nu is also written more regularly in later than in earlier inscriptions (Maassen 1881; Sommer 1907; Lademann 1915; Henry 1967). Forms allowing movable nu may alternatively be elided in verse

τέθνηχ᾽ ὁ μέλλων *Alcestis* 527; contrast τέθνηκεν
ἀντ᾽ ἐμοῦ *Alcestis* 434.

In the dedications from the Athenian acropolis (Raubitschek 1949), formulaic ανεθεκε(ν) and similar forms are predominantly written with movable nu; over half the cases without nu are from verse inscriptions, including one (*DAA* 296) with elision. Movable nu may be orthographically omitted where it is presumably metrically necessary

μ᾽ ανεθεκε υπερ *CEG* 342

and added where it is metrically impossible

ανεθεκεν δε μ᾽ Ευπολις αυτει *CEG* 407.

Movable nu can also appear in verse making position before a word beginning with a consonant

ἤντησεν πατρί *Ion* 802.

Preconsonantal movable nu becomes progressively less common through time in epic (Isler 1908). In the orthography of prose manuscripts, elision of verbal forms allowing movable nu, apart from ἐστί, is less common than spelling with movable nu. An early Ionic inscription shows both treatments within two lines

> ανεθηκεν ωμφιννεω : *Psamm.* 2
> εδωϙ' ωιγυπτιος : *Psamm.* 4.

An antihiatic *s* is found in *οὕτω(ς)* and antihiatic *κ* in the negative *οὐ(κ)*, in both of which the form with final consonant predominates prevocalically and a following vowel is not prodelided after these words.

Difficult clusters

When difficult or unacceptable consonant clusters arise across a word boundary, the structure of the offending onset or coda can be improved by deleting a consonant or by inserting a vowel. For instance, in the Catalan dialects of the Balearic islands, three segment consonant clusters of sonorant plus stop plus consonant (NT.C) are phonotactically ill-formed, and the plosive is deleted; the same occurs when they arise in sandhi: *verd fosc → ver fosc* 'dark green' (Wheeler 1986). In Greek, cluster simplification in sandhi is responsible for the preconsonantal forms of ἐξ (ἐκ, dialect ἐς) and of τούς in Cretan: τος καδεστανς as compared with τονς ελευθερονς.

Hiatus

Hiatus denotes a situation where a syllable ending in a vowel stands before a syllable beginning with a vowel, particularly if a word boundary intervenes between the two syllables; the result is a sequence of sounds both of which have the degree of sonority normally associated with syllable nuclei. A sequence of two contiguous nuclei in fluent speech does not conform to the preferential structure of syllable sequences, in which nuclei are separated by margins. Contiguous vowels within the word may be pronounced as separate syllables in deliberate speech and contracted to a single syllable in fast speech, as in Kalkatungu (Queensland) and Macedonian (Hayes 1981). In some languages hiatus is frequent both within the word and across word boundaries; Gokana (Nigeria: Hyman 1982, 1985, 1990) allows strings of identical vowels. However, there are various strategies that languages can adopt to eliminate hiatus and thereby improve lexically determined sequential syllable structure.

Hiatus within the word is not uncommon in Greek: *θεός, ῥοή, ὄγδοος, ἀήρ, ἐλάα, ἔλεος, νεανίας, τιθέασι, ἕως*; hiatus is analogically reintroduced at the morpheme boundary in Cretan τριυνς; it can occur at the compound seam with original digamma in the second element as in *ὀρθοέπεια* (Brugmann 1913). Across word boundary, hiatus is permitted in verse between stichoi subject to varying syntactic constraints (p. 426), but within the stichos in drama it is limited to a few cases including interjections, *τί, περί, ὅτι* and a couple of fixed phrases, namely forms of *οὐδὲ/μηδὲ εἷς* and of *εὖ οἶδα* (Moorhouse 1962)

> *παπαῖ, οἷον τὸ πῦρ* Agamemnon 1256
> *τί εἶπας;* Philoctetes 917
> *εὖ γ' ὅτι ἐπείσθης* Clouds 866
> *ὅτι ἔστ' ἄβρωτα* Dyscolus 452
> *ἢ περὶ ἄκραν* Acharnians 96
> *εὖ ἴσθ' ἐκεῖνον* O. T. 959
> *ὑγιὲς μηδὲ ἓν* Plutus 37.

This restriction of hiatus to fixed phrases and appositive groups in phonological environments excluding elision indicates that hiatus was less unacceptable at weak junctures where the syllable organization most resembled that found word internally.

Avoidance of hiatus is not only a feature of verse; it also characterizes much Greek prose, particularly in the oratorical style (Benseler 1841; Blass 1892). In Isocrates, there is a strong tendency to exploit word order and choice of words in order to avoid hiatus not only within the major phrase but even across phrase boundary. Additionally, Isocrates avoids crasis and tends to restrict elision to the appositive group (p. 262). The exceptional strictness of this style was remarked on in antiquity (Cicero *Orator* 151; Dionysius of Halicarnassus *De Compositione Verborum* 23.119 UR; Quintilian 9.4.35), and apparently reflects a desire to control for potential hiatus at any rate of speech: elision within the minor phrase is constrained because at slow rates of speech it might fail to apply (leading to hiatus), and hiatus between major phrases is constrained because at rapid rates of speech pause might be eliminated (again leading to a hiatus). The style of Demosthenes is somewhat less strict: hiatus is allowed at major phrase boundary and elision of lexicals outside the appositive group is admitted. The manuscript tradition hands down various instances of major phrase internal hiatus (p. 263), but since these disproportionately involve elidable vowels, the normal assumption is that the hiatus is not phonetic but merely orthographic (Benseler 1841), and modern texts of Demosthenes tend to print the elided form in these cases. By contrast, unelided forms are printed in texts of Thucydides, since hiatus in the manuscript tradition of Thucydides is more evenly distributed between elidable and unelidable vowels. This prose evidence does not yield a clear picture of the extent of interword hiatus in colloquial Greek speech. Since Isocrates avoids not only hiatus but also crases and elisions that are reasonably reconstructed for spoken Greek, it becomes unclear to what extent the avoidance of unelidable hiatus in prose is actually avoidance of synizesis. The question can be resolved on the assumption that the restrictions on synizesis found in verse are just those that applied in spoken Greek, but this assumption is not necessarily warranted.

Another aspect that is unclear is whether the avoidance of hiatus in both verse and prose is simply and directly avoidance of hiatus as such, that is avoidance of difficult sequential syllable structure, or whether it is avoidance of boundary marking properties that are potentially an indirect reflex of hiatus. The former assumption is theoretically quite acceptable: in postmedieval French verse hiatus is avoided, probably on the model of Latin verse. However, if hiatus between lexical words were consistently eliminated by elision, prodelision and synizesis within a prosodic domain, then its occurrence would signal a boundary between domains, which is the hypothetical premise of the latter theory. This theory receives support but hardly confirmation from language such as the following: σιωπῆς τινος ἀξιολόγου διειργούσης τὰ φωνήεντα ἀπ᾽ ἀλλήλων Dionysius of Halicarnassus *De Demosthene* 38.211UR; οὐκ ἐῶντα τὴν ἀκρόασιν ἑνὸς κώλου συνεχοῦς λαβεῖν φαντασίαν id. *De Compositione Verborum* 22.110UR. There is a clear case of orthographic hiatus in a phrase punctuating inscription, which would indicate that hiatus is not a fatal obstacle to minor phrase formation

: ε Ναυπακτο ανχορεοντα : *Naup.* 19;

however, it is not clear whether the orthographic hiatus represents a phonetic hiatus or is simply a citation form spelling.

Gliding and shortening

One strategy for remedying hiatus is postlexical glide development, by which one of the two vowels separated by a word boundary changes to a consonant. This change is more likely to affect the first vowel than the second and occurs most often with high vowels, since their articulatory gestures are closest to those of glides, and less often with mid vowels. In Rumanian, final *i, u, e* and *o* can become glides before an initial open vowel in certain syntactic environments (Avram 1986). An alternative strategy is to keep both vowels vocalic but to make one, usually the first or both (Kaisse 1982), hypershort, often uniting the two vowels into a single syllable nucleus. Such sandhi diphthongs occur commonly in fairly rapid speech in Mexican Spanish (Harris 1970; Cloward 1984); further weakening of the hypershort vowel leads to elision. At least from a synchronic point of view, elision is distinct from gliding and shortening in that it is an abrupt rather than a gradual process, involving the deletion of one vowel and the retention of the other unshortened (Kaisse 1982). Gliding, shortening and elision represent three different strategies for accommodating contiguous vocalic gestures to a timing scheme having some degree of coalescence across word boundary. Glide development and hypershortening can be optional variants, as in Modern Greek and Puerto Rican Spanish (Kaisse 1985). When long vowels are shortened in hiatus, it is sometimes possible to interpret the process as elision or gliding of the second mora of the vowel. In Classical Persian verse, final long high vowels are shortened before a word beginning with a vowel; the rule is often blocked by metron diaeresis (Heny 1981).

In Greek, vowel shortening without consequent diphthong formation occurs in the correptio epica, which is paralleled in Vedic (Allen 1987); it is also found in lyric and in the catalectic anapaestic tetrameters of comedy

> πορδὴ ὁμοίω *Clouds* 394
> τουτὶ φέρω. ἀλλ᾿ ἐπαναίρου *Knights* 784.

Correption appears in the lexical phonology of colloquial Attic in forms like αὑτῇί *Clouds* 201. The linguistic basis for correptio epica has been the subject of considerable dispute (Sjölund 1938). Gliding of the second element of a prevocalic word final short diphthong as in ἄνδρα μοj ἔννεπε is also found in epic and in lyric sections of drama (Allen 1987). In Attic, in the fixed phrase εὖ οἶδα, the first syllable remained heavy

> εὖ εἰδῇ *Wasps* 425,

which indicates that even if there was a transitional glide, the first syllable was diphthongal (Moorhouse 1962). Shortening is presumably a feature of synizesis in Greek (p. 268).

Elision and contraction

When the vowels at the end of the first word and the beginning of the second word are identical, they tend to coalesce into a single syllable nucleus, which may, but need not necessarily, be long or somewhat lengthened, according to the influence exerted by the timing scheme of the uncontracted sequence. If the underlying mora count is preserved, identical vowel coalescence is a type of contraction, if not, it is a type of elision. Identical vowel coalescence produces a slightly lengthened vowel in Tokyo Japanese except in the most rapid speech, but not in Puerto Rican Spanish or Modern Greek (Kaisse 1985). In the sandhi of identical vowels in Sanskrit, the coalescence of two short vowels results in a long vowel, but the coalescence of a short and a long vowel or of a long and a long vowel results in a long vowel, not a superlong vowel. There is some evidence that vowel coalescence between words and between two elements of a compound could be blocked in Vedic if it would have resulted in a superheavy syllable (Brugmann 1913; Allen 1962); in Modern Greek, vowel coalescence is avoided if it results in a stress clash (Nespor 1987).

Glide development, diphthongization and identical vowel coalescence can be viewed as changes in the way segments are mapped onto the syllable template, which is why they are conveniently represented in some form of autosegmental framework (Schane 1987). Unlike these, contraction and elision involve the outright deletion of one of a sequence of two nonidentical segments, and in this sense they represent a more drastic strategy. In contraction, the underlying mora count is preserved, in elision it is reduced; if the quality of the second vowel consistently predominates, as in Haya (Tanzania: Byarushengo 1977), contraction is behaving segmentally like elision but prosodically like contraction. More typically, the quality of the output vowel in contraction is a derivative or a compromise of the quality of both input vowels, so that the process is bidirectional. In some languages contraction yields only monophthongs, in others both monophthongs and diphthongs, and in yet others monophthongs if the left input vowel is short and diphthongs if it is long (de Haas 1988). Contraction often competes with elision; for instance, Zulu (S. Africa: Doke 1926) has elision, prodelision and contraction; contraction involves $a + i \rightarrow e$, $a + u \rightarrow o$, as well as $a + a \rightarrow a$. Identical vowel coalescence and elision of one of a pair of nearly identical vowels are more likely than elision of one of a pair of vowels that share few features: in Puerto Rican Spanish, unstressed e is lost only before e and i, unstressed o only before o and u. Italian has *c'insegna* 'he teaches us' but *ci avvisa* 'he advises us.' In Tokyo Japanese, identical vowel coalescence occurs both word internally and between words, whereas contraction of nonidentical vowels is word internal only and sociolectally very limited (Hasegawa 1979). In Attic lexical phonology, the prefix περι- can lose its final vowel before another ι in the participial forms of εἶμι giving περιών, περιόντες, but not before other vowels as in περιέχων. Elision of the final vowel of the first word (elision proper) is more common than elision of the initial vowel of the second word (prodelision). In Icelandic, where elision is common in colloquial speech, it is the first vowel that is lost (Pétursson 1986). In Modern Greek, it is always the first of two vowels that is elided, except that a vowel following a clitic may be prodelided (Kaisse 1982, 1985).

Not all vowels are equally prone to elision. In Mexican Spanish, hiatus was found to occur more frequently if the first vowel was a front vowel (Cloward 1984). In Modern Greek, high vowels are not elided except in clitic groups and o is particularly resistant to elision in certain syntactic environments; in Puerto Rican Spanish, unstressed a may be elided before any vowel, but unstressed e and o are elided only as specified above; similarly in Chicano Spanish (Clements et al. 1983). The nature of either or both vowels in the hiatic sequence can condition the occurrence of elision: in one type of elision in Modern Greek, e may be deleted before *o, a, u, i* but *a* only before *o*. In another type, the clitic elision just mentioned, there seems to be a computation of the relative strength of the two vowels: if the second vowel is more resistant than the first, elision occurs, whereas if the first vowel is more resistant, prodelision occurs: *με οδηγεί* → *μ' οδηγεί* 'he leads me,' but *το έχω* → *τό 'χω* 'I have it' (Kaisse 1985). In Kabyle Berber (Algeria: Bader 1983), for the marked word order subject plus verb the first vowel is always elided, but for the normal word order verb plus subject there is a hierarchy $u > i > a$, such that *a* is always lost whether by elision or prodelision, and *u* is always preserved whether it is the first or the second vowel. In Eastern Catalan dialects, ə is elided both word finally and word initially; the Western Catalan dialects, which have little or no centralization of unstressed vowels, probably have less elision (Wheeler 1986). It is reasonably safe to conclude that, in general, elision is favoured the more features are shared by the elidable vowel with the surviving vowel and the more the elidable vowel is shortened, centralized, and weakly articulated. The converse of this latter conclusion is well supported: stressed vowels are generally more resistant to elision than unstressed vowels. In Modern Greek, under certain conditions stress blocks coalescence and most types of elision (Kaisse 1982; Nespor 1987; Condoravdi 1990). When a stressed vowel is elided, stress need not be lost, but can remain in the original sequential position, now mapped onto its new vocalic occupant: Chicano Spanish *vendrá Inéz* → *vendr' Ínéz* 'Ines will come'; similarly Puerto Rican Spanish *podrá iniciár* → *podr' íniciár* 'he will be able to begin'; with prodelision, Modern Greek *τό 'χω* just cited. Similarly, in tone languages the tones of final elided vowels can be reassociated with the first vowel of the next word as in KiRundi (Burundi: Goldsmith 1990); in Efik (Nigeria: Simmons 1980), when vowels are elided in sandhi, if the tones of the contiguous vowels are different, contour tones result on the unelided vowel; in other words, the segmental properties are elided but the tonal properties are not, a situation that is again conveniently represented in an autosegmental framework.

The postlexical status of elision has a number of important consequences. Like resyllabification, elision can apply after major allophonic rules. In Modern Greek, the palatalization and rounding of consonants in the environment of front and rounded vowels respectively remains a property of the consonant even if the vowel is then elided and the newly contiguous vowel is not front or, respectively, round (Kaisse 1985; Condoravdi 1990). In Maasai (Kenya: Tucker et al. 1955), a Low tone vowel may contribute to the environment triggering tonal catathesis even if it is elided. Word internal processes of vowel deletion may be more constrained than those found in sandhi: this is the case for identical vowel

coalescence in Modern Greek and Italian (Nespor 1987). Root syllables can be particularly resistant to vowel loss, whereas inflectional
syllables are prone to all sorts of reductions (Gauthiot 1913). In Auca
(Ecuador: Pike 1964), a sequence of two vowels is heterosyllabic in the
root but homosyllabic in the suffix. Word internal vowel coalescence and
elision can also involve rules not identical to the sandhi rules: in Castilian
Spanish 'alcohol' is *alcól* with a lengthened vowel in slow speech and *alcól*
with a vowel of normal length in fast speech, whereas 'four eyes' is always
cuatr' ójos with a vowel of normal length. Vowel contraction in Classical
Persian verse affects lefthand short front vowels at clitic boundaries only;
it does not apply either between two lexical items or between root and
suffix. Contraction, coalescence and elision in Bantu languages such as
Zulu are distributed according to lexical and syntactic criteria, with variation from one language to another (Doke 1926). In Kinyarwanda, elision
applies between words in the domain of the major phrase (Chambon
1991); in Kinyarwanda verse, elision applies consistently not only line
internally but also across lines, and line initial vowels do not contribute
to the mora count (Coupez et al. 1970).

Elision in Greek

Elision in Greek conforms to a number of the crosslinguistic trends just
surveyed. For a vowel to be elided in Greek (Lobeck 1804; Kühner et
al. 1890; Brugmann 1913; Maas 1962; West 1982), it has to meet a
number of different criteria: phonological criteria relating to the quantity and quality of the vowel, morphological and lexical criteria specifying whether a word or an ending belongs to the class of elidables, and
prosodic domain criteria requiring that elision occur within and not
between domains largely determined by syntactic constituency. Elision
is not blocked by a rough breathing (p. 20).

Long vowels are not elided. Elision of mid and low vowels is relatively unrestricted; of the high vowels -*υ* is never elided in Attic, -*ι* is
elided in certain words and categories only. The elision of -*αι* in certain
verbal endings is well attested in comedy

> κολάσ' ἔξεστι *Clouds* 7
> γῆμ' ἐπῆρε *Clouds* 43;

in tragedy, manuscript readings such as

> λειφθήσομ' ἤδη *Philoctetes* 1071
> σῴζεσθ' αὐτός *I. T.* 679

are emended. Elision of -*αι* apparently involves loss of intervocalic glide,
as in some types of crasis, followed by elision of *a* (Allen 1973); elision
of -*αι* is avoided by Demosthenes (Sommerstein 1973).

Elision of monosyllabic words is restricted: σά is not elided by itself but it may be elided in the composite τά σά *O. T.* 405. -ι is elided in verbal endings; in the dative endings of the third declension it is elided in Homer but not in Attic (Lobeck 1804). Prepositions ending in -ι such as ἀντί, ἐπί elide in Attic, but περί does not. In the Attic prose inscriptions δέ and οὐδέ elide more readily than τε and οὔτε (Threatte 1980).

The orthographic representation of elision involves omission of the elided vowel; the most straightforward interpretation of this fact is that an elided vowel was completely deleted at normal speech rates. Reduction to a hypershort vowel rather than total deletion may have occurred at slower speech rates as a transitional stage between unreduced citation form pronunciation in artificially slow speech and complete deletion in normal speech. The degree of reduction may also have varied according to the domain boundary between the two words. However, there is a long tradition of scholars who assume that at normal speech rates, even within the domain of the minor phrase, elision involved hypershortening and not complete deletion (Markland on Eur. *Supplices* 901; Ahrens 1845; Meyer 1896; Rossi 1969; Ruijgh 1981). The fact that elision can occur at the caesura and at change of speaker within the line is not necessarily an argument in favour of this position: resyllabification and rhythmic mapping also continue through caesura and antilabe. Elision at the diaeresis in the trimeter does constitute a permissible form of caesura, but the phonetic implications of this phenomenon are unclear (Allen 1973:21). If the elided vowel after a voiceless stop consonant before a word with a rough breathing is not completely deleted, then the delay in voice onset must be assumed to pass back into the hypershortened vowel. The interpretation of Hegelochus' speech error at *Orestes* 279 is further complicated if γαλήν᾽ and γαλῆν are not segmentally identical; this also applies to puns involving elided nonlexicals: γ᾽ἔρανον–γέρανον Athenaeus 8.338, τήνδ᾽ἐμοῦσαν–τήνδε μοῦσαν Athenaeus 14.616, ἀπ᾽ὄνου –ἀπὸ νοῦ scholiast on *Clouds* 1273. The musical settings generally treat elision as complete deletion of the final vowel: the elided vowel is not written, and no separate note is assigned to it (ME 6.1–2). Nevertheless, there are two instances in settings of iambotrochaic metre in which

ME 6.1   ν ά μ α τ᾽ ἐ π ι ν ί σ ε τ α ι   *Ath.* 7

ME 6.2   ν] η ν έ μ ο υ ς δ᾽ ἔ σ χ ε ν   *Lim.* 9

a metrically elided vowel is written on the papyrus and assigned a note of its own (ME 6.3–4). In neither case is there any indication of the

TABLE 6.8
Elided word ends as a percentage of all word ends
in the trimeter (data from van Raalte 1986)

	Elided word ends %
Semonides	10.91
Sophocles	15.29

ME 6.3 $\overset{\mathsf{M\ P\ \overline{PC}}}{\delta\grave{\epsilon}\ \acute{o}\mu o\tilde{\upsilon}}$ *DAM* 37.16

ME 6.4 $\underset{\eta\grave{\upsilon}\tau\acute{\epsilon}\kappa\nu\eta\sigma\alpha\ \grave{\epsilon}\gamma\acute{\omega}}{]\ \mathsf{P\ M:\overline{MZ}}}$ *DAM* 38.ii.3

rhythmical status of the elided and following vowels. In each case, the syllable following the elision must be light, so that if the musical rhythm did not depart substantially from the metre, the elided vowel was presumably treated as hypershort, and perhaps the following vowel too, yielding a musical ornament (West 1992).

Elision is a postlexical rule that causes connected speech to deviate from a string of citation forms. Although, in principle, words in context are more intelligible than citation forms while words excised from their context are less intelligible than citation forms (Oakeshott-Taylor 1980), elision presumably adds a degree of complexity to speech processing; and, at least in its more extended domains, elision may also carry with it the associations of style and register that typically characterize conversational speech. Either or both of these factors could explain why elision overall, expressed as the percentage of all word ends that are elided,

TABLE 6.9
Elided word ends as a percentage of all word ends
in the fifth longum of the trimeter
(data from van Raalte 1986)

	Elided words ends in fifth longum %
Semonides	2.43
Aeschylus	3.66
Sophocles	12.46

is constrained in the stricter styles of the trimeter (Table 6.8). Elision of a word ending in fifth longum is even more strongly avoided in the stricter styles of the trimeter, indicating an additional level of constraint in the metrically sensitive coda (Table 6.9).

Domain of elision

The domain of elision is another area in which there is some degree of prima facie contradiction between metrical evidence and orthographic practice. In principle, both nonlexical and lexical words can be elided throughout the verse line. Elision of lexicals is permitted at the caesura

> ἡγεῖσθ᾽ ἀνόσιον *Orestes* 595
> κατθανούμεθ᾽ ἀξιώτατα *Orestes* 1061

even across a major syntactic boundary

> δεδράκασ᾽· οἷς Ὀλύμπιοι θεοὶ *Philoctetes* 315.

It has been noted that elision is relatively less frequent at the caesura in the hexameters of Callimachus and in the stricter styles of the trimeter (Descroix 1931; van Raalte 1986). However, what is avoided at the caesura in the trimeter is just what can appear at bridges and consequently is internal to the appositive group: single elided (and unelided) appositives and elided nonlexical trochee-shaped words (p. 310); the rate of elided lexicals at the caesura is not lower than the rate within the hemistich (Hedin 1994). In Homer, unelided short vowels in hiatus are found most commonly at major metrical or syntactic boundaries (Ahrens 1848; Shewan 1923). This metrical evidence suggests that the domain of elision is the major phrase, bounded by the metrically defined pause of line end. Elision is more sensitive to potential prosodic boundaries within the line, as evidenced by the results of syntactic constituency tests (p. 384), and elision across major phrase boundary within the line is an artificiality arising from the metrical restructuring of major phrases into verse lines. But elision of lexical words within the major phrase would be, on the evidence of verse, a normal property of connected speech in Greek. This assumption is corroborated by the fact that in Demosthenes, although hiatus is avoided relative to its incidence in Thucydides, elidable lexical word junctures are not (Hedin 1994). Elision of lexical words is avoided in the verse of Callimachus (Maas 1962) and in the prose of Isocrates (Blass 1893): this suggests that in deliberate speech, elision was mainly confined to the appositive group.

By contrast, in most prose inscriptions elision of lexical words is unusual, particularly before another lexical word; elision mainly affects nonlexicals (Lademann 1915; Henry 1964, 1967). In the manuscript tradition of prose authors, insofar as elision is orthographically noted, it is likewise predominantly in the domain of the appositive group, much more rarely in the domain of the minor phrase. In Demosthenes, many, but not all, of the instances of elision between two lexical words in modern texts lack manuscript authority. The appropriate editorial practice for elision in general was the subject of some dispute even in the early nineteenth century: "Reiskius... pro arbitrio in Demosthenem elisiones innumeras intulit" (Wunderlich 1810). It appears on the basis of some samples that the manuscripts of Demosthenes agree with each other in having elision or scriptura plena in any particular case about 80% of the time, and that the papyri agree with the manuscripts about 90% of the time, although there are cases of elided spellings corrected into scriptura plena on papyri (McCabe 1981). It is not clear to what extent this relative unity of orthographic practice is a useful guide regarding the occurrence of elision in the oral delivery of Demosthenes' speeches. As already noted, it is traditionally argued that if hiatus in the manuscript tradition of an author is largely confined to instances involving elidable vowels, then the hiatus is orthographic and not phonetic, even if later grammarians in antiquity can interpret unelided spellings literally (Dionysius of Halicarnassus *De Demosthene* 43; Reeve 1971).

The orthographic and the metrical evidence on the domain of elision can be reconciled by assuming that either or both have deviated from the faithful representation of ordinary speech. The free extension of elision to all words including lexicals throughout the stichos could be a poetic artificiality like the extension of vowel harmony from the word to the line in Kalmyk verse (Russia) and the obligatory archaic *e*-muet in French verse (Jakobson et al. 1979), or the extensive recourse to epenthetic vowels in Ponapean verse (Fischer 1959). Elision and apocope are partially conventionalized in Finnish verse (Leino 1986). Alternatively, the widespread orthographic reluctance to elide outside the appositive group could merely reflect the tendency for the orthography to spell lexical words in citation forms. The latter assumption has to be made in any case for scriptura plena in verse (Allen 1885; Threatte 1977)

παιδα ολοφυρομενος *CEG* 14
τοδε ιδεν I².987.

Such spellings indicate that elision need not be represented in the orthography, but it does not necessarily follow that the domains of elision were identical in verse and in prose. Elision is orthographically represented more readily in verse inscriptions than in prose inscriptions. This does not necessarily indicate that elision was more common in verse than in prose; it could simply be the case that the metrical requirement for elision and connected speech within the stichos discouraged word by word citation form spelling. The Cretan Gortyn code is a prose inscription which transmits the phonetics of connected speech in some detail; in addition to a variety of consonant sandhi phenomena, it provides a few cases of elided lexical words

> τα γραμματ᾽ εγραψε
> γυνα κερευονσ᾽ αι αποβαλοι
> ταν γυναικ᾽ απομοσαι.

The phrase punctuating inscriptions (p. 388) naturally do not elide across interpuncts

> επιτυχοντα : αι κα δειλεται *Naup.* 3
> ανχορεοντα : εν Λοϙρους *Naup.* 20
> καδαλεοιτο : αιτε *Her.* 8.

Between interpuncts, elision can occur, although *Oeanth.* elides only nonlexicals including lower numerals. In a couple of instances, an adverb is elided before its verb in a verb or participial phrase

> : τοι 'νταυτ᾽ εγραμενοι *Her.* 10
> ενθαδ᾽ εσταθησαν : *Eph. Art.* A.5,

but in a third instance elision fails when the adverb is in the subject phrase

> αι ενθενδε εσταθησαν *Eph. Art.* A.4.

Elision of lexicals, including higher numerals, is quite well represented in these inscriptions

> : ϙωι βασιλευς εδωϙ᾽ ωιγυπτιος : *Psamm.* 4
> : αι δειλετ᾽ ανχορειν *Naup.* 7
> : εν τριαϙοντ᾽ αμαραις : *Naup.* 42
> τριαϙοντ᾽ αμαραι : *Naup.* 42.

The placement of the interpuncts in

> καταλειπον : τα εν ται ιστιαι *Naup.* 7

is prima facie evidence for elision across minor phrase boundary. Apart from this instance, *Naup.* elides both nonlexicals and lexicals with consistency between interpuncts, that is within the minor phrase (it does not elide vowels before *h*). *Psamm.*, an archaic Ionic inscription, consistently applies the rules of connected speech between interpuncts — elision, crasis, assimilation of final nasals, movable nu. The inscriptional evidence just cited suggests that in ordinary speech elision was regular at least within the domain of the minor phrase. Only in deliberate speech would elision be restricted to the domain of the appositive group. Therefore, the orthography of prose texts commonly underrepresents the incidence of elision in normal speech. Furthermore, as already argued, it is reasonable to assume on the basis of the metrical evidence and of the practice of Demosthenes that, at least in fluent speech, elision was not restricted to the minor phrase but applied in the domain of the major phrase. That elision applied more easily within the syntactic phrase than across the boundary between syntactic phrases is established by additional data cited in Table 8.2.

Elision and the accent

When an accented vowel is elided, the accent is not deleted but retracted to the preceding syllable provided the elided word is not one of the socalled proclitics. There are no cases preserved of the settings of elided oxytones that are not proclitics, so that it cannot be determined whether the music treated the retracted accent as an acute in all cases (following the normative rule), as an acute over a short vowel and a circumflex over a long vowel or diphthong (thereby providing a tone bearing unit in the elided word for the accentual fall), or as a grave in place of an acute. There is some disagreement in the ancient grammatical tradition. If retraction to the first mora of long vowels was the norm or an acceptable variant and perceptually identical to the regular circumflex, it would follow that there was no accentual component in Hegelochus' speech error (p. 239).

The musical settings of elided paroxytones are so few that statistical inferences cannot be reliably drawn about the effect of elision on the accentual excursion. It appears that the interval of rise to the peak and the interval from the peak to a following unaccented word initial syllable were comparable to those found in unelided paroxytones in the case of lexical words, but that in the case of nonlexical words there was considerable reduction of the accent. In ME 6.5, there is continued pitch

ME 6.5 Ath. 5

ἔ-δραν ἄμ' [ἀ]-γα-κλυ-ται-εῖς

fall from the final syllable of ἔδραν to ἄμ' of an interval of 1.5 tones, so that ἄμ' is treated more like an enclitic than an accented prepositive. Similarly, elided ὅδ' is set an octave lower than orthotone ἔστ' in ME 6.9 below. By contrast, in ME 6.6 the pitch relations are compatible with those of a proper name paroxytone.

ME 6.6 Lim. 14

'Ατ-[θ]ίδ' ἐ - πὶ γ\α/ - α - λ[όφωι

Elision does not seem to affect pitch movement in elided proparoxytones. In the Delphic hymns, the fall from the pitch peak to the following syllable is very close to that found in unelided proparoxytones: the mean for elided proparoxytones is 1.20 tones, and that for unelided proparoxytones (not under emphasis, not initial or final in the clause and not in proper names) is 1.29 tones. This means that elision does not occasion any compensation for the further pitch fall (a semitone on the average) that would have occurred on the final vowel in the absence of elision; this fits with the idea that the further fall is demarcative rather than a component of the accent. ME 6.7–8 are examples of elided proparoxytones from musical settings that respect the accent.

ME 6.7

νά - ματ' ἐ - πι - νί - σε-ται   *Ath.* 7

ME 6.8

αὖ - ξετ' ἀ - γη - ρά - τωι   *Lim.* 39

Of the seven elided proparoxytones with heavy accented syllable that are well enough preserved to tell, only one, συύριγμ' *Lim.* 30, bears a melism on the accented syllable. There are only two cases of elided paroxytones with heavy accented syllable, both ἔστ', ME 6.9 and *DAM* 39.11: in both cases ἔστ' is set to a falling melism. If this small dataset

ME 6.9

ὅδ' ἔστ' 'Α - χιλ - [λέως παῖς   *DAM* 37.18

could be taken as representative, then the association of melisms with elided paroxytones would be significant; there is only a probability of less than $p = 0.042$ (7!3!/9!2!) that a divergence this great would arise in samples of respectively seven and two proparoxytones and paroxytones. This suggests that there was some form of compensation for the postpeak fall that would otherwise be lost when the final vowel was elided in paroxytones. It is also interesting, although it cannot be proven statistically significant, that in musical settings that respect the accent only nonlexical paroxytones are elided before a word begininng with an accented vowel: if this is a real constraint, at least for elided pyrrhic-shaped paroxytones, it could conceivably suggest a phonological constraint on elision in slow speech designed to preserve the full High-Low movement of the accent in lexical words. That elided high frequency disyllabic lexicals like πόδ' and even ἦλθ' can become rhythmically prepositive at more fluent speech rates is indicated by some metrical data (p. 325).

Crasis

Greek also has vowel contraction across word boundary, which differs from elision both phonologically and morpholexically. In some cases, two nonhigh vowels are contracted into a single long vowel which belongs to the inventory of lexically occurring long vowels; this sort of contraction is termed crasis

τἀπολολοτα I².74.17
τὠφθαλμώ *Clouds* 362
θὦπλ᾽ *Birds* 449
ἐγὠνταμειβόμην *Cologne Epode* 6.

The long vowel resulting from crasis may be the first element of a long diphthong

τᾱὐτ᾽ II².5673
ἠυσέβεια *I. T.* 1202.

The phonological rules for this postlexical contraction are in principle the same as those for lexical contraction, except that Attic tends to preserve the quality of the first vowel of the second word

ἀνήρ *Bacchae* 848
τἀπόλλωνος *Birds* 982; contrast τὀπολλονι *LSAG* 51.6,
τὀπελονι XIV.1,

just as in certain lexical contractions the quality of the vowel of the ending is allowed to predominate, as in *ἁπλᾶ*. Such forms may have encouraged a reanalysis of crasis as elision with vowel lengthening (Schwyzer 1959)

χἰκετεύετε *Helen* 1024
θὔδωρ *Crates* 17.5KA
χὐοι *CEG* 42.

An intervocalic glide may be dropped resulting in crasis with a following vowel

κἀμάτευες *O. T.* 1052
ἀρχαί *Clouds* 1197
κἐμι *ABV* 85,

or with two following vowels

μοὐταῖρος *Ecclesiazusae* 912 ← μοι ὁ ἑταῖρος
χὀλεφας ← καὶ ὁ ἐλέφας *LSAG* 16.4.

Contraction of two monophthongal vowels in sandhi can also result in a diphthong which belongs to the inventory of lexically occurring diphthongs; this sort of contraction may be called phonological synaeresis

θοἰμάτιον *Clouds* 179
θαἰμάτια *Wasps* 408.

In other cases contraction of monophthongal vowels or diphthongs apparently results in a new type of diphthong or triphthong which does not belong to the underlying phonological inventory, or at least does not pattern with the lexically occurring diphthongs; this sort of contraction may be called phonological synizesis

> μὴ ἄλλην *Thesmophoriazusae* 476
> ἦ οἰχόμεσθ᾽ *Trachiniae* 85
> ἐπεὶ οὐδ᾽ *Philoctetes* 948.

It is not clear from the orthography to what extent such prima facie synizeses could actually be pronounced as crases, elisions or prodelisions, particularly in rapid speech; the same holds for lexical synizeses such as τειχέων Eur. *Electra* 615. For μὴ plus alpha privative, the orthography usually indicates synizesis

> μὴ ἀδικεῖν *Eumenides* 691
> μὴ ἀμαθεῖς *Troades* 981

but for μὴ plus prefixal ἀπο-, the manuscripts vary, for whatever reason (Scheindler 1896; Platnauer 1960)

> μὴ (ἀ)πολακτίσῃς *P.V.* 651 (Dawe 1964:226)
> μὴ ἀπολείπεσθαι Soph. *Electra* 1169; ἀ- is partly erased
>   in L (Jebb ad loc.).

The above phonological classification of contractions crossclassifies to some extent with the traditional orthographic classification; a case like

> εἰ δὲ μή, ἡμεῖς *Thesmophoriazusae* 536

is an orthographic synizesis, but since identical vowels can easily coalesce, it may be a phonological crasis.

The environments of contraction and elision in Attic are practically mutually exclusive. Contraction is basically an extension of a lexical rule, and its domain is a subset of those structures that can form an appositive group, namely those appositive groups that are the most cohesive for phonological or syntactic reasons or because of their high discourse frequency (Ahrens 1845); other appositives, like nonappositives, elide rather than contract. The article and the relative contract, but other determiners elide

> τοὔνειδος *I.A.* 305
> τοῦτ᾽ ὄνειδος *Alcestis* 721
> ἀπόνησα *H.F.* 259.

καὶ contracts, but ἀλλά elides

> κἀναθήματα *Antigone* 286
> ἀλλ᾽ ἀνδρὸς *Andromache* 872.

Disyllabic prepositions elide rather than contract

> κατ᾽ ἄκρων *Phoenissae* 1176
> ὑπ᾽ αὐτὴν *Phoenissae* 1178.

Contraction can occur, though less frequently, between a lexical word and a postpositive

> δοῦνᾰν ἐμαυτῆς *Lysistrata* 116
> οἰμώξετᾰρ᾽ *Thesmophoriazusae* 248.

Crasis between two lexical words is quite unusual

> : εξ Αιγυπτώγαγων : *Psamm.* 3,

except in lexicalized phrases

> τύχἀγαθῇ *Birds* 436
> ὁσημέραι *Plutus* 1006.

The style of Herodas is marked by a high incidence of synizesis including instances not in an appositive group

> τῆς ληκύθου ἡμέων 3.8
> παῦσαι· ἱκαναὶ 3.81
> λέγω, αὕτη 4.42
> βίου ὄνησις 7.34.

These may represent an artificial Hellenistic extension of the metrical practice of Hipponax, but it does not necessarily follow that these forms would also have been linguistically artificial in archaic Ionic. Synizesis between lexical words is also found in Aeolic verse

> ὠράνω αἴθερος *Sappho* 1.11.

Prodelision

When a word ends in a long vowel, that vowel cannot be elided; but if the next word begins with a short vowel, that short vowel can be elided under certain conditions: this is termed prodelision (Ahrens 1845; Lucius 1885; Platnauer 1960). In prodelision, the principle that the weaker of two vowels is elided takes precedence over the principle that the lefthand vowel is preferentially elided. Prodelision is comparatively rare after diphthongs; the vowels *o*, *ι* and *υ* are not prodelided. Prodelision may apply to the first vowel of nonlexical or lexical words, but in a lexical word the prodelided vowel is predominantly the vowel of a prefix such as the augment or a prepositional prefix

> μόχθου 'πικουφίζουσαν Eur. *Electra* 72
> παγκοίνῳ 'δάμη *Septem* 608
> με 'ποσταμεν *Naup.* 11.

Prodelision of a nonprefixal vowel in a lexical word is less common

> μή 'σθιε *Knights* 1106
> καλή 'χουσ᾽ *Lysistrata* 646
> φθιμενη 'χω II².10650

ε 'δελφεον *Naup.* 7
ε 'χεπαμον *Naup.* 16.

In drama, prodelision affects ἐξ more commonly than ἐς, and ἀπό and ἀνά are prodelided, but not ἀντί, ἀμφί or ἄνευ. Prodelision is also found with polysyllabic nonlexicals, including nonprefixed words in comedy

μὴ 'νταῦθα *I. T.* 1322
: τοι 'νταυτ' *Her.* 10
μὴ 'τέρωσε *Acharnians* 828
φράσω· 'πειδὴ *Clouds* 1354.

The use of prodelision is constrained in the stricter styles of verse: its incidence per thousand lines ranges from 4 in Aeschylus to 13 in Sophocles and 23 in Aristophanes (Platnauer 1960).

Prodelision is a phonological process distinct from crasis: prodelision is deletion of the second vowel, crasis is contraction of the vowel sequence into a long vowel or diphthong. A degree of indeterminacy arises because in many environments the output of both rules would be segmentally identical, so that it might appear that prodelision is simply crasis in a subset of its environments

ἡπίνοια − ἡ 'πίνοια *Antigone* 389.

However, the two processes can often be distinguished in terms of their environments and of their outputs. When the righthand word is a lexical word, in crasis there is no restriction on its structure, whereas in prodelision, as just noted, the prodelided vowel is predominantly the first vowel of a prefix. When the lefthand word is a lexical word, for crasis the second word is as a rule nonlexical

κλαύσἄρα←κλαύσῃ ἄρα *Peace* 532,

whereas for prodelision it may be a lexical beginning with a prefix

σκυτίνη 'πικουρία *Lysistrata* 110.

There is also a potential normative difference in the accentuation of the output: in crasis, a lefthand nonlexical loses its orthographic accent, whereas in prodelision it maintains the accent

κἀπικούρησιν *Andromache* 28
ἢ 'πικουρία *Hecuba* 872.

It is possible that a grave is changed to an acute if the prodelided vowel was accented (Postgate 1924)

μή 'θιγες *Antigone* 546; see also *Knights* 1106, *Lysistrata* 646 cited above.

Finally, there are some environments in which the segmental output of crasis is not identical to that of prodelision: *-οι, -αι* and *-ῳ* in crasis lose the glide and contract

μούγκώμιον ← μοι ἐγκώμιον *Clouds* 1205
ἀρχαὶ ← αἱ ἀρχαὶ *Clouds* 1197
τὸπιϜοιϙοι *Naup.* 34,

whereas in prodelision, to the extent that they could occur, these diphthongs presumably remained intact

κελητίσαι 'κέλευον *Wasps* 501
περιόψομαι 'πελθόντ' *Frogs* 509.

These last instances are indeterminate between prodelision and crasis, the latter being rare between two lexical words.

RHYTHM IN CONNECTED SPEECH

A valuable body of experimental data has been established relevant to the temporal properties of prosodic units larger than the foot, but some degree of caution is necessary on the part of the reader in the interpretation of these results. In the first place, a distinction needs to be made between results derived from test sentences and results derived from connected discourse (Harris et al. 1974). Experiments using connected discourse afford a fairly reliable indication of the effects of rhythm in ordinary, random speech, but the variables are very difficult to control. Use of frame or carrier sentences controls for many of the variables, but constant repetition of such sentences, some of which are actually constructed so as to scan like verse, leads to a high degree of rhythmicization. Consequently, the results may have to be interpreted as indicating only the effects that rhythm can have under particularly favourable circumstances. There are also various other complications that arise from time to time in some publications. Apart from elementary problems like comparing open syllables to closed syllables ending in a voiced stop, some studies fail to distinguish foot rhythm from word rhythm, word rhythm from phrase rhythm, and prepausal lengthening from nonprepausal lengthening. Although these qualifications are mentioned at this point, they apply equally to some of the studies cited in other chapters. It is likely that the domains of rhythm are hierarchically organized with respect to one another, and that the lower ordered units have a reduced degree of the same properties that characterize the higher order units (p. 411), but this assumption is not always unambiguously demonstrated by the experimental results.

Up to this point, the temporal relations of syllables have been analyzed largely from the relatively static perspective of citation forms; it will also be necessary to investigate them from the dynamic point of view of connected speech. At a very slow dictation speed, each word is an autonomous rhythmic unit and is separated from contiguous words by pauses.

But, as has already been pointed out, when speech becomes more rapid and more fluent, rhythmic organization is assigned to domains greater than the individual word. Extending the domain of rhythmicization involves various modifications to the temporal relations of syllables generated by the rules of demarcation, of foot structure assignment and of mapping. The relevant processes, which will be referred to as readjustment of final lengthening, refooting and remapping, respectively, can apply separately or in conjunction with one another.

Readjustment of final lengthening

Evidence has already been cited (p. 148) that the amount of final lengthening is related to the hierarchy of prosodic domains; evidence has also been cited that in fluent speech prosodic domains encompass a larger span of phonosyntactic substance than in slow speech (p. 225); it follows from these two premises that final lengthening is not merely physically reduced as speech becomes more fluent but is also adjusted to reflect the progressively more extensive prosodic domains. This argument may be restated in concrete terms as follows. It was found that nonbranching subject noun phrases in simple sentences had less final lengthening than branching subject noun phrases, which suggests that, at normal rates of speech, the nonbranching noun phrase was not processed as a separate phonological phrase but was joined with the following verb phrase into a single phonological phrase, whereas the branching noun phrase was accorded the status of an autonomous phonological phrase (Goldhor in Klatt 1976). Final lengthening was less at the ends of words that were not the last word of the phonological phrase. To the extent that this branching distinction governs phonological phrasing at normal rates of speech but not at slow rates of speech, it illustrates the mechanism of readjustment.

Refooting

Like initial and final syllable structure, initial and final foot structure cannot always be optimized in citation forms; stray syllables have to be adjoined, which can result in surface amphibrach feet. In connected speech, too, foot structure is initially assigned within the domain of the word, a limitation which creates the potential for remedial reorganization particularly at the edges. Just as syllable structure can be improved by resyllabification, so foot structure can be improved by refooting. Refooting is a process by which a syllable is transferred from the word in which it belongs to a foot of a contiguous word in order to improve or regularize the rhythm. Refooting does not necessarily imply resyllabification; each rule has its own domain. A good illustration of refooting in English is provided by two rules of progressive vowel reduction, namely trochaic and dactylic shortening (Huggins 1975). These processes belong to the group of prosodic rules designed to minimize durational differences between feet. In an experiment already cited in Chapter 3 (Fowler 1977), in which the design may have encouraged rhythmical reading, the duration of the stressed vowel of the proper name in the sentence "Dave signed the paper" was 132 msec; in "Davis signed the paper" it was 120 msec; and in "Davidson signed the paper" it was 87 msec. The durational difference between the vowel of the monosyllabic foot *Dave* and the first vowel of the trochaic foot *Davis* is a highly significant auditory cue, as shown by reiterant speech experiments (Nakatani et al. 1978). When the sentence "Dave has signed the paper" is spoken at slow dictation speed, the surface foot structure will be "Dave | has signed |," as dictated by the syntax. But at the fairly rapid rate of speech used in the experiment, the duration of the stressed vowel of the first foot in "Dave has signed" was not the same as that in "Dave signed": in fact, it was hardly different from that in "Davis signed" (122 msec); similarly "Jan is running" and "Janice running." The only possible explanation is that the first syllable of the second foot, the syntactic proclitic *has*, became rhythmically enclitic by being transferred to the preceding foot, and consequently triggered trochaic shortening in the first foot. Similarly, dactylic shortening in the stressed syllable of the verb of "I notice Alicia" (90 msec) versus trochaic shortening in "I notice Lisa" (100 msec) involves refooting of the initial unstressed syllable of *Alicia*. This sort of result has been replicated in a more recent study (Fourakis et al. 1988). Refooting likewise explains why the duration of the word *speed* is greater in the sentence "Speed kills" than in the sentence "Speed increases" (Lehiste 1972; Cooper et al. 1980). Refooting seems to be a factor in slips of the ear like *the script of linguistics* for *descriptive linguistics* (Bond et al. 1980). The effect emerged both in spontaneous slips of the ear like *Sheila Fishley* for 'she'll officially' and in laboratory induced misperceptions of faintly presented speech like *music seen in phases* for 'music's even paces' (Cutler et al. 1992). In a gating experiment, in which the second half of a sentence was presented to subjects in incremental segments, refooting seems to underly erroneous perceptions such as *plumber* for *plum on [the tree]* (Grosjean 1985). Refooting is also presupposed by puns such as *Laura Norda* for 'law and order'; in British English *cuppa* 'cup of [tea],' the refooted form has actually become lexicalized. In Danish, the addition of an unstressed prefix to a nonsense word had a shortening effect on the preceding word, which suggests refooting (Fischer-Jørgensen 1982). Evidence for refooting has also been found in Swedish (Strangert 1985). It was noted above that resyllabification does not necessarily produce syllables identical to word internal syllables; transitional stages can occur. This is probably also true of refooting. Despite other potentially disturbing factors in the test sentences, the available data (Fowler 1977; Rakerd et al. 1987) suggest that trochaic and dactylic shortening can be weaker with refooting than word internally. It would follow in general that refooted feet need not be absolutely identical to the corresponding word internal feet resulting from the application of the lexical rules of foot structure assignment.

One important result of the study of refooting is that it can apply across a subject phrase–verb phrase boundary even when a stressed syllable preceding the boundary has undergone phrase final lengthening; a stressed syllable was found to be lengthened by about 45 milliseconds phrase finally, while both phrase medial and phrase final stressed syllables were shortened about 7 milliseconds by a following unstressed syllable in the next word: the phrase final lengthening did not eliminate or diminish the trochaic shortening due to refooting (Rakerd et al. 1987). This result, which was not evident from earlier studies (Cooper et al. 1980), suggests that the domain of footing can cross a phrase boundary; this has direct implications for the Greek metrical caesura, which is a foot internal phonological phrase boundary (p. 399).

Evidence was cited in the preceding paragraph suggesting that an English utterance such as "Dave has signed the paper" can be trochaic not only in verse but also in fairly rapid conversational speech. Consequently, refooting is not simply an artificiality of versification, but rather a natural process in the rhythmic production of ordinary speech, even if its domain can be artificially extended in verse. Both in English and in Swedish, the speaker has the option to refoot, but is not obliged to do so. There is no reason not to assume the same for refooting in Greek. For instance, in a series of amphibrach words (#ŠŠŠ#) spoken at a slow rate of speech, each word is demarcated from the next word and the contiguous light syllables cannot be mapped onto the same arsis. In more fluent speech, demarcation is more likely to be reduced and refooting (and remapping) can apply. The more the underlying word based rhythm is iterated, the more difficult it is for refooting to negate it. This is probably one component of the defective rhythm in the notorious line

ἣ δὲ χίμαιραν ἔτικτε πνέουσαν... Hesiod *Theogony* 319.

In iambic verse, there are very rigid constraints on refooting to a disyllabic arsis. The socalled split anapaest rule, as it applies to Aristophanes, states that a disyllabic arsis in iambic metre may not consist of the unelided final syllable of a word and the initial syllable of the next word, if both words are lexical or if either word is a nonlexical not cohering with the other: an instance like κροκωτὰ φοροῦσαι *Lysistrata* 44 Rav.

violates this rule. While the split anapaest rule could simply reflect the additional cost and complexity of refooting, it probably also indicates that, at least at certain rates of speech, a refooted disyllabic arsis involving two lexical words was not identical to a word internal disyllabic arsis, presumably because some form of demarcation persisted after refooting. In English verse too, the weight of the syllables filling the weak positions of an anapaest are much more strictly regulated in iamboanapaestic verse than in pure anapaests (Hanson 1992).

It is reasonable to assume that for Greek too a measurable result of refooting was a change in the absolute and relative durations of the syllables in the foot. This was probably the case not only when refooting resulted in a change from underlying rising rhythm to surface falling rhythm or vice versa, for instance an iamb-shaped word in a trochaic tetrameter as in

ἵεται ξίφος κελαινὸν... *Bacchae* 628,

but also when the effect of refooting was to change a monosyllabic arsis to a disyllabic arsis, as when iamb- and trochee-shaped words occur in dactylic or anapaestic rhythm.

Although refooting as a general phenomenon is well supported typologically, it is not necessarily the case that in any particular language refooting generates rising and falling rhythm in speech with equal facility. In English speech, refooting is principally associated with falling rhythm, that is with left dominant feet. Various factors might contribute to this situation in English. Trochaic rhythm is more suited to rapid speech than iambic rhythm. Iambic foot structure is comparatively rare in lexical words (Cutler et al. 1992), and consequently refooting to trochaic structure increases conformity with the canonical lexical stress template. A preference for trochaic foot structure is also a factor conditioning the omission of unstressed syllables in lexical words and in clitic groups in English child language, where it is more common in iambic than in trochaic feet (Gerken 1991). The rhythm of Greek conversational speech is reported by ancient authorities to have been basically iambic (p. 117), and this may suggest that refooting of arsis (or stray) syllables left to right was more natural in Greek speech than refooting right to left. At least in principle, some caution is necessary when extrapolating from refooting in verse to refooting in speech: verse may have involved more consistent ῥυθμοποιία through more extensive domains. It has been asserted that in a preponderantly trochaic language the existence of iambic verse is a poetic artificiality having no counterpart in speech (Nord et al. 1989). This view, which implies that refooting is obligatory at all speech rates, has not been supported by empirical evidence. If refooting in speech was preferentially unidirectional, and if refooting is characteristic of fluent speech, it would follow that the rhythm of fluent speech would have been rather different and more uniform than that of slow speech. These questions are so basic that it is worth at least speculating about the implications of different assumptions. In English, a simple utterance like "Mary married Arthur Fowler" has trochaic rhythm both in slow speech and in rapid speech. But a simple utterance like "The book is on the shelf" has iambic surface rhythm at slow dictation speed, but in fluent conversational speech one possible version would be trochaic with refooting.

Remapping

Whereas refooting involves associating arsis or stray syllables with a thesis in a different word, remapping is a process in which the thesis-arsis relations assigned to the word in isolation by the lexical rules of rhythmic organization are modified to take account of the rhythmic environment of contiguous words in the domain and repair defective prominence alternation at some level in the hierarchy. Remapping is illustrated by the so-called rhythm rule (Liberman et al. 1977; Kiparsky 1979; Selkirk 1984; Giegerich 1985; Shattuck-Hufnagel 1988). In English, in very general terms remapping reverses the strength relations in the sequence secondary stress foot + primary stress foot when another primary stress foot follows. Provided the words are not pronounced with intervening phonological phrase boundary or with focus accent on the first word, *Chinése expert* will be pronounced *Chínese expert* if it means 'an expert who is Chinese.' The syllables potentially affected by the English rhythm rule can be neither too weak nor too strong. The rhythm rule cannot shift primary stress onto an unstressed syllable (Kaisse 1987): it is not possible to remap *revéred expert* → *révered expert*. Conversely, the syllable that is weakened cannot be one that is the strongest in its domain, as would be the main stress of a major phrase or the primary stress in a compound phrase: *Chinése expert* is unaffected by the rhythm rule if it means 'an expert on China,' since in such "compound" phrases the main stress is on the first word. The rhythm rule applies more easily when the stresses are contiguous than when they are separated by unstressed syllables. It can also apply throughout the phrasal domain: many speakers will say "to counteráct the interféring accelerátion" but "to cóunteract the ínterfering fórce" (Bolinger 1986). Like many rules of connected speech, the rhythm rule in English is apparently sensitive to lexical frequency and to speech rate.

Similar stress reversals occur in many other languages, for instance German and Amuesha (Peru: Fast 1953). In the standard Italian of northern Italy, the stress can be remapped onto a lexically unstressed syllable if the word has no available secondary stress, perhaps because unstressed syllables are less reduced in Italian than they are in English: so not only *ònoró Búdda* → *ónoro Búdda* 'he honoured Buddha,' but also *metá tórta* → *méta tórta* 'half a cake' (Nespor et al. 1986). Where remapping does not occur, the durational interval between the contiguous stresses is increased. In Tuscan Italian this durational increment can make a consonant with raddoppiamento sintattico even longer (Nespor 1990); consequently remapping applies after resyllabification. Similarly in Greek remapping applies to resyllabified structures.

Since remapping modifies or actually reverses the underlying rhythmic prominence relations in a word, it is a fairly drastic process, and the evidence of Greek verse suggests that remapping is rather severely constrained in anything except fluent speech. Table 6.10 compares the incidence of tribrach- and fourth paeon-shaped words, expressed as percentages of all resolutions of each word shape, located before and after the penthemimeral caesura in the trimeter of Euripides. Tribrach-shaped words are admitted, although with some degree of constraint, before the caesura even in the Severior and Semiseverus styles

> ὅσιος αὐτὸς *Heraclidae* 719
> ἄδικα *Hecuba* 801,

whereas fourth paeon-shaped words are excluded before the caesura until the Liber style

> ἑλομένη *Helen* 294
> ἀνοσίῳ *Helen* 869.

The precaesural avoidance of the fourth paeon-shaped word is not merely an effect of the well documented preference for locating resolution at the beginning of the hemistich; some additional factor is causing a greater degree of constraint on the fourth paeon-shaped word relative to the tribrach-shaped word. That additional factor is the cost of remapping Š̂ŠŠŠ to Š̌ŠŠŠ when the preceding word ends in a thesis.

TABLE 6.10
Tribrach- and fourth paeon-shaped words
before and after the caesura

	ŠŠ|₃Š %	ŠŠŠ|₃Š %	ŠŠ|₄Š %	ŠŠ|₄ŠŠ %
Severior	4.50	0.00	70.07	74.71
Semiseverus	11.03	0.00	75.06	63.46
Liber	9.62	5.62	62.34	65.26
Liberrimus	13.77	20.83	52.04	53.57

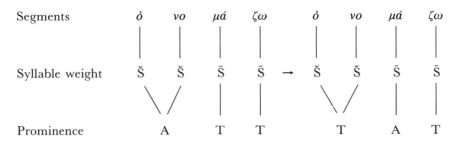

FIGURE 6.9
Remapping in the ionic a minore word shape

   In the case of the fourth paeon-shaped word, remapping involved shifting the matrix from lexical thesis to arsis. In the case of the ionic a minore
word shape (ŠŠŠŠ), remapping changes the initial disyllabic arsis into
a thesis through matrix formation and the following thesis into arsis
through subordination, as illustrated in Figure 6.9. The phrasally organized rhythm triggers the combined application of two subsidiary mapping
rules resulting in a particularly radical departure from lexical rhythm.
Table 6.11 gives the rate of occurrence per thousand trimeters of ionic
a minore-shaped words beginning in second and fourth longum respectively

θεραπεύειν μέλη *Orestes* 222
ἐπιβᾶσαι πέτραν *Bacchae* 1097.

In contrast to many other word shapes which show significant growth
in the rate of resolution with each style change (Table 3.3), resolution
in the ionic a minore word shape shows no significant growth prior to
Euripides Liber: this reflects the complexity of the remapping in this
word shape.

TABLE 6.11
Rate per thousand trimeters
of ionic a minore word shape

	Beginning in second longum	Beginning in fourth longum
Aeschylus	0.00	0.47
Sophocles	0.13	0.27
Severior	0.00	0.68
Semiseverus	0.36	0.36
Liber	0.41	5.83
Liberrimus	2.09	12.20

In the fourth paeon and ionic a minore word shapes, remapping involves the application of matrix formation or subordination or both to syllables within the word to which these subsidiary mapping rules did not apply in the lexical rhythm: in neither case was the final syllable of the word affected. As a consequence of the principle of final syllable prominence (p. 124), final syllables are more resistant than internal syllables to the reductions occasioned by remapping. When a word consists of or ends in two light syllables, the final syllable is rhythmically stronger than the penultimate syllable in the citation form. In dactylic verse, the final syllable can be weakened and remapped to become the second syllable of a disyllabic arsis, but this is forbidden in iambic verse by the socalled divided anapaest rule. The divided anapaest rule, as it applies to Aristophanes, states that with very few exceptions a disyllabic arsis in iambic metre may not consist of the last two syllables of a lexical word (not including high frequency pyrrhic-shaped imperatives) if there is no elision and if the following word is not a nonlexical cohering to the left; some pyrrhic-shaped lexical words occur line initially in Menander

> πάθος ἐμπεσεῖν *Aspis* 402
> ὄχλος ὡς ἔοικε *Dyscolus* 405
> ἀγρὸν εὐσεβέστερον *Georgus* 35.

While the divided anapaest rule could simply reflect the additional cost and complexity of remapping, it probably also indicates that, at least for certain rates of speech, a remapped disyllabic arsis was not identical to a word internal disyllabic arsis. Remapping involving matrix formation and subordination in appositive groups is analyzed below (p. 308).

Remapping involving subordination of the final heavy syllable of a lexical word not standing before a postpositive is strictly forbidden in tragedy by Porson's bridge; even an example with two proper names

> Ἀριόμαρδος Σάρδεσιν *Persae* 321

has not been accepted by all editors. This constraint is very significantly relaxed in comedy

> τοὺς πολίτας σώσετε *Ecclesiazusae* 414
> λοιδορῆσαι βούλομαι *Lysistrata* 1128
> ἐραστὴν πραγμάτων *Clouds* 1459

and in Hipponax and Herondas

> προσδέκονται χάσκοντες Hipponax 9.1 (Haslam 1986)
> κἀποτάκτους λωβεῦμαι Herodas 3.69
> τὸν σίδηρον τρώγουσιν Herodas 3.76.

The related constraint in the hexameter against word end after contracted biceps in the fourth foot is likewise relaxed in the mime section of

Theocritus 15 (DS 1984), and Rupprecht's bridge in the catalectic anapaestic dimeter of tragedy is relaxed in comedy

μηδ' ἄκων ἐγκαθεδεῖται *Frogs* 1523.

This extension of subordination to the final syllable of lexical words in the less formal styles of verse might merely be ascribed to less stringent metrical practice in the less formal styles of verse. However, it is also possible to assume that it reflects the more fluent phrasing of less formal speech. The fact that punctuation and even change of speaker (as at *Ecclesiazusae* 755) can occur at long third anceps in comedy is not a very strong argument against a linguistic basis for the violation of Porson's bridge in comedy, since elision and resyllabification, which have an undisputed linguistic basis, can also occur across change of speaker; for instance, *Clouds* 849 has elision across a divided anapaest with change of speaker.

There is some revealing evidence from Aristophanes which illustrates how major phrase or sentence boundary can be used to prevent remapping and to maintain a rhythm closer to the basic lexical rhythm. In the trimeter of Aristophanes, an anapaest following a resolved longum is strongly avoided except bridging the boundary of the first metron (Stephens 1988b), and in this location the anapaest is almost always preceded by a major syntactic boundary (Pongratz 1902): either a new sentence, with change of speaker at *Birds* 108, or a clause containing a finite verb begins with the anapaest

ἀλλ' ἀθάνατος. ὁ γὰρ Ἀμφίθεος *Acharnians* 47
ὥσπερ κέραμον, ἵνα μὴ καταγῇ *Acharnians* 928
καὶ θοἰμάτιον· ὅτε δὴ δ' ἐκεῖνο *Ecclesiazusae* 315.

Despite the small number of examples available, it is possible to show that this constraint is genuine and noncoincidental. The data in Table 6.12 show that in a sample consisting of the *Acharnians* and the *Lysistrata*

TABLE 6.12

Major syntactic boundary
after word final resolved second longum

	With boundary %	Without boundary %	N
Disyllabic anceps	80.00	20.00	5
Monosyllabic anceps	11.86	88.14	59

$$\omega = 29.71, \ p[k \rangle 1] = 0.0024$$

the rate of major syntactic boundaries after a word final resolved second longum is significantly greater when the following anceps is disyllabic than when it is monosyllabic. The odds for a boundary are almost thirty times greater before disyllabic anceps; the observed difference or a more extreme one has a chance of less than one in four hundred of arising by chance in comparisons of this size. Similar significant results are found when the test is made against the frequency of major syntactic boundaries before disyllabic anceps preceded by unresolved second longum. It follows that, in the absence of a boundary, the syllable sequence would not have been metrical in iambic rhythm. Perhaps it would have been organized trochaically with the resolution matrix on the first two light syllables of the tribrach and prolongation of the first syllable of the anapaest. The effect of the boundary is to block this syntagmatic mapping and allow the anapaest to retain its underlying lexically assigned rising rhythm.

Domain of remapping

Unlike resyllabification and elision, whose domains extend to the phrase, the rules of remapping mainly involve the appositive group (p. 308). In split resolutions, the first syllable of the matrix is typically a nonlexical, while the second syllable either is another nonlexical or belongs to the lexical host word of the appositive group

> τίς ὁ τρόπος *H.F.* 965
> τίς ὄλεθρος *Orestes* 1126.

When resolution occurs such that the matrix consists of a disyllabic word, particularly in the stricter styles the word is preferentially elided, nonlexical or followed by a postpositive

> πατέρ᾽ ἀποιμώξῃ *Medea* 31
> διὰ φόνου *Andromache* 175
> γόνυ σὸν Eur. *Supplices* 165.

Likewise, in split and divided anapaests both syllables typically belong to an appositive group

> τὰ μέτωπ᾽ *Knights* 631
> μετὰ τἀνδρὸς *Ecclesiazusae* 243,

although trochee-shaped nonlexicals are comparatively rare

> τόνδε λέβητα *Cyclops* 343.

There is an interesting parallel in Finnish iamboanapaestic verse, where, if the arsis is disyllabic, both syllables must be nonlexical words (Hanson 1992). For subordination at Porson's bridge, the subordinated syllable and, in the case of a prepositive, the following word, or, in the case of a postpositive, the preceding word belong to an appositive group

καὶ συμφοράς *Orestes* 677
ἄρχειν γὰρ νεὼς *Helen* 1552.

In the appositive group, a heavy monosyllabic nonlexical does not head its own foot, as it would in the citation form of the nonlexical, but is allowed to become part of a foot including adjacent material. The appositive group requirement does not exhaust the syntactic account of Porson's bridge, which is syntactically constrained also at the phrasal level, since, as will be shown later (p. 334), prepositions subordinate preferentially in head interrupted structures. In more rapid and less formal styles of speech, the domain of subordination encompasses more extended appositive groups (satyric: p. 323) and even the juncture between lexical words in the phrase (comedy: p. 279).

Remapping and demarcation

The fact that in deliberate speech subordination applies word internally but fails to apply between lexical words suggests that for a syllable to subordinate, it must have maximum temporal adjacency to the subordinating environment; final lengthening at the end of lexical words creates a temporal separation that hinders remapping. Nonlexicals reduce their demarcation from the host word; consequently, with little or no intervening temporal separation, subordination is free to apply. The constraints against split resolution can be interpreted in similar terms. The final syllable of a lexical word is temporally separated from the initial syllable of a following lexical word to such an extent that the two syllables cannot be processed together as a matrix. But a matrix can be formed with an appositive whose temporal adjacency to the other syllable in the matrix is more like that of contiguous word internal light syllables. In the case of the split anapaest, there is a metrical requirement that in iambic rhythm the two syllables of the disyllabic arsis have maximum temporal adjacency; this metrical requirement is fulfilled either word internally or in an appositive group.

The gradient philological evidence of verse is in principle open to two interpretations. One interpretation simply assumes that to the parameter established by the philological evidence there corresponds a phonetic parameter of temporal adjacency. On this approach, the extension of the domains of the subtractive mapping rules in less formal styles of verse reflects an increasing latitude in the degree of temporal separation admissible with remapping; the filter becomes less fine and lets more structures through. The other interpretation assumes that it is not so much the filter that changes as the substance being filtered: as the temporal separations get progressively reduced in more rapid speech, more and more of them fall through the mesh of the filter. Similarly, experimen-

tal results can be misleadingly interpreted as supporting a ternary classification when the average is taken from measurements varying between
binary categories.

It is not clear whether the second interpretation can be carried to its
logical conclusion of making no more than a binary metrically relevant
distinction in degree of final lengthening. This would entail the assumption that insofar as nonlexicals could appear at bridges, they had no final
lengthening at all and were in this respect identical to word internal syllables. A problem arises when the evidence of Knox's bridges is integrated
with the evidence for remapping and split anapaests. It is difficult to
see what factor other than reduction of demarcation within the appositive group could account for the admissibility of nonlexical structures
at Knox's iamb and trochee bridges (p. 151) in cases such as

> ἐν δίκῃ χρόνου Solon 36.3
> ἀλλὰ μυρίαι Semonides 1.20
> περὶ στόμα Archilochus 44.

By contrast, subordination of nonlexicals at Porson's bridge is not permitted in the iambographers and severely constrained in the early plays
of Euripides. Split resolution after a trochee-shaped nonlexical is also
rare outside line initial position

> οὐχὶ διὰ τοῦτον *Plutus* 171
> μηδὲν ὑπὸ τηθίδος *Dyscolus* 386
> ἀλλὰ τί φέρω *Periciromene* 522.

The problem is how to explain a ternary classification with a binary durational feature. A possible solution is to assume that loss of demarcation
applies automatically in the appositive group, but that subordination
and matrix formation do not necessarily apply whenever their phonological environments are satisfied in the appositive group; they constitute further steps in the rhythmical organization of the appositive group.
Subordination implies reduction of demarcation, but reduction of demarcation does not necessarily imply subordination. In deliberate speech,
appositive groups could have reduced demarcation and some mapping
other than subordination and matrix formation. However, this line of
argument cannot apply to anapaests in the trimeter if these simply involve
disyllabic arses and not a separate rule of subtractive mapping. Trochee-
shaped nonlexicals in split anapaests are rare in the rapid and informal
speech of comedy despite the fact that they can appear at Knox's bridge
in the iambographers, the rhythm of whose verse is based on quite
deliberate speech. If final lengthening in trochee-shaped nonlexical (prepositive) words is eliminated completely in the language of the iambographers, it is difficult to see why trochee-shaped words are so constrained

in split anapaests in comedy. Conversely, if trochee-shaped nonlexical words have final lengthening in the language of comedy, it is difficult to see why they should be permitted at Knox's bridge in the iambographers. Consequently, it is probably necessary to assume three metrically relevant degrees of temporal adjacency within the phrase, with trochee-shaped nonlexical words having a degree intermediate between that characterizing word internal syllables and that characterizing the juncture between lexical words. The intermediate degree of temporal adjacency is sufficient to permit them to stand at Knox's bridge but insufficient to qualify for a disyllabic arsis in iambic verse. If this ternary classification is admitted in principle, it becomes available to account for other evidence too, for instance the difference between tragedy and comedy in the frequency of pyrrhic-shaped nonlexical words (particularly prepositions) in split resolution and of trochee-shaped nonlexical words in line initial split dactyls, and the inscriptional punctuation of disyllabic forms of the article (p. 328). Although there is not a perfect overlap of rhythmic and accentual classes, the assumption of three metrically relevant degrees of demarcation is supported by the fact that there are three major classes of accentual prominence, associated with enclitics, nonlexicals and lexicals respectively (p. 363).

7 | The Appositive Group

PROSODIC DOMAINS

Before embarking on an analysis of the appositive group, which is the prosodic domain ranked one step above the word, it will be appropriate to consider the theoretical status of the prosodic domain in general and the sort of evidence that can be adduced from speech and from verse in support of particular domains. The rules of connected speech surveyed in Chapter 6—gliding, elision, contraction, resyllabification, refooting, and remapping—apply within domains which, in the present state of knowledge, can usually be stated most easily morphologically or syntactically. However, even in terms of a purely formal and logical analysis, this approach is open to the criticism that it omits an explanatory link. The concept of the domain, in common with all phonological constructs not concerned with ordinal and quantitative relations, arises from the related fundamental organizational principles of classification and abstraction. A domain is a set of syntactic structures within which apply a set of phonological rules; by virtue of the existence of the domain, the syntactic structures and the phonological rules become cooccurrence classes. Unless the classification is accidental, the members of each class can be assumed to share some internal property. In concrete terms, if in a language syntactic phrases are characterized by a conjunction of phrase accent, final lengthening, resyllabification and elision, either this particular combination of phonological properties is quite accidental or it represents the various manifestations of a single shared property, and that shared property must obviously be phonological and not syntactic, since the class of items sharing it is phonological. This interpretation, based on formal analysis, is supported by substantive considerations. In general, the rules of phrase prosody serve to improve the fluency of speech within prosodically demarcated domains. As speech becomes more fluent, the energy and the time allotted to separate syllables is decreased:

to make an extreme comparison, when the durations of vowels in connected discourse are compared with the corresponding durations in citation forms, they are found to be much shorter (Klatt 1975). The degree to which words are shorter in connected speech than in citation forms is correlated with their grammatical category: in one study of Swedish, nouns and adjectives retained about 75% of their citation form duration, as compared with only 21% for articles; other categories fall in between (Fant et al. 1991b). This acceleration has significant effects on the implementation of the arsis-thesis alternation, in that the additive strategies used to achieve rhythm in slow speech tend to be replaced by subtractive strategies in more fluent speech, which results in fewer monosyllabic feet. Moreover, as the pauses separating words are eliminated and final lengthening is reduced, the phonetic obstacles to improving syllable and foot structure are progressively removed. So the domains of the rules of phrase prosody are, ontologically, just as phonetic and natural as the segmental environments of allophonic rules. The domains of prosodic rules are the spans within which their application is motivated by prosodic fluency and across which their application is blocked by prosodic demarcation, and conversely they are the spans whose edges are subject to demarcative rules which are blocked within the span. If the rules of phrase prosody were not natural, then, like the segmental composition of morphemes, they could vary arbitrarily from one unrelated language to another. In fact, like the rules of segmental allophony, they show an underlying crosslinguistic homogeneity.

Variable phrasing

Various empirical arguments have been used to corroborate the idea that the domains of prosodic rules are phonological. Phrasing has been found to depend not only on syntactic structure, but also on phonological factors, specifically phonological length and rate of speech. In the task of counting aloud, the series of numbers is phrased into rhythmically acceptable prosodic chunks: 21–22, 23–24, 25–26, and 25–30, 35–40, but 1321 [thirteen twenty-one], 1322, 1325, 1330. The same syntactic constituent is more likely to be produced as one phonological phrase if it contains relatively few words or syllables and as two phonological phrases if it contains relatively many words or syllables (Nespor et al. 1986). The major pause in a sentence tends to be located so as to divide it into phonologically balanced constituents, even when they do not reflect the major syntactic division (Gee et al. 1983). In Japanese, words can be combined into a single accentual phrase, but this is avoided when a very long phrase would result (Poser 1985). The effects of rate of speech on phrasing are transparent when phrase stress is marked by segmental rules, as happens in various southern Italian dialects in which vowels are diphthongized or otherwise mutated under phrase stress but not under word stress, for instance *u ráisu* 'rice,' but *u rìsu cráudu* 'uncooked rice' in the dialect of Belvedere Marittimo (Cosenza: Rohlfs 1929, 1938). For the dialect of Adernò (Catania: Santangelo 1905), one and the same line of verse, 'I have my heart hung on a nail,' can be pronounced more slowly "Aju lu cori méu mpintu nta nciúovu" with two mutated vowels and optional caesural pause, or more rapidly "Aju lu cori miu mpintu nta nciúovu" with one vowel mutation and no pause.

Readjustment of the syntax

There are also cases in which the prosodic phrasing contradicts or re-adjusts the syntactic structure. In Japanese, the verb at the end of a preposed relative clause frequently forms a single accentual phrase with its following head noun, so that for the prosody the verb is extracted from its parent constituent and adjoined to the head noun (Poser 1985). Syntactic clitics sometimes take phonological hosts at odds with their syntactic connections. This is trivially so for sentential clitics (like Greek δέ, γάρ, δή), which have scope over the whole sentence but are phonologically attached to the first word, the first accented word or the first constituent. Likewise, a preposition may have scope over a branching or conjoined constituent but be prepositive only to the adjacent lexical word. More significant are instances of syntactic proclitics being phonologically enclitic: this occurs in Kwakwala (British Columbia: Anderson 1984) and perhaps Yagua (Peru: Payne 1983), where consequently words seem to be marked not for their own case or deictic status but for that of the following word (Klavans 1985), as illustrated in Figure 7.1. Similarly in Kukuya (Congo: Hyman 1985b), prefixes can be phonologically attached not to their own grammatical word but to the preceding grammatical word. In certain Chinese dialects function words cliticize

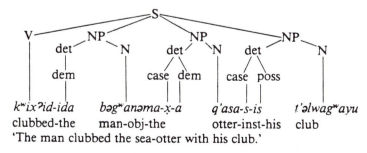

FIGURE 7.1
Prosodic enclisis of syntactic proclitics
in Kwakwala (from Anderson 1984)

to the left irrespective of constituency relations; the beginning of the lexical host word is automatically also the beginning of the clitic group; if no lexical word precedes, function words cliticize to the right by default (Chen 1990; Selkirk et al. 1990). This type of readjustment reflects a tendency for the phonology to generalize enclisis at the cost of ignoring syntactic constituency (Selkirk 1986). The effect this would have in English is illustrated by the propensity to generalize enclisis in the English spoken by native speakers of Malayalam (Kalackal 1985).

In Greek, there is often complete agreement between syntactic cohesion, normative accentual clisis and rhythmic cohesion, as for instance

> ἄκουσόν μου Ion 633

at Porson's bridge. In other cases, there is disagreement. In

> αὖθίς μοι φράσον Helen 471

likewise at Porson's bridge, the leftward prosodic grouping implied by the accentual enclisis and the rhythmic evidence of the bridge is in conflict with the syntactic constituent structure, where μοι φράσον is the immediate constituent. However, there is considerable evidence that normative enclitics do not always cliticize to the left irrespective of constituency relations (p. 365). In the case of the rhythmical composites consisting of prepositive + prepositive (p. 319), the phonological motivation to create a wordlike structure out of two nonlexicals outweighs the requirement of respecting syntactic constituency; a conjunction and an article or preposition can form a composite to the exclusion of the rest of the phrase, and the composite can stand before the caesura

> καὶ τοῖς ἤθεσιν Eur. Electra 385
> πρὸς τοὺς δυσσεβεῖς O.C. 280.

Elision of nonlexicals can be associated with a prosodic link that conflicts with syntactic constituency, as is illustrated by elided forms of ὅδε at Porson's bridge (p. 324):

> τοῦ λόγου τοῦδ᾽ ἐξερῶ O.T. 219
> δωμάτων τῶνδ᾽ ἐκπεσεῖν Andromache 875
> ὀπαδὸν Ἱππολύτου τόνδ᾽ εἰσορῶ Hippolytus 1151.

Such elided forms are only optionally prepositive, since they can also occur before the caesura and diaeresis:

> δόμων τῶνδ᾽ ἐξιόντι Ion 535
> ἡλίου τόδ᾽ εἰσορᾶν ἐμοὶ φάος Philoctetes 663.

Elided ἐστί can cohere to the right in agreement with or in violation of constituency

> ἔστ᾽ ὦ ξέν᾽ Ion 514; Havet's bridge
> ἔστ᾽ ἄξια Bacchae 246; Porson's bridge.

Enclitic ποτε becomes proclitic when elided line initially after brevis in longo in

πoτ' ἄλλoς O. T. 1085

and postcaesurally at *Iliad* 3.205. In one instance

ποῖ σὸν πόδ' ἐπὶ συννοίᾳ κυκλεῖς *Orestes* 632

the elided head of the immediate constituent σὸν πόδ' is, on the evidence of the resolution, prosodically attached to the following constituent and, on the evidence of the caesura, detached from the preceding preposi- tive sequence.

Diagnostics for prosodic domains

For the purposes of this analysis, the term prosodic domain is used in its strict definition, that is a domain of temporal, fundamental frequency or intensity organization. There is a widespread lack of direct experimen- tal data on prosodic domains and particularly their phonological demar- cation. Phonologists often rely on segmental or tonal sandhi rules, clitic placement rules and other nonexperimental evidence as a diagnostic for prosodic domains and subdomains, but this is an indirect source of evidence which sometimes risks begging the question. For instance, in Amoy and Haifeng Chinese major phrase final lengthening and even pause can occur within a lexical tone sandhi domain (Chen 1987), which suggests that for the present state of the language tone sandhi may not be a reliable indication of the durational chunking that constitutes phras- ing in its narrow sense. The potential artificiality of French liaison is indicated by the fact that in some styles the liaison consonant can be followed by a brief pause (Encrevé 1988). A sandhi rule whose domain correlates with a rhythmic, accentual or intonational domain presents no problem: it applies within the same prosodic domain defined by the rhythmic, accentual or intonational rule. However, not all sandhi rules are fully productive; some are liable to various degrees of categorial or lexical constraint. Consider the processes of gemination and latent seg- ment insertion. The Italian raddoppiamento sintattico occurs whenever its segmental specification is met within its domain. An intermediate degree of morpholexical saturation is shown by Greek movable nu, whose environment must be categorially rather than phonologically specified: contrast dative plural ποσί(ν) with vocative singular πόσι. At the other end of the spectrum lies the alternation between *a* and *an* in English, which, since it only affects this one word, cannot be a phonological rule at all but must be a rule of allomorph selection, and is obviously not evidence for its own separate prosodic domain. Despite such differences in lexical saturation, productivity and degree of grammaticalization (Rotenberg 1978; Hayes 1990), there is an essential unity not only in the nature of the phonetic processes themselves but also in the various factors potentially conditioning them — the syntactic factors that determine their domains, the additional factors that further constrain them and the phonostylistic factors that cause variation along those parameters. The conditioning factors seem mainly to involve syntactic cohesion, phonological substance and the text frequency of a morpheme, word or locution, all of which are ultimately manifested by phonetic adjacency and fluency of production. At least diachronically, the constraints on nonproductive prosodic rules can still be interpreted as phonetic and natural. So while some degree of caution is needed in using sandhi rules as a diagnostic of synchronically valid prosodic domains, information about the syntactic conditioning of prosodic domains may be drawn not only from fully productive phonological rules, but also from rules of allomorphy or of lexical selection, and intermediate stages between these two endpoints: the factors conditioning the different types of rules are very comparable and fossilized sandhi is one source of allomorphy.

Instead of using sandhi rules to discover prosodic domains, it is possible to slow speech down to artificially deliberate rates at which auditory differences in the duration of pause and final lengthening can be used to identify the demarcation and hierarchization of prosodic domains. For instance, such a procedure will reveal that ceteris paribus there is a deeper prosodic divide between subject noun phrase and predicate than between verb and object noun phrase. The same strategy can actually be used in normal speech to achieve disambiguation, as with [old] [men and women] vs. [old men] [and women] (p. 416). But it introduces all the problems associated with the descriptive account of variation and leaves unanswered the question whether at normal rates of speech the differences in demarcation are completely eliminated or whether ghost differences can remain, thereby changing the correlations under investigation.

These are old and familiar topics in Greek metre. On the basis of very gross rules stated in the simple binary terms of occurring versus not occurring at metrical bridges, it is easy to elicit the commonly accepted lower level prosodic units, the word (type λόγων) and the appositive group (type τῶν λόγων); a larger domain which will be shown to be the minor phrase (type καλοῖσιν ὑμεναίοισιν Orestes 1210) can be elicited from the conventions of punctuation in certain inscriptions and is the prototypical hemistich in the trimeter and the hexameter (p. 398). The problem is that as soon as the data are expanded to include even relatively coarse grained philological evidence, the possibility of multiple subcategories arises. For instance, appositive groups containing the article may be metrically different from those containing other nonlexicals (p. 341); the sequence τὸν ἐμόν may be metrically different from other articular phrases having the same syllable structure (p. 331), and so on. As already remarked (p. 282), one interpretation of this type of evidence is that, phonologically, there are only two categories, word and appositive; the more rapid and the less formal the style of speech, the more likely words are to become phonologically appositive (DS 1978). The other interpretation is that, at any given rate and style of speech, sufficiently detailed phonetic evidence would indicate that some or all of the lexically and syntactically different categories are also phonetically distinct in ways that cannot be predicted purely in terms of phonological environment. Given this ambiguity, it is often more convenient to discuss the environments of the rules of prosody directly in terms of their conditioning syntactic factors, provided it is understood that those factors actually operate through the medium of a hierarchy of prosodic domains.

THE PROCESSING OF FUNCTION WORDS

Over and above the familiar categorial classification of words as nouns, verbs, conjunctions, etc., it is usual to distinguish two supercategories—content words, also termed lexical words, and function words, also termed nonlexical words. Content words are nouns, verbs, adjectives and many adverbs, particularly those derived from adjectives. Function words, or functors, include determiners, modal and auxiliary verbs, negatives, pronouns, conjunctions, complementizers, particles and many underived adverbs. Content words prototypically express referential meaning, while functors prototypically share with inflectional affixes the role of defining phrase and sentence structure, expressing grammatical relations among content words and conveying pragmatic and discourse related features, for instance discourse structure above the level of the sentence (γάρ, οὖν), emphasis (δή), and the speaker's attitude to the utterance or his interlocutors. Functors are not uniformly nonreferential: pronouns can be referential, but deictically or anaphorically rather than in the usual manner of direct primary reference. Just as pronouns can be seen as non-lexical nouns, so auxiliaries and modals are nonlexical verbs and words like ποῖος are nonlexical adjectives; prepositions also range from the primarily grammatical like *of* to semantically substantial words like *beyond* (Emonds 1985).

Functors other than prepositions differ from content words in syntactic terms in not being expandable into phrases which they head containing their own specifiers, modifiers and arguments, or, in those syntactic theories that posit functor headed phrases, in being expandable in a more limited way. Consequently content words are sometimes called major category words and functors minor category words. Another distinction is that major categories like nouns contain a vast number of different members and can be added to by neologism, while minor categories like determiners contain relatively few members; new functors arise not by neologism but rather as a result of the semantic bleaching of erstwhile content words. Accordingly content words are often called open class words and functors closed class words. However, in some languages adjectives clearly constitute a closed class: Igbo (Nigeria), for instance, is said to have only eight adjectives. Functors can inflect and even form compounds with each other, as English *somewhere*, Greek οὐδεπώποτε, but they often do so differently from content words (Golston 1991): for instance there may be specific functor endings, as in Sanskrit *te, tāsām*, Latin *illius*, or word internal inflection, as in Greek τῶνδε, ὧντινων, Latin *cuilibet, quemquem*. As discussed in greater detail below, functors are also phonologically distinct from content words in not being subject to prosodic minimality requirements (Golston 1991), and in being very susceptible to reduction in continuous speech: *some* is commonly reduced to *sm̩* but *sum* is not; *can* and *will* are commonly reduced to *cn̩* and *'ll* when they are auxiliary verbs but not when they are nouns meaning 'tin' and 'testament.'

Reading, evoked potentials

Functors have been found to elicit different responses from content words in reading. When subjects were asked to cross out target letters in a text, they were more apt to notice and cancel the letters in content words than in functors (this result was not an artefact of text frequency or syllable stress); subjects who were warned in advance to pay special attention to functors did not perform any better than those who were not (Schindler 1978; Haber et al. 1981; Rosenberg et al. 1985). Anything that retards the reading process, like mixing upper case and lower case letters in the stimulus, diminishes this effect (Drewnowski et al. 1977). It is probable that, for whatever reason, function words are more likely than content words to be read holistically and recognized as a single indivisible orthographic unit. When words were presented very briefly to one visual field only (tachistoscopic hemifield word recognition), function words were reported less accurately than content words when presented to the right visual field but not when presented the left visual field; this suggests that there is differential recognition of the two types of words but only in the left hemisphere (Bradley et al. 1983). Functors are also particularly liable to omission, substitution or duplication in writing: even though in English all but one of the 60 most commonly occurring words are functors, accounting for over forty per cent of all word tokens, in a number of different classes of writing errors the proportion of functors was significantly greater. The difference between slips of the tongue and slips of the pen probably relates in some way to the need for message segments to be retained in short term memory for a longer period for writing (Hotopf 1983).

In another type of experiment, the electrical activity (evoked potentials: Picton et al. 1984) elicited in the brain by word presentation was recorded via electrodes placed on the scalp; when the words of sentences were presented sequentially on a video screen, different patterns of event related potentials were elicited by content words and functors, perhaps reflecting a different amount or duration of processing for the two word types (Kutas et al. 1983; Garnsey 1985; van Petten et al. 1991).

Speech errors

Another valuable source of evidence is speech errors. The errors all of us make now and again in speaking are not random; their regularities reflect the regularities of normal language production (Fromkin 1971, 1973; Shattuck-Hufnagel 1979; Garrett 1975, 1980). The type of mislocation error which involves exchanging the position of constituents of the same syntactic category affects predominantly content words: "They *left* it and *forgot* it behind"; "The one I kept pinned on the *room* to my *door*"; "I left the *briefcase* in my *cigar*." In some cases complete noun phrases can be located in erroneous destinations: "I got into *this guy* with *a discussion*." But more often than not functors and the specification for inflections are not moved together with their "head" words and remain stranded (Garrett et al. 1980; Stemberger 1985; Berg 1987): "You have to *square* it *face*ly"; "You *order*ed up *end*ing"; "Seymour sliced the *knife* with a *salami*." This speech error evidence dissociates the processes involved in generating a syntactically correct phrase structure, that is generating a grammatical frame, from the insertion of content morphemes. The phenomenon of stranding implies that the phrase is correctly constructed but that there has been a breakdown in getting the correct lexical item into one of two simultaneously available and usually categorially identical slots. Inflectional affixes and functors are not affected because they are not being linked to slots in this phase: either they are already in place at this point, or conceivably they are inserted at a later stage. Functors can undergo exchanges with a member of the same class — pronouns with pronouns, prepositions with prepositions, but functors do not exchange with content words: "He taught *us* to *it*"; "...which was parallel *to* a certain sense *in* an experience of..."; this indicates that lexical insertion and nonlexical insertion occur at different stages (Golston 1991). Priming experiments suggest that what the frame contains is a categorial specification rather than a specific member of the class of functors (Bock 1989). Functors can also simply get misplaced and inflections attached to the wrong host, which suggests that functor insertion is an independent process.

Word games

The separate status of grammatical frame and lexical insertion can be exploited in word games. In one type of word game, the frame is kept intact but the lexicals are replaced with nonsense morphemes. The Jabberwocky poem is a celebrated example: "'Twas *brill*ig and the *slith*y *tov*es...." When subjects were asked to monitor an utterance for a target word, their response times were more rapid for normal speech than for Jabberwocky speech, and more rapid for Jabberwocky than for randomly jumbled speech, whether the target was directly specified or indirectly conveyed in terms of another word rhyming with the target or in terms of a semantic class (Marslen-Wilson et al. 1980). Not only the rhythmical regularity of the verse form but also the possibility of a syntactic analysis make Jabberwocky easier to learn and to recall than strings of nonsense words without supporting grammatical formatives. It has been shown experimentally that the presence of functors makes it easier for subjects to learn both phrase-like and sentence-like strings of nonsense syllables (Epstein 1961; Glanzer 1962); this is presumably because structured stimuli are easier to remember than unstructured stimuli. Another example is "railway slang" (Driver 1990): *Muddle and Get Nowhere* 'Midland and Great Northern [Railway]'. When asked to segment a sentence into words, children tend, for whatever reason, to disregard function words (Ehri 1975). In a child's version of Pig Latin, function words were not transformed like lexical words nor were proclitic function words treated as an unstressed part of the following lexical word (Cowan 1989). Similarly in French "langage à l'envers," most function words are unaffected, although some pronouns are variably affected (Sherzer 1982). The converse of Jabberwocky is the telegraphic language of telegrams, classified advertisements and early child language, in which in English the lexical words are strung together without a grammatical frame (Ferguson et al. 1977).

Agrammatism

While the evidence adduced so far establishes that grammatical frame construction and lexical insertion are separate processes, it does not indicate in what way they are separate. It might be that one simply occurs prior to the other in the sequence of events involved in sentence production. More concretely, a grammatical frame is established before a content word is inserted into it but its output morphophonological shape is "accommodated" (Berg 1987) after lexical insertion: note the form of the indefinite article and the possessive suffix in *a money's aunt* [an aunt's money] (Garrett 1975). It is also possible that the two processes represent rather different cognitive operations, perhaps making different demands on the speaker's attention and capabilities. It is often assumed that when some type of behaviour has to be executed frequently and routinely, a rapid automated procedure tends to be created for it; so the processing of functors, a class of words having particularly high frequency, may have been associated with a separate access, retrieval or processing mechanism. If grammatical frame construction is functionally distinct from lexical insertion along these lines, function words and content words (and/or the way they are used) could in one way or another be neuroanatomically discrete. In order to follow this intriguing line of enquiry, we need to shift our attention from normal speech to impaired speech, that is to aphasia.

Total loss of speech in aphasia is not very common and often only temporary. Dr. Johnson's famous case of aphasia in 1783 was transitory (and did not severely impair his faculty for writing or for Latin verse composition). Typically some aspects of language are retained while other aspects are impaired, and, despite an initially disconcerting degree of variation from one patient to another, a number of fairly regular patterns across patients emerge, although their precise classification has been disputed ever since the birth of aphasiology (de Bleser 1987). This selective impairment of linguistic ability suggests that language is organized by the nervous system into functionally discrete modules which correlate to some degree and in some potentially quite complex ways (Shallice 1988) with anatomically discrete localization in the brain. So neurological disease provides an insight into the organization of language in normal disease free speakers.

Agrammatism, or Broca's aphasia, is a type of aphasia in which functors and inflections are particularly affected and speech is halting and laboured. In the most severely impaired patients, speech is fragmented and consists largely of serial naming; functors tend to be simply omitted, except perhaps for conjunctions. In less severely impaired patients, functors are partially preserved or a different functor is substituted for the target functor. Agrammatism is traditionally associated with anterior lesions; there were few exceptions to this general conclusion in a study of over two hundred patients with a brain scan technique called computerized tomography (Basso et al. 1985). It has been found that not only extensive lesions but also relatively small lesions in different cortical locations can cause agrammatism (Vanier et al. 1990), which supports the idea that interpatient variability in aphasia is due not only to difference in the site, extent and aetiology of the lesion but also to the fact that different individuals can have differently localized language functions, contributing to a general picture of selective deficits within an overall clinical syndrome (Caplan 1991). This conclusion is also suggested by electrical stimulation studies, in which there is the focal application of a small electrical current to particular cortical sites for a period of about 4–12 seconds during surgical treatment of epilepsy under local anaesthesia (Mateer et al. 1989).

There is some disagreement as to whether, or at least to what extent, agrammatic speech is a direct reflex of the primary deficit or the result of a strategy adopted by the patient to compensate for his deficit. This latter approach takes two forms. The most radical claims that agrammatics have some general problem with speech that makes it particularly effortful and they compensate for this overloading of the system by concentrating on content words, with the consequence that functors are omitted or carelessly selected (Kolk et al. 1985). Although this is also what happens when one writes a telegram, the "telegraphic" utterances of agrammatic speakers are, for whatever reason, rather different from written telegrams (Tesak et al. 1991). The less radical view allows that the deficit selectively impairs language as suggested by agrammatic speech, but interprets the oscillation between omission and misselection as resulting not from different degrees of impairment but from different strategies of compensation for the deficit, thereby eliminating one of the classical distinctions between agrammatic (nonfluent) and paragrammatic (fluent) aphasia (Heeschen 1985). The more radical form of compensation theory would undermine the neuroanatomical interpretation of the selective impairment of functors. The theory is in principle not implausible. A patient suffering not apparently from Broca's aphasia but from laryngeal apraxia (impairment of the coordination and timing of movements of the laryngeal muscles in speech resulting from brain damage) used what seemed to be a compensatory strategy including omission of functors inter alia and misselection from morphological paradigms: these effects disappeared completely from this patient's speech when he started to use an electronic artificial larynx (Marshall et al. 1988). On the other hand, one electrical stimulation study produced sentences in which a functor was replaced by a semantically or phonologically heavier functor (Mateer et al. 1989): "If my son *is* late" → "If my son *will getting* late"; "If you *are* serious" → "If you *gonna* serious." Given the circumstances under which they were produced, these errors are more likely to be a direct reflex of the applied current than the result of a compensation strategy for effortful speech. Agrammatics often try to improve on their first attempts and in general give the impression of striving for more adequate speech production rather than having deliberately adopted a strategy of paying little attention to grammar morphemes. Both agrammatic and paragrammatic signing have been found in left hemisphere lesioned deaf patients who use American Sign Language to communicate (Poizner et al. 1991).

Although agrammatics often have rather parallel problems in producing and understanding speech, there are documented cases of patients who are agrammatic in speech but not in auditory comprehension or vice versa (Miceli et al. 1983; Schwartz et al. 1985; Nespoulos et al. 1988). There are also cases of patients who are agrammatic in speech but not in writing (Italian: Miceli et al. 1983; Japanese: Goodglass 1990), but in English it is usually the other way around (Bub et al. 1982; Howard 1985). This potential dissociation across tasks and/or modalities — the same patient may be anomic in one task and agrammatic in another — indicates that agrammatism can reflect failure of some modality specific processing module and need not imply the erasure of all linguistic knowledge. This interpretation is strengthened by the evidence of the dissociation of the spontaneous speech of agrammatics from their often good performance in offline metalinguistic tasks like repeating sentences, judging the grammaticality of sentences or filling in missing functors in sentences. For instance, patients can often judge the grammaticality of sentences that they find difficult to comprehend (Linebarger et al. 1983; Kolk et al. 1985; Wulfeck 1988). Agrammatics are also surprisingly good at judging the grammaticality of sentences with erroneous or missing functors or inflections (Saffran et al. 1980) or even at correcting transcripts of their own erroneous speech and inserting omitted functors (Goodglass 1990). In a sentence reading task in which the words were printed vertically (one above the other), the patient showed no agrammatism for the first few words, but agrammatism set in as soon as it was realized that the words formed a sentence (Stark 1988; Nespoulous et al. 1989). Such evidence suggests that the linguistic knowledge is not obliterated: it is accessed or used differently in spontaneous speech and in metalinguistic tasks. Maybe the difference is between a conscious, controlled and deliberate offline use in metalinguistic tasks versus a more automatic use in spontaneous speech (Stark 1988); as already noted, the distinction between controlled and automatic processing is well established in psychology (Shiffrin et al. 1977).

Phonology

The problems that agrammatics have with functors point to a selective breakdown in some linguistic subcomponent, but there has been little agreement as to which specific subcomponent is involved. According to one view (Kean 1979; see Garman 1982), the functor problem is phonological; it is certainly the case that agrammatic speakers have more overall problems with pronunciation, particularly of consonants, than paragrammatic speakers. Phonological alexics, that is patients who can read real words but not nonwords because their phonological reading route is impaired, often have some difficulty with functors and affixes (Patterson 1982). Some purely phonological factors conditioning functor omission in agrammatism have been identified. For instance, if the prosodic prominence of functors is artificially augmented, comprehension on the part of agrammatics is improved (Harris 1988). Sentence initial unstressed functors were repeated with greater difficulty than sentence initial stressed functors and than sentence internal unstressed functors by agrammatics (Goodglass et al. 1967). The syllabic plural, as in *houses*, is better preserved than the asyllabic plural, as in *dogs*. It is perhaps easier to think how a phonological problem could cause omission than misselection, but it has been found that even a postlexical rule, namely liaison in French, can trigger misselection as an avoidance strategy, as when *les éléphants* is produced as *les l'éléphant* or *le éléphant* in order to suppress the liaison (Kehayia et al. 1990). However, the deficit is not phonological in any simple and direct way. It is not the case that unstressed syllables of content words are omitted at the same rate as identical unstressed functors: *a tack* is much more likely than *attack* to be produced without the first syllable, despite the fact that they are homophonous. One phonological alexic had more difficulty reading productively autonomous affixes than affixes that have lost their transparency, for instance *rapidly* versus *hardly* (Coslett in Friedman 1988). Moreover, functors which are often relatively unreduced are liable to omission too, while homophonous content words are far less likely to be affected: French *car* and *or* caused difficulty for an agrammatic reader when they meant 'since' and 'now' but not when they meant 'coach' and 'gold' (Andreewsky et al. 1975); similarly in English, discounting the fact that overlearned snippets of verse tend to be relatively well preserved, *to be or not to be* is more difficult for agrammatics than *two bee oar knot two bee* (Gardner et al. 1975). In fact, one and the same German preposition caused more problems as a purely syntactic argument marker ("Peter hofft auf den Sommer" 'Peter hopes for the summer') than it did as a locative preposition ("Peter steht auf dem Stuhl" 'Peter stands on the chair') (Friederici 1982, 1985). It seems that the agrammatic is sensitive to the same factors that cause functors to be treated as a separate phonological class rather than to the phonological reduction per se; inflections, which in some languages can carry the word stress, as in Italian *cantiámo* 'we sing', are easier to integrate with functors on this approach.

Morphology

The evidence from the morphology of agrammatics is rather less ambiguous. Although both functors and inflections serve to signal syntactic structure, syntax and morphology were dissociated in two Italian agrammatics (Miceli et al. 1983): one patient was severely impaired for inflections but had relatively unimpaired syntax, while the other had a severe syntactic deficit but performed better with inflections. This dissociation suggests that the morphological deficit is autonomous and not simply the reflex of a purely syntactic deficit (Saffran et al. 1980). Another revealing aspect of agrammatic morphology is the dissociation of inflectional and derivational morphology: in one study inflectional errors were more common than derivational errors and an inflectional affix was never substituted for a derivational one or vice versa (Miceli et al. 1988). This fits with the overall pattern of agrammatic errors, since derivational morphology tends to have a higher level of semantic content than inflectional morphology and to be less involved in the computation of syntactic structure. Derivational errors were less common than inflectional errors also in the reading of phonological dyslexics (Coslett in Friedman 1988). The reason why functors can be either omitted or misselected while inflections are mainly misselected is that agrammatics tend not to produce illegal words: in English, omission of the plural suffix results in a legal word, *dog* for *dogs* for instance, but in Italian it would leave a bare stem, *can* for *cani* for instance, which is a possible form in some dialects but not in the standard language. A few instances are recorded of patients who systematically omit inflections even though this can result in illegal words, as happened in the case of a Finnish patient (Niemi et al. 1990).

Syntax

The syntax of agrammatic speech is in general less complex than normal syntax; coordination tends to replace subordination, and branching noun phrases having two content words are difficult to produce, leading to the omission of modifying adjectives and possessives: when asked to repeat sentences containing prenominal adjectives in subject or object noun phrases, agrammatics tended to omit the adjectives or make them predicates (Schwartz 1987). Impaired syntactic comprehension in agrammatics is well documented (Caramazza et al. 1976; Grodzinsky 1986, 1990). Bitransitive sentences, that is sentences having both a direct and an indirect object, are difficult for agrammatics not only in German, where interpretation often depends on exact processing of the case inflection of the definite article (Stark et al. 1988), but also in English, perhaps because the sequence of two noun phrases represents marked word order. Passive sentences with a *by* agent phrase are also poorly understood:

where animacy is not an indication of semantic roles, that is where agent and patient are both animate or both inanimate, agrammatics perform randomly on passive sentences; apparently they assign agent status to the first noun phrase and to the *by* phrase as well. Local syntax seems to be easier for the agrammatic than syntax spanning the sentence (Linebarger et al. 1983; Tyler 1985). The pattern of spared affixes and functors—derivational affixes, discourse particles and coordinating and subordinating conjunctions are relatively spared—suggests that what is impaired is relational meaning and what is preserved is referential and pragmatic meaning. But it does not necessarily follow that the deficit arises from the use of this subset of functors in syntactic computation rather than from the storage or retrieval of this subset in the lexicon, and there is some evidence that does not fit with the purely syntactic interpretation of the functor deficit. The dissociation between inflection and syntax noted above for some Italian agrammatics applied equally between functors and syntax; the same dissociation was found for English agrammatics (Berndt 1987). Moreover, in those instances in which an agrammatic substitutes an erroneous functor rather than omitting the functor completely, a syntactic slot must have been computed for the functor even though the slot was wrongly filled. Instances are reported from Serbocroatian in which the inflected case form is correct even when the verb is omitted, and from Polish in which case marking was correct when a preposition was omitted (Menn et al. 1990). This suggests that inflectional and functor impairment is in principle separate from syntactic impairment: if they tend to cooccur, that could be because they are sited contiguously so as to be liable to be affected by the same lesion.

Category and lexicon

It has also been established that specific properties of an individual word can affect its use by aphasics—the phonological length or weight of the word, its frequency of usage, its grammatical category and its semantic definition. Anomic patients have particular difficulty with nouns and little problem with verbs and functors. The neologisms characteristic of Wernicke's aphasia occur predominantly in nouns, more rarely in adjectives and verbs and practically never in functors. Agrammatics both in Italian (Miceli et al. 1984) and in English (Zingeser et al. 1990) find verbs more difficult than nouns and functors more difficult than verbs. However in Icelandic verbs were not avoided more than nouns, possibly because nominal morphology is quite complex in this language (Menn et al. 1990). The relative susceptibility of verbs could be interpreted as a reflex of a syntactic impairment, either because verbs carry more relational meaning than nouns or because they require the computation of agreement in a broad sentential domain. When verb inflection is mis-selected, there is often a preference, in some but not all patients (Miceli et al. 1989), for nominal forms like participles or infinitives; this could also be due to a desire to avoid agreement computation or to a prefer-ence for unmarked or citation forms, but these approaches are not supported by the fact that in Polish the past tense is preferred to the presumably unmarked present tense because it is a participial form, despite the fact that the past tense requires gender agreement. The categorial hierarchy noun > verb > functor should probably be inter-preted lexically, rather than syntactically, as reflecting ultimately the degree to which a word has concrete semantic content: one agraphic showed just the above hierarchy when writing to dictation with the addi-tional explicitly documented distinction that concrete nouns were writ-ten better than abstract nouns (Bub et al. 1982). Deep dyslexics have particular difficulty reading functors, and they can also have more difficulty reading verbs than nouns. Both effects have been ascribed to lack of concrete imageable referents (Morton et al. 1980; Allport et al. 1981): the more concrete and imageable categories and/or individual lexical items have more easily accessible semantic representations. In one case of acquired dysgraphia (Baxter et al. 1985), nouns were spelled more accurately than adjectives, adjectives more accurately than verbs and verbs more accurately than functors, and the hierarchy was reported to be categorial and not merely a direct reflection of the level of concrete-ness or imageability of the word. In single word repetition by an Italian agrammatic, there was a preference for citation forms of nouns and adjec-tives: this probably indicates that there was a particular problem with grammatical morphemes even when they were not being used for syntac-tic computation; in other words that there was a specifically lexical prob-lem with these morphemes. Such a problem could arise in a number of different ways. For instance, the meaning of functors and inflections could be degraded in the lexicon, or there could be a problem in access-ing them ("looking them up"). It is also theoretically possible that their storage in the lexicon and access to them could be unimpaired and that they could be liable as a class to a glitch in the way they are temporarily stored for sentence production in working memory; but this is less likely, since the problem seems to lie in the correct selection of one member of the subcategory: the look-up mechanism succeeds in accessing the correct subcategory but cannot reach down to the level of the individual item (Lapointe 1985). This aspect of agrammatism is nicely described by the introspective report of a French patient (Nespoulous et al. 1989): "Even though I know perfectly well that it is a preposition or an article that I need, several words of these categories come up in my mind and

I never know for sure which one to choose." The degradation of specific semantic features and the preservation of more general classifications is also found in one type of deep dyslexia in which the patient reads *admiral* as *colonel* and *turtle* as *crocodile* and has similar problems when matching words to pictures (Coltheart 1987). Separation of categorial and semantic definitions in the lexicon is also indicated by the case of a transcortical sensory aphasic who recognized the category of words he did not understand, since he completed sentences with grammatically appropriate but semantically inappropriate items (Berndt et al. 1987). While agrammatics have a general problem with functors and inflections as a class, they still tend to retain access to the categorial label (determiner, auxiliary, preposition, pronoun etc.) of particular items, although the semantic distinction between different items of the same category is blurred.

The difficulties agrammatics have with online access to functors and inflections suggest that these items are stored or accessed separately from content words in the lexicon (Garrett 1975; Lapointe 1985; Golston 1991), and it is this separate routine that is impaired in agrammatics. While this hypothesis remains a very plausible one, the evidence produced to support it is the subject of ongoing dispute. This evidence pertains to the relationship between the frequency of a word and the time it takes someone to recognize whether the word exists or not in his language (Bradley et al. 1980; Bradley 1983). Subjects react faster to *dog* than to *elk* in this recognition task; they also reject complete nonwords like *spoardlan* faster than nonwords starting with an existing word like *strandlan*. It was claimed that for normal speakers these effects applied only to content words and not to functors, whereas for agrammatics they applied to all words. This claim seemed to substantiate the idea that normal speakers, but not agrammatics, had a special fast access to functors for construction of the grammatical frame. But these results have turned out to be difficult to replicate (Gordon et al. 1982; Segui et al. 1982; Kolk et al. 1985b; Garnsey 1985; Petocz et al. 1988; Matthei et al. 1989; Dell 1990), although the effort devoted to this goal testifies to the theoretical import of the dispute. It is difficult to test the hypothesis because there are not many content words that have the same frequency as ordinary high frequency functors. It is suggestive that in the letter cancellation task reported above (p. 292), there were two conditions under which functors were not treated differently from content words: one was when the text was scrambled, and the other was when the subject was agrammatic (Rosenberg et al. 1985).

At the present state of our knowledge, it is reasonable to conclude that functors are processed separately from content words in sentence production, and that certain types of aphasia arise from damage to areas of the brain specifically involved in one or more aspects of the storage or processing of functors and other grammatical morphemes. It is a fascinating thought that the "exceptions" to the metrical bridges which played such a central role in traditional philological scholarship should turn out to have some sort of neuroanatomical basis.

THE APPOSITIVE GROUP

Syntactic clisis

Whereas some functors, like definite articles or complementizers in Greek, have a syntactically determined position in which they stay, others tend to congregate in a specifically clitic slot (Klavans 1985), often sentential second position, either because they have sentential scope and are consequently assigned to such a slot or because they are moved into that slot out of the phrasal constituent in which they would have remained had they been nonclitic words (Taylor 1990; Garrett 1990; Halpern 1992). For instance, in Czech, clitics cluster in a fixed order (question particle – auxiliary, reflexive – dative pronoun – accusative pronoun) after the first constituent of the sentence irrespective of its categorial or functional nature; clitic clusters are phonologically enclitic, but proclitic after a major phrase boundary; metri gratia rearrangement of the word order is acceptable in verse (Toman 1986). In Homeric Greek, sentence connective clitics like τε and δέ appear after the first word of the sentence including any topicalized constituent, whereas second position pronominal clitics appear after the complementizer position.

Correlation of levels

As just noted, not all nonlexical words are syntactic clitics. Conversely, not all syntactic clitics are phonologically clitic. In Bikol (Philippines: Zwicky 1977), monosyllabic syntactic clitics are phonologically clitic, but disyllabic words sharing some properties of syntactic clitics are phonologically independent words. In Luganda (Uganda: Hyman et al. 1987), not all syntactic clitics are phonological clitics for the purposes of the vowel shortening rule. In Greek, a number of accented particles are located in sentential second position: μέν, δέ, γάρ, ἄρα, οὖν. Not all nonlexicals are phonologically clitic: for instance, disyllabic functors are not fully destressed in English; and not all phonological clitics are nonlexical: verbs were generally unaccented under certain conditions in Indo-European. Apparently, the prototypically low informational content or concreteness of nonreferential words, and to a lesser degree of verbs as against nouns, causes them to be herded into prosodically unobtrusive slots, and additionally causes their prosodic prominence to be diminished. But different factors condition this tendency at different levels, so that an imperfect correlation results.

Phonological clisis

Nonlexicals are characterized by a tendency to have higher frequency than lexicals and less phonological substance, even in their basic un-reduced lexical representations. In Greek, both nonlexical and lexical words can be monosyllabic — δή/γῆ, ἐξ/κρέξ, τούς/βοῦς, but monosyllabic words ending in a short vowel can only be nonlexical — με, σε, ἐ, σφε, γε, τε, τι, δέ, ὁ, τό, τά, σύ, ἄ, πρό. Final consonants are "extrametrical," so that CV̆C is fine for nonlexicals, as in ἐν, ἄν, πρός, but marginal for lexicals: θέν, στάν, δός (p. 80, 102). Similarly in Pitjantjatjara (Australia: Bowe 1990), many clitic pronouns are monomoraic, whereas the minimal content word form is bimoraic. Nonlexical words are allowed to contravene the minimal word weight rule (p. 93) because, at least in their noncitation forms, they naturally form feet with their host words. The dynamic correlate is the reduction of nonlexicals in stress languages: English be→bi but not bee→*bi. So what characterizes nonlexicals at the phonological level is a tendency to lose some or all of the distinguishing properties of autonomous words and become part of a host word which is generally, but not exclusively, a content word.

In some languages, it is possible to discriminate nonlexicals from lexicals in spectrally distorted speech or in hummed phrases (Nooteboom et al. 1978): for instance, spectrally distorted "Hoist the load to your left shoulder" was perceived as "Turn the page to the next lesson" (Blesser in Martin 1972); the syntactic structure was correctly extracted from the prosody. The phonological processes involved include loss of accentual prominence with potential segmental weakenings particularly in stress languages, resyllabification, refooting, remapping, and reduction of final lengthening, as well as extension of the word internal rules of segmental phonology. The progressive application of these processes is apparent from a diachronic perspective, since nonlexical words and suffixes can originate from lexicals: for instance, but 'from outside,' not 'NEG ever thing,' -ly 'having the body of.' In such developments, there is often a correlation of semantic bleaching with phonological reduction. The shortening of final vowels in Latin verb forms occurs earlier where these forms have been bleached and demoted to the status of discourse particles (cavĕ, pută, putŏ) and particles of request or interrogation (quaesŏ, orŏ, rogŏ) than in corresponding semantically full verb forms (Stephens 1985). Three stages are seen in the development of the future tense in

Romance from infinitive plus *habeo*, where *habeo* is progressively demoted from content word to function word to inflectional suffix; the phonological reduction is aligned with the progressive semantic reduction and generalization entailed by the process of grammaticalization (Bybee et al. 1989). The phonological weakening of nonlexicals can be illustrated by instances of lexical and nonlexical words derived from the same root. The following pronunciations are reported for the southern Italian dialect of Vico del Gargano (Foggia: Rohlfs 1929): *u proimə* 'the first' (*il primo*) with diphthongization under phrase stress; *u primə misə* 'the first month' (*il primo mese*) with normal vocalism under word stress; *prəmə də pənsá* 'before thinking' (*prima di pensare*) with vowel centralization under low stress in a nonlexical. In Shanghai Chinese, the words meaning 'a' and 'some' are clitics, but the same words can also mean 'one' and 'two' respectively, in which case they are not clitics (Selkirk 1990). In Chonnam Korean, the word *saaram* forms its own accentual phrase when it means 'man' but not when it means 'someone' (Jun 1990). In Isthmus Zapotec (Mexico: Mock 1985), most prepositions are originally body part nouns; in the former function they are unstressed, in the latter they are stressed: for instance *lu* 'before,' *lú* 'face.'

A variety of Greek evidence attests the propensity of the article and prepositions to undergo phonological reduction that is not found with lexical words. Reduction of long diphthongs may have occurred earlier in the forms of the article (Bechtel 1921:45; Schwyzer 1959:201). Contraction tends to occur earlier in the feminine article than in *ā*-stem nouns, as in Boeotian

> ταν υπεραμεριαων *DGE* 523.14
> των φυλεων *DGE* 701.14.

Elean rhotacism may have started in nonlexical forms (Bechtel 1923). The disyllabic prepositions ἀνά, παρά, κατά, ποτί are widely reduced to monosyllabic forms, and the resulting final consonants are subject to assimilation (Bechtel 1923; Rüsch 1914)

> αμ ποταμον Cretan
> παρ τας πολιος Aetolian
> κατ τον νομους Phocian
> ποτ ταν πολιν Argolic.

In Elean, certain phonologically heavy forms of the article can be reduced to the onset dental stop before a vowel (Bechtel 1923:845); there is no reason to assume that the phenomenon is merely orthographic

> τ' ιαρο
> τ' Ολυμπιοι
> τορ ιαρομαορ τ' Ολυμπιαι.

Appositives

Just as many nonlexicals have a lexically assigned accent which can be reduced in fluent speech, so at least those nonlexicals that do not violate the minimal word weight rule can be regarded as lexically demarcated words whose demarcation is reduced in fluent speech. Even nonlexicals that are never demarcated in ordinary speech are more autonomous than bound morphemes, in the sense that they are more likely to be demarcated in slow dictation. In Greek, nonlexicals tend to lose the status of autonomous words having their own thesis and come to be treated more as part of a contiguous word. As a result, extended domains are created for the rules of rhythm, including but not limited to demarcation: particularly obvious departures from underlying word rhythm are noticeable when final syllables become medial in the extended domain. As just remarked, not all nonlexicals lose their rhythmical autonomy, and those nonlexicals that do lose rhythmical autonomy do not necessarily do so for all the different rules of rhythmic prosody or in all environments or at all rates and styles of speech, nor do they all have an equal propensity to do so other things being equal. The term appositive is commonly used to refer to the class of nonlexicals that have the potential for losing some degree of rhythmical autonomy, or to this class of words when they actually do lose rhythmical autonomy in any particular instance. A prepositive is an appositive which, when it is not autonomous, coheres rhythmically with what follows, and a postpositive is an appositive which, when it is not autonomous, coheres rhythmically with what precedes. The direction in which appositives cohere rhythmically with contiguous words is normally, but not uniformly, the same as that in which they cohere syntactically. The term appositive group properly refers to a prosodic structure that is made up of a host word, usually a lexical, and one or more nonlexicals, and that is not rhythmically identical either to the word or to the minor phrase. However, the term is also used more loosely to refer to such a structure whether or not it is rhythmically identical to the word at any particular rate of speech; similarly, in English *a rise* is often called a clitic group even when it is phonetically undistinguishable from *arise* at the rate of speech described. The appositive group is distinguished from the phonological phrase in having a higher degree of the postlexical counterparts of lexical rules, that is, it has more word prosody than phrases (but less than simple words). For instance, subordination tends to be more constrained in the appositive group than in the word, but less constrained than in the phrase where it is found to apply between lexical words only in colloquial speech. It is important to distinguish between the syntactic constituent or prosodic domain to which clitics or appositives attach (Zec et al. 1991) and the prosodic domain that results from their being hosted by a contiguous word: for instance, a clitic may be attached to some type of phrase but form a clitic group with its host word only.

In Greek, where accent and rhythm are not as highly correlated as in English, it is useful to distinguish the appositive group as a rhythmic domain from the clitic group as an accentual domain. Not all rhythmic appositives are accentual clitics and not all accentual clitics are fully appositive rhythmically. Similarly in Luganda, rules for tone lowering can under certain conditions apply within the phrase and be blocked within the clitic group, which results in a noncorrelation between demarcation rules governing vowel quantity and tone rules of an accentual nature governing pitch fall (Hyman et al. 1987).

The theory of Greek appositives is also supported by evidence from the word order of particles. This evidence does not necessarily indicate syntactic cohesion, since the placement of clitics can reflect phonological conditions (Zec et al. 1990). Postpositive particles are as a very general rule placed after the first word or, less commonly, after the first constituent of the clause. In the latter case, the constituent sometimes consists of two lexical words

γυναῖκα πιστὴν δ' *Agamemnon* 606
φλογὶ φέγγεται δὲ λειμών *Frogs* 344

but, particularly in prose, the majority of instances involves article, preposition or negative (Denniston 1934)

ἐν δημοκρατίᾳ δὲ *Republic* 564d
τοὺς ἀνθρώπους δὲ *Parmenides* 128c
ἐπὶ τῇ κεφαλῇ δὲ *Anabasis* 5.4.13.

This evidence distinguishes the appositive group from other phrases as a preferential environment for postponed particles.

Syllable restructuring

In addition to their particular rhythmical properties, many nonlexicals in Greek show their own specific behaviour with regards to the various rules of syllable phonology, such as resyllabification, gemination and elision. It was demonstrated in Chapter 6 that the appositive group is a particularly favourable environment for coda to onset resyllabification, onset to coda resyllabification, and $\dot{p}$-gemination; furthermore, with onset to coda resyllabification, the steeper the sonority slope of the cluster, the less likely resyllabification is to occur in structures other than the appositive group.

Metrical evidence

Metrical evidence for appositive groups must be interpreted in the framework of covarying access to two parameters. The first parameter is metrical environment or position in the line: what is evidence for appositive status line internally may not be evidence at all line initially or even postcaesurally, and the line internal positions are themselves ordered into a hierarchy of constraint (DS 1984). Particularly in comedy, major syntactic boundaries and change of speaker within the line are likewise locations of greater licence, with the qualification that some nonlexicals, particularly sentential second position particles, are automatically attracted to the vicinity of postpausal metrical locations. Postpausal metrical licence is a well established feature in many metrical systems (p. 145). The second parameter involves the stylistic differences among the genres: nonlexicals or semilexicals that are appositive in comedy are not necessarily so in tragedy. The second parameter reflects the different rates and styles of speech to which comedy, satyric and tragedy have access. In fluent, colloquial speech a greater number of nonlexicals in a greater variety of syntactic contexts are appositive than in slow, deliberate speech. Since comedy has easier access to colloquial speech than tragedy, it offers a greater variety of appositives with less syntactic constraint. This is documented at various points in the ensuing analysis. Access to one parameter covaries with that to the other, because satyric and comedy also relax the constraints of position in the line as compared with tragedy.

Š-prepositives

A single light monosyllabic prepositive, that is a prepositive consisting of a syllable light by nature or by position and not contiguous to another appositive, is strongly avoided before the caesura in all styles of the trimeter. This indicates that such prepositives did not have the durational demarcation characteristic of full words. It remains open whether in certain styles of speech they could have a reduced degree of demarcation (appositive demarcation) or whether they simply had no demarcation at all (p. 283). In the latter case, they would not differ in demarcation from nonfinal syllables of lexical words. The evidence from precaesural location is confirmed by the distribution of these forms at bridges. Such forms do not violate Hermann's bridge in the hexameter

> καὶ ἀδευκέα πότμον *Odyssey* 10.245
> ἐν ἀγῶνι πεσόντα *Iliad* 15.428, 16.500
> τὸν ἄριστον ἁπάντων *Odyssey* 14.19
> ὅς ἐναίσιμος εἴη *Iliad* 6.521, *Odyssey* 10.383.

Unlike the final syllable of a lexical word, a prepositive consisting of a light syllable may be remapped onto a matrix in the style of language to which tragedy has access

> ὁ κακός, ὁ προδότης *Orestes* 1057
> τὸν ἀσεβῆ *O.C.* 823, *O.T.* 1382, 1441
> τίς ὀνομάζεται *Phoenissae* 124;

with elided disyllabic nonlexical

> τίν' ἐπικουρίαν *Orestes* 266
> ἐπ' ὀλέθρῳ *Phoenissae* 534
> ἵν' ἀκοῦσαι *Bacchae* 475.

S̄-prepositives

A single heavy monosyllabic prepositive is also strongly avoided before the caesura in all styles of the trimeter. An emendation that introduces one, such as the insertion of ἐν before the caesura at *Orestes* 88, is to be regarded with suspicion on metrical grounds. If a heavy monosyllabic prepositive stands before a lexical iamb-shaped word followed by a lexical disyllable at the end of the trimeter

> ἐν δόμοις ἰδών Semonides 7.29
> ἐν δίκῃ χρόνου Solon 36.3,

the resulting structure does not violate Knox's iamb bridge. A heavy monosyllabic prepositive is allowed to stand before Porson's bridge in tragedy

> τοῖς δύσφροσιν *Agamemnon* 608
> ἐν σπαργάνοις *Agamemnon* 1606
> οὐ βούλομαι Soph. *Electra* 1043
> καὶ πλούσιον *Andromache* 640

but not in Archilochus, Semonides and Solon. Table 7.1 compares the incidence of syntagmatic tetrasyllables with prepositive before Porson's bridge (#S̄#S̄S̄S̄#, type just cited) and asyntagmatic tetrasyllables (#S̄S̄S̄S̄#, type τητωμένη *Helen* 274) at the end of the trimeter in the iambographers and in the *Helen*. The results indicate that the absence of the syntagmatic type in the iambographers is statistically significant. Furthermore, prepositives before Porson's bridge are comparatively rare in the strictest styles of tragedy too; this constraint is progressively relaxed in the later plays of Euripides, as is evidenced by the data in Table 7.2. Loss of demarcation after καί is independently suggested by the pun on καὶ νοῦ and καινοῦ Diogenes Laertius 2.118, 6.3. An elided trochee-shaped nonlexical is also allowed before Porson's bridge

δεῦρ᾽ ἱκόμην O. T. 318
ἀλλ᾽ ἐννοεῖς O. T. 330, cp. 831
ἀντ᾽ εὐσεβοῦς Helen 1029
ἔστ᾽ ἄξια Bacchae 246, cp. Orestes 615
κᾆτ᾽ ἔκπιε Cyclops 563.

Loss of demarcation after an elided nonlexical is independently suggested by the pun on τήνδ᾽ἐμοῦσαν and τήνδε μοῦσαν (p. 239, 260); the reported ambiguity of ἀνθ᾽ ὧν and ἀνθῶν Etymologicum Magnum 108.53 could be purely orthographic.

This difference in the admissibility of prepositives before Porson's bridge between stricter and less strict metrical styles of the trimeter can be interpreted as reflecting a difference in the fluency or informality of the speech styles which they permit themselves to access. It would follow that heavy monosyllabic prepositives are not subordinated in this phonological environment in deliberate speech, but become progressively more liable to subordination as the style of speech becomes more fluent: similarly in Madurese (Java: Stevens 1968), proclitics are independent words in slow speech and part of a larger phonological word in fast speech. At the slow speech end of the parameter, the syntagmatic tetrasyllable with the prepositive was less likely to undergo subordination than the asyntagmatic tetrasyllable: subordination before another heavy syllable in the same word is easier than subordination consequent on appositive boundary reduction.

A heavy syllable prepositive before a spondee-shaped word ending in fifth longum does not constitute an absolute violation of Wilamowitz's bridge in the iambographers

ἐξ οἴκου βάλοι Semonides 7.60

but the resulting syntagmatic molossus structure is more constrained than the asyntagmatic molossus, type ἀνθρώποις. The syntagmatic molos-

TABLE 7.1
Syntagmatic and asyntagmatic line final tetrasyllables
in the iambographers and in tragedy

	Syntagmatic tetrasyllable	Nonsyntagmatic tetrasyllable
Archilochus, Semonides, Solon	0	12
Helen	24	72

$p = 0.041$, $\omega = 8.448$

TABLE 7.2

Rate per thousand trimeters in Euripides
of heavy monosyllabic unelided prepositive
at Porson's bridge

Severior except *Rhesus*	
and *Alcestis*	3.31
Semiseverus	12.61
Liber	21.99
Liberrimus	32.77

sus represents 34.81% of all molossus structures in Euripides' *Helen* but only 7.5% in Archilochus, Semonides and Solon, a difference which is statistically significant ($\chi^2 = 11.661$). These data suggest that although a heavy syllable prepositive can create the environment for subordination of the first syllable of a following spondee-shaped word, it could also remain rhythmically autonomous in slow and careful speech. Similarly, matrix formation is more constrained in a syntagmatic dactyl structure, type τὸν πόδα, than it is in a lexical dactyl-shaped word, type μητέρα. In Euripides Liberrimus, the syntagmatic type is a little more common than the asyntagmatic type, but in Euripides Liber it is only half as common: this means that in the Liber style resolution is more constrained in the syntagmatic type than in the simple lexical dactyl-shaped word; this constraint was then relaxed in the Liberrimus style.

Ŝ- and S̄-postpositives

In the case of prepositives, the nonlexical itself suffered loss of durational demarcation, opening up the way to subordination of the nonlexical before Porson's bridge and subordination of the first syllable of the following spondee-shaped word at Wilamowitz's bridge. In the case of postpositives, boundary weakening occurs to the left of the nonlexical, because the domain of rhythmic organization joins the nonlexical with the preceding lexical. The final syllable of the lexical word is not a trigger for subordination but itself the target; it loses demarcation, thereby creating an environment for remapping. Similarly in Luganda, enclitics create an environment in which final vowel shortening does not apply (Hyman et al. 1987). On the other hand, in Modern Hebrew rhythmically motivated stress shift across words affects nonlexical words only (Bolozky 1982).

A single monosyllabic postpositive consisting of a light syllable which does not cohere to the right for syntactic reasons or because of elision is regularly placed before rather than after the feminine caesura in the hexameter. A single light postpositive is found rarely after the first syllable of a resolution

> ποτὲ μὲν ἐπ᾽ ἦμαρ *Phoenissae* 401
> ὀψέ γε φρονεῖς εὖ *Orestes* 99
> ἴσα γὰρ ἀληθῶς *Birds* 1167.

A single monosyllabic postpositive consisting of a heavy syllable may stand after the caesura in the trimeter, as

> κἀγώ 'ξελέγξαι μὲν ξένους *I. T.* 955
> παρέξω γὰρ δέρην *Hecuba* 549,

with resyllabification

> δυοῖν γερόντοιν δὲ στρατηγεῖται *Heraclidae* 39.

Such lines are far more common than they would be if they were merely lines with medial diaeresis which happened to have postpositives in third longum, since medial diaeresis is otherwise rare in Euripides. On the other hand, they are not as common as they would be if postpositives were no less acceptable than lexical monosyllables and prepositives after the caesura. It is not clear whether these postcaesural postpositives were rhythmically autonomous, or simply changed from postpositive to prepositive status as is assumed for postcaesural enclitics (p. 365). There are no cases in the iambographers of a single monosyllabic postpositive following a lexical trochee-shaped word ending in third anceps: the structure

> ἄνδρα γὰρ χρεών *Heraclidae* 390

does not occur in Archilochus, Semonides or Solon. All cases of a postpositive in this context involve a preceding nonlexical trochee-shaped word

> οὐδέ μιν κακῶν *Semonides* 7.8
> οὔτε γὰρ κακὸν *Semonides* 7.22
> ταῦτα μὲν κράτει *Solon* 36.15.

Although the incidence is too low for a statistical proof, it is likely that a postpositive in this position did not by itself prevent a violation of Knox's trochee bridge. Taken together, the evidence from the distribution of single postpositives indicates that those consisting of a light syllable caused loss of demarcation, while those consisting of a heavy syllable were less likely than lexical monosyllables to be rhythmically autonomous, but more likely than light syllable postpositives and more likely than light and heavy syllable prepositives to be rhythmically autonomous.

Single postpositives consisting of a heavy syllable are quite rare at Porson's bridge particularly after a lexical word in all styles of the trimeter

> θνητοῖς γὰρ γέρα *P. V.* 107

μισεῖς μὲν λόγῳ Soph. *Electra* 357
δόξῃ γοῦν ἐμῇ *Trachiniae* 718
σωτὴρ νῷν βλάβης *Heraclidae* 640 MSS
ἄρχειν γὰρ νεὼς *Helen* 1552.

Although single postpositives following a lexical word are not common after short third anceps either, they are particularly constrained after long third anceps. This indicates that in fluent speech a heavy postpositive could create the environment for the subordination of the final syllable of a preceding lexical word but that the resulting syntagmatic molossus was more constrained than the corresponding asyntagmatic molossus.

S̆S̆-appositives

There is a considerable body of evidence indicating that disyllabic non-lexicals can be appositive under certain conditions. There are a few cases of a resolution split after a nonlexical pyrrhic-shaped word

παρὰ λόγον *Bacchae* 940
τίνα λόγον *Ion* 931
τίνα τρόπον *Birds* 180
ὅθεν ὁ πατρῷος *Birds* 1527
περὶ γυναικὸς *Birds* 1639
πόθεν ἔχεις *Epitrepontes* 864
μόλις ἀνακύπτοντ' *Dyscolus* 537.

There is a split before the nonlexical in

δορὸς ὑπὸ πολεμίου τυπείς *Acharnians* 1194;

this instance involves a head interrupted prepositional phrase, as does

Ἑλικῶνος ὑπὸ ζαθέοιο *Theogony* 23

with iamb-shaped preposition at Hermann's bridge. A pyrrhic-shaped postpositive is found in

λαβὼν ταχὺ πάνυ *Thesmophoriazusae* 916.

It may be that these split resolutions tend to involve high frequency lexical words following the disyllabic nonlexical, or that they tend to be common syntagms. ἐμός can be appositive in common syntagms, as perhaps English *mə boy* versus *my buoy*

ἐμὸς ἀνὴρ *Lysistrata* 102
ὁ μὲν οὖν ἐμὸς υἱός Alexis Arnott 1957:n.4;

monosyllabic and trochee-shaped forms of this word arising by prodelision and crasis respectively can also be appositive

τῇ 'μῇ μωρίᾳ *Ichneutae* 353
οὑμὸς ἀνὴρ *Lysistrata* 838.

When filling a resolved longum in the trimeter, nonlexical pyrrhic-shaped words

> περὶ νεκροῖς *Phoenissae* 881
> δύο λόγω *Phoenissae* 559

are less constrained than lexical ones

> πόλιν ἀποστερῶν *Phoenissae* 993
> ψόγος ἐς ῞Ελληνας *Bacchae* 779.

The data presented in Table 7.3 indicate that, particularly in Aeschylus and Sophocles, lexical words are constrained in this position as compared with the practice in later Euripides. In resolved fourth longum lexical pyrrhic-shaped words are strictly avoided, elided tribrach-shaped words are rare, but nonlexicals are admitted in the later styles; in resolved second longum only nonlexicals are permitted.

If an anapaest at the beginning of the trimeter is divided after a pyrrhic-shaped word, the pyrrhic-shaped word is always nonlexical in tragedy and overwhelmingly so in Aristophanes, and the following word is commonly nonlexical

> ἐπὶ τοῖσδε Eur. *Electra* 1030
> μετὰ ταῦτ' *Frogs* 143
> ἀτὰρ ἥτις *Ecclesiazusae* 1067, cp. *Lysistrata* 65, 450.

Examples with a following lexical word are

> ἐπὶ δαῖτα *Bacchae* 1247
> ἐπὶ συμφοραῖς *Knights* 655
> ἵνα θοἰμάτιον *Ecclesiazusae* 544
> ἐμὸν ἔργον *Thesmophoriazusae* 1172.

The proportion of pyrrhic-shaped nouns dividing initial anapaests in Aristophanes is only 1.5% as compared with almost 15% in Menander. A possible interpretation of this evidence is that, in agreement with the principle of final syllable prominence, the underlying or lexical rhythm

TABLE 7.3
Lexical pyrrhic-shaped words as a percentage
of all pyrrhic-shaped words in resolved longum

Aeschylus	8.57
Sophocles	13.89
Severior	30.00
Semiseverus	23.26
Liber	39.33
Liberrimus	31.31

of the pyrrhic-shaped word is iambic; mapping of the two light syllables onto arsis would then represent remapping in connected speech. Nonlexical pyrrhic-shaped words are less resistant to remapping than lexicals. Loss of demarcation may be indicated by the reported ambiguity of κατὰ φέροντος and καταφέροντος Apollonius Dyscolus II.435.6 Uhlig and by the pun on ἀπ' ὄνου and ἀπὸ νοῦ according to the scholiast on *Clouds* 1273 (p. 239, 260).

S̄S̆-appositives

Reduction of demarcation after nonlexical trochee-shaped words is indicated by their occurrence ending in third anceps in the trimeter of the iambographers, where lexicals are constrained because of Knox's trochee bridge. While a structure like

ῥᾷστος ἀνδρὶ δυστυχεῖ *Hippolytus* 1047

is not possible in the iambographers, structures like

ἀλλὰ μυρίαι Semonides 1.20
οὐδὲ πάρδαλιν Semonides 14.2
ἄλλον ἐκδίκως Solon 36.9
οὔτε πεμμάτων Solon 38.3

are permissible. In more fluent speech, nonlexical trochee-shaped words can also undergo remapping, so that their final syllable forms a matrix with the initial syllable of a following nonpostpositive word; in tragedy, there are only a couple of examples of such dactyls in Euripides Liberrimus

οὐδὲ πάθος *Orestes* 2
ὥστε διὰ τοῦτον *Bacchae* 285.

The structure is found in

αὐτὸς ἔχ' *Cyclops* 270

and is well documented in Aristophanes

ὥσπερ ἀδικηθεὶς *Birds* 138
ἀλλὰ δόλιον *Plutus* 1157
ταῦτα καταθείμην *Ecclesiazusae* 795.

In Menander, trochee-shaped lexicals are permitted in initial dactyls

πτωχὸς ἀδικηθείς *Dyscolus* 296
πρᾶξιν ἰδίαν *Heros* 46

and major syntactic boundaries sometimes occur after them, which may be a metrical artificiality. The data are presented in Table 7.4. The steady diachronic and stylistic trend in the table indicates that this type of remapping was not readily admitted in the styles of speech on which tragedy

TABLE 7.4

Line initial dactyls split after a nonlexical
trochee-shaped word without punctuation
as a percentage of all line initial dactyls

Liber	0.00
Liberrimus	1.52
Aristophanes	7.50
Menander	10.29

is based. An anapaest is split after a nonlexical trochee-shaped word more
rarely than a dactyl, partly because this combination cannot begin the line

> τόνδε λέβητα *Cyclops* 343
> τούσδε παιανιστάς *Dyscolus* 230 Pap.
> ὡς κεῖνος ἀναιδέως *Peace* 48
> ἀλλὰ καλοῦμαι *Clouds* 1221
> δὴ ʼντεῦθεν ἐλοιδορούμεθα *Clouds* 62 (δʼ ἠντεῦθεν Rav.)
> μήτε δάκνειν *Birds* 442.

A monosyllabic lexical word is subordinated at Porson's bridge before
a syntactically left cohering trochee-shaped nonlexical in

> παῖς ἥδε μοι Eur. *Supplices* 1098.

When an initial anapaest in the trimeter is divided, it is relatively rare,
even in Menander, for the first two syllables to constitute a lexical pyrrhic-
shaped word not followed by a postpositive. Four cases involve lexical
words followed by ἐστί

> λάλος ἐστὶν Euripides Frag. 112.2 Nauck
> τρόπος ἔσθʼ Menander Frag. 407.7 Körte
> πάθος ἐστί *Aspis* 286
> ξένος ἐστὶν *Misumenus* 270.

These examples suggest that this enclitic trochee-shaped word could also
cohere rhythmically with a preceding pyrrhic-shaped lexical word; it
coheres to the right as well as to the left in

> τουτὶ τί ποτʼ ἐστὶ τὸ θηρίον; *Birds* 93.

Elided ἐστʼ occurs at Porson's bridge in late Euripides (p. 310).

S̆S̄-appositives

Reduction of durational demarcation after a right-linking nonlexical
iamb-shaped word is indicated by the occurrence of such words ending
in fifth longum in the trimeter of the iambographers, where lexical iamb-

shaped words are constrained because of Knox's iamb bridge. While a structure like

> στυγεῖ πόσις *Andromache* 205

is not possible in the iambographers, structures like

> ὅκῃ θέλει Semonides 1.2
> ὑπὸ χθονός Semonides 1.14

are permissible. However, the resulting syntagmatic structure is more constrained than the corresponding asyntagmatic structure, since the syntagmatic diiamb represents 8.14% of all diiambs in the iambographers as compared with 20.93% in Euripides' *Helen* ($\chi^2 = 6.351$). A violation of Wilamowitz's bridge in a tetrameter is avoided through the preceding iamb-shaped prepositive in

> καὶ περὶ κνήμας ἰδεῖν Archilochus 114.3.

There is some evidence from the hexameter that ἐών can be postpositive

> καὶ ἐσθλὸς ἐὼν ἀγορεύεις *Iliad* 16.627, *Odyssey* 17.381
>   Hermann's bridge
> ἀλλ᾽ ἔτι παιδνὸς ἐὼν Callimachus *Hymns* 1.57 Meyer's
>   bridge.

The other examples of word boundary at Meyer's bridge in Callimachus' *Hymns* and *Epigrams* have trochee-shaped nonlexicals preceding the bridge. The sequence nonlexical trochee-shaped word plus nonlexical iamb-shaped word splits an anapaest in

> δεῦρο πάλιν βαδιστέον *Frogs* 652, 658.

S̄S̄-appositives

The spondee-shaped word has the greatest phonological substance of all the disyllabic word shapes, and nonlexical spondee-shaped words are consequently less likely to be appositive than lighter shapes, other things being equal. A spondee-shaped nonlexical ending in fifth longum does not prevent a violation of Wilamowitz's bridge: a structure like

> καίπερ τρέμων *Andromache* 717

is not permitted in the iambographers. The corresponding asyntagmatic tetrasyllabic structure

> μωμήσεται Semonides 7.113

does occur, although it is constrained. The manuscripts offer a few possible cases of a morphologically uncompounded spondee-shaped nonlexical word before Porson's bridge

> ἀλλὰ ψεύσεται *Andromache* 346
> οὕτω γίγνεται *I. T.* 580.

Morphologically complex spondee-shaped nonlexicals (p. 342) are rather better attested before Porson's bridge

> οὐδεὶς βούλεται *Alcestis* 671; contrast οὐδεὶς ἀντερεῖ
> *Alcestis* 615 with intervening caesura
> οὐδεὶς ἠδίκει *Cyclops* 672, cp. 120
> οὐδὲν θάτερον *Phoenissae* 747
> οὐδὲν γίγνεται Eur. Frag. 494.1 Nauck
> οὐδὲν δεῖ πονεῖν *O.C.* 1022
> οὐδὲν δεῖ φίλων *H.F.* 1338
> οὐδὲν δεῖ θεῶν Eur. Frag. 154.4 Austin.

Although δεῖ is prepositive at *Orestes* 1035 and postpositive at *Isthmiastae* 7, its direction of coherence often seems to depend on the syntax, so it probably does not cohere to the left in these two instances; οὐδὲν δεῖ may be a fixed phrase. It is also likely that spondee-shaped nonlexicals could be postpositive on the evidence of a few divided anapaests

> ἀλλ᾽ ἔμπορος εἶναι *Ecclesiazusae* 1027
> βεβρεγμένος ἥκω Eubulus 123.2KA
> ἐπίσκοπος ἥκω *Birds* 1022;

in the last two examples the verb seems to have been semantically bleached almost to the status of an auxiliary.

Trisyllabic appositives

Even with trisyllabic words, nonlexical status favours rhythmic coherence. The tribrach-shaped word πότερον, -α represents 50% of all line initial tribrachs in Euripides Severior, as compared with only 12.5% in Euripides Liberrimus. The discrepancy may simply be due to the basic syntactic need for this word in a style which significantly constrains the overall incidence of resolution, but it is also possible that its non-lexical status and high text frequency encouraged matrix formation on the word final syllables. In

> ποτέρας τῆς χερός; *Cyclops* 681

ποτέρας stands before Porson's bridge followed by the definite article, where a lexical anapaest-shaped word would not be acceptable. The non-lexical status of the dactyl-shaped word αὐτίκα as well as of the following pyrrhic-shaped word apparently contribute to the acceptability of split resolution in the fixed phrase

> αὐτίκα μάλα *Frogs* 785, *Lysistrata* 744
> αὐτίκα μάλ᾽ *Knights* 746, *Peace* 367, *Birds* 202,
> *Lysistrata* 739.

An amphibrach-shaped nonlexical stands before Hermann's bridge in
ἄνευθε πόνου καὶ ἀνίης *Odyssey* 7.192.

Composites

Sequences of nonlexicals can join together into a single lexicalized accentual unit (p. 342), but even when they do not do so they still have a
tendency to form autonomous rhythmic units. It is often found that a
sequence of two appositives may stand before a bridge: whereas this might
not seem particularly remarkable in the case of two prepositives, it is
equally true of the sequence prepositive plus postpositive. Furthermore,
sequences of two appositives are also found before the caesura, where
single prepositives are strongly avoided. For instance, in the *Orestes* when
a single prepositive stands in second anceps, there is always an alternative metrical division (hephthemimeral caesura or medial elision), but
when a sequence of two prepositives ends in second anceps, in two thirds
of the instances the following penthemimeral division is the only possible caesura ($p = 0.0015$). Before a bridge, the appositive sequence forms
a single undemarcated sequence with the following word; on the other
hand, precaesural location implies word demarcation. The apparent
contradiction is easily resolved by the assumption that the appositive
sequence was a rhythmically autonomous composite at slower rates of
speech but lost its autonomy in more rapid speech; the variation in verse
indicates that verse had access to both rates of speech. This evidence
for appositive sequences in Greek is paralleled in Ilocano (Philippines:
Bloomfield 1942), where a proclitic like *kas* 'as' followed by an enclitic
like *la* 'only' becomes a proclitic sequence, and proclitic *kas* 'as' followed
by proclitic *ta* 'that' results in *kasta*, which varies between proclitic and
autonomous word. When a clitic composite becomes an autonomous
word, it can move to a nonclitic position, as happens with sentence initial
clitic clusters in Warumungu (Australia: Simpson et al. 1986). In a final
stage, the composite can develop into a single lexical item like French
du and *des*. In Byzantine Greek, appositive sequences are more readily
stressed than single appositives and less readily stressed than disyllabic
nonlexical words (Stephens 1988).

There may also be some syntactic evidence for the composite. There
are a few instances in which a particle, instead of being placed after the
first word or after the first constituent, is inserted between the branching nodes of a noun phrase that does not begin the clause (Denniston
1934)

ἐν τοῖς γὰρ οἰκείοισιν *Antigone* 661
δεῖ τᾶς γὰρ εἰράνας *Lysistrata* 144
περὶ τῶν δὲ κορῶν *Lysistrata* 593

> ἡ τῶν γὰρ ἀνδρῶν Alexis 150.6KA
> ἐν τῷ γὰρ αἰσχρῷ Plato *Symposium* 209b
> ὑπὸ τοῦ γε λιμοῦ *Peace* 483
> ἐν τῇ δὲ ἐσθῆτι Herodotus 2.159.

One possible explanation of such instances is that the particle is here placed after the first prosodic word, which is the composite made up of nonlexical plus article.

S̆S̆-composites

A pyrrhic-shaped sequence of prepositive plus prepositive does not yield an unacceptable split resolution when the second appositive is the first syllable of the matrix

> τίς ὁ τρόπος *Phoenissae* 390
> τίς ὁ πόθος *Philoctetes* 601.

The sequence prepositive plus postpositive may also be metrically located in this way

> τὸ δὲ πλέον Eur. *Supplices* 158
> τὸ γὰρ ἴσον *Phoenissae* 538.

Some degree of potential autonomy for such structures is suggested by their occasional occurrence at the end of the trimeter in comedy

> τό τε *Samia* 235
> τί δὲ *Samia* 307.

All examples of articles at the end of the line in the εἶδος Σοφόκλειον with the exception of *Antigone* 409 involve some form of appositive sequence

> τό τε *O.T.* 995
> τὸ γὰρ *Trachiniae* 434
> τὰ σὰ *Antigone* 453.

S̄S̆-composites

Trochee-shaped sequences consisting of two prepositives or of prepositive plus postpositive are permitted to occur before Knox's trochee bridge in the trimeter of the iambographers

> οἱ μὲν ἡμέρην Semonides 1.7
> οὐδ' ἐς οἰκίην Semonides 7.106
> οἱ δὲ σίλφιον Solon 39.1.

Such sequences can also stand before the caesura as rhythmical composites

> τοὺς μὲν Ἀΐδης Semonides 7.117
> τὴν δὲ τουτέρου Semonides 7.113.

In drama, a trochee-shaped prepositive plus prepositive sequence does not yield an unacceptable split resolution in

> μὴ τὸ κράτος Bacchae 310
> καὶ τὸ μανιῶδες Bacchae 299.

Such structures can also appear as a composite before the caesura

> ἢ τὸν αὐτάδελφον Antigone 503
> οὐ πρὸς ἡδονὴν λέγω τάδε; Soph. Electra 921
> κἂν ἐν ἡμέρᾳ γνοίης μιᾷ O.T. 615.

A trochee-shaped prepositive plus postpositive sequence does not yield an unacceptable split resolution in

> οὐ γὰρ ἔνι τούτοις Lysistrata 163
> εἰ δὲ παραβαίην Lysistrata 235;

there is a case in tragedy with a following postpositive

> εἰ δέ τι κόρης σῆς I.A. 498.

This structure can also appear as a composite before the caesura

> εἰ δὲ δυστυχεῖ Orestes 484
> τὰς γὰρ ἐν μέσῳ σιγῶ τύχας Orestes 16
> ἔκ τε τειχέων Phoenissae 1103.

SS-composites

The variable application of remapping just noted for resolution also motivates the metrical treatment of spondee-shaped sequences of two appositives at Porson's bridge. Like single monosyllabic prepositives, and unlike spondee-shaped nonlexicals for the most part, these sequences can stand before Porson's bridge. Unlike single monosyllabic prepositives, and like spondee-shaped nonlexicals, these sequences can stand before the caesura. Prepositive plus prepositive stands before Porson's bridge in cases like

> ἢ τοῖς δρωμένοις O.C. 1144
> ἐς τὴν εὔβοτρυν Philoctetes 548
> ἐκ τῆς ποντίας Philoctetes 269
> εἰ μὴ τοῦ θεοῦ O.T. 1438.

Very comparable sequences stand before the caesura as composites

> καὶ τοῖς ἤθεσιν Eur. Electra 385
> πρὸς τοὺς δυσσεβεῖς O.C. 280
> ἐκ τῆς αἰχμαλωτίδος Ajax 1228
> εἰ μὴ τὰς φρένας Hippolytus 1014.

The phonological attraction of the two appositives into a composite can overcome syntactic constituency, so that a determiner is detached from its noun and attached to a preceding conjunction or preposition.

Prepositive plus postpositive stands before Porson's bridge less commonly

ἐν γὰρ τῷ μαθεῖν *O.C.* 115.

This structure is well attested before the caesura

ἐν γὰρ τοῖς πόνοισιν Eur. *Supplices* 323.

When the appositive sequence stands before Porson's bridge, the second appositive is subordinated in the syntagmatic molossus that results from joining the appositive sequence to the following cretic word in a single domain. When the appositive sequence stands before the caesura, it must be an autonomous rhythmical composite. Once again it is necessary to assume variation in the language, with the versification of the tragedians having access to both variants. The appositive sequence stands midway in the hierarchy of autonomy between single prepositives and disyllabic nonlexicals. An additional step on the hierarchy is represented by structures in which the second appositive is a prodelided nonlexical

τῇ 'μῇ μωρίᾳ *Ichneutae* 353 Radt.

Extended composites

There is some evidence that even disyllabic nonlexicals followed by a postpositive can join with a following word to constitute a single word-like rhythmic domain. Knox's iamb bridge is apparently not violated by

κάρτα γὰρ κακῶς ῥιγῶ Hipponax 32.2
οὐδέ οἱ γέλως μέλει Semonides 7.79;

in the Semonides line there may be the added motivation that οἱ μέλει is a syntactic constituent. Further evidence comes from the data on split anapaests in comedy

οὐδὲν γὰρ ἄνευ σοῦ *Birds* 847
ἀφ' οὗ γὰρ ὁ Πλοῦτος *Plutus* 1173
καίτοι γε ταλάντου *Clouds* 876
καὐτὴ γὰρ ἔγωγ' *Thesmophoriazusae* 469.

Such cases seem to be an extension of the right cohering properties of the composite noted above in which the postpositive follows a monosyllabic prepositive, which likewise yield acceptable split anapaests

καὶ γὰρ ἐγὼ *Thesmophoriazusae* 173, *Ecclesiazusae* 998.

In principle, it could be assumed that in these structures the postpositive simply becomes prepositive, as happens in the case of syntactically motivated prepositive enclitics (p. 365), without the creation of an extended domain including the preceding disyllabic nonlexical. However, such an interpretation does not account for the parallel nature of the evidence for morphologically simplex nonlexicals (type ἀλλά), morphologically complex nonlexicals (type οὐδέ), composites with monosyllabic first element (type εἰ δέ) and composites with polysyllabic first element (type κάρτα γάρ). Since the noncomposites can only cohere to the right in their entirety, it is simpler to assume that the composites also form a single right cohering rhythmical structure.

In satyric, a nonlexical spondee- or anapaest-shaped word may stand before Porson's bridge provided it is followed by the definite article

> τάχα τις ὑμῶν τῷ ξύλῳ *Cyclops* 210
> ποτέρας τῆς χερός *Cyclops* 681
> πρὸς αὐτῇ τῇ πέτρᾳ *Cyclops* 682
> αὐτῇ τῇ κλο[πῇ] *Ichneutae* 341 Radt;

there is a single instance in tragedy

> κἄνευ τῆς ἐμῆς *O.C.* 664.

These instances indicate that a polysyllabic nonlexical was more liable to remapping with subordination of its final heavy syllable if a form of the article followed; remapping presupposes a single wordlike rhythmic domain. These instances differ from the composites in anapaests just discussed, in that it is the final syllable of the polysyllabic nonlexical, rather than the following monosyllabic postpositive, that is remapped.

Bidirectional appositives

Postpositives are occasionally found before Hermann's bridge between lexical words; although many cases have syntactic motivation for cohering to the right, or occur after a nonlexical iamb-shaped word and so belong with the composites, or both

> ἐπεί σε φυγὼν ἱκέτευσα *Odyssey* 15.277
> ἐπεί κε τέκωσι, τοκῆες *Odyssey* 8.554,

a substantial number of instances occur after lexical words and have no overt syntactic motivation

> Διός γε διδόντος ἀρέσθαι *Odyssey* 1.390
> φέρειν δὲ γύην ὅτ' ἂν εὕρῃς *Works and Days* 427
> τροχαλὸν δὲ γέροντα τίθησιν *Works and Days* 518
> λαιοῦ δὲ κεράατος ἄκρον *Phaenomena* 174.

Similarly, there are a number of instances of postpositives making acceptable split anapaests in comedy; although some are apparently syntactically motivated, others are parallel to the Hermann's bridge examples just cited

> ὑπὸ τῶν γλαυκῶν γε τάλαιν' ἀπόλλυμαι *Lysistrata* 760
> καὶ νῦν πορίζεταί γε τὰ δεῖπν' *Alexis* Arnott 1957:n.11.

There is also a case of a postpositive before rather than after Porson's bridge

τῶν κακῶν γὰρ μητέρων *Andromache* 230.

The conjunction τε is found cohering to the right before Hermann's bridge

Τρωσίν τε καὶ Ἕκτορι δίῳ *Iliad* 17.719

σύας τε κύνας τ' ἀπερύκων *Odyssey* 18.105;

and καί seems to be acceptable in a divided anapaest in

ὦ τύμπανα καὶ κύφωνες *Plutus* 476

τριχίδια καὶ σηπίδια Alexis Arnott 1957:n.6.

Although some of these cases may again reflect a simple change from postpositive to prepositive, it is probable that in many instances the rules of word rhythm are extended to the phrasal domain in fluent speech, so that the appositive coheres both to the left and to the right. This interpretation is supported by one instance

κήρυκα δὲ πέμψον *Birds* 843

in which postpositive δέ would give a divided anapaest and prepositive δέ a split anapaest; only bidirectional cohesion gives a wellformed anapaest.

Elision and remapping

The occurrence of elision presupposes cohesive phonological phrasing. In Zulu, elision causes two words to be treated as a single stress domain; when elision fails, each word preserves its original primary stress with intervening hiatus (Doke 1926). In Greek, verse and prose evidence combine to suggest that the domain of elision was the major phrase; it would follow that in speech elision was effectively blocked by pause. Conversely, elision is favoured by cohesive syntactic structures (p. 262), particularly when nonlexicals are present: the proportional incidence of elision in Attic prose inscriptions of the fourth century is particularly high for disyllabic prepositions such as ἀντί, ἀπό, κατά, for the negatives οὐδέ and μηδέ, and for the deictic-anaphorics οἵδε and τάδε (Threatte 1980); subordination of elided forms of ὅδε is well attested at Porson's bridge, as already noted (p. 288)

ξένος μὲν τοῦ λόγου τοῦδ' ἐξερῶ *O.T.* 219

τῆσδ' ἔξομαι *Hecuba* 398

τούσδ' εἰδέναι *Hecuba* 1006

ἢ μόνῳ τῷδ' εὐτυχεῖς; *Ion* 1426 (see app. crit.).

In comedy, elision of polysyllabic nonlexicals is found in divided anapaests

κοὐδεμί' ἔκφορος λόγου *Thesmophoriazusae* 472

οὐδέποτ᾿ ἤλπισα *Birds* 956
οὐδέποθ᾿ ἡμέρα γενήσεται; *Clouds* 3.

When elision occurs, rhythmic cohesion can be increased to the point
at which rules of word rhythm, specifically matrix formation and subordination, can replace the rules of phrase rhythm expected with lexical
words. There are a few examples in resolution or at Porson's bridge of
an elided disyllabic lexical word before a nonlexical other than a postpositive: with resolution

πόδ᾿ ἐπὶ συννοίᾳ κυκλεῖς *Orestes* 632;

at Porson's bridge

καὶ πέρα γ᾿ ἴσθ᾿ ἢ λέγω *Philoctetes* 1277
οὐκ οἶδ᾿ ἐξ ὅτου *Cyclops* 639
πῶς ἐμὰς ἦλθ᾿ ἐς χέρας *Bacchae* 1286 Musurus.

The acceptability of a longer lexical word elided before a nonlexical word
other than a postpositive at Porson's bridge is less well established textually

κατάρχεσθ᾿ εἰ *Heraclidae* 529
σήμαιν᾿ εἶτ᾿ ἔχει *Philoctetes* 22
ἀπείρηκ᾿ ἐν κακοῖς *Orestes* 91;

in

παῖδ᾿ ὄντα *P. V.* 986 FTri

the second word is probably a disyllabic postpositive.

When elision occurs between two lexical words, each word normally
remains a separate domain for the application of the rules of word
rhythm. However, there is some evidence to suggest that word domain
rules could sometimes apply across such elisions. Instances where elision
prevents a split resolution or a split or divided anapaest (Bernhardi
1872:276) include

τὸ στόμ᾿ ἐπιβύσας *Plutus* 379
ἢ μέγ᾿ ἐνορῶ βούλευμ᾿ *Birds* 162
ξυστίδ᾿ ἔχων *Clouds* 70
τὸν πατέρ᾿ ἐλαύνεις *Clouds* 29
τὸν πατέρ᾿ ἐπέταξε *Wasps* 69
ἠργάσατ᾿ ἀνήρ *Frogs* 488
τἀμπόρι᾿ ἀνεῳγμένα *Birds* 1523
τὰ χοιρίδι᾿ ἀπέδου *Acharnians* 830 MSS.

Elided lexical or semilexical disyllabic words occasionally occur before
Hermann's bridge

μέγ᾿ ἀμείνονα φῶτα *Iliad* 2.239
στόμ᾿ ἔχων *Iliad* 2.250

> ἐπὶ δ' οὔατ' ἀλεῖψαι ἑταίρων *Odyssey* 12.47
> λάχ' ἐλαυνέμεν ἵππους *Iliad* 23.357.

In the fourth foot of the tragic trimeter, elided tribrach-shaped words are allowed rarely but lexical pyrrhic-shaped words are forbidden

> ὄνομ' *Ion* 1594, *Helen* 490, *Phoenissae* 553,
> *I.A.* 962.

In

> ἐχήρωσ' Ἑλλάδα *Cyclops* 304

the proper name and the more fluent phrasing of satyric probably combine with elision to render the structure acceptable at Porson's bridge. Instances at Porson's bridge in tragedy are textually questionable

> ἡγεῖτ' οἴκοθεν *Ajax* 1101
> νώτοισ' οὐρανὸν *Ion* 1 Witte (Page 1961; Luppe 1983).

Inscriptional evidence

The complex of metrical evidence just assembled indicates that between the prosodic domain of the word and that of the minor phrase, Greek had a prosodic domain here termed the appositive group. This metrically based hypothesis of an appositive group is independently confirmed by epigraphic evidence, specifically by the placement of interpuncts in punctuating inscriptions. There are a number of inscriptions of more than minimal length that punctuate words (rather than phrases) with a sufficient degree of consistency to permit a useful analysis. These include *IGA* 497, *SEG* 31.984–5 (T.D.); *SEG* 11.314 (*Arg.*); *IGA* 499 (*Eph. Aug.*) and a related fragment Sokolowski 1955:n.30B (*Eph. Frag.*); I³.1.5 (*Eleus.*); IV.554, Jameson 1974 (*Hal.*) is essentially word punctuating with the addition of some minor phrases, as are many of the inscriptions in the Cyprian syllabary including *ICS* 217 (*Id.*). Although it is convenient to refer to these inscriptions as word punctuating, the domain that they are actually punctuating is the appositive group. These inscriptional punctuations are clearly intended to demarcate phonological domains and not syntactic constituents: punctuation is sometimes placed after a composite consisting of two prepositives, which makes good phonological sense but no syntactic sense at all, since in such cases a determiner is typically detached from its noun and attached to a preceding preposition or conjunction.

In the following analysis, punctuation is uniformly transcribed by the colon irrespective of the number and type of interpuncts actually used in the inscription. Punctuation is often not written at the end of the inscriptional line; omission in this location is not evidence for phrase punctuation. The different editions of these inscriptions often vary in their readings of punctuation, partly through editorial decision and partly through typographical error.

Punctuation is almost always omitted between single monosyllabic appositives and their host word

> : ho παις : καλος : ναι : *ARV* 1.26
> : το προτον : *DAA* 61
> : τα γεγραθμενα : *T.D.* d.15
> : τα ποιϜεματα : *Arg.* 2

> : εν Αβδηροισιν : *T.D.* d.5
> : ες γην : *T.D.* A.6
> : εκ γης : *T.D.* B.22
> : εν τῆπαρηι : *T.D.* B.34
> : ες πολιος : *LSAG* 31.2.3
> : συμ πολλοισιν *T.D.* a.24

> : με χρε[σ]θο : *Arg.* 6
> : το λοιπο : *T.D.* B.8
> : ου στησω *T.D.* a.23
> : η τεχνηι : *T.D.* A.8
> : τας θιο : *Arg.* 6
> : τας κορας : *LSAG* 53.1
> : και γενος : *T.D.* A.5
> τοις Αργειοις : *SEG* 13.239
> : καν αποκρυψει : *Eph. Aug.* 4
> : χὸ βομος : *SEG* 32.356, *LSAG* 16.4
> : τος ηιεροποιος : *Eleus.* 2

> : τοδ᾽ α⟨γ⟩αλμα : *DAA* 336.

The article becomes appositive more readily when it goes with a nonbranching constituent

> : τον γρασσματον : *Hal.* 4
> θεσαυρον : τον : τα(:)ς :: Αθαναιας : *Hal.* 1
> ε ταν βολαν : ταν : ανϙ᾽ Αρισστονα : *Hal.* 2.

Otherwise punctuated appositives are quite rare and often doubtful (*SEG* 35.479; *LSAG* 26.4; contrast *LSAG* 26.6; *LSAG* 51.6 [τον: ?]; *DAA* 339). και: and : δε (unelided) are found in structures involving proper names (*LSAG* 11.14, 71.43–4; I².660 ?; *LSAG* 4.31), where the visual effect of setting off the proper names is achieved by accessing an artificially slow rate of speech at which appositives are demarcated from their host words.

Pyrrhic-shaped appositives are not separated by punctuation from their host words

: επι Τηιοισιν : *T.D.* A.2
: επι δυναμει : *T.D.* B.31, cp. d.17
επι τονδεονεν : *Arg.* 1
: περι Τηιων : *T.D.* B.24
: hοτε Παραιβατες [:] *Eleus.* 1.

In Mycenaean, disyllabic prepositions are usually separated from the noun they govern by the word divider, but the word divider is sometimes omitted (Davies 1987).

Inscriptional punctuation of phonologically heavier disyllabic non-lexicals is variable, depending on the rate of speech accessed by the text and on the particular word in question

: ουδε ποιησω : ουδε λυησω : ουδε διωξω : *T.D.* a.12
ουτε : συμ πολλοισιν *T.D.* a.24
: οστις : *T.D.* A.6, B.8 cp. A.1, B.3
: τοισι : χρεμασι : τοισι : χρεστερμοισι : τοισι : τας θιιο : *Arg.* 5
: ταδεν : τα ποιϜεματα : *Arg.* 2.

In the above, the complex nonlexical *οὐδέ* is appositive in *T.D.* where *ὅστις* is not; nor is the trisyllabic plural

: οιτινες : *T.D.* B.29;

and in the examples from *Arg.* a distinction is made between monosyllabic forms of the article which are prepositive and the heavier trochee-shaped *τοῖσι* which is not. Forms of the verb *to be* are generally punctuated whether they follow a focused word or not

: εμι : *LSAG* 53.1
: εμεν : *SEG* 13:239
: εοντος : *SEG* 32:356
: ειμι : *LSAG* 71.44.

Sequences of nonlexicals become appositive more readily than polysyllabic single word nonlexicals of the same shape

: και τα χρεματα τε : *Arg.* 3
: hοιζ δε δαμιοργος : *Arg.* 12
αι δε σιναιτο : *Arg.* 11

: η προς βαρβαρους : *T.D.* B.26
: και τοι δεμοι : *Eleus.* 1
: η κατ' ηπειρον : *T.D.* A.9

: εν ηισιν ηπαρη : *T.D.* B.36
: η κατα θαλασσαν : *T.D.* A.8
: οστις δε τιμοχεων *T.D.* d.12.

The last example supports the metrical evidence for extended appositive groups (p. 322) and their interpretation as a single domain including the host word. The metrical evidence indicated that sequences of nonlexicals can also become composites, that is they can function as autonomous rhythmic domains; this variant phonological organization is also confirmed by inscriptional punctuations

: εν τει : εορτει *Eleus.* 5
και τος : ηιεροποιος : I³.1.244.C.3
: εν τοι : πολεμοι : I².929
: και το : ιρεως : *MDAII* 30:167
: και τεν : Νικεν : *LSAG* 51.6
: ηενεκα τας : καταθεσιος : ε τας : αλιασσιος : *Hal.* 4
: απο τον : πολεμιον : *DAA* 135 ?; 135b is a late copy
επι τες : τριτες I³.1.261.

In the inscriptions in the Cyprian syllabary, even disregarding prepositives in final -ς which tend, for whatever reason (Davies 1987), to be autonomous except when followed by enclitics (*ka-sa-pa-i Id.* 4, *ta-sa-ke Id.* 29), there is ample evidence for the composite

ǀ ι(ν) ται ǀ μαχαι ǀ *Id.* 3
ǀ εξ τοι ǀ Fοικοι ǀ *Id.* 5
ǀ απυ ται ǀ ζαι ǀ *Id.* 8, 17
ǀ εξ τοι ǀ χοροι ǀ *Id.* 11

varying with the extended appositive group

ǀ εξ ται πτολιFι ǀ *Id.* 6
ǀ τον ι(ν) Σιμιδος ǀ αρουραι *Id.* 20
ǀ ι(ν) τα(ν) θιον ǀ *Id.* 27.

Eph. Aug. and *Eph. Frag.* punctuate after prepositive + postpositive unless the prepositive is the article

: ημ μεν : ιθυς : *Eph. Aug.* 7
: ην δε : την δεξιην [:] *Eph. Aug.* 8
ην δε : οι δικαζον:τες *Eph. Frag.* 5
: εγ δε : της αριστερης : *Eph. Aug.* 5
: τον δε καπρον : *Eph. Frag.* 4.

Eph. Aug. and *Eph. Frag.* do not punctuate after preposition plus article

: ες την δεξιην : *Eph. Aug.* 6
: επι τοις δικαζοσιν : *Eph. Frag.* 1.

The evidence of these Ephesus inscriptions suggests that rhythmically autonomous composites are more readily formed if neither appositive is the determiner. Variation in punctuation after ἄν seems to be partly due to the weight of the preceding nonlexical

: ος αν τιμην : *T.D.* a.5
: ος αν τας (σ)τηλας : *T.D.* B.35

οστις αν : με ποιει : *LSAG* 5.9
: hοπος αν : δραπετες I³.1.45.3
: hοπος αν : εντος I³.1.45.11.

In the light of the parallel metrical treatment of composites (p. 321), it is mistaken to regard the inscriptional punctuation of composites as ornamental or as an inscriber's error, a view sometimes taken in earlier work (Kaiser 1887; Larfeld 1914). Extended appositive groups can occur in word punctuating inscriptions

: εαν δε τι πασχω *LSAG* 71.44;

in phrase punctuating inscriptions, fairly long sequences of nonlexicals can combine with a host word to count as two appositive groups for the purposes of minor phrase formation (p. 388)

: hοτι με μετα Λοϙρον *Naup.* 10
: αι τις hυπο τον νομιον *Naup.* 27
: hον ποτ' ενι προμαχοις : *CEG* 27.

FACTORS CONDITIONING APPOSITIVE STATUS

It is not the case that all nonlexicals have an equal tendency to become appositive; a variety of factors combine to condition the degree to which the rules of word prosody may be extended to phrasal domains in any particular structure. This is why detailed analysis of the phonology of nonlexicals generally reveals a hierarchy. The English auxiliaries *has, have* and *will* can undergo two types of reduction. Strong reduction eliminates everything except the coda consonant and the result is 's, 've, 'll [-s/z, -v, -l]. Weak reduction optionally eliminates the onset, shortens and centralizes the vowel, but does not destroy syllabic status: the result is əz, əv, əll. Strong auxiliary reduction is more constrained for *have, will* and *are* than it is for *has* and *is*: the former have strong reduction only in a subset of the environments in which the latter reduce, namely after pronouns ending in a vowel: "He's got it," "Lee's got it"; "We've got it", "The Cree əv got it" (Zwicky 1970; Kaisse 1985).

Similar hierarchies can be found in the Greek evidence. For instance, not all prepositives are equally permissible in split resolutions. The data presented in Table 7.5 show the change through time of three variables in the trimeter of Euripides: the proportion of all resolutions in third longum that are split, the proportion of all split resolutions in third longum that are articular phrases, and the proportion of articular phrases splitting resolved third longum that are just the phrase τὸν ἐμόν. The growth through time in the first column indicates the metrical cost and

TABLE 7.5
Split resolutions in third longum in Euripides

	Split as % of all resolved third longum	Articular phrase as % of column 1	τὸν ἐμόν as % of column 2
Severior, Semi-severus	3.16	100.00	60.00
Liber	5.72	65.31	15.63
Liberrimus	9.28	53.06	7.69

hence the prosodic complexity of remapping. The decrease through time in the second column indicates that an articular phrase

> ὁ νόμος *Ion* 643
> τὸν ἴσον *Phoenissae* 487

is easier to remap than a comparable phrase with a different determiner

> τίς ὄλεθρος *Orestes* 1126

or with a preposition

> ἐς ἐλάτην *Bacchae* 1061

or a less cohesive structure

> σὺ πάλιν *I.A.* 843.

The decrease through time in the third column indicates that the articular phrase τὸν ἐμόν, which has relatively high text frequency and an appositive second word, is easier to remap than other articular phrases; it may be on its way to becoming lexicalized.

Syntax

Although nonlexical words tend to cliticize relatively easily to contiguous host words, much the same syntactic factors can constrain clitic group formation as constrain phonological phrase formation (p. 377). The close syntactic attachment of determiners is illustrated by the palatalization rule of Cibaeño Spanish (Dominican Republic: Harris 1983): *el aviso* 'the advice' but *ei avisa* 'he advises.' Similarly in French, liaison with a variety of specifiers is more consistent than liaison with the copula, modals and certain prepositions (de Jong 1990). The effect of scope on cliticization is illustrated by English auxiliary reduction. Strong auxiliary reduction does not apply if the host is a conjunct: "Jacqueline, I've been to London" is fine, but *"Jack and I've been to London" is not (Kaisse 1985). In Danish, the object pronoun is unstressed in *han sér mig* 'he sees me,' but stressed in the coordinate *han sér míg og Péter* 'he sees me and Peter' (Rischel 1983). Whatever the formal means chosen to diagram it, the syntactic complexity resulting from coordination results in a prosodic structure that blocks strong reduction in English and destressing in Danish. Movement and trace can also affect cliticization. Preposing a participle can create conditions that block strong auxiliary reduction in English, just like coordination above: "Jack's been our star reporter" is fine, but *"Speaking tonight's been our star reporter" is not unless S.T. was the reporter's name; strong auxiliary reduction of *has* requires the host to be the subject noun phrase (Kaisse 1985). In Irish, the interrogative particle *an* nasalizes a following verb but not a following noun with the verb *to be* understood; likewise, the negative particle *ni* 'not' lenites a following verb but not a following noun when it means 'is not' (Rotenberg 1978). Similarly, in Welsh *nid* 'not' can be reduced to *ni* before a following consonant when, as in the normal sentence pattern, it is followed by an inflected verb, but not in cleft negative sentences (Awbery 1986).

Depth of attachment

When they stand at Porson's bridge, monosyllabic and elided disyllabic conjunctions, such as εἰ, ἤ, καί, ὡς, ἀλλ᾽, and their crasis forms, such as κεἰ, κἄν, are sensitive to the depth of the following syntactic division, that is to the number of following opening brackets. In the Severior and Semiseverus styles of Euripides, if a conjunction introduces a clause or verb phrase (higher level conjunction) rather than simply connecting nouns, adjectives or adverbs (lower level conjunction), then the conjunction must be the first element of an appositive composite; the second element of the composite is a prepositive or postpositive (p. 319) or a monosyllabic form of a verb which is enclitic somewhere in its paradigm and which forms a complete parenthetical phrase with the conjunction

> καὶ μὴ μόλῃ *Alcestis* 850
> εἰ μὴ θέλει *Heraclidae* 435
> καὶ γὰρ πνοὰς *Hecuba* 1289
> τῆς ἐμῆς, ὡς φῄς, χερὸς *Hecuba* 273.

In contrast, when the conjunction connects nouns or adjectives, it may be followed not only by a nonlexical

> ἀλλ᾽ ἐκ θεῶν *Andromache* 680
> καὶ τοῖσι σοῖς *Andromache* 750,

but also by a polysyllabic lexical

> καὶ μητέρα *Alcestis* 646
> καὶ πλούσιον *Andromache* 640.

The data are presented in Table 7.6. The decrease in the number of high level conjunctions forming composites in later Euripides is statistically significant; there is no significant difference for the lower level

TABLE 7.6
High and low level conjunctions in composites at Porson's bridge

	High level conjunction		Low level conjunction	
	In composite %	Not in composite %	In composite %	Not in composite %
Severior, Semiseverus	100.00	0.00	25.00	75.00
Liber, Liberrimus	52.17	47.83	45.00	55.00
	$\omega = \infty$, $p = 0.039$		$\omega = 0.041$, $p = 0.296$	

conjunction between the two style periods. This test shows that the subordination of heavy, monosyllabic conjunctions is less likely when these conjunctions introduce higher level syntactic structures, since in that case they are syntactically more separated from the material to their right. Composite formation introduces a phonological factor which mitigates the depth of the following syntactic division: consequently, in the stricter styles higher level conjunctions can be subordinated only if they are elements of a composite.

Marked word order

There is evidence that in Greek departure from basic word order within constituents may result in rhythmic autonomy of normative prepositives. This is the case with the possessive pronoun σός which is prepositive

σῷ συγγόνῳ *Helen* 978 [Porson's bridge].

In trimeters with no potential hephthemimeral caesura or medial elision, heavy monosyllabic forms of σός that are attributive and not preceded by a prepositive may stand before the penthemimeral caesura only if they are postposed to their noun

μηδὲν κακῶν σῶν *Hippolytus* 714
πρὶν μὲν τέκνων σῶν *Medea* 1145
'Αργοῦς κάρα σὸν *Medea* 1387
δόμους δ' ἔχειν σοὺς *Orestes* 1146.

This restriction indicates that when postposed, the possessive pronouns were rhythmically demarcated on their right. They did not necessarily become postpositive since they may stand after the sole possible caesura even when they are postposed to their head noun standing in the first hemistich

τήνδ', ἢ πύλαισι σαῖς *Hippolytus* 101

> εἰ δυσμενείᾳ σῇ *Hippolytus* 965
> σκῆψίν τιν᾽ ἐχθροῖς σοῖς *Medea* 744.

The relative frequency of this phenomenon was analyzed in a sample from the *Medea, Hippolytus, Orestes* and *Bacchae*: in the position preceding the penthemimeral caesura there were 7 instances of σός postposed to its head noun and none preposed, and in the position following the penthemimeral caesura there were 5 instances postposed as compared with 10 preposed. These figures indicate that σός did not become phonologically postpositive when syntactically postposed to its head noun ($p = 0.0046$). This conclusion is confirmed by the observation that, unlike enclitic forms of the personal pronouns, forms of σός never stand after Porson's bridge unless preceded by a prepositive.

Head interrupted prepositional phrases

In Greek verse, prepositions may precede a continuous or discontinuous noun phrase

> πρὸς πλουσίαν τράπεζαν *Helen* 295

or they may occur in anastrophe, which is relatively rare with branching noun phrases

> βασιλικῶν δόμων ὕπερ *Phoenissae* 1326

or the noun phrase may be interrupted by the preposition, with the head of the noun phrase either preceding or, far more usually, following the preposition

> πόλισμ᾽ ἐς Παλλάδος *I. T.* 1014
> πωλικῶν ἐξ ἀντύγων *Rhesus* 567.

For this test, head interrupted prepositional phrases [N P N]$_{PP}$ in which the preposition is preceded by a lexical word belonging to the noun phrase

> νερτέρων ἐκ δωμάτων *Alcestis* 1073
> συμφορᾶς ἐς τοὔσχατον *Orestes* 447

were compared with head flanking branching prepositional phrases [[P] [NP]]$_{PP}$ not having enjambement of any material in the dominated branching noun phrase, which means mainly prepositional phrases in which the noun phrase consisted of article plus noun or noun plus possessive pronoun

> ἐκ τῶν φίλων *H.F.* 1234
> ἐς παῖδ᾽ ἐμόν *H.F.* 223.

Crasis forms in which the article is not a separate syllable are very rare and have been omitted from the test. The results are presented in Table 7.7; a heavy monosyllabic preposition at Porson's bridge is not allowed to stand before a branching noun phrase in the earlier style periods of

TABLE 7.7

Comparison of the frequencies of the head interrupted and
head flanking structures of prepositional phrases at Porson's bridge
in earlier and later styles of Euripides

	$[N\ P\ N]_{PP}$	$[P\ NP]_{PP}$
Severior, Semiseverus	7	0
Liber, Liberrimus	7	10
$p = 0.0099$		

Euripides — if the preposition governs a branching noun phrase, only
the head interrupted type of structure occurs. By contrast, in the later
style periods, the head flanking type $[P\ NP]_{PP}$ actually becomes more
frequent than the head interrupted type. The exclusion of the type [P
NP]$_{PP}$ where NP branches from the earlier styles is statistically significant: the value of p, calculated by the hypergeometric distribution,
means that there is slightly less than one chance in a thousand that this
exclusion could result from random factors. There is not enough variation in the use of the article between the earlier and later styles of Euripides to account for the observed difference without reference to the
syntactic difference.

It has been shown that the head interrupted structure provides an
easier environment for subordination than the head flanking structure
in branching prepositional phrases. It can be shown that the head interrupted structure also provides an easier environment for subordination
of the preposition than the simple nonbranching prepositional phrase:
$[N\ P\ N]_{PP}$ is easier than $[P\ N]_{PP}$. This test, which employs the same
sampling criteria as the preceding test, compares head interrupted
prepositional phrases as above

ὀλβίοις ἐν δώμασιν Eur. *Supplices* 5

with nonbranching prepositional phrases

ὡς βάλῃς ἐς Τάρταρον *Orestes* 265
πνεῦμ᾿ ἀνεὶς ἐκ πλευμόνων *Orestes* 277.

Table 7.8 compares the proportions of the two types in the earlier styles
of Euripides with their proportions in the later styles. The odds ratio
ω shows that the odds for the nonbranching type $[P\ N]_{PP}$ in the later
styles are over seven times as great as they are in the earlier styles. This
difference is statistically significant, so that it must be concluded that
the $[P\ N]_{PP}$ type is constrained in the earlier styles, though not so
strongly as to be completely excluded. However, it is worth remarking

TABLE 7.8

Comparison of the rates of occurrence of preposition
plus nonbranching object and head interrupted prepositional phrase
at Porson's bridge in earlier and later styles of Euripides

	[P N]$_{PP}$	[N P N]$_{PP}$
	%	%
Severior, Semiseverus	36.36	63.64
Liber, Liberrimus	80.56	19.44

$\omega = 0.14$, $\chi^2 = 7.85$

that of the four instances in the Severior, one involves the idiom ἡμέραν
ἐξ ἡμέρας *Rhesus* 445 and the other three are from the prosatyr play *Alcestis*
which is much less restrictive in its treatment of Porson's bridge than
the tragedies of the Severior group (p. 234). The results presented in
Table 7.8 reflect the fact that the head interrupted type [N P N]$_{PP}$ has
the lowest ranking syntactic boundary possible before the preposition
that must be subordinated, whereas with the [P N]$_{PP}$ type the boundary before the preposition is always a greater one, that is it separates
the preposition from some element which is not part of the prepositional
phrase. Subordination is sensitive to the strength of the lefthand syntactic
boundary because, as argued in Chapter 2, it is a process that applies
prototypically to the central syllable of a molossus, that is, it has both
a lefthand and a righthand phonological environment.

a-interrupted phrases

In the case of the prepositional phrases just analyzed, the preposition
was the head of the discontinuous constituent. Intuitively, the special
status of the head interrupted structure compared to its head flanking
counterparts is motivated not by the fact that it is a phrasal head qua
head that intervenes between two elements which belong to a phrasal
complement of that head—rather, the salient property is the intercalation of some element a between two others β_1 and β_2 which, if contiguous, would form a constituent to which a does not belong but which
would form a larger constituent with a. Accordingly, the head interrupted structure [...Y X^{head} Y...]$_{XP}$ where the two Y elements would
form a complement of the head X^{head} may be regarded as a special case
of the more general structure [...β_1 a β_2...]$_{XP}$, such that XP is the
smallest phrase containing a but a need not necessarily be the head of
XP and β_1 and β_2 are constituents of some BP also belonging to XP.
The structure[...β_1 a β_2...]$_{XP}$ (from now on simply [β_1 a β_2]$_{XP}$) there-

fore unites phrasal heads, $a = X^{head}$, and what are traditionally defined as nonphrasal elements such as specifiers and complementizers, $a \neq X^{head}$, since if a were phrasal and belonged to XP and $a \neq X^{head}$, XP would not be the smallest phrase containing a.

The first test of the hypothesis that the more general a-interrupted structure also promotes heavy syllable subordination more effectively than the a-flanking counterparts in appositive groups is designed to hold the syntactic category of XP constant. In Greek, articular noun phrases with the definite article $= a \neq X^{head}$ constitute the single XP which occurs frequently enough at Porson's bridge to permit such a test. The a-flanking class consists of articular phrases with nonbranching or, more rarely, branching NP, which, in addition to a noun, may be a substantival adjective, a genitive, a substantivized adverb and so on

> τὴν πρόσπολον *I. T.* 798
> τῶν ἐξόδων *H.F.* 623
> τῷ Πηλέως χάριν γενέσθαι παιδὶ *Hecuba* 383.

The a-interrupted class includes instances in which material up to the length of a cretic intervenes between β_1 and a

> τύχαις ταῖς οἴκοθεν *Andromache* 979
> ἡμέραν τὴν κυρίαν *Alcestis* 158
> παῖδ' ἔχεις τὸν Πηλέως *Rhesus* 119.

When the noun phrase contains an adjective in this class, the serialization can only be [N (S̄S̄S̄) Art Adj]$_{NP}$, since the adjective would be predicative in the order Adj (S̄S̄S̄) Art N; if the noun phrase contains a genitive, either serialization is possible, but the genitive preceding the article is quite rare. Both test classes are limited to instances in which the article is immediately preceded and followed by a lexical word. The results of the test are presented in Figure 7.2, from which it is clear that there is a steep and steady decline in the rate of occurrence of the article interrupted structure of articular noun phrases. This effect cannot be explained as a side effect of any trends involving enjambement or use of the definite article. When the Severior and Semiseverus data are combined to increase sample size, $\chi^2 = 7.7215$, so that there is less than one chance in one hundred that a value as great or greater could have arisen by chance.

A second test involves the negative particles οὐ, μή, which also may occur as a in the a-interrupted structure. When a = negative, β_2 is generally the head of the minimal containing phrase XP and β_1 is the complement of β_2. When β_2 is a verb, β_1 may be an infinitive or participle

> λέγειν οὐκ ἄζομαι *Alcestis* 326
> φροῦδος ὢν οὐ φαίνεται *Rhesus* 865

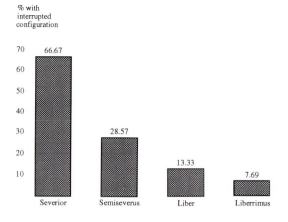

FIGURE 7.2

Article interrupted noun phrases as a percentage
of articular noun phrases at Porson's bridge
through the style periods of Euripides

or a substantive complement, such as an accusative direct object

δεσπότας δ' οὐ λοιδορῶ *Hecuba* 1237

or partitive genitive complement

νέων δὲ πημάτων οὐχ ἅπτεται *Hecuba* 675.

When β_2 is an adjective, β_1 may be an infinitive

γαμεῖν οὐκ ἄξιον *Alcestis* 628

or a genitive of comparison

στεμμάτων δ' οὐκ ἥσσονας *Andromache* 894;

certain prepositions also occur as β_2

σῶν φρενῶν οὐκ ἔνδον ὢν *Heraclidae* 709.

The extent of the available data permits a more stringent test of negative interrupted phrases than the one just presented for article interrupted phrases. Only instances in which β_1 appears immediately before the negative are assigned to the a-interrupted class: cases with any intervening material are assigned to the other class. Furthermore, β_1 must be a complement for which β_2 is strictly subcategorized: instances with adverbial adjuncts, for instance, are not classed as a-interrupted. If β_1 belongs to a branching phrase, it must be the head of that phrase: structures such as

γονέας ὑβρίζειν τοὺς ἐμοὺς οὐκ ἠξίου Eur. *Electra* 257

TABLE 7.9

Negative interrupted phrases at Porson's bridge

	a-interrupted %	Other types %
Severior, Semiseverus	57.14	42.86
Liber, Liberrimus	23.53	76.47

$$\omega = 4.33, \; \chi^2 = 6.35$$

are not classed as a-interrupted. Instances in which a single prepositive precedes the negative are excluded. The results of the test are presented in Table 7.9. The odds for a negative at Porson's bridge to be in the a-interrupted structure are over four times greater in the earlier styles than in the later styles; the difference is statistically significant. This test is also important in that taken together with the test on articular phrases it shows that the evidence for a-interrupted phrases is crosscategorial. Since the phrases in the test of articular phrases are noun phrases and the phrases in the test of the negatives are almost never noun phrases, being typically verb phrases or adjective phrases, the effect of the a-interrupted structure is independent of the syntactic category of the XP as well.

The above analyses of head and nonhead a-interrupted structures at Porson's bridge indicate that subordination, which is a prosodic process dependent on both a lefthand and a righthand environment, applies more readily in a-interrupted structures than in a-flanking structures and also more readily in a-interrupted branching structures than in nonbranching structures. When a is prepositive, the a-interrupted structure yields a particularly cohesive prosody, and domain boundaries that could block the prosodic processes tested are less likely to occur in the a-interrupted structure.

Category

There is considerable crosslinguistic regularity in the categories of appositive and clitic words. For instance, the following categories are usually unstressed in Isthmus Zapotec unless under contrastive focus: anaphoric pronouns, deictics, negative marker, interrogative particle, subordinate clause marker, prepositions, attitudinal particles, conjunctions (Mock 1985). The list of categories exhibiting accentual clisis or rhythmic appositive status in Greek is very similar: it is presented with some parallels from other languages in Table 7.10.

TABLE 7.10
Appositives and clitics (from DS 1983)

Category	Greek		Other Languages[a]
	Orthographi-cally clitic	Orthotonoumena metrically permissible at prosodic bridge	Loss of phonological autonomy
Pronouns	μου, μοι, σε, σοι, νιν	σῷ *Hel.* 978; οὕς *Hipp.* 1063; ἐμός *Lys.* 102; ἐμόν *Thesm.* 1172	Germanic, Romance, Fula,[b] Uto-Aztecan,[c] Madurese,[d] Ilocano,[e] Warramunga[f]
Demonstratives		τόνδ' *Hipp.* 1151; τόνδε *Cyc.* 343; τοῦτ' Soph. *El.* 409; ἥδε E. *Supp.* 1098	Syrian Arabic, Fula
Articles	ὁ, ἡ, οἱ, αἱ,	τῆς *Aj.* 90; τῇ *Bacch.* 1148	Germanic, Romance, Syrian Arabic, Shuswap[g]
Indefinites	τις, τι, που, ποτε		Ilocano
Interrogatives		πόθεν *Epit.* 864; τίς *Av.* 1021; ποῖ *Alc.* 943	Hmong,[h] Fula
Numerals		τρεῖς *IA* 49; ἕν *Tro.* 425; δέκα *Thesm.* 741; ἐννέα *Thesm.* 637	Fula, Italian, Madurese
Conjunctions	εἰ, ὡς, τοι, τε, ἀλλ'	καί *Andr.* 640; [ἀλλ' *Phil.* 9]; ἀλλά *Andr.* 346MS, Sem. 1. 20, *Nub.* 1221	Spanish, Syrian Arabic, Madurese, Ilocano, Shuswap
Prepositions	ἐν, ἐς, εἰς, ἐκ, ὡς	πρός *Phoen.* 413; παρά *Bacch.* 940; ἀπό (SS̄) Sem. 7. 63	Spanish, English, Czech, Lithuanian, Syrian Arabic, Ulithian,[i] Madurese, Shuswap
Emphasizing particles	γε	πάνυ *Av.* 1458	Shuswap
Modal particles		ἄν *Andr.* 935	Luiseño,[j] Hmong, Madurese, Shuswap
Negatives	οὐ, μηδ'	μή *HF* 197	Lithuanian, Hmong, Madurese
Adverbials		δεῦρ' *OT* 318; δεῦρο πάλιν *Ran.* 652; εἶτ' *Cyc.* 563; εἶτα *Thesm.* 414	English, Tagalog, Madurese
Copula	ἐστι, εἰσι	[ἔστ' *Bacch.* 246 prepos.]	English, Czech
Imperatives		δός *IT* 501; θένε *Av.* 54	Tagalog

[a] Accentual or segmental evidence for optional or obligatory loss of phonological independence by nonlexicals.
[b] West Africa
[c] Western North America
[d] Java
[e] Philippines
[f] Australia
[g] Western North America
[h] Southeast Asia
[i] Micronesia
[j] Western North America

Prepositions are included because phonologically they often behave like nonlexicals, at least with their unmarked word order. For instance, in Irish initial mutation is induced by various nonlexicals including degree modifiers, verbal particles, complementizers and quite a few preposi-tions (Rotenberg 1978). Syntactically a preposition is generally regarded as a phrasal head. Like lexicals, prepositions can undergo exchange in speech errors: "Send for tickets *at* two *for* the box office"; but unlike lexicals they tend not to be involved in spoonerisms (Garrett et al. 1980). As already noted (p. 298), agrammatic speakers have greater problems with prepositions that function as case assigners like *of* [possessive] and *to* [dative] than they do with prepositions that have a more lexical semantic content like *in* and *on* (Friederici 1982, 1985; Bennis et al. 1983; Grodzinsky 1988).

It is not yet clear to what extent specifically categorial factors influence cliticization and appositive status of nonlexicals, since prima facie categorial differences can turn out to be differences of constituency, frequency or phonological substance. For instance, a difference between specifiers and complementizers could be interpreted in terms of the degree of attachment to the following constituent (Hayes 1989). A categorial hierarchy of function words seems to be a factor in the accentuation of strings of nonlexical words in English (Giegerich 1985). The evidence from agrammatism for a categorially defined hierarchy of nonlexicals is difficult to interpret. In a crosslinguistic study it was found that auxiliaries are particularly susceptible to omission and that articles are quite resistant (Menn et al. 1990). However, there is considerable variation, not only from one language to another, but also from one speaker to another within the same language. For instance, one Italian patient made errors (combined omissions and substitutions) on 6.2% of auxiliary verbs and 61.5% of clitic particles, whereas another made errors on 52.6% of auxiliary verbs and only 25% of clitic particles (Miceli et al. 1989). If this variation is statistically significant, it could be interpreted as evidence of selective impairment of different categories of the functors in the lexicon (or in the way the lexicon is used) or varying postincident success in developing strategies to bypass a processing impairment (Caplan 1991). An earlier study found that agrammatic speakers of both Italian and Dutch omitted nonlexicals in the following descending order of frequency: determiners, auxiliaries, prepositions, pronouns, connectives (Caramazza et al. 1985).

Differential application of the mapping rules provides prima facie evidence for a categorial hierarchy among nonlexicals in Greek. In Aeschylus (excluding the *Prometheus*), approximately 70% of all instances of word end at Porson's bridge involve articles or prepositions, as compared with 42% in Sophocles and 44% in Euripides. The additional level of constraint in Aeschylus indicates that he is favouring the more readily subordinable categories; articles and prepositions do not constitute a class definable in terms of constituent structure to the exclusion of other nonlexicals that can be appositive, and it is not immediately clear how these data could be reanalyzed to exclude categorial distinctions.

Morphology

Disyllabic nonlexicals in Greek may be either morphologically simplex or morphologically complex. There are three, overlapping, diagnostic criteria for synchronic complexity. The first criterion is violation of the trochee rule of accentuation, whereby accented long vowels or diphthongs in the penultimate syllable are circumflex if the vowel of the final is short or the diphthong is -αι or -οι not in the locative or optative: εἴπερ, οὔτε, ὥσπερ, ὥστε, τήνδε, τούσδε. The second criterion is internal or double inflection: ὅστις, οἵτινες, ᾗτινι; ὅδε, τοῦδε, τῷδε. The third criterion is derivability from independently existing words via productive phonological rules: ὅστις < ὅς + τις, οὐδείς < οὐδ᾽ εἷς < οὐδὲ εἷς (*εἷς). By these diagnostics, nonlexicals such as αὐτός, εἶτα, οὗτος are classified as synchronically simplex, although from an Indo-European perspective they are morphologically analyzable. There is considerable evidence that the complex type of nonlexical is more acceptable at metrical bridges than the simplex type. In tragedy, seven of the nine more securely attested spondee-shaped nonlexicals at Porson's bridge not followed by postpositives are either forms of οὐδείς (p. 318) or crasis equivalents of the spondee-shaped word

> κἄνευ τῆς ἐμῆς O.C. 664
> κᾆτα ψεύδομαι I.A. 530.

In contrast to the tragic rate of 77.8% for complex or crasis nonlexicals, in a sample from Aristophanes (*Acharnians, Peace* and *Frogs*) only 26.09% of the spondee-shaped nonlexicals ending in third anceps were morphologically complex or crasis forms, and no form of οὐδείς was observed.

Complex nonlexicals are also preferred in line initial split dactyls. Trochaically split line initial dactyls do not occur in the extant tragedies of Aeschylus, Sophocles or in those of the Severior, Semiseverus and Liber styles of Euripides. In Euripides Liberrimus there are two instances not followed by a postpositive, and both are morphologically complex

> οὐδὲ πάθος Orestes 2
> ὥστε διὰ τοῦτον Bacchae 285.

In Aristophanes 45.45% of the trochaically split line initial dactyls are split after a morphologically complex nonlexical, 48.48% are split after a morphologically simplex nonlexical, and a few others are split after a lexical word. In Menander, the relative frequency of the complex type declines further to 30.16% as lexicals and even major syntactic boundaries are admitted more freely in line initial split dactyls. The fact that the complex nonlexical type is the class of trochee-shaped word first admitted in split dactyls and the steady diachronic and stylistic decline in their relative frequency indicates that the complex type was initially less constrained (DS 1983)

Among elided trochee-shaped nonlexicals like ἀλλ᾽, δεῦρ᾽, τοῦδ᾽, οὐδ᾽, the morphologically complex type is disproportionately represented at Porson's bridge with 83.33% of such forms having complex or crasis structure in the extant tragedies of Euripides

> εἶτ᾽ εὐτυχὴς *Alcestis* 685
> οὐδ᾽ Ἑλλάδος *Andromache* 367
> τούσδ᾽ εἰδέναι *Hecuba* 1006
> τἀφ᾽ Ἑλλάδος *I. T.* 540.

In contrast, in the Aristophanes sample just noted only 7.69% were of the complex type and no crasis forms were observed: this is a highly significant difference with $\chi^2 = 19.6576$. In Aeschylus and Sophocles, the rate of the elided simplex type is higher than in Euripides, but elided simplex forms are followed by monosyllabic nonlexicals far more frequently than are elided complex forms

> ταῦτ᾽ ὦ τέκνα Aesch. *Supplices* 753 MS
> ἀλλ᾽ ἐκ βροτῶν *O. T.* 831
> ἀλλ᾽ εἰ παρὼν *Philoctetes* 410.

Elided forms of ὅδε are strikingly frequent: 62.5% of all elided trochee-shaped nonlexical words before Porson's bridge not followed by a post-positive in Euripides were forms of ὅδε, whereas elided forms of οὗτος are very rare and sometimes emended, as at Aesch. *Supplices* 753 above. In contrast, in the Aristophanes sample only one form of elided ὅδε was observed, as compared with four elisions of οὗτος.

Semilexicals

Some categories of words occupy a borderline position between the lexicals and the nonlexicals. In Irish, the lower numerals induce initial mutation, the higher numerals do not. Imperatives are more liable to prosodic and segmental reduction than other verb forms: reduced forms of the imperative occur in Tagalog and are particularly marked in colloquial Icelandic (Orešnik 1980). In some types of English verse, most of the instances of phrase final stress in metrically weak position involve semantically general or bleached words like *thing* and *man* (Tarlinskaja 1989). In Greek, accentual clisis in φημί could involve word order and the low intonation of parentheticals; clisis in the verb *to be* is subject to semantic conditions. The appositive status of certain numerals is fairly well attested

> ἓν ἀπέχθημα *Troiades* 425
> τρεῖς παρθένοι *I.A.* 49 Porson's bridge
> πέντε ταλάντοις *Acharnians* 6
> δέκα μῆνας *Thesmophoriazusae* 741
> μίαν ηῦρον *Clouds* 76
> ἐννέα παίδων *Thesmophoriazusae* 637.

Elision is relatively common with the lower cardinal numerals in fourth century Attic prose inscriptions (Threatte 1980). That certain lexical imperatives can behave rhythmically like nonlexicals is also fairly well established. δός appears before Porson's bridge in

τοῦτο μὲν δὸς τῇ τύχῃ I. T. 501

where it is preceded by a nonlexical composite and followed by the definite article; δὸς is one of a few verb forms that violate the rule that the minimal weight for a lexical word in Greek is bimoraic (p. 93). Unelided lexicals are strongly avoided in divided anapaests in Aristophanes: however, pyrrhic-shaped imperatives are well attested, ranging from semantically bleached extraparadigmatic forms like φέρε Knights 145 and ἄγε Knights 155, usually followed by postpositives such as νυν or δή, to semantically full lexicals. In the latter class, some are followed by postpositives like

λαβέ νυν Knights 1190

others by prepositives or trochee-shaped nonlexicals

φέρε τοὺς ὀβελίσκους Acharnians 1007

θένε τὴν πέτραν Birds 54

ἄφες ἀπὸ βαλβίδων Knights 1159

λαβὲ καὶ ταδί νυν Knights 1183

λαβὲ τόνδε τὸν ἀλάβαστον Lysistrata 947

φέρε δεῦρο Ecclesiazusae 738, Thesmophoriazusae 1115.

Elided tribrach-shaped words also occur, but in this class too imperatives predominate

ὕπεχ' Acharnians 1063, Thesmophoriazusae 756

πάριτ'/πάριθ' Acharnians 44, Ecclesiazusae 129

ἄφετ' Lysistrata 1166.

A number of monosyllabic semilexical words from categories other than the imperative are attested at Porson's or Havet's bridge

εὖ κείμενα Choephori 693

εὖ πράξομεν Ion 518 tetrameter

φωνῆς δεῖ μόνον Isthmiastae 78a.7 Radt

διὰ σὲ κεῖνον δεῖ δραμεῖν I.A. 1455 MSS;

instances of δεῖ after a morphologically complex nonlexical have already been noted (p. 318); with elided appositive

δεῖ δ' ἢ βρόχους Orestes 1035

χρή μ' ἀθλίαν I.A. 1026.

In Mycenaean, omission of the word divider is well attested in the common phrase pa-si-te-o-i 'to all gods' (Davies 1987); πάντα is a borderline appositive in two instances (one elided) in a Cyprian metrical inscription which punctuates high end appositive groups and one phonologically light phrase

> | πα(ν)τ' ακοραστος *ICS* 264.2
> | κυμερεναι πα(ν)τα | *ICS* 264.4.

Subordination of monosyllabic nouns — in environments other than before a postpositive (Eur. *Supplices* 267, *Hecuba* 592) — is occasionally found; the following word is nonlexical in all cases, and there tend to be additional contributing factors

> παῖς ἤδε μοι Eur. *Supplices* 1098
> παῖδ' ὄντα με *P. V.* 986;

in the second example, elision is a subsidiary factor;

> οὐκ ἔχει νοῦν οὐδένα *Antigone* 68
> νοῦν οὐκ ἔχον/ἔχων *Bacchae* 252, 271;

contrast at the caesura

> νοῦν οὐκ ἔχειν *Andromache* 252;

the examples with *νοῦς* are probably fixed phrases.

Phonological substance

The factor of phonological substance has a number of different manifestations. If clitics have a preferential or canonical shape, it is likely to have less phonological substance than that of lexicals; and the more frequent the clitic, the less its phonological substance tends to be. Clitics also sometimes have a phonological structure that violates canonical word shape rules applicable to lexicals, which is the case in Greek (p. 304) as it is with Latin *-que* and *-ve*. In general, clitics tend to be monosyllabic; disyllabic clitics exist in some languages, for instance Tagalog; Ngiyambaa (New South Wales: Klavans 1982) has trisyllabic clitics. The structure of the syllables of clitics can also be impoverished: in Chrau (Vietnam: Zwicky 1977), sentence final clitics, which are mostly monosyllabic, cannot have consonant clusters in the syllable onset. Phonological substance is also a major factor conditioning the degree to which nonlexicals are liable to prosodic and segmental reduction. In English, many monosyllabic nonlexicals can destress but disyllabic ones cannot: *have* can become *həv* but *having* cannot become *həving*; the only exception is *any* with its V̆CV̆ structure, which can become *n̩ni* in fluent speech. In Danish, light syllable prepositions are more likely to be unstressed than heavy syllable prepositions and monosyllabic ones than disyllabic ones: *ved åen* 'at the river,' *bágved húset* 'behind the house' (Rischel 1983). Similarly, in Russian monosyllabic prepositions are clitic and block final devoicing, disyllabic prepositions are tonic and have final devoicing. In Amoy Chinese, monosyllabic postpositions enter into a tone group with a preceding complement, but disyllabic postpositions do not (Chen 1987). In French, monosyllabic prepositions show more liaison than disyllabic prepositions (Morin et al. 1982; de Jong 1990). The syllable count of the host rather than that of the preposition is the determining factor for linking *r* in Walloon, which appears after certain prepositions before monosyllabic pronouns but not before disyllabic pronouns (Francard et al. 1986). The English monosyllabic nonlexicals are not all equally liable to destress. The most important conditioning factor within the subclass of monosyllabic nonlexicals is the structure of the syllable rhyme. The further the rhyme is down the hierarchy $\breve{V}$, $\breve{V}R$ (R = resonant), $\breve{V}C$, $\breve{V}CC$, $\bar{V}$, $\bar{V}C$, the less likely it is to destress; frequency is probably also relevant (Selkirk 1984).

The analysis of appositives at bridges in the preceding section was designed to illustrate the fact that Greek nonlexicals of various shapes and syllable numbers can become appositive; differences in frequency of occurrence were not emphasized. However, it is intuitively clear that as the number of morae and syllables in the word increases, so the number of attested instances at bridges decreases. While there is an abundance of examples of monosyllabic nonlexicals at bridges, this abundance is reduced to a trickle for spondee-shaped nonlexicals, and the evidence for trisyllabic nonlexicals at bridges is quantitatively comparable to that for monosyllabic and elided disyllabic lexicals. However, this situation does not result solely from the direct conditioning effect exerted by phonological substance on the rules of phrase rhythm. Nonlexical words with less phonological substance also tend to have a higher text frequency than longer and heavier words, and so are more available to appear at bridges; high text frequency is also itself a factor encouraging phonological reduction, as noted below. Words with less phonological substance also tend to have less semantic substance and consequently exert less resistance to phonological reduction in fluent speech. Notwithstanding these qualifications, other factors being equal greater phonological substance does imply greater resistance to reduction in phrase rhythm. This can be demonstrated explicitly in Greek, holding constant the factor of syntactic category. Monosyllabic personal pronoun forms are relatively well attested at Porson's bridge

> παραινεῖς μοι καλῶς *Choephori* 903
> διὰ μάχης σῷ συγγόνῳ *Helen* 978
> σωτὴρ νῷν βλάβης *Heraclidae* 640
> ἄκουσόν μου, πάτερ *Ion* 633

but, excluding two cases followed by a postpositive (*Heraclidae* 303, *O. T.* 142), there is no certain instance of a disyllabic personal pronoun form with an unambiguously heavy final syllable at Porson's bridge (see *O. T.* 1482, *Philoctetes* 222, *Isthmiastae* 78a.23 Radt). A sequence like ἡμῖν κύριον, which is normal line internally as at *Orestes* 1035, is rare or nonoccurring line finally in tragedy. Similar evidence is provided by prepositions. Monosyllabic heavy syllable prepositions like ἐκ, ἐν, εἰς, πρός are well attested before Porson's bridge

> ἐκ χείματος *Agamemnon* 900
> ἐν σπαργάνοις *Agamemnon* 1606, *Choephori* 755
> πρὸς τέρμασιν *Andromache* 1081;

also found is elided ἀντί *Helen* 1029; πλήν occurs as a conjunction (*Andromache* 905, *Orestes* 1615). Disyllabic improper prepositions like ἐκτός, ἐντός, εἴσω, ἔξω, χωρίς, ἐγγύς have a much lower text frequency than the monosyllabic type, but their occurrence ending in long third anceps is restricted to a single instance of ἄνευ with crasis before the article

> κἄνευ τῆς ἐμῆς *O.C.* 664.

A sequence like ἔξω δωμάτων, which is normal line internally as at *Alcestis* 508, is not allowed line finally in tragedy. The almost complete exclusion of the disyllabic type before Porson's bridge reflects its greater phonological substance.

Frequency

Frequency is a pervasive conditioning factor in phrase phonology. In one study, the occurrence of fast speech rules in several hours of natural speech was analyzed and a systematic correlation was found between the application of a rule and the frequency of the word operated on by the rule (Johnson in Kaisse 1985). Final dental palatalization in English illustrates the frequency factor: it was found that palatalization was over three times as common in "The scientist *had utensils* in his lab" as in "The scientist *had euglena* in his lab" (Cooper et al. 1980). Final dental palatalization is very common before nonlexical *you* and *your*, fairly acceptable before *yet* and *yesterday*, but disfavoured before less frequent words: compare "This fact will complicač your holidays" with "This fact will complicate urology" (Rotenberg 1978). Among French disyllabic prepositions, liaison can occur with relatively frequent items such as *après* 'after,' *durant* 'during,' but hardly with a rare item like *hormis* 'except' (Morin et al. 1982). Very generally, the rate of articulation increases with practice and familiarity of the material (Goldman-Eisler 1961).

Any test of frequency as a factor conditioning appositive status in Greek will have to control for other potentially interacting factors such as phonological substance, syntactic constituency and syntactic category. These controls can be maintained by testing the class of monosyllabic prepositions of the canonical structure (C)V̆C at Porson's bridge. By definition words of this class belong to the same syntactic category; they have the same distributional possibilities; and there is a substantial gradient of text frequency among them. In Euripides including the fragments, ἐν has a total frequency of 1362 as compared with only 214 for σύν/ξύν. These prepositions are distributionally comparable within the stichos since they both govern only the dative; the only factor not controlled for by the comparison is their phonological difference, particularly the presence or absence of an onset. 1.61% of the occurrences of ἐν (22 instances) are located before Porson's bridge, whereas there are no cases of σύν/ξύν at Porson's bridge. Since the sample size is quite large, this difference is statistically significant ($p = 0.0039$): there are less than four chances in a thousand that σύν/ξύν should be excluded before Porson's bridge if it were actually just as acceptable as ἐν. It is possible to control for the presence of the syllable onset by comparing πρός with σύν/ξύν. In Euripides πρός occurs 817 times, nearly four times as often as σύν/ξύν. 1.71% of the occurrences of πρός are before Porson's bridge, which is again significantly higher than the rate for σύν/ξύν ($p = 0.0371$). σύν/ξύν is also constrained before Porson's bridge in Aeschylus and Sophocles, who only allow it in this position if it is the first element of a composite appositive structure

> σὺν τῷ τρίτῳ *Choephori* 244
> ὡς σὺν σοὶ κάτω Soph. *Electra* 1166.

This constraint does not apply to ἐν and πρός in Aeschylus or to ἐκ/ἐξ in Aeschylus and Sophocles. These data indicate that the text frequency of a preposition is a factor conditioning its liability to the heavy syllable subordination rule.

Fixed phrases

Not all speech is generated ex novo every time we speak; some of what we say comes in preassembled phrasal units, including but not limited to cliches, idioms and slogans (Vihman 1982). Phrase phonology is conditioned not only by the frequency of a lexical item but also by the frequency of the locutions in which it occurs. Common syntagms become fixed phrases and fixed phrases become lexical units. French liaison is more common in an expression such as *premier étage* 'first floor' than in a fully generated syntagm like *singulier ami*; liaison is obligatory in completely lexicalized expressions such as *accent aigu* and *fait accompli* (Zwicky 1972). French liaison is rare between *comment* 'how' and a following verb except in the fixed expressions *comment est-ce que* and *comment allez-vous* (Morin et al. 1982). In Danish, most noun phrases do not have a single phrasal accent, but fixed phrases are an exception: *hjerter dáme* 'Queen of Hearts' (Rischel 1983). Common expressions are more likely to show proclitic accent retraction in Serbocroatian and Slovenian (Vermeer 1986). In English, compare *thiŝ year* with *this yeast* and "Gimme that flower" with "Sieve me that flour"; similar contractions and constraints occur in Icelandic (Pétursson 1986). Agrammatic patients have relatively little difficulty with overlearned discourse idioms like *I see, I dunno*; a Chinese agrammatic omitted the attribution functor *de/zhi* consistently except once in her street address (Menn et al. 1990).

In Greek, a number of cases of split resolution or divided anapaest involve what are probably common syntagms, fixed phrases, idioms and oaths

ἀκούετε λεῴ *Acharnians* 1000, *Peace* 551, *Birds* 448
τἄδικα λέγων *Clouds* 884
κακὸν ἐργάσασθαι *Plutus* 465
πολλὰ κακά *Ecclesiazusae* 436
πολὺ μᾶλλον *Plutus* 195, 867.

These fixed phrases become domains for word prosody rather than phrase prosody; consequently, nonfinal lexical items within the phrase lose their demarcation, and final syllable constraints on matrix formation and on disyllabic arsis no longer apply.

Figures of speech

In Greek, figures of speech involving repetition of a word with the same or different inflections involve a high degree of cohesion; they have a greater than expected frequency among the instances of postponed particle (Denniston 1934)

φόνον φόνου δὲ *Philoctetes* 959
βᾶτε βᾶτε δ' ἐς δόμους *Helen* 331
ἴτω ἴτω δὲ *Birds* 856
κακῷ κακὸν γὰρ *Troades* 621
ἄτοπος ἄτοπα γὰρ *Ion* 690.

Fixed or lexicalized phrases with repeated words for 'every day' and 'every year' have been found written without the word divider: Mycenaean *we-te-i-we-te-i*, Cyprian *a-ma-ti-a-ma-ti* in an otherwise fairly regularly word divided inscription (Davies 1987). In light of the above evidence, there is less justification for dismissing rhythmically difficult mappings of such figures of speech as simply metri gratia. For instance, there is a rule prescribing that a tribrach-shaped word may not end in resolved fourth longum in the trimeter unless it is preceded by a prepositive

καὶ χάριτας *Orestes* 244;

there are no examples with a preceding lexical word except for the figure

χάριν ἄχαριν *I. T.* 566.

The split anapaests

> μεθεῖτε μεθεῖτε *Frogs* 1393 MSS
> κάτησο κάτησο *Thesmophoriazusae* 1184 (*Τοξότης*)

are supported by the comparable instances of postponed particle just cited. Further evidence for word internal phonology in this type of figure of speech is afforded by the hiatus in

> ἴδε ἴδ᾽ ὦ φίλα γύναι *Trachiniae* 222
> ὁρῶ ὁρῶ *Persae* 1019.

ACCENT

Polytonicity

Elements that from a morphological point of view are components of words can have their own accent in addition to, and often subordinate to, the main word accent. It is not uncommon in stress languages for some affixes to receive optional or obligatory secondary stress, as is the case with certain derivational suffixes and verbal endings in Anglo-Saxon (Campbell 1959). Morpheme accent can also occur in pitch accent languages. In Japanese, a few morphemes best categorized as prefixes can have their own pitch accent not only when under contrastive focus but under other conditions as well (Poser 1985). Although Greek affixes are not always fully integrated segmentally (*δύσνοος, δύσμεικτος* but *ἔννυμι, εἰμί*), there is no evidence for any lack of accentual integration from the orthography, the accounts of the grammarians or the musical records (ME 7.9, 7.11).

The accentuation of compounds is also potentially variable. In a number of languages, compounds are divided into two classes according to whether they have a single accent or an accent on each element, a distinction that tends to correlate with the degree to which a compound is morphosyntactically generated or an established monolithic lexical item. For instance, in Dakota (Chambers et al. 1980; Shaw 1985), Welsh (Allen 1975) and Anglo-Saxon (Bliss 1967), productive or semantically transparent compounding is multiaccentual, whereas opaque or lexically fixed compounds are monoaccentual. The latter also tend towards adopting word internal segmental phonology — *lamppost* with one *p*, *lamp-pole* with geminate *p*, and unit morphology — *ἐκαθήμην, ἐκάθιζον*. In Japanese, there is some variation between mono- and biaccentual compounds depending on syntactic composition, rate of speech, idiolectal text frequency and focus (Kubozono 1987). In Malayalam (S.W. India: Mohanan 1982), dvandva compounds are multiaccentual, others monoaccentual. In the Greek musical records, three of the comparatively few words whose setting violates the basic rule that the accented syllable is not set lower than any other syllable in the word are compounds; in all three cases, these compounds would conform to the basic rule if their constituents were individually accented on the analogy of the independent components (ME 7.1–3). Evidence for the rhythmic autonomy of compound

ME 7.1   φερ- ό-   πλοι- ο   *Ath.* 10

ME 7.2   δι - κό - ρυ- φον   *Lim.* 2

ME 7.3   φα- εσ - φό - ρα   *DAM* 34.2

elements has already been cited (p. 150). Both the accentual and the rhythmic evidence may pertain only to slow, deliberate speech. In ME 7.2 the first element of the compound is nonlexical and both pitch peaks are on the lexical element, perhaps sound symbolically given the meaning 'two-peaked' (Reinach 1911).

Atonicity

Conversely, items that from a syntactic point of view are independent words can be unaccented. This applies in principle not only to nonlexical grammatical function words, but also to lexical words such as verbs, adjectives and nouns. Some stress languages are reported as having unaccented lexical words (Hyman 1977), and the phenomenon is clearly attested for pitch accent languages by Japanese. In this language, lexical words may be accented, in which case there is a fall from high to low pitch on one of the syllables of the word; or words may be post-accented, in which case the pitch fall is on an enclitic following the word; or they may be unaccented, in which case there is a pitch fall neither on any syllable of the word nor on a following enclitic. In Japanese, as in Greek, the location of the accent is more regular and patterned in verbs than in nouns. The diachronic explanation for this in Greek is that verbs appear to have been classed with certain nonlexical words as unaccented under certain conditions in Indo-European: in Vedic, the finite verb of a main clause lacked a word accent except initially in the sentence or verse line. This prosodic characteristic of the verb may find a parallel in tone languages: in proto-Bantu, tone patterns were more restricted in verbal stems than in nominal stems (Odden 1985), and there may be a tendency, at least in some languages, for accent to develop from tones earlier in the verbal system than in the nominal system (Clements et al. 1984). Such phenomena lend considerable support to the view that prominence (and demarcation) in the word are ontologically related to prominence (and demarcation) in the utterance (Hyman 1977, 1978b); the prosodic prominence of nouns may be related to the comparatively high informational content of nontopic noun phrases. In Greek, a few verb forms are clitic but there are no clitic noun forms. In Hungarian, verbs can be destressed when preceded by a verbal modifier. In Danish, phrasal destressing affects verbs far more than nouns and adjectives (Rischel 1983). In both Anglo-Saxon (Kuhn 1933) and Modern English sentences, nouns tend to receive stronger or preferential stress as compared with verbs; although some of these effects are due to factors of word order and constituency (Sorensen et al. 1978), verb destressing seems ultimately to reflect informational content (Rochemont 1986; Bolinger 1989). The same hierarchy appears in diachronic change: Latin dative and ablative -$\bar{o}$ are more resistant to shortening than verbal -$\bar{o}$. It has already been noted (p. 300) that for agrammatic speakers nouns are often better preserved than verbs, and nominal forms of verbs like participles and infinitives are often substituted for finite verbal forms.

A lexical word can become weakly accented or unaccented and combine with a contiguous word into a single accentual phrase not only in stress languages but also in pitch accent languages. This is a common occurrence in Japanese (Poser 1985; Beckman et al. 1986; Vance 1987), where two words such as adjective and noun or noun plus governing verb or family name plus surname can be pronounced with separate accents on each word or with one accent on the whole phrase. In the latter case, if the first word is an accented word, the accent of the second word is not realized. The combination of Japanese words into single accentual phrases depends on speech tempo and is constrained phonologically, syntactically and semantically (Selkirk et al. 1988); the process is dialectally variable, applying more easily in the dialect of Tokyo than in the dialect of Osaka (Pierrehumbert et al. 1988). Similarly in Digo (Kenya: Kisseberth 1984), in a phrase consisting of a verb with a single High tone followed by a Low-toned noun, the High tone is shifted from the verb to the noun. There is no evidence in the musical settings for deaccenting of lexical words in the Greek phrase.

Clisis

While atonicity tends to be restricted and exceptional for lexical words, it is widespread and typical for nonlexical words, which are consequently often referred to as clitics. It is useful to distinguish syntactic clisis from phonological clisis (p. 303). The former typically involves particular word order constraints on a class of nonlexical words that need not be exclusively atonic. Phonological clisis in turn requires a distinction between accentual clisis and rhythmic clisis, that is between words that are atonic and words that are appositive. Some accentual clitics occur only in an atonic form, like Latin -*que*. Other words appear in atonic or tonic form, depending on a number of syntactic and semantic factors. The atonic forms may be transparently derived from the tonic forms by productive segmental rules affecting atonic syllables in general, or they may be to one degree or another segmentally distanced from the tonic form in a unique and idiosyncratic way, as the Serbocroatian enclitic *im* 'to them' is from *njima*. The existence of tonic forms alternating with atonic forms has suggested three possible descriptive approaches to accentual clisis. In some cases, it seems best to list both forms in the lexicon, in others to derive the atonic form from the tonic form by a destressing or deaccentuation rule, and in others again to derive the tonic form from the atonic form by a surface accenting rule. It does not appear useful to attempt to generalize any one of these approaches to all instances.

Enclitics

The following forms are enclitic in Greek (Postgate 1924; Vendryes 1945).

1. The oblique cases of the singular personal pronouns are enclitic, when they are unemphatic

> μου, μοι, με
>
> σε, σου, σοι
>
> ἑ, οὑ, οἱ.

The selection of orthotonic and enclitic personal pronoun forms is largely determined by focus, as discussed in Chapter 10, and by phrasing, as discussed in Chapter 9. It is not necessary to analyze the unemphatic forms of the first and second persons plural ἡμᾱς, ἡμῶν, ἡμῖν, ὑμᾱς, ὑμῶν, ὑμῖν as synchronic enclitics: a final acute becomes a grave before these forms as before orthotone words, and their invariably paroxytone accentuation cannot be explained as a variant of enclitic accentuation conditioned by the long vowels of their penultimate syllables, since the length of penultimate vowels otherwise has no effect on the limitation of accent recession (Allen 1973). According to Herodian I.558 Lentz, the first and second person dual forms νῶϊν, σφῶϊν are always orthotonic; but the third person dual and plural forms in σφ- are enclitic when unemphatic. Apollonius Dyscolus I.26 Schneider and Herodian I.558, II.82 Lentz state that the accusative singular αὐτόν in its anaphoric usage is enclitic too, but modern editors do not follow this rule.

Herodian gives a rule for the accentuation of pronouns after prepositions that recalls the disjunctive pronouns of French and Italian: αἱ μετὰ προθέσεως δὲ ἀεὶ ὀρθοτονοῦνται, διὰ σέ, περὶ σοῦ, κατ'ἐμέ, ἐπὶ σοί I.559 Lentz.

However, there is considerable variation in the manuscripts, and πρός με is regular (Postgate 1924). The paroxytone accentuation of the unemphatic plurals of the personal pronouns ἥμων, ὕμων, ἥμιν, ὕμιν, ἥμας, ὕμας is accounted for by phonological substance (Vendryes 1945). All these forms have four morae while no enclitic has more than three morae: τὸ μέγιστον μέγεθος τῶν ἐγκλιτικῶν τρίχρονόν ἐστι Apollonius Dyscolus II.186.4 Uhlig.

2. The indefinite pronoun and its cognate indefinite adverbs (words in *kʷ-) are enclitic

τις, τινα, τινος, τινι, τινες etc.

πη, ποι, που, ποθεν, ποτε, πω, πως etc.

The contrast between indefinite enclitic τις and interrogative orthotonic τίνος is reflected in the musical settings of ME 7.4–5: in ME 7.4 the

ME 7.4   εἰ τις   DAM 38.2.6

ME 7.5   ἤ τί-νος   DAM 39.2

enclitic induces an acute on the proclitic conjunction εἰ from which the pitch falls to τις, whereas in ME 7.5 pitch rises steeply to the peak of interrogative τίς.

3. The conjunction τε, the modal κε(ν), the focus particles γε, περ, and the asseverative and discourse cohesive particles θην, νῦν, ῥα, τοι are all enclitic.

As already noted, not all postpositives are enclitic. The grammarian at Anecdota Bekker III.1156 and the scholiast on Dionysius Thrax 466.18 Hilgard claim that the postpositives μέν, δέ, γάρ are enclitic. Some support for this tradition is found in manuscript accentuations such as ἐγώ μεν, σύ δε, ἄλλοί γαρ and the accentuation of the univerbated composite τοίγαρ (Vendryes 1945). The musical documents do not support a general application of this doctrine, but indicate that these postpositives have grave accents with the regular lowering on nonlexicals (p. 364). The difference between the pitch excursion associated with the enclitic conjunction τε and that associated with the orthotonic conjunction δέ is illustrated in ME 7.6–7: in ME 7.6 the acute of λιγύ is changed into a grave which is assigned the same pitch as that assigned to the grave of δὲ, and the latter in turn is assigned the same pitch as the following word initial Mid tone of λωτὸς, whereas ME 7.7 shows the acute on τάν and a substantial fall of two whole tones to the Low tone on enclitic τε. Since grave accents are part of the rising trajectory, the point at which the

ME 7.6   *Ath.* 14

λι - γὺ δὲ λω - το-ὸς

ME 7.7   *Lim.* 38

τάν τε δο - ρίσ[

trajectory turns from falling to rising lies between the end of the word and the postpositive and consequently splits the appositive group. This absence of coordination of rhythm and accent is not really problematic, since under certain conditions the turning point in the trajectory can actually occur within a lexical word (secondary rise). It is possible that the doctrine of enclitic *μέν, δέ, γάρ* refers to a less deliberate rate and style of speech than that reflected in the musical settings; this would be evidence that pitch excursions on some orthotone nonlexical words were liable to be reduced to the point of enclisis in fast speech. It is also possible that under strong contrastive focus in the type *ἐγὼ μὲν... σὺ δὲ,* the pitch pattern was interpreted as Mid High Low and equated with that of *ἐγώ τε* due to the special pitch obtrusion assigned to the pronoun and perhaps some additional postfocus pitch lowering on the particle. This interpretation receives some late musical support from a setting in Mesomedes' Hymn to the Sun (ME 7.8).

ME 7.8   *DAM* 4.17

σοὶ μέν χο - ρὸς

4. The indicative forms of *εἰμί* and *φημί* are enclitic under certain circumstances, except for the second person singular forms *εἶ* and *φῄς* (but not Homeric *ἐσσί* nor the modernization *εἶς* Herodian II.503.29, 950.4 Lentz).

According to Herodian I.553 Lentz and the *Etymologicum Magnum* 301.2 (cf. Ἀρκαδίου περὶ τόνων 142.13, 147.23 Barker; scholiast on *Iliad* 1.63), the normative clitic *ἐστί* is paroxytone at the beginning of a clause or verse and when it follows *οὐκ, μή, ὡς, ἀλλά, καί* and *τοῦτο*; it should not be enclitic to zero or to certain other nonlexical words. This tradition is corroborated by the setting of *οὐκ ἔστ'* in ME 7.9, where the melism

ME 7.9   *DAM* 39.11

οὐκ ἔστ' ἀ - έλπ - του τέρ - ψις

set to *ἔστ'* is higher than the melism set to the accented syllable of *ἀέλπτου* and presupposes paroxytone accentuation of the unelided form, since enclitic accentuation would require the pitch peak to occur on *οὐκ* rather than on *ἔστ'*. The setting of *ἔστ'* in ME 7.10 suggests that *ἐστί* may have

ME 7.10   ὅδ' ἐστ' 'Α - χιλ - [λέως παῖς   *DAM* 37.18

been paroxytone after a wider class of demonstratives; for if ἔστ' were unaccented, it would be unusual for it to be set so much higher than the following word initial midtone of *Ἀχιλλέως*. If this setting does in fact reflect acute accentuation of ἔστ', then it would follow that the paroxytonesis claimed by Herodian in *τοῦτ' ἔστιν ἁμάρτημα* did not have to result from perseveration of the high pitch induced on *-o* by enclisis (Vendryes 1945). It is also widely accepted that when ἐστί is semantically existential or expresses possibility, it is always paroxytone regardless of its position in the sentence (Hermann 1801)

> *κεῖσε μὲν ἔστι καὶ ὕστερον ὁρμηθῆναι Iliad* 14.313
> *ἔστι δ' ὅπη νῦν ἔστι Agamemnon* 67.

Hermann's rule is followed by modern editors, but it is not mentioned by ancient grammarians and has been disputed (Vendryes 1945). The setting of the clause in the eighth and ninth lines of the Seikilos inscription (ME 7.11), where there is no semantic objection to taking ἔστι as

ME 7.11   πρὸς ὀ - λί - γον ἐ - στὶ τὸ ζῆν,   *DAM* 18.8

existential, corroborates Hermann's rule: the setting either reflects paroxytone accentuation or is a mismatch. *πρὸς ὀλίγον ἐστὶ* cannot be interpreted as a single accentual word (Sommerstein 1973), for it is an exceptionless rule of this inscription, as of the Delphic hymns, that after the first postpeak fall in pitch in an accentual unit pitch never rises and then falls again.

Proclitics

Whereas the ancient grammarians, particularly Apollonius Dyscolus, Herodian and Charax, devoted extensive discussion to the enclitics, they did not recognize a class of proclitics

> *πᾶν ἄρθρον ὀξύνεται χωρὶς τῶν γενικῶν καὶ δοτικῶν· αὗται γὰρ περισπῶνται* Herodian I.473 Lentz
> *τὸ ὡς ὀξύνεται κἂν ἐν ἀρχῇ κἂν ἐν μέσῳ κἂν ἐν τέλει ἢ πλὴν μόνον ὅτε σημαίνει τὸ ὅμως* Herodian II.160 Lentz
> *τοῦτο* (scilicet οὗ) *δὲ καὶ ἐν τῇ συνεπείᾳ ὀξύνεται* Herodian I.504 Lentz.

The existence of enclisis was highlighted by a number of semantic and pragmatic contrasts signalled by the distinction between enclitic and orthotonic forms, but any such contrasts there could have been between

proclitic and orthotone may have been less salient and more comparable to those between focused and unfocused words in general. However,
the main reason why the grammarians do not recognize proclisis is that,
as will be argued below, proclisis does not involve complete atonicity
but is merely one manifestation of a quite general tendency to reduce
and compress accentual excursions in nonlexical words: proclitics were
tonic.

It is the practice of the manuscripts to write eleven prepositive nonlexical words without accents

> the monosyllabic vowel initial forms of the article ὁ, ἡ,
> οἱ, αἱ
> the monosyllabic vowel initial conjunctions εἰ, ὡς
> the monosyllabic vowel initial prepositions ἐ(ι)ν, ἐ(ι)ς,
> ἐκ/ξ, ὡς
> the monosyllabic vowel initial negative οὐ(κ) in normal
> syntactic contexts.

The term proclitics was coined for these forms in the early nineteenth
century (Hermann 1801). It is generally assumed that there is no basis
in the language for treating the forms of the article with τ- as orthotone
and those without τ- as atonic. The practice of the manuscripts is interpreted as a purely orthographic convention, serving to distinguish ὁ,
ἡ, οἱ, αἱ, ἐξ, εἰ, εἰς, ἐν, οὐ, ὡς from ὅ, ἤ, οἵ, αἵ, ἔξ, εἴ, εἷς, ἔν, οὔ, ὧς, as well as
affording an economy in the writing of high frequency forms. But on the
basis of a variety of other evidence it is widely assumed that Greek did
have a class of proclitics which included several other forms in addition
to those that are written unaccented in the manuscripts (Wackernagel
1914). This class of proclitics includes

> Prepositions: ἀνά, ἀπό, διά, ἐκ/ξ, ἐν(ι), ἐ(ι)ς, ἐπί, κατά, μετά, παρά,
> περί, πρό, πρός, ξ/σύν, ὑπέρ, ὑπό, ὡς, perhaps ἀμφί, ἀντί
> Conjunctions: ἀλλά, ἀτάρ, εἰ, ἐπεί, ἤ, ἠδέ, ἠμέν, καί, οὐδέ,
> μηδέ, φή, ὡς
> Negatives: οὐ(κ), μή
> Adverb: ἰδού.

There is disagreement regarding proclisis of forms of the article: according
to one view, no forms of the article are proclitic (Vendryes 1945); but
it has also been suggested that all forms of the article, including those
in τ-, were proclitic (Sommerstein 1973). However, rhythmic clisis, that
is appositive status, does not necessarily imply accentual clisis. The
evidence of the musical settings does not support any posited difference
between forms with and without τ-. There are two instances of the article
in clause internal position in the Seikilos epitaph (ME 7.12): there is

ME 7.12

DAM 18.8–11

no difference between the form with τ- and the form without; the excursion from ό to the peak of the following lexical word χρόνος is the same as that from τό to ζῆν. (In clause initial position, the article in τὸ τέλος is treated similarly to the monosyllabic preposition πρός in πρὸς ὀλίγον [p. 430]).

The generally assumed underlying or contextual atonicity of the class of proclitic is difficult to reconcile with the statements of the grammarians. It has been argued that the grammarians extrapolated from the secondary induced accentuation of proclitics before an enclitic (Allen 1973). It has also been supposed that the grave was a Low tone and the equivalent of no accent at all, so that within the phrase a final underlying acute would surface as zero accent phonetically identical to proclisis; this idea is refuted by the musical evidence presented in Chapter 4.

One item of evidence adduced in favour of this posited class of proclitics is that in Aeolic, practically all words (West 1970) have fully recessive accentuation, except for prepositions and certain conjunctions, which keep their oxytone accents: πᾶσα γὰρ λέξις ὑπὲρ μίαν συλλαβὴν παρ' ἡμῖν ὀξυνομένη παρὰ τοῖς Αἰολεῦσι βαρύνεται,... χωρὶς τῶν προθέσεων καὶ τῶν συνδέσμων· ἐπὶ τούτων γὰρ φυλάττουσι τὴν ὀξεῖαν τάσιν, οἷον ἀνά, κατά, διά, μετά, αὐτάρ, ἀτάρ Choeroboscus Anecdota Bekker III.1203. However, it is not clear why explicit statements that Aeolic 'preserves the oxytone' should be taken to mean that "there was no accent at all" (Postgate 1924). Such an interpretation is only possible on the assumption that the grave is the same as no accent, that is that the grave represents a Low tone, which is not the case. The failure of barytonesis in proclitics in Aeolic is better explained as due to the fact that proclitics always form part of the rising pitch trajectory: if the accent were retracted, this would create a High-Low movement that would disrupt that trajectory.

Another item of evidence is that, according to the grammarians, there is no difference in accentuation between a preposition or a preverb in tmesis and its corresponding prefix within a compound verb: τὸ δὲ καταγράφω εἴτε δύο μέρη λόγου ἐστὶν εἴτε καὶ ἕν, οὐκ ἐνδείκνυται διὰ τῆς τάσεως. καὶ τὰ τούτοις ὅμοια, τὸ ἀποίκου, καταφέροντος, ἅπαντα τὰ τοιαῦτα, τῆς αὐτῆς ἔχεται ἀμφιβολίας Apollonius Dyscolus II.435.4 Uhlig. This is true in the sense that the pitch excursion over proclitics up to the accentual peak of the following lexical word is part of the rising trajectory. The mean

rise from the first syllable of a disyllabic proclitic such as ἐπί to the peak
of the full accent of the following lexical is 1.14 tones in the Delphic
hymns, which is indistinguishable from the mean rise within words from
an initial unaccented syllable over at least two syllables to the peak of
the full accent, which is 1.00 tone (p. 186). However, disyllabic proclitics
show a rise from their initial to their final syllables of only 0.07 tones
on the average as compared to 0.25 tones for the rise from the first to
the second syllable in words with at least three syllables before a full
accent, and 0.59 tones from the pre-preaccentual to the immediately
preaccentual syllable within words. This tendency for proclitics to have
a flatter internal trajectory than word internal preaccentual syllables is
illustrated by a number of settings of ἀνά and ἐπί as proclitics and as
preverbs in the Delphic hymns (ME 7.13–18), where the prepositions

are set to level pitch and the preverbs to rising pitch with the exception
of ἐπινίσεται. Of all the proclitics in the Delphic hymns, only one, ἐπί
in ME 7.19, is set with a rise from the first to the final syllable. Although

the tendency towards a pitch plateau over proclitics is not statistically
significant given the small amount of data preserved, it is continued in
later documents (ME 7.20); the pitch plateau can include a preceding
grave on a lexical or nonlexical word (ME 7.33).

ME 7.20  *DAM* 38.2.6

κα - τὰ σ|τέ|-γας

A third item of evidence is that when most oxytone words are elided, the accent is retracted to the preceding syllable (p. 265)

πολλὰ ἔπαθον → πόλλ᾽ ἔπαθον,

but this does not apply to prepositions and conjunctions

παρ᾽ ἐμοῦ
ἀφ᾽ ἑαυτοῦ
ἀλλ᾽ ἐγώ
οὐδ᾽ ἐμοί.

It is incorrect to equate these elided proclitics with elided enclitics that would bear a secondary accent, merely because the accent is not retracted (Vendryes 1945). Enclitics are always part of the falling pitch trajectory following the peak of the preceding word accent; but proclitics are always part of the rising trajectory that moves up to the full accent of the next word, as illustrated by ME 7.21–22 where ἀπ᾽ is both times set higher

ME 7.21 ἐ - κεί - νας ἀπ᾽ ἀρ - χᾶς *Lim.* 19

ME 7.22 σ]υ-ύ - ριγμ᾽ ἀπ᾽ ε[ὐ-] [νω]- ῶν[*Lim.* 30

than the final unaccented syllable of the preceding word and at the same level or slightly lower than the following word initial unaccented syllable. Moreover, in the Delphic hymns monosyllabic and elided disyllabic proclitics have on the average only about half the rise to an initial full accent on a following lexical word (0.33 tones) as an immediately prepeak word internal syllable (0.70 tones). In ME 7.23, the orthographically

ME 7.23 ἐς [᾿Ο] - λ[υ]μ-πον *Ath.* 13

atonic preposition ἐς is set at exactly the same pitch as the full accent of the following proper name; the steepest rise of this type in the Delphic hymns is of only one tone from the conjunction ὡς to the peak of the circumflex on the following verb in ME 7.24. This phenomenon is probably related to the plateau tendency just noted for disyllabic proclitics.

ME 7.24 ὡς ει- εί - [λες, *Ath.* 21

The ancient treatment of elided disyllabic proclitics as atonic may simply reflect the fact that they never have higher pitch than a following unaccented syllable and are never themselves followed by a fall in pitch. If it were statistically significant, the 0.33 tone difference between the average pitch of monosyllabic and elided disyllabic proclitics and that of the following full accent peak would indicate grave accentuation. The evidence of the musical settings does not require that monosyllabic or disyllabic proclitics be interpreted as either underlyingly or contextually atonic; their settings are in conformity with the reduction of phrase medial pitch excursions in shorter and nonlexical words and the integration of those words into the rising pitch trajectory to a following lexical accent.

In sentence initial position, a proclitic may be set with a very great pitch excursion, an octave over Ἀλλὰ *Lim.* 26 and 2.5 tones over Ἀμφὶ *Lim.* 23. In both cases, the greatest portion of the rising interval takes place within the proclitic, and the final syllable of the proclitic, like that of other grave words, is set quite close in pitch to the initial syllable of the following word (p. 430).

The foregoing considerations suggest that the traditional class of proclitics was not completely atonic and so not the precise counterpart in the rising pitch trajectory of the enclitics in the falling trajectory.

Other nonenclitic nonlexicals

Some right linking nonlexical words are not proclitic but have full accents; such words, particularly the heavier word shapes, tend to have an internal High-Low movement as opposed to the plateau tendency of the proclitics. In the musical documents, trochee-shaped paroxytone and perispomenon right linking nonlexicals are regularly set with a High-Low accentual excursion, even though their peaks are subordinated to the peaks of their host words (ME 7.25). Pyrrhic-shaped paroxytone right link-

ME 7.25   *Ath.* 19

τόν - δε πά-γον,

ing nonlexicals may be set either with a High-Low pitch movement (ME 7.26–29) or with a plateau (ME 7.30–31). Furthermore, these nonlexicals behave quite differently from lexical words in regard to catathesis: the accent of a lexical word depresses the accent of a following lexical word (see Chapter 9), but the accent of a nonlexical word has no such effect.

ME 7.26   *Lim.* 13

Τό - τε

ME 7.27   ὅ - τι   νό - ωι   *Lim.* 18

ME 7.28   ὅ - τε [τε] - ὀμ   μαν - τό-συ[νον]   *Lim.* 32

ME 7.29   τά - δ[ε π]αρ - όν - τα   *DAM* 39.14

ME 7.30   ἱ - να   *Ath.* 3

ME 7.31   τά - δε   λέ - γεις   ποτ [α   *DAM* 39.3

There are six cases in the hymns of a nonlexical word bearing the acute or circumflex and standing before a lexical word (not a proper name) also bearing the acute or circumflex within a downtrend domain (one with intervening enclitic, another with intervening proclitic). Table 7.11 compares the rate of 100% at which the peak of a nonlexical is set lower than or equal to the peak of its immediately following lexical with the corresponding, and much lower, rate at which the peak of the first lexical word in pairs of immediately successive lexical words, neither of which is a proper name, is so set. The value $p = 0.0089$ is calculated by the hypergeometric distribution and means that there is only a chance of about nine in a thousand that the exclusion of pitch fall from a nonlexical accentual peak to a lexical accentual peak could arise at random in samples of the same size and marginal frequencies. The same principle of the subordination of nonlexical acute and circumflex accents to following lexical acute and circumflex accents also holds without exception when grave accents intervene and when the following lexical is a proper name. As would be expected, the lexical peak tends more often

TABLE 7.11
Nonlexical acute or circumflex
compared with lexical acute or circumflex
before a following lexical acute or circumflex

	$P_1 > P_2$	$P_1 \leq P_2$
Nonlexical + Lexical	0.00%	100.00%
Lexical + Lexical	58.33%	41.67%
$p = 0.0089$		

to be higher than the nonlexical peak if the lexical is a proper name or if a grave intervenes, whereas when these factors are absent the lexical peak is more often at the same level as the nonlexical peak.

The subordination of the acute and circumflex accents of nonlexical words represents in principle the accentual correlate of rhythmic appositive status. The magnitude of accentual excursions to the acute and circumflex of nonlexicals is reduced as compared with that of lexicals of the same length (see Table 4.10), and nonlexical acutes and circumflexes do not trigger catathesis in a following lexical word. Right linking nonlexicals form a tonal domain with their host lexicals. Unlike structures of grave plus fully accented lexical, however, they do not form part of a single accentual trajectory: the High-Low movement of the nonlexical accent is reduced but not eliminated.

While a sequence of lexical graves tends to have an upward trajectory, as in ME 7.32 where there is a rise of 2.5 tones from the first to

ME 7.32   θυρ - σο-πλή[ξ   ἑσμὸς ἰ] - ε - ρὸς   *Lim.* 20

the third grave, in sequences of lexical grave plus left linking or right linking nonlexical grave there is regularly a pitch plateau over the two graves in the Delphic hymns (ME 7.33, 7.6 above). In ME 7.6, a non-

ME 7.33   Δελ - φὸν ἀ - νὰ   *Ath.* 7

lexical grave occurs between two lexical graves, and there is a plateau covering the first grave and the nonlexical followed by a rise to the third grave. This evidence indicates that grave depression is a general feature of nonlexical words, and that the phenomenon of proclisis needs to be interpreted in this wider context.

Conclusion: The accentuation of proclitics and nonenclitic nonlexicals

It may be concluded from the above analysis that the theory of proclitics cannot be maintained in its current form. Proclitics are not atonic. Although they are part of the rising trajectory, they are more comparable to lexical grave accented words than to preaccentual word internal syllables, because monosyllabic and elided disyllabic proclitics are set closer to a following peak than word internal preaccentual syllables and disyllabic proclitics have a flatter internal trajectory than word internal preaccentual syllables. In sentence initial position, proclitics can have a steep pitch rise to the grave, which resembles the rise to a lexical grave, with the final syllable of the proclitic set quite close to the initial syllable of the following word. Proclitics are also not so much a special class of word different from tonic words, as assumed by the current theory of proclitics, but rather merely one rather strong manifestation of the phenomenon of accentual reduction in nonlexical words. The degree to which accentual excursions are lowered and compressed in nonlexical words depends on the length (number of syllables) and the heaviness (phonological substance) of the nonlexical word in question. Monosyllabic nonlexicals have more accentual reduction than disyllabic nonlexicals, and pyrrhic-shaped nonlexicals have more reduction than trochee-shaped nonlexicals. This parameter of accentual reduction affects nonlexicals with circumflex and (nonfinal) acute accents as well as those with a grave accent, so that paroxytone right linking nonlexicals can also be reduced to a plateau phrase medially. The idea of the subordination of nonlexical pitch accents is parallelled mutatis mutandis in Japanese: in sequences of an accented lexical word plus an accented particle, such as *róndon-máde* 'as far as London,' the particle is not always completely deaccented but can show varying degrees of accentual reduction (Kubozono 1987).

Anastrophe

Most of the disyllabic proper prepositions and cognate preverbs of Greek descend from adverbs that were paroxytone in Indo-European: *ἀπό, παρά, περί, ὑπό*, Sanskrit *ápa, pára, pári, úpa*; the original accentuation of *ἀνά, κατά* is probably preserved in *ἄνω, κάτω*. Greek retained the older paroxytone accentuation in certain syntactic relic constructions. It is called anastrophe by the grammarians, who analyzed it as the recession of the basically oxytone accent in marked word orders. The following are the more significant structures in which anastrophe occurs.

1. When only the preverb is expressed and the verb itself is deleted

    ἐπεὶ οὔ τοι ἔπι δέος Iliad 1.515 (*ἔπι = ἔπεστι*).

2. When the preverb immediately follows the verb

    ἔχεν κάτα γαῖα μέλαινα Iliad 2.699.

When one or more words intervene between the verb and the following preverb, the grammarians disagree as to the application of anastrophe.

3. When the preposition follows the head of the noun phrase which it governs, that is in the structures [N Prep], [X N Prep] and [N Prep X] where X is a complement or adjunct of N: *πᾶσα πρόθεσις εἴτε μονοσύλλαβος εἴτε δισύλλαβος ὀξύνεται, εἰ μὴ κατὰ ἀναστροφὴν παραληφθῶσι· τότε γὰρ βαρύνονται αἱ δισύλλαβοι οἷον ἄστυ κάτα Ξάνθοιο* Herodian I.479 Lentz. Anastrophe is blocked if the governed word is separated from the preposition even by an elided monosyllabic nonlexical. On *Iliad* 7.163, Herodian observes *τῷ δ' ἐπί: οὐκ ἀναστρεπτέον τὴν πρόθεσιν· μεταξὺ γὰρ πέπτωκεν ὁ δέ*

σύνδεσμος Scholia on the *Iliad* II.257 Erbse. The accentuation of prehead prepositions in the head interrupted structure [X Prep N] was disputed by the grammarians: on

ἐμῷ ὑπὸ δουρὶ *Iliad* 18.92

a scholiast reports τὴν δὲ ὑπό οἱ μὲν συντάσσοντες τῷ δουρί ὀρθοτονοῦσιν, οἱ δὲ τῷ ἐμῷ ἀναστρέφουσιν Scholia on the *Iliad* IV.451 Erbse. The grammarians also vary in their treatment when X is a genitive noun, as

λᾶος ὑπὸ ῥιπῆς *Iliad* 12.462,

where Herodian disputes Tyrannion's anastrophe (Scholia on the *Iliad* III.386 Erbse). Manuscript accentuation of [X Prep N] structures can also vary (Vendryes 1945)

τοῦ γυναικείου περὶ/πέρι νόμου *Republic* 457b.

The musical settings show that anastrophe could occur in structures such as interrogative plus preposition plus noun, as in ME 7.34 where the fall in pitch from ἐ- to -πι in ἔπι indicates anastrophe; this contrasts with ἐπὶ without anastrophe in ME 7.19 above. Another example is ME 7.35, which has the structure adjective₂ plus preposition plus noun₁ plus noun₂ (the indices denote agreement and the preposition governs noun₁).

ME 7.34   τίν' ἔ - πι   τό-π[ον]   *DAM* 40.19

ME 7.35   λευ - κῶν   ὑ - πὸ σύρ - μα - σι   μό - σχων·   *DAM* 4.23

Direction of clisis

The effect of syntactic factors on the rhythmic cohesion of normative accentual enclitics is most readily demonstrated by an analysis of post-caesural instances of the enclitic pronouns μου, μοι, σου, σοι, νιν, τις, του, τῳ in the spoken trimeters of extant tragedies. The effect is clearly illustrated by high frequency syntagms of pronoun plus verb when the clitic follows the caesura

οὐχ ἧσσον εὐδάκρυτά μοι λέγεις τάδε *Choephori* 181
οὖτοι καμοῦμαί σοι λέγουσα τἀγαθά *Eumenides* 881
ἀλλ᾽ εἰ μὲν ἄνδρα σοι δοκεῖ σῶσαι ξένον *Helen* 954.

Contrast the reverse word order with the clitic after the verb and preceding the caesura

Φθίαν, δοκεῖ μοι ξυγγενοῦς μαθεῖν πέρι *Andromache* 887
καὶ δὴ λέγω σοι πᾶν ὅσον κατειδόμην Soph. *Electra* 892
ἄρχειν παρόν μοι, τῷδε δουλεύσω ποτέ; *Phoenissae* 520.

In general, a normatively enclitic pronoun follows the caesura of a spoken tragic trimeter under one of two syntactic conditions. Under the first condition, its governing word or phrase follows the enclitic, so that it coheres syntactically to its right

> τόσον γε μέντοι σοι προσημαίνω, γύναι *Medea* 725
> οὐκ ἔστιν ὅστις σοι προφητεύσει τάδε *Ion* 369
> ἃ δ’ ἦλθον ἤδη σοι θέλω λέξαι, πάτερ *O.C.* 1291.

The first condition also covers noun phrases of the structure adjective plus pronoun plus noun

> θνῄσκω. σὲ δ’ ἄλλη τις γυνὴ κεκτήσεται *Alcestis* 181
> ῥάκη, βαρείας του νοσηλείας πλέα *Philoctetes* 39.

Contrast the reverse serialization with the enclitic before the caesura

> ἥκω φέρων σοι τῶν ἐμῶν βοσκημάτων Eur. *Electra* 494
> κατεύχομαί σοι, καὶ σὺ κλῦθί μου, πάτερ *Choephori* 139.

Under the second condition, the pronoun is followed by a modifier in its pronominal phrase

> θεοὺς ἀτίζων τις βροτῶν δώσει δίκην Aesch. *Supplices* 733
> ἀλλ’ αὐτόχειρί μοι μόνη τε δραστέον Soph. *Electra* 1019.

Contrast the reverse serialization modifier plus pronoun with the enclitic before the caesura

> αἰτουμένῳ μοι δὸς κράτος τῶν σῶν δόμων *Choephori* 480.

In a small number of cases the enclitic pronoun coheres syntactically both to the left and to the right, as when it belongs simultaneously to two structures

> πῶς οὖν κελεύει νιν μολεῖν ἐσταλμένον *Choephori* 766.

In a number of other instances a postcaesural second person pronoun is in focus, often contrastive or otherwise emphatic, and so orthotone rather than enclitic

> οὐκ ἔστι πέρσαι σοὶ τὸ Δαρδάνου πέδον *Philoctetes* 69;
>   Webster ad loc.
> ἐγὼ δ’ ἀδελφὴ σοὶ προσηυδώμην ἀεί Soph. *Electra* 1148
> ἐγὼ προφήτης σοὶ λόγων γενήσομαι *Bacchae* 211.

Failure of rhythmic cohesion to the left in normative accentual enclitics is rare when the syntactic cohesion is to the left

> ἀρκεῖν ἔοικέ σοι παθεῖν, δρᾶσαι δὲ μή *Rhesus* 483
> ἀλλ’ ὧδε δαίμων τις κατέφθειρε στρατόν *Persae* 345,

and seems to be associated with verses having a strong syntactic break suggesting median diaeresis

ὀργὰς ξυνοίσω σοι· γεραιτέρα γὰρ εἶ *Eumenides* 847
ἔλθω κομιστήν σου· τὸ γὰρ πεπρωμένον *Andromache* 1268.

Once cases of emphasis and prima facie median diaeresis have been excluded, the direction of syntactic cohesion of all types of postcaesural enclitics may be statistically tested directly against the direction of syntactic cohesion of prepenthemimeral enclitics. The sample of postcaesural enclitics for this test was based on the list provided by Descroix (1930: 284); the control sample of prepenthemimeral enclitics was taken from the *Choephori*, *Eumenides*, *Philoctetes*, *Andromache* and Euripides' *Electra*. The results are given in Table 7.12. The odds for a postcaesural accentual enclitic pronoun to cohere syntactically to its right, that is in the direction opposite to that of its normative enclisis but in agreement with its metrical location, are over four and a third times as great as the odds for a precaesural enclitic pronoun to cohere to its right. The tendency for postcaesural normative enclitics to cohere to the right is also greater than the tendency for precaesural normative enclitics to cohere to the left, which indicates that rhythmic cohesion to the right requires more syntactic support than rhythmic cohesion to the left, the unmarked condition.

The strong association of postcaesural enclitic pronouns with rightward syntactic cohesion indicates that they were both rhythmically prepositive and accentually proclitic: the latter would entail their becoming part of the rising trajectory towards the peak of the following lexical word. The evidence cannot be explained in purely metrical terms as due to a weakened caesura or, in Aeschylus and Sophocles, a median diaeresis, since there would be no reason for a metrical licence to be invoked only in such strong association with syntactic structure. Therefore, postcaesural enclitics must be rhythmically demarcated to the left. Since rhythmical demarcation to the left is not compatible with accentual enclisis, these pronouns must be either orthotonic or proclitic. There is

TABLE 7.12
Syntactic cohesion of pre-
and postcaesural enclitic pronouns

	Right cohering %	Left cohering %
Postcaesural	73.53	26.47
Precaesural	38.88	61.11

$$\omega = 4.365, \ \chi^2 = 8.506$$

no particular linguistic or metrical reason for orthotonicity; the examples are not restricted to initial position in the clause, and in tragedy neither postcaesural position nor even stichos initial position is by itself a sufficient condition for orthotonicity. Since these postcaesural pronouns can be neither enclitic nor orthotonic, it follows that they are proclitic. This conclusion is supported by some instances in which normatively enclitic words cohere to the right across bridges. This occurs at Porson's bridge

> πάλλεταί μου καρδία Aesch. *Supplices* 785
> τὶς πείσεται *Phoenissae* 885
> σοι βοστρύχων *Troades* 1182,

and with a few split anapaests in comedy (Sobolevski 1964)

> δειπνεῖν με δίδασκε *Frogs* 107
> τῆς ὁδοῦ τι λέγει πέρι *Birds* 23 MSS.
> ᾤμην σε γαλῆν λέγειν Strattis 60.2 Kock.

A syntax driven variation in the direction of rhythmical cohesion is also found with ἄν, which can be postpositive

> τἄμ᾽ ἐκαρποῦτ᾽ ἄν λέχη *Andromache* 935; Porson's bridge

or prepositive

> ἀλλ᾽ οὐχ ὁμοίως ἄν ὁ θεὸς τιμὴν ἔχοι *Bacchae* 192;
> resolution.

In many cases, the phrasing of ἄν is affected by additional factors analyzed later (p. 422): *Ajax* 526 (cp. *Orestes* 360), *Ecclesiazusae* 95, 1087, *Thesmophoriazusae* 8, *Clouds* 1250, *Birds* 1126. Evidence has already been cited (p. 324) suggesting that at least the anapaest examples may involve bidirectional rhythmic cohesion.

Secondary accentuation

It is not the case that all (unfocused) clitics are always atonic in their pronunciation, that is in their surface phonetic representation; even inherently atonic forms can become accented by postlexical rules. In the simplest situation, the accent location rule applies to the clitic group: for instance, in Hixkaryana (Carib: Klavans 1982), stress occurs on the final syllable of the phrase except at the end of the sentence or utterance; since enclitics can and often do appear at the end of phrases, they can be stressed by this rule. Contrast Standard Italian, where the location of the accent is not changed when clitics are added to a word: *cárica* 'load,' *cáricamecelo* 'load it on it for me'; similarly in Auca (Ecuador: Pike 1964) and in Spanish *castígue* 'punish,' *castíguesemelo* 'punish him for it for me' (Harris 1983). Consequently, there is a prosodic difference between simple Italian words in which by and large the location of the accent is limited to one of the three last syllables and the group consisting of word plus enclitics, to which the accent limitation rule does not apply. However, in a number of Southern Italian dialects, longer clitic groups are subject to a reaccentuation rule that shifts the accent to the (heavy) penultimate syllable, so that the accentuation of clitic groups conforms to the common penultimate accent of simple words: Standard Italian *risparmiátevele*, Neapolitan dialect *sparagnatavélle*; from a diachronic perspective, such forms probably reflect shift of primary stress from the verb to the clitic and consequent preservation of the geminate consonant. In modern Greek, lexical stress cannot occur further back than three syllables from the end of the word: when the addition of an enclitic would cause this constraint to be violated, the lexical stress is reduced to a secondary stress and a new postlexical primary stress is placed two syllables to the right of the lexical stress (Newton 1972; Arvaniti 1992).

In Greek, although the word accent is never moved from its lexically determined position in clitic groups, clitics have the property of potentially throwing back an accent onto the last syllable of the host word or of taking on an accent themselves, under various conditions. These secondary accents have the effect of reducing the degree to which clitic groups deviate from the basic accent limitation rule that applies to lexical words. The rules for the accentuation of orthotone word plus single enclitic are summarized in Table 7.13, which uses sample words for the various orthotonic words and clitic word shapes. The following are the most important generalizations that emerge from the table (Allen 1973; Steriade 1988; Sauzet 1989; Golston 1989).

1. The basic accent of the orthotonic word is never changed; the lexically assigned peak is not shifted to a different syllable nor to a different mora of the same syllable: φῶς τινων. The fact that the acute does not become a circumflex in clitic groups satisfying the quantitative requirements of circumflex accentuation is one of the clear differences between the accentuation of words and that of clitic groups: ἀνήρ τις.

2. The accent induced by the enclitic on the orthotonic word can occur only on a light syllable, and there must be at least one mora of pitch fall between the orthotonic accent and the accent induced by the enclitic

δῆμός τις
ἄνθρωπός τις
*ξένός τις
*δαίμών τις.

The exclusion of the type *δαίμών τις despite the fact that the two acutes are separated by the first mora of the long vowel in the final syllable means that a clitic may not induce an intranuclear Low-High tone movement. πόλεώς τινος is not an exception even in synchronic terms, since

TABLE 7.13
Accentuation of orthotone plus single enclitic

Orthotone word	Clitic word shape			
	Š	S̄	ŠŠ/S̄Š	Š-CV̄(C)
Oxytone	ἀγαθός τις	ἀγαθός μου	ἀγαθός τινος ἀγαθός ποτε ἀγαθός ἐστι ἀγαθός φησι	ἀγαθός τινων
Perispomenon	φῶς τι	φῶς μου	φῶς τινος φῶς ποτε φῶς ἐστι φῶς φησι	φῶς τινων
Paroxytone	ξένος τις	ξένος μου	ξένος τινός ξένος ποτέ ξένος ἐστί ξένος φησί	ξένος τινῶν
	Ἕλλην τις	Ἕλλην μου	Ἕλλην τινός Ἕλλην ποτέ Ἕλλην ἐστί Ἕλλην φησί	Ἕλλην τινῶν
Properispomenon in -V̆C	δῆμός τις	δῆμός μου	δῆμός τινος δῆμός ποτε δῆμός ἐστι δῆμός φησι	δῆμός τινων
Properispomenon in -V̆(C)CC	κῆρυξ τις	κῆρυξ μου	κῆρυξ τινός κῆρυξ ποτέ κῆρυξ ἐστί κῆρυξ φησί	κῆρυξ τινῶν
Proparoxytone	ἤκουσέ τις	ἤκουσέ μου	ἤκουσέ τινος ἤκουσέ ποτε ἄνθρωπός ἐστι ἄνθρωπός φησι	ἤκουσέ τινων

the first mora of the final vowel could have had rising rather than falling pitch. It is interesting that in Japanese heavy syllables in which the second mora is a sonorant, but not those in which it is an obstruent, reduce and retract the phrase initial Low tone, thereby avoiding an intranuclear Low High sequence in which each tone is linked to its own mora (p. 211). The grammarians claim that trochee-shaped paroxytones take an enclitic induced accent on their final syllable just like properispomena: κἂν παροξύνοιτο τροχαϊκὴ οὖσα ἀλλός τις, ἐστί τις, ἔνθά ποτε, Λάμπέ *τε, φύλλά τε καὶ φλοιόν, τυφθέντά τε* Herodian I.563.2 Lentz. Such accentuations are found in manuscripts of Homer such as the Venetus

> *πύργόν τε* Iliad 22.462
> *ὄφρά σ'* Iliad 22.282
> *ὅσσά τ'* Iliad 22.115

and the Syrian palimpsest

> *ἐνθάτις* Iliad 16.209
> *ὀφράτις* Iliad 12.317;

they also occur in some manuscripts of classical authors such as the Laurentianus of Sophocles. The accentuation rule for trochee-shaped paroxytones is generally assumed to be a simple overgeneralization by the grammarians from paroxytones with resonant coda consonants, type *πύργόν τε* (Vendryes 1945; Allen 1973), where it was phonetically motivated. However, there is some evidence that onset as well as coda resonants could be perceived as tone bearing for the purposes of song (p. 193), so perhaps the *ὄφρά σ'* type too could have some basis in Greek speech at slow rates, despite the usual constraint against tone-bearing onsets (p. 56). The slower the rate of speech, the less, presumably, the coarticulation of the vowel gesture with the onset consonant(s) and consequently the more likely the latter are to achieve independent moraic status. Although the type *ὅσσά τ'* does not contain a resonant, voiceless fricatives have comparatively great intrinsic duration and the tonal excursion might have been perceptually interpolated through the prolonged period of voicelessness.

3. The induced accent can fall no further back than the final rhythmic mora of the orthotonic host; the postaccentual fall has to be on the first or only mora of the clitic and cannot be on or even through the last mora of the lexical word; consequently, the lexical word can have two accentual High tones postlexically but only one postaccentual fall. The weight of the final syllable of the lexical word is computed according to the same citation form rule as applies for accent recession, even though the enclitic is being joined with the lexical word into a single domain for the purpose of the rule, so that CV̆C is light and CV̆CC is heavy. It follows that properispomena in -ξ and -ψ cannot receive an induced accent, since their final rhythmic mora is not a tone bearing unit

> *δῆμός τις*
> **κῆρύξ τις.*

4. The quantity of the final syllable of an enclitic has no effect on the location of the induced accent

> *ἤκουσέ τις*
> *ἤκουσέ μου*

ἤκουσέ τινος
ἤκουσέ τινων.

The quantity of the initial syllable of an enclitic, whether measured in rhythmic morae or tone bearing units, has no effect on the location of the induced accent; ἐστι and εἰσι, φημι and φησι pattern just like ποτε

ἄνθρωπός ποτε
ἄνθρωπός ἐστι
ἄνθρωπός φησι.

5. A clitic is in principle subordinate in accentuation to an orthotone. It is unnecessary to accent a clitic at all unless its final syllable is separated by two syllables from the orthotonic accent

ξένος τινῶν
φῶς τινων.

Monosyllabic clitics never take an accent, and disyllabic clitics are accented only on their final syllable; this accent is the grave (within the phrase) if the final nucleus contains a short vowel and the circumflex if it contains a long vowel; the latter is the only condition under which an accentual High followed by a postaccentual fall is induced within the clitic word by secondary accentuation

ξένος τινός
ξένος τινῶν.

The quantities of the syllables of the enclitic have no effect on its accentuation

ξένος ἐστί
ξένος φησί
ξένος ποτέ.

The continuous pitch fall over paroxytone and perispomenon plus enclitic is illustrated by the musical settings in ME 7.36–37. Enclitic accentuation induced on a properispomenon is illustrated by ME 7.38, where

ME 7.36   DAM 39.2
τίς εἶ ποτ'

ME 7.37   DAM 39.3
λέ-γεις ποτ [α

ME 7.38   DAM 39.9
]γης δεῦ - ρό μοι.

the peak of the melism assigned to -ρό in δεῦρό is set to the same pitch as that assigned to amelismatic δεῦ-; this pattern contrasts with that found with a properispomenon followed by an orthotonic interrogative, which is illustrated by ME 7.39 where pitch continues to fall over the final syllable of -θε in ἦλθε with a rise on the following interrogative.

ME 7.39 DAM 40.24

Synenclisis

When more than one enclitic follows a word, the grammarians claim that each enclitic except the last bears the acute. Both Herodian I.563 Lentz and Apollonius Dyscolus I.249 Schneider accentuate νυ and σε in

ἤ νύ σέ που δέος ἴσχει Iliad 5.812,

and Herodian adds the example

εἴ πέρ τίς σέ μοί φησί ποτε.

This rule of the grammarians is generally rejected as an artificiality or a purely orthographic device (Vendryes 1945; Barrett 1964:426). Herodian himself does not apply the rule in all cases, and a scholiast on *Odyssey* 1.62 accents

τί νυ οἱ,

claiming οὐκ ἐγείρει τὸν τόνον (Postgate 1924:74; Vendryes 1945:89). The objection that the rule violates the constraint against acutes on consecutive morae is not well founded, as it may merely indicate a level pitch plateau over the string of prefinal enclitics, possibly a Mid tone plateau after a fall from the peak and before a final fall to the valley on the last enclitic. This possibility is supported by the fact that a Mid tone plateau is attested in the rising trajectory for series of grave accented nonlexical words (p. 359). Manuscript practice varies; the Venetus B of the *Iliad* accents alternate enclitics beginning with the second from the end

ἤ νυ σέ που.

There is little musical evidence bearing on the issue, and none from the earlier documents. In Mesomedes' *Hymn to the Sun*, a sequence of two enclitics is set on a plateau (*DAM* 4.24), but since the plateau extends all the way back through a postpositive to the accentual peak of the preceding acute accent, there are little grounds for confidence that this setting faithfully reflects linguistic pitch relations.

A level High or Mid tone that spreads back over a series of clitics may seem surprising in Greek, where, in contrast to Tokyo Japanese, accentual prominence is culminative. But this sort of tone assimilation can occur even in a basically culminative system. In Swedish, it was found that a disyllabic clitic is high toned when it stands between the high tone of a sentence accent and the high tone of an immediately following word accent (Bruce 1977). In many northern Norwegian dialects such as the dialect of Narvik (which have a pitch differentiated stress accent with the high tone dislocated to the poststress syllable in accent 2 words), in compounds with primary accent 2 the dislocated high tone spreads rightward until it reaches the secondary stress (Lorentz 1984).

Accentual composites

The tendency just illustrated for the sequence host plus clitic not to deviate too far from the normal accentual pattern of simple lexical words carries with it the implication that the longer the string of clitic syllables, the greater the likelihood of reaccentuation. A related phenomenon is the tendency for sequences of two or more clitics to combine to form autonomous accentual (and rhythmic: p. 319) words. In English sentences like 'You could have called,' either *you* or *could* is stressed in normal pronunciations. In Serbocroatian, if the conjunctions *ali* and *pa* are followed by enclitics, they are accented; otherwise, they may themselves be proclitic (Inkelas et al. 1988). Furthermore, clitics that occur frequently together in a fixed word order can easily combine into portmanteau forms through the application of segmental morphological rules, for instance the combinations of preposition and definite article in Portuguese or Italian. In Greek, traditionally univerbated composites consisting of proclitic plus enclitic follow the rule for the orthographically separate type; consequently the proclitic bears the acute even in violation of the trochee rule: *εἴτε, καίτοι, οὔτε, οὔτις, ὥσπερ, ὥστε*. Similarly in composites with enclitics, the original accent of orthotone words remains unchanged even in violation of the limitation rule: *ᾧτινι, ὧντινων*. Univerbated composites consisting of two enclitics show more variation: *τοιγάρ – τοίγαρ*. Appositive composites not involving enclitics follow the usual rule that a final acute becomes grave, but no other changes are indicated. In the musical settings, as expected for a sequence of nonlexical graves, they are set on a pitch plateau (ME 7.40) or on a shallow rise up to their lexical host (ME 7.41–42). In initial position in a sentence or clause, a composite

ME 7.40   Καὶ γὰρ δει-λαὶ   *DAM* 36.8

ME 7.41   ὑ - πὸ σὸν τρο- χὸν   *DAM* 5.7

ME 7.42  *DAM* 5.19

consisting of monosyllabic proclitic plus postpositive such as *ὁ δὲ Ath.* 16 (ME 9.6) may have a steep excursion to the grave of the postpositive with only a shallow rise to the peak of the following lexical; this setting of the composite is very comparable to that of the noncomposite *Ἀλλὰ Lim.* 26 (ME 9.8: p. 361, 430).

8 | The Minor Phrase

Constituency

The information carried by a labelled bracketing or tree structure is of two kinds: the labels carry categorial information, which specifies the parts of speech and the different categories of constituents they form, and the bracketing or tree geometry specifies the constituents and indicates whatever degree of hierarchical relationship they may have to one another. Constituents are groups of words that go together to make grammatical and semantic units of some kind, for instance a prepositional phrase or a noun phrase. Constituency is hierarchical in the sense that, for instance, a prepositional phrase may consist of a preposition plus a noun phrase which in turn may consist of an article plus an adjective phrase plus a noun, and the adjective phrase may itself consist of an adverb phrase plus an adjective, and so on. Not just any string of contiguous words forms a constituent; for instance, in a prepositional phrase, preposition plus article does not form a constituent, since the article does not belong with the preposition to the exclusion of the noun. In this work, the term constituent is used in a broad sense that includes combinations forming a semantic unit whose elements are not necessarily syntactically contiguous. In a language with relatively free word order like Greek, syntactic constituents are not infrequently discontinuous, that is interrupted by some other word or phrase.

In addition to not having an explicit principle of hierarchization, the syntactic terminology of traditional grammar tends to lose sight of the distributional commonalities across the categorial nomenclature. This makes it unsuitable for analyzing phrasal prosody, since phrasal prosody is much more sensitive to tree geometry than it is to categorial distinctions. For instance, in Gilyak (Siberia: Kaisse 1985), word initial obstruents become voiced after nasals and become spirants after vowels in the following structures: noun plus noun compounds, adjective plus modified noun, possessive pronoun plus modified noun, direct object

plus governing verb; initial consonants remain unaffected between subject
and object, subject and verb, direct object and indirect object. In a theory
of syntax that recognizes a parallelism in the internal structure of phrases,
it is possible to abstract away from specific categorially defined environments and to restate the sandhi rule with greater simplicity and generality as applying to the head of a phrase when preceded by its modifiers
(used here as a cover term for complements including the object of a
verb, attributes and adjuncts). Such a formulation has the advantage
of not suggesting that it is purely accidental which structures do and
which do not allow sandhi, but rather that the phonology is reflecting
some shared syntactic property. This irrelevance of categorial distinctions is a common, but not exceptionless, feature of such rules. In
Kimatuumbi (Tanzania: Odden 1987; Hayes 1990), there is a vowel
shortening rule that applies to a variety of categorially distinct constituents such as noun phrase, adjectival phrase, prepositional phrase, verb
phrase. However in Isthmus Zapotec (Mexico: Mock 1985), destressing applies to noun plus adjectival modifier but not to noun plus possessive modifier. In general, it is not surprising that phonological phrasing
is more sensitive to constituency than it is to category: phrasing involves
segmenting phonological substance into chunks which largely correspond
to syntactic chunks, so it relates more to the beginnings and ends of structures than it does to their internal composition.

Whereas the appositive group serves to join nonlexical words with
a host word into a single prosodic unit, the minor phonological phrase
serves to unite certain combinations of lexical words and clitic groups
into a single prosodic unit. Minor phonological phrases are not constructed randomly out of any adjacent words, but, as might be expected,
they are made up of syntactically related words, typically the syntactic
head and its modifiers as just defined. Various factors condition this process. The phonology will tend to phrase adjacent items together provided
that neither of them belongs more closely to a third item. This intuition
underlies the well known effect of syntactic branching on phonological
phrasing. In Mende (Sierra Leone: Cowper et al. 1987), according to
one interpretation, initial consonant mutation applies to the second item
in structures such as noun plus adjective, preposition plus noun, possessive plus noun, and also subject plus intransitive verb, provided that
the second node does not branch, as would be the case if the intransitive verb were followed by an adverb or the preposition by a branching
noun phrase rather than by a single noun. In some approaches, many
branching constraints are stated less directly in terms of structural relations obtaining between syntactic constituents (Kaisse 1985) or in terms
of the beginnings or ends of constituents (Selkirk 1986). Another potential
constraint is illustrated by Ewe (Ghana: Clements 1978), where tonal

sandhi applies to two nouns when they are in a possessive phrase but not when they are two separate verbal complements: the two verbal complements do not form an immediate constituent by themselves and cannot be phrased with each other to the exclusion of the ultimate head of the phrase. Similarly, in Hausa there is typically a phonological phrase boundary between the two objects of double object constructions (Inkelas et al. 1990). Even in the absence of branching, too deep a break between constituents is a bar to phonological phrasing. For instance, while Mende permits sandhi across the relatively deep constituent break between subject and predicate, Gilyak and Kimatuumbi, cited in the preceding paragraph, do not. The phrasal boundary Low tone appears at normal speech rates between subject and verb but not between verb and object in Slave (British Columbia: Rice 1989b). Carrier deaccenting applies between object and transitive verb but not between subject and intransitive verb (Story 1989).

Word order

According to one formulation, minor phonological phrases tend to be formed from the head of a syntactic phrase plus material on that side of the head on which complements do not freely occur — under certain conditions, material on the other side of the head may also be included (Nespor et al. 1986; Hayes 1989). Head relative directionality results in a number of instances of asymmetry in the phrasing of prehead and posthead modifiers, which can sometimes be interpreted as evidence for two different degrees of phonological phrase. In colloquial French, liaison applies between preposed adjective plus noun, but not between noun plus postposed adjective. In Vedic, internal sandhi applies in the structure possessive plus noun, external sandhi in the structure noun plus possessive (Hale 1988). In Papago (Arizona: Hale et al. 1987), tonal phrasing reflects the serial order of head and modifier/argument (including the subject of a verb): prehead modifiers are included within the tonal phrase but posthead modifiers are not. In modern Greek, one elision rule applies between words up to the head and a different elision rule applies between the head and material following it in the same syntactic phrase (Condoravdi 1990). Some theories of syntactic phrase structure make a hierarchical distinction between prehead and posthead modifiers (Selkirk 1986).

Complement and adjunct

In Amoy Chinese, an adverb forms a tone group with its following verb and an adjective with its following noun, but a noun does not form a tone group with its following disyllabic postposition nor a direct object with its following verb; here the phonology seems to be reflecting the functional syntactic distinction between adjunct/attribute and complement (Chen 1987; 1990). This distinction can also regulate phrase stress in Danish: *han faldt i vandet* with unstressed verb means 'he fell in the water,' with stressed verb it means 'he fell, (while) in the water' (Rischel 1983); in English, the adjunct is more likely than the complement to be a separate major phonological phrase in such sentences. The phonology is reflecting the fact that in sentences like this the adjunct attributes a separate semantic property, an additional piece of information. Some theories of syntactic phrase structure make a hierarchical distinction between complement and adjunct. A similar distinction between unitary and multiple semantic properties seems to subdivide the class of complements in the Danish rule whereby, in verb phrases consisting of verb plus object not having focus, the verb does not have separate stress unless the noun is articulated: *køb hús* and *køb et hús* both mean 'buy a house,' but the former is closer to 'do the act of housebuying' (interpretation as a single event), the latter to 'do the act of buying on an object that is a house' (autonomy of event and role player); branching of the object phrase is not relevant to the latter condition and an adverbial phrase may stand between the verb and the object (Rischel 1983). A similar semantic distinction is noted in some studies of noun incorporation (Mithun 1984).

Scope

Constraints on phonological phrase formation often involve the scope of a specifier or modifier. Coordination, which obviously entails the introduction of some form of syntactic complexity, results in broad scope and its absence in narrow scope. Under certain conditions French liaison fails when the righthand word is conjoined and the lefthand word has scope over only the first conjunct: "Jean est [très intelligent] et [modeste]" 'John is very intelligent and (he is) modest' has liaison of *très* with *intelligent*, but "Jean est très [intelligent et modeste]" 'John is very intelligent and (very) modest' does not. However, liaison does not fail if the syntactic complexity is introduced to the left of the head rather than to its right, so that the last of a series of prenominal adjectives can have liaison with the following noun (Rotenberg 1978). In Japanese, the scope of a modifier can be a factor determining phrasing: if a modifier has narrow scope it may form an accentual phrase with the following word, but, if it has wide scope, it may not do so to the exclusion of the remainder of the constituent; but the last of a series of adjectives often combines with a following noun into an accentual phrase (Poser 1985). In Italian, the scope of a postnominal adjective can condition the application of raddoppiamento sintattico, which is consequently more likely to apply to *una palla di cauccù giallo* 'a ball of yellow rubber' than to *una palla di cauccù gialla* 'a yellow ball of rubber' (Chierchia in Selkirk 1984). In English, greater final lengthening and pitch fall can occur before a prepositional phrase if it modifies the whole verb phrase rather than just the noun phrase dominated by that verb phrase, as in "Lieutenant Baker instructed the troop with a handicap" ['His instruction was handicapped' versus 'The troop was handicapped'] (Cooper et al. 1980; Cooper et al. 1981). Similar differences result from the scope of negation (Liberman 1979). In Italian, broad scope of a prepositional phrase can block raddoppiamento sintattico, as in "Ho picchiato il re con lo scettro" 'I hit the king with a sceptre' ['I did it with a sceptre' versus 'The king had a sceptre'] (Selkirk 1984).

Movement and trace

Other forms of syntactic complexity can also influence minor (or major) phonological phrase formation. Preposing the object of a transitive verb blocks consonant mutation in Mende (Cowper et al. 1987); preposed sentence initial objects are followed by a phrasal break in Chizigula (Tanzania: Kenstowicz et al. 1990). Preposed topic constituents have phrase final Low tone in Slave (Rice 1989). Cleft constructions in Hausa introduce a phrase boundary (Inkelas et al. 1990). In English, traces from verb and noun gapping can be marked by increased pitch fall and by durational increment, as in "The porter took your bags and Wade your luggage" versus "Roberta took your bags and weighed your luggage" (Cooper et al. 1980; Cooper et al. 1981). A trace left by a deleted verb or noun can also block sandhi. Final dental palatalization is reduced before a trace in English (Cooper et al. 1980). Raddoppiamento sintattico can be blocked at traces in Italian, as in "Mio fratello mangiò le fragole e Fifì tutto il resto" 'My brother ate the strawberries and Fifì [ate] everything else' versus "Mio fratello mangiò le fragole e finì tutto il resto" 'My brother ate the strawberries and finished everything else' (Chierchia in Selkirk 1984).

Word order and phrase structure

Languages can differ quite strikingly in the degree to which word order is fixed. English is an example of a language that has relatively fixed word order in the phrase and relatively fixed phrase order in the sentence. In Makua (Tanzania: Stucky 1982, 1983), word order is fixed within the noun phrase but noun phrases may appear anywhere in the sentence: noun phrase order is syntactically free and may therefore be exploited for discourse functions. In Hungarian, noun phrases have fixed word order; phrase order is fixed in so-called "neutral" sentences but free in other sentences (Horvath 1986; Kenesei 1986). In Polish, phrase order in the sentence is quite free; word order in a noun phrase consisting of a noun plus modified adjunct [XYY] is free except that discontinuous constituents [YXY] are excluded (Gorecka 1988). Finally, certain Australian languages such as Dyirbal (Dixon 1972) and Warlpiri (Hale 1983; Laughren 1989) are reported as having few if any constraints on the order of words in the sentence.

Although not all languages with a rich inflectional morphology have free word order, languages with free word order often have a rich inflectional or affixal morphology: constituency and grammatical function are signalled by rection and concord rather than by word order; in one sample, it was found that, at the least, the person of the subject of the clause is formally indicated by agreement (Steele 1978). Where other factors such as inflection, concord and animacy fail to disambiguate grammatical relations, word order tends to become fixed as in the Latin accusative and infinitive construction in which both subject and object are in the accusative case and the subject regularly precedes the object, or in Dakota where the order of subject and object is not automatically prescribed unless there would be ambiguity, in which case the subject obligatorily precedes the object (Andrews 1985). Conversely in Kanuri (Nigeria: Hutchison 1986), overt case marking of the subject and object phrase is obligatory in clauses that would otherwise be ambiguous but is normally omitted in clauses with canonical word order and a human subject and a nonhuman object. There is apparently an association between a case system marking grammatical relations and subject-object-verb word order (Greenberg 1963; Mallinson et al. 1981). Free word order does not imply random word order: in free word order languages, word order is largely controlled by pragmatic needs including the newness or oldness of the information being conveyed (Firbas 1971; Panhuis 1982; Payne 1992). These pragmatic factors are theoretically distinct from any properly syntactic devices that may be used to implement them, such as focalization and topicalization. Conversely, in English with its fixed word order the prosody plays a larger role in signalling pragmatic factors.

There are various approaches to the description of free word order. According to one approach, free word order languages have little or no hierarchical surface phrase structure, and in particular they lack verb phrases (Chomsky 1981; Hale 1982, 1983; Bouchard 1984; Whitman 1987); this assumption allows surface word order to be represented in two-dimensional tree diagrams without crossing branches. In languages with pronominal affixal or clitic arguments, lexical arguments can be interpreted as coindexed adjuncts (Jelinek 1984, 1989). In a second approach, which posits different levels of phrase structure related by mapping, it is assumed that one word order is basic and that other word orders are derived from it by scrambling rules — with obvious limits on scrambling between coordinate structures or between clauses (Ross 1986) — or by a more limited and constrained set of mainly pragmatically motivated movements. However, some languages apparently do not have any basic word order defined in syntactic rather than purely pragmatic terms (Mithun 1992). A third approach allows hierarchical phrase structure without specific linear serialization (Pullum 1982; Stucky 1982). Classical Greek, while basically a subject-object-verb language, permits considerable variability in word order, particularly in verse. Many constituents are discontinuous, interrupted not only by enclitics, particles, and other nonlexical words, but also by lexical words belonging to other syntactic constituents. The relative freedom of word order in verse is often noted in language descriptions. In Turkish, adjectives precede the noun they modify: in verse, but not in speech or written prose, they can also occur to the right of their noun (Kornfilt 1990). In Finnish, which is a highly inflected language, word order is fairly free in speech, and even more so in verse which is also less constrained in its use of discontinuous constituents (Leino 1986). In modern Georgian, discontinuous noun phrases are mainly restricted to poetic language (Boeder 1989). The intuitive notion of phrasal category remains definable in terms of case marking, agreement, subcategorization and semantics generally. Rules for the location of clitics have been exploited as evidence of phrasal structure in Greek (Taylor 1988, 1990; Garrett 1989; Halpern 1992) as in Ngiyambaa (Australia: Klavans 1982), another language with fairly free word order, where clitics can occur after any first word or any first two or more words providing those words are a constituent. So it is a meaningful question to ask whether and, if so, how prosodic processes in Greek may be affected by the serialization of words relative to their phrasal constituencies. Some of the data presented in this chapter and in Chapter 6 indicate that verbs cohere phonologically more with their objects than with their subjects; if this is evidence for the syntactic verb phrase in Greek, it would follow that Greek had a hierarchical phrase structure; a similar line of reasoning has been used to argue for the verb phrase in Slave (Rice 1989).

The general proposition that the prosody of Greek is sensitive to constituency relations despite the comparatively free word order of Greek — in other words, that Greek prosody does not interpret Greek syntax as a string of configurationally unrelated words — is confirmed by some additional data on the domains of resyllabification and elision, which will be presented in the following sections. It will be shown that these rules of connected speech apply within prosodic domains that reflect syntactic structure.

Interphrasal environment

Data have already been presented in Table 6.3 showing that in Euripides onset to coda resyllabification of initial clusters of the type *s* + stop is permitted between a verb and the following word if the second word belongs to the verb phrase, but avoided if it belongs to the subject noun phrase. A similar distinction between intraphrasal and (syntactically) interphrasal application can be established for onset to coda resyllabification in syntagmata not involving verbs. Included in the intraphrasal class for this test are heads with nonbranching modifiers

> μέλανα στολμὸν *Alcestis* 216,

heads with branching modifiers

> ἔν τ' ὄμμασι σκυθρωπόν *Bacchae* 1252 (Dodds ad loc.)
> τῶν κατθανόντων γ' ἀκροθίνια ξένων *I. T.* 75

and two modifiers not forming a constituent together, but each modifying the same head

> σεμνὰ στεμμάτων μυστήρια Eur. *Supplices* 470.

The interphrasal class includes contiguous phrases neither of which is the head of a larger phrase containing both

> τοῖσι πράγμασι σκότον *Ion* 1522 noun phrase plus
>   noun phrase
> ἱππείοις δ' ἐν δίφροισι ψαμάθων Αὐλίδος ἐπέβασαν *I. T.*
>   214 prepositional phrase plus noun phrase;

it also includes conjuncts

> ἐλάταισι στεφανώδει τε χλόᾳ *I.A.* 1058

and vocatives

> θεοῦ τις, ὦ ξένε, βλάβη *Ion* 520.

In the interphrasal instances of onset to coda resyllabification, it is more common, particularly in the trimeter, for at least one of the two syntactic phrases to be nonbranching as at *Ion* 1522 and *I.A.* 1058 above. The distribution of the two classes in the earlier and later plays of Euripides is presented in Table 8.1. Despite the small number of cases in the earlier plays, the exclusion of resyllabification in the interphrasal class is statistically significant, with only about three chances in a hundred of arising from random variation.

The phonological sensitivity to the distinction between intra- and interphrasal environment is also evidenced by elision. This can be demonstrated by comparing lexical words elided onto the vowel initial prepositions ἐς/εἰς, ἐκ/ἐξ and ἐν with lexical words ending in a phonologically and morphologically elidable vowel before the consonant initial

TABLE 8.1

Increase in interphrasal sequences as a percentage of all cases
of onset to coda resyllabification in Euripides (nonverb categories)

	Inter-phrasal %	Intra-phrasal %	Sample size
Severior, Semiseverus	0.00	100.00	6
Liber, Liberrimus	48.39	51.61	31
	$p = 0.0321$		

prepositions διά, πρός and σύν. (Instances in which the elided word is
a semantically bleached pyrrhic-shaped imperative such as φέρ᾽ *Phoenissae* 276 are excluded, since these function pragmatically as interactional
discourse particles.) The elided and nonelided classes are crossclassified
as intra- or interphrasal sequences. Examples of the intraphrasal type are

λειμῶν᾽ ἐς Ἥρας *Phoenissae* 24 prepositional phrase
ἐφθέγξατ᾽ εἰς ἡμᾶς *Phoenissae* 475 verb phrase
ἀπόντ᾽ ἐκ δωμάτων *Orestes* 573 participial phrase
κρύπτ᾽ ἐν πέπλοισι *Orestes* 1125 adjective phrase
πέσημ᾽ ἐκ δίφρου *Orestes* 1548 noun phrase.

Examples of the interphrasal type are

εἰς ἔμ᾽ ὄμματ᾽ ἔς τ᾽ ἐμῶν παίδων βίον *Phoenissae* 1613
ἐπεὶ δὲ κατθανούμεθ᾽, ἐς κοινοὺς λόγους *Orestes* 1098
τὴν Ἑλλάδος μιάστορ᾽ εἰς Ἅιδου βαλεῖν *Orestes* 1584.

The results for all instances in the *Phoenissae* and the *Orestes* are presented
in Table 8.2. The value of the odds ratio ω means that the odds for interphrasal sequences are over five times greater when elision is not involved
than when it is. The value of χ^2 shows that this difference is very significant statistically. It follows that elidability is conditioned by syntactic
structure and that interphrasal sequences inhibit elision as compared
to intraphrasal structures.

Branching

Phonological sensitivity to syntactic branching in Greek can be demonstrated from data involving onset to coda resyllabification. Instances of
resyllabification from a lexical word back onto a preceding verb within
the same clause can be classified into three structural types. Class 1
contains verb plus nonbranching modifier (complement or adjunct),
many cases involving sister nodes

λείπετε στέγας *Medea* 894
πάραγε πτέρυγας *Ion* 166.

Class 2 contains verb plus branching modifier: in most cases, particularly in the trimeter, the constituent following the verb is a subconstituent of the smallest intermediate constituent to which the verb belongs

σχήσετε στερρὸν δόρυ Eur. *Supplices* 711
σέμν' ἀφαιρεῖτε στέφη Eur. *Supplices* 359.

Class 3 contains verb plus some element of the subject noun phrase

ὤλλυτο πτόλις *Hecuba* 767
εἰσελήλυθε ξένος *Bacchae* 233.

The resyllabified clusters were classified into two classes according to their sonority slope: κτ-, πτ-, ξ- and ψ were assigned to the class with the flatter sonority slope, σκ-, σπ-, βλ-, γλ- and γν- to the class with the steeper sonority slope. The relative frequencies for the two classes of clusters in the three different structures are presented in Figure 8.1. These data show that the steeply sloped clusters have a higher frequency of the syntactically most cohesive structures Class 1 than the clusters with flatter slopes, and, conversely, the more steeply sloped clusters do not resyllabify at all in the least cohesive structure Class 3; whereas the clusters with flatter slopes have a higher rate of Class 3 than of Class 1 structures. The value of $\bar{r}$ indicates that the odds are approximately three to one that onset to coda resyllabification of steeper sonority slope clusters will occur in more cohesive structures than resyllabification of flatter sonority slope clusters. The value of z indicates that the observed differences are statistically significant. The less prone a cluster is to resyllabify, the less likely is it that those instances in which it does resyllabify will involve branching or interphrasal syntactic contexts.

TABLE 8.2

Comparison of the proportions of intraphrasal and interphrasal
sequences of lexical word plus preposition
between elided and nonelided instances

Following preposition	Inter-phrasal %	Intra-phrasal %	Sample size
Vowel initial	17.50	82.50	40
Consonant initial	52.00	48.00	25

$$\omega = 5.1071, \ \chi^2 = 8.5941$$

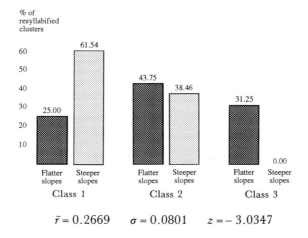

$$\bar{r} = 0.2669 \qquad \sigma = 0.0801 \qquad z = -3.0347$$

FIGURE 8.1

Interaction of sonority slope and syntactic structure for onset
to coda resyllabification between a verb and the next word

Verb plus subject

Up to this point, it has simply been assumed that the sequence verb
plus subject is unlikely to form a phonological phrase, since the divide
between subject and verb phrase is generally assumed to be the deepest
in the sentence. However sandhi processes such as resyllabification do
apply between verb and a following subject, and it is important to establish exactly what are the syntactic conditions under which they can apply.
In the tragic trimeter resyllabification between verb (V) and subject (S)
is practically limited to fourth and fifth longum; in these metrical positions the following constraints apply:

1. The subject of VS does not branch to the right whether within the
verse or onto the next line

2. The verb is either preceded by another element of the subject
phrase, optionally followed by a monosyllabic nonlexical word or an
elided conjunction such as δ', giving the discontinuous structure S_1VS_2
(see Chapter 10)

Θρῇξ νιν ὤλεσε ξένος *Hecuba* 774

or VS is initial in its clause (Cl), optionally preceded by a nonlexical
word (generally a conjunction), giving the structure $_{Cl}[VS]$

οὐδ᾽ ἐφρουρεῖτο στρατὸς *Rhesus* 764
ἡνίκ᾽ ὤλλυτο πτόλις *Hecuba* 767.

This constraint does not apply in the less strict satyric style

ἄλλοι πρὸς ἄντρα σοῦσαφίκοντο ξένοι *Cyclops* 252.

There are also constraints on the resyllabification of verb plus some element other than the subject (X) in the same metrical positions, but these contraints are weaker than those applying to verb plus subject. The counterpart of constraint 2 is considerably weakened: 66.66% of the instances of resyllabification between verb and some element other than the subject involve either discontinuous X_1VX_2 or are clause initial $_{Cl[}VX$. These structures are prima facie proportionally more frequent than when resyllabification does not apply in these positions in the trimeter. In the remaining 33.33% of the cases, the lexical material preceding the verb does not form a constituent with it to the exclusion of X, or if it does then it is an immediately branching phrase. The counterpart of constraint 1 does not apply to VX

σέμν' ἀφαιρεῖτε στέφη μητρός Eur. *Supplices* 359
εἰ μὴ σχήσετε στερρὸν δόρυ Eur. *Supplices* 711.

The higher level of constraint on resyllabification in verb plus subject than in verb plus some element other than the subject is not the result of accidental nonattestation. In the extant tragedies of Aeschylus, Sophocles and Euripides, when resyllabification occurs in fourth or fifth longum, 100% of the VS instances conform to the above constraints, but, as just noted, 33.33% of the VX instances do not. The difference is statistically significant (by the hypergeometric distribution $p = 0.0288$).

These results indicate that if VS is to be encompassed within a prosodic domain cohesive enough for onset to coda resyllabification to apply, the verb must be in sole contact with the subject phrase and not in contact on its left with any lexical element of the verb phrase; furthermore a subject noun undergoing resyllabification must not be followed by any element of the subject phrase. These severe limitations suggest that the formation of a minor phonological phrase over (S)VS is a default process; it does not happen if there are any alternative phrasal combinations for V and S. Specifically, V and S must be (lexical) sister nodes immediately dominated by the clause node if they are to be phrased together. Even then, phrasing is more difficult than within the verb phrase (p. 246). The possibility of subject-verb phrasing is confirmed by the evidence of phrase punctuating inscriptions (p. 391). The differential syntactic affiliation of the subject with the verb in transitive and intransitive clauses is also evidenced in discontinuous noun phrases (p. 485).

Participial phrases

Onset to coda resyllabification of participle plus some lexical word was also analyzed for the same metrical positions in the trimeter. The element following the participle (X) is always a complement of the participle, never its subject and never a member of a higher syntactic phrase. Like verb X, participle X is not subject to the constraints applying to verb plus subject. Since participial phrases are generally short, having only one noun phrase subconstituent which is frequently nonbranching, the commonest condition is for the participle to be phrase initial

κἀξισώσαντε ζυγὰ Soph. *Electra* 738

τοῖς ἐφεστῶσι σφαγῇ *I. T.* 726.

When there is resyllabification between participle and X, the syntactic cohesion immediately to the left of the participle is never greater than that to the right with X.

Phrase punctuating inscriptions

The metrical evidence just analyzed was designed to establish the significance in Greek of syntactic constituency as a factor conditioning the application of rules of connected speech. This metrical evidence remains a rather veiled and imprecise basis for a definition of the phonological minor phrase: it establishes principles and tendencies without necessarily leading to an exhaustive phrasing of any particular stretch of text. Fortunately, there is substantial evidence from inscriptional punctuation for the temporal chunking of speech at a level between the appositive group and the major phrase. The inscriptional evidence corroborates and amplifies the metrical evidence in such a way that each provides substantial independent confirmation of the conclusions based on the other. It is a reasonable assumption that chronological and regional differences in inscriptional evidence for phrasing generally reflect varying orthographic practice rather than real differences in language. In the following analysis, punctuation is again uniformly transcribed by the colon, irrespective of the number and type of interpuncts actually used in the inscription; I is used for the word divider in the Cyprian syllabary.

Whereas one class of inscriptions punctuates exclusively or almost exclusively appositive groups (p. 326), there is another class that punctuates phrases, often with a sufficient degree of consistency to permit a useful analysis. These include I^3.1.45, Hill 1951:B.45 (*Call.*); IX^2.1.718, Meiggs et al. 1980:n.20 (*Naup.*); *LSAG* 42.6, Meiggs et al. 1980:n.17 (*Her.*); *LSAG* p. 481 add. to p. 473, Masson et al. 1988 (*Psamm.*); *LSAG* 66.53, Reinach *REG* 22:311 (*Eph. Art.*); IX^2.1.717, *LSAG* 15.4 (*Oeanth.*); and *DGE* 725, *LSAG* 64.33 (*Milet.*). Although inscriptions in which there is a formalized use of punctuation to demarcate the items in a list are excluded from this corpus of texts, *Milet.* has been included since it is phrase punctuated throughout and shows how list punctuation originates from consistent phrase punctuation—items in a list, even when they comprise only a single word, are separated from each other by phrase boundary and in many languages also intonationally demarcated (p. 413).

Phonological phrasing in any language tends to be quite variable, depending on rate of speech and discourse factors as well as semantic, syntactic and phonological properties (p. 286); in Tokyo Japanese, minor phrases (as defined by initial lowering) may consist of from one to three words and the same sentence can have alternative phrasings, particularly at different rates of speech (Selkirk et al. 1988; Selkirk 1990). There is no reason to think that Greek should be an exception; although much apparent variation in inscriptional punctuation is motivated by constituency or by focus, there are instances that appear to be random

> εχσεναι θοαν I³.1.4b.7
> εχσεναι : θοαν I³.1.4b.12.

This variability naturally inherent in phonological phrasing is compounded by epigraphical and editorial "noise": the evidential value of any inscriptional instance of punctuation rests on the assumption that it is neither an inscriber's error nor a false transcription. There are a remarkable number of cases of the latter category of error, partly because interpuncts can be difficult to recognize on damaged stone surfaces, and partly because the importance of punctuation for an understanding of Greek phrasing has been generally underestimated. Editorial error can involve omission (*LSAG* 3.20, 4.31, 16.4) or addition (*SEG* 30.1283); but the assumption of widespread inscriber's error is methodologically dangerous. There are apparently absurd word internal punctuations of the type

> : οι δικαζον : τες *Eph. Frag.* 5
> Ταλειδες π:οιες *JHS* 52.pl.VII.2

but not even all of these are outright errors. Problems with a nail hole explain the oddity of

> : τα:ς :: Αθαναιας : *Hal.* 1

(Jameson 1974); two other instances seem to involve vacillation between punctuating word end and syllable end in the presence of elision

> καταλειπον:τα εν ται ιστιαι *Naup.* 7; other factors have
> been suggested (Kent 1926); the expected location
> for the punctuation is after ιστιαι
> : μ' α:νεθεκε : *LSAG* 55.3.

More troublesome is the apparent tendency for some inscriptions to vary between minor phrase punctuation and major phrase punctuation. *Oeanth.* B seems to start out with word punctuation, proceed to minor phrase punctuation and end up with major phrase punctuation; the length of the punctuated segments also tends to increase towards the end in

Eph. Art.; other inscriptions just lose interest in punctuation as the text proceeds (*LSAG* 42.8; Jameson et al. 1994). This inscriptional variation between smaller and larger domains interestingly reappeared when a seven year old Norwegian boy, who could not read or write, pretended to write ten sentences as he spoke them aloud; he systematically paused between sections of his speech and left corresponding white spaces between his scribbles. At the outset of the game, the demarcations fell at syllable end or at word end (and as in inscriptions resyllabification was ignored), but towards the end of the game the average length of the section increased and demarcation was omitted at some word ends (Borgström 1954).

Since word punctuation systematically reflects prosodic structure, it is unlikely that phrase punctuation should simply be random, haphazard and linguistically unmotivated. The phrase punctuating inscriptions form a substantial body of text, so that it is possible, with the above qualifications, to reconstruct at least the outline of an algorithm for the formation of the phonological minor phrase in Greek on the basis of the system of punctuation they use. It should be noted that in some inscriptions punctuation may be omitted at the end of a major phrase (*Naup.* 12; *Oeanth.* 3; *LSAG* 71.43–44.19); in others, minor phrases are punctuated by a single row of interpuncts and major phrases by multiple rows, as in *Eph. Art.* and I³.1.4 (p. 429). Apart from this latter device, the all-or-nothing nature of inscriptional punctuation precludes representation of any higher level hierarchical prosodic structure. That the class of phrase punctuating inscriptions is systematically different from the class of word punctuating inscriptions is well illustrated by differences in the punctuation of precompiled phraseology

> : η τεχνηι : η μηχανηι : *T.D.* A.8
> : τεχναι και μαχαναι : *Naup.* 38
>
> : και αυτον : και γενος : *T.D.* B.27
> : αυτον και το γενος : *Naup.* 4.

One interpretation of word punctuation is that it is simply phrase punctuation at a rate of speech at which every appositive group is a separate minor phrase, as it might be in slow dictation.

Phrasing algorithm

The first step in the phrasing algorithm is to form phrases out of phonologically binarily branching constituents, that is out of contiguous appositive groups that make a syntactic constituent. There is no reason to suspect that this premium on binary structures is a mechanical and artificial epigraphical feature; some analyses of Japanese phrasing (Selkirk

1990) have suggested just such a preference for binary structures, particularly in slower speech

: ταλαντον κ' αργυρο : *Her.* 5
: τυρον αγνον : *Milet.* 4
: διφασια μελιχματα : *Milet.* 2
: ες βασιλεως διδοται : *Milet.* 3
: εκ πολεως ηνειχτθησαν : *Eph. Art.* 2
: εν τριαϞοντ' αμαραις : *Naup.* 42
: το 'ν Ναυπακτον Ϝοικεοντος : *Naup.* 29
: τον ξενον με hαγεν : *Oeanth.* 1
: αι ψευδεα προξενεοι : *Oeanth.* 8.

A minor phrase can be formed whether the modifier precedes the head or follows it

: ε Ναυπακτο ανχορεοντα : *Naup.* 19 [PP V]
: καρυξαι εν ταγοραι : *Naup.* 20 [V PP],

but there may be a preference for phrasing prehead modifiers with the head when both a prehead and a posthead modifier are present: in

: αι κα hυπ' ανανκας απελαονται : ε Ναυπακτο : *Naup.* 8

the prehead adjunct is phrased with the head and the posthead complement is orphaned. Proper names having the structure head plus modifier tend to constitute fixed phrases in phrase punctuating inscriptions

: τοι Δι Ολυνπιοι : *Her.* 6
: τοι Ζι τολυνπιοι *IGA* 111.4
Αθεναιηι Πατροιηι : *EG* IV. Fig. 5
: Απολλωνος Δελφινιο *Milet.* 12
Απολλωνι Δελφινιωι : *LSAG* 65.50;

sometimes also in word punctuating inscriptions

: Ηερμει Εναγονιοι : *Eleus.* 3.

Unarticulated forms probably have a stronger tendency to lack internal punctuation. In Serbocroatian, second position clitics may not be placed between the two elements of a proper name: *taj je pesnik* 'that-AUX poet,' *Lav Tolstoj je* 'Leo Tolstoi-AUX' (Halpern 1992).

A nonbranching subject or the head of a discontinuous branching subject phrase may be phrased with a verb, at least when the verb is intransitive or when, for whatever reason, the verb's complement is not phrased with the verb

: δραπετες με εσιει : *Call.* 4
: hα δε βολα ποτελατο : *Hal.* 6
: και χρεματα παματοφαγεισται : *Naup.* 40, 44
: εορτη κηρυσσεται : *Milet.* 12.

In the Hekatompedon inscription (I³.1.4), which uses a notably restrained version of phrase punctuation, when the subject of an imperatival infinitive is postverbal backgrounded information and the object is a preverbal topic, the subject is phrased separately

: γρα[φσα]σθαι : τος ταμιας I³.1.4.B3
: ανοιγεν : [τος] ταμιας : I³.1.4.B18.

These data support the conclusion based on the metrical evidence already presented (p. 386) that the verb is phrased with the subject only by default, at least in the absence of interfering factors. In one case where a subject seems to be phrased with the indirect object in a dedication, the inscriber left space for the missing punctuation (*DAA* 220). Quite similarly, in Korean sentences with fronted objects, the rule of obstruent voicing indicates that the subject can be phrased with the verb but not if the verb is modified by an adverb (Cho 1990). A prototypical situation in which the object of a transitive verb and the subject of an (active or stative) intransitive verb are classed together as opposed to the subject of a transitive verb represents an ergative organization. Ergativity is a widespread principle of grammatical organization. In some languages, like Wichita (Rood 1971; Dahlstrom 1983) and Chuckchee (Polinsky 1990), it applies in an area of morphosyntax that is in some ways analogous to phonological phrasing, namely noun incorporation (Mithun 1984; Rosen 1989; Baker 1988, 1994). Objects of transitive verbs and subjects of intransitive verbs (preferentially but not exclusively limited to unaccusatives) may be incorporated within the verbal complex, but not subjects of transitive verbs. The same restriction tends to apply to the formation of discontinuous noun phrases in Greek (p. 485). When the intransitive verb exhausts the verb phrase, the verb is a sister node to the subject and consequently there is no obstacle in the tree geometry to prevent its being phrased with the subject.

In Cyprian, apart from a few instances with phonologically heavy nonlexicals

| Ϝρετας τασδε | *Id.* 29
| α(ν)τι το μισθον | *Id.* 5

and a few fixed phrases with proper names

| τα(ν) πτολιν Εδαλιον | *Id.* 1
| τον Ονασικυπρον τον ιγατεραν | *Id.* 2
| ο Παφο βασιλευς | *ICS* 6, cp. 15, contrast 7,

most of the clear cases of the divider sign punctuating phrases involve a verb phrased with its subject or complement

| κατεϜοργον Μαδοι | *Id.* 1
| ανογον Ονασιλον | *Id.* 2

| πεισει Ονασιλοι | *Id.* 12, 25
| ο Αρμανευς εχε | *Id.* 21
| ανοσιγα Ϝοι γενοιτυ *Id.* 29
| οικο(ν) ναον *ICS* 306.4.

The preponderance of verbs in Cyprian punctuated phrases may indicate that in this dialect particularly verbs lacked prosodic salience (p. 352). The nonverbal element in the phrase tends to be free of appositives. The high incidence of proper names could be a pragmatic phenomenon or it could be a reflex of the constraint on appositives. In the latter case, it follows that for the easiest and most restrictive type of phrasing, the simple lexical word phrases more readily than the group consisting of lexical word plus appositive(s).

However, in general it is clear that the minor phrase is based on a phonologically branching structure, not on a syntactically branching structure (unless formulated in terms of lexical categories excluding prepositions). The phrasing algorithm is largely blind to appositives. Simple two word constituents can become a phonological phrase

: προσταταν καταστασαι : *Naup.* 34
: διομοσαι ηορϙον : *Naup.* 45,

but so can syntactically much more complex structures, such as a branching prepositional phrase with articulated noun and articulated modifier plus any additional appositive material such as a conjunction

: εκ τες φυλες τες πρυτανευοσες *Call.* 16
: αι τις ηυπο τον νομιον τον επιϜοιϙον : *Naup.* 27.

The importance of syntactic constituency in the phrasing algorithm is illustrated by cases in which a nonbranching constituent is flanked by two branching constituents, for example NP V NP

: ταλαντον κ' αργυρο : αποτινοιαν : τοι Δι Ολυνπιοι :
Her. 5
: τοις αυτον νομιοις : χρεσται : κατα πολιν Ϝεκαστους :
Naup. 28.

If in these instances the phrasing had been completely random, constituency relations would not have been reflected by punctuation at a greater than chance rate. If the phrasing had simply paired appositive groups from left to right, the verb would have been phrased with the first following appositive group of the right hand noun phrase; if the phrasing had simply paired appositive groups from right to left, the verb would have been paired with the second element of the left hand noun phrase, again violating constituency. The verbs are left unpaired because the algorithm, on its first pass, paired appositive groups according to constituency (αυτον is not appositive). Other instances of phonologically nonbranching constituents phrased separately from flanking branching constituents are the second prepositional phrase in

: αι κα hυπ' ανανκας απελαονται : ε Ναυπακτο : Λοqροι
τοι Ηυποκναμιδιοι : *Naup.* 8

and the phrasing of the modifiers in

: οις λευκη : εγκυαρ : λευκωι αναβεβαμενη : *Milet.* 6

where εγκυαρ modifies the noun phrase οις λευκη to form a constituent that is itself modified by the following participial phrase. Contrast

: δυο γυλλοι εστεθμενοι : *Milet.* 2

with prepositive δυο and nonbranching participial phrase.

It should be noted that some of the usual approaches to phrasing are too directional in character to handle the Greek data. An approach in which phrases are built from the head and material on the nonrecursive side of the head privileges the nonrecursive side to a degree that appears unwarranted in Greek. An approach that phrases right-branching structures with a lefthand node, or vice versa, but allows a new phrase to start only at the end, or respectively at the beginning, of a constituent, cannot account for data which allows inclusion of nonbranching nodes from both the left and the right; for instance, a verb can be joined to a prepositional phrase from either the left or the right.

The limitation of first pass phrasing to two appositive groups per phrase means that (phonologically) branching constituents can be phrased differently from their nonbranching counterparts

: θυειν και λανχανειν : *Naup.* 3
: οσια λανχανειν : και θυειν : *Naup.* 2

: το τες Νεμεσεος αργυριο : I³.1.248.3
: το δε αλλο αργυριο : το τες Νεμεσεος : I³.1.248.9

: Λοqρον τον Ηυποκναμιδιον : *Naup.* 26, 34
: επιϜοικους Λοqρον : τον Ηυποκναμιδιον : *Naup.* 5

ε Ναυπακτο ανχορεοντα : *Naup.* 19
: εν Ναυπακτοι : καρυξαι εν τἀγοραι : *Naup.* 20
: αι τις hυπο τον νομιον τον επιϜοικον : ανχορεει *Naup.* 27.

Since the first pass pairs only contiguous items forming a constituent, some sequences of appositive groups will remain unpaired after the initial pass. These may optionally be paired in a second pass through the unpaired material. This phonological pairing in the absence of syntactic motivation is also found in the phrasing of unaccented words in Japanese, where optionally indirect object and direct object may be paired without the intervening initial lowering that demarcates the left edge of the minor phrase (Selkirk 1990)

τον hορϙον εξειμεν : *Naup.* 12
: τον Λοϙρον τὀπιϜοιϙοι : *Naup.* 34
: αι κα με γενος εν ται ιστιαι : *Naup.* 16
: Ϝεκαστον νομος εστι : *Naup.* 30.

But there is apparently some resistance to joining either a direct object or an indirect object to its verb to the exclusion of the other complement

: τὀνκαλειμενοι : ταν δικαν : δομεν τον αρχον : *Naup.* 41
: αι κα με διδοι : τοι ενκαλειμενοι : ταν δικαν : *Naup.* 43.

The next step is to phrase single appositive groups that have been orphaned by the preceding steps. This may be accomplished by allowing the orphans to stand as autonomous phrases

: ταλαντον κ' αργυρο : αποτινοιαν : *Her.* 5
: τοι Δι Ολυνπιοι : τοι καδαλεμενοι : *Her.* 6
: εν υδριαν : ταν ψαφιξιν ειμεν : *Naup.* 45
τεκναι και μαχαναι : μεδεμιαι : Ϝεϙοντας *Naup.* 12
: τονκαλειμενοι : ταν δικαν : *Naup.* 41, cp. 43
: εν Ναυπακτοι : καρυξαι εν τὰγοραι : *Naup.* 20
: με φαρειν : εν Λοϙροις τοις Ηυποκναμιδιοις : *Naup.* 5.

Alternatively, the orphan appositive group may be adjoined to a preceding or following phonological phrase according to its syntactic constituency relations: this solution may have been favoured when one of the three appositive groups was phonologically light or lacked appositives. In the phrasing of Japanese accented words into major phrases, a ternary branching subject phrase may optionally be treated as a single catathesis domain; and in the phrasing of Japanese unaccented words into minor phrases, an object noun following a branching subject phrase is optionally joined to the latter without initial lowering (Selkirk 1990)

: επαγεν μετα τριακοντα Ϝετεα : *Naup.* 13
: ενορϙον τοις επιϜοικοις εν Ναυπακτον : *Naup.* 11
: hοπος αριστα και ευτελεστατα σκευασαι : *Call.* 8
: ειν τωι πρωτωι χρυσωι ηνειχτθησαν : *Eph. Art.* 3
τα ξενικα ε θαλασας hαγεν : *Oeanth.* 3
: ερδεται τὠτερων ετως τελη : *EG* IV. Fig. 5.

In an early fourth-century Boeotian inventory with list punctuation (*SEG* 24.361), simplex numerals are adjoined to a preceding branching phrase

: λανπτερωχοι σιδαριοι τρις : 20
: χαλκια πλατεα πεντε 7

but in one case a complex numeral is phrased separately

: Ϝοινοχοια χαλκια : πεντεκαιδεκα : 13.

Scope affects phrasing, since scope affects constituency and constituency affects phrasing

> : οσια λανχανειν : και θυειν : *Naup.* 2;

if the punctuation were after οσια rather than after λανχανειν, the phonology would have indicated that οσια was the complement of both verbs. When a phonologically heavy preposition has scope over two conjuncts, there may be some preference for not linking the first conjunct with the preposition to the exclusion of the second conjunct

> : εχθος προξενο και Ϝιδιο ξενο : *Oeanth.* 11 (και begins
> a new inscriptional line)
> : ανευς : βολαν : και ζαμον πλαθυοντα *IGA* 111.8.

Although articulated modifiers can follow the basic rules of phrase formation as in various examples already cited, in certain contexts they can also show some degree of prosodic autonomy. A probably branching articulated modifier is phrased separately from its noun in an example involving a head interrupted verb phrase

> εν τέπιαροι κ᾽ ενεχοιτο : τοι ᾽νταυτ᾽ εγραμενοι *Her.* 10;
> the punctuation is partly worn but clearly visible
> (A. Johnston pers.comm.).

There are a couple of cases where an articulated modifier is located between two elements of a noun phrase; the articulated modifier is not phrased with either element of the noun phrase to the exclusion of the other

> : Χαλειεοις : τοις συν Αντιφαται : Ϝοικεταις *Naup.* 47
> και Ναυπακτιον : τον επιϜοιϟον : πλεθαι : *Naup.* 40.

The separate phrasing of articulated modifiers can result in a prima facie violation of constituency

> : επιϜοικους Λοϟρον : τον Ηυποκναμιδιον : *Naup.* 5
> : διομοσαι ηορϟον : τον νομιον : *Naup.* 45.

The most likely explanation for the separate phrasing of articulated modifiers is that they reflect a degree of focus, since they specify a subset of the preceding noun phrase, the latter being more generic and topic-like: this results in prosodic autonomy. This approach is supported by the parallel phrasing of noun phrases with resumptive deictics

> : αι δε τιρ τα γραφεα : ται καδαλεοιτο : *Her.* 7
> | τον α(ν)δριγα(ν)ταν | το(ν)δε κατεστασε | *ICS* 220
> τον α(ν)δρια(ν)ταν [space] τον(ν)υ | εδωκεν [end line]
> κας | ονεθεκεν [space] *ICS* 215; phrase end
> is denoted by space, word end by the divider.

There remain some cases in which constituency is disregarded in favour of phonologically balanced phrasing

: αργυραι πεντε : και ειϟοσ⟨ι⟩ μνεαι : *Eph. Art.* 2;
: χρεματα τοις Ηυποκναμιδιοις : νομιοις χρεσται : *Naup.* 25

or when a numeral is phrased with a preposition and separated from its noun

: εντος ηεχσεκοντα : εμερον : *Call.* 12
μεχρι τριον : οβελον : I³.1.4.B12.

This restructuring is another indication that inscriptional punctuation is an orthographic representation of phonological and not syntactic structure.

Conjuncts and disjuncts are regularly phrased together

: αιτε Ϝεπος αιτε Ϝαργον : *Her.* 3
: τα τ' αλ⟨α⟩ και παρ πολεμο : *Her.* 4
: κὲ δαμο κὲ ϟοιναϝον : *Naup.* 4
: τεχναι και μαχαναι : *Naup.* 38, cp. 12.

Second position clitic placement rules in some languages provide clear evidence for the constituency of conjuncts: for instance, in Pitjantjatjara (Australia: Bowe 1990), second position clitics, which appear after the first constituent, are located at the end of sentence initial conjuncts whether they are paratactic or linked by a conjunction; similar evidence is found in Pashto (Pakistan: Kaisse 1981), Serbocroatian and Luiseño (Halpern 1992). Pairing of conjuncts and disjuncts proceeds left to right, so that a third item is phrased separately, if

: αιτε Ϝετας αιτε τελεστα : αιτε δαμος : *Her.* 8

is interpreted as a ternary structure; but it is also possible that the first two disjuncts are a binary structure which is a sister to the third. A recurrent feature of the phrasing of conjuncts and disjuncts is disregard for constituency

: τρετο και δαμευεσσθο : ενς Αθεναιαν : *Hal.* 5
: ε τας Χαλειδος : τον Οιανθεα μεδε τον Χαλειεα : ε τας
Οιανθιδος : *Oeanth.* 2
: Ηοποντιον : τε χιλιον : πλεθαι και ΝαϜπακτιον :
τον επιϜοιϟον : πλεθαι : *Naup.* 39.

It is not clear whether this violation of constituency is due to restructuring or simply to the mechanical application on the part of inscribers of a rule requiring conjuncts to be phrased together.

Sandhi evidence

The orthographic representation of the assimilation of final -ρ and -ς to initial δ- between lexical words in the Cretan Gortyn Code (Baunack et al. 1885; Brause 1909) provides independent support for some aspects of the above analysis of Greek phrase formation. The domain of this assimilation, which is probably the same for both consonants, extends to the minor phrase. Assimilation is orthographically represented between subject and nonbranching verb phrase

> ο πατεδ δοει VI.2, (IX.41)
> ο ανεδ δοι III.20, III.29
> πατροδ δοντος V.2, but πατρος δοντος VIII.20,

but not between subject and branching verb phrase

> ο δε δικαστας δικαδδετο πορτι τα αποπονιομενα IX.30
> ο δ' αμπαναμενος δοτο ται εταιρειαι X.37,

nor in a variety of other, mostly but not exclusively, nonphrasal environments (II.27, III.14, IV.49, V.38, VIII.45, X.22). Other factors, such as phonological substance and text frequency, may also have a role.

In Attic inscriptions, assimilation of a final nasal to a following initial consonant is particularly common at the end of the fifth century and in the first half of the fourth century (Threatte 1980). Such assimilation occurs most often in appositive groups, but it is also comparatively well established for the domain of the minor phrase by a number of examples of assimilation in lexical words before καί, in branching noun and verb phrases, verb plus subject and other minor phrase structures

> ακοντομ Μεθοναιον I².57.23
> ηιερογ χρεματον I².251; cp. I².304.2
> διαλυεμ προς αλλελος I².116.21
> ανεθηκεγ Καλλιον II².1400.42
> πατροθεγ και II².1237.119; but πατροθεν και ibid. 120.

Verse structure

The inscriptional evidence for minor phrase formation collected above confirms the natural intuition that, while the verse stichos represents the prototypical major phrase, the hemistich is the prototypical minor phrase. Similar observations can be made about verse in other languages too. In English nursery rhymes like "Doctor Foster went to Gloucester" or "Humpty Dumpty sat on a wall," there is a major phrase which consists of two minor phrases, and each minor phrase consists of two linguistic feet; the feet are either lexical words or refooted clitic groups. The hemistich in the metre of Dante's *Commedia*, which consists of two or three feet, has been analyzed as prototypically a phonological phrase (Nespor et al. 1986). One way of measuring the phonological weight of a metrical unit in Greek is purely by the number of appositive groups it contains, irrespective of their constituency relations. Although the hemistich of the trimeter may consist of one appositive group (or extended appositive group)

καὶ πολυφραδεστάτας Semonides 7.93

κακοφραδής τε Solon 36.21

or of three appositive groups

πῖαρ ἐξεῖλεν γάλα Solon 37.8 (head interrupted),

the hemistich containing two appositive groups is, particularly in the iambographers, easily the most common type

δαιμόνων Ὀλυμπίων Solon 36.4

τῷ κακῷ τε κἀγαθῷ Solon 36.18

ἥδ᾽ ἐχηρώθη πόλις Solon 36.25.

The hemistich with three appositive groups is more frequent in tragedy than in the iambographers, at least in part due to the relaxation of the constraints of Knox's bridges in the second hemistich

ἀλκίμου μάχης φίλοις Heracleidae 683

κἀμπύρων μισθοὺς φέρειν Bacchae 257.

If the three appositive groups form a constituent, they can be interpreted as a minor phrase with adjoined element. Table 8.3 gives the relative frequencies of the number of appositive groups in the first hemistich of the iambic trimeter of Semonides and Solon as compared with Euripides *Electra*. Since a hephthemimeral caesura increases the hemistich by a trochee, it increases the chances for an additional appositive group as compared with the penthemimeral caesura. To control for this effect, the data are reported separately for trimeters according to caesural type; medial elision and certain ambiguous verses have been excluded. No trimeters were observed with unambiguous penthemimeral caesura that contained three appositive groups in the first hemistich; similarly, no trimeters were observed with unambiguous hephthemimeral caesura that contained a single appositive group in the first hemistich. The great preference for two appositive groups in both caesural types and in both the archaic and late classical styles is apparent. In the later style, the

TABLE 8.3

Number of appositive groups in the first hemistich of the trimeter

	Penthemimeral			Hephthemimeral		
Appositive groups in first hemistich	1 %	2 %	3 %	1 %	2 %	3 %
Semonides, Solon	10	90	0	0	83	17
Euripides *Electra*	2	98	0	0	76	24

three appositive group hemistich does become more frequent if there is a hephthemimeral caesura. In both the archaic and late classical samples, the ratio of penthemimeral to hephthemimeral caesura was 2:1, reflecting in part the preference for the length of two appositive groups.

In some Homeric hexameters, the longer hemistich has three appositive groups and the shorter hemistich has two

> ἀγχίμολον δὲ σύες τε καὶ ἀνέρες ἦλθον ὑφορβοί *Odyssey* 14.410
> κλαγγὴ δ᾽ ἄσπετος ὦρτο συῶν αὐλιζομενάων *Odyssey* 14.412,

while in others, for instance, both hemistichs have two appositive groups

> ὤπτησάν τε περιφραδέως ἐρύσαντό τε πάντα *Odyssey* 14.431.

These tendencies support the intuition that the hemistich is prototypically a minor phrase, but it is obviously mistaken to assume that every hemistich must be a minor phrase, just as it is not the case that every stichos is a major phrase. Monotonous versification is avoided by introducing some degree of mismatch between prosodic domain and corresponding metrical domain. Consequently, a hemistich may contain more than one minor phrase

> πρᾶξιν, κακοῖσιν *Trachiniae* 152,

or a minor phrase may straddle the boundary between hemistichs

> ἀσήμων ὀργίων *Antigone* 1013.

In metrical inscriptions, punctuation is based on a variety of principles (all references are to *CEG*). In some inscriptions, punctuation marks the end of the stichos (13; 68; 69), but in others it is linguistically based, as demonstrated by

> : Οινανθες : θεκεν μνεμα : καταφθιμενες : 54

where punctuation marks the phrasing but not the diaeresis. Some metrical inscriptions punctuate words and appositive groups

> : μοιραν : εχων 170, cp. 243, 287;

in others, the punctuated element may be not only a word or appositive group but also an extended appositive group or an easily formed minor phrase

> : αυτικα κενον 454
> hος δ᾽ αν τοδε πιεσι : 454
> : hον ποτ᾽ ενι προμαχοις : 27
> hιμερος hαιρεσει : 454
> | Ϝεπο(μ) μεγα | *ICS* 264.

Orphans tend not to be adjoined but remain autonomous phrases

> : σεμα Θρασονος : ιδον 28
> : φρασιν : αλα μενοινον : 28
> : θετο δ᾽ αυτον : αδελφε : 37.

The punctuation of these metrical inscriptions apparently accesses a slower rate of speech in which single words are less readily joined into minor phrases. There are also instances in which the more fluent phrasing evidenced by many of the punctuated prose inscriptions is the basis for punctuation, with the result that interpuncts demarcate the hemistich

τοδ' Αρχιο 'στι σεμα : κἀδελφες φιλες : 26
σεμα τοδ' ενγυς hοδο : 39
: φιλα Ϝεργασατο ματερ 138; discontinuous.

One reason why hemistich punctuation is not more common is that the first word of the line tends to be set off by punctuation, probably because it is focused and so constitutes an autonomous phrase (p. 478). This is common with metrically perfect or metrically imperfect proper names

: Οινανθες : 54
Χαιρεδεμο : τοδε σεμα : 14
Αντιλοχο : 34
Δαμοτιμοι : τοδε σαμα : 138;

initial punctuation is also found with other words

στεθι : και οικτιρον : 27
: στελεν : δ' επ' αυτοι : θεκε Φαιδιμοσοφος 26.

Line initial focus has the effect of dividing the first hemistich into two minor phrases, which does not preclude a hierarchically higher phrase boundary (intermediate phrase boundary) at the caesura. Conversely, proper names can be punctuated also line medially

θορος : Αρες 27
: Φαιδιμος : εργασατο 18.

The punctuation of proper names is a feature that survives in a stylized form into later unpunctuated inscriptions. While focus prevents words being phrased together, elision probably encourages it

ανθροπε hος (σ)τειχεις : 28
: παιδα ολοφυρομενος [:] 14.

Phrase final lengthening

Evidence has already been cited (p. 274) that a minor phrase boundary may be foot internal, and that there is no necessary theoretical conflict between lengthening at the end of the minor phrase and foot structure assignment in the domain of the major phrase. Not only are longer items preferentially located at the end of domains (*tit for tat*, etc.: p. 50), but phrase final lengthening tends to be proportionately greater on intrinsically or contextually long segments than on short ones: lengthening before voiced consonants in English is greatly exaggerated in prepausal position; compare "...on his back." with "...on his bag." (Klatt 1976). It follows that any trend to prefer intrinsically longer syllable structures in metrical positions corresponding to the end of the minor phrase can be taken as evidence of phrase final lengthening. By the second half of the third century B.C. a long-term diachronic trend is discernible for increasingly strict regulation of the syllable structure preceding the caesura and diaeresis. The fact that this trend is hard to identify in earlier texts is a reflection of the generally more stringent rules of Hellenistic and later versification and probably has no diachronic linguistic implications. It is first encountered as an increasing preference for $C\bar{V}(C)$- over $C\breve{V}C$-syllables (as defined after resyllabification) before the diaeresis of the pentameter. In Theocritus, Callimachus, Asclepiades, Posidippus, Hermesianax, Anyte and Leonidas (all from the first half of the third century B.C.), the average rate of $C\breve{V}(C)$ in that position is 14.4%, but this drops to 8.6% in Dioscorides (second half of the third century B.C.), 6.9% in Antipater of Sidon (late second century B.C.), 2.1% in Antipater of Thessalonica (first century A.D.) and 0% in Philip of Thessalonica (first century A.D.) (West 1982). Before the masculine caesura of the hexameter there is a similar trend to prefer $C\bar{V}(C)$-syllables; both chronologically and in strength it lags somewhat behind the trend at the diaeresis of the pentameter, which is to be expected given that the diaeresis tends to be a stronger metrical boundary than the caesura. In genuine Theognis the rate of $C\breve{V}C$ before the masculine caesura is 23.68%. The average rate in Hellenistic epigrams down through Meleager (probably late second to early first century B.C.) decreases to 17.72%, with 24.17% in Meleager himself (Gow et al. 1968); Asclepiades has 19.64%, Dioscorides only 9.52% and Antipater of Sidon 17.95%. In the epigrams of the *Garland* (covering material from c. 100 B.C. to 40 A.D.) of Philip of Thessalonica (first century A.D.), the average rate drops to 11.77% with 2.59% in Philip himself (Gow et al. 1968); Antiphilus has 14.78%, Antipater of Thessalonica 12.00%, Argentarius 11.63% and Philodemus 8.1%. Dioscorides and Philip have a stronger preference for superheavy syllables (42.86% and 44.83% respectively) than Asclepiades and Antiphilus (28.57%). Later, significant preference for $C\bar{V}(C)$ is also found before the masculine caesura in paroxytonetic dactylic hexameters such as *GDK* 7, Pseudo-Lucian *Tragodopodagra* 312–24, and the end-accented miuric hexameters of *GDK* 9.16–20 (third century A.D.). Later still, the hexameters of Nonnus strongly avoid $C\breve{V}C$-syllables before a masculine caesura (Tiedke 1873; Keydell 1959).

ACCENT

Now that the syntactic constituency of the Greek minor phrase as a domain of temporal demarcation has been analyzed in detail, it remains to establish what, if any, accentual properties were specific to the minor phrase. It is theoretically possible either that downtrends proceeded regularly throughout the major phrase without regard for intervening minor phrase boundaries; alternatively, it is possible that minor phrase structure was signalled by some specific tonal adjustment. This latter situation has been discerned in Japanese, where, for instance, in right branching phrases consisting of accented words of the type [big] [farm owner] the initial rise in pitch to the second peak is greater than in left branching phrases of the type [big farm] [owner]; this phrase initial pitch boost reflects prosodic structure rather than syntactic structure directly, since it applies also to domains that are rhythmically rather than syntactically motivated; the effect of the boost is not limited to the phrase initial accent but causes a general raising of pitch values throughout the phrase (Kubozono 1987, 1989, 1992; Selkirk et al. 1988, 1991; Selkirk 1990). A similar intermediate resetting of downtrends within the major phrase was found in Chonnam Korean (Jun 1990). Phrase initial boost is used as a descriptive term: it can be interpreted phonologically either as a boost computed from the last peak of the preceding phrase or as a phrasal downstep computed from the first peak of the preceding phrase (van den Berg et al. 1992); either computation could produce a hierarchization between major phrase "reset" and minor phrase "boost," reflecting the underlying syntactic hierarchy.

By analyzing the relative magnitudes of the peak to peak intervals in the musical settings of the Delphic hymns, it is possible to show that within catathesis domains, which basically coincide with major phonological phrases (p. 441), the progressive lowering of the pitch of accentual peaks is regulated by the articulation of the major phrase into constituent minor phonological phrases. In order to avoid any potential indeterminacy associated with the application of the phrasing algorithm established above, the analysis will be presented in the first instance purely in syntactic terms.

The analysis is based on sequences of three lexical words (excluding proper names) within a catathesis domain, each of which has an acute or circumflex accent and which are not separated from each other by grave or nonlexical accents. Such a string of lexical words is denoted by $L_1L_2L_3$, and the pitches of the accentual peaks of L_1, L_2 and L_3 are denoted by P_1, P_2 and P_3 respectively. Excluding for the moment head interrupted constituents and structures in which two modifiers precede or follow the head, it is the case that if L_2 and L_3 belong to a syntactic constituent to which L_1 does not belong, denoted L_1 [L_2L_3, then P_2 is not lower relative to P_1 than P_3 is relative to P_2. Conversely, if L_1 and L_2 belong to a constituent to which L_3 does not belong, denoted L_1L_2] L_3, then P_2 is lower relative to P_1 than P_3 is relative to P_2. If the intervals between the successive peaks are denoted as P_1P_2 and P_2P_3 and measured in semitones and tones, and if for the purposes of this test (and related tests in Chapters 9 and 10) falling intervals, being the norm between peaks, are defined as positive (>0) and rising intervals as negative (<0), these rules may be represented as follows:

$$1.1 \ L_1 \ [L_2L_3 \ \Rightarrow \ P_1P_2 \leq P_2P_3$$
$$1.2 \ L_1L_2] \ L_3 \ \Rightarrow \ P_1P_2 > P_2P_3.$$

The definition of falling intervals as positive and rising intervals as negative is purely a convention with no empirical effect. Subrule 1.1 implies that, for example, in structures of branching genitive phrase plus noun phrase consisting of noun and adjective, if there are two unequal falling intervals between the peaks, the greater fall will occur between the noun and the adjective of the noun phrase and the smaller fall between the last word of genitive phrase and the noun of the noun phrase. An example of this interval relation, $P_1P_2 < P_2P_3$, in this structure is given in ME 8.1 in which there is a falling interval of a whole tone from P_2 θύ- to P_3 -ώ-, but a smaller falling interval of only a semitone from P_1 -βρό-

ME 8.1      *Ath.* 2

ἐ[ρι] - βρό-μου-ου   θύ-γα-τρες εὐ - ώ - λ[ενοι,]

to P_2 θύ- across the constituent boundary. Similarly, subrule 1.1 predicts that in a structure in which the first lexical word is a verb and the second and third are the adjective and noun of an instrument adjunct phrase, if there is a level interval and a falling interval, the level interval will occur between the peak of the verb and the peak of the following adjective and the falling interval between the peak of the adjective and the peak of its head noun. An example of this is presented in ME 8.2, in which -πέ- and -δά- are set to the same pitch but there is a fall of 3.5 tones from -δά- to -νῷ.

ME 8.2

ἐπ - έχ - εις   ά - δά - μαν - τι   χα - λι - νῷ

DAM 5.4

Subrule 1.2 implies that, for instance, in a structure of branching genitive phrase plus verbal form (with a direct object modified by the genitive phrase following the lexical triple), if there are two unequal intervals between the peaks, the larger interval will occur within the genitive phrase and the smaller interval will occur between the last word of the genitive phrase and the verbal form. This interval relation, $P_1P_2 > P_2P_3$, is illustrated by ME 8.3 in which there is a falling interval

ME 8.3   γλαυ - κα-[α̃]ς ἐ - λαί - ας θι-γου-οῦσ'   *Lim.* 6

of 2 tones between the peak of -ᾶς and -λαί- within the genitive phrase, but a smaller falling interval of only a semitone between -λαί- and the peak of -γοῦσ'. Similarly, subrule 1.2 predicts that in a structure of branching direct object noun phrase plus verb, if there is one falling interval and one zero interval between the peaks, the falling interval will occur between the noun and its modifier and the zero interval between the final word of the noun phrase and the verb. This is illustrated by ME 8.4, in which there is a falling interval of two tones between

ME 8.4   αἲ νι - φο-βό - λους πέ-τρας ναί - εθ'   *Lim.* 3

P_1 -βό- and P_2 πέ- but no difference in pitch between P_2 πέ- and P_3 ναί-. Likewise, in a structure of branching indirect object noun phrase plus verb, if there is one falling and one rising interval between the peaks, the falling interval will occur within the noun phrase and the rising interval between the last word of the noun phrase and the verb. This is illustrated by ME 8.5 in which there is a falling interval of 1.5 tones between

ME 8.5   πᾶ - σι θνα - τοι-οῖς προ-φαί - νει - [εις   *Ath.* 20

the accentual peaks of πᾶ- and -τοῖς but a rising interval between the peak of -τοῖς and -φαί-, so that as predicted $P_1P_2 > P_2P_3$. Finally, in a structure $L_1L_2]$ L_3 with both intervals rising, the larger rise will be across the constituent boundary, as with the direct object noun phrase plus verb in ME 8.6; and in a structure L_1 [L_2L_3, subrule 1.1 permits equal intervals, as with verb plus branching noun phrase in ME 8.7 and last word of a noun phrase plus branching adjective phrase in ME 8.8.

ME 8.6   [τρ]ί- πο-δα μαν - τεῖ- εῖ - ον ὡς εἰ - εἴ - [λες,   *Ath.* 21

ME 8.7   αι - εἲ - θε(ι) νέ - ων μῆ - ρα   *Ath.* 12

ME 8.8   τεχ- νι - τω-ῶν ἐν - οι- κο - ος πό - λει   *Lim.* 20

Rules 1.1 and 1.2 must be tested statistically to ensure that they reflect a real constraint on interval relations and are not merely an observational coincidence such as is likely to occur in a small data set. Table

TABLE 8.4
Correlation of interval relations between accentual
peaks with constituent structure

	$P_1P_2 > P_2P_3$	$P_1P_2 < P_2P_3$
$L_1 [L_2L_3$	0	6
$L_1L_2] L_3$	6	1
	$p = 0.0041$	

8.4 presents the data for the Delphic hymns on all strings of three fully accented lexical words, except proper names, that are not interrupted by grave or nonlexical accents, and which occur within catathesis domains (defined as finite clauses and branching participial phrases). The two cases of head interrupted structures and the one case of modifier plus modifier plus head are omitted. The distribution observed is highly significant. Even though there are only 13 lexical triples that meet the structural description of rules 1.1 and 1.2, there is only a chance of about one in two hundred and forty-four that the distribution of the magnitudes of the intervals between accentual peaks would accord with the syntactic structure as prescribed by the rules purely as a result of random coincidence. The single exception to a perfect bidirectional implication is in ME 8.9, where the greater interval fall occurs between the direct

ME 8.9   ε - οὐ - ύ-δρου   νά - ματ' ἐ - πι - νί - σε-ται,   Ath. 7

object noun (P_2) and the verb (P_3) rather than between the adjective of the genitive phrase modifying the noun (P_1) and the noun (P_2). However, this exception is probably not a real exception but a side effect of the test having been set up in syntactic terms rather than in terms of the directly motivating prosodic structure, since according to the proposed phrasing algorithm (p. 390), νάματ' (L_2) would have been detached from its modifying phrase (L_1) and paired with the following verb (L_3). Where phonological minor phrases are determined by factors in addition to simple constituency relations, the minor phrase boundary need not coincide with the single observable constituent boundary in the triple.

The treatment of head interrupted structures in the Delphic hymns is different from that of structures having a more strongly differentiated internal constituency. In head interrupted structures there is apparently no constraint on the locations of the greater and the smaller peak to peak intervals. In ME 8.10 $P_1P_2 < P_2P_3$, whereas ME 8.11 has just the opposite relation, $P_1P_2 > P_2P_3$. If these head interrupted structures constituted single phonological minor phrases as suggested by some inscriptional evidence (p. 493), then there would be no internal minor phrase boundary within the lexical triple and the interval relations would not be subject to the constraint imposed by membership in different minor phrases.

ME 8.10

μα-αν- τει - εἶ - ον ἐφ-ἐ- - πων πά -γον.   *Ath.* 8

ME 8.11

νέ - ων μῆ - ρα τα-οὐ- ρων·   *Ath.* 12

The syntactically formulated rules 1.1 and 1.2 may be translated directly into rules based on minor phonological phrases. If L_2 and L_3 belong to a minor phrase to which L_1 does not belong, then the peak of L_2 is not lower relative to the peak of L_1 than the peak of L_3 is relative to the peak of L_2; and conversely if L_1 and L_2 belong to a minor phrase to which L_3 does not belong, then the peak of L_2 is lower relative to the peak of L_1 than the peak of L_3 is relative to the peak of L_2:

2.1 $L_1 \: [L_2L_3 \Rightarrow P_1P_2 \leq P_2P_3$

2.2 $L_1L_2] \: L_3 \Rightarrow P_1P_2 > P_2P_3$

where [and] now represent the beginning and the end of a minor phonological phrase respectively. Informally, these rules mean that in the settings of the Delphic hymns within a minor phonological phrase the pitch of accentual peaks falls more or respectively rises less than across the boundary between minor phrases. This formulation may be tested against all pairs of uninterrupted fully accented lexical words, excluding proper names, in the Delphic hymns, once they have been cross-classified as belonging to the same minor phrase or belonging to two different minor phrases. This procedure has the effect of greatly increasing the size of the data set beyond that available in Table 8.4. The results are presented in Table 8.5. Within minor phrases the mean fall was found

TABLE 8.5

Mean interval in tones between accentual peaks within and across minor phrases

Within phrases	Across phrases
$P_1P_2] = 1.12$	$P_1] \: [P_2 = 0.00$
$s = 1.00$	$s = 1.11$
$P_1P_2] > P_1][P_2: \: t = 3.68, \: df = 46$	
$p < 0.005$	

to be just over a whole tone, whereas across minor phrase boundary the mean fall was observed to be zero. The parsing into minor phrases employed for this test is not the only one compatible with the phrasing algorithm proposed above; other parsings will yield different means, but all parsings compatible with the algorithm will result in differences in the same direction, $P_1P_2] > P_1] [P_2$.

The interval relations elicited by this analysis indicate that while catathesis operates over the domain of the major phrase, a slight boost in pitch is applied at the beginning of minor phrases within the catathesis domain. As a result of this phrase initial boost, the pitch of the first full accent in a minor phrase is not as much lower than the last peak in the preceding minor phrase as it would have been in the absence of a minor phrase boundary; in fact, it may be slightly higher than the last peak in the preceding phrase. The effect of phrase initial boost is illustrated in Figure 8.2. In the Delphic hymns, the pitch boost at the beginning of the minor phonological phrase is just enough to make the mean interval between accentual peaks across minor phrase boundaries equal to zero, that is to block, but not to reverse, catathesis. In contrast, reset at the beginning of a major phonological phrase, that is at the beginning of a new catathesis domain, induces a rise of just over a whole tone from the phrase final to the phrase initial full accent peak in the musical settings of the Delphic hymns. The series of peak to peak intervals $1.14 > 0.00 > -1.05$ gives a rough indication of the progression from minor phrase internal downtrend to minor phrase initial boost to major phrase reset; major phrase reset is about twice as great as minor phrase boost in the Delphic hymns. Minor phrase boost may be interpreted as a hierarchically reduced version of reset (p. 440).

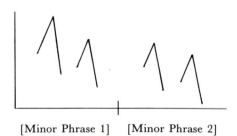

[Minor Phrase 1]   [Minor Phrase 2]

FIGURE 8.2
Minor phrase initial boost

9 | The Major Phrase and Utterance

Phonology and syntax

Given that certain aspects of the prosody of a sentence reflect its grammatical structure, it might be thought that they could be accounted for in the simplest and most straightforward manner by computing measured intonational, durational and intensity relations directly from the surface syntactic structure. However, as has already been pointed out, there are good grounds for assuming that between syntax and the phonetics of prosody there lies a level of properly phonological prosodic organization. One of the arguments used to support such a level was the independence of the units of prosody from the syntactic constituents onto which they are mapped. For instance, in the artificially slow dictation of polysyllabic words, feet and even syllables within a foot can be pronounced with a continuation pitch rise and an intervening pause; that is, feet and syllables can be pronounced with the intonational and durational features normally associated with major phrases. Conversely, in breathless colloquial speech, the syntactic sentences "I'm sorry. I'm late. I got held up" can be pronounced as a single prosodic sentence, that is with the intonational and durational characteristics of one sentence (Crystal 1969). Within the spectrum of normal speech rates, too, the same sentence can often be pronounced equally naturally with and without internal pauses and intonational phrase boundaries. The melodies and rhythms of phrases and sentences evidently have their own autonomous existence and structure. They are autonomous not only from the syntax, as just noted, but also from the segmental phonology: when words are exchanged in speech errors, the phrase stress stays put, as in "I kept it pinned on the ròom to my dóor" or the stranding exchange "You have to squàre it fácely" (Garrett et al. 1980). The autonomy of intonational melodies is a logical prerequisite for exploiting the Greek musical records as evidence for the intonation of Greek speech.

It is probably a general rule that the larger the verse structure, the more likely it is to end with a major syntactic boundary. In particular, sentence end is common at the end of stichoi and even more so at the end of couplets and stanzas, and conversely less common in other positions than it would be with random distribution. In a study of Finnish verse, a main clause boundary was found at the end of 98% of the quatrains, 88% of the couplets and 47% of the lines. Conversely, a phrase consisting of attribute plus headword is overwhelmingly more likely to occur within the line than across line boundary (Leino 1986). At the level of performance, pauses tend to be introduced at the end of verse lines which are not present when the same text is read as prose (Lieberman et al. 1972; Lehiste 1987). It is not the syntactic unit (sentence, clause, etc.) but its implementing phonological unit, or more precisely prosodic unit, that is involved in the rule constraining mismatch of verse unit and syntactic unit. This rule, which is naturally liable to artistic manipulation by the poet, is related to the disruption caused by pause and its associated prosodic features when verse unit and linguistic unit are mismatched, as is quite clear at the paragraph–stanza level, particularly in sung verse. In a hymn, for instance, considerable disruption results from a sentence ending two words into the first line of the following stanza rather than at the end of the last line of its own stanza. On the other hand, such a situation would not be a mismatch at all but the norm in an artificial language in which pause and its associated prosodic features were regularly implemented two words before the end of the syntactic sentence or paragraph. In a perceptual experiment using sentences with mismatched prosodic and syntactic boundaries, it was found that listeners made more recognition errors immediately preceding the prosodic boundary than immediately following it (Darwin 1975). Presumably, listeners tend to discard prosodic cues to syntactic boundaries immediately after another prosodic boundary, since the likelihood of a prosodic boundary increases as the phonological distance from the preceding boundary grows. This may be one of the reasons why those bridges in Greek verse which constrain false division of the stichos are less strictly observed at the beginning of the line. Major phrases are apparently important not only as phonological cues to syntactic, and consequently semantic, structure, but also as cues to processing units. Our brains seem to process the utterances we hear in clausal chunks: it has been found that the last word of the penultimate sentence of a message is much less likely to be recalled than the first word of the final sentence, while contiguous sentence internal words are more or less equally well recalled (Jarvella 1971; Flores d'Arcais 1978). Verbal memory seems to be replaced by semantic memory clause by clause.

Gradience

It is unlikely that prosodic units are processed entirely in terms of the numerical values characterizing their phonetic output. There is some evidence that durational increments at phrase boundaries can be phonologically organized in terms of units of rhythm, rather like musical rests (p. 434); this would be compatible with foot rhythm continuing across certain syntactic boundaries. Likewise, according to one tradition of intonational analysis, behind the intonational contour lies a phonological organization in terms of sequences of High and Low tones associated with accents and boundaries (Pierrehumbert 1980; Pierrehumbert et al. 1989). The phonological analysis of phrase prosody is rendered especially difficult not only by the problem of variability and optionality of the mapping of prosodic categories onto syntactic structure, but also by the problem of gradience in the phonetic actuation of both prominence and boundary demarcation. Feet are composed of strong and weak syllables, metra of strong and weak feet; words, minor phrases and major phrases are characterized by different degrees of stress. The additional duration characteristic of the end of a sentence may (Oller 1979), but need not (Klatt 1975), be greater than that associated with phrase end and less than that associated with paragraph end; in general, the gradience of final lengthening is less rigorous when other cues like intonation and pause are available (Wightman et al. 1992). A similar hierarchy is found with pauses (Goldman-Eisler 1972; Lehiste 1980b); in Swedish, the silent interval at the end of sentences is about 60% of that at the end of paragraphs, and that at the end of clauses about 20% (Strangert 1991). At the end of an intonationally demarcated major phrase in a declaration, pitch falls to a lower point than after a word accent within the phrase, but often not as low as at the end of a sentence; and at the end of a sentence, often not as low as at the end of a paragraph. Laryngealization is stronger and more frequent at higher ranked boundaries (Strangert 1991). In French, the increase in duration and rise in pitch associated with minor phrase boundary is smaller than those associated with major phrase boundary (Delattre 1966b; Rossi 1979; Fletcher 1991). Finally, the degree of resetting of downtrend seems to reflect phrasal hierarchy (Kubozono 1987, 1992; Ladd 1988); in Japanese by and large the deeper the syntactic division, the greater the phrase initial boost. It might follow that prosodic distinctions are theoretically n-ary, that prosodic structure is recursively hierarchical, and that the speaker can make as many distinctions as required for the optimum phonological implementation of the utterance. For instance, data on final lengthening might be best accounted for by positing two levels of minor phrase and two levels of major phrase (Ladd et al. 1991). However, prosodic structure can be flatter than syntactic structure. For instance, the number of different stress levels within the phrase may be limited (Bierwisch 1968) and the infinite embedding of the syntax, as in "This is the cat that caught the rat that ate the cheese...", may not be fully reflected prosodically. Apart from this issue, the problem remains that the hierarchies of phrasal prosody are implemented largely in quantitative rather than in qualitative terms, and presumably perceived by the listener largely in relational rather than in absolute terms. The situation is further complicated by the fact that in addition to these hierarchical relations, true gradience also exists reflecting different degrees on the pragmatic continuum of emphasis or of finality and the degree of speaker arousal and involvement (p. 474).

It should be noted that in simple sentences the major phrase coincides with the sentence and potentially with the utterance; this results in some terminological indeterminacy in the literature, which has been allowed to continue in the ensuing discussion. In its narrow sense, the major phrase is part of a sentence containing more than one major phrase; in its broad sense, the term includes major phrases that are also prosodic sentences. This indeterminacy reflects a general principle of prosodic structure according to which the utterance is exhaustively parsed on every prosodic level; consequently, a minor phrase may also be a major phrase, and a prosodic sentence may also be a prosodic paragraph.

Major phrase

The end of a major phrase is reliably associated with a number of different prosodic attributes. Final lengthening (p. 146) is reported for various languages (English: Klatt et al. 1975; Dutch: de Rooij 1979; Serbocroatian: Lehiste et al. 1986; Chichewa: Kanerva 1990); measurements for German suggested increases in duration for phrase final syllables over phrase medial syllables ranging from approximately 50% to 175% (Zinglé 1978). Phrase final lengthening tends to be greater in reading than in conversation; true pause (nonarticulatory silence) may also occur. However in Japanese, while there is some final lengthening especially prepausally in conversational speech, a study of reading actually found final shortening (Takeda et al. 1989). In Dutch, final lengthening is a more effective cue to major phrase boundary than intonation, and in situations with an artificial experimentally induced conflict between the two cues, final lengthening overrides intonation (de Rooij 1979). Intensity is generally falling at the end of the major phrase, just as it is rising at the beginning: in experiments with singing, it was found that synthesized tones sounded unrelated to each other if they did not form part of a long-term amplitude event (Sundberg 1978). A relatively steep fall in pitch characterizes major phrase boundary in declarative sentences in English (O'Shaughnessy 1979) and often in Dutch (Collier et al. 1975). In Japanese, the boundary between conjoined clauses was found to be marked by final lengthening and a resetting of catathesis at the beginning of the second clause; pause may also occur (Uyeno et al. 1981). In Hausa, tonal downstep is reset in clauses beginning with the conjunction *àmmaa* 'but,' and the phrase final tonal sequences Low High and Low Low are realized as Low Low-level and Low Low-falling respectively (Meyers 1976; Schuh 1978).

When syntactic units of the same type — words in lists, phrases, clauses — are conjoined, a major phrase boundary at the end of the first unit is often additionally marked by a rise in pitch on the last syllable, known as a continuation rise, which indicates to the listener that the information conveyed by the phrase is not yet completed and that more related matter will follow. Continuation rise is different from question rise: it is generally smaller and located on the preboundary syllable, while question rise is larger and starts on the stressed syllable (O'Shaughnessy 1979). The interval of the rise is roughly equal to that of an accentual rise but it is timed differently relative to its host syllable, reaching its peak with the end of voicing in the preboundary syllable (Collier 1991). Other major phrase boundaries, such as those between a main clause and a following dependent clause, frequently show no continuation rise. When a syntactic parallelism is indicated lexically, as in *both A and B* rather than simply *A and B*, pitch was found to rise on *A* and the fall and continuation rise were eliminated. A continuation rise in Dutch is illustrated in Figure 9.1. In Serbocroatian, a pitch differentiated stress language, intonationally marked phrase boundaries can have raised pitch,

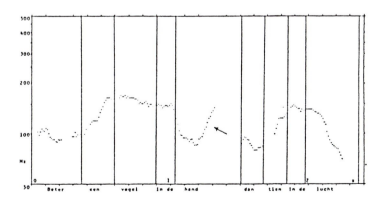

FIGURE 9.1
Continuation rise in Dutch (from Willems 1982)

signalling incompleteness like the English continuation rise; the pitch level of the last word is raised and the intervals of fall within the word are reduced, whereas at the end of a sentence pitch falls (Lehiste et al. 1986). Continuation rises are reported for stress languages from many different parts of the world, such as Azerbaijani (Householder 1965), Iai (Ouvea: Tryon 1968), Maidu (California: Shipley 1964), Khasi (N.E. India: Rabel 1961) and Swahili (Polome 1967). Continuation rises in chunked telephone numbers were found in English but not in the tone language Mandarin Chinese nor in the pitch accent language Osaka Japanese (Tsukuma et al. 1991).

Whether or not a major phrase boundary occurs at any particular point in the speech stream depends on a variety of conditioning factors, such as syntactic constituency, phonological length or heaviness of the constituents, focus and rate of speech (Bierwisch 1966). For instance, the sentence "Prof. Jones will arrive tomorrow" is liable to be produced as a single major phrase in fluent speech, but as two major phrases in deliberate speech. If the heaviness of the subject phrase is increased as in "Prof. Sir Gerald Anstruther Parkhurst-Jones will arrive tomorrow," or if there is contrastive focus as in "Prof. JONES is arriving tomorrow [but Prof. Smith is here already]," the likelihood of major phrase boundary after the subject phrase goes up. In one study, Dutch proverbs containing syntactic clause boundaries were read aloud, and there was considerable variation in whether the syntactic boundary was intonationally marked or not ('t Hart et al. 1973). In addition to variation between presence and absence of major phrase boundary, it is reasonable to assume the existence of an intermediate phrase boundary, characterized by less exaggerated pitch movements, absence of continuation rise and a lesser degree of temporal disjuncture. Intermediate phrase boundary too may vary with major phrase boundary on the one hand and presumably with minor phrase boundary on the other; variation between phrase boundaries with and without continuation rise in the same syntactic structure is found both in English (Beckman et al. 1986) and in Dutch ('t Hart et al. 1990).

Syntactic correlates

Notwithstanding the variability just noted, it is possible to make some generalizations concerning the syntactic structures that typically trigger major phrase boundary. Major phrase boundary is often signalled orthographically by a comma and is sometimes informally called comma intonation. Conjoined clauses typically show major phrase boundary, while conjoined noun phrases are less likely to do so: average pitch fall before *and* was greater in "I decided to go to the party this weekend with

Steve and Tina is planning to go with Tom" than in "I decided to go to the party this weekend with Steve and Tina if Patty will go with Tim" (Cooper et al. 1981). In various languages, an intonational break between conjoined noun phrases is less likely if they represent a conceptual unit and perhaps a fixed phrase, such as *bow and arrow*, than if they constitute a diversified list such as *bow and rifle* (Mithun 1988). When conjoined main clauses are compared with main clause plus complement clause or restrictive relative clause, as in "Anthony was surprised and Raymond became upset" versus "Anthony was surprised Andréa became upset," greater average pitch fall was found in the former, suggesting that complement clauses and restrictive relative clauses tend not to be separated by major phrase boundary; there was no major reset of downtrend between the conjoined main clauses, which indicates that boundary pitch fall and downtrend reset may be independent parameters (Cooper et al. 1981). These major phrase boundaries are also cued by durational differences (Cooper et al. 1980), although many studies fail to factor out the potential effects of refooting and consequent trochee shortening. Embedded conjoined clauses are less likely to be separated by major phrase boundary than nonembedded conjoined clauses, as in "Billy thought his father was a merchant and his mother was a secret agent" versus "Billy thought his father was a merchant and his father was a secret agent" (Lakoff in Downing 1973). Nonrestrictive relative clauses and parentheticals tend to be set off by preceding and following major phrase boundaries. An analysis was made of a series of conjoined center embedded relative clauses in Japanese, in the sentence "My brother [topic, subject] him who is the painter of the Mona Lisa, who studied the principles of blood circulation,... who is called the founder of modern science, Da Vinci [object] respects": each relative clause represented a separate catathesis domain and was separated from the preceding clause by a pause averaging about 340 milliseconds (Uyeno et al. 1981). Dislocated constituents are also commonly set off by major phrase boundary (p. 461). Intermediate phrase boundary is plausibly suggested as typical at normal speech rates between sequences of phonologically heavy parallel modifiers, as in "a round-windowed sun-illuminated room," and before vocatives and question tags (Beckman et al. 1986).

Intermediate and, for even greater explicitness, major phrase boundary are commonly exploited by speakers to disambiguate lexically identical sequences with differing constituency (Price et al. 1991); Figure 9.2 illustrates an instance in which the intermediate phrase boundary cues the broad scope of the modifier *pale* in "a pale [orange and yellow] ballgown." In another study, major phrase boundary was used to cue the scope of the adverb in the ambiguous sentence "He speaks English

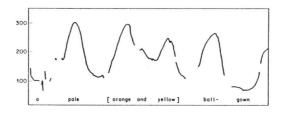

FIGURE 9.2

F_0 contour with intermediate phrase boundary
after broad scope modifier (from Beckman et al. 1986)

naturally"; when the adverb had scope over the whole sentence, there
was a steep fall in pitch on *English* followed by a significant pause, features
that were absent when the adverb had scope only over the verb phrase
(O'Shaughnessy 1979). Some level of major phrase boundary, that is
pitch fall and increased duration, is also used to disambiguate sentences
like "Steve or Sam and Bob will come" and "A plus E times O" (Lehiste
1975; Lehiste et al. 1976; Streeter 1978; O'Shaughnessy 1979). The durational component of the boundary cue by itself is sufficient to disambiguate such sentences, but pitch by itself is not (Lehiste 1980c). In whispered
speech, which has overall greater duration than phonated speech, speakers
do not compensate for the missing pitch cues by exaggerating the durational cues (Lehiste 1983). In these cases use of the major phrase boundary is not an automatic reflex of the need for inspiration after a certain
period of speech activity nor is it an automatic correlate of the syntactic
structure; rather, it is under the active control of the speaker and deliberately used for the purpose of disambiguation in structures which would
have no major phrase boundary if there were no potential for ambiguity,
as in "Three plus two makes five." Perceptually identifiable prosodic
disambiguation occurs not only when ambiguous sentences are read in
contrastive pairs, but also when the experimental design ensures that
each member of the pair is read in a different session (Price et al. 1991).
A variety of structures disambiguated by pause and catathesis reset have
also been analyzed in Japanese (Uyeno et al. 1981). In the chunking
of telephone numbers, Japanese, unlike English and Chinese, makes
little use of final lengthening but relies on catathesis reset and pause
(Tsukuma et al. 1991). The insertion of pauses at phrase boundaries
has been found to improve language comprehension for Wernicke's
aphasics (Blumstein et al. 1985).

Parentheticals

The term parentheticals is here used loosely as a cover term for a class
of expressions external to the main sentence, sometimes referred to as
"Outside" or "O" expressions (Bing 1979); as such, parentheticals are

not restricted to sentence medial position. This class of expressions includes vocatives, epistemic verbs like *I wonder*, direct quotation verbs like *he said*, sentence adverbials like *obviously*, tag questions, interjections and expletives. In Pitjantjatjara (Australia: Bowe 1990), vocatives and exclamations are outside the domain of pronominal clitic placement rules. These expressions often relate to discourse factors involving the relationship between the interlocutors or their attitude to the main sentence, rather than making a contribution to the cognitive message of the main sentence. The placement of parentheticals is sensitive to constituency: compare "He dispelled, I fear, her illusions of wealth" with *"He deprived, I fear, her children of wealth" (Emonds 1973). Explicitly contrastive parentheticals are inserted according to the scope of the contrast: "He dispelled HER, not MY, illusions of wealth" (Zwicky 1978). In a number of languages — English, Dutch, Russian — certain interjections are sentence external: they may be placed sentence finally, or sentence initially or after a left dislocated constituent, but not after a subject phrase nor after a fronted (undislocated) topic (Greenberg 1984). The placement of parentheticals can be used by the speaker as a pragmatic device to set off and therefore further highlight focused items (Dooley 1982): "And THAT — in short/to my surprise/so I am told/as on many other occasions — was the essence of Prof. Smith's lecture." It is important to note that the existence of a phrase boundary after the constituent preceding the parenthetical does not imply that there would be a phrase boundary in the same position in a corresponding sentence lacking a parenthetical, such as "And THAT was the essence of Prof. Smith's lecture," since focused constituents not followed by a parenthetical are not automatically set off by phrase boundary.

As compared with their main clauses, parentheticals have low intensity and are often said to be unaccented; when accented, they have Low tone. If they have a downtrend pattern, it is separate from that of the main clause; the downtrend pattern of the main clause is interrupted by the parenthetical and resumed after its completion; parentheticals are set off by pauses before and particularly after the parenthetical (English: Cooper et al. 1981; Kutik et al. 1983; Rumanian: Dascălu 1974). Appositions are also set off by pauses but they are not Low-toned: compare "My neighbours, the Finks, keep stopping by" (accented apposition) with "My neighbours, the finks, keep stopping by" (Low-toned parenthetical) (Ladd in Bing 1979). Final vocatives are preceded by a boundary implemented by a sharp fall in pitch with no continuation rise; the vocative itself often has low level pitch with slight terminal rise (O'Shaughnessy 1979); the intonational characteristics of vocatives are influenced by the intonation of the main clause (Ladd 1986). When they are placed sentence initially, parentheticals like vocatives and direct quotation verbs are regularly accented, and not Low-toned as sentence medially. Some medially placed parentheticals, particularly epistemic verbs and sentence adverbials, can receive a High tone: compare "She already knows, apparently/I imagine" with "She already knows, APPARENTLY/I IMAGINE"; the High tone in the latter versions contributes a separate qualification comparable to a right dislocated afterthought (Bing 1979). Parenthetical sentences in paragraphs also have lower intensity and pitch than sentences that advance the discourse.

Sentence

Resyllabification, elision, sandhi and similar rules are usually thought of as sentence internal rules; coarticulation involving anticipatory nasalization (McClean 1973) and consonant clusters (Hardcastle 1985) is reduced before major syntactic boundaries at normal speech rates. Yet under certain conditions sandhi rules can apply across sentence boundary, as is reported for voicing assimilation in Mexican Spanish, identical vowel coalescence in Italian and Modern Greek, and for flapping and linking *r* in English (Nespor et al. 1986, Nespor 1987). The domain of such rules can include more than one sentence provided that the sentences share a broadly defined semantic unity and provided that there are no phonological factors militating against a single domain. This latter phonological condition implies that a single domain is only constructed when the sentences are relatively short and no pause intervenes between them. The general semantic condition has various semantic, syntactic and pragmatic implications. The two sentences have to be spoken by the same speaker and to the same interlocutor: compare the application of final dental palatalization in English "[to Jack] Try ič. You'll like the taste" versus its absence in "[to Jack] Try it. [to Jill] You'll like the taste." Syntactic relationships involving ellipsis and anaphora encourage a single domain for English linking *r*: "What a nice sofa[r]. Is it new?". The logical relations 'and,' 'therefore,' 'because' favour a single domain: English flapping applies across sentence boundary in "Turn up the heat. I'm freezing" but not in "Turn up the heat. I'm Frances" (Nespor et al. 1986). The degree to which differences in intonation and demarcation also distinguish such sentences merits detailed investigation, since the application of segmental sandhi would be understandable if the syntactic sentence boundary were implemented by a prosodic phrase boundary.

As a phonological unit, the sentence is demarcated by features of duration, intensity and pitch. Lengthening of the final syllable of the sentence has been noted in various modern European languages (Delattre 1966). In English the durational increment is quite large: in a sentence consisting of four monosyllabic feet such as "Jack's aunt likes cats" uttered as one of a list of sentences, the duration of the feet were 350, 320, 355 and

700 msec (Lehiste 1973). In some other languages, the effects are smaller, or, as in Finnish and Estonian, hardly significant. In French, sentence final lengthening was found to be less than major phrase final lengthening, but the sum of final lengthening and the following pause was greater at the end of a sentence than at the end of a major phrase (O'Shaughnessy 1984). The onset of the final syllable, as well as its vowel and coda consonant(s), can undergo lengthening. Sentence final lengthening can extend further back than the final syllable of the phrase (Kloker 1975): lengthening effects have been found in the penultimate syllable (Klatt 1975), the last stressed syllable, the last foot and the last word (Lehiste 1975; Umeda et al. 1981). Listeners expect the last foot of an English sentence to be longer than earlier feet (Lehiste 1975). Intensity rises steeply at the beginning of an utterance and then declines as the utterance progresses, falling off quite steeply at the end (Pierrehumbert 1979; Nishinuma 1979). Pause over 200 msec was the strongest cue to sentence end (Strangert 1991).

Various effects of the overall number of words, morae or stresses in the major phrase or sentence have been reported. In Japanese, it was found that the greater the number of morae, the lower the duration of each mora (Nishinuma 1979); in recited Japanese verse, average mora duration was slightly lower in hypermetric lines having an additional mora than in regular lines (Homma 1991). In Yoruba and West Greenlandic Eskimo, the average duration of the mora (light syllable) fell from about 180 msec for short utterances to about 120 msec for long utterances (Nagano-Madsen 1992). For Swedish, the duration of the stressed vowel of the first word was not or only slightly dependent on the number of following words, but the duration of the stressed vowel of the last word was notably influenced by the number of preceding word stresses; this contrasts with the word level at which, as in Dutch (Nooteboom 1972), the effect of the number of syllables in the word following the stress on the duration of the stressed vowel is greater than that of the number of syllables preceding the stress (Lyberg 1977; Lindblom et al. 1981). In English, when different test words were read embedded in frame sentences of different lengths, it emerged that the longer the frame sentence, the shorter the duration of the test word and vice versa (Lehiste 1980).

Paragraph

The end of a paragraph can be signalled by an increase both in the number and in the degree of possible sentence end cues (Lehiste 1979; Bruce 1982b; Kreiman 1982). Laryngealization is more frequent at paragraph end than at sentence end and it tends to last longer. The pitch fall is likely to be deeper and the pause longer (Lehiste 1980b; Fant et al. 1989). In reading, the last sentence of a paragraph also tends to be longer in duration than the same sentence occurring paragraph medially (Lehiste 1975b). A macrodowndrift in the domain of the paragraph has been reported for some tone languages (Bolinger 1978). Paragraph domain downtrend has been found in Danish (Thorsen 1986, 1987), and in Swedish where, when a single sentence was compared with a three sentence paragraph, it was found that the peaks and valleys of the single sentence were lower than those of the initial sentence of the paragraph and higher than those of the final sentence (Bruce 1982b). Paragraph beginnings are signalled by abrupt rises in pitch and intensity. Figure 9.3 diagrams the pitch of the first vowel of 42 sentences belonging to seven paragraph-sized news items in a Finnish newscast read by a male speaker: pitch rises abruptly when the first word of a sentence is also the first word of a paragraph; intermediate pitch level characterizes the first word of a subparagraph (compare sentences 7 and 10).

THE MAJOR PHRASE IN GREEK

Ancient punctuation

The simplest and probably oldest system of ancient punctuation distinguished complete from incomplete structures — τελεία στιγμή (*finalis*) and ὑποστιγμή (*subdistinctio*) — with the possibly later addition of a μέση στιγμή (*media*) associated with a breathing pause in theoretical discussions (Dionysius Thrax 7 Uhlig; Blank 1983; Habinek 1985). That the punctuation is not purely a syntactically based device for textual interpretation and disambiguation but includes a prosodic element is indicated by its association with ἀνάγνωσις in Dionysius Thrax and with *lectio* in

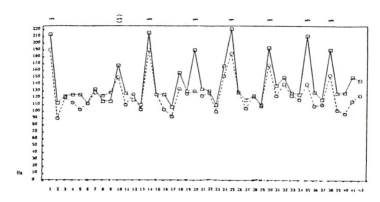

FIGURE 9.3
F₀ of the first vowel of 42 Finnish sentences
in seven paragraphs spoken by a male newscaster.
○: initial F₀. □: peak F₀ (from Iivonen 1984)

the Roman grammatical tradition, as well as by the fact that some scholia attribute relative durations to the different marks: according to the grammarian Heliodorus (scholia on Dionysius Thrax 314 Hilgard), ἡ μὲν γὰρ τελεία τέσσαρας ἔχει χρόνους σιωπῆς, ἡ δὲ μέση ἕνα, ἡ δὲ ὑποστιγμὴ ἥμισυν. An elaborated system based on an eight-point hierarchy is associated with Nicanor, known as ὁ Στιγματίας 'The Punctuator,' a grammarian of the second century A.D., whose influence is prominent in the scholia on the *Iliad*. The application of ancient doctrines of punctuation to the Iliad can be tracked in Friedländer's collection (1850) and via the entry *Interpunctio* in the index to the recent edition of the Iliad scholia (Erbse 1988:135). The following describes Nicanor's system of punctuation in descending rank order as reported by a scholium on Dionysius Thrax 26.4 Hilgard, with the hierarchy of pause durations reconstructed on the basis of various *Iliad* scholia (Friedländer 1850; Blank 1983):

1. τελεία στιγμή – 4 χρόνοι: used between two sentences in asyndeton and after initial vocatives or exclamations

2. ὑποτελεία στιγμή – 3 χρόνοι: used between sentences when the second has a connective such as δέ, γάρ, ἀλλά, αὐτάρ

3. πρώτη ἄνω στιγμή – 2 χρόνοι: used between contrastive clauses with μέν... δέ, οὐκ... ἀλλά and disjunctive ἤ... ἤ

4. δευτέρα ἄνω στιγμή – 1 χρόνος: used between independent clauses connected by the conjunction καί

5. τρίτη ἄνω στιγμή – 1 χρόνος: used between independent clauses connected by the conjunction τε

6. ὑποστιγμὴ ἐνυπόκριτος – 1 χρόνος: not a breathing pause; used between correlative clauses such as ὅτε... τότε, ἕως... τέως; intonationally marked: "grammaticus nescioquis... καταβιβάζοντες inquit ἐμφαντικώτατα τὴν φωνὴν ζητητικὴν αὐτὴν κατασκευάζομεν τῶν ἑξῆς" (Friedländer 1850:59)

7. ὑποστιγμὴ ἀνυπόκριτος – 1 χρόνος: used with parenthetical material

8. ὑποδιαστολή – 1 χρόνος: used between relatives and their antecedents and for phrasal disambiguation.

Nicanor's system needs to be interpreted in the overall context of ancient grammatical doctrine. Apart from the general idea of a detailed hierarchy of syntactic domains as a basis for phrasing, the system is interesting for its measurement of pause in rhythmic units, which anticipates modern phonetic observations and phonological constructs (p. 434), and in the evidence it apparently provides for a continuation rise in Greek correlative clauses. The precise meanings of ὑπόκρισις and καταβιβασμός in this context are not entirely clear. Both ὑπόκρισις and ὑποκριτική include various aspects of prosody (τῆς φωνῆς ποιότητι ἐμφαντική ἐστι τῶν τῆς ψυχῆς παθημάτων, scholiast on Dionysius Thrax 477.22 Hilgard). καταβιβασμός is used at the lexical level to refer to a shift of the accent (Apollonius Dyscolus I.178 Schneider, II.300 Uhlig). Some sort of intonational peak seems to be implied, which, given its syntactic environment, suggests a continuation rise. The intonational overlay of a continuation rise on the word accentual excursion could be one basis for the report of three different types of circumflex by Glaucus of Samos (Sturtevant 1940:100; Sealey 1963).

Particles

In Serbocroatian, as in a number of other languages, clitics appear in socalled sentential second position, specifically after the first word or the first constituent of the sentence: "Taj mi je pesnik napisao pesmu" or "Taj pesnik mi je napisao pesmu" 'That poet wrote me a poem.' Fronted topicalized constituents separated from the rest of the sentence by a pause lie outside the domain within which second position is computed: "Ove godine, taj pesnik mi je [or taj mi je pesnik] napisao pesmu" 'This year, that poet wrote me a poem.' Domain external constituents consist of at least two phonological words, that is they must be phonologically branching, and the heavier a fronted constituent is, the more likely it is to be outside the clitic domain. These phonological conditions suggest that the clitic domain is computed in terms of phonological major phrases rather than in terms of syntactic structure (Corbett 1990; Halpern 1992).

In Greek, the particle ἄν appears either next to the verb or in sentential second position. In Greek too, certain structures can remain outside the domain over which second position is computed and consequently may be interpreted as separate major phrases; they include the following (Fraenkel 1964):

1. Genitive absolute phrases

   [Ἀθηναίων δὲ αὐτὸ τοῦτο παθόντων] διπλασίαν ἄν... Thucydides 1.10.2

2. Nonattributive participial phrases

   [καὶ μὴ ἀπειρίαν τοῦ ἀνδρείου παρόντος προβαλλομένους] εἰκότως ἂν ἔν τινι κακοὺς γενέσθαι Thucydides 2.87.3

3. Topicalized phrases

   [καὶ πρὸς μὲν τοὺς τρόπους τοὺς ὑμετέρους] ἀσθενὴς ἄν μου ὁ λόγος εἴη Thucydides 6.9.3

   [περὶ δὲ τειχῶν, ὦ Μέγιλλε,] ἔγωγ' ἂν τῇ Σπάρτῃ συμφεροίμην Plato Laws 6.778d (with parenthetical)

[τῷ τοίνυν πατρὶ τῷ ἐμῷ] ἀλλὰ μὲν ἄν τις ἔχοι ἐπικαλέσαι ἴσως, εἰς
χρήματα δὲ... Lysias 19.60

4. Constituents with contrastive focus

[ἡμῖν δ᾽] ἐκ πολλῆς ἂν περιουσίας νεῶν μόλις τοῦτο ὑπῆρχε
Thucydides 7.13.1

ἐν μὲν τῷ τέως χρόνῳ... [νῦν δὲ] πάντας ἂν ὑμᾶς βουλοίμην...
Lysias 7.12.

Parentheticals

Although parentheticals respect constituency and serve pragmatically
to highlight focused items, as already noted it cannot be assumed that
the phonological phrasing would be same in the absence of the parenthetical. Nevertheless, parentheticals in Greek gravitate to those positions established as likely, or at least potential, major phrase boundaries
by other criteria. The placement of vocatives, for instance, is typically
associated with the following structures (Fraenkel 1965):

1. Genitive absolute

προϊόντος δὲ τοῦ χρόνου, ὦ ἄνδρες, ἧκον... Lysias 1.11

2. Nonattributive participial phrases

τοιαύτας ἔχοντες προφάσεις καὶ αἰτίας, ὦ Λακεδαιμόνιοι καὶ
ξύμμαχοι, ἀπέστημεν Thucydides 3.13.1

3. Topicalized phrases and/or phrases with informational or contrastive focus

περὶ δὲ ψυχήν, ὦ ἄριστε, οὐχ ὁ αὐτὸς τρόπος; Plato *Gorgias* 505b
ὥστε πολλῶν ἕνεκα, ὦ ἄνδρες δικασταί, προσῆκέ μοι... Lysias
10.5
οὔτ᾽ ἐν τῷ πρὸ τοῦ χρόνῳ, ὦ ἄνδρες Πλαταιῆς,... οὔτε νῦν...
Thucydides 2.73.3
μεγάλ᾽, ὦ ἄνδρες Ἀθηναῖοι, δείγματα... Demosthenes 2.20
οὐ συνειδότα ἐκείνοις, ὦ ἄνδρες Ἀθηναῖοι, οὐδέν Lysias 13.18
[before right dislocated focus].

4. Complement infinitive clauses

φασὶ δ᾽ οἱ σοφοί, ὦ Καλλίκλεις, καὶ οὐρανὸν καὶ γῆν... τὴν κοινω-
νίαν συνέχειν Plato *Gorgias* 507e
Σωκράτη δ᾽ ἐγὼ ἐπαινεῖν, ὦ ἄνδρες, οὕτως ἐπιχειρήσω Plato
Symposium 215a.

Orthotonic pronominal forms are used after certain Greek parentheticals (p. 428); this indicates that some parentheticals were prosodically
demarcated in such a way as to make it impossible for a clitic group

to be formed across the parenthetical boundary. Initial vocatives can be external to the main sentence in Greek as in Vedic (Allen 1973:253).

Hiatus in prose

Nonelidable vowel junctures are avoided in Demosthenes except "quum verbum in vocalem desinens post pausam quandam, quae fieri debet in loquendo et quam plerique interpunctione significare solemus, excipitur a verbo cum vocali incipiente" (Benseler 1841:62). Instances of hiatus such as the following in the *De Corona* (Hedin 1994) are probably licensed by major phrase boundary

[πάσαις δ᾽ αἰτίαις καὶ βλασφημίαις ἅμα τούτου κεχρημένου] ἀνάγκη κἀμοὶ... ἀποκρίνασθαι 34; genitive absolute

[οἷς καὶ δικαίως καὶ προσηκόντως ὀργιζόμενοι] ἑτοίμως ὑπηκούσατε τῷ Φιλίππῳ 20; participial phrase

[εἰ τῷ τιν᾽ ἀρχὴν ἄρχοντι] ἢ διδόναι τῇ πόλει τὰ ἑαυτοῦ διὰ τὴν ἀρχὴν μὴ ἐξέσται, ἤ... 114; fronted topic plus disjuncts

οὐ γὰρ ἐζήτουν οἱ τότ᾽ Ἀθηναῖοι [οὔτε ῥήτορ᾽ οὔτε στρατηγὸν] 205; disjuncts

τὰς αὐτὰς συλλαβὰς καὶ ταὐτὰ ῥήματ᾽ ἔχει [ἅπερ... 223; restrictive relative clause (complex)

τοσαύτῃ γ᾽ ὑπερβολῇ συκοφαντίας οὗτος κέχρηται [ὥστε... 212; consecutive clause (complex).

There is also a fairly systematic avoidance of hiatus in many other authors (Kühner et al. 1890:198); a detailed study of the practice in the novelists again shows hiatus clustering at likely major phrase boundaries as in the following examples from Heliodorus (Reeve 1971):

1. Before the conjunctions ἀλλά, ἤ, οὐδέ, second οὔτε and εἴτε
2. Topicalized phrase
   [ὀφθαλμοὺς δ᾽ ἐκείνου] οἱ μὲν πόνοι κατέσπων, ἡ δ᾽ ὄψις τῆς κόρης ἐφ᾽ ἑαυτὴν ἀνεῖλκεν 1.2.3
3. Participial phrase
   τὸν ὄντα [ὅστις ἐστὶν ὁ ξένος ἐρωτωμένη] ἀγνοιεῖν ἔλεγεν 10.22.2
4. Subordinate clauses including relative clauses and conditionals
   ἡ ἀληθῶς σοφία [ἧς αὕτη παρωνύμως ἐνοθεύθη] 3.16.4
5. Parentheticals including vocatives
   χαίροντά μοι τοῦτον, ὦ βασιλεῦ, ἀντίπεμψον 10.34.4

Verse correlates

It is intuitively natural to see the stichos as the prototypical verse correlate of the major phrase or simple utterance, an idea which is corroborated by the phenomenon of stichomythia and by the clustering of all punctuation, and particularly major punctuation, at line end. The percentages of each type of punctuation occurring internal to the stichos or lyric colometry in tragedy and the *Cyclops* is given in Table 9.1; idiosyncratic differences in editorial practice are unlikely to be a seriously disturbing factor in this sort of massive statistical analysis.

With only two exceptions, punctuation marks lower on the hierarchy, that is further to the right in Table 9.1, show higher proportions of occurrence in internal positions. If the rows and columns of the table are indexed beginning with (1,1) in the upper left and ending with (9,4) in the lower right, there is the very strong tendency in the rank ordering of the proportions

$$P(i,j) < P(i,k) \text{ for } j < k \text{ and all } i.$$

The higher rate of internal periods in satyric is a significant marker of genre, and the higher rates in Euripides as compared to Aeschylus, Sophocles and the *Rhesus* are a significant criterion for stylistic differentiation. The higher rates in the *Liber* and *Liberrimus* styles of Euripides as compared to the *Severior* and *Semiseverus* reflect the evolution of Euripides' versification. The stricter the genre and the stricter the style within a genre, the greater the tendency for punctuation to be line final, that is the greater the tendency for the stichos to coincide with the major phrase. It is remarked by Dionysius of Halicarnassus that phrasing which did not coincide with verse structure made the metre less transparent: διαχέουσι καὶ ἀφανίζουσι τὴν ἀκρίβειαν τοῦ μέτρου *De Compositione Verborum* 26.

The distribution of hiatus also supports an interpretation of the stichos as prototypically a major phrase or simple utterance. With a few exceptions (p. 254) hiatus is not permitted line internally in the trimeter; this recalls the practice of certain prose writers just discussed, where the

TABLE 9.1
Proportions of internal incidence of punctuation marks

	Period %	Query %	Colon %	Comma %
Aeschylus	34.47	37.28	62.82	71.97
Rhesus	31.58	34.15	69.77	76.20
Sophocles	34.34	37.66	70.66	79.78
Severior	35.72	39.21	70.86	76.54
Semiseverus	35.95	40.65	69.12	72.65
Liber	40.09	41.75	73.74	76.75
Liberrimus	37.33	42.63	76.88	74.82
Cyclops	39.19	42.00	87.13	78.95

domain within which hiatus is avoided is identified as the major phrase. In practice, not all stichoi would be prose major phrases; consequently hiatus sometimes occurs in verse in locations that are internal to the prose major phrase. The percentage of stichos pairs with interlinear hiatus within the major phrase and across the boundary between major phrases (as plausibly stipulated by Stinton 1977) is presented in Table 9.2 for the trimeters of selected plays of Euripides and Aristophanes. The general trend is for the incidence of interlinear hiatus of both types to increase as one proceeds from the stricter to the less strict styles of Euripides and from tragedy to comedy, which implies that interlinear hiatus is avoided in the stricter styles. The odds ratio in the third column shows that the constraint is stronger on major phrase internal hiatus than on hiatus across major phrase boundary, and that as it is progressively relaxed the odds for the former become closer to those for the latter, even surpassing them in one play.

The phenomenon of brevis in longo (p. 79) implies final lengthening, at least of certain prepausal short vowels, in Greek. There is also a variety of evidence in the musical records pointing to the lengthening of some line final syllables in the musical settings, and these lengthenings could have correlates in spoken verse and ultimately reflect lengthening at the end of the major phrase in prose speech. As already noted (p. 116), lengthening of a phrase final thesis is indicated by a number of instances in which a length mark, triseme or diseme functioning as a mark of lengthening, is used at the end of trimeters or lecythia. In

TABLE 9.2
Proportions of interlinear hiatus
in the trimeter (based on Stinton 1977)

Play	Within major phrases %	Between major phrases %	Odds ratio
Euripides			
Medea	3.40	16.98	0.1721
Heraclidae	5.65	17.82	0.2762
Andromache	2.94	24.08	0.0955
Ion	6.40	23.82	0.2187
Helen	16.44	28.16	0.5019
Aristophanes			
Knights	31.63	23.47	1.5290
Acharnians	18.82	24.54	0.7129
Clouds	27.27	33.52	0.7436

the Oslo papyrus the diseme is used inconsistently to mark single notes mapped onto heavy syllables and consistently to mark multiple notes mapped onto heavy syllables; the triseme has been identified by some editors once in the anapaests on ἐλθ[*DAM* 36.2 (unexplained) and three times on the last syllable of a trimeter (ME 9.1–3) (Winnington-Ingram

ME 9.1   P P̄C̄   *DAM* 37.16
ὁ μ ο ῦ

ME 9.2   M C̄   *DAM* 37.17
τ έ χ ν η ν

ME 9.3   M Ι Ι Ῑ   *DAM* 37.18
ἠ ρ γ ά ζ ε τ ο̣

1955; Pappalardo 1959). The leimma indicating pause time after catalexis probably needs to be distinguished from the triseme indicating final rallentando in acatalectic verse. In the Michigan papyrus, a diseme is followed by an upward-slanting line on ἐμποεῖ *DAM* 39.15 and on λέγεις *DAM* 39.17, and in both instances the end of a trimeter is suspected; therefore they could be trisemes indicating line final lengthening. Of the other possible trisemes in this text, two actually stand before leim-mata and most of the remainder are at least not incompatible with the end of some type of metrical unit. In *DAM* 38 the diseme on one of a pair of notes assigned to the final syllable of a lecythion in two instances may be interpreted as a mark of final lengthening (ME 9.4–5) (Turner ad loc.).

ME 9.4   Ū ? [   ] P M : M̄Z̄   *DAM* 38.ii.3
μ ᾶ λ λ ο ν η ὐ τ έ κ ν η σ α ἐ γ ώ

ME 9.5   ] Ι M M Ȯ Ξ Ι Ξ C C̄Φ̄   *DAM* 38.ii.4
τ] ῶ ν κ α κ ῶ ν χ ο ρ ε ύ σ α τ ε·

In the hexameter of Callimachus, when there is a word boundary after third biceps, that is when the line could be interpreted as having a medial diaeresis, it must have not only a regular caesura but also a bucolic diaer-esis, and, additionally, there must be a syntactic boundary at either the caesura or the bucolic diaeresis that ranks higher than the boundary after third biceps and that is potentially a major phrase boundary — a combi-nation of requirements that effectively precludes medial diaeresis (Bulloch 1970). Consequently, a line such as

ἤδη γὰρ δηρὸν χρόνον ἀλλήλων ἀπέχονται *Iliad* 14.206

would not be permitted in Callimachus.

Orthotonic pronouns

In the absence of focus, phrasing can be an indirect determinant of the form of the pronoun. At the beginning of a clause even unfocused pronouns are orthotonic: αἱ κατ' ἀρχὴν τιθέμεναι, κἂν μὴ ἔχωσιν ἀντιδιαστο-λὴν, διὰ τῶν ἀρκτικῶν τόπων ὀρθοτονοῦνται Herodian I.560 Lentz. Apollonius Dyscolus I.39.21 Schneider contrasts

> ἐμὲ δ᾽ ἔγνω καὶ προσέειπε *Odyssey* 11.91

with the clause medial enclitic in

> ἔγνω δὲ ψυχή με ποδώκεος Αἰακίδαο *Odyssey* 11.471.

Certain nonfinite structures also select the orthotonic forms in initial position. This is regular in the genitive absolute

> ἐμεῦ ἀπομηνίσαντος *Iliad* 19.62
> ἐμοῦ θανόντος *Trachiniae* 1222,

and participial phrases when semantically equivalent to finite subordinate clauses

> πιστὸς δ᾽ ἀδελφὸς ἦσθ᾽, ἐμοὶ σέβας φέρων *Choephori* 243.

The orthotonic forms also appear after certain parenthetical material

> θέλοντι δ᾽, εἴπερ οἶσθ᾽, ἐμοὶ φράσον τάδε *Choephori* 522,

and noun phrases in apposition

> ἄνθος, στρατοῦ δώρημ᾽, ἐμοὶ ξυνέσπετο *Agamemnon* 955.

A clitic group cannot be formed across major phrase boundary, so only the orthotonic form is possible. Since phonological phrasing is variable, it is not surprising that there is variation between enclitic and orthotonic pronouns in certain syntactic environments, for instance after vocative phrases

> δέσποιν᾽, ἐμοί τοι συμφορὰ μὲν ἀρτίως *Hippolytus* 433
>> τί δῆτ᾽ ἔτερψας, ὦ τάλαινά, με
> ἐλπὶς τότ᾽
>> *Heraclidae* 433.

Enclitics after a vocative are especially associated with syntactic structures in which they are final, so that a phonological phrase ends with the enclitic; the example above from the *Heraclidae* is an extension of this principle from the major phonological phrase to the metrical stichos. Conversely, orthotonic forms stand at the beginning of the stichos, which corresponds to the beginning of the major phrase, even when not in focus and not clause initial, particularly in Homer

> ἦ τάχα χήρη
> σεῦ ἔσομαι·
>> *Iliad* 6.408.

In tragedy, there is a closer congruence of stichos and major phrase in this regard, so that stichos initial pronouns are almost always either in focus or clause initial.

Inscriptional punctuation

A few inscriptions use a hierarchical system of interpuncts, which is direct evidence for different levels of phrasing and discourse structure. In the Hekatompedon inscription (I^3.1.4; Jordan 1979), which is written stoichedon, a single row of interpuncts fitted between letters is used for a conservative version of minor phrase punctuation, and three rows of interpuncts (some editorially restored) filling a letter space are used to separate sections or paragraphs. The silver plaque from Ephesus (*Eph. Art.*) uses a ternary system: a single row of interpuncts marks the minor phrase; two rows mark sentence end, but their use is not consistent and subject to uncertainties of interpretation; three rows apparently signify a higher ranked discourse structure such as a section. *Milet.* (*LSAG* 64.33) uses hierarchical punctuation to distinguish list items from sections.

Initial rise and terminal fall

In addition to the global downward slope of declination and catathesis, the utterance is also locally demarcated by intonational boundary features, so that pitch tends to be rising at the beginning of the utterance and to fall sharply to the baseline at or towards the end of a declaration (Cohen et al. 1982; Liberman et al. 1984). Although apparently lacking in some languages — Copenhagen Danish has no overt terminal fall (Grønnum 1990) — these features of the pitch contour of sentences are widely reported both for stress languages and for languages having lexical tone or a pitch accent. In Serbocroatian, the fundamental frequency peak in disyllabic words with falling accent occurs closer to the end of the syllable nucleus when such words occur at the beginning of the utterance than when they occur utterance medially; at the end of an utterance in disyllabic words with rising accent the fundamental frequency of the second syllable is comparatively low and in words with falling accent the fundamental frequency of the second syllable tends to fall to the point of laryngealization (Lehiste et al. 1986). In English, the initial rising intonation can have the effect of postponing the pitch peak of the first stress unless it is focused (O'Shaughnessy 1979; Eady et al. 1986). The terminal fall can be distributed over the posttonic syllables of the last word as in Zuni (New Mexico: Newman 1965). In Bambara (Mali: Mountford 1983), an inital Low tone and the last High tone in the sentence are generally lower than they would be in the absence of boundary effects. In Hausa, an utterance initial High tone is often realized as a rising tone and there is a strong tone lowering tendency in utterance final position (Meyers 1976). In Haya (Tanzania: Hyman 1978b) and in Kinyarwanda (Furere et al. 1985), both prepausal and postpausal High tones can become Low tones under certain conditions. Phrase final tone lowering occurs in Slave (British Columbia: Rice 1989b) and in West Greenlandic Eskimo final High tone is lowered to Mid in absolute terminal position (Nagano-Madsen 1993). Tone languages having little or no downdrift can still modify the final tone of a clause or sentence, as happens in Wobe (Ivory Coast: Bearth 1980). In Chinese, a sentence final rising tone becomes a relatively uncontoured low tone. Japanese has a specifically terminal pitch fall (Poser 1985; Pierrehumbert et al. 1988).

It is normal in European song for there to be a considerable degree of correlation between musical phrase end and major syntactic constituent boundary. Similar matching rules are found in African music, for instance (Nketia 1974). In the Ewe drum language (Dahomey: Locke et al. 1980), which reproduces the rhythm of a spoken or sung text for dancing, short rests in the master drum rhythms mostly fall at syntactic constituent boundaries. An extreme case of disregard for the correlation of musical and linguistic phrasing is the deliberate liturgical distortion of the Indian Samavedic chants, in which periods can begin in the middle of a word. A falling melody at the end of major syntactic constituents is common in European song; a high incidence was found in an analysis of a Purcell song (Rohrer 1983).

The existence of initial rise and terminal fall in Greek speech is indicated by the distribution of intervals greater than or equal to an octave within words or appositive groups in the Delphic hymns; these often coincide with the beginnings or ends of melodic sections. All rises of an octave or more (ME 9.6–8) occur at the beginning of sentences or

ME 9.6 *Ath.* 16

ME 9.7 *Lim.* 13

ME 9.8 *Lim.* 26

after potential major phrase boundaries. The latter are defined as including whole participial phrases, clauses that are grammatically complete in terms of concord, rection and subcategorization, and coordinate major noun phrases containing branching adjective phrases. The octave rises to the grave in ME 9.6 and 9.8, and the rise of two and a half tones in 'Aμφὶ *Lim.* 23, which occur at the beginning of sentences and melodic sections, contrast with an average rise to the grave major phrase internally of less than a third of a tone. Some falls of an octave or more occur at the beginning of sentences or major phrases, where they reflect the accentual fall uncompressed by catathesis; others occur at the ends of periodic sentences or at locations that are potential major phrase ends (ME 9.9–12), where they reflect terminal fall. There are no octave intervals in locations that are unarguably major phrase medial, even though the odds for medial occurrence are greater than the odds for initial or final occurrence, since there are far more settings preserved in medial position than in either initial or final position.

ME 9.9 — *Lim.* 19
αὐ - [το] -χθό-νων

ME 9.10 — *Lim.* 13
να - ἇ - σον

ME 9.11 — *Lim.* 21
Κε - κρο - πί - αι.

ME 9.12 — *Lim.* 23
φιλ - έν - θεον.

Final oxytones

According to the grammarians, oxytones receive the grave accent ἐν τῇ συνεπείᾳ, ἐν τῇ συμφράσει (Vendryes 1945:37, 237), which may plausibly be interpreted as major phrase internally. In phrase final oxytones in the Delphic hymns, tone either rises from (ME 9.13) or is set level with (ME 9.14) the preceding syllable; cp. κλειτύν (melism) *Lim.* 2, Ὠκεανός *Lim.* 11. Due to the size and character of this sample, it is hard to say whether phrase final oxytones are more like phrase final nonoxytones or

ME 9.13 — *Lim.* 35
θε - ά

ME 9.14 — *Ath.* 9
'Aθ - θίς

phrase internal lexical graves. In Mesomedes' Hymn to Nemesis, which is later, sentence and melody section final acute in ῥοπά is set lower than the preceding syllable. The final acute has been interpreted as evidence for the existence in Greek of an intonational terminal High tone which was phonetically latent except on oxytones and perhaps on other accentual patterns where it did not conflict with the accentual fall (Trubetzkoy 1969:238; Allen 1973). This hypothesis is difficult to reconcile with the evidence cited above for terminal fall in nonoxytone words. In Osaka Japanese (p. 181), an accent in a Low-beginning word on the final mora of an utterance, as in citation forms, is produced by some speakers as a High-Low movement with accompanying lengthening of the final mora, but by other speakers as a High tone without a fall and without final lengthening (Kori 1987; Pierrehumbert et al. 1988). So Greek might conceivably have had an optional High-Low movement in major phrase final acute syllables. Final lengthening allows more phonological space for an accentual fall, relieving the need for compression of the accentual excursion to a grave. In the Delphic hymns, θηήρ Lim. 29 (ME 4.7) apparently has a falling melism on a phrase final acute, possibly supported in the later settings by φωνή DAM 36.9, but not by the rising melisms on Ἀχιλλεύς DAM 36.8 and ἐγώ DAM 38.2.3

Pause

A not inconsiderable share of the overall duration of speech is occupied by silence. A proportion of this silence is associated with the articulation of stop consonants, while other periods of silence consist of pauses. Pauses typically occupy about 18% of speech duration in reading (Huggins 1964) and as much as 50% in conversation (Klatt 1976; Autesserre et al. 1989); no difference was found between English and French radio interviews, each having 17% silence (Grosjean et al. 1975). Nongrammatical pauses or hesitation pauses located just before lexical words (MacClay et al. 1959) may occur as a focus cue (Fant et al. 1989) or as a result of difficulty in finding a word. Pauses may also arise from a change in the planning of a sentence; final lengthening or drawling may be substituted for a true pause. Grammatical pauses occur between prosodic units, generally of the rank of the phrase or higher.

The occurrence (Bierwisch 1966) and duration of a grammatical pause depend among other factors on the hierarchy of prosodic domains as it reflects the hierarchy of syntactic structure (Goldman-Eisler 1972; Duez 1982; Gee et al. 1983). In Estonian, pauses within the sentence tend to be shorter than pauses between sentences, and the latter in turn shorter than pauses between paragraphs (Lehiste 1980). In Danish text which was read aloud, it was found that sentence boundaries were always accompanied by a pause averaging 1040 msec, while only about half of the sentence internal clause boundaries were accompanied by pause, which averaged 460 msec (Thorsen 1987). In a corpus of English speech,

66% of all sentence transitions were marked by pauses ranging from 50 msec to 5 seconds, with the longest pauses marking paragraph-like discourse transitions (Deese 1984). Inhalation requires more time than simply ceasing phonation, and consequently breathing pauses have greater duration than nonbreathing pauses, approximately twice the duration at most rates of speech; since longer pauses occur at deeper constituent boundaries, respiration occurs preferentially at major syntactic divisions (Grosjean et al. 1979). When subjects read aloud a Hungarian story, 87.5% of the inhalations occurred at sentence end, the remainder at clause or phrase end (Fónagy et al. 1960). In balanced rhythmical reading in Swedish, 70% of pause time was located between sentences; most of the breathing occurred at the boundaries between sentences or major clauses, and breathing was correlated with longer pauses (Fant et al. 1989). The occurrence of pause and of respiration also depends in part on the distance from the preceding respiration (Fujisaki et al. 1971). Speakers prefer to balance the phonological length of constituents in the output (Grosjean et al. 1979), which can introduce a disparity between syntactic and prosodic domains. Subjective listening often leads to perceived pauses when there is no actual pause, merely phrase final lengthening (Martin 1970). Both normal and time compressed speech is easier to understand when pauses are inserted at syntactic boundaries than when they are inserted periodically without reference to syntactic structure, even in the absence of other phrasal prosodic cues (Wingfield et al. 1984).

As speech rate is increased, pausing is curtailed; although the duration of pauses is reduced, the main strategy is to eliminate pauses at relatively less important constituent breaks. In slow reading at 75 words per minute one pause occurred every 2.3 words, whereas in fast reading at 391 words per minute this dropped to one pause every 33 words; breathing pauses and nonbreathing pauses, as measured by rib cage expansion, were approximately equal in number at the slow rate; at a normal rate, a fifth of all pauses were nonbreathing pauses; and at the fast rate nonbreathing pauses had practically disappeared (Grosjean et al. 1979). In Swedish, perceptible pauses, including "filled pauses," were about four times as frequent in slow speech as in fast speech (Strangert 1991). The distribution of pauses at various constituent boundaries is illustrated in Figure 9.4.

Domain of podic rhythm

There is some evidence that in ordinary speech it is the major phrase that constitutes the basic domain of podic rhythm, the prosodic unit within which foot structure is assigned (Donovan et al. 1979). Percep-

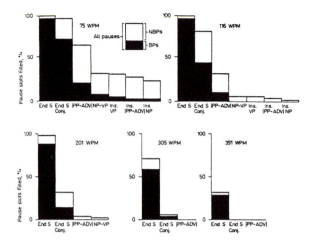

FIGURE 9.4

Syntactic distribution of breathing and nonbreathing pauses
according to speech rate (from Grosjean et al. 1979)

tual experiments show that, once rhythm is established, strong rhythmic expectancies arise in the listener as the utterance proceeds (Martin
1979; Buxton 1983); not all studies were able to replicate this result (Mens
et al. 1986). Final lengthening at certain phrase boundaries seems to
disturb the rhythm and make timing judgements more difficult for the
listener (Klatt et al. 1975). However, when there is refooting across phrase
boundary, trochee shortening applies equally to finally lengthened syllables, an observation that is relevant for the interpretation of the verse
caesura (p. 274; Rakerd et al. 1987). The localized ritardando of final
lengthening can extend into the unstressed beginning of the word following the boundary (Kloker 1975; Lea 1977); in Swedish, there was a small
postpausal initial lengthening effect of about 20 msec on the consonant
onset of the first syllable of the next foot (Fant et al. 1989). This is another
factor that may be relevant for an understanding of how foot rhythm
is continued across a verse caesura. Data have also been cited suggesting that on the average interstress durations, including pause time, double
at major phrase boundaries and triple at sentence boundaries (Lea 1980).
In some drum language surrogates, extra beats or separate tones can
be used to signal phrase boundary (Torday et al. 1922; Clarke 1934;
Carrington 1949; Stern 1957; Rialland 1974). A correlation between
the duration of pause plus prepausal final lengthening and average foot
duration was found for English, French and Swedish; it occurred in both
prose and verse reading (Fant 1991; Fant et al. 1991). In Swedish (Fant
et al. 1989), the sum of final lengthening plus pause between sentences
equalled two or three stress feet in duration in normal rhythmical read-

ing, but not in other styles of reading, and there was a negative correlation between final lengthening and pause duration: this result recalls the continuity of rhythm across pause in musical performance, and confirms an intuition of phonological theory (Selkirk 1984) which, as noted above, goes back to the ancient grammarians. Lower ranked phrasal final lengthening occurred without pause and did not consist of an extra foot's duration; this observation too is relevant for an understanding of the verse caesura. In verse reading, pause between lines added the duration of a foot, except that if there was a catalectic syllable, then the combination of that syllable plus pause added up to the duration of a foot (Kruckenberg et al. 1991). The fact that in prose as well as in verse the combination of pause and final lengthening can be assigned a duration that is a whole figure multiple of foot duration indicates that rhythmic measurement can continue even through boundaries marked by pause (Cutler et al. 1979; Fant et al. 1988).

DOWNTRENDS

In declarative utterances, when other pitch modifying features are factored out, all or almost all languages have an overall downtrend in pitch from the beginning to the end of the utterance (Cohen et al. 1982). The phenomenon seems to be more marked in sentences read under experimental conditions than in connected discourse (Cooper et al. 1985), perhaps because experimental sentences are treated as separate paragraphs; however, the suggestion that there is no preterminal downtrend in spontaneous speech has not been widely accepted (Repp 1985; Lieberman 1986). This downtrend is the result of a combination of sequential local adjustments in fundamental frequency triggered by High-Low accentual or tonal movements (catathesis), an independent global decline in fundamental frequency over the course of the utterance (declination), and a more localized fall in fundamental frequency at the end of the utterance (terminal fall), potentially developing into laryngealization, which has already been discussed (p. 429). Electronically generated intonation contours sound unnatural if they have no downtrend or even if they have catathesis but lack declination ('t Hart et al. 1990). Listeners expect downtrends and partially correct for them in perception both in stress languages (Pierrehumbert 1979; Leroy 1984; Terken 1991) and in pitch accent languages (Shimizu et al. 1981). When instructed to produce equal accents, Dutch speakers made the second accent 6.5 Hz lower (Gussenhoven et al. 1988).

The apparent universality of downtrend suggests that, even though it may be linguistically controlled, it has some ultimate physiological basis, and considerable effort has been devoted to discovering whether that basis lies in the respiratory system or in the laryngeal musculature or both (Collier 1987; Gelfer 1987; 't Hart et al. 1990); there is also a correlation with the height of the speaker's larynx (Maeda 1976; Petersen 1985). The relatively steep and rapid fundamental frequency excursions associated with pitch accents and focus accents are too large to be accounted for purely in terms of cooccurring changes in subglottal pressure (p. 14) and are related to significant activity of the cricothyroid muscle; by contrast, as is particularly clear from reiterant speech using the syllable *ma*, in stretches of unaccented syllables between accents, fundamental frequency and subglottal pressure decline slowly but cricothyroid activity is largely suppressed (Gelfer 1987). It would follow that catathesis is mainly associated with laryngeal activity and declination mainly with progressively falling subglottal pressure. Declination has been estimated to contribute to downtrend at a very approximate rate of 10 Hz per second (Pierrehumbert et al. 1988). It has been suggested that the phenomenon of catathesis may be related to the fact that raising pitch requires more time and effort than letting it fall (Ladd 1984). It has been argued that progressively declining subglottal pressure is not simply a passive reflex of airflow from the lungs (p. 10) but reflects some form of overall control by the speaker, and that declination is the indirect consequence of this strategy; on this view, speakers regulate subglottal pressure but not to the extent of maintaining it level. It is possible actively to maintain constant subglottal pressure during the prolonged utterance of a sustained vowel regardless of decreasing lung volume (Strik et al. 1989); and when utterances were deliberately produced on a monotone, subglottal pressure remained constant (Collier 1987). There is increasing evidence that the energy allotted to articulatory gestures also declines as the utterance progresses (Krakow et al. 1991).

The effects of catathesis and declination are found in simple stress accent languages like English, in dislocated stress languages like Danish (Figure 9.5) and in pitch differentiated stress languages such as Serbocroatian (Figure 9.6). In the pure pitch accent language Japanese (Figure 9.7), the rate of pitch fall is far greater following a minor phrase having an accentual pitch fall than following an unaccented minor phrase; however, pitch does decline in sequences of unaccented minor phrases too, which establishes declination as a factor separate from catathesis (Poser 1985); this distinction is also indicated by the fact that the number of syllables separating two accentual peaks can influence the height of the second peak (Pierrehumbert et al. 1988). The effects of downtrend are such that both in stress languages and in pitch accent languages an accented syllable late in the sentence may have lower pitch than some or all unaccented syllables early in the sentence. In many, but not all, lexical tone languages, in sentences with alternating High and Low tones,

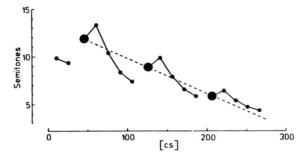

FIGURE 9.5
Schema for downtrend in Danish terminal declarations.
Large dots: stressed syllables. Small dots: unstressed syllables
(courtesy of N. Grønnum)

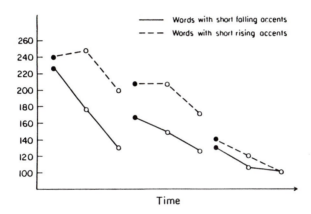

FIGURE 9.6
Downtrend in sentences consisting of three trisyllabic words
in Serbocroatian (from Lehiste et al. 1986)

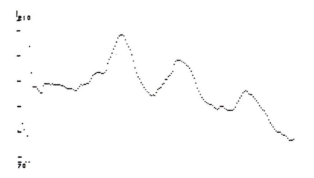

FIGURE 9.7
Downtrend in the Japanese declaration
Sore wa nurúi umái nomímono (from Poser 1985)

pitch drifts downwards as the sentence progresses, with the High tones falling more rapidly than the Low tones (Figure 9.8). Consequently, the absolute pitch of a High tone late in the sentence can be the same as, or lower than, that of a Low tone earlier in the same sentence. Sequences of Low tones without an intervening High tone also drift downwards. However, sequences of High tones without an intervening Low tone may fall little or not at all, in the latter case possibly to prevent misinterpretation of a lowered High tone as a Mid or Downstepped tone (Hombert 1974).

Catathesis has been viewed as an iterative downward assimilation of a following High tone to a preceding Low tone. In fact, the falling movement onto the Low tone is deeper than the preceding one and the rise to the following peak is shallower than the preceding one. This is because catathesis does not only lower absolute frequencies but also compresses the frequency range of accentual excursions; the High tones fall more rapidly than the Low tones, so that a line drawn through the High tones (the topline) would not be parallel to a line drawn through the Low tones (the bottomline, as distinguished from the baseline which is the lowest pitch used by the speaker). Some of this compression is absorbed with conversion from a linear frequency scale in Hertz to a logarithmic pitch scale in semitones or to a percentage measure (Fujisaki et al. 1979), but a significant difference can remain, as is seen in Figure 9.5 which has a semitone scale. In Hausa a High-Low interval of as much as 20 Hz was found at the beginning of an utterance and only 2–3 Hz at the end of an utterance (Meyers 1976; Pierrehumbert 1980). It is often the case that the topline is not straight but has a steeper slope in its initial section (Gelfer 1987) also on a logarithmic scale ('t Hart et al. 1990). Downtrends are also significantly influenced by focus, which tends to have the effect of raising the focused High tone and lowering postfocus tones (p. 466). In English, focus interacts systematically with downtrend, so

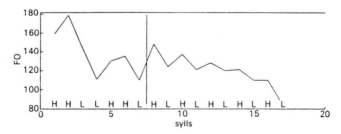

Yaa aikàa wà Maanii / làabaarin wannàn yaaròn alàrammà

FIGURE 9.8
Tonal downtrend in a Hausa declaration
(from Inkelas et al. 1990)

that a late focused High tone can be slightly lower than an early un-focused High tone (Pierrehumbert 1980). Downtrend measurements are also conditioned by the overall pitch range or register chosen by the speaker. When subjects are instructed to "speak up," reflecting a greater degree of overall emphasis or arousal, not only do the absolute values of accentual peaks increase, but the intervals between consecutive peaks, expressed logarithmically, also increase (Pierrehumbert 1980). The longer the sentence, the slower the rate of downtrend (Maeda 1976; Cooper et al. 1981; Collier et al. 1984). This correlation is reported for languages such as English, Dutch, Swedish (Bruce 1982) and Hausa (Lindau 1985). In principle, downtrend could be anchored to the beginning of the slope, the end of the slope, or neither. Languages seem to differ in this regard. In English, as in Swedish, the end point is fairly stable, and the pitch of the first accented syllable tends to vary according to the length of the sentence, being higher in longer sentences according to most studies; there is variation among speakers in this regard and the same speaker can adopt different strategies (Gelfer 1987). The terminal fall to the base-line in English is not affected by different degrees of emphasis (Pierre-humbert 1980). There is also some evidence for length of the domain affecting downtrend in Japanese (Poser 1985); however in Japanese the endpoint is more variable and sensitive to preceding catathesis (Pierre-humbert et al. 1988). In one study of Hausa the pitch of the first high tone showed little variation in sentences of different lengths (Silverstein 1976). In Danish, increased sentence length resulted in higher initial pitch, a lower endpoint and a more gradual slope (Thorsen 1986).

Reset

In longer sentences, downtrend can be reset at the boundary between main clause and subordinate clause or vice versa or at the boundary between coordinate clauses: the fact that such reset has been found to cooccur with final lengthening and pause indicates that reset occurs at prosodic phrase boundary. A perceptual experiment in which reset was manipulated to differentiate the ambiguous sentence "They decorated the girl with the flowers" suggested that reset on the prepositional phrase favoured its interpretation as modifying the verb phrase, which would indicate that reset was a cue to major phrase boundary ('t Hart et al. 1990); in a similar experiment in Japanese, reset was a more important boundary cue than pause (Azuma et al. 1991). Reset does not necessar-ily entail inhalation, and inhalation can occur at locations not showing reset ('t Hart et al. 1990). The results of different studies of reset are rather variable; this is partly due to different speech materials and vari-able speaker strategies and partly to the number of different ways in which reset can be defined and measured. Some studies found complete or almost complete reset at clause boundary (Bruce 1982; Collier 1987), while most studies found that at the beginning of a second clause downtrend is reset to start significantly lower than its sentence initial value, so that the second clause is in a lower pitch range than the first (Thorsen 1985, 1986; Gelfer 1987; Ladd 1988; Appels in 't Hart et al. 1990). Since terminal fall is distinct from catathesis and declination, it is important to factor out terminal fall if the bottomline is used to measure the degree of downtrend reset; some English speakers allow an internal clause final terminal fall to the baseline before reset (Ladd 1988). Reset has been found in English, Dutch (Collier 1987), Danish (Thorsen 1985, 1986; Bannert et al. 1986), Hausa (Silverstein 1976; Inkelas et al. 1990), Japanese (Fujisaki et al. 1984) and Korean (Lee 1989). In the laboured speech of Broca's aphasics, reset applies to smaller domains than in normal speech, but syntactic structure continues to be respected (Danly et al. 1982). Like declination and catathesis, terminal fall seems to have a physiological basis, and this idea is corroborated by the observation that declination and terminal fall occur in the vocal productions of vervet monkeys (Hauser et al. 1992). The fact that they do not occur randomly throughout the utterance but are patterned in such a way as to signal prosodic and ultimately syntactic strucure indicates that they have been grammaticalized.

It has already been noted that the term major phrase is a cover term for a potential hierarchy of prosodic domains including at least the intermediate phrase and the major phrase proper, and that its implementing phonetic properties tend to be higher gradient values of properties also characterizing the minor phrase (p. 411). Downtrend reset fits well into this overall picture. The comparatively small boost in fundamental frequency that is characteristic of the intermediate phrase in Japanese (p. 403: Kubozono 1987, 1992; Selkirk et al. 1988) corresponding to what is here termed the minor phrase in Greek, can be interpreted as a minimal degree of downtrend reset. Hierarchical prosodic structure among major phrases can feature gradient values of downtrend reset: in sentences like "Allen has more popular policies, and Warren is a stronger campaigner, but Ryan has a lot more money," it was found that downtrend was reset at the end of each clause but resetting was greater before *but* than before *and* both for the order *A and B but C* and for the order *A but B and C* (Ladd 1988). At the upper end of the scale, gradient downtrend has been found among sentences in the paragraph (p. 420).

Downtrend in song

In Subsaharan Africa, where most tone languages have downdrift, musical melodies are often reported to be characterized by a predominantly downward slope, as for instance in Zulu song (Cope 1959), in Igbo (Ekwueme 1974, 1980) and in Lingala (Carrington 1966). The highest note in a typical Igbo melody is the first high tone, after which the tune works its way down to the end. There is one type of chant, sometimes termed singsong, in which the rhythms and lexical tones, if any, of speech are preserved in a regularized or stylized form, but the intonation is deliberately eliminated, as is exemplified by the cries of some Chinese street vendors (Chao 1956). The recitation of the Zulu Izibongo praise poems is a type of singsong: downdrift is absent and the fall in pitch occurs all at once on the last two syllables of the stanza (Rycroft 1960).

Catathesis in Greek

In the Delphic hymns, it is typical for a major phrase to have its highest pitch on the first lexical nongrave accent, after which the pitch of the peaks and the valleys falls all the way to the end of the major phrase. When proper names are excluded, out of all the major phrases in the two hymns in which the setting of the first lexical acute or circumflex is preserved, that pitch is the highest in the phrase 71% of the time. At the beginning of the next major phrase, the pitch level is reset, often somewhat lower in successive major phrases within the same periodic sentence, so that periodic sentences often consist of hierarchically structured downtrend domains. A simple and well preserved example of downtrend within a major phrase is the clause beginning with proleptic συνόμαιμον in ME 9.15.

ME 9.15

Ath. 3

The major prerequisite for a controlled and unbiased test of the claims made in the preceding paragraph is an explicit specification of the domain of downtrends in syntactic terms, for it would obviously be circular to define the domains by the points at which there occurs a rise from one accentual peak to the next. For the present, only the minimal assumption is made that the beginnings and ends of downtrend domains coincide with the beginings and ends of the simple sentence, of finite clauses such as final clauses, relative clauses, coordinate clauses with connective particles like δέ, καί, and of complex branching participial phrases; infinitive phrases do not occur in the hymns. Minor phrase initial boost (p. 403) is disregarded at this stage of the analysis, as is the possibility that more than one downtrend domain may occur within the syntactic structures specified. Consequently, the resulting tests will be conservative and biased against the hypothesis that the musical settings respect linguistic downtrends, since any instances of domain internal pitch reset will be counted as exceptions to downtrend.

The first test of downtrends in the hymns involves calculating the mean interval between the accentual peaks of acute and circumflex syllables in pairs of immediately successive words within the domain as just defined. Since nonlexical words and proper names have special accentual properties, they are excluded from the test. These mean intervals, denoted P_1P_2 are reported separately for *Ath.* and *Lim.* in Table 9.3. Each hymn shows a statistically significant tendency for the accentual peak to fall from the first to the second of two lexical words in immediate succession. The difference between the mean falls in the two hymns is not significant, and the grand mean is just a little over a semitone.

Downtrend can also be observed in the pitch valleys of successive lexical words within the above syntactically specified domain. The corresponding means for the interval between the lowest postpeak pitches of successive words, denoted V_1V_2, are given in Table 9.4, which uses the same sampling criteria as for Table 9.3, but excluding word pairs the last of which is final in its clause, so as not to incorporate any contribution from terminal fall. In neither hymn is the mean interval between successive valleys significantly less than zero. The means do not differ between the two hymns. The difference between the grand mean, 0.41, and zero is just at the 0.05 level of significance ($t = 1.69$, $df = 39$). The valley to valley grand mean is also not significantly different from the peak to peak grand mean, but especially in view of the data from *Lim.* it seems that the tendency for the pitch of successive valleys to fall is not so strong as for successive peaks. In other words, the topline probably fell more steeply than the bottomline.

Data on preaccentual Mid tones in two successive fully accented lexical words, excluding proper names, are much less extensive than for

TABLE 9.3

Mean interval in tones
between successive accentual peaks

Ath.	*Lim.*
$P_1P_2 = 0.44$	$P_1P_2 = 0.60$
$s = 1.18$	$s = 1.27$
$P_1P_2 > 0$: $t = 1.81$, $df = 23$	$P_1P_2 > 0$: $t = 2.33$, $df = 23$
$p < 0.05$	$p < 0.025$

TABLE 9.4

Mean interval in tones
between pitch valleys in successive words

Ath.	Lim.
$V_1V_2 = 0.57$	$V_1V_2 = 0.24$
$s = 1.39$	$s = 1.66$
$V_1V_2 > 0$: $t = 1.06$, $df = 19$	$V_1V_2 > 0$: $t = 0.62$, $df = 18$
$p > 0.05$	$p > 0.25$

accentual peaks and valleys, so that a test for preaccentual Mid tones similar to that presented above for peaks and valleys would be more subject to statistical noise. Nevertheless, the mean difference between the pitches of the lowest tones of the immediately prepeak syllables of two successive lexical words is significantly greater than zero. So it may be concluded that catathesis lowers all the pitches of a word following a full accent, initial Mid tones as well as accentual peaks and valleys.

As noted above, catathesis does not merely lower pitch levels but also progressively compresses the range of accentual excursions; the peak to valley measurements will be smaller farther into a catathesis domain than at the beginning. This effect of catathesis is most clearly demonstrated by comparing the maximum peak to valley interval for lexical words excluding proper names which stand in absolute initial position in downtrend domains with the corresponding interval for lexical words that follow them immediately with no intervening accent of any kind. The beginnings of melodic sections are excluded from this test, so as not to incorporate any purely musical effect associated with this position. The mean peak to valley intervals in tones for the first (P_1V_1) and the second (P_2V_2) fully accented nongrave word of the domain are reported in Table 9.5. The mean peak to valley excursion for domain initial lexical words is over twice as great as the mean for lexical words

TABLE 9.5

Compression of peak to valley interval
in catathesis domain

$P_1V_1 = 2.31$	$P_2V_2 = 1.06$
$s = 1.60$	$s = 0.86$
$P_1V_1 > P_2V_2$: $t = 2.01$, $df = 19$	
$p < 0.05$	

which immediately follow them. As the *t*-test shows, a difference this great or greater has less than one chance in twenty of arising at random. The compression effect holds true also when the accentual fall is measured from the peak to the Low of the following syllable or of the second mora of the circumflex if set to a melism, that is when the additional pitch fall over the final syllable of proparoxytones and properispomena with melisms is discounted. The mean rise to the accentual peak shows a parallel difference. All the preserved words in question have only one unaccented syllable preceding the accentual peak. The mean rise for lexical words in absolute initial position is 1.61 tones, but the mean rise for an immediately following lexical word is 0.64 tones. Since there are fewer preserved cases of rise to accentual peaks, this difference cannot be shown to be statistically significant.

The preserved data are such that when measurements are extended to the third fully accented lexical word of a string uninterrupted by grave and nonlexical accents, there is evidence for a chaining effect of lowering but not of compression: the lowering but not the compression of accentual excursions after n uninterrupted full accents is greater than after $n - 1$ for $n \geq 3$. One factor influencing this result may be reset between minor phrases, which was analyzed at the end of Chapter 8.

It is the High-Low movement of the acute or circumflex that triggers catathesis. The effect of catathesis in a pair of trisyllabic words having their accent on the medial syllable may be represented schematically as in Figure 9.9. C_H represents the effect of catathesis in lowering the peaks, C_L its effect in lowering the valleys, and C_U the word internal effect of lowering the postpeak valley relative to the word initial unaccented syllable. The fall from the first accentual High tone H_1 triggers a lowering of the tones to the right of H_1. The result is the catathesis factor $C_H = H_1 - H_2$ tones for accentual peaks and $C_L = L_1 - L_2$ tones for valleys. Since $C_H > C_L$, the effect will be to compress the interval of pitch excursion in the second word by $C_H - C_L$ tones. Catathesis can be

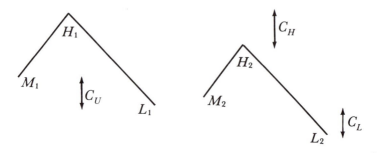

FIGURE 9.9
Schema for catathesis in Greek

regarded as applying within the High-Low sequence of the accent. This interpretation has the advantage of explaining, at least in large part, why preaccentual syllables appear as Mid tones. Both the pre- and the postaccentual syllables (or morae) may be regarded as phonologically Low toned. Catathesis lowers the postaccentual Low by the factor C_U, making the preaccentual syllable seem to be a Mid tone in relation to it: $M = L + C_U$.

Effect of the grave on catathesis

The grave accent, particularly in nonlexical words, behaves quite differently from the acute and circumflex accents of lexical words in regard to catathesis. The results presented in Table 4.6 established that the grave accent has a lower pitch than the subsequent nongrave accent; this means that the grave does not trigger catathetic lowering; only the High-Low movement of full accents, the acute and the circumflex, causes such lowering. Less trivially, the grave also blocks the lowering effect of catathesis that would be expected to be caused by a High-Low accentual movement in the word preceding the grave. In the Delphic hymns, even within a downtrend domain, the tendency is for the pitch of accentual peaks not to fall if a grave intervenes between them. Instances of rise (ME 9.16) and level accentual peaks (ME 9.17) in pairs of lexical words separated by a grave outweigh cases of pitch fall, which are regular when no grave intervenes (ME 9.18–19). Table 9.6 compares the mean interval between the accentual peaks of fully accented High-Low pairs of words

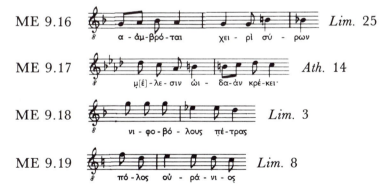

in immediate succession within the major phrase, A_1A_2, and the corresponding mean in pairs separated by a grave, A_1gA_2, in the Delphic hymns. Both lexical and nonlexical graves are included in the test; proper names are excluded from the peak to peak measurements. The results of the comparison confirm the hypothesis that an intervening grave blocks downtrend. In fact, this accentual configuration is associated with a mean rise of a semitone between the first and second peaks of the two full

TABLE 9.6

Mean interval in tones between successive peaks
of full accents without and with an intervening grave

A_1A_2	A_1gA_2
$P_1P_2 = -0.52$ (fall)	$P_1gP_2 = +0.52$ (rise)
$s = 1.22$	$s = 2.49$

$P_1P_2 < P_1gP_2$: $t = 1.99$, $df = 57$
$p < 0.05$

accents. Although not all possible effects of focus are excluded from Table 9.6, the overall mean rise cannot be entirely reduced to a reflex of focus. Further, it appears that the grave accent of nonlexical words such as αἳ, δὲ, ἐπὶ, σὺ, has a stronger blocking effect on catathesis than the grave of lexical words such as χειρὶ. When a nonlexical grave separates two fully accented lexical words, the peak of the second accent averages 0.83 tones higher than the peak of the first, but when a lexical grave intervenes the second peak is only 0.10 tones higher than the first. This difference includes a substantial contribution from minor phrase initial boost. It is instructive also to compare these results with the observed mean falling interval between the first and third accentual peaks in strings of three uninterrupted, fully accented lexicals excluding proper names (ME 9.20), where $P_1P_3 = 1.33$ ($s = 1.57$, $df = 14$). This fall of one and a third

ME 9.20

γλαυ - κα - [ᾶ]ς   ἑ - λαΐ - ας   θι - γου - οῦφ'   Lim. 6

tones crossing a full lexical accent is a significant lowering as compared to the rise of 0.10 tones crossing a lexical grave ($t = 1.75$, $df = 18$, $p < 0.05$). This difference between full and grave lexical accents cannot be ascribed to a difference in syntactic structure: the data sets for both the sequence of second plus third fully accented lexical and the sequence of grave lexical plus fully accented lexical consist primarily of noun plus modifier or complement plus verb in either order; nor can the difference be ascribed to the effects of focus.

The sample is too small to make a reliable inference concerning the effect of an intervening grave on the interval between the valleys in successive High-Low word pairs, since damage to the inscriptions disproportionately affects the settings of the postpeak valleys in these accentual configurations. Nevertheless, it may be noted that an intervening grave seems to reduce the mean fall between successive valleys to zero, as compared to the mean fall of 0.41 tones between the valleys of immediately successive peak-valley pairs. It is possible, therefore, that the major effect of an intervening grave is on the topline, with a smaller effect on the bottomline slope.

Parallel to its blocking effect on the catathetic lowering of accentual peaks, we would also expect the grave accent to have an inhibiting effect on catathetic compression of peak to valley excursions within words, and this is certainly true of the grave accent of nonlexical words. Inhibition of catathetic compression by the nonlexical grave can most conveniently be tested by measuring the immediate postaccentual fall, that is the interval from the accentual peak to the Low of the following syllable or of the second mora for a circumflex set to a melism; only lexical words which are not proper names and which do not stand in final position are included in the test. The mean of this interval for words preceded by the grave of a nonlexical word, gHL_1, is compared with the mean for words preceded by a lexical acute or circumflex, AHL_1, in Table 9.7. The mean pitch fall from the accentual peak to the first Low following it is over a semitone greater when a nonlexical grave precedes than when a lexical full accent precedes. As the t-test shows, this difference is statistically significant. The inhibition of catathetic compression by nonlexical graves is not caused by averaging in the effect of proclitic graves such as ἀνά, ἐπί, and ἠδέ: when proclitic graves are excluded, gHL_1 increases to 1.92 tones. In contrast to the grave of nonlexical words, the grave of lexical words has no demonstrable effect on catathetic compression: the mean when a lexical grave (G) precedes, GHL_1, is 1.06, which is indistinguishable from $AHL_1 = 1.02$.

The general inhibiting effect of the nonlexical grave on catathetic compression established in Table 9.7 can be articulated into two components, as was the case with catathetic lowering. In the first place, nonlexical graves do not themselves trigger catathesis. This can be seen by

TABLE 9.7

Interval in tones of postaccentual pitch fall
with and without preceding nonlexical grave

Nonlexical grave precedes	Lexical full accent precedes
$gHL_1 = 1.69$	$AHL_1 = 1.02$
$s = 1.59$	$s = 0.95$
$gHL_1 > AHL_1$: $t = 2.00$, $df = 60$	
$p \approx 0.025$	

comparing the mean interval from the accentual peak to the first following Low for lexical words excluding proper names which are preceded by just one lexical word having an acute or circumflex at the beginning of downtrend domains, $[AHL_1$, with the mean for the same interval in lexicals preceded by one or two nonlexicals bearing the grave likewise at the beginning of downtrend domains, $[(g)gHL_1$: $[AHL_1 = 1.06$ but $[(g)gHL_1 = 2.01$. The difference is nearly a whole tone, and the mean for lexicals preceded by nonlexical graves is only slightly less than the mean for the total peak to valley interval of lexical words in absolute domain initial position, which is 2.31 (see Table 9.5). So it may be concluded that the High-Low movement of full accents is required to trigger catathetic compression. Secondly, not only do nonlexical graves fail themselves to trigger catathetic compression, they also actually block the compression that a preceding full lexical accent would trigger in the absence of an intervening grave. In the string consisting of fully accented lexical plus nonlexical grave plus fully accented lexical, the mean HL_1 for the second lexical is 1.90, which is significantly greater than the mean $AHL_1 = 1.02$ from Table 9.7 ($t = 1.89$, $df = 49$, $p < 0.05$).

The effect of the grave accent on catathesis in a string consisting of trisyllabic paroxytone plus disyllabic grave plus trisyllabic paroxytone words may be represented schematically as in Figure 9.10. (The figure is not drawn to scale and no attempt is made to reproduce the varying steepness among the slopes of the lines.) Tones with a subscript 2 represent the pitches that the second trisyllabic word would have had if no grave word intervened; tones with a suprascript + represent the higher pitches occasioned by the intervening grave word. The initial unaccented syllable of the second trisyllabic word is represented as slightly higher than the grave, since it is on the average a little less than a quarter tone higher, although it is frequently set to the same pitch as the grave.

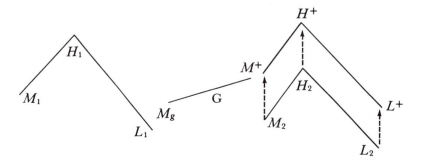

FIGURE 9.10
Schema for the effect of the grave accent on catathesis in Greek

The grave does not trigger catathesis because it is not a full accent; it lacks the fall to a Low tone in the same word. More problematic is why the grave seems to block the effect of catathesis that a preceding accentual High-Low movement would be expected to have, and in fact reverses the movement from downtrend to uptrend. The simplest hypothesis is that, at least under certain circumstances, a word bearing the grave accent combines with a following fully accented word in the same downtrend domain to form a single accentual trajectory. Such a process would parallel the tendency in Japanese for an unaccented word, that is a word with no High-Low fall, to be merged into a single minor phrase with the word following it. The hypothesis of a single accentual trajectory would explain why an initial, unaccented syllable of a following lexical word is almost never lower than the preceding grave, but, as just noted, on the average a quarter of a tone higher. The rising trajectory counting from the first syllable of the grave word obviously covers more syllables and morae than would be the case if there were no grave word, and the normal rising trajectory is augmented by the additional rise from the valley of the preceding accented word to the grave.

It was noted above that nonlexical graves boost the following accentual peak to a greater degree than lexical graves. Furthermore, all the nonlexical graves in the grave plus lexical strings whose pitches are preserved in the Delphic hymns are prepositives, although only a minority are proclitics, with the single exception of δὲ, which may cohere bidirectionally (p. 323) since it occasionally stands before Hermann's bridge. So the nonlexical grave words in the dataset are just those that would be expected to enter into phonological processes with a following word. Since on average lexical grave words also block downtrend to some extent, they too apparently permit the formation of a single accentual trajectory. This hypothesis is somewhat corroborated by the observation that eight of the nine preserved cases with lexical grave involve the more cohesive syntactic structures that, on the evidence of data presented in Chapter 6, promote sandhi processes, namely phrases consisting of noun and modifier (in either order) or of object and verb.

Reset

If domain initial catathesis reset is respected in the musical settings, the interval between the (nongrave) accentual peak of the last word of a major phrase (here defined conservatively as a finite clause or a complex participial phrase) and the accentual peak of the first word of a subsequent major phrase within a periodic sentence should show a significant tendency to rise, in contrast to the established tendency for the interval between two contiguous accentual peaks to fall within the major phrase.

TABLE 9.8

Rising peak to peak interval in tones
across major phrase boundary

$$P_f][P_i = -1.05$$
$$s = 2.38$$

$$P_f][P_i < 0: \ t = 1.97, \ df = 19$$
$$p < 0.05$$

The test of this effect is limited to lexical words, but in order to obtain an adequate sample size proper names are included; this does not bias the test in favour of the hypothesis, since five of the six proper names occur at the end of the first domain rather than at the beginning of the second; instances in which two lexical words are separated by one or more nonlexical words are included; instances involving the ends of periodic sentences and melodic sections are, of course, excluded. The mean observed interval in tones between the major phrase final and major phrase initial peaks, $P_f][P_i$, the standard deviation and the relevant test statistics are reported in Table 9.8. The results confirm the hypothesis that the pitch of the first lexical acute or circumflex accent in a major phrase is reset higher than the acute or circumflex at the end of the preceding major phrase. Out of the twenty cases in the dataset, only three show a falling peak to peak interval: two of them fall by only a semitone, and the third (ME 9.21) with a fall of an octave is a special case probably

ME 9.21  Lim. 22

reflecting deaccentuation of an elided imperative, since loss of prosodic autonomy in elided imperatives is indicated by metrical data (p. 344); if this last case is excluded as an outlier, the mean interval of reset greatly increases.

The musical settings provide examples of catathesis reset at the sorts of major phrase boundary within sentences established by the evidence of ἄν and parentheticals above. Reset is particularly clearly evidenced with nonattributive participial phrases in the Delphic hymns. When the participial phrase precedes the main verb and its arguments and adjuncts, reset occurs immediately after the participial phrase, as in ME 9.22 where

ME 9.22

λι - γὺ δὲ λω - το-ὸς βρέ-μων   α - εἰ - όλ - οι-οις

μ[έ] - λε - σιν ὠι - δα-ὰν κρέ-κει·   Ath. 14

there is a rise of a semitone from the peak of the phrase final participle to the peak of *αἰόλοις*, the modifier of the instrument adjunct of the main verb. Conversely, when the nonattributive participial phrase follows the main clause of its sentence, reset occurs at the beginning of the participial phrase, as at ME 9.23 where there is a rise of three tones from the peak

ME 9.23

of the direct object *ὄπα* of the preceding main verb to the peak of the participle. Parenthetical vocatives, if short, do not show reset; rather, pitch continues to fall from the preceding word, as at ME 9.24. Longer, predicative, vocative phrases, however, do trigger catathesis reset, as at ME 9.25. The two types cooccur in ME 9.26, where the imperative

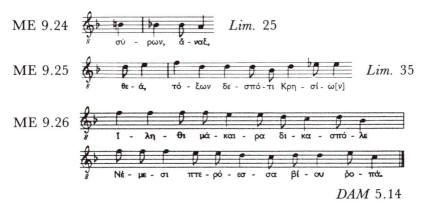

ME 9.24

ME 9.25

ME 9.26

DAM 5.14

verb and the first vocative phrase form one catathesis domain, after which catathesis is reset on the proper name, from which the accentual peaks of the following epithets fall, first by a semitone, then by a tone and a tone again.

Loss of classical system of pitch accent catathesis

The later musical documents offer little or no evidence for catathesis, a fact that is evidently related to the progressive disintegration of the structure of the pitch accent system of Classical Greek and sensitivity to it in musical settings. It is not evidence for the absence of any form of downtrend in the later language. In the Delphic hymns, the mean interval between the pitch peaks of full accents in successive lexical words internal to the major phrase is a clearly falling one of about a semitone; within the minor phrase, the interval of fall is even greater, 1.12 tones. In contrast, in the Hymn to Nemesis *DAM* 5, the major phrase internal peak to peak interval is only 0.09 tones, and the mean including major phrase final pairs is nearly identical. In the Christian hymn *DAM* 34, the mean including major phrase final pairs is only 0.04 tones. The other documents have too few pairs of lexical accents preserved for reliable evidence. Within the minor phrase, however, the later documents continue to reflect catathesis, although to a considerably reduced extent. In the Hymn to Nemesis, the average interval between the peaks of contiguous lexical words (not proper names) in all types of minor phonological phrases is a fall of 0.7 tones. In the Christian hymn, the interval between successive accentual peaks is still sensitive to catathesis within the minor phrase. Between the sister nodes of binarily branching structures (all of which consist of noun plus adjective in either order), that is within putative prosodic minor phrases, there are five instances of peak to peak pitch fall and only one instance of a rise, on the theonym χἄγιον πνεῦμα, which can be explained as a focus pitch obtrusion. By comparison, between words that are not sister nodes of binarily branching phrases there are six cases of peak to peak rise or level tone and only one fall. The difference (fall:rise = 5:1 versus 1:6) is statistically significant ($p = 0.0251$). No such correlation obtains in the Hymn to Nemesis.

Sentence type

Questions (Ultan 1969) can be classified into three groups according to the type of response expected: yes–no questions (ἄρα...), information questions containing a question word (τίς, ποῦ, etc.), and alternative questions (πότερον... ἤ...). Various syntactic and lexical devices are commonly used to indicate a question. For instance, the normal declarative order of constituents can be inverted in a question; and question words tend to occupy the initial position in the sentence or the focus position. All languages have question words, and many use interrogative particles or affixes such as ἄρα and Latin -ne either only in yes–no questions or in all types of questions. Interrogative particles tend to occur at the beginning or end of a question or enclitic to the initial constituent. Although intonation is the normal phonological device for indicating a question, a few languages have idiosyncratic features such as final glottalization or voicing. In some languages, questions can differ from statements in overall duration; they are ten percent shorter in Hausa (Lindau 1985). In Japanese, the final vowel of a yes–no question without a question particle shows significant lengthening, probably to accommodate interrogative rising pitch (Nishinuma 1979); similarly, in Serbocroatian questions tend to have greater final lengthening than declarations (Lehiste et al. 1986). In some West African tone languages, questions are signalled by High or Low tone that is added to or replaces the last tone; this phenomenon arises when sentence final question morphemes lose their segmental features (Williamson 1979).

In almost all languages some form of raised pitch is associated with at least some types of questions (Hermann 1942; Ultan 1969). This distinction between the intonation of questions and that of statements seems to rest on the grammaticalization of the association of rising pitch with an attitude of incompleteness, suspension and doubt and of falling pitch with an attitude of finality and conclusiveness. The precise nature of the pitch raising in questions varies from one language to another. For instance, the higher pitch may be on the last syllable or towards the end of the question, or, as in Finnish, at the beginning of the question (Lehtinen 1964), or starting with the focused word or the first stressed syllable (Norlin 1989), or on a question word irrespective of its position in the sentence; it may or may not be followed by a fall in pitch, and the register or absolute pitch of questions may be higher than that of statements. Question words may be distinguished from homophonous indefinites by High tone only, as in Korean *nuku* 'who?/someone,' *əti* 'where?/somewhere' (Cho 1990). In tone languages, downtrends can be partially or totally eliminated in questions, as in Hausa (Lindau 1985) and Chinese (Gårding 1987; Poser 1985). The last high tone is also raised in Hausa. Surprised interrogation in Luganda involves lengthening of the final vowel and a terminal rise on the added mora (Lindsey 1985). In Zulu, a declaration can be changed into a question (or into a sarcastic declaration meaning the opposite of the overt message) merely by tonal modification, with no syntactic or lexical change (Doke 1926): therefore, even in a tone language interrogation can be signalled by intonation alone. In the pitch accent language Japanese, a sharp rise in pitch was found on final syllables in yes–no questions, as opposed to the normal terminal fall in declarative utterances (Poser 1985), and, perhaps as a reflex of an attitudinal difference, in general women tended to use pitch rise to mark questions more than men (Oishi in Poser 1985). Question intonation in Hausa and Japanese is illustrated in Figures 9.11–12.

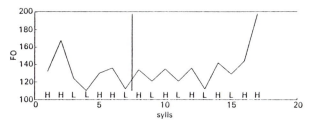

Yaa aikàa wà Maanii / làabaarìn wannàn yaaròn alàramma?

FIGURE 9.11
Question version of Hausa sentence in Figure 9.8 (from Inkelas et al. 1990)

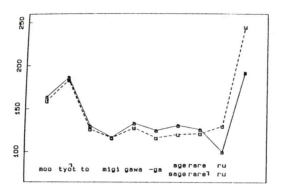

FIGURE 9.12
Question in Japanese. Dashed line: unaccented verb.
Solid line: accented verb (from Pierrehumbert et al. 1988)

While almost all languages have either rising pitch or some form of higher pitch in yes–no questions, question word questions are not so consistently associated with rising pitch; in one sample (Bolinger 1978) 14 out of 17 languages had the same kind of terminal pitch fall in question word questions as in statements. A pitch rise in questions containing a question word can also be optional in a language; or the pitch slope may be somewhere between that of statements and that of yes–no questions. Such is the case in Hausa, where downdrift is found in question word questions with alternating High and Low tones, but the slope is less than that in statements and raising of the last High tone is less common than in yes–no questions.

Genuine commands that call for immediate obedience are associated with falling pitch in many languages, such as English, Japanese (Abe 1955) and Swahili (Ashton 1947). Exclamations in Japanese have rising pitch (Sakiyama 1981); in some West African tone languages, they are indicated by cancellation of downdrift, by the raising of all tones or of the High tones only, or by the exaggeration of tones, that is the raising of High tones and the lowering of Low tones, as in Igbo (Williamson 1979). Exaggerated pitch movements are found in exclamatory particles like *kalau* 'extremely' in Hausa (Meyers 1976; Inkelas et al. 1990). A wider pitch range and increased duration are used to signal surprise, wonder and incredulity in various languages including English and German.

There is direct evidence for prosodic cues distinguishing statements, questions and commands in Greek from two passages in Aristotle's *Poetics*, in which it is stated that these categories are distinguished in ὑποκριτική (1456b.10) and that the pronunciation of the same utterance is distinguished according as it is a question or a command (1457a.21). High tone on the question word in Greek is indicated by the fact that it is only in the interrogatives τίς, τί that a final acute remains unchanged rather than turning into a grave within the phrase: πᾶσα λέξις ὀξύτονος ἐν τῇ συνεπείᾳ... κοιμίζει τὴν ὀξεῖαν εἰς βαρεῖαν, χωρὶς τοῦ τίς ἐρωτηματικοῦ Choeroboscus (scholia on Dionysius Thrax 127.32 Hilgard). The retention of the acute is illustrated in ME 9.27, where the pitch of the acute on τίς is a whole tone higher than that on the following word νόστος.

ME 9.27   τίς νόσ - τος   *DAM* 39.8

10 | Topic and Focus

Topic and focus are important factors in prosodic analysis, since they can affect both the relative prosodic prominence of individual constituents and their phonological phrasing. The prosodic differentiation of topic and focus makes a significant contribution to the efficiency with which the hearer interprets the information conveyed by a sentence; in one study, focusing new information and not focusing old information resulted in shorter comprehension times than vice versa (Bock et al. 1983). Topic and focus have antecedents in the "psychological subject and predicate" of nineteenth-century studies (Weil 1878; Paul 1909) and in the "theme and rheme" of the Prague school and other functional theories (Mathesius 1928; Firbas 1964, 1966; Halliday 1967). Although they are pragmatic categories related to the way information is classified and organized in discourse, in some cases they can affect the cognitive meaning of a sentence as well as its informational content. For example, the referent of the anaphoric pronoun in "John hit Peter and then he/HE hit Bill." varies according as the pronoun is focused or not: unfocused *he* is coreferential with John, focused *he* is coreferential with Peter (Oehrle 1981; Reinhart 1982).

Topic

Topic (Vallduví 1992; Chafe 1976; Li et al. 1976; Reinhart 1982; Gundel 1974, 1987; Dooley 1982; Hannay 1985) is best understood as the entity about which the sentence is designed to convey information. In most discourse contexts, a sentence like "Prof. Jones is very fond of red wine" will be interpreted as conveying information about Prof. Jones. On the analogy of a paper filing system (Vallduví 1992), the topic is the name on the file in which the new information is to be placed. The speaker encodes the topic so that the hearer knows which file to retrieve or activate for the addition or updating of information. The referential status of an expression indicates whether a file already exists for the entity in question either from the hearer's pre-existing knowledge or from anterior stages of the discourse, and use of a pronoun indicates that the file is currently active. Although a single sentence can sometimes require the hearer simultaneously to create a new file and store information in it, topics normally activate already existing files. This is why topics often involve old or predictable information either already established or entailed by the discourse or shared among the interlocutors in their immediate consciousness and attention. Proper names, like *Prof. Jones* in the example above, have readily identifiable referents and so make excellent topics. Nongeneric indefinite noun phrases make poor topics: *"A cat, it's under the table" is an example of an indefinite left dislocated topic. A specific indefinite can occur as a topic if it is anchored in something definite and identifiable to the interlocutors: "A cat under the table down there, they gave it the leftover fish" (Gundel 1985). According to the understanding of topic outlined above, the status of information as new or old is not the same thing as its topicality, and the former does not define the latter. The topic can involve new information, as just noted, and not all old information need be topical. For instance, the topic marking particle *wa* in Japanese has the function of creating, maintaining and retrieving a discourse topic (Uyeno 1987). In the narrative sequence, "A child came walking. There came a dog running. And then the dog bit the child," if the third sentence is viewed as a third discrete event of a sequence, *wa* is not used to mark *dog* even though it is old information, but if the third sentence is viewed as asserting additional information about the previously mentioned dog, then *wa* is used (Shibatani 1990).

In the most usual type of topic situation, the topic is first established and then an assertion is made about it. In many languages, including English, the topic tends to be encoded as the subject. In such languages, object topics can be avoided by passivization or sometimes by lexical choice. "As for Jack, Mary gave him a book" can be rephrased "As for Jack, he was given a book by Mary" or "As for Jack, he received a book from Mary." One reason why passivization may be less used in spoken English than in written English is that in the former the phonology differentiates topic and focus. The term topic as used here refers to the sentence topic. Longer segments of discourse, such as the paragraph or the narrative, can also have topics, which may be called discourse topics or macrotopics. The topic of any sentence within the longer discourse structure may or may not be identical to the discourse topic.

Focus

Focus (Rochemont 1986; Culicover et al. 1983; Dik et al. 1981; Rochemont et al. 1990; Huck et al. 1990; Vallduví 1992) is best understood as a parameter of informational salience. Information can be accorded salient status in a sentence for a variety of different informational reasons. But since the linguistic, and particularly the prosodic, implementation of the different categories tends to be in terms of different degrees of the same property, it is reasonable to assume that the different categories share some common property at the informational level also; otherwise their prosodic relationship would be coincidental. At the low end of the parameter, focus is simply the new information the sentence is designed to convey, the speaker's contribution to the ongoing progression of the conversation. The new information is neutrally provided by the speaker for inclusion in the file; this may be termed informational focus. In other cases, the information provided serves to correct information already in the file. When there is overt correction of a previous assertion or supposition of the hearer, this may be termed counterassertive focus, as in "No, it's RED wine that Prof. Jones is very fond of." In yet another type of focus, namely contrastive focus, a variable is specifically contrasted with another potentially applicable variable without counterassertion, as in "Prof. Jones likes RED wine better than WHITE wine." Sometimes the contrast is between the entities specified and all other potentially applicable entities; this is termed exhaustive listing focus, as in "It's CHIANTI that Prof. Jones is very fond of." Even when exhaustive listing is not linguistically encoded, it can be conversationally implied by simple informational focus, as in "Prof. Jones worked on Tacitus today," which is usually taken to imply that he did not work on anything else. Presentational focus, as its name suggests, occurs in sentences like "Here comes the bride." Finally, according to the prevalent opinion, interrogative words are focused, although they need not be the only focused item in the sentence; interrogative words can ask for simple information, for contrastive information or for exhaustive listing.

The scope of focus varies from one sentence to another. When most or all of the material in the sentence is new information and so is focused, focus is said to have broad scope (Gundel 1985), as sometimes in answers to the question "What happened?" or in out-of-the-blue remarks. In a sentence like "A dog bit a cat," about the only information that could qualify as topical is the implied spatiotemporal context ("in the park yesterday") in the absence of which events are difficult to interpret. In such sentences, choice of the subject, which is the grammatical topic and agent, can be governed by factors such as empathy or even proximity of a participant to the speaker. Broad scope focus on the complete sentence is not very common in transitive sentences in ordinary conversational speech, which prefers to introduce new information at the rate of one item per clause and to assign it to the object (du Bois 1987). Narrow scope focus applies to one or more constituents or subconstituents of the sentence; items with narrow scope focus are set in capital letters in some of the examples above.

It is not uncommon to find some degree of terminological confusion between topic and focus in the literature. This is probably because languages often exploit rather similar highlighting strategies to implement marked topic and focus, and because topic and focus are not mutually exclusive. For instance, it may be pragmatically appropriate to highlight what would otherwise be background information, either to direct the listener's attention more strongly to the topic status of an expression, or because the topic is itself focused, as when it is newly introduced into the discourse, thereby contrasting with the previous topic, or reactivated after a lapse, or when it is contrastive with other material in the immediate discourse context (Ward 1988).

Informational articulation

It is a common intuition that simple sentences are articulated into complementary informational segments, but the exact structure of such an articulation is quite problematic (C. Smith 1991; Vallduví 1992). On a binary articulation, focus, or more precisely its informational component, corresponds to the new information contributed by the sentence and topic to the subject about which the information is supplied. It would follow that when the subject is the topic, the whole verb phrase is a broad scope focus, and when the subject is the (only) focus, the whole verb phrase is a broad scope topic. The idea of a broad scope topic implies, on the filing analogy, that information is not necessarily filed under individual entities prototypically corresponding to noun phrases, but that files can represent whole situations minus a single (narrow focus) item of information. This problem is avoided by positing two separate and potentially overlapping articulations of the sentence into topic versus comment and focus versus presupposition respectively. For instance, in a sentence such as "Prof. Jones works on Tacitus," *works* is old information since the hearer presumably knows that professors work on something. So on the first articulation *Prof. Jones* is seen as the topical entity and *works on Tacitus* as the comment; and on the second articulation *Prof. Jones works* is seen as presupposition and *on Tacitus* as focus. In a third approach, topic and focus (now including contrastive focus) are independent features in a single articulation that combines the topic and focus articulations; in addition to being either topical and unfocused or untopical and focused, constituents can be topical and focused, like contrastive topics, or untopical and unfocused, like *works* in the above example; *works* is included in the sentence not because it is either topic or focus but because nonfragmentary sentences require certain material to be present if they are to be grammatical and easily interpreted.

Topic and focus markers

For the specific marking of topic and focus in nonneutral or nondefault sentences, different languages use different combinations of devices — phonology; morphology, affixes and particles; word order; special constructions. Different devices cooccur in the same language to express different types and degrees of topic and focus. For instance, Aghem (Cameroon: Watters 1979; Dik et al. 1981) uses word order, verb morphology, particles and cleft construction to distinguish unmarked sentences, informational focus, counterassertive focus and exhaustive listing, and to distinguish broad scope and narrow scope focus.

Verbal morphology and particles

Verbal morphology is exploited to differentiate neutral sentences from sentences with a focused constituent in Noni (Cameroon: Hyman 1981b) and Aghem; in Efik (de Jong 1981), it is used to indicate whether it is a preverbal or a postverbal constituent that is focused and to distinguish informational and contrastive focus. In Bemba (Tanzania: Givon 1972), verbal morphology signals the scope of focus, wide scope on the whole verb phrase and narrow scope on the complement of the verb only. English exploits the dummy auxiliary *do* for counterassertive focus. In Wambon (Irian Jaya: de Vries 1985), verbal suffixes are used to indicate whether the subject of the following clause will or will not involve a different topic already established in the discourse. Use of particles, such as the topic particle *wa* in Japanese and *nɨn* in Korean, and the focus particle *ni* in Yoruba and *tar* in Marathi, is widespread. In a sample of thirty languages from across the world, it was found that some languages have only topic markers, some only focus markers, some both and some neither (Gundel 1987). Focus markers fall into two classes, those that mark any constituent including the whole sentence and those that mark only narrow nominal focus (Gundel 1987). Navajo (Arizona: Schauber 1978; Barss et al. 1989) has focus particles like *ga'* (focus), *hanii* (counterassertive negative focus), *ndi* 'even.' Various Greek particles involve focus marking, including *γε, δή, μέν, μήν*.

Word order

Some languages assign a fixed position in the word order of their sentences to focus and/or topic. New or contrastive topics tend to go first in languages of all types; in Subject-Verb-Object and Subject-Object-Verb languages, other topics tend to occupy the subject slot and focus the object slot; languages in which the verb precedes the subject prefer focus to precede topic (Herring 1990). Not only is the topic correlated with the subject, which is not surprising since the subject is a grammatical topic, but focus is correlated with the object; this is presumably because, especially in the absence of adjuncts, the object often carries the nucleus of new information (Harlig et al. 1988; Kim 1988). Hungarian (Kenesei 1986; Kiss 1987; Moravcsik 1990) provides a good illustration of the use of word order in pragmatically nonneutral sentences. In Hungarian, the topic is sentence initial and the focus preverbal, or more precisely prepredicate; the interaction of these two slots and focus accent implements a variety of pragmatic distinctions (the English constructional translations are more marked than the originals; the macron is used for vowel length and the acute for focus accent): "Jānos Máriāt szereti" 'As for John, it is Mary he loves'; "Jānos Máriāt széreti" 'As for John, as for Mary, he loves her'; "Máriāt János szereti" 'As for Mary, it is John who loves her'; "Máriāt széreti Jānos" 'As for Mary, John loves her'; "Máriāt szereti Jānos" 'It is Mary that John loves'; and so on (Kiss 1987).

Word order variation can be pragmatically exploited not only in languages with comparatively free word order but also in languages with quite fixed word order like English. This feature ranges parametrically from regular and systematic variation to highly marked reordering with low text frequency. In Podoko (Cameroon: Jarvis 1991), a Verb-Subject-Object language, every main clause with an imperfective transitive verb has a postverbal focus position; if there are no focus distinctions in the clause, the object is placed in the focus slot. On the other hand, in Vute (Cameroon: Thwing et al. 1987), focus is expressed by verbal morphology and sentential particles, and word order is not used apart from some cleftlike constructions. Presentational sentences are particularly associated with Subject-Verb inversion, as in Guaraní (Brazil: Dooley 1982) and in the English socalled stylistic inversions of the type "On the platform sat Prof. Jones." In Navajo, Subject-Object inversion in sentences in which both arguments are human is used to topicalize the object (Barss et al. 1989). Swahili has Subject-Verb-Object order for neutral sentences, Verb-Object-Subject order when the subject is emphasized. More marked is the English fronting of focused topics known as Y-movement: "Cicero I can read easily, but Tacitus I find difficult." It is reasonable to assume that the departure from unmarked word order attracts the attention of the interlocutor more efficiently to the pragmatic relations the speaker wishes to convey.

Dislocation

It is useful to distinguish simple constituent order variation from those left and right movements in which the moved argument is in some way syntactically and/or phonologically external to the main clause. Such movements are often called dislocations. The main clause may have a resumptive pronoun and the dislocated element can fail to preserve the case of the clause internal argument, as in Icelandic (Zaenen 1980). In Haya (Tanzania: Byarushengo et al. 1976; Tenenbaum 1977) there are two types of dislocation; in left dislocation, used for old or new topics, no tonally manifested phrase boundary intervenes between the dislocated material and the main clause: "Abakázi Kakúlw' óbugoló babumúha" 'The women, Kakulu, the snuff, they give it to him.' In right dislocation, which backgrounds old information in contexts such as counterassertion, there is a tonally manifested phrase boundary (#) before each right dislocated constituent: "Abubóná # Kakulw' # óbugólo" 'He sees it, Kakulu, the snuff.' In both left and right object dislocation the verb carries the object pronoun. This is not unlike the situation in Catalan, which has potentially multiple left dislocation of topics and right dislocation of unfocused untopical material; coreferential clitics on the verb mark both types, and right dislocated material is prosodically external to the main clause (Vallduví 1992). Left and right dislocated subjects with coreferential pronominal clitics occur in Genoese Italian, giving sentences like "The Catherine, she sells the fish at Genoa" and "It sells the fish at Genoa, the Catherine" respectively (Pullum 1977). In Wambon, there are two types of topicalization, a simple fronting with no following intonational boundary and a more marked construction which does have an intonational boundary. In Hungarian, contrastive topics, unlike regular topics, are phrased separately from the main clause (Kiss 1987). In Japanese, the topic phrase with *wa* is generally set off from the rest of the sentence by a major phrase boundary and so constitutes a separate catathesis domain (Poser 1985).

English makes a distinction between simple topics, as in A. "What do you think about John?" B. "John, I don't like (him)" with major phrase boundary after the topic, and focused topics (with the focus specifying the subset of a topical set), as in A. "Is there anybody you don't like?" B. "John I don't like" where, depending on its phonological length or heaviness, the topic can be phonologically integrated with the rest of the sentence (Gundel 1974; Rochemont et al. 1990). The phonological implementation of the phrase boundary after Y-moved and left dislocated constituents has been studied experimentally by comparison with the potential absence of a boundary in comparable simple sentences (O'Shaughnessy 1976; Cooper et al. 1980; Cooper et al. 1981). Some of this evidence is difficult to evaluate, since it is not always possible to factor out potentially confounding effects such as trochee shortening across phrase boundary or categorily or pragmatically motivated stress differences; and since the results are often presented as averages, it is not possible to distinguish parametric differences from variation of the presence versus the absence of a single property. However, it is clear that for many speakers, depending on other conditioning factors, left dislocated constituents and longer Y-moved constituents tend to have phrase final lengthening, pause, a somewhat steeper fall in pitch, and a continuation rise. Similar results were obtained for preposed prepositional phrases of the type "At Brockton's city park, Cher scolded the children" as compared to "The owner of the park shows gold to the children."

Clefts

Constructions like cleft ("It was Mary who found the cat") and pseudo-cleft ("What Mary found was the cat") are among the most marked instantiations of pragmatic differences. They typically involve some form of equational construction combined with a relative clause (Harries-Delisle 1978). These constructions, which are used in different discourse contexts (Hetzron 1975; Prince 1978; Gundel 1985), serve to highlight the informational content of one element in a proposition by radically separating it from backgrounded material. Pseudocleft results in more topicalization of the nonhighlighted material and is more appropriate discourse initially: "What I'm going to talk about is the trimeter" is a more appropriate opening to a lecture than *"It's the trimeter that I'm going to talk about." In *it*-clefts, the subordinate clause may contain either presupposed old information or backgrounded new information, and such information can also be partially located in an unfocused segment of the predicate, as in "It was UNDER the table that she found the cat"; the focused element may serve to exclude all other candidates (exhaustive listing: "It is only...") or a single possible alternative ("It is rather...") or merely to underscore the noteworthiness of the focused element without much thought for the exclusion of alternative candidates ("It is precisely...") (Borkin 1984). Cleft type constructions can also be used in questions: "What was it that Mary found?". In Temne (Sierra Leone: Hutchinson 1969) both questions and answers are regularly cleft constructions. There are also highly marked topic constructions serving various discourse functions, such as "As for...", and "Speaking of...".

Phonology of focus

In English, the additional prominence associated with focus accent falls on the lexically accented syllable, even in compounds with contrasted second element: "We didn't find any blúeberries, but we did see some blúebirds." Focus accent on syllables other than the syllable bearing the word stress tend to be restricted to contexts of repair and the like, as in "I didn't say bluebérry, I said bluebírd" (Rochemont et al. 1990). Focus accent in English is assigned to the rightmost lexical category of a focused constituent, except in compound phrases. For instance "The man in the blue hát left" could answer "Who left?", "Which man left?", or "Which man in blue left?" (Rochemont 1986), and, for reasons to be explained in the next paragraph, also "What happened?". In a study of focused and unfocused compound and noncompound phrases like *Itálian teacher* and *Itàlian téacher* respectively, it emerged that the peak fundamental frequency may actually be lower in the rightmost constituent of noncompound phrases too, even though the rightmost constituent is still perceived as accented, since it has increased duration and the direction of pitch movement is rising rather than level or falling; there may also have been a perceptual correction for catathesis (Farnetani et al. 1988).

Insofar as major phrases having broad focus can be pronounced neutrally without any internal focus distinctions, if the rule just given were extended to broad focus, it would generate a main stress on the rightmost lexical category of the entire major phrase. A number of languages including English and German, but not Danish, have a tendency for relative prominence to be assigned to the rightmost of otherwise equal stresses (Bruce 1977; Selkirk 1984). A much discussed exception to this generalization is that in English the main accent is often retracted from an intransitive predicate (that is not contrastively or counterassertively focused) to a preceding nonpronominal subject, as in "The pláne crashed" (Ladd 1990). Every major phrase in English has a major phrase accent, which is often called the sentence accent in sentences having only one major phrase. Consequently, a constituent can carry a default major phrase accent if it is the rightmost constituent of the major phrase, even if it does not have narrow focus. However, the phonetic implementation of the default major phrase accent in broad focus sentences is liable to be different from that of narrow focus on the same word: when sentences like "Jeff gave the ball to the cat" were spoken as neutral assertions with broad focus on the whole sentence, as assertions having broad focus on the verb phrase only and as assertions having narrow focus on *cat*, it was found that the narrow focus version had higher pitch and greater duration on the focused word than the other versions; the main effect of broad focus on the verb phrase was to introduce a separate major phrase boundary after the subject (Eady et al. 1986; Swedish: Grønnum 1990).

Pitch obtrusion is the most obvious exponent of the focus accent. In English, focus accent may involve a High tone or a Low tone, which become respectively even higher or lower under increased emphasis (Pierrehumbert 1980). The Low tone is often used in yes-no questions such

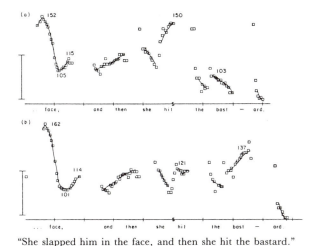

"She slapped him in the face, and then she hit the bastard."

FIGURE 10.1
Disambiguating focus accent. (a): with coreference.
(b): without coreference (from O'Shaughnessy 1979)

as "Does JACK like TACITUS?", types of contradictions such as "I DON'T like TACITUS" and, as already noted, in parentheticals (Pierrehumbert et al. 1990). Pitch tracks for a well known example of focus accent disambiguation are given in Figure 10.1; fundamental frequency on *bastard* is low if it is coreferential with *him* and if *hit* is new information, but high if *bastard* contrasts with *him* and *hit* contributes little that has not already been established by *slapped*. Actual peak measurements for differently focused versions of the same utterance are given in Table 10.1: new information is focused and has pitch obtrusion, old information is unfocused and therefore liable to accent reduction (if not pronominalized or simply deleted). In German, previously established, new, and emphatic information are differentiated by the timing of the pitch peak relative to the stressed syllable (Kohler 1987). The distinction between word accent and sentence accent is particularly clear in the case of Swedish: in one type of Swedish, sentence accent simply involves a larger excursion for the word accent, but, in another type, in simplex words sentence accent induces a second rise to High tone following the accentual fall and in compound words the word accent is realized on the first element of the compound but the sentence accent on the second element (Bruce 1977, 1983).

Increased duration and intensity are commonly subsidiary features of focus accent; however, in one study of English stress, no significant difference was found between sentence stress and word stress for intraoral air pressure and for airflow values, although both are normally correlated with intensity (Brown et al. 1974). Focused words were found to have

TABLE 10.1

Comparative fundamental frequencies in Hz for the stressed syllables
in the sentence "The farmer was eating the carrot"
(based on O'Shaughnessy 1979)

	farmer	eating	carrot
1. What was the farmer doing?	158	166	130
2. Who was eating the carrot?	164	105	100
3. What was the farmer doing with the carrot?	142	166	106
4. What was the farmer eating?	131	135	147
5. What was happening?	191	132	148

increased duration in Czech, Finnish and Swedish (Engstrand 1986).
The durational increment in Dutch was not confined to the accented
syllable but in some degree affected all other syllables of the word too;
the increment was not extended to other words in a focused constituent, a fact that confirms the importance of the word as a domain of
temporal as well as accentual organization (Eefting 1991).

The stresses of unfocused words often have little or no pitch obtrusion, particularly following a focused stress; the shrinking of preceding
and following pitch excursions serves further to highlight the focused
stress. This phenomenon has been observed in a variety of languages
(Thorsen 1980; Eady et al. 1986b; Yokoyama 1986; Vogel et al. 1987;
Botinis 1989). In Danish, to the extent that pitch is used at all to signal
focus, it is mainly by the attenuation of neighbouring stresses rather
than obtrusion of the focused stress (Grønnum 1990). In Chonnam
Korean, a focused word has higher pitch and greater duration and intensity; it starts a new accentual phrase and deaccents subsequent material
within the major phrase (Jun 1990). In Chinese, tonal excursions are
compressed after focus (Gårding 1987). In Japanese initial lowering can
be eliminated following a focused minor phrase (Kubozono 1987). Some
evidence has also been found for shortening of prefocus (Grønnum 1990)
or postfocus durations (Weismer et al. 1979; Eady et al. 1986b; Gårding
1987).

Sentences in which focus (new information) was not implemented by
pitch obtrusion were rated as unacceptable by Dutch listeners (Nooteboom et al. 1987; in a letter describing task, the probability of deaccentuation increased with the uninterrupted repetition of the same
referent (Nooteboom et al. 1982). Comparable results have been obtained
when duration was measured (Fowler et al. 1987). The duration of the
stressed vowel in the word *father* reduced drastically starting from its

second occurrence in a discourse (Umeda 1975); analysis of a twenty-minute radio broadcast of a short story showed durational reduction of both nouns and pronouns, with resetting at major breaks in the narrative (Campbell 1991). Mere repetition of a word in a list is not sufficient to produce the same shortening found in discourse repetition, and homophones in discourse do not trigger shortening (Fowler 1988).

Typology of focus markers

In English and Dutch, pitch obtrusion is a stronger cue to focus than syntactic devices like passivization (to produce a topic subject and a focus agent) and fronting (Nooteboom et al. 1981; Bock et al. 1983). Focus accent has been found to be used for new information even by two-year-old children (Wieman 1976). However, this does not necessarily mean that it will be the preferential implementation of focus in all languages: prosody may be expected to play a less important focus marking role in languages which have free word order or which use focus morphemes and particles or in which pitch movement has other crucial functions, that is in languages having lexical tone or a pure pitch word accent. In a contrastive study of various linguistic actuations of givenness and newness of information among preschool children and adults in three different languages, it was found that contrastive stress is used more in English than in Italian, and more in Italian than in Hungarian where it is comparatively rare; use of contrastive stress in English increased with age among preschool children (MacWhinney et al. 1978). The conclusions of this study may be supplemented by further crosslinguistic evidence. The elastic word order of Czech and Slovak is exploited for pragmatic purposes, with the focus generally appearing after the topic; the intonation of Czech sentences is more stable and uniform than in English (Daneš 1972). In Breton informational (noncontrastive) focus may be syntactically fronted without also being additionally stressed (Anderson et al. 1977). However, focus accent for contrastive focus is well established in free word order languages, as in Russian, which is a stress language. In Serbocroat, which is a pitch differentiated stress language, pitch obtrusion is mainly used for contrastive focus; old or contrastive information is preverbal, the latter being distinguished from the former by contrastive focus (Lehiste et al. 1978; Gvozdanović 1981); the interval between the peak frequency of an accented first syllable and the terminal frequency of the postaccentual syllable in the second word of a sentence increased from 40 Hz without emphasis to 130 Hz with maximum emphasis; emphasized words also had greater duration and intensity (Lehiste et al. 1986). In Hungarian, constituents placed in the preverbal focus position can carry contrastive stress; contrastive stress in other positions is mainly for contexts of repair like correcting mispronunciations or replies to echo questions (Horvath 1986). Word order and particles are the main exponents of focus in Finnish (Lehtinen 1964), but pitch obtrusion is found with contrastive focus and to some extent also with informational focus (Iivonen 1987). In Navajo, focus is implemented by particles (Schauber 1978), while inverted Subject-Object word order is used to topicalize the object (p. 461).

A number of languages are reported as having no prosodic exponent of focus at all, or even hardly any intonation: Amharic and Mohawk (Harries-Delisle 1978), Aghem (Watters 1979), Awiya and Somali (Hetzron 1969). However, pitch obtrusion as one implementation of contrastive focus is well established in tone languages such as Zulu (Doke 1926), Thai (Abramson 1962) and Chinese (Chang 1958). In Hausa, emphasis is implemented by raising the first High tone in the emphasized word along with any adjacent High tone to the right in the same phrase, and focus probably triggers a preceding phrase boundary; see Figure 10.2 (Inkelas et al. 1990). A suggestive difference is reported between two Ivory Coast languages: in Toura, which does not make extensive use of word order to mark focus, tonal modification is an important focus marking device, but in Wobe, which fronts focused material, tonal modification is less significant (Bearth 1980). In the pitch accent language Japanese, word order and particles play a larger focus marking role than in English; however prosodic exponents of focus are also well documented. A difference of approximately 20 Hz for the male voice was found between emphasized and unemphasized words in one study, and duration (particularly of consonants) and intensity can also be increased (Abe 1972; Umeda et al. 1975; Aizawa 1981; Matsunaga 1984; Poser 1985; Kori 1987, 1989; Pierrehumbert et al. 1988). Contrastive focus not only raises fundamental frequency in Japanese but also affects phrasing: in adjective-noun-*wa* structures, contrastive focus on the noun

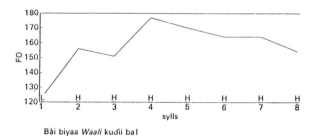

Bài biyaa *Waali* kuɗii bal

FIGURE 10.2
High tone raising with emphasis in Hausa
(from Inkelas et al. 1990)

almost always resulted in an intermediate phrase boundary between the adjective and the noun, marked by final lengthening and blocking of catathesis; this boundary was not observed when contrastive focus was on the adjective or when there was no focus. In West Greenlandic Eskimo, which is also a pitch accent language, focused words can be phrased separately from surrounding material and produced with expanded pitch range (Nagano-Madsen 1993). On the basis of the evidence collected, it is safe to conclude that, even though Greek has a pitch accent and makes extensive pragmatic use of particles and word order, there is no typological reason for excluding a priori the possibility that focus, and particularly contrastive focus, could have been marked prosodically in Greek by pitch obtrusion and by phrasing effects.

Affective prosody

It emerged quite clearly from the above survey of the prosodic implementation of focus that foregrounded information is accorded exaggerated prosodic properties and backgrounded information attenuated prosodic properties, a correlation that is evidently iconic in origin (Bolinger 1978). Since prosodic prominence lends physical salience to the segmental material that carries it, it is natural to find it used to convey informational salience and conversely to find some or all of the prosodic features of neighbouring material to be made less prominent. The association of stress with content words and lack of stress with functors is also presumably iconic in origin. Both normal speakers and agrammatic aphasics identify target words more quickly when they carry sentence stress (Swinney et al. 1980), and exaggerated stress facilitates comprehension for aphasics (Pashek et al. 1982); it is conceivable that one function of the durational component of stress is to add extra time needed to process new, as opposed to old and predictable, information. The problem is that exaggerated prosody can reflect not only focus but also emphasis and register; before attempting to disentangle the various factors contributing to prosodic prominence, it will be convenient to pause and review the general question of affective prosody and its grammaticalization.

Even though the display of emotion in general is constrained by the norms and conventions of different societies and cultures (Ekman 1972), it is fairly clear that the vocal expression of emotion is not merely a learned cultural signalling system: it shows some degree of phylogenetic continuity and it is ultimately physiologically based, as already discerned by Charles Darwin (1872/1965). A survey of the vocalizations of over fifty different birds and animals, ranging from the pelican and the sandpiper to the elephant and the rhinoceros, has found that harsh, lower frequency sounds consistently indicate hostility, while higher frequency, more tone-like sounds suggest fear or friendliness (Morton 1977). The sexual dimorphism in the vocal anatomy of humans and many other species manifested by the lower pitch of the male voice and the higher pitch of the voices of women and children could be ethologically explained as the result of millennia of evolution affecting the length and the mass of the vocal cords according as the primary need was to express aggression or to induce protection (Morton 1977; Ohala 1983). Other things being equal, the larger the animal, the larger its vocal anatomy and the lower the frequency it can produce. In aggressive encounters it is a useful strategy to suggest large bodily mass auditorily through low frequency vocalization (and visually through piloerection). Conversely, infants, being smaller than adults, can be expected to vocalize higher in the frequency range of their species. So a higher frequency signal presumably suggests smaller bodily mass and therefore less danger of harm from aggression.

When in an emotional state, both humans and other species exhibit endocrine and muscular activities resulting in observable changes in their outward appearance, in recognizable facial, gestural and postural movements, and often in particular types of vocalization (Scherer 1981). Humans as well as animals express their emotional state by uttering nonlinguistic sounds, as when they laugh, cry, moan or shriek. Emotions such as anger and fear are associated with increased activation of the sympathetic nervous system, which prepares the body for action in an emergency, and consequently with increased heart rate, pupillary dilation, and distribution of blood to the exterior muscles. Emotions such as tranquil happiness and sadness are associated with activation of the parasympathetic nervous system, which is responsible for rest and recovery, and consequently with decreased heart rate and diversion of blood away from the exterior muscles. These physiological effects can have a direct influence on the respiratory, phonatory and articulatory movements involved in speech, particularly when strong emotional states occasion a disturbed respiratory pattern, tremor and decreased smoothness of motor control (Williams et al. 1972, 1981).

A number of studies suggest that prosodic expressions of emotion fall into two preliminary classes of covarying features (Scherer 1981). Energized arousal, including emotions such as anger and fear, is in principle associated with a high pitch register, a wide pitch range, high intensity and fast speech rate. The absence of physiological arousal, including emotions such as boredom, pleasantness and sadness, is in principle associated with low pitch, narrow pitch range, low intensity and slow speech rate. Anger can trigger sudden peaks in fundamental frequency and intensity, and fear is associated with some degree of fluctuation in fundamental frequency; the speech rate for sorrow was about half the neutral rate (Williams et al. 1972; Hansen 1988). Anger can be characterized by rapid and exaggerated articulatory gestures, tenderness by slow, gliding articulations (Fónagy 1976). The more rapid falling rhythms are more suited to emotions associated with a higher general level of muscular activity (Sundberg 1982). There can also be significant differences in voice quality (Fónagy 1962; Crystal 1975). Figure 10.3 shows register differences when three professional actors simulated various emotional attitudes in the performance of a short play having identical test phrases embedded in the dialogue (Williams et al. 1972). These experimental results are corroborated by the study of voice recordings obtained in real-life emotional situations. One study (Williams et al. 1969) analyzed the recording of a conversation between an aircraft controller and a pilot which ended in the pilot losing control of his plane and fatally crashing. The pitch of the pilot's voice rises steadily as he becomes more aware of the danger; just before the crash, when the pilot is presumably terror-stricken, the pitch is extremely high and undergoes large fluctuations; similar effects appear in the analysis of other aircraft accidents (Kuroda et al. 1976). Establishing the exact combination of prosodic signals that serve as cues to various specific emotions has proved a difficult undertaking (Uldall 1960, 1964; Crystal 1969). For instance, both boredom and sadness seem to be associated with low pitch and slow tempo; likewise anger, elation and fear are not very well discriminated. In order to elicit judgements of attitude uninfluenced by the content of the message, investigators have used electronic manipulation and splicing (Scherer 1971) or synthesized tones (Scherer et al. 1977). It is also known that the same prosodic signals can receive quite different interpretations according to the discourse context (Hadding-Koch 1961), and that similar emotional situations can have diverse prosodic expressions (Disner 1982).

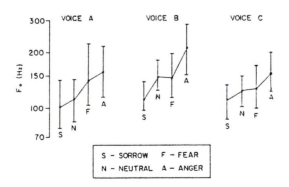

FIGURE 10.3
Median F_0 and range of F_0 for three actors
simulating various emotions (from Williams et al. 1972)

Involuntary, physiologically based prosodic features can be mimicked or feigned not only by professional actors (Williams et al. 1972) and singers (Kotlyar et al. 1976) but also obviously by participants in ordinary discourse. This is equally so for the facial and other bodily gestures that convey attitude either by themselves or in conjunction with vocal signals—smiling, shrugging the shoulders, assuming the expression of ὑπόδρα ἰδών, and so on. In such cases, prosody and gesture have the function of conveying the intended affective meaning, as opposed to the linguistic meaning, of the message. For instance, the interpretation of sentences such as "That was an earthshaking experience" as sarcastic or neutral can depend critically on intonation as well as discourse context. One study, involving reaction to sentences read by actors so as to evoke any of eight different emotions (love, happiness, sarcasm, fear and so on) found that the language and cultural origin of the listener did not affect his judgement (Sedlacek et al. 1963). However, it is often noted that intonation is exploited more extensively to convey attitude and information structure in languages like English than in some other languages. In English, in addition to the use of Low tone for some types of focus accent, there are fairly subtle intonational differences which appear to relate to the speaker's understanding of his interlocutor's beliefs about the status of the information being communicated (Pierrehumbert et al. 1990; Hobbs 1990). The rather striking variability in the pitch movements associated with the English stress accent as it interacts with intonation is not found in the Japanese pitch accent (Beckman et al. 1986). In tone languages, such as Taiwanese, Mandarin and Thai, the use of local variation in pitch movement to express affective meaning is constrained compared with its use in English, presumably so as to avoid interference with its lexical function, but intensity and duration, as well as register (average absolute pitch level), are exploited freely as in English (Ross et al. 1986). At very early stages in the acquisition of tone languages, prior to the use of adult lexical items, attitudinal factors predominate: in Thai and Mandarin, very young children tend to use high or rising pitch for requests or demands and to express unusual interest, and mid, low or falling pitch for responses and comments (Clumeck 1980). Raised register and exaggerated intonation are used in the speech of parents addressed to children to elicit attention, modulate arousal, communicate affect and facilitate language comprehension (Fernald et al. 1989); this is true both for stress languages such as English, German and Italian and for the pitch accent language Japanese, as illustrated in Figure 10.4.

There are many similarities between the way emotion is conveyed in speech and the way it is conveyed in instrumental and vocal music; in the latter, melody, dynamics and rhythm are all involved (Gundlach

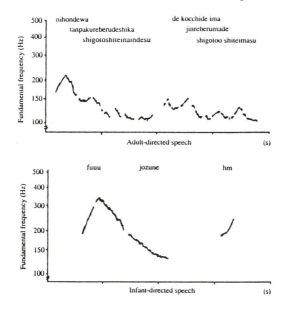

FIGURE 10.4

F_0 contours in adult- and infant-directed speech
of a Japanese father (from Fernald et al. 1989)

1932; Fónagy et al. 1963). High pitch and large pitch intervals are considered to be animated; low pitch and smaller intervals are judged sombre. In a sample of Hungarian folksongs, it was found that in those with tender texts all intervals were a fourth or less, whereas in those with angry texts 72% were a fourth or more. Similarly fast tempi are judged animated and slow tempi sombre.

Just as attitudinal vocalizations can become lexicalized as interjections (for instance αἰαῖ, ὀτοτοῖ, φεῦ, cp. αἰάζω, ὀτοτύζω, φεύζω), so the prosodic expression of emotion can become grammaticalized. It is probably useful to distinguish the attitudinal and the grammatical functions of prosody, even though it is difficult to define the boundary between them (Cruttenden 1970). For instance, rising intonation is a signal of unfinished discourse and of curiosity, falling intonation of finality and dogmatism (Cruttenden 1981). The greater the curiosity of a question, the more its pitch rises; the more peremptory a command, the steeper its fall in pitch. This attitudinal use of pitch is evidently grammaticalized in the use of rising intonation to signal the grammatical distinction between questions on the one hand and statements and commands on the other. While affective pitch is parametric—the higher the pitch, the stronger the emotion conveyed thereby, grammaticalized pitch probably functions in terms of categorial distinctions (Scherer et al. 1984; Ladd et al. 1985). Although the lexica of unrelated languages throughout the world are quite arbitrary and therefore mutually unintelligible, their intonational systems are far more comparable (Bolinger 1978, 1986, 1989), because, although they operate in terms of language specific rules (Ladd 1990), in large part they ultimately reflect shared nonlinguistic behaviour.

Focus accents in utterances like "Lower your voice!" or "Speak softly!" are still implemented by prosodic prominence; while prosodic prominence in such cases could simply be due to the need to attract attention, it is probably due more to its grammaticalization as a focus marker. Rather similarly, in American Sign Language, the sign for *slow* is made by passing one hand slowly across the back of the other hand; to indicate *very slow* the same gesture is performed more quickly (sic) (Klima et al. 1979).

Focus, emphasis and register

Consider now the theoretical problems associated with the analysis of focus in the light of the above brief excursus on affective prosody. Focus is ultimately iconic in origin and it is largely implemented by quantitative rather than qualitative differences, but neither of these facts implies that focus cannot be phonologically categorial. However, in addition to the binary distinction between focused and unfocused, it has been noted that different types of focus are implemented by different degrees of prosodic prominence; in particular, counterassertive focus is stronger than contrastive focus which is stronger than simple informational focus. For instance, in Spanish focused preverbal objects have greater prosodic prominence if they are counterassertive than if they are informational (Silva-Corvalán 1983). The same hierarchy seems to apply morphosyntactically; verbal reduplication is contrastive in Efik (de Jong 1981) and cleft constructions in English can be counterassertive. Focus is a localized prosodic exaggeration. This local exaggeration is overlaid on the register chosen for the whole utterance, which reflects the overall degree of speaker arousal and involvement. While register could itself be treated categorially by distinguishing normal register, attenuated register and amplified register, an additional parametric factor is still involved, since within each category different degrees of speaker arousal correspond to different levels of prosodic register. The situation is further complicated by the fact that in addition to these hierarchical and gradient relations, there is also a localized gradience: different degrees on the pragmatic continuum of emphasis can be reflected in different degrees of increment in intensity and duration and in different degrees of the height to which fundamental frequency rises or the depth to which it falls on any focused tone. The listener is apparently able to decode the physical signal in terms of these varying contributory factors while also making allowances for differences due to downtrends, phrasing, vowel height and perturbations from surrounding consonants.

TOPIC AND FOCUS IN GREEK

Personal pronouns

In Greek, there are parallel orthotonic and enclitic forms for all the personal pronouns. In the second and third persons and in the plural of the first person, the only difference is the presence versus the absence of the accent or its location, for instance σου - σοῦ, οὐ - οὔ, ἤμων - ἡμῶν. In the first person singular, the orthotonic forms begin with ἐ-, which is absent in the enclitic forms: ἐμέ - με, ἐμοῦ - μου, ἐμοί - μοι. The selection of orthotonic and enclitic personal pronoun forms is largely determined by focus, which is the primary explanation given by the grammarians for orthotonicity (Laum 1928). When in focus (ἔμφασις), particularly contrastive focus (ἀντιδιαστολή), the pronouns are orthotonic; when not in focus (ἀπόλυτος), they are enclitic subject to certain conditions noted below. αἱ μὲν οὖν ἐγκλινόμεναι τῶν ἀντωνυμιῶν αὐταί εἰσιν, αἵτινες ὀρθοτονού-μεναι μὲν ἀντιδιαστολὴν ἔχουσιν ἑτέρου προσώπου, ἐμοῦ ἤκουσας, οὐκ ἄλλου· ἐμοὶ ἔδωκας, οὐκ ἄλλῳ· ἐμὲ ἐδίδαξας, οὐκ ἄλλον. ἐγκλινόμεναι δὲ ἀπόλυτα πρόσωπα δηλοῦσιν, ἤκουσά σου, ἔδωκά σοι Herodian I.559 Lentz; similarly Apollonius Dyscolus I.61.24 Schneider. For example, σοί is orthotonic in

ε ἰ δὴ σοὶ πᾶν ἔργον ὑπείξομαι Iliad 1.294

where the scholia state οὕτως ὀρθοτονητέον τὴν ἀντωνυμίαν· ἀντιδιασταλτικὴ γάρ ἐστιν, and σέο is orthotonic in

οἵ σέο φέρτεροί εἰσι Iliad 2.201,

as again noted by the scholia. On the other hand, σε is enclitic in

οἵ τέ σε πεφρίκασι Iliad 11.383,

where the scholia state οὐκ ἀναγκαῖον δὲ ἀντιδιαστέλλειν... δύναται γὰρ καὶ ἀπόλυτος εἶναι, and εὐ is enclitic in

εἴ πώς εὐ πεφίδοιτο Iliad 20.464,

as again noted by the scholia. The accentuation of σέο differs in the two instances of the repeated line Iliad 3.446/14.328; the scholia on 3.446 attribute ἀντιδιαστολή to the latter but not to the former.

The accentual difference between focused and unemphatic personal pronouns is illustrated by their contrasting treatment in the musical settings. κἀμὲ in ME 10.1 is set to a rising third, and the pitch of -μὲ is not only higher than that of the immediately following grave, as would

ME 10.1 *DAM* 36.9

Κά-μὲ γλυ-κε-ρὰ βαί-νει φω-νή

be expected, but also higher than the acute of *βαίνει*. By contrast, unfocused *νιν* in ME 10.2 is treated exactly like an unaccented word final
syllable, and the setting of the acute of *δέ* is what would be expected
for a word internal acute rather than a grave, since it is higher than
the peak of the circumflex of the nonlexical *ὁμοῦ*.

ME 10.2 *Ath.* 13

ὁ-μου-οῦ δέ νιν Ἄ-ραψ

It follows from the general principle that focused pronouns are orthotonic that the nominative forms are never enclitic, since in a PRO-drop
language like Greek overt expression of a subject pronoun will almost
always involve some sort of focus: *καὶ ἡ μὲν γενικωτάτη αἰτία τῆς ὀρθῆς
τάσεως ἡ ἀντιδιαστολὴ τοῦ προσώπου* Herodian I.559 Lentz; *καὶ καθόλου
πᾶσα ἀντωνυμία ὀρθῆς πτώσεως ἐγκλιτικῆς συντάξεως ἀπαράδεκτός ἐστιν, οὐ
μόνον τῆς χρήσεως τὸ τοιοῦτον ἐπιδειξαμένης, ἀλλὰ καὶ τῆς φωνῆς συνεπισχυούσης
τῇ χρήσει* Apollonius Dyscolus II.167 Uhlig. Contrastive focus is seen
in the reversal of agent and patient with rightward verb gapping and
juxtaposed pronouns

> *ἤ μ᾿ ἀνάειρ᾿, ἤ ἐγὼ σέ Iliad* 23.724
> *ἔγειρ᾿ ἔγειρε καὶ σὺ τήνδ᾿, ἐγὼ δὲ σέ Eumenides* 140
> *ἤ κέν με δαμάσσεται, ἤ κεν ἐγὼ τόν Iliad* 21.226.

Other examples have simple focus on the subject

> *μή σε, γέρον, κοίλῃσιν ἐγὼ παρὰ νηυσὶ κιχείω Iliad* 1.26
> *τοιγὰρ ἐγώ τοι ταῦτα μάλ᾿ ἀτρεκέως ἀγορεύσω Odyssey* 1.179.

Similarly, the third person singular is orthotone when reflexive

> *ἤ ὀλίγον οἷ παῖδα ἐοικότα γείνατο Τυδεύς Iliad* 5.800,

as noted by the scholia. Intensive *αὐτός* as a focus device selects the
orthotonic forms of pronouns: *αἱ μετὰ τῆς ἐπιταγματικῆς ἀντωνυμίας τῆς αὐτός
ἀεὶ ὀρθοτονοῦνται* Herodian I.560 Lentz. This applies with some exceptions (Kühner et al. 1890.1:347, 1890.2:558) also when the pronoun
is not reflexive but, for instance, in contrastive focus

> *οὐ γὰρ ὅπως τοῖς παροῦσιν... ἀλλ᾿ ὅπως αὐτῷ ἐμοὶ* Plato
> *Phaedo* 91a.

καί 'too, also' selects the orthotonic form when its scope is over the
pronoun, type *εἰπὲ καὶ ἐμοί*. When the scope of *καί* is wide, the enclitic
form of the pronoun may follow: *καί μοι τοῦτ᾿ ἀγόρευσον* [*Odyssey* 4.645]

ἐγκλίνεται οὐ συμπλακέν, τοῦ ἑξῆς ὄντος καὶ τοῦτό μοι ἀγόρευσον Apollonius Dyscolus I.40.20 Schneider. The rules for the accentuation of a pronoun coordinated with another pronoun or a noun are also given by Apollonius Dyscolus: εἰ ἐκτὸς τῆς συμπλοκῆς ἡ ἀντωνυμία γένοιτο, πάντως τότε καὶ ἀπόλυτος γενήσεται, δός μοι καὶ 'Απολλωνίῳ· εἰ δὲ ἀντιστραφήσεται, πάντως καὶ ὀρθοτονηθήσεται, δός 'Απολλωνίῳ καὶ ἐμοί I.40.16 Schneider. Exceptions to this word order constraint (Kühner et al. 1890:346) are rare

> ἀσπαστὸν ἐμοὶ καὶ παιδὶ *Odyssey* 19.569
> ἐχθίστους ἐμοὶ καὶ σοὶ *Troades* 404.

Appositive group

Focus is the converse of predictability and has just the opposite prosodic effects. It tends to inhibit phrasing both at the level of the minor phrase and at the level of the clitic group. Focus prevents destressing in English: "Jack's got sm money" but "Jack's got SOME money" scilicet "but not much." Focus prevents deaccentuation in the formation of the accentual minor phrase in Japanese (Poser 1985); and it blocks the shift of the word accent from the lexical word to a proclitic in Serbocroat: *zà sîna* 'for the son' but *za bràta, a ne za sîna* 'for the brother, but not for the son' with contrastive focus (Lehiste et al. 1986). In Danish prepositional phrases with a pronoun, the preposition gets the stress if the pronoun is anaphoric, but the pronoun gets the stress if it is deictic: *méd ham* 'with him' but *med hám* 'with him [over there]' (Rischel 1983). The application of sandhi rules also tends to be obstructed by focus: the likelihood of final dental palatalization in English has been found to be somewhat reduced if the word preceding the pronoun is focused and very significantly reduced if the pronoun itself is focused, as in *aid YOU soon* versus *aidž you soon* (Cooper et al. 1980). In Amoy Chinese tone sandhi, pronouns enter into a tone group with what follows except under focus (Chen 1987). Focus encourages just those properties, namely prosodic prominence and articulatory precision and integrity, that the fluency and rapidity of phrase prosody tend to diminish wherever possible.

In Greek, there may be a rhythmic effect associated with contrastive focus as indicated by the particle μέν. Both μέν and γάρ are found after Porson's bridge; if μέν follows the contrasted word, that word is not a polysyllabic lexical (*O.T.* 142, *Alcestis* 165, 323, *Hecuba* 903, Eur. *Supplices* 267); in

> μισεῖς μὲν λόγῳ... ἔργῳ δὲ Soph. *Electra* 357

the contrastive word follows, as it does after a monosyllabic lexical in

> εἰ γῆ μὲν κακή... χρηστὴ δ' *Hecuba* 592.

No similar apparent restriction applies to γάρ, which appears comparatively freely after polysyllabic lexicals (*Trachiniae* 932, *Philoctetes* 466, *Helen* 1552, *I. T.* 678). So it may be that contrastive focus makes the final syllable of a lexical word resistant to subordination before a postpositive. μέν also appears to behave differently from γάρ in split anapaests in Aristophanes, where unlike γάρ it does not occur in composites with disyllabic first element or as a binding appositive.

Minor phrase

The need to highlight focused material can inhibit minor phrase formation; this is a well documented crosslinguistic tendency, attested for Hausa (Inkelas 1989), Japanese (Poser 1985; Pierrehumbert et al. 1988; Selkirk et al. 1991), Korean (Cho 1990; Jun 1990), West Greenlandic Eskimo (Nagano-Madsen 1993), Shanghai Chinese (Selkirk et al. 1990) and Chichewa (Malawi: Kanerva 1990). The likelihood that focused constituents will form a separate minor phrase in Greek may explain certain apparent anomalies of punctuation in phrase punctuating inscriptions, but this approach is circular to the extent that the discourse structure assumed cannot be independently motivated. Constituents that are contrastive or focused, particularly at the beginning of a paragraph, tend to appear as phrases consisting of one appositive group only

> : κα τονδε : hα ᾽πιϜοικια : *Naup.* 1
> : ΛοϘρον τον : Ηυποκναμιδιον : *Naup.* 1; elsewhere mostly
>   unpunctuated
> : ΠερϘοθαριαν : και Μυσαχεον : *Naup.* 22; unpunctuated
>   in line 27
> : κεν ΛοϘροις : τοι⟨ς⟩ Ηυποκναμιδιοις : *Naup.* 21; contrastive
>   with εν Ναυπακτοι in line 20.

Major phrase

A number of syntactic criteria, many of which have already been noted in Chapter 9, point to potentially separate phrasing of fronted topic and focus material (Fraenkel 1964, 1965; Hale 1987; Taylor 1990; Garrett 1993)

> 1. Position of interrogatives
>
>   δολόμητιν δ᾽ ἀπάταν θεοῦ τίς ἀνὴρ θνατὸς ἀλύξει; *Persae* 107 (93)
>   τὰ δὲ τούτου τοῦ ἀγῶνος πῶς ἔχει; Demosthenes 25.4
>   τὰς εἰσφορὰς πότερον τὰ κτήματ᾽ ἢ τὰ σώματ᾽ ὀφείλει
>   Demosthenes 22.54

2. Position of particles and parentheticals

   τοὺς μὲν Λακεδαιμονίους, ὦ ἄνδρες ξύμμαχοι, οὐκ ἂν ἔτι αἰτιασαίμεθα Thucydides 1.120.1

   Κλεοφῶντος τοίνυν, ὦ ἄνδρες δικασταί, ἕτερα μὲν ἄν τις ἔχοι κατηγορῆσαι Lysias 30.12

3. Second position for pronominal clitics

   τοὺς τέσσερας μῆνας τρέφει μιν ἡ Βαβυλωνίη χώρη Herodotus 1.192.1

4. Resumptive pronouns

   τὴν γὰρ μαρτυρίαν, ἣν ᾤμην εἶναι..., ταύτην οὐχ ηὗρον ἐνοῦσαν ἐν τῷ ἐχίνῳ Demosthenes 45.57.

Musical evidence

Pitch rise induced by emphatic focus can be seen quite clearly in the Delphic hymns, particularly as a dampening or reversal of downtrend within downtrend domains. As is appropriate in hymns that also celebrate cult places, theonyms and toponyms are systematic exceptions to downtrend, and their nongrave accents tend to be set higher, not lower than or even equal to, the nongrave accents of an immediately preceding lexical word. It is this special, emphatic status of proper names that necessitated their exclusion from several tests of downtrend in Chapter 9. Table 10.2 compares the mean interval between the accentual peaks of lexical words in immediate succession within a downtrend domain neither of which is a proper name ($-PN$ $-PN$) with the mean interval between a nonproper name lexical and a proper name ($-PN$ $+PN$). Cases with intervening graves are excluded. The ends of melody sections are also excluded. The results show that there is a mean rise between the accentual peaks of a nonproper name lexical word and a proper name of over four tenths of a tone, whereas there is a fall of about a semitone

TABLE 10.2

Pitch rise from nonproper name to proper name

$-PN$ $-PN$	$-PN$ $+PN$
$m(-PN) = 0.52$	$m(+PN) = -0.42$
$s = 1.22$	$s = 1.34$
$m(+PN) > m(-PN)$: $t = 2.33$, $df = 58$	
$p = 0.025$	

from the first to the second of two nonproper name lexicals, and the difference is statistically significant. This result indicates that emphatic focus was signalled by an increase in pitch level large enough to convert the prevailing downtrend into uptrend on focused or additionally emphasized words.

After a focus obtrusion on a proper name within a syntactic structure that normally corresponds to a downtrend domain, downtrend starts over from the higher focus pitch, as in ME 10.3. In other words, if there

ME 10.3   Ath. 10

Τρι - τω-ω- νί - δος   δά-[πε]-δον

is an unusual degree of pitch obtrusion internal to a normal downtrend domain, pitches following that obtrusion do not fall to a level calculated from the previous unfocused material, but to a level calculated from the new high.

In *DAM* 32 and 36 and in *POxy* 3161, mythological names are also marked by elaborate melisms and by durational protraction (West 1992), which may be taken as evidence for a durational component in the prosodic implementation of emphatic focus in Greek speech (as in many other languages).

Discontinuous noun phrases

Although left and right movement of complete constituents is found in many languages, discontinuous noun phrases in which the modifier is separated from its head are not particularly common in the languages of the world. The phenomenon is well established in some Algonquian languages—Cree (Starks 1987), Fox and Ojibwa (N. Central USA, Canada). In Fox (Dahlstrom 1987), discontinuous noun phrases regularly have the pattern Y_1XY_2, where Y_1 is the modifier and Y_2 the head of the phrase YP, and X is the ultimate head of the superordinate phrase XP and serves as a pivot around which the components of the discontinuous constituent are arranged. X is normally the verb or other predicate, while Y_1 can be a demonstrative or quantifier or a possessor. If there are two modifiers, they may both be placed in the Y_1 position or they may be split between Y_1 and Y_2, giving word orders of the type *"These four* are used *songs"* or *"These* are used *four songs."* Syntactic material belonging to the verb may occur adjacent to the verb in the X position, as in sentences of the type *"Many* were carried out from that place *people."* A Fox verb cannot be surrounded by two intertwined discontinuous noun phrases, as commonly in Latin verse, but separable verbal prefixes and modifiers can appear in intertwined constituents in the order Preverb Modifier Verb Noun ($PreXY_1XY_2$). The pragmatic function of discontinuity in Fox is to focus the modifier Y_1: fronted deictics in discontinuous structures are used to pick out one member of a previously mentioned set, and fronted quantifiers to pick out a subset (Dahlstrom pers. comm. 1991). In Ojibwa (Tomlin et al. 1979), focused quantifiers are fronted from postverbal noun phrases to a slot at the beginning of the clause immediately after any clause initial function words, giving structures like "And *all* they took from them their *sugar*."

Discontinuous noun phrases are also attested in a number of Australian languages (Blake 1977) such as Kalkatungu (Blake 1983), Nyangumarda (Geytenbeek 1980) and Yidin (Dixon 1977). In Kalkatungu, a deictic, quantifier or focused adjective can be fronted, in which case it is likely to bear strong stress: "*A big* bit me *spider*"; if the modifier is Y_2, as in "*A spider* bit me *(a) big (one)*," the construction may be related to amplification constructions of the type "*Meat* I kill *kangaroo*" in which the general information precedes the specific.

In a number of native American languages fronted quantifiers preferentially or obligatorily modify the object rather than the subject of a transitive verb, as in Pima (Arizona: Munro 1984), Tzotzil (Mexico: Aissen 1984) and Halkomelem (British Columbia: Gerdts 1984). In Japanese, postposing a modifier out of a topic phrase is much less natural than out of a nontopic phrase (Simon 1989), and for whatever reason (Whitman 1987), a subject is allowed to stand between an object and its quantifier but not an object between a subject and its quantifier. Pima allows two preposed quantifiers, for instance one modifying a direct and one an indirect object, in which case chiastic order is not permitted; also in Pima, the object constraint is stronger for numerals than for logical quantifiers ('many,' 'all,' etc.). Numeral modifiers of subjects in Pima cannot be fronted in clauses having transitive verbs but only in clauses having a restricted group of intransitive verbs; similarly and more generally in Tzotzil and Halkomelem, quantifiers modifying subjects may be fronted in intransitive clauses but not in transitive clauses.

In Tzotzil, the material between the fronted quantifier and the modified noun is always the predicate; it may be a simple verb or a complement predicate as in "*Many* I want to eat *sweets*." Further evidence for discontinuous noun phrases comes from Hungarian. In one type of Hungarian possessive construction, the possessor can become detached from the possessed, so that, for instance, either the latter or the former can stand as a single constituent in focus position (Szabolcsi 1981, 1983). Hungarian also allows adjectives and numerals to be detached from their head noun and postposed; this order is used for amplifications, but it can also be used to emphasize the postposed modifier (Kiss 1987; Moravcsik pers. comm. 1991). In Latin prose, head interrupted genitive phrases and verb phrases are well evidenced: *clarissimae testis victoriae, De Officiis*

1.22.75; *ad exitus pervehimur optatos*, *De Officiis* 2.6.19. In Horace, discontinuity of adjective and noun is extremely common: *Virtus repulsae nescia sordidae / intaminatis fulget honoribus*, *Odes* 3.2.17; the adjective, which tends to carry the foregrounded information, comes first in almost 85% of the instances (Naylor 1922). The construction also appears in Old Norse ("Goðan eigum vér konung" 'Good have we a king': Faarlund 1991) and is common in Old Georgian (Boeder 1989).

The floated quantifiers of modern European languages like English "The boys have all left," "He gave the boys all a book" and French "Les enfants ont tous vu ce film" 'The children have all seen this film' are sometimes confused with fronted quantifiers but they represent a different phenomenon. Floated quantifiers are not preferentially associated with objects—in fact it was suggested that they are most easily launched by subjects (Keenan 1976) — and the resulting construction has an individuating and distributive function that is lacking in the unfloated counterpart (O'Grady 1982, 1991; Sportiche 1988).

A number of fairly clear tendencies emerge from the above survey. The preferred structure has the ultimate head as the pivot which is straddled by the discontinuous constituent. The ultimate head is preferentially the predicate (simple verb or, less commonly, complex predicate), and the discontinuous constituent is preferentially the object noun phrase. The fronted item is more usually the modifier than the head of the noun phrase. The modifier can be an ordinary adjective, but is preferentially a deictic or quantifier; deictics and numerals are probably more marked than logical quantifiers. The pragmatic function of the construction is commonly associated with focus. This is hardly surprising given the nature of the modifiers typically involved. In a study of fundamental frequency in English, it was found that words which are the most consistently assigned focus accent include those which indicate the speaker's commitment to the truth value of the sentence, like negatives, sentential adverbs and restrictive modals, and those like quantifiers and deictics which restrict the set of items for which the proposition is true or false (O'Shaughnessy et al. 1983).

In principle, discontinuous noun phrases could be generated *in situ*, or could arise by movement of the modifier or the head, or could be due to intercalation of the interrupting material. The idea that fronting in general implies movement, as its traditional name suggests, is supported by languages in which fronted material can leave behind a pronominal copy in the basic word order slot as in Breton (Anderson et al. 1977) and by languages in which, at least on a purely syntactic analysis, clitics are attached to the initial constituent discounting fronted material, as in Gurindji (Australia: McConvell 1980) and various other languages (p. 422).

Discontinuous phrases straddling a nonlexical word have already been illustrated with reference to appositive group formation in Chapter 7 (p. 334). The following discussion is restricted to pivot elements that are not appositive. In the most common form of discontinuity in Greek lexically branching phrases, the head of what, abstracting away from purely distributional criteria, would correspond to a phrase XP occurs between elements of a branching phrase YP dominated by XP. This head interrupted structure may be represented as $[...YX^{head}Y...]_{XP}$, where X^{head} is the head of XP, Y is understood as any element of YP, and ... indicates that $YX^{head}Y$ does not necessarily exhaust XP. For the purposes of the ensuing discussion, this notation will be simplified to just $[YXY]_{XP}$. Typical examples are

> καινὸν ἀγγέλλεις ἔπος *Troades* 55 $[Adj \ V \ N]_{VP}$
> νόστον ἐμβαλεῖν πικρόν *Troades* 66 $[N \ V \ Adj]_{VP}$
> ἐπ᾽ ἀκτὰς ἤλυθον Σκαμανδρίους *Troades* 374 $[P \ N \ V \ Adj]_{VP}$.

A sample from the *Troades* of verb phrases containing at least one branching complement phrase and in which the verb is not separated from at least one element of that complement phrase by other material not belonging to the verb phrase reveals a frequency of over 29% for the $[YVY]_{VP}$ structure, which is almost equal to the respective individual frequencies of the left and right flanking alternative structures, $[VYY]_{VP}$ and $[YYV]_{VP}$ respectively. Discontinuous constituents of this type belong to the class of syntactic structures to which the ancient grammarians assigned the term "hyperbaton" (Quintilian 8.6.62) and which were studied at the turn of the century under the heading of "Spaltung" or "Sperrung." Use of interrupted constituents is a typical feature of verse word order and is also well attested in classical prose, becoming a stylistic feature of later authors like Polybius and Dionysius of Halicarnassus and particularly Theodorus (Lindhamer 1908). According to one view, use of interrupted constituents is a purely literary artificiality (Denniston 1952), yet interrupted constituents are found in texts which, whatever degree, if any, of literary pretension they may have, are unlikely to use stilted or otherwise artificial word order (Havers 1912; Chantraine 1952). So it is probably safe to assume that this typical feature of verse word order has a basis in ordinary speech. Since hyperbaton often seems to involve the comparatively unstructured strategies of placing the most important information first or adding an afterthought to a syntactically complete sentence, it can equally well be associated with an informal and unplanned speech style; and in point of fact, in Warlpiri (Australia: Andrews 1985) continuous noun phrases are preferred in writing and discontinuous noun phrases in spoken language.

Discontinuous noun phrases in Greek largely conform to the various crosslinguistic tendencies established above (DS 1994). For the modifier in the Y phrase, there is a preference hierarchy ranging from quantifiers, deictics and pronominals as the preferred categories through restrictive modifiers to nonrestrictive modifiers and expressions of speaker evaluation, which are avoided. The modifier in the Y phrase is usually in the Y_1 position and the head in the Y_2 position

> ταύταις ἐχρήσαντο ταῖς συμφοραῖς Aeschines 1.88.

Modifiers can also occur in the Y_2 position, probably often reflecting postnominal location in the underlying continuous structure

> ἔτη δὲ εἶναι τὰς σπονδὰς πεντήκοντα Thucydides 5.18.3, cp.
> σπονδὰς ποιήσασθαι ἔτη πεντήκοντα id. 5.41.2
> ἐπιστολὰς δὲ σιγῶ ψευδεῖς Aeschines 3.225.

The interrupting pivot element is preferentially a verb form, either the verb of the clause containing the noun phrase or the matrix verb

> οἶμαι μέγιστον ὑμῖν ἐρεῖν σημεῖον Demosthenes 29.19
> μεγάλα τούτων οἶμαι σημεῖα δείξειν ὑμῖν Aeschines 3.177.

Occasionally it is some other generally predictable item that does not form a superordinate phrase with YP — some other often nonlexical element of the verb phrase, the subject or a parenthetical

> πολλὴν ὁ δῆμος πρόνοιαν ἐποιεῖτο ὑπὲρ αὐτοῦ καὶ τῶν θεῶν
> Demosthenes 59.92.

Nonlexicals, predictable material and parentheticals all tend to have low prosodic prominence.

The pragmatic function of discontinuity in Greek noun phrases follows from the above properties and is illustrated by its distribution in Thucydides 5.31-32 (Lindhamer 1908)

> ἐς Ἄργος ἐλθόντες... Ἀργείων ξύμμαχοι ἐγένοντο 5.31.1
> σφῶν τε καὶ Ἀργείων γίγνεσθαι ξυμμάχους 5.32.5
> εἴπερ Λακεδαιμονίων εἰσὶ ξύμμαχοι 5.32.6;

the only continuous, uninterrupted instance, 5.31.1, does not involve new information but information predictable from the preceding text. The Y_1 modifier mostly appears at the front of the phrase and frequently of the clause, a position often associated with focus, and it belongs preferentially to a class of words that restrict the range over which a proposition is true and which, as just noted, are especially associated with focus. Verbs, the most common X element, are in general less likely to be focused than nouns, and in some languages are particularly liable to destressing or are unaccented in most environments (p. 352). The head noun tends to have comparatively low informational content, the point often being to identify or quantify a relatively predictable entity or property. In principle, focus could apply to a binarily branching noun phrase in four different ways: narrow focus on the modifier, narrow focus on the head noun, broad scope focus on the whole noun phrase, double focus (narrow focus on each constituent); the discontinuous YXY structure typically serves to implement the first of these focus distributions.

The following constraints emerged from a sample of Attic prose consisting of the speeches of Aeschines. The object phrase is the most common discontinuous noun phrase, probably in part reflecting the fact that prototypically the object is the argument that carries the informational focus of the simple sentence

ἕτερον νικᾷ ψήφισμα Δημοσθένης Aeschines 3.68

πονηρὰ φύσις... δημοσίας ἀπεργάζεται συμφοράς Aeschines 3.147.

However, both subject phrases and complement ôr adjunct oblique and prepositional phrases are well attested straddling the verb in intransitive clauses

βραχύς μοι λείπεται λόγος Aeschines 3.175

πρὶν ἐπὶ τὴν ὑστέραν ἀπαίρειν πρεσβείαν... Δημοσθένην Aeschines 3.73,

but hardly ever in transitive clauses having lexical direct objects

ἐκ τούτου τὴν μορίαν ἀφανίζειν ἐπεχείρησα τοῦ χωρίου Lysias 7.28.

A prepositional phrase can be discontinuous when an intransitive clause contains a subject, but the converse is poorly attested: in the sample, prepositional phrases with SVS were probably external to the verb phrase. Nonlexical arguments are invisible in this calculus. Many but apparently not all intransitive verbs straddled by their subject phrases are passive or unaccusative. X is usually the sister of the YP node in the underlying structure and surfaces between Y_1 and Y_2, although in some instances Y_1 or Y_2 itself branches and X may appear within the lower branching phrase. In complement infinitive clauses, the matrix verb can appear alongside or in place of X. First branching node c-command is not a sufficient condition for the structures typically underlying discontinuity (a subject alone straddled by the object phrase is rare) but it is a necessary condition. A formulation in terms of government is more difficult, since in intransitive clauses government would extend to the subject apparently even when it is agentive, whereas in transitive clauses it would be limited to the first branching NP node of the underlying verb phrase structure (adverbs are invisible).

These restrictions on discontinuous noun phrases recall the rules for noun incorporation in some languages (p. 392) and the rules for phonological phrasing (p. 377, 386). Similar constraints can apply to floated quantifiers. In Hindi, both in perfective clauses (which have ergative verb agreement) and in imperfective clauses (which do not), a quantifier can float to the right of the direct object or the subject of an intransitive verb but not the subject of a transitive verb; this distribution has been explained as a constraint against floating a quantifier into a position where it could be interpreted as modifying the wrong nominal (Pandharipande et al. 1977). Some Korean speakers allow the object to intervene between the subject and its floated quantifier, provided the quantifier is overtly case marked (O'Grady 1991).

Another question is how discontinuous noun phrases are best analyzed in theories of syntax that allow movement rules. Given a basic YYX word order, and sidestepping the problem of a basic order for modifier and head in noun phrases in general and in noun phrases with focused modifiers in particular, it would follow that discontinuity involves movement to the right of X (Taylor 1990). This clearly accounts for preverbal noun phrases with Y_1 modifiers, as the following stepwise progressions illustrate

> ἱκανὸν τεκμήριον παρέχεται Plato *Menexenus* 237e
> μέγα δὲ τεκμήριον τῷ λόγῳ αὐτὸς παρέχεται Plato *Symposium* 195a
> ἱκανὸν ἐρῶ τεκμήριον Isaeus 6.1
> μέγα ὑμῖν τεκμήριον ἐρῶ Lysias Frag. 398.14 Albini
> μέγα ὑμῖν ἐρῶ τεκμήριον Demosthenes 49.48

> μέγα τεκμήριόν ἐστιν Plato *Protagoras* 341d
> μέγα τεκμήριον ὑμῖν ἔστω Demosthenes 47.77
> μέγιστον ὑμῖν ἔστω τεκμήριον Demosthenes 53.1
> μέγιστον μέν ἐστιν αὐτῷ τῷ ἔχοντι κακόν Demosthenes 25.32
> μεγάλ᾽, ὦ ἄνδρες Ἀθηναῖοι, κατ᾽ ἐκείνου φαίνοιτ᾽ ἂν ὀνείδη
>   Demosthenes 2.4.

Right movement is intuitively attractive for amplificatory Y_2 modifiers

> δωρεὰς καὶ προδόσεις δοὺς ἑκάστῳ αὐτῶν μεγάλας Demosthenes 50.7,
>   cp. 50.12,

but it is counterintuitive for fronted Y_1 modifiers, since the point of the discontinuous structure is evidently to highlight the modifier rather than to cast a shadow over the remaining material; the simplest and most direct account of fronting is obviously movement to the front. It is also mechanically simpler in cases when the modifier is fronted ahead of the subject or out of a complement clause *τὴν μεγίστην ἂν αὐτὸν δικαίως οἶμαι δίκην δοῦναι* Demosthenes 21.202

πολλὴν γὰρ πάνυ κατέλιπεν ὁ πατὴρ αὐτῷ οὐσίαν Aeschines 1.42

and where the position of the modifier is formally comparable, though not necessarily identical, to that of the fronted interrogative

μεγάλοις ὑμᾶς τεκμηρίοις διδάξω Isaeus 10.16

ποίῳ δύναιτ' ἂν τις τεκμηρίῳ τοῦτο σαφῶς ἐπιδεῖξαι
    Aeschines 2.162.

It was noted above that interrogative words probably represent at least one component of the total focus material in a question, and the fronting of interrogative words can be interpreted as a focus driven fronting (Sasse 1977; Blake 1983). So some of the evidence points to right movement and some to left movement. One way of reconciling these conflicting indications is to separate fronting from discontinuity and order the former before the latter. First the complete phrase containing the focused modifier is fronted to the left edge, and then the unfocused head noun is moved to the right, thereby further highlighting the Y_1 modifier by making it more independent of its head noun. Either process can also occur independently of the other, that is phrases can be fronted and remain continuous, and Y_2 can be right moved in phrases that have not themselves undergone fronting.

Phrasing of YXY

The discontinuous head interrupted structure just described has a tendency to promote the application of certain types of sandhi and prosodic processes more strongly than the continuous head flanking structures. This can be demonstrated by calculating the relative frequency of head interrupted and head flanking structures for onset to coda resyllabification and $ρ$-gemination as compared to elision in verse, while holding constant the direction of application relative to the head of the XP. In other words, the relative frequency of $[Y\text{-}XY]_{XP}$ is treated as a proportion of $[Y\text{-}XY]_{XP} + [YP\text{-}X]_{XP}$, and the relative frequency of $[YX\text{-}Y]_{XP}$ is treated as a proportion of $[YX\text{-}Y]_{XP} + [X\text{-}YP]_{XP}$, where the hyphen indicates the location of the sandhi or elision. It is known from other evidence that resyllabification and $ρ$-gemination apply in tighter domains than elision. The data for the test were all cases in the extant tragedies of Euripides of $ρ$-gemination and onset to coda resyllabification of the clusters $πτ\text{-}, κτ\text{-}, στ\text{-}, σπ\text{-}, σκ\text{-}, ξ\text{-}, ψ\text{-}, βλ\text{-}, γλ\text{-}, γν\text{-}$ in verb phrases between lexical words and in metrically unambiguous locations; the sample for elision was drawn from the *Medea* and the *Troades*. Resyllabification in $[Y\text{-}XY]_{XP}$ is illustrated by

μητέρα κτείναντα σήν Eur. *Electra* 1251

θυγατέρα κτανεῖν ἐμήν *I.A.* 96
ἐπὶ κάρα στέψουσι καλλικόμαν *I.A.* 1080.

Resyllabification in [YX-Y]$_{XP}$ is illustrated by

ἱερούς ἀνέσχε πτόρθους *Hecuba* 459
σέμν' ἀφαιρεῖτε στέφη Eur. *Supplices* 359
πολλούς ὤλεσε στρατηλάτας Eur. *Supplices* 162 MSS.

Resyllabification in [YP-X]$_{XP}$ is illustrated by

λογχοποιῶν ὄργανα κτᾶσθαι *Bacchae* 1208.

Resyllabification in [X-YP]$_{XP}$ is illustrated by

σχήσετε στερρὸν δόρυ Eur. *Supplices* 711.

The results are presented in Figure 10.5; they show that when onset to coda resyllabification or ρ-gemination applies between a verb and a word belonging to a branching complement phrase on its right, the head interrupted structure is far preferred both in absolute terms and in comparison to elision in the same direction. When the sandhi process applies between a verb and a word belonging to a branching complement phrase to the left of the verb, the frequency of the head interrupted type is reduced, but it still remains more frequent in resyllabification and ρ-gemination than in elision. The statistics d_R and d_L are the standardized differences between the relative frequencies of the [YXY]$_{XP}$ structure in onset to coda resyllabification/ρ-gemination and in elision

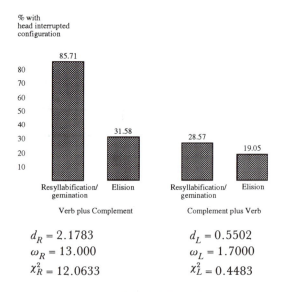

% with
head interrupted
configuration

$d_R = 2.1783$ $d_L = 0.5502$
$\omega_R = 13.000$ $\omega_L = 1.7000$
$\chi^2_R = 12.0633$ $\chi^2_L = 0.4483$

FIGURE 10.5

Comparison of head-interrupted to right and left head-flanking structures for resyllabification/ρ-gemination and elision

for, respectively, application to the right and to the left of the verb. They are a measure of association reflecting how strongly syntactic structure is correlated with phonological process. More intuitive as a measure of association is the odds ratio ω. The value of ω_R means that the odds for the head interrupted structure in left to right application is thirteen times greater in onset to coda resyllabification and p-gemination than the odds for it in elision. The value of ω_L is considerably less than that of ω_R, but still reflects a correlation in the same direction. The χ^2_R is highly significant and means that the correlation in left to right application cannot be explained as the result of chance variation in the distribution of the syntactic structures. The value of χ^2_L is not significant. It cannot, however, be safely concluded that the correlation of structure with type of phonological process obtains only if the direction of application of the latter is rightward from the verb. A difference in the strength of a correlation, as measured by d_R and d_L, is assessed by the test statistic χ^2_{homog}; since the value of this statistic for Figure 10.5 is not significant at the 0.05 confidence level, the difference in strengths of the correlations between rightward and leftward applications could fairly easily have arisen by chance, even if it were in reality of the same strength in the two directions.

The interpretation of Figure 10.5 is as follows: the relative frequency of the head interrupted structure $[YXY]_{XP}$ as compared to the head flanking types $[X\ YP]_{XP}$ and probably $[YP\ X]_{XP}$ among instances of onset to coda resyllabification and p-gemination is greater than its relative frequency among instances of elision; since resyllabification and p-gemination are phonological processes that occur in tighter domains than elision, Y_1X or XY_2 of the discontinuous structure is more suitable for the tighter phonological phrasing than are the corresponding continuous structures.

Internal prosodic structure of YXY

In Warlpiri (Laughren 1989), the location of the clitic auxiliary complex is sensitive to focus. Noun plus unfocused modifier is a single phrase for auxiliary placement, with primary stress on the noun and secondary stress on the modifier. But focused modifier plus noun is two phrases, so that the auxiliary complex follows the focused modifier and both modifier and noun have primary stress. Focus makes the modifier a more independent item of information, whether clitic placement is computed simply in terms of prosodic domains or in terms of some sort of syntactic-informational entities that correlate with prosodic entities. Conversely, low informational content or lack of definiteness or specificity can affect prosody in the opposite direction, as already noted in the case of destressing in Danish (p. 379). Noun incorporation too preferentially applies to indefinite and unfocused items. When the noun is not seen as a separate and independent item of information, it is liable to reduction rules at various levels of linguistic organization. Since in Greek Y_1 is typically focused and Y_2 typically carries rather topical or predictable information, it should follow that Y_1 has the greater claim to prosodic independence, that if X is phrased together with one element of the Y phrase to the exclusion of the other, then that element should be the unfocused one. One way of testing this is to analyze all instances from the tragic trimeter in which there is onset to coda resyllabification or p-gemination between Y_1 and the verb or between the verb and Y_2. Both complement and subject YPs were included in this test. When resyllabification takes place in a discontinuous YXY structure between the verb and a following element of the noun phrase (denoted by the hyphen V-N_2), N_2 is the head of the noun phrase 91.7% of the time. In the remaining 8.3%, only two instances, N_2 is a genitive modifier, each time χθονός

κλήρους δ' ἐμβατεύσετε χθονὸς *Heraclidae* 876

αὐτόματον, ἢ νιν σεισμὸς ἔστρεψε χθονός; *I.T.* 1166.

In both instances, it is the head noun in the N_1 position and not the genitive modifier in the N_2 position that is focused or conveys the informational nucleus; both κλῆρος and σεισμός imply the presence of χθών in the situation. That there is a genuine constraint on the formation of cohesive phonological phrases in discontinuous structures to the effect that N_2 must be the head noun when there is V-N_2 resyllabification is proved by a test against a control sample of discontinuous structures with no positional lengthening from the tragic trimeter, where the rate is much lower as shown in Table 10.3. The value of the odds ratio, 8.942, means that the odds for the head noun to occur in the N_2 position are nearly nine times greater when V and N_2 necessarily enter into a minor phrase than when they do not; the chi square shows that the correlation is statistically significant. Conversely, when the onset to coda resyllabification takes place between N_1 and V (denoted N_1-V), N_1 is the head noun of the noun phrase 78% of the time, a rate considerably exceed-

TABLE 10.3
Internal structure of discontinuous noun phrases

	N_2 = head %	$N_2 \neq$ head %
V-N_2	91.67	8.33
Verse control	55.17	44.83

$\omega = 8.942$, $\chi^2 = 8.615$

ing the 45% rate at which N_1 is the head in the control sample, although due to the small size of the available dataset the difference is not statistically significant. Furthermore, if positionally lengthened N_1 is a modifier, it is always nonlexical and consequently more likely to be phrased with the verb regardless of the syntactic structure

τόσα κτᾶσθαι κακά Medea 1047.

Phrasing of SVS

In Pima, a fronted quantifier modifying the object can be treated as a single constituent with a following verb for the purposes of computing second position for the clitic auxiliary complex, but a fronted quantifier modifying the subject in a transitive sentence cannot be linked to a following verb but must be treated as an independent constituent for auxiliary placement. Greek too had rather strict constraints on the phrasing of discontinuous subject phrases. It has already been noted that when the discontinuous phrase is the subject phrase, there is a preference in both prose and verse for structures in which the interrupting verb is a sister of the subject phrase in terms of lexically branching underlying constituency relations. Verse instances of SVS do sometimes occur that fail to meet this requirement, both with a lexical direct object

ἐρημία γὰρ πόλιν ὅταν λάβῃ κακή Troades 26

and with a complement or adjunct prepositional phrase

ἀλλ᾽ ἐκ λόγου γὰρ ἄλλος ἐκβαίνει λόγος Troades 706.

It should also be noted that S_2 may branch

πᾶς δ᾽ ὑφηγεῖται τρόπος μορφῆς Eumenides 192.

However, in the subset of all SVS structures in which coda to onset resyllabification indicates tight phrasing, the requirement for sisterhood is exceptionless, on the evidence of a dataset consisting of all instances of lexical coda to onset resyllabification of all types of clusters in fourth and fifth longum in the tragic trimeter — an easily controlled environment and the only one where such lexical resyllabification is usably frequent. If the verb is not intransitive, resyllabification occurs only if the direct object is an enclitic pronoun, whether it intervenes between S_1 and V

Θρῇξ νιν ὤλεσε ξένος Hecuba 774

or precedes the S_1VS_2 structure

ἤ νιν σεισμὸς ἔστρεψε χθονός I. T. 1166.

In fact, there are even more stringent conditions: if coda to onset resyllabification occurs in S_1VS_2, then not only must the verb be intransitive, or if transitive have only an enclitic pronoun direct object, but also

1. There must be no other lexical constituents of the clause containing S_1VS_2 besides those belonging to S_1, V, and S_2

2. Although S_1 may be branching, S_2 may not be branching

3. S_2 is overwhelmingly the head of the subject phrase, as demonstrated above.

These constraints mean that it is not simply the interrupted structure S_1VS_2 in any sentential context that promotes the formation of a cohesive prosodic domain, but just the short clause of the lexical structure $[S_1VS_2]_{Cl}$ where S_2 does not branch and is normally the head. These constraints ensure that those S_1VS_2 strings showing onset to coda resyllabification satisfy at the level of lexical words the motivating criteria for discontinuity: in such short clauses S_1 and S_2 form a subject phrase to which the verb does not belong but with which the verb forms a larger constituent, namely the entire short clause itself.

The constraints requiring $[S_1VS_2]_{Cl}$ structure for resyllabification to apply are not merely the result of the accidental absence of the excluded types in a small dataset. A judgment sample of 14 S_1VS_2 structures not involving coda to onset resyllabification was taken from the *Eumenides, Troades* and *Phoenissae* in the identical location at the end of the trimeter: 7 were found to conform to the short clause constraint but 7 violated it. The difference between 0 violations out of 7 and 7 violations out of 14 is statistically significant (by the hypergeometric distribution $p = 0.0295$). These results suggest that in a verb interrupted subject phrase the verb could be phonologically phrased together with the subject phrase element to its right or it could be phrased separately from it, and that the former outcome was more likely when the constraints just established were met than when they were not met.

It is also possible to show that the $[S_1VS_2]_{Cl}$ structure promotes the formation of a resyllabification domain more than the corresponding short clause with flanking structure verb plus subject phrase $[V\ SP]_{CL}$

οὐδ' ἐφρουρεῖτο στρατὸς *Rhesus* 764

or the extended interrupted type S_1XVS_2 where X contains one or more lexical words

ἄλλοι πρὸς ἄντρα σοὐσαφίκοντο ξένοι *Cyclops* 252;

this latter type does not occur in tragedy. In the fourth and fifth longum of the tragic trimeter, there are only 3 cases of the flanking structure (and, as just noted no case of the extended interrupted structure) with resyllabification as compared to 7 of the $[S_1VS_2]_{Cl}$ type. The odds of 7:3 in favour of the short clause structure when resyllabification occurs are obviously much greater than the odds for the short clause at the end of the trimeter in general. The flanking and the extended interrupted types are also constrained in that neither the subject phrase in the flanking type nor S_2 in the extended interrupted type may be branching (whereas a head may be resyllabified before a branching complement).

Inscriptional punctuation of discontinuous structures

In phrase punctuating inscriptions, a discontinuous structure consisting of three appositive groups can be treated as a single minor phrase

Πηδωμ μ᾽ ανεθηκεν ωμφιννεω : *Psamm.* 1
: ϙωι βασιλευς εδωϙ᾽ ωιγυπτιος : *Psamm.* 3
: το παρα τοισι τας διακοσιας δραχμας οφελοσι I³.1.248.5;
    articulated participial phrase.

While not precluding some form of internal prosodic constituency, as indicated by the metrical evidence cited above, the *Psamm.* punctuations attest the prosodic unity of the simple N_1VN_2 structure.

General properties of YXY phrasing

On the basis of the various items of evidence just presented, and of the appositive group evidence presented in Chapter 7, it would be a reasonable hypothesis that an interrupted constituent is always more cohesive than its flanking counterparts, more precisely that in any interrupted structure of a given category and lexical content, YXY, whatever the syntactic status of X and its relation to YP, a prosodic domain of a given level would be more readily formed over YX or XY or both than over its flanking counterparts X YP or YP X. This hypothesis is difficult to prove. There are a number of instances in which a semilexical word intercalated within a syntactic phrase shows coda to onset resyllabification at the end of the trimeter

τὸν πατρῷον ἡνίκα στόλον *Trachiniae* 562,

but, since resyllabification is also quite frequent in comparable non-interrupted structures

ἡνίκα ξὺν Ἡρακλεῖ *Heraclidae* 741,

it is not clear that the intercalation of the semilexical promotes resyllabification. When the intercalated element is lexical, the hypothesis is very difficult to test with any rigorous level of control. It is comparatively rare in Greek, even in verse, to find the interweaving of two or more branching constituents that do not stand in a head to complement/adjunct relation, a feature that is so common with noun phrases in the Latin pentameter

alba procellosos vela referre Notos Ovid *Heroides* 2.12.

Resyllabification is found though rarely when a nonbranching element other than the superordinate phrasal head is intercalated *ἐντύναθ' ἵππους ἅρμασι ζυγηφόρους Hippolytus* 1183,

but in the trimeter resyllabification does not have greater absolute frequency in such intercalated structures than in their flanking counterparts

      περικαλύψαι τοῖσι πράγμασι σκότον Ion 1522.

Such structures, both flanking and interrupted, are subject to the constraint that in the trimeter both of the constituents involved cannot simultaneously be branching.

    Another question is whether the syntactic relation of the interrupting element to the interrupted constituent influences the extent to which a prosodic domain of a given level can be formed. In the absolute sense, the answer is affirmative: resyllabification in S_1VS_2 has been shown to be subject to the severe constraint that the structure completely exhaust a short clause except for nonlexicals and S_2 not branch. Such a constraint does not hold when the verb is intercalated within a constituent of the verb phrase

      σέμν' ἀφαιρεῖτε στέφη μητρός Eur. *Supplices* 359.

In its relative sense, the question asks whether, as compared with its flanking counterpart, an interrupted structure always increases the probability of domain formation at a given level of cohesion to the same degree. This question is almost impossible to answer by a direct statistical test, since there are so many different factors that influence the relative frequencies of the variant orders of different syntactic categories, but the following rather intricate reasoning suggests that the answer is negative: the lexically exhaustive clause $[S_1VS_2]_{Cl}$ is favoured to a higher degree (70% to 30%) over all other verb plus subject possibilities with resyllabification than $[X_1VX_2]$ lexically exhaustive of its clause or participial phrase where X is an element other than the subject is favoured over other verb plus X possibilities (24.24% to 75.76%: $\chi^2 = 7.0739$). It follows that the interrupted structure is a more important factor in the phonological phrasing of syntactically difficult sequences.

Musical evidence

Unfortunately, in the Delphic hymns the settings of discontinuous noun phrases are too poorly preserved to permit fully adequate control for interacting factors, but there is some tonal evidence supporting the foregoing conclusion on the phrasing of YXY. In the two instances of $N_1(X)VN_2$ structures (proper names excluded), when N_2 is the head, there is a fall in pitch from the accentual peak of the verb to that of N_2 (ME 10.4-5). The substantial pitch falls between the peaks of the verb and N_2 exclude any focal pitch obtrusion on the N_2s and accord with

ME 10.4   [πρ]ω - ῶ -   να μα-αν-   τει - εῖ - ον   ἐφ- ἑ- - πων   πά-γον   *Ath.* 8

ME 10.5   ἱερουί   -   καισιν εὐμε]νεῖς   μό- λ[ε] - τε

προσ - πό - λοι - σ⟨ι⟩   *Lim.* 37

the assumption that the verb and N_2 belonged to the same minor phonological phrase. Furthermore, in ME 10.4 there is a rise of a tone and a half from the peak of πρῶνα to that of μαντεῖον; although reset may be a factor here, this rise would also accord with focus motivated pitch obtrusion on μαντεῖον. In the single case where N_2 is the modifier (ME 10.6), there is a very large pitch rise to the peak of N_2, even when the

ME 10.6   συ - υ-   ρίγ - μαθ' ι - ἰ-   εἰς   ἀ - θώ   -   πε [υτ'   *Ath.* 24

effect of the grave accent of the participle is factored out. This rise is the musical reflection of the focal pitch obtrusion assigned to ἀθώπευτ'. These three instances are consistent with the hypothesis that in discontinuous structures of the type $N_1(X)VN_2$, if N_2 is the head it is usually unfocused and phrased with the verb, whereas if N_2 is the modifier, then N_2 is focused and not necessarily phrased with the verb. There is only one usable instance of a YXY structure in which X is not the verb (ME 10.7). In this instance, pitch falls from the peak of the verb governing

ME 10.7   αι - εῖ - θε⟨ι⟩   νέ - ων   μῆ - ρα   τα-ού- ρων·   *Ath.* 12

the whole YXY structure to Y_1; this pitch fall excludes any focus motivated pitch obtrusion on νέων, and the rise from the peak of X to that of Y_2 reflects its focal status, which is concordant with its placement in absolute final position of its clause.

Mesomedes' Hymn to the Sun and Hymn to Nemesis only weakly reflect the classical system of catathesis, and in them the treatment of pitch relations in discontinuous structures is the reverse of that just analyzed. In N_1VN_2 structures where N_2 is the head, there are 3 cases of pitch rise from the peak of the verb to the peak of N_2 and none of fall; where N_2 is the modifier, there is one case of pitch fall from the verb to N_2 and none of rise. In the one instance of Y_1XY_2 in which X is not the verb, there is a fall from X to Y_2 (the head) despite the fact that Y_2 is a proper name.

In a couple of instances in the Delphic hymns, a continuous noun phrase containing an emotively loaded word is moved into an initial focus slot ahead of a subordinating conjunction. In ME 10.8, the accentual

ME 10.8  *Ath.* 21

[τρ]ί- πο-δα μαν - τει- εῖ - ον ὡς ει - εῖ - [λες

peak of *μαντεῖον* is not affected by catathesis but is a tone higher than that of its preceding head noun, and its initial unaccented syllable is 5 semitones higher than the first postpeak syllable of the noun, which is consequently set with secondary rise (p. 189). Secondary rise on the preceding modifier of such a fronted constituent also occurs in ME 10.9.

ME 10.9   *Lim.* 32

ὁ βάρ] - βα - ρος ἄ - ρης ὅ - τε

Not all instances of movement around a conjunction involve a whole phrase; such movement can cooccur with discontinuity when only one constituent of the phrase is fronted. There are two instances in the Delphic hymns of this sort of fronting of the modifier only, with the noun left stranded after the verb in clause final position (ME 10.10–11). Both instances involve a nonrestrictive adjective, that is an adjective which does not serve to distinguish the noun from other members of a set but rather is a descriptive amplification. In ME 10.10, the accentual peak

ME 10.10

'Αλ-[λὰ χρηη - σμ]ωιδὸν ὃς ἔ - χει - εις τρί - πο - δα

Lim. 21

ME 10.11   *Ath.* 21

ἐχ - θρὸς ὅν ἐ - φρ]ου-ού- ρει - ει δρα-κων

of the stranded N_2 is a semitone higher than the peak of the verb; there is also a secondary rise on the verb, as there is in ME 10.11; in both instances, the settings indicate focus on N_2. A stranded adjective does not necessarily have marked pitch obtrusion. In ME 9.15 above, *χρυσεοκόμαν* is separated by the verb and its means complement from *Φοῖβον* and stranded at the end of the clause, but it conforms to the usual catathetic lowering and compression; perhaps as an ornamental epithet it is treated as unemphatic amplificatory material. Conversely, focus can occur on an emphatic word in final position that is not stranded due to prolepsis or hyperbaton. In ME 10.12, the emphatic adverb *ἀσέπτως*

ME 10.12

τάνδ' ὃς ἐπὶ γαῖα]ν ἐπέ-   ρα-ασ' ἀ - σέπ - τ[ως,

Ath. 26

is placed in clause final position. Although much of the preceding musical setting is lost, it is clear that ἀσέπτως received pitch obtrusion sufficient to induce a secondary pitch rise on the postaccentual syllable of the preceding verb.

| Bibliography

Aaltonen, O., E. Vilkman and I. Raimo. 1988. Laryngeal adjustments or subglottal pressure? Studies on sentence stress production with excised human larynges. *Journal of Phonetics* 16:349.

Abd-El-Jawal, H. and I. Abu-Salim. 1987. Slips of the tongue in Arabic and their theoretical implications. *Language Sciences* 9:155.

Abe, I. 1955. Intonational patterns of English and Japanese. *Word* 11:386.

Abe, I. 1972. Tone-intonation relationships. *Proceedings of the Seventh International Congress of Phonetic Sciences*: 820. The Hague.

Abel, S. 1972. Duration discrimination of noise and tone bursts. *Journal of the Acoustical Society of America* 52:1219.

Abraham, R.C. 1941. *A Modern Grammar of Spoken Hausa.* London.

Abramson, A.S. 1962. *The Vowels and Tones of Standard Thai.* Bloomington.

Abramson, A.S. 1978. Static and dynamic cues to distinctive tones. *Language and Speech* 21:391.

Adams, C. 1979. *English Speech Rhythm and the Foreign Learner.* The Hague.

Adams, C.D. 1917. Demosthenes' avoidance of breves. *Classical Philology* 12:271.

Ades, A.E. 1974. How phonetic is selective adaptation? Experiments on syllable position and vowel environment. *Perception and Psychophysics* 61:66.

Ahrens, H.L. 1845. *De Crasi et Aphaeresi.* In *Kleine Schriften,* ed. C. Haeberlin: 52. Hannover (1891).

Ahrens, H.L. 1848. De hiatu apud elegiacos Graecorum poetas antiquiores. *Philologus* 3:223.

Ainsworth, W.A. 1972. Duration as a cue in the recognition of synthetic vowels. *Journal of the Acoustical Society of America* 51:648.

Ainsworth, W.A. 1974. The influence of precursive sequences on the perception of synthesized vowels. *Language and Speech* 17:103.

Ainsworth, W.A. 1986. Pitch change as a cue to syllabification. *Journal of Phonetics* 14:257.

Aissen, J. 1984. Themes and absolutives: Some semantic rules in Tzotzil. *Syntax and Semantics* 16:169.

Aizawa, K. 1981. Lengthening of sounds for emphasis of intensity. *Bulletin of the Phonetic Society of Japan* 167:5.

Allen, F.D. 1885. On Greek versification in inscriptions. *Papers of the American School of Classical Studies at Athens* 4:30.

Allen, G.D. 1972. The location of rhythmic stress beats in English. *Language and Speech* 15:72, 179.

Allen, G.D. and S. Hawkins. 1978. The development of phonological rhythm. *Syllables and Segments,* ed. A. Bell and J.B. Hooper: 173. Amsterdam.

Allen, G.D. and S. Hawkins. 1980. Phonological rhythm: Definition and development. *Child Phonology I,* ed. G.H. Yeni-Komshian, J.F. Kavanagh, C.H. Ferguson: 227. New York.

Allen, J.W.T. 1971. *Tendi.* New York.

Allen, M.R. 1975. Vowel mutation and word stress in Welsh. *Linguistic Inquiry* 6:181.

Allen, T.W., K. Walker, L. Symonds and M. Marcell. 1977. Intrasensory and inter-sensory perception of temporal sequences during infancy. *Developmental Psychology* 13:225.

Allen, W.S. 1950. Notes on the phonetics of an Eastern Armenian speaker. *Transactions of the Philological Society* 1950:180.

Allen, W.S. 1962. *Sandhi.* The Hague.

Allen, W.S. 1967. Correlation of tone and stress in ancient Greek. *To Honor Roman Jakobson* 46. The Hague.

Allen, W.S. 1973. *Accent and Rhythm.* Cambridge.

Allen, W.S. 1983. Some reflections on the penultimate accent. *Illinois Classical Studies* 8:1.

Allen, W.S. 1987. *Vox Graeca.* Third edition. Cambridge.

Allen, W.S. 1987b. The development of the Attic vowel system: Conspiracy or catas-trophe? *Minos* 20–22:21.

Allport, D.A. and E. Funnell. 1981. Components of the mental lexicon. *Philosophical Transactions of the Royal Society of London,* Series B 295:397.

Alstermark, M. and Y. Erikson. 1971. Swedish word accent as a function of word length. *Quarterly Progress and Status Report, Speech Transmission Laboratory, Royal Institute of Technology, Stockholm* 1971.1:1.

Anceaux, J.C. 1965. *The Nimboran Language: Phonology and Morphology.* The Hague.

Ancher, G.-P. 1978. Coupe morphologique et coupe syllabique en Attique. *Revue de Philologie* 52:66.

Anderson, S.R. 1984. Kwakwala syntax and the government-binding theory. *Syntax and Semantics* 16:21.

Anderson, S.R. and S. Chung. 1977. On grammatical relations and clause structure in verb-initial languages. *Syntax and Semantics* 8:1.

Andreewski, E. and X. Seron. 1975. Implicit processing of grammatical rules in a clas-sical case of agrammatism. *Cortex* 11:379.

Andrews, A. 1985. The major functions of the noun phrase. *Language Typology and Syntactic Description I,* ed. T. Shopen: 62. Cambridge.

Anttila, R. 1989. Spoonerizing double-entendre in Finnish. *Virittäjä* 93:370.

Anusiene, L. 1991. Rhythmical model of a phonetical word of present-day Lithuanian utterances. *Proceedings of the XIIth International Congress of Phonetic Sciences IV*: 250. Aix-en-Provence.

Aoki, H. 1970. *Nez Perce Grammar.* Berkeley.

Arnott, W.G. 1957. Split anapaests, with special reference to some passages of Alexis. *Classical Quarterly* 51:188.

Arvaniti, A. 1992. Secondary stress: Evidence from Modern Greek. *Papers in Labora-tory Phonology II,* ed. G.J. Docherty and D.R. Ladd: 398. Cambridge.

Ashton, E.O. 1947. *Swahili Grammar.* London.

Auer, P. 1989. Some ways to count morae. *Linguistics* 27:1071.

Aujac, G. and M. Lebel. 1981. *Denys d'Halicarnasse: Opuscules rhétoriques.* Paris.

Autesserre, D., Y. Nishinuma and I. Guaitella. 1989. Breathing, pausing, and speak-ing in dialogue. *Eurospeech 89 II*: 433.

Avram, A. 1986. Sandhi phenomena in Romanian. *Sandhi Phenomena in the Languages of Europe*, ed. H. Andersen: 551. Berlin.

Awbery, G.M. 1986. Survey of sandhi types in Welsh. *Sandhi Phenomena in the Languages of Europe*, ed. H. Andersen: 415. Berlin.

Azuma, J. and Y. Tsukuma. 1991. Role of F_0 and pause in disambiguating syntactically ambiguous Japanese sentences. *Proceedings of the XIIth International Congress of Phonetic Sciences III*: 274. Aix-en-Provence.

Bader, Y. 1983. Vowel sandhi and syllable structure in Kabyle Berber. *Studies in the Linguistic Sciences* 13:1.

Baer, T. 1979. Reflex activation of laryngeal muscles by sudden induced subglottal pressure changes. *Journal of the Acoustical Society of America* 65:1271.

Bailey, C.J.N. 1978. *Gradience in English Syllabization and a Revised Concept of Unmarked Syllabization*. Bloomington.

Bailey, R.W. and J.L. Robinson. 1973. *Varieties of Present-Day English*. New York.

Bailey, T. 1976. Accentual and cursive cadences in Gregorian psalmody. *Journal of the American Musicological Society* 29:463.

Baken, R.J. 1987. *Clinical Measurement of Speech and Voice*. Boston.

Baker, M. 1988. *Incorporation: A Theory of Grammatical Function Changing*. Chicago.

Baker, M. 1994. *The Polysynthesis Parameter*. Oxford.

Balasubramanian, T. 1980. Timing in Tamil. *Journal of Phonetics* 8:449.

Balasubramanian, T. 1981. Emphasis in Tamil. *Journal of Phonetics* 9:139.

Balasubramanian, T. 1981b. Duration of vowels in Tamil. *Journal of Phonetics* 9:151.

Bannert, R. 1982. Temporal and tonal control in German. *Working Papers, Institute of Linguistics and Phonetics, Lund University* 22:1.

Bannert, R. 1986. Independence and interdependence of prosodic features. *Working Papers in General Linguistics and Phonetics, Lund University* 29:31.

Bannert, R. and A.-C. Bredvad-Jensen. 1975. Temporal organization of Swedish tonal accents. *Working Papers in General Linguistics and Phonetics, Lund University* 10:1.

Bannert, R. and N.G. Thorsen. 1986. Acoustic-phonetic investigations of the intonation of German and Danish. *Annual Report, Institute of Phonetics, University of Copenhagen* 20:45.

Barker, M.A.R. 1964. *Klamath Grammar*. Berkeley.

Barrett, W.S. 1964. *Euripides. Hippolytus*. Oxford.

Barry, M.C. 1985. A palatographic study of connected speech processes. *Cambridge Papers in Phonetics and Experimental Linguistics* 4.

Barss, A., K. Hale, E.T. Perkins and M. Speas. 1989. Aspects of logical form in Navajo. *Athapaskan Linguistics: Current Perspectives on a Language Family*, ed. E.D. Cook and K.D. Rice: 317. Berlin.

Bartoli, M.G. 1930. Ancora una deviazione del greco all' ossitonia ario-europea. *Rivista di Filologia e Istruzione Classica* 58:24.

Bartoňek, A. 1966. Development of the long-vowel system in ancient Greek dialects. *Opera Universitatis Purkynianae Brunensis, Facultas Philosophica* 106. Prague.

Basso, A., A.R. Lecours, S. Moraschini and M. Vanier. 1985. Anatomoclinical correlations of the aphasias as defined through computerized tomography. *Brain and Language* 26:201.

Bates, E., A. Friederici and B. Wulfeck. 1987. Grammatical morphology in aphasia: Evidence from three languages. *Cortex* 23:545.

Bauer, H.R. 1988. Vowel intrinsic pitch in infants. *Folia Phoniatrica* 40:138.

Baunack, J. and T. Baunack. 1885. *Die Inschrift von Gortyn*. Leipzig.

Baxter, D.M. and E.K. Warrington. 1985. Category specific phonological dysgraphia. *Neuropsychologia* 23:653.

Bearth, T. 1980. Is there a universal correlation between pitch and information value? *Wege zur Universalienforschung*, ed. G. Brettschneider and C. Lehmann: 124. Tübingen.

Beazley, J.D. 1956. *Attic Black-Figure Vase-Painters*. Oxford.

Beazley, J.D. 1963. *Attic Red-Figure Vase-Painters I*. Second edition. Oxford.

Bechtel, F. 1921–1924. *Die griechischen Dialekte I–III*. Berlin.

Beckman, M.E. 1982. Segment duration and the "mora" in Japanese. *Phonetica* 39:113.

Beckman, M.E. 1986. *Stress and Non-Stress Accent*. Dordrecht.

Beckman, M.E. and J.B. Pierrehumbert. 1986. Intonational structure in Japanese and English. *Phonology Yearbook* 3:255.

Beckman, M.E. and J. Edwards. 1990. Lengthenings and shortenings and the nature of prosodic constituency. *Papers in Laboratory Phonology I*, ed. J. Kingston and M.E. Beckman: 152. Cambridge.

Beckman, M.E., J. Edwards and J. Fletcher. 1992. Prosodic structure and tempo in a sonority model of articulatory dynamics. *Papers in Laboratory Phonology II*, ed. G.J. Docherty and D.R. Ladd: 68. Cambridge.

Beddor, P.S., R.A. Krakow and L.M. Goldstein. 1986. Perceptual constraints and phonological change: A study of nasal vowel height. *Phonology Yearbook* 3:197.

Beekes, R.S.P. 1971. The writing of consonant groups in Mycenaean. *Mnemosyne* 24:337.

Behrens, S. 1985. The perception of stress and lateralization of prosody. *Brain and Language* 26:332.

Behrens, S. 1989. Characterizing sentence intonation in a right-hemisphere-damaged population. *Brain and Language* 37:181.

Belis, A. 1988. A proposito degli "inni delfici" ad Apollo. *La musica in Grecia*, ed. B. Gentili and R. Pretagostini: 205.

Belis, A. 1992. *Les Hymnes à Apollo*. Corpus des inscriptions de Delphes III. Paris.

Bell, A. 1970. *A State-Process Approach to Syllabicity and Syllable Structure*. Ph.D. dissertation. Stanford.

Bell, A. 1971. Some patterns of occurrence and formation of syllable structures. *Working Papers on Language Universals, Stanford University* 6:23.

Bell, A. 1977. Accent placement and perception of prominence in rhythmic structures. *Studies in Stress and Accent*, ed. L. Hyman: 1. Los Angeles.

Bell, A. and J.B. Hooper. 1978. Issues and evidence in syllabic phonology. *Syllables and Segments*, ed. A. Bell and J.B. Hooper: 3. Amsterdam.

Bell, H. 1968. The tone system of Mahas Nubian. *Journal of African Languages* 6:26.

Bell-Berti, F., S. Regan and M. Boyle. 1991. Final lengthening: Speaking rate effects. *Journal of the Acoustical Society of America* 90:2311.

Bendor-Samuel, J.T. 1969. Yakur syllable patterns. *Word* 25:16.

Bengtsson, I. and A. Gabrielsson. 1983. Analysis and synthesis of musical rhythm. *Studies of Musical Performance*, ed. J. Sundberg: 27. Stockholm.

Benguerel, A.-P. and J. D'Arcy. 1986. Time-warping and the perception of rhythm in speech. *Journal of Phonetics* 14:231.

Bennis, H., R. Prins and J. Vermeulen. 1983. *Lexical-Semantic versus Syntactic Disorders in Aphasia: The Processing of Prepositions*. Publikaties van het Instituut voor Algemene Taalwetenschap 40.

Benowitz, L., D. Bear, M. Mesulam, R. Rosenthal, E. Zaidel and R. Sperry. 1984. Contributions of the right cerebral hemisphere in perceiving paralinguistic cues of emotion. *Cognitive constraints on Communication*, ed. L. Vaina and J. Hintikka: 75. Dordrecht.

Benseler, G. 1841. *De Hiatu in Oratoribus Atticis et Historicis Graecis*. Freiberg.

Berdan, R. 1983. The necessity of variable rules. *Variation in the Form and Use of Language*, ed. R.W. Fasold: 63. Washington D.C.

Berendsen, E. 1987. Schwa deletion in Dutch cliticization. *Phonologica 1984,* ed. W.U. Dressler, H.C. Luschützky, O.E. Pfeiffer and J.R. Rennison: 13. London.

Berg, T. 1987. The case against accommodation. *Journal of Memory and Language* 26:277.

Berinstein, A.E. 1979. *A Cross-Linguistic Study on the Perception and Production of Stress.* Working Papers in Phonetics, University of California, Los Angeles 47.

Berkovits, R. 1993. Progressive utterance-final lengthening in syllables with final fricatives. *Language and Speech* 36:89.

Berndt, R.S. 1987. Symptom co-occurrence and dissociation in the interpretation of agrammatism. *The Cognitive Neuropsychology of Language,* ed. M. Coltheart, G. Sartori and R. Job: 221. London.

Berndt, R.S., A. Basili and A. Caramazza. 1987. Dissociation of functions in a case of transcortical sensory aphasia. *Cognitive Neuropsychology* 4:79.

Bernhardi, K. 1872. De incisionibus anapaesti in trimetro comico graecorum. *Acta Societatis Philologicae Lipsiensis* 1:245.

Bertinetto, P.M. 1989. Reflections on the dichotomy "stress-" vs. "syllable-timing." *Revue de Phonétique Appliquée* 91:99.

Bertinetto, P.M. and C.A. Fowler. 1989. On sensitivity to durational modifications by Italian and English speakers. *Rivista di Linguistica* 1:69.

Best, C.T., H. Hoffman and B.B. Glanville. 1982. Development of infant ear asymmetries for speech and music. *Perception and Psychophysics* 31:75.

Bharucha, J.J. and J.H. Pryor. 1986. Disrupting the isochrony underlying rhythm: An asymmetry in discrimination. *Perception and Psychophysics* 40:137.

Bierwisch, M. 1966. Regeln für die Intonation deutscher Sätze. *Untersuchungen über Akzent und Intonation im Deutschen,* ed. M. Bierwisch: 99. Berlin.

Bierwisch, M. 1968. Two critical problems in accent rules. *Journal of Linguistics* 4:173.

Bijeljac-Babic, R., J. Bertoncini and J. Mehler. 1993. How do 4-day-old infants categorize multisyllabic utterances? *Developmental Psychology* 29:711.

Bing, J.M. 1979. *Aspects of English Prosody.* Ph.D. dissertation, University of Massachusetts.

Birnbaum, D.J. 1981. Rising diphthongs and the Slovak rhythm law. *Harvard Studies in Phonology* 2:1.

Black, H.A. 1991. The phonology of the velar glide in Axininca Campa. *Phonology* 8:183.

Black, J.W. 1970. The magnitude of pitch inflections. *Proceedings of the Sixth International Congress of Phonetic Sciences*: 171. Prague.

Blake, B.J. 1977. *Case Marking in Australian Languages.* Canberra.

Blake, B.J. 1983. Structure and word order in Kalkatungu: The anatomy of a flat language. *Australian Journal of Linguistics* 3:143.

Blank, D.L. 1983. Remarks on Nicanor, the Stoics and the ancient theory of punctuation. *Glotta* 61:48.

Blass, F. 1892, 1893. *Die attische Beredsamkeit II, III.1.* Second edition. Leipzig.

Blass, F. 1899. Neuestes aus Oxyrhynchos. *Neue Jahrbücher für das Klassische Altertum* 3:30.

Blight, R.C. and E.V. Pike. 1976. The Phonology of Tenango Otomi. *International Journal of American Linguistics* 42:51.

Bliss, A.J. 1967. *The Metre of Beowulf.* Second edition. Oxford.

Blood, D.L. 1967. Phonological units in Cham. *Anthropological Linguistics* 9.8:15.

Bloomfield, L. 1942. Outline of Ilocano syntax. *Language* 18:193.

Blumstein, S. 1988. Approaches to speech production deficits in aphasia. *Handbook of Neuropsychology I,* ed. F. Boller and J. Grafman: 349. Amsterdam.

Blumstein, S. and W.E. Cooper. 1974. Hemispheric processing of intonation contours. *Cortex* 10:146.

Blumstein, S., B. Katz, H. Goodglass, R. Shrier and B. Dworetsky. 1985. The effects of slowed speech on auditory comprehension in aphasia. *Brain and Language* 24:246.

Boas, F. and E. Deloria. 1939. *Dakota Grammar*. Washington.

Bock, J.K. and J.R. Mazzella. 1983. Intonational marking of given and new information. *Memory and Cognition* 11:64.

Bock, K. 1989. Closed-class immanence in sentence production. *Cognition* 31:163.

Bodendorff, M. 1880. *Das rhythmische Gesetz des Demosthenes*. Dissertation, Königsberg.

Boeckh, A. 1811. *Pindari Opera I.2*. Berlin.

Boeder, W. 1989. Verbal person marking, noun phrase and word order in Georgian. *Configurationality: The Typology of Asymmetries*, ed. L. Marácz and P. Muysken: 159. Dordrecht.

Bolinger, D. 1962. Binomials and pitch accent. *Lingua* 11:34.

Bolinger, D. 1978. Intonation across languages. *Universals of Human Language II*, ed. J.H. Greenberg: 471. Stanford.

Bolinger, D. 1986. *Intonation and Its Parts*. Stanford.

Bolinger, D. 1989. *Intonation and Its Uses*. Stanford.

Bolozky, S. 1982. Remarks on rhythmic stress in Modern Hebrew. *Journal of Linguistics* 18:275.

Bolton, T.L. 1894. Rhythm. *American Journal of Psychology* 6:145.

Bond, Z.S. and S. Garnes. 1980. Misperceptions of fluent speech. *Perception and Production of Fluent Speech*, ed. R. Cole: 115. Hillsdale.

Booij, G. and J. Rubach. 1987. Postcyclic versus postlexical rules in lexical phonology. *Linguistic Inquiry* 18:1.

Bopp, F. 1856. *A Comparative Grammar of the Sanscrit, Zend, Greek, Latin, Lithuanian, Gothic, German and Sclavonic Languages*. Translated by E.B. Eastwick. London.

Borchgrevink, H.M. 1982. Prosody and musical rhythm are controlled by the speech hemisphere. *Music, Mind, and Brain*, ed. M. Clynes: 151. New York.

Borg, A. 1973. The segmental phonemes of Maltese. *Linguistics* 109:5.

Borgström, C.H. 1954. Språkanalyse sam barnelek. *Norsk Tidsskrift for Sprogvidenskap* 17:484.

Boring, E.G. 1942. *Sensation and Perception in the History of Experimental Psychology*. New York.

Borkin, A. 1984. *Problems in Form and Function*. Norwood.

Botinis, A. 1989. *Stress and Prosodic Structure in Greek: A Phonological, Acoustic, Physiological and Perceptual Study*. Lund.

Bouchard, D. 1984. *On the Content of Empty Categories*. Dordrecht.

Bowe, H.J. 1990. *Categories, Constituents and Constituent Order in Pitjantjatjara*. London.

Bower, G.H. and D. Winzenz. 1969. Group structure, coding, and memory for digit series. *Journal of Experimental Psychology* Monograph 80.2.2.

Bowers, D., H.B. Coslett, R.M. Baven, L.J. Spreedie and K.M. Heilman. 1987. Comprehension of emotional prosody following unilateral lesions. *Neuropsychology* 25:317.

Bradley, D. 1979. Speech through music: The Sino-Tibetan gourd reed-organ. *Bulletin of the School of Oriental and African Studies* 62:535.

Bradley, D.C. 1983. *Computational Distinctions of Vocabulary Type*. Bloomington.

Bradley, D.C., M.F. Garrett and E.B. Zurif. 1980. Syntactic deficits in Broca's aphasia. *Biological Studies of Mental Processes*, ed. D. Caplan: 269. Cambridge, Mass.

Bradley, D.C. and M.F. Garrett. 1983. Hemisphere differences in the recognition of closed and open class words. *Neuropsychologia* 21:155.

Bradley, D.C., R.M. Sánchez-Casas and J.E. García-Albea. 1993. The status of the syllable in the perception of Spanish and English. *Language and Cognitive Processes* 8:197.

Brambach, W. 1869. *Metrische Studien zu Sophocles.* Leipzig.

Brambach, W. 1871. *Rhythmische und metrische Untersuchungen.* Leipzig.

Brandt, K. 1902. Metrische Zeit- und Streitfragen. *Jahresbericht der königlichen Landes-schule Pforta* 1902:8.

Brause, J. 1909. *Lautlehre der Kretischen Dialekte.* Halle.

Bright, W. 1957. *The Karok Language.* Berkeley.

Bright, W. 1957b. Singing in Lushai. *Indian Linguistics* 17:24.

Bright, W. 1965. Luiseño phonemics. *International Journal of American Linguistics* 31:342.

Brookshire, R. 1972. Visual and auditory sequencing by aphasic subjects. *Journal of Communication Disorders* 5:259.

Browman, C.P. 1978. Tip of the tongue and slip of the ear: Implications for language processing. *Working Papers in Phonetics, University of California, Los Angeles* 42.

Browman, C.P. and L. Goldstein. 1988. Some notes on syllable structure in articulatory phonology. *Phonetica* 45:140.

Browman, C.P. and L. Goldstein. 1990. Gestural specification using dynamically-defined articulatory structures. *Journal of Phonetics* 18:299.

Browman, C.P. and L. Goldstein. 1990b. Tiers in articulatory phonology, with some implications for casual speech. *Papers in Laboratory Phonology I,* ed. J. Kingston and M.E. Beckman: 341. Cambridge.

Brown, G., K.L. Currie and J. Kenworthy. 1980. *Questions of Intonation.* London.

Brown, R. and D. McNeill. 1966. The "tip of the tongue" phenomenon. *Journal of Verbal Learning and Verbal Behavior* 5:325.

Brown, W.S. Jr. and R.E. McGlone. 1974. Aerodynamic and acoustic study of stress in sentence production. *Journal of the Acoustical Society of America* 56:971.

Bruce, G. 1977. *Swedish Word Accents in Sentence Perspective.* Lund.

Bruce, G. 1982. Developing the Swedish intonation model. *Working Papers, Department of Linguistics, Lund University* 22:51.

Bruce, G. 1982b. Textual aspects of prosody in Swedish. *Phonetica* 39:274.

Bruce, G. 1983. Accentuation and timing in Swedish. *Folia Linguistica* 17:221.

Bruce, G. 1984. Rhythmic alternation in Swedish. *Nordic Prosody III,* ed. C.-C. Elert, I. Johansson and E. Strangert: 31. Stockholm.

Bruce, G. 1986. On the phonology and phonetics of rhythm: Evidence from Swedish. *Phonologica 1984,* ed. W.U. Dressler, H.C. Luschützky, O.E. Pfeiffer and J.R. Rennison: 21. London.

Brugmann, K. 1913. Zur Geschichte der hiatischen (zweisilbigen) Vokalverbindungen in den indogermanischen Sprachen. *Berichte über die Verhandlungen der königlich Sächsischen Gesellschaft der Wissenschaften zu Leipzig, Philologisch-Historische Klasse*: 141.

Brugmann, K. 1930. *Vergleichende Laut-, Stammbildungs- und Flexionslehre der indogermanischen Sprachen.* Second edition. Berlin.

Bub, D. and A. Kertesz. 1982. Deep agraphia. *Brain and Language* 17:146.

Buck, C.D. 1955. *The Greek Dialects.* Chicago.

Bulloch, A.W. 1970. A Callimachean refinement to the Greek hexameter. *Classical Quarterly* 20:258.

Buxton, H. 1983. Temporal predictability in the perception of English speech. *Prosody: Models and Measurements,* ed. A. Cutler and D.R. Ladd: 111. Berlin.

Byarushengo, E.R. 1977. Preliminaries. *Southern California Occasional Papers in Linguistics* 6:1.

Byarushengo E.R., L.M. Hyman and S. Tenenbaum. 1976. *Tone, Accent, and Assertion in Haya.* Southern California Occasional Papers in Linguistics 3.

Bybee, J.L. and O. Dahl. 1989. The creation of tense and aspect systems in the languages of the world. *Studies in Language* 13:1.

Cairns, C.E. and M.H. Feinstein. 1982. Markedness and the theory of syllable structure. *Linguistic Inquiry* 13:193.

Campbell, A. 1959. *Old English Grammar.* Oxford.

Campbell, W.N. 1989. Syllable-level duration determination. *Eurospeech 89 II*: 698. Edinburgh.

Campbell, W.N. 1990. Shortening of feet in longer articulatory units. *Journal of the Acoustical Society of America* 88:S129.

Campbell, W.N. 1991. Durational shortening and anaphoric reference. *Proceedings of the XIIth International Congress of Phonetic Sciences II*: 286. Aix-en-Provence.

Capell, A. and H.E. Hinch. 1970. *Maung Grammar.* The Hague.

Caplan, D. 1985. Syntactic and semantic structures in agrammatism. *Agrammatism,* ed. M.-L. Kean: 125. Orlando.

Caplan, D. 1991. Agrammatism is a theoretically coherent aphasic category. *Brain and Language* 40:274.

Caramazza, A. and E.B. Zurif. 1976. Dissociation of algorithmic and heuristic processes in language comprehension. *Brain and Language* 3:572.

Caramazza, A. and R.S. Berndt. 1985. A multicomponent deficit view of agrammatic Broca's aphasia. *Agrammatism,* ed. M.-L. Kean: 27. Orlando.

Cardona, G. 1965. *A Gujarati Reference Grammar.* Philadelphia.

Carmon, A. and I. Nachsohn. 1971. Effect of unilateral brain damage on perception of temporal order. *Cortex* 7:410.

Carrington, J.F. 1949. *A Comparative Study of Some Central African Gong-Languages.* Brussels.

Carrington, J.F. 1966. Tone and melody in a Congolese popular song. *African Music* 4:38.

Carrio i Font, M. and A.R. Mestre. 1991. A contrastive analysis of Spanish and Catalan rhythm. *Proceedings of the XIIth International Congress of Phonetic Sciences IV*: 246. Aix-en-Provence.

Carrol, K. 1956. Yoruba religious music. *African Music* 1.3:45.

Carson, J. 1969. Greek accent and the rational. *Journal of Hellenic Studies* 89:24.

Caspers, J. and V.J. van Heuven. 1991. Phonetic and linguistic aspects of pitch movements in fast speech in Dutch. *Proceedings of the XIIth International Congress of Phonetic Sciences V*: 174. Aix-en-Provence.

Cedergren, H. 1973. *Interplay of Social and Linguistic Factors in Panama.* Ph.D. dissertation, Cornell University.

Cedergren, H. and D. Sankoff. 1974. Variable rules: Performance as a statistical reflection of competence. *Language* 50:333.

Chafe, W.L. 1976. Givenness, contrastiveness, definiteness, subjects, topics, and point of view. *Subject and Topic,* ed. C.N. Li: 25. New York.

Chafe, W.L. 1977. Accent and related phenomena in the Five Nations Iroquois languages. *Studies in Stress and Accent,* ed. L.M. Hyman: 169. Los Angeles.

Chailley, J. 1979. *La Musique grecque antique.* Paris.

Chambers, J.K. and P.A. Shaw. 1980. Systematic obfuscation of morphology in Dakota. *Linguistic Inquiry* 11:325.

Chambon, T. 1991. Phonological interpretation of F_0 variations in a Bantu language: Kinyarwanda. *Proceedings of the XIIth International Congress of Phonetic Sciences II*: 218. Aix-en-Provence.

Chang, N.-C. T. 1958. Tones and intonation in the Chengtu dialect (Szechuan, China). *Phonetica* 2:59.

Chantraine, P. 1952. Les recherches sur l'ordre des mots en grec. *Anales de Filologia Clásica* 5:71.

Chao, Y.R. 1956. Tone, intonation, singsong, chanting, recitative, tonal composition, and atonal composition in Chinese. *For Roman Jakobson,* ed. M. Halle, H.G. Lunt, H. McLean and C.H. van Schooneveld: 52. The Hague.

Chatman, S. 1965. *A Theory of Meter*. The Hague.

Chen, M. 1970. Vowel length variation as a function of the voicing of the consonant environment. *Phonetica* 22:129.

Chen, M. 1987. The syntax of Xiamen tone sandhi. *Phonology Yearbook* 4:109.

Chen, M. 1990. What must phonology know about syntax? *The Phonology-Syntax Connection*, ed. S. Inkelas and D. Zec: 19. Chicago.

Chierchia, G. 1986. Length, syllabification and the phonological cycle in Italian. *Journal of Italian Linguistics* 8:5.

Cho, Y.-M.Y. 1990. Syntax and phrasing in Korean. *The Phonology-Syntax Connection*, ed. S. Inkelas and D. Zec: 47. Chicago.

Cho, Y.Y. 1991. Voicing is not relevant for sonority. *Proceedings of the Seventeenth Annual Meeting of the Berkeley Linguistics Society*: 121.

Chomsky, N. 1981. *Lectures on Government and Binding*. Dordrecht.

Christ, W. 1879. *Metrik der Griechen und Römer*. Leipzig.

Chuang, C.K. and W.S. Wang. 1978. Psychophysical pitch biases related to vowel quality, intensity difference, and sequential order. *Journal of the Acoustical Society of America* 64:1004.

Clarke, E.F. 1985. Structure and expression in rhythmic performance. *Musical Structure and Cognition*, ed. P. Howell, I. Cross and R. West: 209. London.

Clarke, R.T. 1934. The drum language of the Tumba people. *American Journal of Sociology* 40:32.

Clements, G.N. 1978. Tone and syntax in Ewe. *Elements of Tone, Stress, and Intonation*, ed. D.J. Napoli: 21. Washington, D.C..

Clements, G.N. 1980. The hierarchical representation of tone features. *Harvard Studies in Phonology II*, ed. G.N. Clements: 50. Bloomington.

Clements, G.N. 1986. Compensatory lengthening and consonant gemination in Luganda. *Studies in Compensatory Lengthening*, ed. L. Wetzels and E. Sezer: 37. Dordrecht.

Clements, G.N. 1990. The role of the sonority cycle in core syllabification. *Papers in Laboratory Phonology I*, ed. J. Kingston and M.E. Beckman: 283. Cambridge.

Clements, G.N. 1992. Comments on Chapter 7. *Papers in Laboratory Phonology II*, ed. G.J. Docherty and D.R. Ladd: 183. Cambridge.

Clements, G.N. and S.J. Keyser. 1983. *CV Phonology: A Generative Theory of the Syllable*. Cambridge, Mass.

Clements, G.N. and S.R. Hertz. 1991. Nonlinear phonology and acoustic interpretation. *Proceedings of the XIIth International Congress of Phonetic Sciences I*: 364. Aix-en-Provence.

Clements, G.N. and J. Goldsmith. 1984. *Autosegmental Studies in Bantu Tone*. Dordrecht.

Clevenger, T. and M. Clark. 1963. Coincidental variation as a source of confusion in the experimental study of rate. *Language and Speech* 6:144.

Cloward, R.A. 1984. *Spanish Vowel Sandhi: Toward a Characterization of Low-Level Processes in Phonology*. Ph.D. dissertation, University of Illinois, Urbana-Champaign.

Clumeck, H. 1980. The acquisition of tone. *Child Phonology I*, ed. G.H. Yeni-Komshian, J.F. Kavanagh and C.F. Ferguson: 257. New York.

Cohen, A., R. Collier and J. 't Hart. 1982. Declination: Construct or intrinsic feature of speech pitch? *Phonetica* 39:254.

Cole, D.T. 1967. *Some Features of Ganda Linguistic Structure*. Johannesburg.

Cole, T. 1988. *Epiploke: Rhythmical Continuity and Poetic Structure in Greek Lyric*. Cambridge, Mass.

Collard, R. and D.-J. Povel. 1982. Theory of serial pattern production: Tree traversals. *Psychological Review* 89:693.

Collier, R. 1987. F_0 declination: The control of its setting, resetting, and slope. *Laryngeal Function in Phonation and Respiration,* ed. T. Baer, C. Sasaki and K.S. Harris: 403. Boston.

Collier, R. 1991. Multilanguage intonation synthesis. *Journal of Phonetics* 19:61.

Collier, R. and J. 't Hart. 1975. The role of intonation in speech perception. *Structure and Process in Speech Perception,* ed. A. Cohen and S.G. Nooteboom: 107. Berlin.

Collier, R. and C.E. Gelfer. 1984. Physiological explanations of F_0 declination. *Proceedings of the Tenth International Congress of Phonetic Sciences*: 354. Dordrecht.

Collinge, N.E. 1985. *The Laws of Indo-European.* Amsterdam.

Coltheart, M. 1987. Functional architecture of the language-processing system. *The Cognitive Neuropsychology of Language,* ed. M. Coltheart, G. Sartori and R. Job: 1. London.

Comotti, G. 1989. Melodia e accento di parola nelle testimonianze degli antichi e nei testi con notazione musicale. *Quaderni Urbinati* n.s. 32:91.

Condoravdi, C. 1990. Sandhi rules of Greek and prosodic theory. *The Phonology-Syntax Connection,* ed. S. Inkelas and D. Zec: 63. Chicago.

Conklin, H.C. 1956. Tagalog speech disguise. *Language* 32:136.

Conklin, H.C. 1959. Linguistic play in cultural context. *Language* 35:631.

Connell, B. and D.R. Ladd. 1990. Aspects of pitch realisation in Yoruba. *Phonology* 7:1.

Cooper, A.M., D.H. Whalen and C.A. Fowler. 1988. The syllable's rhyme affects its P-center as a unit. *Journal of Phonetics* 16:231.

Cooper, W.E. and J.R. Ross. 1975. Word order. *Papers from the Parasession on Functionalism,* ed. R.E. Grossman, L.J. San and T.J. Vance: 63. Chicago.

Cooper, W.E. and J. Paccia-Cooper. 1980. *Syntax and Speech.* Cambridge, Mass.

Cooper, W.E. and J.M. Sorensen. 1981. *Fundamental Frequency in Sentence Production.* New York.

Cooper, W.E., C. Soares, J. Nicol, D. Michelew and S. Goloskie. 1984. Clausal intonation after unilateral brain damage. *Language and Speech* 27:17.

Cooper, W.E., S.J. Eady and P.R. Mueller. 1985. Acoustical aspects of contrastive stress in question-answer contexts. *Journal of the Acoustical Society of America* 77:2142.

Cope, T. 1959. "African music," a lecture given at Natal University. *African Music* 2.2:33.

Corbett, G. 1990. Serbo-Croat. *The World's Major Languages,* ed. B. Comrie: 391. New York.

Corssen, W. 1870. *Ueber Aussprache, Vokalismus und Betonung der lateinischen Sprache II.* Second edition. Leipzig.

Coulon, V. 1953. Notes critiques et exégétiques. *Revue des Etudes Grecques* 66:34.

Counts, D.R. 1969. *A Grammar of Kaliai-Kove.* Honolulu.

Coupez, A. and T. Kamanzi. 1970. *Littérature de cour au Rwanda.* Oxford.

Courtenay, K. 1974. On the nature of the Bambara tone system. *Studies in African Linguistics* 5:303.

Cowan, H.K.J. 1965. *Grammar of the Sentani Language.* The Hague.

Cowan, N. 1989. Acquisition of Pig Latin: A case study. *Journal of Child Language* 16:365.

Cowper, E.A. and K.D. Rice. 1987. Are phonosyntactic rules necessary? *Phonology Yearbook* 4:185.

Crothers, J.H. 1979. Nez Perce. *Handbook of Phonological Data from a Sample of the World's Languages,* ed. J.H. Crothers, J.P. Lorentz, D. Sherman, M.H. Vihman: 780. Stanford.

Crusius, O. 1894. Zur neuesten antiken Musikresten. *Philologus* 52:160.

Crusius, O. 1894b. *Die delphischen Hymnen*. Göttingen.

Crusius, O. 1897. *Babrii Fabulae Aesopeae*. Leipzig.

Cruttenden, A. 1970. On the so-called grammatical function of intonation. *Phonetica* 21:182.

Cruttenden, A. 1981. Falls and rises: Meanings and universals. *Journal of Linguistics* 17:77.

Crystal. D. 1969. *Prosodic Systems and Intonation in English*. Cambridge.

Crystal, D. 1975. *The English Tone of Voice*. London.

Crystal, D. 1991. *A Dictionary of Linguistics and Phonetics*. Third edition. Oxford.

Crystal, T. and A. House. 1982. Segmental durations in connected speech signals: Preliminary results. *Journal of the Acoustical Society of America* 72:705.

Culicover, P.W. and M. Rochemont. 1983. Stress and focus in English. *Language* 59:123.

Cunningham, I.C. 1971. *Herodas: Mimiambi*. Oxford.

Cutler, A. 1980. Syllable omission errors and isochrony. *Temporal Variables in Speech: Studies in Honour of Frieda Goldman-Eisler*, ed. H.W. Dechert and M. Raupach: 183. The Hague.

Cutler, A. 1986. Phonological structure in speech recognition. *Phonology Yearbook* 3:161.

Cutler, A. and D.J. Foss. 1977. On the role of sentence stress in sentence processing. *Language and Speech* 20:1.

Cutler, A. and S.D. Isard. 1979. The production of prosody. *Language Production I*, ed. B. Butterworth: 245. New York.

Cutler, A., S. Butterfield and J.N. Williams. 1987. The perceptual integrity of syllabic onsets. *Journal of Memory and Language* 26:408.

Cutler, A. and B. Butterfield. 1992. Rhythmic cues to speech segmentation. *Journal of Memory and Language* 31:218.

Dahlstrom, A. 1983. Agent-patient languages and split case marking systems. *Proceedings of the Ninth Annual Meeting of the Berkeley Linguistics Society*: 37.

Dahlstrom, A. 1987. Discontinuous constituents in Fox. *Native American Languages and Grammatical Typology*, ed. P.D. Kroeber and R.E. Moore: 53. Bloomington.

Dalby, J.M. 1986. *Phonetic Structure of Fast Speech in American English*. Bloomington.

Dale, A.M. 1968. *Lyric Metres of Greek Drama*. 2nd edition. Cambridge.

Dale, A.M. 1969. *Collected Papers*. Cambridge.

Daneš, F. 1972. Order of elements and sentence intonation. *Intonation: Selected Readings*, ed. D. Bolinger: 216. Harmondsworth.

Danly, M. and B. Shapiro. 1982. Speech prosody in Broca's aphasia. *Brain and Language* 16:171.

Darkins, A.W., V.A. Fromkin and D.F. Benson. 1988. A characterization of the prosodic loss in Parkinson's disease. *Brain and Language* 34:315.

Darwin, C. 1872/1965. *Expression of the Emotions in Man and Animals*. Chicago.

Darwin, C.J. 1975. On the dynamic use of prosody in speech perception. *Structure and Process in Speech Perception*, ed. A. Cohen and S.G. Nooteboom: 178. Berlin.

Darwin, C.J. and A. Donovan. 1979. Perceptual studies of speech rhythm: Isochrony and intonation. *Spoken Language Generation and Understanding*, ed. J.C. Simon: 77. Dordrecht.

Dascălu, L. 1974. On the "parenthetical" intonation in Romanian. *Revue Roumaine de Linguistique* 19:231.

Dauer, R.M. 1983. Stress-timing and syllable-timing reanalyzed. *Journal of Phonetics* 11:51.

Davidsen-Nielsen, N. 1974. Syllabification in English words with medial sp, st, sk. *Journal of Phonetics* 2:15.

Davies, A.M. 1987. Folk-linguistics and the Greek word. *Festschrift for Henry Hoenigswald*, ed. G. Cardona and N.H. Zide: 263. Tübingen.

Davies, A.M. 1987b. Mycenaean and Greek syllabification. *Tractata Mycenaea*, ed. P.H. Ilievski and L. Crepajac: 91. Skopje.

Davis, S. 1985. *Topics in Syllable Geometry.* Ph.D. dissertation, University of Arizona.

Davis, S. 1988. Syllable onsets as a factor in stress rules. *Phonology* 5:1.

Davis, S. 1989. Stress, syllable weight hierarchies, and moraic phonology. *Proceedings of the Sixth Eastern States Conference on Linguistics*: 84.

Davis, S. 1989b. On a non-argument for the rhyme. *Journal of Linguistics* 25:211.

Dawe, R.D. 1964. *The Collation and Investigation of Manuscripts of Aeschylus.* Cambridge.

Dawes, R. 1745. *Miscellanea Critica.* Cambridge.

de Bleser, R. 1987. From agrammatism to paragrammatism. *Cognitive Neuropsychology* 4:187.

de Chene, B.E. 1985. *The Historical Phonology of Vowel Length.* New York.

de Haas, W. 1988. *A Formal Theory of Vowel Coalescence: A Case Study of Ancient Greek.* Dordrecht.

de Jong, D. 1990. The syntax-phonology interface and French liaison. *Linguistics* 28:57.

de Jong, J. 1981. On the treatment of focus phenomena in Functional Grammar. *Perspectives on Functional Grammar*, ed. T. Hoekstra, H. van der Hulst and M. Moortgat: 89. Dordrecht.

de Jong, K. 1989. Initial prominence and accent in Seoul Korean prosody. *Journal of the Acoustical Society of America* 85:S98.

de Rooij, J.J. 1979. *Speech Punctuation.* Ph.D. dissertation, University of Utrecht.

de Saussure, F. 1884. Une loi rythmique de la langue grecque. *Mélanges Graux. Recueil de travaux d'érudition classique dédié à la mémoire de Charles Graux*: 737. Paris.

de Saussure, F. 1916. *Cours de linguistique générale.* Lausanne.

de Saussure, F. 1922. *Recueil des publications scientifiques.* Lausanne.

de Vries, J. 1938. *Untersuchungen über die Sperrung von Substantiv und Attribut in der Sprache der attischen Redner.* Ph.D. dissertation, Göttingen.

de Vries, L. 1985. Topic and focus in Wambon discourse. *Syntax and Pragmatics in Functional Grammar*, ed. A.M. Bolkestein, C. de Groot and J. Mackenzie: 155. Dordrecht.

Deese, J. 1984. *Thought into Speech: The Psychology of a Language.* Englewood Cliffs.

Delattre, P. 1963. Comparing the prosodic features of English, German, Spanish and French. *International Review of Applied Linguistics* 1:193.

Delattre, P. 1964. Comparing the consonantal features of English, German, Spanish and French. *International Review of Applied Linguistics* 2:155.

Delattre, P. 1966. A comparison of syllable length conditioning among languages. *International Review of Applied Linguistics* 4:183.

Delattre, P. 1966b. Les dix intonations de base du français. *French Review* 40:1.

Delattre, P. 1968. An acoustic and articulatory study of vowel reduction in four languages. *International Review of Applied Linguistics* 7:295.

Dell, F. and M. Eldmedlaoui. 1988. Syllabic consonants in Berber: Some new evidence. *Journal of African Languages and Linguistics* 10:1.

Dell, G.S. 1988. The retrieval of phonological forms in production: Test of predictions from a connectionist model. *Journal of Memory and Language* 27:124.

Dell, G.S. 1990. Effects of frequency and vocabulary type on phonological speech errors. *Language and Cognitive Processes* 5:313.

den Os, E.A. 1988. *Rhythm and Tempo of Dutch and Italian: A Contrastive Study.* Ph.D. dissertation, University of Utrecht.

Denniston, J.D. 1934. *The Greek Particles.* Oxford.

Denniston, J.D. 1939. *Euripides. Electra.* Oxford

Denniston, J.D. 1952. *Greek Prose Style.* Oxford.

Derwing, B.L. 1992. A "pause-break" task for eliciting syllable boundary judgments from literate and illiterate speakers. *Language and Speech* 35:219.

Descroix, J. 1931. *Le Trimètre iambique.* Mâcon.

Deutsch, D. 1986. Recognition of durations embedded in temporal patterns. *Perception and Psychophysics* 39:179.

di Cristo, A. and D.J. Hirst. 1986. Modeling French micromelody: Analysis and synthesis. *Phonetica* 43:11.

Diggle, J. 1981. *Studies on the Text of Euripides.* Oxford.

Dihle, A. 1954. Die Anfänge der griechischen akzentuierenden Verskunst. *Hermes* 82:182.

Dik, S., M.E. Hoffmann, J.R. de Jong, S.I. Djiang, H. Stroomer and L. de Vries. 1981. On the typology of focus phenomena. *Perspectives on Functional Grammar,* ed. T. Hoekstra, H. van der Hulst and M. Moortgat: 41. Dordrecht.

Disner, S.F. 1982. Stress evaluation and voice lie detection: A review. *Working Papers in Phonetics, University of California, Los Angeles* 54:78.

Dixit, R.P. 1989. Glottal gestures in Hindi plosives. *Journal of Phonetics* 17:213.

Dixon. R.M.W. 1972. *The Dyirbal Language of North Queensland.* Cambridge.

Dixon, R.M.W. 1977. *A Grammar of Yidiɲ.* Cambridge.

Dobree, P.P. 1820. *Ricardi Porsoni Notae in Aristophanem.* Cambridge.

Dogil, G. 1984. Grammatical prerequisites to the analysis of speech style: Fast/casual speech. *Intonation, Accent, Rhythm,* ed. D. Gibbon and H. Richter: 91. Berlin.

Doke, C.M. 1926. *Phonetics of the Zulu Language.* Johannesburg.

Donegan, P.J. and D. Stampe. 1983. Rhythm and the holistic organization of language structure. *The Interplay of Phonology, Morphology and Syntax,* ed. J.F. Richardson, M. Marks, A. Chukerman: 337. Chicago.

Donovan, A. and C.J. Darwin. 1979. The perceived rhythm of speech. *Proceedings of the Ninth International Congress of Phonetic Sciences II:* 268. Copenhagen.

Dooley, R.A. 1982. Options in the pragmatic structuring of Guaraní sentences. *Language* 58:307.

Dowling, W.J. 1973. Rhythmic groups and subjective chunks in memory for melodies. *Perception and Psychophysics* 14:37.

Downing, B.T. 1973. Parenthesization rules and obligatory phrasing. *Papers in Linguistics* 6:108.

Draper, M., P. Ladefoged and D. Whitteridge. 1959. Respiratory muscles in speech. *Journal of Speech and Hearing Research* 2:16.

Drerup, P. 1929. Das Akzentuationsproblem im Griechischen. *Neophilologus* 14:291.

Dresher, B.E. and A. Lahiri. 1991. The Germanic foot: Metrical coherence in Old English. *Linguistic Inquiry* 22:251.

Dressler, W. 1973. Pour une stylistique phonologique du latin: A propos des styles négligents d'une langue morte. *Bulletin de la Société de Linguistique de Paris* 68:129.

Dressler, W. 1974. Desaktivierung und phonologische Nachlässigkeit. *Wiener Linguistische Gazette* 6:20.

Dressler, W. 1976. Inhärente Variation und variable Regel. *Soziolinguistik,* ed. A. Schaff: 53. Vienna.

Drewitt, J.A.J. 1908. Some differences between speech scansion and normal scansion in Homeric verse. *Classical Quarterly* 2:94.

Drewnowski, A. and A.F. Healy. 1977. Deletion errors on "the" and "and": Evidence for reading units larger than the word. *Memory and Cognition* 5:636.

Drewnowski, A. and B.B. Murdock Jr. 1980. The role of auditory features in memory span for words. *Journal of Experimental Psychology: Human Learning and Memory* 6:319.

Driver, C. 1990. Laying it on the line. *Manchester Guardian Weekly* 143–21:28.

DS. See p. 561.

du Bois, J.W. 1987. The discourse basis of ergativity. *Language* 63:805.

Duez, D. 1982. Silent and nonsilent pauses in three speech styles. *Language and Speech* 25:11.

Duysinx, F. 1981. Accents, mélodie et modalité dans la musique antique. *L'Antiquité Classique* 50:306.

Dyhr, N. 1990. The activity of the cricothyroid muscle and the intrinsic fundamental frequency in Danish vowels. *Phonetica* 47:141.

Eady, S.J. and W.E. Cooper. 1986. Speech intonation and focus location in matched statements and questions. *Journal of the Acoustical Society of America* 80:402.

Eady, S.J., W.E. Cooper, G.V. Klouda, P.R. Mueller and D.W. Lotts. 1986b. Acoustical characteristics of sentential focus. *Language and Speech* 29:233.

Edmonds, J.M. 1957. *The Fragments of Attic Comedy I.* Leiden.

Edwards, J. and M.E. Beckman. 1988. Articulatory timing and the prosodic interpretation of syllable duration. *Phonetica* 45:156.

Edwards, J., M.E. Beckman and J. Fletcher. 1989. Final lengthening: A local tempo change. *Journal of the Acoustical Society of America* 85:S27.

Edwards, J., M.E. Beckman and J. Fletcher. 1991. The articulatory kinematics of final lengthening. *Journal of the Acoustical Society of America* 89:369.

Eefting, W. 1991. The effect of "information value" and "accentuation" on the duration of Dutch words, syllables, and segments. *Journal of the Acoustical Society of America* 89:412.

Eek, A. 1987. The perception of word stress: A comparison of Estonian and Russian. *In Honor of Ilse Lehiste,* ed. R. Channon and L. Shockey: 19. Dordrecht.

Ehri, L.C. 1975. Word consciousness in readers and prereaders. *Journal of Educational Psychology* 67:204.

Ehrlich, H. 1912. *Untersuchungen über die Natur der griechischen Betonung.* Berlin.

Ehrlich, S. 1958. Le mécanisme de la synchronisation sensorimotrice. *L'Année Psychologique* 58:7.

Ehrlich, S., G. Oléron and P. Fraisse. 1956. La structure tonale des rythmes. *L'Année Psychologique* 56:27.

Einarsson, S. 1949. *Icelandic Grammar, Texts, Glossary.* Baltimore.

Ekblom, R. 1925. *Quantität und Intonation im Zentralen Hochlitauischen.* Uppsala.

Ekblom, R. 1933. *Die lettischen Akzentarten.* Uppsala.

Ekman, P. 1972. Universal and cultural differences in facial expression. *Nebraska Symposium on Motivation,* ed. J.R. Cole: 207. Lincoln, Nebr.

Ekwueme, L.E.N. 1974. Linguistic determinants of some Igbo musical properties. *Journal of African Studies* 1:335.

Ekwueme, L.E.N. 1980. Analysis and analytic techniques in African music. *African Music* 6:89.

Elert, C.-C. 1964. *Phonologic Studies of Quantity in Swedish.* Stockholm.

Eliasson, S. 1986. Sandhi in Peninsular Scandinavian. *Sandhi Phenomena in the Languages of Europe,* ed. H. Andersen: 271. Berlin.

Ellis, A.J. 1873. On the physical constituents of accent and emphasis. *Transactions of the Philological Society* 1873-4:113.

Elwell-Sutton, L.P. 1976. *The Persian Metres.* Cambridge.

Emeneau, M.B. 1944. *Kota Texts.* Berkeley.

Emmorey, K.D. 1987. The neurological substrates for prosodic aspects of speech. *Brain and Language* 30:305.

Emonds, J. 1973. Parenthetical clauses. *You Take the High Node and I'll Take the Low Node,* ed. C. Corum, T.C. Smith-Stark and A. Weiser: 333. Chicago.

Emonds, J. 1985. *A Unified Theory of Syntactic Categories.* Dordrecht.

Encrevé, P. 1988. *La liaison avec et sans enchaînement.* Paris.

Engstrand, O. 1986. Durational correlates of quantity and sentence stress: A cross-linguistic study of Swedish, Finnish and Czech. *Working Papers in Phonetics, University of California, Los Angeles* 63:1.

Engstrand, O. 1988. Articulatory correlates of stress and speaking rate in Swedish VCV utterances. *Journal of the Acoustical Society of America* 83:1863.

Ephron, H.D. 1961. Mycenaean Greek: A lesson in cryptanalysis. *Minos* 7:63.

Epstein, W. 1961. The influence of syntactical structure on learning. *American Journal of Psychology* 74:80.

Erbse, H. 1988. *Scholia Graeca in Homeri Iliadem VII.* Berlin.

Eriksson, A. 1987. Rhythm in recited poetry. *Nordic Prosody IV,* ed. K. Gregersen and H. Basbøll: 127. Odense.

Eriksson, A. 1991. *Aspects of Swedish Rhythm.* Lund.

Essens, P.J. 1986. Hierarchical organization of temporal patterns. *Perception and Psychophysics* 40:69.

Essens, P.J. and D.-J. Povel. 1985. Metrical and nonmetrical representations of temporal patterns. *Perception and Psychophysics* 37:1.

Everett, D. and K. Everett. 1984. On the relevance of syllable onsets to stress placement. *Linguistic Inquiry* 15:705.

Ewan, W.G. 1979. Can intrinsic vowel F_0 be explained by source/tract coupling? *Journal of the Acoustical Society of America* 66:358.

Ewan, W.G. and R. Krones. 1974. Measuring larynx movement using the thyro-umbrometer. *Journal of Phonetics* 2:327.

Faarlund, J.T. 1991. The unaccusative hypothesis and configurationality. *Papers from the 27th Regional Meeting of the Chicago Linguistic Society:* 141.

Fairbanks, C. 1981. *The Development of Hindi Oral Narrative Meter.* Ph.D. dissertation, University of Wisconsin, Madison.

Fant, G. 1991. Units of temporal organization: Stress groups versus syllables and words. *Proceedings of the XIIth International Congress of Phonetic Sciences I:* 247. Aix-en-Provence.

Fant, G. and A. Kruckenberg. 1988. Stress and interstress intervals in reading. *Journal of the Acoustical Society of America* 84:S98.

Fant, G. and A. Kruckenberg. 1989. *Preliminaries to the Study of Swedish Prose Reading and Reading Style.* Quarterly Progress and Status Report, Speech Transmission Laboratory, Royal Institute of Technology, Stockholm 1989:2.

Fant, G., A. Kruckenberg and L. Nord. 1991. Durational correlates of stress in Swedish, French and English. *Journal of Phonetics* 19:351.

Fant, G., A. Kruckenberg and L. Nord. 1991b. Temporal organization and rhythm in Swedish. *Proceedings of the XIIth International Congress of Phonetic Sciences I:* 251. Aix-en-Provence.

Farnetani, E. 1990. V-C-V lingual coarticulation and its spatiotemporal domain. *Speech Production and Speech Modelling,* ed. W.J. Hardcastle and A. Marchal: 1. Dordrecht.

Farnetani, E. and S. Kori. 1986. Effects of syllable and word structure on segmental durations in spoken Italian. *Speech Communication* 5:17.

Farnetani, E., C.T. Torsello and P. Cosi. 1988. English compound versus noncompound phrases in discourse. *Language and Speech* 31:157.

Farnetani, E. and S. Kori. 1990. Rhythmic structure in Italian noun phrases: A study on vowel durations. *Phonetica* 47:50.

Fast, P.W. 1953. Amuesha (Arawak) phonemes. *International Journal of American Linguistics* 19:191.

Fay, D. and A. Cutler. 1977. Malapropisms and the structure of the mental lexicon. *Linguistic Inquiry* 8:505.

Feaver, D.D. 1960. The musical setting of Euripides' *Orestes*. *American Journal of Philology* 81:1.

Ferguson, C.A. and C.E. DeBose. 1977. Simplified registers, broken language and pidginization. *Pidgin and Creole Linguistics,* ed. A. Valdman: 99. Bloomington.

Fernald, A., T. Taeschner, J. Dunn, M. Papousek, B. de Boysson-Bardies and I. Fukui. 1989. A cross-language study of prosodic modifications in mother's and father's speech to preverbal infants. *Journal of Child Language* 16:477.

Ferrein, A. 1741. De la formation de la voix de l'homme. *Histoire de l'Académie Royale des Sciences de Paris* 51:409.

Fidelholtz, J.L. 1975. Word frequency and vowel reduction in English. *Papers from the Eleventh Regional Meeting of the Chicago Linguistic Society*: 200.

Firbas, J. 1964. On defining the theme in functional sentence analysis. *Travaux Linguistiques de Prague* 1:267.

Firbas, J. 1966. Nonthematic subjects in contemporary English. *Travaux Linguistiques de Prague* 2:239.

Firbas, J. 1971. On the concept of communicative dynamism in the theory of functional sentence perspective. *Sborník Prací Filosofické Fakulty Brněnske University* A19:135.

Fischer, J.L. 1959. Meter in Eastern Carolinian oral literature. *Journal of American Folklore* 72:47.

Fischer-Jørgensen, E. 1982. Segment duration in Danish words in dependency on higher level phonological units. *Annual Report, Institute of Phonetics, University of Copenhagen* 16:137.

Fischer-Jørgensen, E. 1990. Intrinsic F_0 in tense and lax vowels with special reference to German. *Phonetica* 47:99.

Fischer-Jørgensen, E. and H.P. Jørgensen. 1970. Close and loose contact (Anschluss) with special reference to North German. *Annual Report, Institute of Phonetics, University of Copenhagen* 4:43.

Fix, T. 1843. *Euripidis Fabulae I.* Paris.

Flanagan, J.L. and M.G. Saslow. 1958. Pitch discrimination for synthetic vowels. *Journal of the Acoustical Society of America* 30:435.

Flege, J.E. 1988. Effects of speaking rate on tongue position and velocity of movement in vowel production. *Journal of the Acoustical Society of America* 84:901.

Flege, J.E. and W.S. Brown Jr. 1982. Effect of utterance position on English speech timing. *Phonetica* 39:337.

Fleiss, J.L. 1973. *Statistical Methods for Rates and Proportions.* New York.

Fletcher, J. 1987. Some micro-effects of tempo change on timing in French. *Proceedings of the XIth International Congress of Phonetic Sciences III*: 129. Tallinn.

Fletcher, J. 1991. Rhythm and final lengthening in French. *Journal of Phonetics* 19:193.

Flores-d'Arcais, G.B. 1978. The perception of complex sentences. *Studies in the Perception of Language,* ed. W.J.M. Levelt and G.B. Flores d'Arcais: 155. Chichester.

Fokes, J. and Z.S. Bond. 1993. The elusive/illusive syllable. *Phonetica* 50:102.

Fónagy, I. 1962. Mimik auf glottaler Ebene. *Phonetica* 8:209.

Fónagy, I. 1976. La mimique buccale. *Phonetica* 33:31.

Fónagy, I. and K. Magdics. 1960. Speed of utterance in phrases of different lengths. *Language and Speech* 3:179.

Fónagy, I. and K. Magdics. 1963. Emotional patterns in intonation and music. *Zeitschrift für Phonetik, Sprachwissenschaft und Kommunikationsforschung* 16:293.

Foster, M.L. 1969. *The Tarascan Language.* Berkeley.

Fourakis, M. 1986. An acoustic study of the effects of tempo and stress on segmental intervals in Modern Greek. *Phonetica* 43:172.

Fourakis, M. and C.B. Monahan. 1988. Effects of metrical foot structure on syllable timing. *Language and Speech* 31:283.

Fowler, C.A. 1977. *Timing Control in Speech Production.* Bloomington.

Fowler, C.A. 1979. "Perceptual centers" in speech production and perception. *Perception and Psychophysics* 25:375.

Fowler, C.A. 1981. A relationship between coarticulation and compensatory shortening. *Phonetica* 38:35.

Fowler, C.A. 1983. Converging sources of evidence for spoken and perceived rhythms of speech: Cyclic production of vowels in sequences of monosyllabic stress feet. *Journal of Experimental Psychology: General* 112:386.

Fowler, C.A. 1986. An event approach to the study of speech perception from a direct-realist perspective. *Journal of Phonetics* 14:3.

Fowler, C.A. 1987. Consonant-vowel cohesiveness in speech production as revealed by initial and final consonant exchanges. *Speech Communication* 6:231.

Fowler, C.A. 1988. Differential shortening of repeated content words produced in various communicative contexts. *Language and Speech* 31:307.

Fowler, C.A. 1992. Vowel duration and closure duration in voiced and unvoiced stops: There are no contrast effects here. *Journal of Phonetics* 20:143.

Fowler, C.A. and L. Tassinary. 1981. Natural measurement criteria for speech: The anisochrony illusion. *Attention and Performance IX,* ed. J. Long and A. Baddeley: 521. Hillsdale.

Fowler, C.A. and J. Housum. 1987. Talkers' signaling of "new" and "old" words in speech and listeners' perception and use of the distinction. *Journal of Memory and Language* 26:489.

Fowler, C.A., D.H. Whalen and A.M. Cooper. 1988. Perceived timing is produced timing: A reply to Howell. *Perception and Psychophysics* 43:94.

Fox, R.A. 1987. Perceived P-center location in English and Japanese. *Working Papers in Linguistics, Ohio State University* 35:11.

Fox, R.A. and I. Lehiste. 1987. Discrimination of duration ratios by native English and Estonian listeners. *Journal of Phonetics* 15:349.

Fox, R.A. and I. Lehiste. 1987b. The effect of vowel quality variations on stress-beat location. *Journal of Phonetics* 15:1.

Fox, R.A. and I. Lehiste. 1989. Discrimination of duration ratios in bisyllabic tokens by native English and Estonian listeners. *Journal of Phonetics* 17:67.

Fraenkel, E. 1950. *Aeschylus. Agamemnon.* Oxford.

Fraenkel, E. 1964. Kolon und Satz II. *Kleine Beiträge zur klassischen Philologie I*: 93. Rome.

Fraenkel, E. 1965. Noch einmal Kolon und Satz. *Sitzungsberichte, Bayerische Akademie der Wissenschaften, Philosophisch-Historische Klasse* 2.

Fraisse, P. 1946-47. Mouvements rythmiques et arythmiques. *L'Année Psychologique* 47-48:11.

Fraisse, P. 1956. *Les Structures rythmiques: Etude psychologique.* Louvain.

Fraisse, P. 1966. L'anticipation de stimulus rythmiques. *L'Année Psychologique* 66:15.

Fraisse, P. and G. Oléron. 1954. La structuration intensive des rythmes. *L'Année Psychologique* 54:35.

Fraisse, P. and C. Voillaume. 1971. Les repères du sujet dans la synchronisation et dans la pseudo-synchronisation. *L'Année Psychologique* 71:359.

Francard, M. and Y.-C. Morin. 1986. Sandhi in Walloon. *Sandhi Phenomena in the Languages of Europe,* ed. H. Andersen: 453. Berlin.

Friederici, A. 1982. Syntactic and semantic processes in aphasic deficits: The availability of prepositions. *Brain and Language* 15:249.

Friederici, A. 1985. Levels of processing and vocabulary types. *Cognition* 19:133.

Friedländer, L. 1850. *Nicanoris Περὶ Ἰλιακῆς Στιγμῆς Reliquiae Emendatiores*. Königsberg.

Friedman, R.B. 1988. Acquired dyslexia. *Handbook of Neuropsychology I*, ed. F. Boller and J. Grafman: 377. Amsterdam.

Frøkjaer-Jensen, B., C. Ludvigsen and J. Rischel. 1973. A glottographic study of some Danish consonants. *Annual Report, Institute of Phonetics, University of Copenhagen* 7:269.

Fromkin, V. 1971. The nonanomalous nature of anomalous utterances. *Language* 47:27.

Fromkin, V. 1973. *Speech Errors as Linguistic Evidence*. The Hague.

Fry, D.B. 1955. Duration and intensity as physical correlates of linguistic stress. *Journal of the Acoustical Society of America* 27:765.

Fry, D.B. 1958. Experiments in the perception of stress. *Language and Speech* 1:126.

Fudge, E. 1987. Branching structure within the syllable. *Journal of Linguistics* 23:359.

Fujimura, O. 1990. Methods and goals of speech production research. *Language and Speech* 33:195.

Fujimura, O. and J. Lovins. 1978. Syllables as concatenative phonetic units. *Syllables and Segments*, ed. A. Bell and J.B. Hooper: 107. Amsterdam.

Fujimura, O. and J. Lovins. 1982. *Syllables as Concatenative Phonetic Units*. Bloomington.

Fujisaki, H. and T. Omura. 1971. Characteristics of durations of pauses and speech segments in connected speech. *Annual Report, Engineering Research Institute, University of Tokyo* 30:69.

Fujisaki, H., K. Nakamura and J. Imoto. 1975. Auditory perception of duration of speech and nonspeech stimuli. *Auditory Analysis and Perception of Speech*, ed. G. Fant and M.A.A. Tatham: 197. New York.

Fujisaki, H., K. Hirose and K. Ohta. 1979. Acoustic features of the fundamental frequency contours of declarative sentences in Japanese. *Annual Bulletin, Research Institute of Logopedics and Phoniatrics* 13:163.

Fujisaki, H. and N. Higuchi. 1979. Temporal organization of segmental features in Japanese disyllables. *Proceedings of the Ninth International Congress of Phonetic Sciences II*: 275. Copenhagen.

Fujisaki, H. and H. Hirose. 1984. Analysis of voice fundamental frequency contours for declarative sentences in Japanese. *Journal of the Acoustical Society of Japan* 5:233.

Furere, R. and A. Rialland. 1985. Tons et accents en Kinyarwanda. *African Linguistics: Essays in Memory of M.W.K. Semikenke*, ed. D.L. Goyvaerts: 99. Amsterdam.

Gabrielsson, A. 1974. Performance of rhythm patterns. *Scandinavian Journal of Psychology* 15:63.

Gandour, J. 1974. Consonant types and tone in Siamese. *Working Papers in Phonetics, University of California, Los Angeles* 27:92

Gandour, J. 1977. On the interaction between tone and vowel length. *Phonetica* 34:54.

Gandour, J. and B. Weinberg. 1980. On the relationship between vowel height and fundamental frequency. *Phonetica* 37:344.

Gandour, J. and R. Dardarananda. 1983. Identification of tonal contrasts in Thai aphasic patients. *Brain and Language* 18:98.

Gandour, J. and R. Dardarananda. 1984. Prosodic disturbance in aphasia: Vowel length in Thai. *Brain and Language* 23:206.

Gandour, J., S.H. Petty and R. Dardarananda. 1988. Perception and production of tone in aphasia. *Brain and Language* 35:201.

Gårding, E. 1967. *Internal Juncture in Swedish.* Lund.

Gårding, E. 1987. Speech act and tonal pattern in Standard Chinese: Constancy and variation. *Phonetica* 44:13.

Gårding, E., O. Fujimura and H. Hirose. 1970. Laryngeal control of Swedish word tones. *Annual Bulletin, Research Institute of Logopedics and Phoniatrics* 4:45.

Gårding, E., O. Fujimura, H. Hirose and Z. Simada. 1975. Laryngeal control of Swedish word accents. *Working Papers in General Linguistics and Phonetics, Lund University* 10:53.

Gårding, E. and J. Zhang. 1987. Tempo and prosodic pattern in Chinese and Swedish. *Working Papers in General Linguistics and Phonetics, Lund University* 34:116.

Gardner, H. and E.B. Zurif. 1975. "Bee" but not "be": Oral reading of single words in aphasia and alexia. *Neuropsychologia* 13:181.

Garman, M. 1982. Is Broca's aphasia a phonological deficit? *Linguistic Controversies*, ed. D. Crystal: 152. London.

Garner, W.R. 1974. *The Processing of Information and Structure.* New York.

Garnes, S. and Z.S. Bond. 1975. Slips of the ear: Errors in perception in casual speech. *Papers from the Eleventh Regional Meeting of the Chicago Linguistic Society*: 214.

Garnica, O. 1977. Some prosodic and paralinguistic features of speech to young children. *Talking to Children: Language Input and Language Acquisition,* ed. C. Snow and C. Ferguson: 63. Cambridge.

Garnsey, S.M. 1985. *Function Words and Content Words: Reaction Time and Evoked Potential Measures of Word Recognition.* Ph.D. dissertation, University of Rochester.

Garrett, A. 1989. Ergative case assignment, Wackernagel's Law, and the VP base hypothesis. *Proceedings of the 19th Annual Meeting of the North Eastern Linguistics Society*: 113.

Garrett, A. 1990. *The Syntax of Anatolian Pronominal Clitics.* Ph.D. dissertation, Harvard University.

Garrett, A. 1993. Variation and explanation in syntactic change. Manuscript.

Garrett, M.F. 1975. The analysis of sentence production. *Psychology of Learning and Motivation* 9:133.

Garrett, M.F. 1979. Word and sentence perception. *Handbook of Sensory Physiology VIII: Perception,* ed. R. Held, H.W. Leibowitz and H.L. Teuber: 611. Berlin.

Garrett, M.F. 1980. Levels of processing in sentence production. *Language Production I,* ed. B. Butterworth: 177. London.

Garrett, M.F. and M.-L. Kean. 1980. Levels of representation and the analysis of speech errors. *Juncture,* ed. M. Aronoff and M.-L. Kean: 79. Saratoga.

Gauthiot, R. 1913. *La Fin de mot en indo-européen.* Paris.

Gay, T. 1978. Effect of speaking rate on vowel formant movements. *Journal of the Acoustical Society of America* 63:223.

Gay, T. 1979. Coarticulation in some consonant-vowel and consonant cluster-vowel syllables. *Frontiers of Speech Communication Research,* ed. B. Lindblom and S. Öhman: 69. London.

Gee, J. and F. Grosjean. 1983. Performance structures: A psycholinguistic and linguistic appraisal. *Cognitive Psychology* 15:411.

Gelfer, C.E. 1987. *A Simultaneous Physiological and Acoustic Study of Fundamental Frequency Declination.* Ph.D. dissertation, City University of New York.

Gelfer, C.E., K.S. Harris and T. Baer. 1987. Controlled variables in sentence intonation. *Laryngeal Function in Phonation and Respiration,* ed. T. Baer, C. Sasaki and K.S. Harris: 422. Boston.

Gentil, M. 1990. Organization of the articulatory system: Peripheral mechanisms and central coordination. *Speech Production and Speech Modelling,* ed. W.J. Hardcastle and A. Marchal: 1. Dordrecht.

Gentner, D. 1987. Timing of skilled movements: Test of the proportional duration model. *Psychological Review* 94:255.

Gerdel, F. 1973. Paez phonemics. *Linguistics* 104:28.

Gerdts, D.B. 1984. A relational analysis of Halkomelem causals. *Syntax and Semantics* 16:169.

Gerken, L. 1991. The metrical basis for children's subjectless sentences. *Journal of Memory and Language* 30:431.

Geytenbeek, H. 1980. Continuous and discontinuous noun phrases in Nyangumarda. *Papers in Australian Linguistics* 12:23.

Giannini, A. 1987. On the relationship between coarticulatory effect of lip rounding and syllabic boundary in French. *Proceedings of the XIth International Congress of Phonetic Sciences II*: 299. Tallinn.

Giegerich, H. 1985. *Metrical Phonology and Phonological Structure*. Cambridge.

Gignac, F. 1976. *A Grammar of the Greek Papyri of the Roman and Byzantine Periods.* Milan.

Givon, T. 1972. *Studies in ChiBemba and Bantu Grammar.* Studies in African Linguistics, Supplement 3.

Glanzer, M. 1962. Grammatical category: A rote learning and word association analysis. *Journal of Verbal Learning and Verbal Behavior* 1:31.

Glanzer, M. and S.L. Ehrenreich. 1979. Structure and search of the internal lexicon. *Journal of Verbal Learning and Verbal Behavior* 18:381.

Glenberg, A.M., S. Mann, L. Altman, T. Forman and S. Procise. 1989. Modality effects in the coding and reproduction of rhythms. *Memory and Cognition* 17:373.

Goldman-Eisler, F. 1961. The significance of changes in the rate of articulation. *Language and Speech* 4:171.

Goldman-Eisler, F. 1968. *Psycholinguistics: Experiments in Spontaneous Speech.* London.

Goldman-Eisler, F. 1972. Pauses, clauses, sentences. *Language and Speech* 15:103.

Goldmann, F. 1867. *De Dochmiorum Usu Sophocleo I.* Halle.

Goldsmith, J. 1984. Tone and accent in Tonga. *Autosegmental Studies in Bantu Tone,* ed. G.N. Clements and J. Goldsmith: 19. Dordrecht.

Goldsmith, J. 1990. *Autosegmental and Metrical Phonology.* Oxford.

Goldsmith, J. and G. Larson. 1990. Local modeling and syllabification. *Papers from the 26th Regional Meeting of the Chicago Linguistic Society II: Parasession on the Syllable in Phonetics and Phonology*: 129.

Goldstein, L. 1992. Comments on chapters 3 and 4. *Papers in Laboratory Phonology II,* ed. G.J. Docherty and D.R. Ladd: 120. Cambridge.

Golston, C. 1989. Floating H (and *L) tones in Ancient Greek. *Proceedings of the Arizona Phonology Conference* 3:66. Coyote Papers, University of Arizona.

Golston, C. 1991. *Both Lexicons.* Ph.D. dissertation, University of California, Los Angeles.

Golston, C. 1993. Tone sandhi and the OCP in Ancient Greek. Phonology Conference, Holland Institute for Generative Linguistics, University of Leiden.

Goodglass, H. 1990. Inferences from cross-modal comparisons of agrammatism. *Agrammatic Aphasia: A Cross-Language Narrative Sourcebook II,* ed. L. Menn and L.K. Obler: 1365.

Goodglass, H., I.G. Fodor and C. Schulhoff. 1967. Prosodic factors in grammar: Evidence from aphasia. *Journal of Speech and Hearing Research* 10:5.

Goodwin, W.W. and C.B. Gulick. 1930. *Greek Grammar.* Boston.

Gopal, H.S. 1990. Effects of speaking rate on the behavior of tense and lax vowel durations. *Journal of Phonetics* 18:497.

Gordon, B. and A. Caramazza. 1982. Lexical decision for open- and closed-class items. *Brain and Language* 15:143.

Gordon, B. and A. Caramazza. 1983. Closed- and open-class lexical access in agrammatic and fluent aphasics. *Brain and Language* 19:335.

Gordon, H.W. and J.E. Bogen. 1974. Hemispheric lateralization of singing after intracarotid sodium amylobarbitone. *Journal of Neurology, Neurosurgery, and Psychiatry* 37:727.

Gorecka, A. 1988. Polish word order and its relevance for the treatment of free word order phenomena. *Papers from the 24th Annual Regional Meeting of the Chicago Linguistic Society*: 176.

Gow, A.S.F. and D.L. Page. 1968. *The Greek Anthology. The Garland of Philip.* Oxford.

Greenberg, G.R. 1984. Left dislocation, topicalization, and interjections. *Natural Language and Linguistic Theory* 2:283.

Greenberg, J. 1941. Some problems in Hausa phonology. *Language* 17:316.

Greenberg, J. 1960. A survey of African prosodic systems. *Culture in History,* ed. S. Diamond: 925. New York.

Greenberg, J. 1963. Some universals of grammar with particular reference to the order of meaningful elements. *Universals of Language,* ed. J. Greenberg: 73. Cambridge, Mass.

Greenberg, J. 1965. Some generalizations concerning initial and final consonant sequences. *Linguistics* 18:5.

Greenberg, J. 1970. Some generalizations concerning glottalic consonants — especially implosives. *International Journal of American Linguistics* 36:123.

Greenberg, J. and D. Kaschube. 1976. Word prosodic systems: A preliminary report. *Working Papers on Language Universals* 20:1.

Grégoire, A. 1899. Variation de la durée de la syllable française. *La Parole* 1:161.

Grodzinsky, Y. 1986. Language deficits and the theory of syntax. *Brain and Language* 27:135.

Grodzinsky, Y. 1988. Syntactic representations in agrammatic aphasia: The case of prepositions. *Language and Speech* 31:115.

Grodzinsky, Y. 1990. *Theoretical Perspectives on Language Deficits.* Cambridge, Mass.

Grønnum, N. 1990. Prosodic parameters in a variety of regional Danish standard languages with a view towards Swedish and German. *Phonetica* 47:182.

Grosjean, F. 1979. A study of timing in a manual and spoken language: American Sign Language and English. *Journal of Psycholinguistic Research* 8:379.

Grosjean, F. 1985. The recognition of words after their acoustic offset. *Perception and Psychophysics* 38:299.

Grosjean, F. and A. Deschamps. 1975. Analyse contrastive des variables temporelles de l'Anglais et du Français. *Phonetica* 31:144.

Grosjean, F. and M. Collins. 1979. Breathing, pausing and reading. *Phonetica* 36:98.

Guarducci, M. 1967–1978. *Epigrafia greca I–IV.* Rome.

Gundel, J.K. 1974. *The Role of Topic and Comment in Linguistic Theory.* Ph.D. dissertation, University of Texas, Austin.

Gundel, J.K. 1985. "Shared knowledge" and topicality. *Journal of Pragmatics* 9:83.

Gundel, J.K. 1987. Universals of topic-comment structure. *Another Indiana University Linguistics Club Twentieth Anniversary Volume*: 37. Bloomington.

Gundlach, R. 1932. A quantitative analysis of Indian music. *American Journal of Psychology* 44:133.

Gupta, A. 1987. Hindi word stress and the obligatory branching parameter. *Papers from the 23rd Annual Regional Meeting of the Chicago Linguistic Society II*: 134.

Gussenhoven, C. 1984. *On the Grammar and Semantics of Sentence Accents.* Dordrecht.

Gussenhoven, C. and A.C.M. Rietveld. 1988. Fundamental frequency declination in Dutch: Testing three hypotheses. *Journal of Phonetics* 16:355.

Gvozdanović, J. 1981. Word order and displacement in Serbocroatian. *Predication and Expression in Functional Grammar,* ed. A.M. Bolkestein et al.: 125. London.

Gvozdanović, J. 1986. Phonological domains. *Sandhi Phenomena in the Languages of Europe,* ed. H. Andersen: 27. Berlin.

Haber, R.N. and R. Schindler. 1981. Errors in proofreading: Evidence of syntactic control in letter processing? *Journal of Experimental Psychology: Human Perception and Performance* 7:573.

Habinek, T.N. 1985. *The Colometry of Latin Prose.* Berkeley.

Hadding-Koch, K. 1961. *Acoustico-Phonetic Studies in the Intonation of Southern Swedish.* Lund.

Haggard, M. 1973. Abbreviation of consonants in English pre- and post-vocalic clusters. *Journal of Phonetics* 1:9.

Haggard, M., S. Ambler and M. Callow. 1970. Pitch as a voicing cue. *Journal of the Acoustical Society of America* 47:613.

Hale, K. 1982. Preliminary remarks on configurationality. *Proceedings of the 12th Annual Meeting of the North Eastern Linguistics Society*: 86.

Hale, K. 1983. Warlpiri and the grammar of nonconfigurational languages. *Natural Language and Linguistic Theory* 1:5.

Hale, K. and E. Selkirk. 1987. Government and tonal phrasing in Papago. *Phonology Yearbook* 4:151.

Hale, M. 1987. Notes on Wackernagel's Law in the language of the Rigveda. *Studies in Memory of Warren Cowgill,* ed. C. Watkins: 38. Berlin.

Hale, M. 1988. Preliminaries to the study of the relationship between sandhi and syntax in the language of the Rigveda. Manuscript, Harvard University.

Hall, R.A. 1944. *Hungarian Grammar.* Baltimore.

Halle, M. 1990. Respecting metrical structure. *Natural Language and Linguistic Theory* 8:149.

Halle, M. and J. Vergnaud. 1980. Three dimensional phonology. *Journal of Linguistic Research* 1:83.

Hallé, P.A., B. de Boysson-Bardies and M. Vihman. 1991. Beginnings of prosodic organization. *Language and Speech* 34:299.

Halliday, M.A.K. 1967. Notes on transitivity and theme in English, part 2. *Journal of Linguistics* 3:199.

Halpern, A.L. 1992. *Topics in the Placement and Morphology of Clitics.* Ph.D. dissertation, Stanford University.

Hammond, M. 1987. Hungarian cola. *Phonology Yearbook* 4:267.

Handel, S. 1973. Temporal segmentation of repeating auditory patterns. *Journal of Experimental Psychology* 101:46.

Handel, S. 1974. Perceiving melodic and rhythmic auditory patterns. *Journal of Experimental Psychology* 103:922.

Handel, S. and D. Yoder. 1975. The effects of intensity and interval rhythm on the perception of auditory and visual temporal patterns. *Quarterly Journal of Experimental Psychology* 27:111.

Handel, S. and J.S. Oshinsky. 1981. The meter of syncopated auditory polyrhythms. *Perception and Psychophysics* 30:1.

Hannay, M. 1985. Inferrability, discourse-boundness, and sub-topics. *Syntax and Pragmatics in Functional Grammar,* ed. A.M. Bolkestein, C. de Groot and J.L. Mackenzie: 49. Dordrecht.

Hansen, G.C. 1962. Rhythmisches und Metrisches zu Themistios. *Byzantinische Zeitschrift* 55:234.

Hansen, J.H.L. 1988. *Analysis and Compensation of Stressed and Noisy Speech with Application to Robust Automatic Recognition.* Ph.D. dissertation, Georgia Institute of Technology.

Hansen, P.A. 1983. *Carmina Epigraphica Graeca Saeculorum VIII-V A. Chr. N.* Berlin.

Hanson, K. 1992. *Resolution in Some Modern Meters.* Ph.D. dissertation, Stanford University.

Hanssen, F. 1883. Ein musikalisches Accentgesetz in der quantitirenden Poesie der Griechen. *Rheinisches Museum* 38:222.

Haraguchi, S. 1987. The multidimensional grammatical theory. *Issues in Japanese Linguistics,* ed. T. Imai and M. Saito: 129. Dordrecht.

Haraguchi, S. 1991. *A Theory of Stress and Accent.* Dordrecht.

Hardcastle, W.J. 1985. Some phonetic and syntactic constraints on lingual coarticulation during /kl/ sequences. *Speech Communication* 3:279.

Harlig, J. and K. Bardovi-Harlig. 1988. Accentuation typology, word order and theme-rheme structure. *Studies in Syntactic Typology,* ed. M. Hammond, E. Moravcsik and J. Wirth: 125. Amsterdam.

Harrell, R.S. 1962. *A Short Reference Grammar of Moroccan Arabic.* Washington.

Harries-Delisle, H. 1978. Contrastive emphasis and cleft sentences. *Universals of Human Language IV,* ed. J.H. Greenberg: 419. Stanford.

Harris, J.W. 1970. Sequences of vowels in Spanish. *Linguistic Inquiry* 1:129.

Harris, J.W. 1983. *Syllable Structure and Stress in Spanish.* Cambridge, Mass.

Harris, M.S. and N. Umeda. 1974. Effect of speaking mode on temporal factors in speech. *Journal of the Acoustical Society of America* 56:1016.

Harris, R.A. 1988. *Acoustic Dimension of Functor Comprehension in Broca's Aphasia.* Bloomington.

Harris, Z. 1951. *Methods in Structural Linguistics.* Chicago.

Hasegawa, N. 1979. Casual speech vs. fast speech. *Papers from the 15th Regional Meeting of the Chicago Linguistic Society:* 126.

Hasegawa, Y. and K. Hata. 1992. Fundamental frequency as an acoustic cue to accent perception. *Language and Speech* 35:87.

Haslam, M.W. 1974. Stesichorean metre. *Quaderni Urbinati di Cultura Classica* 17:7.

Haslam, M.W. 1976. Texts with musical notation. *The Oxyrhyncus Papyri* 44:67. London.

Haslam, M.W. 1986. Review of West 1982. *Classical Philology* 81:90.

Hata, K. 1986. Intrinsic pitch of vowels in read speech at different speech rates. *Journal of the Acoustical Society of America* 80:S50.

Hata, K. and Y. Hasegawa. 1991. The effect of F_0 fall rate on accent perception in English. *Proceedings of the Seventeenth Annual Meeting of the Berkeley Linguistics Society:* 121.

Hauser, M.D. and C.A. Fowler. 1992. Fundamental frequency declination is not unique to human speech: Evidence from nonhuman primates. *Journal of the Acoustical Society of America* 91:363.

Havers, W. 1912. Zur "Spaltung" des Genetivs im Griechischen. *Indogermanische Forschungen* 31:230.

Havet, L. 1896. *Cours élémentaire de métrique grecque et latine.* Paris.

Hawkins, S. 1979. Temporal coordination of consonants in the speech of children: Further data. *Journal of Phonetics* 7:235.

Hayes, B. 1979. The rhythmic structure of Persian verse. *Edebiyāt* 4:193.

Hayes, B. 1981. *A Metrical Theory of Stress Rules.* Bloomington.

Hayes, B. 1982. Metrical structure as the organizing principle of Yidiny phonology. *The Structure of Phonological Representations I,* ed. H. van der Hulst and N. Smith: 97. Dordrecht.

Hayes, B. 1985. Iambic and trochaic rhythm in stress rules. *Proceedings of the Eleventh Annual Meeting of the Berkeley Linguistics Society*: 429.

Hayes, B. 1988. Final lengthening and the prosodic hierarchy. *Journal of the Acoustical Society of America* 84:S97.

Hayes, B. 1989. The prosodic hierarchy in meter. *Phonetics and Phonology* 1:201.

Hayes, B. 1989b. Compensatory lengthening in moraic phonology. *Linguistic Inquiry* 20:253.

Hayes, B. 1990. Precompiled phrasal phonology. *The Phonology-Syntax Connection,* ed. S. Inkelas and D. Zec: 85. Chicago.

Hedin, B. 1994. *The Domain of Elision in Greek Speech.* Ph.D. dissertation, Stanford University.

Heeschen, C. 1985. Agrammatism versus paragrammatism: A fictitious opposition. *Agrammatism,* ed. M.-L. Kean: 207. Orlando.

Heilman, K.M., D. Bowers, L. Speedie and H.B. Coslett. 1984. Comprehension of affective and nonaffective prosody. *Neurology* 34:917.

Heitsch, E. 1961. *Die griechische Dichterfragmente der römischer Kaiserzeit.* Göttingen.

Henderson, I. 1957. Ancient Greek music. *The New Oxford History of Music I*: 336. London.

Henry, A.S. 1964. Epigraphica. *Classical Quarterly* 14:240.

Henry, A.S. 1967. Notes on the language of the prose inscriptions of Hellenistic Athens. *Classical Quarterly* 17:257.

Heny, J.M. 1981. *Rhythmic Elements in Persian Poetry.* Ph.D. dissertation, University of Pennsylvania.

Herdan, G. 1960. *Type-Token Mathematics.* The Hague.

Hermann, E. 1923. *Silbenbildung im Griechischen und in den andern indogermanischen Sprachen.* Göttingen.

Hermann, E. 1942. *Probleme der Frage.* Göttingen.

Hermann, G. 1801. *De Emendenda Ratione Graecae Grammaticae.* Leipzig.

Hermann, G. 1815. *De Metrorum Quorundam Mensura Rhythmica.* Leipzig.

Hermann, G. 1816. *Elementa Doctrinae Metricae.* Leipzig.

Hermes, D.J. and J.C. van Gestel. 1991. The frequency scale of speech intonation. *Journal of the Acoustical Society of America* 90:97.

Herring, S.C. 1990. Information structure as a consequence of word order type. *Proceedings of the Sixteenth Annual Meeting of the Berkeley Linguistics Society*: 163.

Hertz, S.R. 1990. The Delta programming language. *Papers in Laboratory Phonology I,* ed. J. Kingston and M.E. Beckman: 215. Cambridge.

Herzog, G. 1934. Speech-melody and primitive music. *Musical Quarterly* 20:452.

Hetzron, R. 1969. *The Verbal System of Southern Agaw.* Berkeley.

Hetzron, R. 1975. The presentative movement or why the ideal word order is V.S.O.P. *Word Order and Word Order Change,* ed. C.N. Li: 347. Austin.

Hibi, S. 1983. Rhythm perception in repetitive sound sequence. *Journal of the Acoustical Society in Japan* 4:83.

Higginbottom, E. 1964. Glottal reinforcement in English. *Transactions of the Philological Society* 1964:129.

Hilberg, I. 1879. *Das Princip des Silbenwägung und die daraus entspringenden Gesetze der Endsilben in der griechischen Poesie.* Vienna.

Hilgard, A. 1894. *Grammatici Graeci IV.1.* Prolegomena. Leipzig.

Hill, G.F. 1951. *Sources for Greek History,* ed. R. Meiggs and A. Andrewes. Oxford.

Hinton, L. 1977. *Havasupai Songs: A Linguistic Perspective.* Ph.D. dissertation, University of California, San Diego.

Hirano, M., J. Ohala and W. Vennard. 1969. The function of laryngeal muscles in regulating fundamental frequency and intensity of phonation. *Journal of Speech and Hearing Research* 12:616.

Hirano, M., J. Ohala and W. Vennard. 1970. Regulation of register, pitch and intensity of voice. *Folia Phoniatrica* 22:1.

Hirsch, I.K., C.B. Monahan, K.W. Grant and P.G. Singh. 1990. Studies in auditory timing 1: Simple patterns. *Perception and Psychophysics* 47:215.

Hirst, D. 1981. Phonological implications of a production model of intonation. *Phonologica 1980*, ed. W.U. Dressler, O.E. Pfeiffer and J.R. Rennison: 195. Innsbruck.

Hirt, H. 1902. *Handbuch der griechischen Laut- und Formenlehre.* Heidelberg.

Hiskett, M. 1975. *A History of Hausa Islamic Verse.* London.

Hixon, T.J., M. Goldman and J. Mead. 1973. Kinematics of the chest wall during speech production. *Journal of Speech and Hearing Research* 16:78.

Hixon, T.J., J. Mead and M. Goldman. 1976. Dynamics of the chest wall during speech production. *Journal of Speech and Hearing Research* 19:297.

Hixon, T.J. and collaborators. 1987. *Respiratory Function in Speech and Song.* Boston.

Hobbs, J.R. 1990. The Pierrehumbert-Hirschberg theory of intonational meaning made simple. *Intentions in Communication,* ed. P.R. Cohen, J. Morgan and M.E. Pollack: 313. Cambridge, Mass.

Hock, H.H. 1986. Compensatory lengthening: In defense of the concept "mora." *Folia Linguistica* 20:431.

Hoenigswald, H. 1989. Overlong syllables in Rigvedic cadences. *Journal of the American Oriental Society* 109:559.

Hoenigswald, H. 1990. The prosody of the epic adonius and its prehistory. Manuscript.

Hoequist, C.E. 1983. Syllable duration in stress-, syllable- and mora-timed languages. *Phonetica* 40:203.

Hoequist, C.E. 1985. *A Comparative Study of Linguistic Rhythm.* Ph.D. dissertation, Yale University.

Hogg, R. and C.B. McCully. 1987. *Metrical Phonology.* Cambridge.

Hohepa, P. 1967. *A Profile Generative Grammar of Maori.* Baltimore.

Hoijer, H. and E.P. Dozier. 1949. The phonemes of Tewa, Santa Clara Dialect. *International Journal of American Linguistics* 15:139.

Hollenbach, B. 1988. The asymmetrical distribution of tone in Copala Trique. *Autosegmental Studies in Pitch Accent,* ed. H. van der Hulst and N. Smith: 167. Dordrecht.

Holmer, N. 1949. Goajiro (Arawak) I: Phonology. *International Journal of American Linguistics* 15:45.

Holzinger, K. 1940. *Kritisch-exegetischer Kommentar zu Aristophanes' Plutos.* Sitzungsberichte der Österreischen Akademie der Wissenschaften in Wien, Philosophisch-Historische Klasse 281.3.

Hombert, J.-M. 1973. Speaking backwards in Bakwiri. *Studies in African Linguistics* 4:227.

Hombert, J.-M. 1974. Universals of downdrift: Their phonetic basis and significance for a theory of tone. *Studies in African Linguistics* Supplement 5:169.

Hombert, J.-M. 1976. Perception of tones of bisyllabic nouns in Yoruba. *Studies in African Linguistics* Supplement 6:109.

Hombert, J.-M. 1978. Consonant types, vowel quality, and tone. *Tone: A Linguistic Survey,* ed. V.A. Fromkin: 77. New York.

Hombert, J.-M. 1986. Word games: Some implications for analysis of tone and other phonological constructs. *Experimental Phonology,* ed. J.J. Ohala and J.J. Jaeger: 175. Orlando.

Hombert, J.-M., J. Ohala and W.G. Ewan. 1979. Phonetic explanations for the development of tones. *Language* 55:37.

Homma, Y. 1973. An acoustic study of Japanese vowels. *The Study of Sounds* 16:347.

Homma, Y. 1981. Durational relationship between Japanese stops and vowels. *Journal of Phonetics* 9:273.

Homma, Y. 1991. The rhythm of *Tanka*, short Japanese poems, read in prose style and contest style. *Proceedings of the XIIth International Congress of Phonetic Sciences II*: 314. Aix-en-Provence.

Hooper, J.B. 1976. *An Introduction to Natural Generative Phonology.* New York.

Horvath, J. 1986. Remarks on the configurationality-issue. *Topic, Focus, and Configurationality*, ed. W. Abraham and S. de Meij: 65. Amsterdam.

Horvath, J. 1986b. *Focus in the Theory of Grammar and the Syntax of Hungarian.* Dordrecht.

Hoshiko, M.S. 1960. Sequence of action of breathing muscles during speech. *Journal of Speech and Hearing Research* 3:291.

Hotopf, W. 1983. Lexical slips of the pen and tongue. *Language Production II*, ed. B. Butterworth: 147. London.

House, D. 1990. *Tonal Perception in Speech.* Lund.

Householder, F.W. 1965. *Basic Course in Azerbaijani.* Bloomington.

Howard, D. 1985. Agrammatism. *Current Perspectives in Dysphasia*, ed. S. Newman and R. Epstein: 1. New York.

Huck, G.J. and Y. Na. 1990. Extraposition and focus. *Language* 66:51.

Hudak, T.J. 1986. The Thai corpus of *chăn* meters. *Journal of the American Oriental Society* 106:707.

Hudgins, C.V. and R.H. Stetson. 1937. Relative speed of articulatory movements. *Archives Néerlandaises de Phonétique Expérimentale* 13:85.

Hudson, R.A. 1973. Syllables, moras and accents in Beja. *Journal of Linguistics* 9:53.

Huggins, A.W.F. 1964. Distortion of the temporal pattern of speech: Interruption and alternation. *Journal of the Acoustical Society of America* 36:1055.

Huggins, A.W.F. 1972. Just noticeable differences for segment duration in natural speech. *Journal of the Acoustical Society of America* 51:1270.

Huggins, A.W.F. 1975. On isochrony and syntax. *Auditory Analysis and Perception of Speech*, ed. G. Fant and M.A.A. Tatham: 455. London.

Huggins, A.W.F. 1975b. Temporally segmented speech and "echoic" storage. *Structure and Process in Speech Perception*, ed. A. Cohen and S.G. Nooteboom: 209. Berlin.

Huggins, A.W.F. 1979. Some effects on intelligibility of inappropriate temporal relations within speech units. *Proceedings of the Ninth International Congress of Phonetic Sciences II*: 283. Copenhagen.

Hughes. E.J. and V.J. Leeding. 1971. The phonemes of Nunggubuyu. *Papers on the Languages of Australian Aboriginals*: 72. Canberra.

Hughes, C.P., J.L. Chan and M.S. Su. 1983. Aprosodia in Chinese patients with right cerebral hemisphere lesions. *Archives of Neurology* 40:732.

Hulse, S.W., J. Humpal and J. Cynx. 1984. Discrimination and generalization of rhythmic and arrhythmic sound patterns by European starlings *(sturnus vulgaris)*. *Music Perception* 1:442.

Hunter, L. 1980. Stress in Hausa: An experimental study. *Studies in African Linguistics* 11:353.

Huss, V. 1978. English word stress in postnuclear position. *Phonetica* 35:86.

Hutchinson, L. 1969. *Pronouns and Agreement in Temne.* Ph.D. dissertation, University of Indiana.

Hutchison, J.P. 1986. Major constituent case marking in Kanuri. *Current Approaches to African Linguistics* 3:191.

Huttar, G.L. 1972. Notes on Djuka phonology. *Languages of the Guianas*, ed. J.E. Grimes: 1. Norman.

Hyman, L.M. 1977. On the nature of linguistic stress. *Studies in Stress and Accent,* ed. L.M. Hyman: 37. Los Angeles.

Hyman, L.M. 1978. Tone and/or accent. *Elements of Tone, Stress and Intonation,* ed. D.J. Napoli: 1. Washington.

Hyman, L.M. 1978b. Historical tonology. *Tone: A Linguistic Survey,* ed. V.A. Fromkin: 257. New York.

Hyman, L.M. 1981. Tonal accent in Somali. *Studies in African Linguistics* 12:169.

Hyman, L.M. 1981b. *Noni Grammatical Structure.* Southern California Occasional Papers in Linguistics 9.

Hyman, L.M. 1982. The representation of length in Gokana. *Proceedings of the First West Coast Conference on Formal Linguistics* 198.

Hyman, L.M. 1984. On the weightlessness of syllable onsets. *Proceedings of the Tenth Annual Meeting of the Berkeley Linguistics Society*: 1.

Hyman, L.M. 1985. *A Theory of Phonological Weight.* Dordrecht.

Hyman, L.M. 1985b. Word domains and downstep in Bamileke-Dschang. *Phonology Yearbook* 2:47.

Hyman, L.M. 1990. Non-exhaustive syllabification: Evidence from Nigeria and Cameroon. *Papers from the 26th Regional Meeting of the Chicago Linguistic Society II: Parasession on the Syllable in Phonetics and Phonology*: 175.

Hyman, L.M. 1992. Moraic mismatches in Bantu. *Phonology* 9:255.

Hyman, L.M. and E.R. Byarushengo. 1984. A model of Haya tonology. *Autosegmental Studies in Bantu Tone,* ed. G.N. Clements and J. Goldsmith: 53. Dordrecht.

Hyman, L.M., F. Katamba and L. Walusimbi. 1987. Luganda and the strict layer hypothesis. *Phonology Yearbook* 4:87.

Hyman, L.M. and F. Katamba. 1993. A new approach to tone in Luganda. *Language* 69:34.

Iivonen, A. 1984. On explaining the initial fundamental frequency in Finnish utterances. *Nordic Prosody III,* ed. C.-C. Elert, I. Johansson and E. Strangert: 107. Stockholm.

Iivonen, A. 1987. Paradigm of recurrent accent types of Finnish. *Nordic Prosody IV,* ed. K. Gregersen and H. Basbøll: 115. Odense.

Imaizumi, S., S. Kiritani, H. Hirose, S. Togami and K. Shirai. 1987. Preliminary report on the effects of speaking rate upon formant trajectories. *Annual Bulletin, Research Institute of Logopedics and Phoniatrics* 21:147.

Ingram, D. 1978. The role of the syllable in phonological development. *Syllables and Segments,* ed. A. Bell and J.B. Hooper: 143. Amsterdam.

Inkelas, S. 1989. *Prosodic Constituency in the Lexicon.* Ph.D. dissertation, Stanford University.

Inkelas, S. and D. Zec. 1988. Serbocroatian pitch accent: The interaction of tone, stress, and intonation. *Language* 64:227.

Inkelas, S. and W.R. Leben. 1990. Where phonology and phonetics intersect: The case of Hausa intonation. *Papers in Laboratory Phonology I,* ed. J. Kingston and M.E. Beckman: 17. Cambridge.

Irigoin, J. 1959. Lois et règles dans le trimètre iambique et le tétramètre trochaique. *Revue des Études Grecques* 72:67.

Irigoin, J. 1965. Review of L. Rossi, *Metrica e critica stilistica. Göttingische Gelehrte Anzeigen* 217:284.

Isačenko, A.V. and H.-J. Schädlich. 1970. *A Model of Standard German Intonation.* The Hague.

Isler, F. 1908. *Quaestiones Metricae.* Greifswald.

Isshiki, N. 1964. Regulatory mechanism of voice intensity variation. *Journal of Speech and Hearing Research* 7:17.

Isshiki, N. 1965. Vocal intensity and air flow rate. *Folia Phoniatrica* 17:92.

Itô, J. 1988. *Syllable Theory in Prosodic Phonology.* New York.

Itô, J. 1990. Prosodic minimality in Japanese. *Papers from the 26th Regional Meeting of the Chicago Linguistic Society II: Parasession on the Syllable in Phonetics and Phonology*: 213.

Ivry, R.B. and S. Keele. 1989. Timing functions of the cerebellum. *Journal of Cognitive Neuroscience* 1:136.

Jaeggli, O.A. 1986. Three issues in the theory of clitics: Case, doubled NPs, and extraction. *Syntax and Semantics* 19:15.

Jakobson, R. and L. Waugh. 1979. *The Sound Shape of Language.* Bloomington.

Jameson, M.H. 1974. A treasury of Athena in the Argolid (*IG* IV.554). *Φορος: Tribute to Benjamin Dean Meritt,* ed. D.W. Braden and M.F. McGregor: 67. Locust Valley.

Jameson, M.H., D.R. Jordan and R.D. Kotansky. 1994. *A Lex Sacra from Selinous.* Durham, N.C..

Jarvella, R.J. 1971. Syntactic processing of connected speech. *Journal of Verbal Learning and Verbal Behavior* 10:409.

Jarvis, E. 1991. Tense and aspect in Podoko narrative and procedural discourse. *Tense and Aspect in Eight Languages of Cameroon,* ed. S.C. Anderson and B. Comrie: 213. Arlington.

Jeffery, L.H. 1990. *The Local Scripts of Archaic Greece,* rev. A.W. Johnston. Oxford.

Jelinek, E. 1984. Empty categories, case, and configurationality. *Natural Language and Linguistic Theory* 2:39.

Jelinek, E. 1989. The case split and pronominal arguments in Choctaw. *Configurationality: The Typology of Asymmetries,* ed. L. Marácz and P. Muysken: 159. Dordrecht.

Jernudd, B.H. 1968. Notes on Lithuanian accents. *Melbourne Slavonic Studies* 2:71.

Jespersen, O. 1904. *Lehrbuch der Phonetik.* Leipzig.

Joanette, Y., P. Goulet and D. Hannequin. 1990. *Right Hemisphere and Verbal Communication.* New York.

Johnson, J.W. 1979. Somali prosodic systems. *Horn of Africa* 2.3:46.

Johnson, L. 1976. Devoicing, tone, and stress in Runyankore. *Studies in Bantu Tonology,* ed. L.M. Hyman: 209. Los Angeles.

Johnson, N.F. 1970. The role of chunking and organization in the process of recall. *The Psychology of Learning and Motivation* 4:71.

Johnson, N.F. 1978. The memorial structure of organized sequences. *Memory and Cognition* 6:233.

Johnson, N.F. and D.M. Migdoll. 1971. Transfer and retroaction under conditions of changed organization. *Cognitive Psychology* 2:229.

Johnston, T.F. 1973. Speech-tone and other forces in Tsonga music. *Studies in African Linguistics* 4:49.

Jones, A.M. 1959. *Studies in African Music I.* London.

Jones, A.M. 1964. African metrical lyrics. *African Music* 3.3:6.

Jones, A.M. 1975. Swahili epic poetry: A musical study. *African Music* 5.4:105.

Jones, R.B. 1961. *Karen Linguistic Studies.* Berkeley.

Jordan, B. 1979. *Servants of the Gods.* Göttingen.

Jouannet, F. 1985. *Prosodologie et phonologie non linéaire.* Paris.

Jourdan-Hemmerdinger, D. 1973. Un nouveau papyrus musical d'Euripide. *Comptes Rendus des Séances de l'Académie des Inscriptions et des Belles Lettres*: 292.

Joynt, R. 1964. Paul Pierre Broca: His contribution to the knowledge of aphasia. *Cortex* 1:206.

Jun, S.-A. 1990. The accentual pattern and prosody of the Chonnam dialect of Korean. *Working Papers in Linguistics, Ohio State University* 38:121.

Jusatz, H. 1893. De irrationalitate studia rhythmica. *Leipziger Studien* 14:173.

Jusczyk, P. and E. Thompson. 1978. Perception of a phonetic contrast in multisyllabic utterances by 2-month-old infants. *Perception and Psychophysics* 23:105.

Kahn, D. 1976. *Syllable-based Generalizations in English Phonology.* Ph.D. dissertation, Massachusetts Institute of Technology.

Kaibel, G. 1893. *Stil und Text der Πολιτεία ᾿Αθηναίων des Aristoteles.* Berlin.

Kaiser, R. 1887. *De Inscriptionum Graecarum Interpunctione.* Berlin.

Kaisse, E.M. 1981. Separating phonology from syntax: A reanalysis of Pashto cliticization. *Journal of Linguistics* 17:197.

Kaisse, E.M. 1982. On the preservation of stress in Modern Greek. *Linguistics* 20:59.

Kaisse, E.M. 1985. *Connected Speech: The Interaction of Syntax and Phonology.* Orlando.

Kaisse, E.M. 1987. Rhythm and the cycle. *Papers from the 23rd Annual Regional Meeting of the Chicago Linguistic Society II*: 199.

Kaisse, E.M. 1990. Toward a typology of postlexical rules. *The Phonology-Syntax Connection,* ed. S. Inkelas and D. Zec: 127. Chicago.

Kakita, Y. and S. Hiki. 1976. Investigation of laryngeal control in speech by use of a thyrometer. *Journal of the Acoustical Society of America* 59:669.

Kalackal, T. 1985. *A Contrastive Analysis of the Phonological Systems of English and Malayalam.* Ph.D. dissertation, Northern Illinois University.

Kalema, J. 1977. Accent modification rules in Luganda. *Studies in African Linguistics* 8:127.

Kanerva, J. 1990. Focusing on phonological phrases in Chichewa. *The Phonology-Syntax Connection,* ed. S. Inkelas and D. Zec: 145. Chicago.

Katada, F. 1990. On the representation of moras: Evidence from a language game. *Linguistic Inquiry* 21:641.

Kawakami, S. 1980. Emphasis and restriction. *Bulletin of the Phonetic Society of Japan* 165:5.

Kawasaki, H. 1983. Fundamental frequency perturbation by voiced and voiceless stops in Japanese. *Journal of the Acoustical Society of America* 73:S88.

Kawasaki, H. 1986. Phonetic explanation for phonological universals: The case for distinctive vowel nasalization. *Experimental Phonology,* ed. J.J. Ohala and J.J. Jaeger: 81. Orlando.

Kawasaki, H. and S. Shattuck-Hufnagel. 1988. Acoustic correlates of stress in four demarcative-stress languages. *Journal of the Acoustical Society of America* 84:S98.

Kean, M.-L. 1979. Agrammatism: A phonological deficit. *Cognition* 7:69.

Kean, M.-L. 1980. Grammatical representation and the description of language processing. *Biological Studies of Mental Processes,* ed. D. Caplan: 239. Cambridge, Mass.

Kean, M.-L. 1985. *Agrammatism.* Orlando.

Keating, P.A. 1985. Universal phonetics and the organization of grammars. *Phonetic Linguistics,* ed. V.A. Fromkin: 115. Orlando.

Keele, S.W. and R.I. Ivry. 1987. Modular analysis of timing in motor skill. *The Psychology of Learning and Motivation* 21:183.

Keenan, E.L. 1976. Towards a universal definition of "subject." *Subject and Topic,* ed. C.N. Li: 303. New York.

Keeney, T.J. 1969. Permutation transformations on phrase structures in letter sequences. *Journal of Experimental Psychology* 82:28.

Kehayia, E., G. Jarema and D. Kadzielawa. 1990. Crosslinguistic study of morphological errors in aphasia. *Morphology, Phonology, and Aphasia,* ed. J.-L. Nespoulous and P. Villiard: 140. New York.

Keller, E. 1987. The variation of absolute and relative measures of speech activity. *Journal of Phonetics* 15:335.

Keller, E. 1990. Speech motor timing. *Speech Production and Speech Modelling,* ed. J.W. Hardcastle and A. Marchal: 343. Dordrecht.

Kelso, J.A.S., B. Tuller and K. Harris. 1983. A "dynamic pattern" perspective on the control and coordination of movement. *The Production of Speech,* ed. P. MacNeilage: 137. New York.

Kenesei, I. 1986. On the logic of word order in Hungarian. *Topic, Focus and Configurationality,* ed. W. Abraham and S. de Meij: 143. Amsterdam.

Kenstowicz, M. 1972. The morphophonemics of the Slovak noun. *Papers in Linguistics* 5:550.

Kenstowicz, M. and Y. Bader. 1985. The phonology of state in Kabyle Berber. *African Linguistics,* ed. D.L. Goyvaerts: 319. Amsterdam.

Kenstowicz, M. and C. Kisseberth. 1990. Chizigula tonology: The word and beyond. *The Phonology-Syntax Connection,* ed. S. Inkelas and D. Zec: 163. Chicago.

Kent, R.D. 1984. Brain mechanisms of speech and language with special reference to emotional interactions. *Language Science: Recent Advances,* ed. R.C. Naremore: 281. San Diego.

Kent, R.D. and R. Netsell. 1972. Effects of stress contrasts on certain articulatory parameters. *Phonetica* 24:23.

Kent, R.D. and K.L. Moll. 1972b. Cinefluorographic analysis of selected lingual consonants. *Journal of Speech and Hearing Research* 15:453.

Kent, R.D. and R. Netsell. 1975. A case study of an ataxic dysarthric. *Journal of Speech and Hearing Disorders* 40:115.

Kent, R.D., R. Netsell and J.H. Abbs. 1979. Acoustic characteristics of dysarthria associated with cerebellar disease. *Journal of Speech and Hearing Research* 22:627.

Kent, R.D. and J.C. Rosenbek. 1982. Prosodic disturbance and neurologic lesion. *Brain and Language* 15:259.

Kent, R.G. 1926. *The Textual Criticism of Inscriptions.* Philadelphia.

Key, H. 1961. Phonotactics of Cayuvava. *International Journal of American Linguistics* 27:143.

Keydell, R. 1959. *Nonni Panoplitani Dionysiaca.* Berlin.

Kim, A.H.-O. 1988. Preverbal focusing and type XXIII languages. *Studies in Syntactic Typology,* ed. M. Hammond, E. Moravcsik and J. Wirth: 147. Amsterdam.

Kingston, J.C. 1984. *The Phonetics and Phonology of the Timing of Oral and Glottal Events.* Ph.D. dissertation, University of California, Berkeley.

Kiparsky, P. 1967. A propos de l'histoire de l'accentuation grecque. *Langages* 2:73.

Kiparsky, P. 1973. "Elsewhere" in phonology. *A Festschrift for Morris Halle,* ed. S.R. Anderson and P. Kiparsky: 93. New York.

Kiparsky, P. 1973b. The inflectional accent in Indo-European. *Language* 49:794.

Kiparsky, P. 1979. Metrical structure assignment is cyclic. *Linguistic Inquiry* 10:421.

Kirtley, C., P. Bryant, M. MacLean and L. Bradley. 1989. Rhyme, rime, and the onset of reading. *Journal of Experimental Child Psychology* 48:224.

Kiss, K.É. 1987. *Configurationality in Hungarian.* Dordrecht.

Kisseberth, C.W. 1984. Digo tonology. *Autosegmental Studies in Bantu Tone,* ed. G.N. Clements and J. Goldsmith: 105. Dordrecht.

Klapp, S. 1979. Doing two things at once: The role of temporal compatibility. *Memory and Cognition* 7:375.

Klapp, S. 1981. Temporal compatibility in dual motor tasks. *Memory and Cognition* 9:398.

Klapp, S., M. Hill, J. Tyler, Z. Martin, R. Jagacinski and M. Jones. 1985. On marching to two different drummers. *Journal of Experimental Psychology: Human Perception and Performance* 11:814.

Klatt, D.H. 1973. Discrimination of fundamental frequency contours in synthetic speech. *Journal of the Acoustical Society of America* 53:8.

Klatt, D.H. 1975. Vowel lengthening is syntactically determined in a connected discourse. *Journal of Phonetics* 3:129.

Klatt, D.H. 1976. Linguistic uses of segmental duration in English: Acoustic and perceptual evidence. *Journal of the Acoustical Society of America* 59:1208.

Klatt, D.H. and W.E. Cooper. 1975. Perception of segment duration in sentence contexts. 1975. *Structure and Process in Speech Perception,* ed. A. Cohen and S.G. Nooteboom: 69. Berlin.

Klavans, J.L. 1982. *Some Problems in a Theory of Clitics.* Bloomington.

Klavans, J.L. 1982b. Configuration in nonconfigurational languages. *Proceedings of the First West Coast Conference on Formal Linguistics*: 292. Stanford.

Klavans, J.L. 1985. The independence of syntax and phonology in cliticization. *Language* 61:95.

Klima, E.S. and U. Bellugi. 1979. *The Signs of Language.* Cambridge, Mass.

Kloker, D. 1975. Vowel and sonorant lengthening as cues to phonological phrase boundaries. *Journal of the Acoustical Society of America* 57:533A.

Klouda, G.K., D.A. Robin, N.R. Graff-Radford and W.E. Cooper. 1988. The role of callosal connections in speech prosody. *Brain and Language* 35:154.

Kluender, K.R., R.L. Diehl and B.A. Wright. 1988. Vowel length differences before voiced and voiceless consonants: An auditory explanation. *Journal of Phonetics* 16:153.

Knight, C.M. 1919. The change from the Ancient to the Modern Greek accent. *The Journal of Philology* 35:51.

Knox, A.D. 1932. The early iambus. *Philologus* 87:18.

Kohler, K.J. 1982. F_0 in the production of lenis and fortis plosives. *Phonetica* 39:199.

Kohler, K.J. 1983. F_0 in speech timing. *Arbeitsberichte, Institut für Phonetik, Universität Kiel* 20:55.

Kohler, K.J. 1987. Categorical pitch perception. *Proceedings of the XIth International Congress of Phonetic Sciences V*: 331. Tallinn.

Kohler, K.J. 1990. Macro and micro F_0 in the synthesis of intonation. *Papers in Laboratory Phonology I,* ed. J. Kingston and M.E. Beckman: 115. Cambridge.

Kohno, M., A. Kashiwagi and T. Kashiwagi. 1991. Two processing mechanisms in rhythm perception. *Proceedings of the XIIth International Congress of Phonetic Sciences II*: 86. Aix-en-Provence.

Kolk, H.J., M.J.F. van Grunsven and A. Keyser. 1985. On parallelism between production and comprehension in agrammatism. *Agrammatism,* ed. M.-L. Kean: 165. Orlando.

Kolk, H.J. and L. Blomert. 1985b. On the Bradley hypothesis concerning agrammatism. *Brain and Language* 26:94.

Kopp, A. 1886. Ueber positio debilis und correptio attica im iambischen Trimeter der Griechen. *Rheinisches Museum* 41:247, 376.

Kori, S. 1987. The tonal behavior of Osaka Japanese. *Working Papers in Linguistics, Ohio State University* 36:31.

Kori, S. 1989. Acoustic manifestation of focus in Tokyo Japanese. *Studies in Phonetics and Speech Communication* 3:29.

Kornai, A. and L. Kálmán. 1988. Hungarian sentence intonation. *Autosegmental Studies in Pitch Accent,* ed. H. van der Hulst and N. Smith: 167. Dordrecht.

Kornfilt, J. 1990. Turkish and the Turkic Languages. *The World's Major Languages,* ed. B. Comrie: 619. Oxford.

Koster, W.J.W. 1953. *Traité de métrique grecque.* Second edition. Leiden.

Kotlyar, G.M. and V.P. Morozov. 1976. Acoustical correlates of the emotional content of vocalized speech. *Soviet Physics. Acoustics* 22:208.

Kowal, S., D.C. O'Connell, E.A. O'Brien and E.T. Bryant. 1975. Temporal aspects of reading aloud and speaking: Three experiments. *The American Journal of Psychology* 88:549.

Kowal, S., R. Wiese and D.C. O'Connell. 1983. The use of time in storytelling. *Language and Speech* 26:377.

Krakow, R.A. 1989. *The Articulatory Organization of Syllables: A Kinematic Analysis of Labial and Velar Gestures.* Ph.D. dissertation, Yale University.

Krakow, R.A., F. Bell-Berti and Q. Wang. 1991. Supralaryngeal patterns of declination: Labial and velar kinematics. *Journal of the Acoustical Society of America* 90:2343.

Král, J. 1925. *Beiträge zur griechischen Metrik.* Prague.

Kratochvíl, P. 1968. *The Chinese Language Today.* London.

Krauss, M. 1985. *Yupik Eskimo Prosodic Systems: Descriptive and Comparative Studies.* Fairbanks.

Kreiman, J. 1982. Perception of sentence and paragraph boundaries in natural conversation. *Journal of Phonetics* 10:163.

Kretschmer, P. 1890. Der Übergang von der musikalischen zur expiratorischen Betonung im Griechischen. *Zeitschrift für vergleichende Sprachforschung* 30:591.

Kretschmer, P. 1932. Literaturbericht für das Jahr 1929. *Glotta* 20:218.

Kruckenberg, A., G. Fant and L. Nord. 1991. Rhythmical structures in poetry reading. *Proceedings of the XIIth International Congress of Phonetic Sciences IV*: 242. Aix-en-Provence.

Krueger, J.R. 1962. *Yakut Manual.* Bloomington.

Kubozono, H. 1985. Speech errors and syllable structure. *Linguistics and Philology* 6:220.

Kubozono, H. 1987. *The Organization of Japanese Prosody.* Ph.D. dissertation, University of Edinburgh.

Kubozono, H. 1989. Syntactic and rhythmic effects on downstep in Japanese. *Phonology* 6:39.

Kubozono, H. 1989b. The mora and syllable structure in Japanese: Evidence from speech errors. *Language and Speech* 32:249.

Kubozono, H. 1992. Modeling syntactic effects on downstep in Japanese. *Papers in Laboratory Phonology II,* ed. G.J. Docherty and D.R. Ladd: 386. Cambridge.

Kuehn, D.P. 1973. *A Cinefluorographic Investigation of Articulatory Velocities.* Ph.D. dissertation, University of Iowa.

Kuhn, H. 1933. Zur Wortstellung und Betonung im Altgermanischen. *Beiträge zur Geschichte der deutschen Sprache und Literatur* 57:1.

Kühner, R. and F. Blass. 1890–1892. *Ausführliche Grammatik der griechischen Sprache I.1– 2.* Hannover.

Kuno, S. 1982. The focus of the question and the focus of the answer. *Papers from the 18th Regional Meeting of the Chicago Linguistic Society: Parasession on Nondeclarative Sentences*: 134.

Kuriyagawa, F. and M. Sawashima. 1984. Vowel duration in /húku/ and /hukú/ in Japanese. *Annual Bulletin, Research Institute of Logopedics and Phoniatrics* 18:83.

Kuriyagawa, F. and M. Sawashima. 1987. Word accent and the duration of vowels in /$C^1u^1C^2u^2$/ in Japanese. *Annual Bulletin, Research Institute of Logopedics and Phoniatrics* 21:41.

Kuriyagawa, F. and M. Sawashima. 1989. Word accent, devoicing and duration of vowels in Japanese. *Annual Bulletin, Research Institute of Logopedics and Phoniatrics* 23:85.

Kuroda, I., O. Fujiwara, N. Okamura and N. Utsuki. 1976. Method for determining pilot stress through analysis of voice communication. *Aviation, Space, and Environmental Medicine* 47:528.

Kuryłowicz, J. 1972. L'origine de ν ἐφελκυστικόν. *Mélanges de linguistique et de philologie grecques offerts à Pierre Chantraine*: 75. Paris.

Kutas, M. and S.A. Hillyard. 1983. Event-related brain potentials to grammatical errors and semantic anomalies. *Memory and Cognition* 11:539.

Kutik, E.J., W.E. Cooper and S. Boyce. 1983. Declination of fundamental frequency in speakers' production of parentheticals and main clauses. *Journal of the Acoustical Society of America* 73:1731.

Labov, W. 1972. *Sociolinguistic Patterns*. Philadelphia.

Ladd, D.R. 1980. *The Structure of Intonational Meaning*. Bloomington.

Ladd, D.R. 1983. Phonological features of intonational peaks. *Language* 59:721.

Ladd, D.R. 1984. Declination: A review and some hypotheses. *Phonology Yearbook* 1:53.

Ladd, D.R. 1986. Intonational phrasing: The case for recursive prosodic structure. *Phonology Yearbook* 3:311.

Ladd, D.R. 1988. Declination "reset" and the hierarchical organization of utterances. *Journal of the Acoustical Society of America* 84:530.

Ladd, D.R. 1990. Intonation: Emotion vs. grammar. *Language* 66:806.

Ladd, D.R. 1992. An introduction to intonational phonology. *Papers in Laboratory Phonology II*, ed. G.J. Docherty and D.R. Ladd: 321. Cambridge.

Ladd, D.R. and K.E.A. Silverman. 1984. Vowel intrinsic pitch in connected speech. *Phonetica* 41:31.

Ladd, D.R., K.E.A. Silverman, F. Tolkmitt, G. Bergmann and K.R. Scherer. 1985. Evidence for the independent function of intonation contour type, voice quality, and F_0 range in signaling speaker affect. *Journal of the Acoustical Society of America* 78:435.

Ladd, D.R. and W.N. Campbell. 1991. Theories of prosodic structure: Evidence from syllable duration. *Proceedings of the XIIth International Congress of Phonetic Sciences II*: 290. Aix-en-Provence.

Ladefoged, P. 1962. Subglottal activity during speech. *Proceedings of the Fourth International Congress of Phonetic Sciences*: 73. The Hague.

Ladefoged, P. 1968. Linguistic aspects of respiratory phenomena. *Annals of the New York Academy of Science* 155:141.

Lademann, W. 1915. *De Titulis Atticis Quaestiones Orthographicae et Grammaticae*. Kirchhain.

Lahiri, A. and J. Koreman. 1988. Syllable weight and quantity in Dutch. *Proceedings of the 7th West Coast Conference on Linguistics*: 217.

Lane, H. and F. Grosjean. 1973. Perception of reading rate by listeners and speakers. *Journal of Experimental Psychology* 97:141.

Langdon, M. 1970. *A Grammar of Diegueño: Mesa Grande Dialect*. Berkeley.

Lapointe, S.G. 1985. A theory of verb form use in the speech of agrammatic aphasics. *Brain and Language* 24:100.

Larfeld, W. 1914. *Griechische Epigraphik*. Third edition. Munich.

Larsen, R.S. and E.V. Pike. 1949. Huasteco intonations and phonemes. *Language* 25:268.

Laubstein, A.S. 1988. *The Nature of the "Production Grammar" Syllable*. Bloomington.

Läufer, C. 1985. *Some Language-Specific and Universal Aspects of Syllable Structure and Syllabification: Evidence from French and German*. Ph.D. dissertation, Cornell University.

Laughren, M. 1984. Tone in Zulu nouns. *Autosegmental Studies in Bantu Tone,* ed. G.N. Clements and J. Goldsmith: 183. Dordrecht.

Laughren, M. 1989. The configurationality parameter and Warlpiri. *Configurationality: The Typology of Asymmetries,* ed. L. Marácz and P. Muysken: 159. Dordrecht.

Laum, B. 1928. *Das Alexandrinische Akzentuationssystem.* Paderborn.

Lea, W.A. 1973. Segmental and suprasegmental influences on fundamental frequency contours. *Consonant Types and Tone,* ed. L.M. Hyman: 17. Los Angeles.

Lea, W.A. 1977. Acoustic correlates of stress and juncture. *Studies in Stress and Accent,* ed. L.M. Hyman: 83. Los Angeles.

Lea, W.A. 1980. Prosodic aids to speech recognition. *Trends in Speech Recognition,* ed. W.A. Lea: 166. Englewood Cliffs.

Leben, W.R. 1985. On the correspondence between linguistic tone and musical melody. *African Linguistics,* ed. D.L. Goyvaerts: 335. Amsterdam.

Lee, S.-H. 1989. Intonational domains of the Seoul dialect of Korean. Manuscript. Ohio State University.

Lee, W.R. 1970. Noticing word-boundaries: A brief investigation. *Proceedings of the Sixth International Congress of Phonetic Sciences:* 535. Prague.

Lehiste, I. 1960. *An Acoustic-Phonetic Study of Internal Open Juncture.* Basel.

Lehiste, I. 1962. Study of [h] and whispered speech. *Journal of the Acoustical Society of America* 34:742.

Lehiste, I. 1965. Juncture. *Proceedings of the Fifth International Congress of Phonetic Sciences:* 172. Basel.

Lehiste, I. 1965b. The function of quantity in the phonological systems of Finnish and Estonian. *Language* 41:447.

Lehiste, I. 1966. *Consonant Quantity and Phonological Units in Estonian.* Bloomington.

Lehiste, I. 1970. *Suprasegmentals.* Cambridge, Mass.

Lehiste, I. 1971. Temporal organization of spoken language. *Form and Substance: Phonetic and Linguistic Papers Presented to Eli Fischer-Jørgensen,* ed. L.L. Hammerich, R. Jakobson and E. Zwirner: 159. Copenhagen.

Lehiste, I. 1972. The timing of utterances and linguistic boundaries. *Journal of the Acoustical Society of America* 51:2018.

Lehiste, I. 1973. Rhythmic units and syntactic units in production and perception. *Journal of the Acoustical Society of America* 54:1228.

Lehiste, I. 1974. The syllable nucleus as a unit of timing. *Proceedings of the Eleventh International Congress of Linguists:* 929. Bologna.

Lehiste, I. 1975. The role of temporal factors in the establishment of linguistic units and boundaries. *Phonologica,* ed. W.U. Dressler and F.V. Mareš: 115. Munich.

Lehiste, I. 1975b. The phonetic structure of paragraphs. *Structure and Process in Speech Perception,* ed. A. Cohen and S.G. Nooteboom: 195. Berlin.

Lehiste, I. 1976. Influence of fundamental frequency pattern on the perception of duration. *Journal of Phonetics* 4:113.

Lehiste, I. 1977. Isochrony reconsidered. *Journal of Phonetics* 5:253.

Lehiste, I. 1978. The syllable as a structural unit in Estonian. *Syllables and Segments,* ed. A. Bell and J.B. Hooper: 73. Amsterdam.

Lehiste, I. 1979. Perception of sentence and paragraph boundaries. *Frontiers of Speech Communication Research,* ed. B. Lindblom and S. Öhman: 191. London.

Lehiste, I. 1979b. The perception of duration within sequences of four intervals. *Journal of Phonetics* 7:313.

Lehiste, I. 1980. Interaction between test word duration and length of utterance. *The Melody of Language,* ed. L. Waugh and C.H. van Schooneveld: 169. Baltimore.

Lehiste, I. 1980b. Sentence and paragraph boundaries in Estonian. *Estonian Papers in Phonetics* 1980–81:9.

Lehiste, I. 1980c. Phonetic manifestation of syntactic structure in English. *Annual Bulletin, Research Institute of Logopedics and Phoniatrics* 14:1.

Lehiste, I. 1983. Signalling of syntactic structure in whispered speech. *Folia Linguistica* 17:239.

Lehiste, I. 1985. Rhythm of poetry, rhythm of prose. *Phonetic Linguistics*, ed. V.A. Fromkin: 145. Orlando.

Lehiste, I. 1987. Rhythm in spoken sentences and read poetry. *Phonologica 1984*, ed. W.U. Dressler, H.C. Luschützky, O.E. Pfeiffer and J.R. Rennison: 165. London.

Lehiste, I. 1990. Phonetic investigation of metrical structure in orally produced poetry. *Journal of Phonetics* 18:123.

Lehiste, I. 1990b. Some aspects of the phonetics of metrics. *Nordic Prosody V*, ed. K. Wiik and I. Raimo: 206. Turku.

Lehiste, I. and G.E. Peterson. 1959. Vowel amplitude and phonemic stress in American English. *Journal of the Acoustical Society of America* 31:428.

Lehiste, I. and G.E. Peterson. 1961. Some basic considerations in the analysis of intonation. *Journal of the Acoustical Society of America* 33:419.

Lehiste, I., J.P. Olive and L.A. Streeter. 1976. Role of duration in disambiguating syntactically ambiguous sentences. *Journal of the Acoustical Society of America* 60:1199.

Lehiste, I. and P. Ivić. 1978. Interrelationship between word tone and sentence intonation in Serbocroatian. *Elements of Tone, Stress, and Intonation*, ed. D.J. Napoli: 100. Washington, D.C..

Lehiste, I. and P. Ivić. 1986. *Word and Sentence Prosody in Serbocroatian.* Cambridge, Mass.

Lehtinen, M. 1964. *Basic Course in Finnish.* Bloomington.

Leino, P. 1986. *Language and Metre: Metrics and the Metrical System of Finnish.* Helsinki.

Lejeune, M. 1972. *Phonétique historique du Mycénien et du Grec ancien.* Paris.

Léon, P.R. and P. Martin. 1980. Des accents. *The Melody of Language*, ed. L.R. Waugh and C.H. van Schooneveld: 177. Baltimore.

Leroy, C. 1970. Etude de phonétique comparative de la langue turque sifflée et parlée. *Revue de Phonétique Appliquée* 14–15:119.

Leroy, L. 1984. The psychological reality of fundamental frequency declination. *Antwerp Papers in Linguistics* 40.

Leskinen, H. and J. Lehtonen. 1985. Zur wortphonologischen Quantität in den Sudostdialekten des Finnischen. *Studia Fennica* 28:49.

Lesky, A. 1953. Das hellenistische Gyges-drama. *Hermes* 81:1.

Lester, L. and R. Skousen. 1974. The phonology of drunkenness. *Papers from the Parasession on Natural Phonology*: 233. Chicago Linguistic Society.

Levin, J. 1985. *A Metrical Theory of Syllabicity.* Ph.D. dissertation, Massachusetts Institute of Technology.

Li, C.N. and S.A. Thompson. 1976. Subject and topic: A new typology of language. *Subject and Topic*, ed. C.N. Li: 457. New York.

Liberman, M.Y. 1979. *The Intonational System of English.* New York.

Liberman, M.Y. and A. Prince. 1977. On stress and linguistic rhythm. *Linguistic Inquiry* 8:349.

Liberman, M.Y. and J. Pierrehumbert. 1984. Intonational invariance under changes in pitch range and length. *Language Sound Structure*, ed. M. Aronoff and R.T. Oehrle: 157. Cambridge, Mass.

Liccardi, M. and J. Grimes. 1968. Itonama intonation and phonemes. *Linguistics* 38:36.

Lichtenberk, F. 1983. *A Grammar of Manam.* Honolulu.

Lieberman, M.R. and P. Lieberman. 1972. Olson's projective verse and the use of breath control as a structural element. *Language and Style* 5:287.

Lieberman, P. 1967. *Intonation, Perception, and Language.* Cambridge, Mass.

Lieberman, P. 1986. Alice in declinationland—A reply to Johan 't Hart. *Journal of the Acoustical Society of America* 80:1840.

Lieger, P. 1914. Streifzüge ins Gebiet der griechischen Metrik. *Symbolae Scotenses* 1913–14:5.

Lieger, P. 1930. Das päonische Metrum und sein Verhältnis zu den Dochmien. *Jahresbericht des Schottengymnasiums in Wien* 1930:3.

Lieger, P. 1933. Die Cantica in Sophokles' Antigone. *Jahresbericht des Schottengymnasiums in Wien* 1933:12.

Lindau, M. 1985. Testing a model of intonation in a tone language. *Working Papers in Phonetics, University of California, Los Angeles* 61:26.

Lindblom, B. 1963. Spectrographic study of vowel reduction. *Journal of the Acoustical Society of America* 35:1773.

Lindblom, B. 1978. Final lengthening in speech and music. *Nordic Prosody,* ed. E. Gårding, G. Bruce and R. Bannert: 85. Lund.

Lindblom, B. 1983. Economy of speech gestures. *The Production of Speech,* ed. P.F. MacNeilage: 217. New York.

Lindblom, B. 1990. Explaining phonetic variation. *Speech Production and Speech Modelling,* ed. W.J. Hardcastle and A. Marchal: 403. Dordrecht.

Lindblom, B. and K. Rapp. 1973. *Some Temporal Regularities of Spoken Swedish.* Institute of Linguistics, University of Stockholm, Publication number 21.

Lindblom, B., B. Lyberg and K. Holmgren. 1981. *Durational Patterns of Swedish Phonology: Do They Reflect Short-Term Memory Processes?* Indiana University Linguistics Club.

Lindblom, B., J. Lubker, T. Gay, B. Lyberg, P. Branderud and K. Holmgren. 1987. The concept of target and speech timing. *In Honor of Ilse Lehiste,* ed. R. Channon and L. Shockey: 161. Dordrecht.

Lindhamer, L. 1908. *Zur Wortstellung im Griechischen.* Ph.D. dissertation, Munich.

Lindsey, G. 1985. *Intonation and Interrogation.* Ph.D. dissertation, University of California, Los Angeles.

Lindskog, J.N. and R.M. Brend. 1962. Cayapa phonemics. *Studies in Ecuadorian Indian Languages I,* ed. B.F. Elson: 33. Norman.

Linebarger, M., M. Schwartz and E. Saffran. 1983. Sensitivity to grammatical structure in socalled agrammatic aphasics. *Cognition* 13:361.

Lisker, L. 1974. On "explaining" vowel duration. *Glossa* 8:233.

Lisker, L. and A.S. Abrahamson. 1964. A cross-language study of voicing in initial stops: Acoustic measurements. *Word* 20:384.

List, G. 1961. Speech melody and song melody in Central Thailand. *Ethnomusicology* 5:16.

Lobeck, C.A. 1804. *Initia Doctrinae de Usu Apostrophi ex Tragicorum Reliquiis Ducta.* Wittenberg.

Locke, D. and G.K. Agbeli. 1980. A study of the drum language in Adzogbo. *African Music* 6:32.

Löfqvist, A. 1975. Intrinsic and extrinsic F_0 variations in Swedish tonal accents. *Phonetica* 31:228.

Löfqvist, A. 1990. Speech as audible gestures. *Speech Production and Speech Modelling,* ed. W.J. Hardcastle and A. Marchal: 289. Dordrecht.

Löfqvist, A. and H. Yoshioka. 1984. Intrasegmental timing: Laryngeal-oral coordination in voiceless consonant production. *Speech Communication* 3:279.

Löfqvist, A. and N.S. McGarr. 1987. Laryngeal dynamics in voiceless consonant production. *Laryngeal Function in Phonation and Respiration,* ed. T. Baer, C. Sasaki and K.S. Harris: 391. Boston.

Löfqvist, A., T. Baer, N.S. McGarr and R.S. Story. 1989. The cricothyroid muscle in voicing control. *Journal of the Acoustical Society of America* 85:1314.

Lombardi, L. and J. McCarthy. 1991. Prosodic circumscription in Choctaw morphology. *Phonology* 8:37.

Loos, E. 1969. *The Phonology of Capanahua and its Grammatical Basis.* Norman.

Loots, M.E. 1980. *Metrical Myths.* The Hague.

Lorentz, O. 1984. Stress and tone in an accent language. *Nordic Prosody III,* ed. C.-C. Elert, I. Johansson and E. Strangert: 165. Stockholm.

Loring, D.W., K.J. Meador, G.P. Lee, A.M. Murro, J.R. Smith, H.F. Flanigin, B.B. Gallagher and D.W. King. 1990. Cerebral language lateralization: Evidence from intracarotid amobarbital testing. *Neuropsychologia* 28:831.

Lucius, A. 1885. *De Crasi et Aphaeresi.* Dissertation, Strassburg.

Ludwich, A. 1866. *De Hexametris Poetarum Graecorum Spondaicis.* Halle.

Ludwich, A. 1885. *Aristarchs Homerische Textkritik nach den Fragmenten des Didymos II.* Leipzig.

Luppe, W. 1983. Atlas-Zitate im 1. Buch von Philodems *De Pietate. Cronache Ercolanesi* 13:45.

Lutz, A. 1986. The syllabic basis of word division in Old English manuscripts. *English Studies* 67:193.

Lyberg, B. 1977. Some observations on the timing of Swedish utterances. *Journal of Phonetics* 5:49.

Maas, P. 1901. Metrisches zu den Sentenzen der Kassia. *Kleine Schriften,* ed. W. Buchwald: 420. Munich.

Maas, P. 1903. Der byzantinische Zwölfsilber. *Kleine Schriften,* ed. W. Buchwald: 242. Munich.

Maas, P. 1908. Review of H. Usener, *Der heilige Tychon. Kleine Schriften,* ed. W. Buchwald: 454. Munich.

Maas, P. 1922. Zum Wortakzent im byzantinischen Pentameter. *Byzantinisch-Neugriechische Jahrbücher* 1922: 163.

Maas, P. 1962. *Greek Metre.* Oxford.

Maassen, H. 1881. De littera nu Graecorum paragogica. *Leipziger Studien* 4:1.

Macchi, M. 1988. Labial articulation patterns associated with segmental features and syllable structure in English. *Phonetica* 45:109.

MacClay, H. and C.E. Osgood. 1959. Hesitation phenomena in spontaneous English speech. *Word* 1:19.

Mackay, D.G. 1974. Aspects of the syntax of behavior: Syllable structure and speech rate. *Quarterly Journal of Experimental Psychology* 26:642.

MacNeilage, P.F. and B.L. Davis. 1990. Acquisition of speech production: The achievement of segmental independence. *Speech Production and Speech Modelling,* ed. W.J. Hardcastle and A. Marchal: 55. Dordrecht.

MacNeilage, P.F. and B.L. Davis. 1991. Vowel-consonant relations in babbling. *Proceedings of the XIIth International Congress of Phonetic Sciences I*: 338. Aix-en-Provence.

MacWhinney, B. and E. Bates. 1978. Sentential devices for conveying givenness and newness: A crosscultural developmental study. *Journal of Verbal Learning and Verbal Behavior* 17:539.

Maddieson, I. 1985. Phonetic cues to syllabification. *Phonetic Linguistics,* ed. V.A. Fromkin: 203. Orlando.

Madsen, S.K., R.A. Duke and J.M. Geringer. 1986. The effect of speed alterations on tempo note selection. *Journal of Research in Music Education* 34:101.

Maeda, S. 1976. *A Characterization of American English Intonation.* Ph.D. dissertation, Massachusetts Institute of Technology.

Mallinson, G. and B.J. Blake. 1981. *Language Typology.* Amsterdam.

Malmberg, B. 1955. The phonetic basis for syllable division. *Studia Linguistica* 9:80.

Marantz, A. 1982. Re reduplication. *Linguistic Inquiry* 13:435.

Marchal, A. 1988. Coproduction: Evidence from EPG data. *Speech Communication* 7:287.

Marchand, H. 1951. Esquisse d'une description des principales alternances dérivatives dans le français d'aujourd'hui. *Studia Linguistica* 5:95.

Marcus, S.M. 1981. Acoustic determinants of perceptual center (P-center) location. *Perception and Psychophysics* 30:247.

Marshall, R.C., J. Gandour and J. Windsor. 1988. Selective impairment of phonation. *Brain and Language* 35:313.

Marslen-Wilson, W. and L.K. Tyler. 1980. The temporal structure of spoken language understanding. *Cognition* 8:1.

Martin, J.G. 1970. On judging pauses in spontaneous speech. *Journal of Verbal Learning and Verbal Behavior* 9:75.

Martin, J.G. 1972. Rhythmic (hierarchical) versus serial structure in speech and other behavior. *Psychological Review* 79:487.

Martin, J.G. 1979. Rhythmic and segmental perception are not independent. *Journal of the Acoustical Society of America* 65:1286.

Masaki, S., S. Kiritani, S. Niimi and K. Shirai. 1986. Influences of increase in speaking rate on jaw and tongue positions for vowels in the production of vowel sequence words. *Annual Bulletin, Research Institute of Logopedics and Phoniatrics* 20:33.

Mase, H. 1973. A study of the role of syllable and mora for the tonal manifestation in West Greenlandic. *Annual Report, Institute of Phonetics, University of Copenhagen* 7:1.

Masson, O. 1983. *Les Inscriptions chypriotes syllabiques.* Paris.

Masson, O. and J. Yoyotte. 1988. Une inscription ionienne mentionnant Psammétique Ier. *Epigraphica Anatolica* 11:171.

Mateer, C.A. and P.A. Cameron. 1989. Electrophysiological correlates of language: Stimulation mapping and evoked potential studies. *Handbook of Neuropsychology II,* ed. F. Boller and J. Grafman: 91. Amsterdam.

Mathesius, V. 1928. On linguistic characterology with illustrations from Modern English. *Actes du Premier Congrès International de Linguistes*: 56. The Hague.

Matthei, E.H. and M.-L. Kean. 1989. Postaccess processes in the open vs. closed class distinction. *Brain and Language* 36:163.

Matsunaga, T. 1984. *Prosodic Systems of Japanese: Parametric Approach to the Analysis of Intonation.* Ph.D. dissertation, Georgetown University.

Mavlov, L. 1980. Amusia due to rhythm in a musician with left hemisphere damage. *Cortex* 16:331.

May, J. and E. Loeweke. 1965. The phonological hierarchy in Fasu. *Anthropological Linguistics* 7:89.

Mbonimana, G. 1983. La métrique dans la poésie pastorale au Rwanda. *Le Kinyarwanda: Études de morphosyntaxe,* ed. Y. Cadiou: 151. Louvain.

McArthur H. and L. McArthur. 1966. Aguatec. *Languages of Guatemala,* ed. M.K. Mayers: 140. The Hague.

McCabe, D.F. 1981. *The Prose-Rhythm of Demosthenes.* New York.

McCarthy, J.J. 1982. *Formal Problems in Semitic Phonology and Morphology.* Indiana University Linguistics Club.

McCarthy, J.J. and A.S. Prince. 1986. *Prosodic Morphology.* Manuscript.

McCarthy, J.J. and A.S. Prince. 1990. Foot and word in prosodic morphology: The Arabic broken plural. *Natural Language and Linguistic Theory* 8:209.

McCawley, J.D. 1978. What is a tone language? *Tone: A Linguistic Survey,* ed. V.A. Fromkin: 113. New York.

McClean, M. 1973. Forward coarticulation of velar movement at marked junctural boundaries. *Journal of Speech and Hearing Research* 16:286.

McConvell, P. 1980. Hierarchical variation in pronominal clitic attachment in the Eastern Ngumbin languages. *Papers in Australian Linguistics* 13:31.

McLemore, C.A. 1991. *The Pragmatic Interpretation of English Intonation: Sorority Speech.* Ph.D. dissertation, University of Texas, Austin.

McRoberts, G.W. and B. Sanders. 1992. Sex differences in performance and hemispheric organization for a nonverbal auditory task. *Perception and Psychophysics* 51:118.

Mehler, J., J. Dommergues, U. Frauenfelder and J. Segui. 1981. The syllable's role in speech segmentation. *Journal of Verbal Learning and Verbal Behavior* 20:298.

Meiggs, R. and D. Lewis. 1980. *A Selection of Greek Historical Inscriptions to the End of the Fifth Century B.C.* Oxford.

Meinhold, K. 1972. Allgemeine phonetische Probleme der Sprechgeschwindigkeit. *Zeitschrift für Phonetik* 25:492.

Meister, R. 1894. Zu den Regeln der kyprischen Silbenschrift. *Indogermanische Forschungen* 4:175.

Meisterhans, K. 1900. *Grammatik der attischen Inschriften.* Berlin.

Menn, L. and L.K. Obler. 1990. *Agrammatic Aphasia: A Cross-Language Narrative Sourcebook.* Amsterdam.

Mens, L. and D. Povel. 1986. Evidence against speech rhythm. *Quarterly Journal of Experimental Psychology* 38:177.

Mermelstein, P. 1975. Automatic segmentation of speech into syllabic units. *Journal of the Acoustical Society of America* 58:880.

Meyer, G. 1896. *Griechische Grammatik.* Third edition. Leipzig.

Meyer, W. 1884. Zur Geschichte des griechischen und lateinischen Hexameters. *Sitzungsberichte, Koeniglich-bayerische Akademie der Wissenschaften, Philosophisch-philologische und historische Classe* 1884:979.

Meyer, W. 1905. Der accentuirte Satzschluss in der griechischen Prosa vom VI bis XVI Jahrhundert. *Gesammelte Abhändlungen zur mittellateinischen Rhythmik II*: 202. Berlin.

Meyers, L.F. 1976. *Aspects of Hausa Tone.* Working Papers in Phonetics 32, University of California, Los Angeles.

Miceli, G., A. Mazzucchi, L. Menn and H. Goodglass. 1983. Contrasting cases of Italian agrammatic aphasia without comprehension disorder. *Brain and Language* 19:65.

Miceli, G., M.C. Silveri, G. Villa and A. Caramazza. 1984. On the basis for the agrammatic's difficulty in producing main verbs. *Cortex* 20:207.

Miceli, G. and A. Caramazza. 1988. Dissociation of inflectional and derivational morphology. *Brain and Language* 35:24.

Miceli, G., M.C. Silveri, C. Romani and A. Caramazza. 1989. Variation in the pattern of omissions and substitutions of grammatical morphemes in the spontaneous speech of socalled agrammatic patients. *Brain and Langauge* 36:447.

Miller, D.G. 1976. The transformation of a natural accent system. *Glotta* 54:11.

Miller, G.A. 1956. The magical number seven, plus or minus two. *Psychological Review* 63:81.

Miller, J.L. 1981. Effects of speaking rate on segmental distinctions. *Perspectives on the Study of Speech,* ed. P.D. Eimas and J.L. Miller: 39. Hillsdale.

Miller, J.L., K.P. Greene and A. Reeves. 1986. Speaking rate and segments: A look at the relation between speech production and speech perception for the voicing contrast. *Phonetica* 43:106.

Miller, M. 1984. On the perception of rhythm. *Journal of Phonetics* 12:75.

Mills, L. and G.B. Rollman. 1979. Left hemisphere selectivity for processing duration in normal subjects. *Brain and Language* 7:320.

Mithun, M. 1984. The evolution of noun incorporation. *Language* 60:847.

Mithun, M. 1988. The grammaticalization of coordination. *Clause Combining in Grammar and Discourse*, ed. J. Haiman and S.A. Thompson: 331. Amsterdam.

Mithun, M. 1992. Is basic word order universal? *Pragmatics of Word Order Flexibility*, ed. D. Payne: 15. Amsterdam.

Mitsuya, F. and M. Sugito. 1978. A study of the accentual effect on segmental and moraic duration in Japanese. *Annual Bulletin, Research Institute of Logopedics and Phoniatrics* 12:97.

Miyaoka, O. 1971. On syllable modification and quantity in Yuk phonology. *International Journal of American Linguistics* 37:219.

Mock, C.A. 1985. Relations between pitch accent and stress. *Papers from the General Session at the Twenty-First Regional Meeting, Chicago Linguistic Society*: 256.

Mock, C.A. 1988. Pitch accent and stress in Isthmus Zapotec. *Autosegmental Studies in Pitch Accent*, ed. H. van der Hulst and N. Smith: 197. Dordrecht.

Moen, I. 1991. Functional lateralization of pitch accents and intonation in Norwegian. *Brain and Language* 41:538.

Mohanan, K.P. 1982. *Lexical Phonology*. Indiana University Linguistics Club.

Mohanan, K.P. 1986. *The Theory of Lexical Phonology*. Dordrecht.

Molfese, D.L., R.A. Buhrke and S.L. Wang. 1985. The right hemisphere and temporal processing of consonant transition durations: Electrophysiological correlates. *Brain and Language* 26:315.

Monoson, P. and W.R. Zemlin. 1984. Quantitative study of whisper. *Folia Phoniatrica* 36:53.

Monrad-Krohn, G.H. 1947. Dysprosody or altered "melody of language." *Brain* 70:405.

Monsen, R.B. and A.M. Engebretson. 1977. Study of variations in the male and female glottal wave. *Journal of the Acoustical Society of America* 62:981.

Monsen, R.B., A.M. Engebretson and N.R. Vemula. 1978. Indirect assessment of the contribution of subglottal air pressure and vocal-fold tension to changes in fundamental frequency in English. *Journal of the Acoustical Society of America* 64:65.

Moorhouse, A.C. 1949. The morphology of the Greek comparative system: Its rhythmical and repetitive features. *American Journal of Philology* 70:159.

Moorhouse, A.C. 1962. Εὖ οἶδα and οὐδὲ εἷς: Cases of hiatus. *Classical Quarterly* 12:239.

Moorhouse, A.C. 1982. *The Syntax of Sophocles*. Leiden.

Moravcsik, E. 1978. Reduplicative constructions. *Universals of Human Language III*, ed. J.H. Greenberg: 297. Stanford.

Moravcsik, E. 1990. Review of Kiss 1987. *Studies in Language* 14:234.

Morin, Y.-C. and J.D. Kaye. 1982. The syntactic basis for French liaison. *Journal of Linguistics* 18:291.

Morris, H.F. 1964. *Heroic Recitation of the Bahima*. Oxford.

Morton, E.S. 1977. On the occurrence and significance of motivation-structural rules in some bird and mammal sounds. *American Naturalist* 111:855.

Morton, J. and W. Jassem. 1965. Acoustic correlates of stress. *Language and Speech* 8:159.

Morton, J., S. Marcus and C. Frankish. 1976. Perceptual centers (P-centers). *Psychological Review* 93:457.

Morton, J. and K. Patterson. 1980. A new attempt at an interpretation, or, an attempt at a new interpretation. *Deep Dyslexia*, ed. M. Coltheart, K. Patterson and J. Marshall: 91. London.

Moulton, W. 1986. Sandhi in Swiss German dialects. *Sandhi Phenomena in the Languages of Europe*, ed. H. Andersen: 385. Berlin.

Mountford, J.F. 1929. Greek music in the papyri and inscriptions. *New Chapters in the History of Greek Literature*, ed. J. Powell and E.A. Barber: 146. Oxford.

Mountford, K.W. 1983. *Bambara Declarative Sentence Intonation*. Ph.D. dissertation, Indiana University.

Mueller, C.F. 1866. *De Pedibus Solutis in Dialogorum Senariis Aeschyli, Sophoclis, Euripidis.* Berlin.

Munhall, K., D. Ostry and A. Parush. 1985. Characteristics of velocity profiles of speech movements. *Journal of Experimental Psychology: Human Peception and Performance* 2:457.

Munhall, K. and A. Löfqvist. 1988. Gestural aggregation in speech. *Journal of the Acoustical Society of America* 84:S82.

Munhall, K., C. Fowler, S. Hawkins and E. Saltzman. 1992. "Compensatory shortening" in monosyllables of spoken English. *Journal of Phonetics* 20:225.

Munro, P. 1984. Floating quantifiers in Pima. *Syntax and Semantics* 16:269.

Munro, P. 1985. Chickasaw accent and verb grades. *Studia Linguistica Diachronica et Synchronica,* ed. U. Pieper and G. Stickel: 581. Berlin.

Nagano-Madsen, Y. 1987. Effect of tempo and tonal context on fundamental frequency contours in Japanese. *Working Papers in General Linguistics and Phonetics, Lund University* 31:103.

Nagano-Madsen, Y. 1988. Phonetic reality of the mora in Eskimo. *Working Papers in General Linguistics and Phonetics, Lund University* 34:79.

Nagano-Madsen, Y. 1989. Mora and temporal-tonal interaction in Japanese. *Working Papers in General Linguistics and Phonetics, Lund University* 35:121.

Nagano-Madsen, Y. 1990. Influence of fundamental frequency pattern on the perception of the vowel mora in Japanese. *Report from the 4th Annual Swedish Phonetics Symposium.* Umeå.

Nagano-Madsen, Y. 1990b. Perception of mora in the three dialects of Japanese. *Proceedings of the 1990 International Conference on Spoken Language Processing I*: 25.

Nagano-Madsen, Y. 1990c. Quantity manifestation and mora in West Greenlandic Eskimo: Preliminary analysis. *Working Papers in General Linguistics and Phonetics, Lund University* 36:123.

Nagano-Madsen, Y. 1991. Moraic nasal and tonal manifestation in Osaka Japanese. *Proceedings of the XIIth International Congress of Phonetic Sciences* 2:210. Aix-en-Provence.

Nagano-Madsen, Y. 1992. *Mora and Prosodic Coordination.* Lund.

Nagano-Madsen, Y. 1993. Phrase-final intonation in West Greenlandic Eskimo. *Working Papers in General Linguistics and Phonetics, Lund University* 40:145.

Nagano-Madsen, Y. and L. Eriksson. 1989. The location of the F_0 turning point as a cue to mora boundary. *Quarterly Progress and Status Report, Speech Transmission Laboratory, Royal Institute of Technology*, Stockholm 1:41.

Nakatani, L.H. and K.D. Dukes. 1977. Locus of segmental cues for word juncture. *Journal of the Acoustical Society of America* 62:714.

Nakatani, L.H. and J.A. Schaffer. 1978. Hearing "words" without words: prosodic cues for word perception. *Journal of the Acoustical Society of America* 63:234.

Nakatani, L.H., K.D. O'Connor and C.H. Ashton. 1981. Prosodic aspects of American English speech rhythm. *Phonetica* 38:84.

Naylor, H.D. 1907. Doubtful syllables in iambic senarii. *Classical Quarterly* 1:4.

Naylor, H.D. 1922. *Horace, Odes and Epodes: A Study in Poetic Word-Order.* Cambridge.

Nelson, W.L., J.S. Perkell and J.R. Westbury. 1984. Mandible movements during increasingly rapid articulations of single syllables: Preliminary observations. *Journal of the Acoustical Society of America* 75:945.

Nespor, M. 1987. Vowel degemination and fast speech rules. *Phonology Yearbook* 4:61.

Nespor, M. 1990. On the separation of prosodic and rhythmic phonology. *The Phonology-Syntax Connection,* ed. S. Inkelas and D. Zec: 243. Chicago.

Nespor, M. and I. Vogel. 1986. *Prosodic Phonology.* Dordrecht.

Nespoulous, J.-L., M. Dordain, C. Perron, B. Ska, D. Bub, D. Caplan, J. Mehler and A.R. LeCours. 1988. Agrammatism in sentence production without comprehension deficits. *Brain and Language* 33:273.

Nespoulous, J.-L., M. Dordain and A.R. LeCours. 1989. Agrammatisme dans la production de phrases en l'absence de troubles de la compréhension. *Langages* 96:64.

Newiger, H.-J. 1961. Prokeleusmatiker im komischen Trimeter? *Hermes* 89:175.

Newman, P. 1972. Syllable weight as a phonological variable. *Studies in African Linguistics* 3:301.

Newman, S. 1965. *Zuni Grammar.* Albuquerque.

Newton, B. 1972. *The Generative Interpretaton of Dialect.* Cambridge.

Newton, R.P. 1975. Trochaic and iambic. *Language and Style* 8:127.

Niemi, J. and P. Koivuselkä-Sallinen. 1985. Phoneme errors in Broca's aphasia: Three Finnish cases. *Brain and Language* 26:28.

Niemi, J., M. Laine and P. Koivuselkä-Sallinen. 1990. A fluent morphological agrammatic in an inflectional language? *Morphology, Phonology, and Aphasia,* ed. J.-L. Nespoulous and P. Villiard: 95. New York.

Nishinuma, Y. 1979. *Un modèle d'analyse automatique de la prosodie.* Paris.

Nishinuma, Y., A. di Cristo and R. Espesser. 1983. Loudness as a function of vowel duration in CV syllables. *Speech Communication* 2:167.

Nishinuma, Y. and D. Duez. 1989. Perceptual optimization of syllable duration in short French sentences. *Eurospeech 89 I*: 694. Edinburgh.

Nketia, J.H.K. 1974. *The Music of Africa.* New York.

Nooteboom, S.G. 1972. *Production and Perception of Vowel Duration. A Study of Durational Properties of Vowels in Dutch.* Ph.D. dissertation, University of Utrecht.

Nooteboom, S.G. 1973. The perceptual reality of some prosodic durations. *Journal of Phonetics* 1:25.

Nooteboom, S.G., J.P.L. Brokx and J.J. de Rooij. 1978. Contributions of prosody to speech perception. *Studies in the Perception of Language,* ed. W.J.M. Levelt and G.B. Flores d'Arcais: 75. Chichester.

Nooteboom, S.G., J.G. Kruyt and J.M.B. Terken. 1981. What speakers and listeners do with pitch accents. *Nordic Prosody II,* ed. T. Fretheim: 9. Trondheim.

Nooteboom, S.G. and J.M.B. Terken. 1982. What makes speakers omit pitch accents? *Phonetica* 39:317.

Nooteboom, S.G. and J.G. Kruyt. 1987. Accents, focus distribution, and the perceived distribution of given and new information. *Journal of the Acoustical Society of America* 82:1512.

Nord, L., A. Kruckenberg and G. Fant. 1989. Some timing studies of prose, poetry and music. *Eurospeech 89 II*: 690.

Nord, L., A. Kruckenberg and G. Fant. 1989b. Timing studies of read prose and poetry with parallels in music. *Quarterly Progress and Status Report, Speech Transmission Laboratory, Royal Institute of Technology, Stockholm* 1989.1:1.

Norlin, K. 1989. A preliminary description of Cairo Arabic intonation of statements and questions. *Quarterly Progress and Status Report, Speech Transmission Laboratory, Royal Institute of Technology, Stockholm* 1989.1:47.

Oakeshott-Taylor, J. 1980. *Acoustic Variability and its Perception.* Frankfurt am Main.

O'Connor, J.D. and O.M. Tooley. 1964. The perceptibility of certain word boundaries. *In Honour of Daniel Jones*, ed. D. Abercrombie, D.B. Fry, P.A.D.MacCarthy, N.C. Scott and J.L.M. Trim: 171. London.

Odden, D. 1979. Principles of stress assignment: A crosslinguistic view. *Studies in the Linguistic Sciences* 9:157.

Odden, D. 1985. An accentual approach to tone in Kimatuumbi. *African Linguistics: Essays in Memory of M.W.K. Semikenke*, ed. D.L. Goyvaerts: 345. Amsterdam.

Odden, D. 1987. Kimatuumbi phrasal phonology. *Phonology Yearbook* 4:13.

Oehrle, R.T. 1981. Common problems in the theory of anaphora and the theory of discourse. *Possibilities and Limitations of Pragmatics*, ed. H. Parret, M. Sbisa and J. Verschueren: 509. Amsterdam.

O'Grady, G.N. 1964. *Nyangumata Grammar.* Sydney.

O'Grady, W. 1982. The syntax and semantics of quantifier placement. *Linguistics* 20:519.

O'Grady, W. 1991. *Categories and Case.* Amsterdam.

Ohala, J.J. 1978. Production of tone. *Tone: A Linguistic Survey*, ed. V.A. Fromkin: 5. New York.

Ohala, J.J. 1983. Cross-language use of pitch: An ethological view. *Phonetica* 40:1.

Ohala, J.J. 1983b. The origin of sound patterns in vocal tract constraints. *The Production of Speech*, ed. P.F. MacNeilage: 189. New York.

Ohala, J.J. 1990. Respiratory activity in speech. *Speech Production and Speech Modelling*, ed. W.J. Hardcastle and A. Marchal: 1. Dordrecht.

Ohala, J.J. 1990b. Alternatives to the sonority hierarchy for explaining segmental sequential constraints. *Papers from the 26th Regional Meeting of the Chicago Linguistic Society II: Parasession on the Syllable in Phonetics and Phonology*: 175.

Ohala, J.J. 1992. The segment: Primitive or derived? *Papers in Laboratory Phonology II*, ed. G.J. Docherty and D.R. Ladd: 166. Cambridge.

Ohala, J.J. and H. Kawasaki. 1984. Prosodic phonology and phonetics. *Phonology Yearbook* 1:113.

Ohala, J.J. and B.W. Eukel. 1987. Explaining the intrinsic pitch of vowels. *In Honor of Ilse Lehiste*, ed. R. Channon and L. Shockey: 207. Dordrecht.

Ohala, M. 1975. Nasals and nasalization in Hindi. *Nasálfest. Papers from a Symposium on Nasals and Nasalization*, ed. C.A. Ferguson, L.M. Hyman and J.J. Ohala: 317. Stanford.

Ohala, M. 1977. Stress in Hindi. *Studies in Stress and Accent*, ed. L.M. Hyman: 327. Los Angeles.

Ohde, R. 1984. Fundamental frequency as an acoustic correlate of stop consonant voicing. *Journal of the Acoustical Society of America* 75:224.

Ohde, R. 1985. Fundamental frequency correlates of stop consonant voicing and vowel quality in the speech of preadolescent children. *Journal of the Acoustical Society of America* 78:1554.

Öhman, S. 1967. Word and sentence intonation. *Quarterly Progress and Status Report, Speech Transmission Laboratory, Royal Institute of Technology, Stockholm* 1967.2–3:20.

Ohsiek, D. 1978. Heavy syllables and stress. *Syllables and Segments*, ed. A. Bell and J.B. Hooper: 35. Amsterdam.

Ojamaa, K. 1976. *Temporal Aspects of Phonological Quantity in Estonian.* Ph.D. dissertation, University of Connecticut.

Okell, J. 1969. *A Reference Grammar of Colloquial Burmese.* London.

Oller, D.K. 1979. Syllable timing in Spanish, English, and Finnish. *Current Issues in the Phonetic Sciences*, ed. H. Hollien and P. Hollien: 331. Amsterdam.

Oller, D.K. 1980. The emergence of the sounds of speech in infancy. *Child Phonology I*, ed. G.H. Yeni-Komshian, J.F. Kavanagh and C.A. Ferguson: 93. New York.

Oller, D.K. and B.L. Smith. 1977. Effect of final-syllable position on vowel duration in infant babbling. *Journal of the Acoustical Society of America* 62:994.

Omote, A. and S. Katō. 1978. *Zeami, Zenchiku, Nihon shisō taikei* 24. Tokyo.

O'Neill, E. 1939. The importance of final syllables in Greek verse. *Transactions of the American Philological Association* 70:256.

O'Neill, E. 1942. The localization of metrical word types in the Greek hexameter. *Yale Classical Studies* 8:105.

Orešnik, J. 1980. On the modern Icelandic clipped imperative. *The Nordic Languages and Modern Linguistics IV*, ed. E. Hovdhaugen: 305. Oslo.

O'Shaughnessy, D. 1976. *Modelling Fundamental Frequency and its Relationship to Syntax, Semantics, and Phonetics.* Ph.D. dissertation, Massachusetts Institute of Technology.

O'Shaughnessy, D. 1979. Linguistic features in fundamental frequency patterns. *Journal of Phonetics* 7:119.

O'Shaughnessy, D. 1984. A multispeaker analysis of durations in read French paragraphs. *Journal of the Acoustical Society of America* 76:1664.

O'Shaughnessy, D. and J. Allen. 1983. Linguistic modality effects on fundamental frequency in speech. *Journal of the Acoustical Society of America* 74:1155.

Osser, H. and F. Peng. 1964. A cross-cultural study of speech rate. *Language and Speech* 7:120.

Ostry, D.J. and K.G. Munhall. 1985. Control of rate and duration of speech movements. *Journal of the Acoustical Society of America* 77:640.

Otake, T., G. Hatano, A. Cutler and J. Mehler. 1993. Mora or syllable? Speech segmentation in Japanese. *Journal of Memory and Language* 32:258.

Packard, J.L. 1986. Tone production deficits in nonfluent aphasic Chinese speech. *Brain and Language* 29:212.

Page, D.L. 1961. Various conjectures. *Proceedings of the Cambridge Philological Society* 7:68.

Pakerys, A. 1982. *Lietuvių Bendrinės Kalbos Prosodija.* Vilnius.

Pallier, C., N. Sebastian-Gallès and T. Felguera. 1993. Attentional allocation within the syllabic structure of spoken words. *Journal of Memory and Language* 32:373.

Palmer, F.R. 1957. The verb in Bilin. *Bulletin of the School of Oriental and African Studies* 19:131.

Palmer, F.R. 1958. The noun in Bilin. *Bulletin of the School of Oriental and African Studies* 20:376.

Palmer, F.R. 1959. The verb classes of Agaw. *Mitteilungen des Instituts für Orientforschung* 7:270.

Palmer, F.R. 1962. *The Morphology of the Tigre Noun.* London.

Pandey, P.K. 1984. A metrical analysis of word accent in Hindustani. Manuscript.

Pandey, P.K. 1989. Word accent in Hindi. *Lingua* 77:37.

Pandharipande, R. and Y. Kachru. 1977. Relational grammar, ergativity, and Hindi-Urdu. *Lingua* 41:217.

Panhuis, D.G.J. 1982. *The Communicative Perspective in the Sentence: A Study of Latin Word Order.* Amsterdam.

Pankratz, L. and E.V. Pike. 1967. Phonology and morphotonemics of Ayutla Mixtec. *International Journal of American Linguistics* 3:287.

Pappalardo, V. 1959. Alcune osservazioni sulla notazione ritmica greca et sul suo impiego in relazione al papiro di Oslo N. 1413. *Dioniso* 22:220.

Parker, F. 1974. The coarticulation of vowels and stop consonants. *Journal of Phonetics* 2:211.

Parker, L.P.E. 1968. Split resolution in Greek dramatic lyric. *Classical Quarterly* 18:241.

Parker, L.P.E. 1972. Greek Metric 1957-1970. *Lustrum* 15:37.

Parry, M. 1928. *L'Epithète traditionnelle dans Homère.* Paris.

Pashek, G.V. and R.H. Brookshire. 1982. Effects of rate of speech and linguistic stress on auditory paragraph comprehension of aphasic individuals. *Journal of Speech and Hearing Research* 25:377.

Pate, D.S., E.M. Saffran and N. Martin. 1987. Specifying the locus of the production impairment in conduction aphasia. *Language and Cognitive Processes* 2:43.

Patterson, K.E. 1982. The relation between reading and psychological coding. *Normality and Pathology in Cognitive Functions*, ed. A.W. Ellis: 77. London.

Paul, H. 1909. *Prinzipien der Sprachgeschichte*. Halle.

Payne, D.L. 1981. *The Phonology and Morphology of Axininca Campa*. Dallas.

Payne, D.L. 1992. *Pragmatics of Word Order Flexibility*. Amsterdam.

Payne, T.E. 1983. Yagua object clitics: Syntactic and phonological misalignment and another possible source of ergativity. *Papers from the Parasession on the Interplay of Phonology, Morphology and Syntax*, ed. J.F. Richardson, M. Marks, A. Chukerman: 173. Chicago Linguistic Society.

Pearl, O.M. and R.P. Winnington-Ingram. 1965. A Michigan papyrus with musical notation. *Journal of Egyptian Archaeology* 51:179.

Peasgood, E.T. 1972. Carib phonology. *Languages of the Guianas*, ed. J.E. Grimes: 35. Norman.

Pence, A. 1966. Kunimaipa phonology: Hierarchical levels. *Pacific Linguistics* 1966:49.

Peters, M. 1977. Simultaneous performance of two motor activities. *Neuropsychologia* 15:461.

Pesetsky, D. 1979. Menomini quantity. *Working Papers in Linguistics, Massachusetts Institute of Technology* 1:115.

Petersen, N.R. 1974. The influence of tongue height on the perception of vowel duration in Danish. *Annual Report, Institute of Phonetics, University of Copenhagen* 8:1.

Petersen, N.R. 1978. Intrinsic fundamental frequency of Danish vowels. *Journal of Phonetics* 6:177.

Petersen, N.R. 1985. Fundamental frequency and larynx height in sentences and stress groups. *Annual Report, Institute of Phonetics, University of Copenhagen* 19:95.

Petersen, N.R. 1986. Perceptual compensation for segmentally conditioned fundamental frequency perturbation. *Phonetica* 43:31.

Petersen, N.R. 1988. The role of intrinsic fundamental frequency in the perception of singing. *Working Papers in General Linguistics and Phonetics, Lund University* 34:99.

Peterson, G.E. and H.L. Barney. 1952. Control methods used in the study of vowels. *Journal of the Acoustical Society of America* 24:175.

Peterson, G.E. and I. Lehiste. 1960. Duration of syllable nuclei in English. *Journal of the Acoustical Society of America* 32:693.

Petocz, A. and G. Oliphant. 1988. Closed-class words as first syllables do interfere with lexical decisions for nonwords: Implications for theories of agrammatism. *Brain and Language* 34:127.

Petr, V. 1912. *Über den kyklischen Daktylus und die Logaöden: Eine Untersuchung aus dem Gebiet der antiken Rhythmik*. Nezhin.

Pétursson, M. 1986. Sandhi im modernen Isländischen. *Sandhi Phenomena in the Languages of Europe*, ed. H. Andersen: 251. Berlin.

Pfeiffer, R. 1934. *Die neuen Diegeseis zu Kallimachosgedichten*. Munich.

Pickel, C. 1880. *De Versuum Dochmiacorum Origine*. Strasbourg.

Pickett, J.M. and L.R. Decker. 1960. Time factors in perception of a double consonant. *Language and Speech* 3:11.

Picton, T.W. and D. Stuss. 1984. Event-related potentials in the study of speech and language. *Biological Perspectives on Language,* ed. D. Caplan, A.R. LeCours and A. Smith: 303. Cambridge, Mass.

Pierrehumbert, J. 1979. The perception of fundamental frequency declination. *Journal of the Acoustical Society of America* 66:363.

Pierrehumbert, J. 1980. *The Phonology and Phonetics of English Intonation.* Ph.D. dissertation, Massachusetts Institute of Technology.

Pierrehumbert, J. 1989. A preliminary study of the consequences of intonation for the voice source. *Quarterly Progress and Status Report, Speech Transmission Laboratory, Royal Institute of Technology, Stockholm* 1989.4:23.

Pierrehumbert, J. and M.E. Beckman. 1988. *Japanese Tone Structure.* Cambridge, Mass.

Pierrehumbert, J. and S.A. Steele. 1989. Categories of tonal alignment in English. *Phonetica* 46:181.

Pierrehumbert, J. and J. Hirschberg. 1990. The meaning of intonational contours in the interpretation of discourse. *Intentions in Communication,* ed. P.R. Cohen, J. Morgan and M.E. Pollack: 271. Cambridge, Mass.

Pierrehumbert, J. and D. Talkin. 1992. Lenition of /h/ and glottal stop. *Papers in Laboratory Phonology II,* ed. G.J. Docherty and D.R. Ladd: 90. Cambridge.

Pike, E.V. 1979. Word stress and sentence stress in various tone languages. *Proceedings of the Ninth International Congress of Phonetic Sciences II*: 410. Copenhagen.

Pike, E.V. 1986. Tone contrasts in Central Carrier (Athapaskan). *International Journal of American Linguistics* 52:411.

Pike, K. 1945. *The Intonation of American English.* Ann Arbor.

Pike, K. 1948. *Tone Languages.* Ann Arbor.

Pike, K. 1964. Stress trains in Auca. *In Honour of Daniel Jones,* ed. D. Abercrombie, D.B. Fry, P.A.D. MacCarthy, N.C. Scott and J.L.M. Trim: 425. London.

Pike, K. 1970. The role of the nuclei of feet in the analysis of tone in Tibeto-Burman languages of Nepal. *Studia Phonetica* 3:153.

Pike, K. and G. Scott. 1963. Pitch accent and nonaccented phrases in Fore. *Zeitschrift für Phonetik* 16:179.

Pind, J. 1986. The perception of quantity in Icelandic. *Phonetica* 43:116.

Pipping, H. 1937. *Zur homerischen Metrik.* Helsinki.

Platnauer, M. 1960. Prodelision in Greek drama. *Classical Quarterly* 10:140.

Platt, A. 1921. On Homeric technique. *Classical Review* 35:141.

Pöhlmann, E. 1960. *Griechische Musikfragmente.* Nürnberg.

Pöhlmann, E. 1970. *Denkmäler altgriechischer Musik.* Nürnberg.

Poizner, H., U. Bellugi and E.S. Klima. 1989. Sign language aphasia. *Handbook of Neuropsychology II,* ed. H. Goodglass and A.R. Damasio: 157. Amsterdam.

Poizner, H., U. Bellugi and E.S. Klima. 1991. Brain function for language: Perspectives from another modality. *Modularity and the Motor Theory of Speech Perception,* ed. I.G. Mattingly and M. Studdert-Kennedy: 145. Hillsdale.

Polinsky, M.S. 1990. Subject incorporation: Evidence from Chuckchee. *Grammatical Relations: A Crosstheoretical Perspective,* ed. K. Dziwirek, P. Farrell and E. Mejías-Bikandi: 349. Stanford.

Polome, E.C. 1967. *Swahili Language Handbook.* Washington.

Pompino-Marschall, B. 1989. On the psychoacoustic nature of the P-center phenomenon. *Journal of Phonetics* 17:175.

Pompino-Marschall, B. 1990. *Die Silbenprosodie.* Tübingen.

Pongratz, F. 1902. *De Arsibus Solutis in Dialogorum Senariis Aristophanis.* Munich.

Porson, R. 1802. *Euripidis Hecuba.* Second edition. Cambridge.

Porson, R. 1812. *Adversaria. Notae et Emendationes in Poetas Graecos.* Cambridge.

Port, R.F. 1977. *The Influence of Speaking Tempo on the Duration of Stressed Vowel and Medial Stop in English Trochee Words.* Indiana University Linguistics Club.

Port, R.F., S. Al-Ani and S. Maeda. 1980. Temporal compensation and universal phonetics. *Phonetica* 37:235.

Port, R.F., J. Dalby and M. O'Dell. 1987. Evidence for mora timing in Japanese. *Journal of the Acoustical Society of America* 81:1574.

Poser, W.J. 1985. *The Phonetics and Phonology of Tone and Intonation in Japanese.* Ph.D. dissertation, Massachusetts Institute of Technology.

Poser, W.J. 1988. Durational effects of syllable structure and distinctive length in Japanese. *Journal of the Acoustical Society of America* 84:S97.

Poser, W. 1990. Evidence for foot structure in Japanese. *Language* 66:78.

Postgate, J.P. 1924. *A Short Guide to the Accentuation of Ancient Greek.* London.

Povel, D.-J. 1981. Internal representation of simple temporal patterns. *Journal of Experimental Psychology: Human Perception and Performance* 7:3.

Povel, D.-J. 1984. A theoretical framework for rhythm perception. *Psychological Research* 45:315.

Povel, D.-J. 1985. Perception of temporal patterns. *Music Perception* 2:411.

Povel. D.-J. and H. Okkerman. 1981. Accents in equitone sequences. *Perception and Psychophysics* 30:565.

Prato, C. 1975. Ricerche sul trimetro euripideo. *Ricerche sul trimetro dei tragici greci. Metro e verso,* ed. C. Prato, A. Filippo, P. Giannini, E. Pallara and R. Sardiello: 111. Rome.

Preusser, D., W.R. Garner and R.L. Gottwald. 1970. The effect of starting pattern on descriptions of perceived temporal patterns. *Psychonomic Science* 21:219.

Price, P.J. 1980. Sonority and syllabicity: Acoustic correlates of perception. *Phonetica* 37:327.

Price, P.J., S. Ostendorf, S. Shattuck-Hufnagel and C. Fong. 1991. The use of prosody in syntactic disambiguation. *Journal of the Acoustical Society of America* 90:2956.

Prince, A.S. 1980. A metrical theory for Estonian quantity. *Linguistic Inquiry* 11:511.

Prince, A.S. 1990. Quantitative consequences of rhythmic organization. *Papers from the 26th Regional Meeting of the Chicago Linguistic Society II: Parasession on the Syllable in Phonetics and Phonology*: 355.

Prince, E.F. 1978. A comparison of wh-clefts and it-clefts in discourse. *Language* 54:883.

Pulgram, E. 1970. *Syllable, Word, Nexus, Cursus.* The Hague.

Pulgram, E. 1975. *Latin-Romance Phonology: Prosodics and Metrics.* Munich.

Pulgram, E. 1981. Attic shortening or metrical lengthening? *Glotta* 59:75.

Pullum, G.K. 1977. Word order universals and grammatical relations. *Syntax and Semantics* 8:249.

Pullum, G.K. 1982. Free word order and phrase structure rules. *Proceedings of the 12th Annual Meeting of the North Eastern Linguistics Society*: 209.

Rabel, L. 1961. *Khasi: A Language of Assam.* Baton Rouge.

Radocy, R.E. and J.D. Boyle. 1988. *Psychological Foundations of Musical Behavior.* 2nd edition. Springfield.

Rakerd, B., W. Sennett and C.A. Fowler. 1987. Domain-final lengthening and foot-level shortening in spoken English. *Phonetica* 44:147.

Rand, E. 1968. The structural phonology of Alabaman, a Muskogean language. *International Journal of American Linguistics* 34:94.

Raphael, L. 1972. Preceding vowel duration as a cue to the perception of the voicing characteristic of word-final consonants in American English. *Journal of the Acoustical Society of America* 51:1296.

Rapp, K. 1971. A study of syllable timing. *Quarterly Progress and Status Report, Speech Transmission Laboratory, Royal Institute of Technology, Stockholm* 1971.1:14.

Ratner, N.B. 1986. Durational cues which mark clause boundaries in mother-child speech. *Journal of Phonetics* 14:303.

Rattray, R.S. 1922. The drum language of West Africa. *Journal of the African Society* 22:226.

Raubitschek, A.E. and L.H. Jeffery. 1949. *Dedications from the Athenian Akropolis.* Cambridge, Mass.

Raven, D.S. 1968. *Greek Metre.* Second edition. London.

Reeve, M.D. 1971. Hiatus in the Greek novelists. *Classical Quarterly* 21:514.

Reinach, T. 1898. Les nouveaux fragments rythmiques d'Aristoxène. *Revue des Études Grecques* 11:389.

Reinach, T. 1911. Hymnes avec notes musicales. *Fouilles de Delphes* 3.2:147.

Reinhart, T. 1982. *Pragmatics and Linguistics: An Analysis of Sentence Topics.* Bloomington.

Reisig, K. 1816. *Coniectaneorum in Aristophanem Libri Duo.* Leipzig.

Reitan, R.M. and D. Wolfson. 1989. The Seashore rhythm test and brain functions. *Clinical Neuropsychologist* 3:70.

Repetti, L. 1993. Degenerate syllables in Friulian. *Linguistic Inquiry* 24:186.

Repp, B. 1985. Critique of "Measures of the sentence intonation of read and spontaneous speech in American English." *Journal of the Acoustical Society of America* 78:1114.

Restle, F. 1970. Theory of serial pattern learning: Structural trees. *Psychological Review* 77:481.

Restle, F. 1972. Serial patterns: The role of phrasing. *Journal of Experimental Psychology* 92:385.

Restle, F. and E. Brown. 1970. Organization of serial pattern learning. *The Psychology of Learning and Motivation* 4:249.

Rialland, A. 1974. Les langages instrumentaux sifflés ou criés en Afrique. *La Linguistique* 10:105.

Rialland, A. 1986. Schwa et syllabes en français. *Studies in Compensatory Lengthening,* ed. L. Wetzels and E. Sezer: 187. Dordrecht.

Rice, K.D. 1987. On defining the intonational phrase: Evidence from Slave. *Phonology Yearbook* 4:37.

Rice, K.D. 1989. On eliminating resyllabification in onsets. *Proceedings of the Eighth West Coast Conference on Formal Linguistics*: 331.

Rice, K.D. 1989b. The phonology of Fort Nelson Slave stem tone: Syntactic implications. *Athapaskan Linguistics: Current Perspectives on a Language Family,* ed. E.D. Cook and K.D. Rice: 229. Berlin.

Rietveld, A.C.M. and C. Gussenhoven. 1985. On the relation between pitch excursion size and prominence. *Journal of Phonetics* 13:299.

Rietveld, A.C.M. and C. Gussenhoven. 1987. Perceived speech rate and intonation. *Journal of Phonetics* 15:273.

Rischel, J. 1983. On unit accentuation in Danish and the distinction between deep and surface phonology. *Folia Linguistica* 17:51.

Rischel, J. 1987. Some reflexions on levels of prosodic representation and prosodic categories. *Nordic Prosody IV,* ed. K. Gregersen and H. Basbøll: 3. Odense.

Ritsma, R.J. 1976. Frequencies dominant in the perception of the pitch of complex sounds. *Journal of the Acoustical Society of America* 42:191.

Roach, P. 1982. On the distinction between "stress-timed" and "syllable-timed" languages. *Linguistic Controversies,* ed. D. Crystal: 73. London.

Robb, M.P. and J.H. Saxman. 1990. Syllable durations of preword and early word vocalizations. *Journal of Speech and Hearing Research* 33:583.

Roberts, W.R. 1910. *Dionysius of Halicarnassus: On Literary Composition.* London.

Robins, R.H. and N. Waterson. 1952. Notes on the phonetics of the Georgian word. *Bulletin of the School of Oriental and African Studies* 14:55.

Robinson, G.M. and D.J. Solomon. 1974. Rhythm is processed by the speech hemisphere. *Journal of Experimental Psychology* 102:508.

Rochemont, M.S. 1986. *Focus in Generative Grammar.* Amsterdam.

Rochemont, M.S. and P.W. Culicover. 1990. *English Focus Constructions and the Theory of Grammar.* Cambridge.

Roehl, H. 1882. *Inscriptiones Graecae Antiquissimae.* Berlin.

Rohlfs, G. 1929. Lautwandel und Satzaccent. *Behrens-Festschrift*: 37. Jena.

Rohlfs, G. 1938. Der Einfluss des Satzakzentes auf den Lautwandel. *Archiv für das Studium der neueren Sprachen* 74:54.

Rohrer, K.T. 1983. Interactions of phonology and music in Purcell's two settings of 'Thy genius, lo.' *Studies in the History of Music I*: 155. New York.

Rood, D.S. 1971. Agent and object in Wichita. *Lingua* 28:100.

Rose, P. 1990. Acoustics and phonology of complex tone sandhi. *Phonetica* 47:1.

Rosen, S.T. 1989. Two types of noun incorporation: A lexical analysis. *Language* 65:294.

Rosenbaum, D.A., S.B. Kenny and M.A. Derr. 1983. Hierarchical control of rapid movement sequences. *Journal of Experimental Psychology: Human Perception and Performance* 9:86.

Rosenberg, B., E. Zurif, H. Brownell, M. Garrett and D. Bradley. 1985. Grammatical class effects in relation to normal and aphasic sentence processing. *Brain and Language* 26:287.

Rosenvold, E. 1981 The role of intrinsic F_0 and duration in the perception of stress. *Annual Report, Institute of Phonetics, University of Copenhagen* 15:147.

Ross, E.D. 1981. The aprosodias: Functional-anatomic organization of the affective components of language in the right hemisphere. *Archives of Neurology* 38:561.

Ross, E.D., J.A. Edmondson and G.B. Seibert. 1986. The effect of affect on various acoustic measures of prosody in tone and nontone languages: A comparison based on computer analysis of voice. *Journal of Phonetics* 14:283.

Ross, J.R. 1986. *Infinite Syntax!* Norwood.

Rossbach, A. and R. Westphal. 1887. *Allgemeine Theorie der griechischen Metrik.* Third edition. Leipzig.

Rossbach, A. and R. Westphal. 1889. *Griechische Metrik.* Third edition. Leipzig.

Rossi, L.E. 1969. La *pronuntiatio plena*: Sinalefe in luogo d'elisione. *Rivista di Filologia e di Istruzione Classica* 97:433.

Rossi, M. 1971. Le seuil de glissando ou seuil de perception des variations tonales pour les sons de la parole. *Phonetica* 23:1.

Rossi, M. 1971b. L'intensité spécifique des voyelles. *Phonetica* 24:129.

Rossi, M. 1978. La perception des glissandos descendants dans les contours prosodiques. *Phonetica* 35:11.

Rossi, M. 1978b. Interaction of intensity glides and frequency glissandos. *Language and Speech* 21:284.

Rossi, M. 1979. Le français, langue sans accent? *L'accent en français contemporain*, ed. I. Fónagy and P.R. Léon: 13. Ottawa.

Rossi, M. and D. Autesserre. 1981. Movements of the hyoid and the larynx and the intrinsic frequency of vowels. *Journal of Phonetics* 9:233.

Rostolland, D. 1982. Acoustic features of shouted voice. *Acustica* 50:118.

Rotenberg, J. 1978. *The Syntax of Phonology.* Ph.D. dissertation, Massachusetts Institute of Technology.

Royer, F.L. and W.R. Garner. 1970. Perceptual organization of nine element auditory temporal patterns. *Perception and Psychophysics* 7:115.

Rubach, J. and G. Booij. 1990. Edge of constituent effects in Polish. *Natural Language and Linguistic Theory* 8:427.

Rubin, H.J. 1963. Experimental studies on vocal pitch and intensity in phonation. *Laryngoscope* 73:973.

Ruhm, H.B., E.O. Mencke, B. Milburn, W. Cooper and D.E. Rose. 1966. Differential sensitivity to duration of acoustic stimuli. *Journal of Speech and Hearing Research* 9:371.

Ruijgh, C.J. 1972. Le redoublement dit attique dans l'évolution du système morphologique du verbe grec. *Mélanges de linguistique et de philologie grecques offerts à Pierre Chantraine*: 211. Paris.

Ruijgh, C.J. 1981. Review of Allen 1973. *Mnemosyne* 34:407.

Ruijgh, C.J. 1985. Problèmes de philologie mycénienne. *Minos* 19:105.

Ruijgh, C.J. 1987. Μακρὰ τελεία et μακρὰ ἄλογος. *Mnemosyne* 40:313.

Rumpel, J. 1865. *Quaestiones Metricae*. Insterburg.

Rumpel, J. 1867. Zur Metrik der Tragiker. *Philologus* 25:471.

Rumpel, J. 1869. Der Trimeter des Aristophanes. *Philologus* 28:599.

Rüsch, E. 1914. *Grammatik der delphischen Inschriften*. Berlin.

Russell, R. 1960. Some problems in the treatment of Urdu metre. *Journal of the Royal Asiatic Society* 160:48.

Ryalls, J. and I. Reinvang. 1986. Functional lateralization of linguistic tones: Acoustic evidence from Norwegian. *Language and Speech* 29:389.

Rycroft, D. 1960. Melodic features in Zulu eulogistic recitation. *African Language Studies* 1:60.

Rycroft, D. 1962. Zulu and Xhose praise-poetry and song. *African Music* 3.1:79.

Saffran, E.M., M.F. Schwartz and O.S.M. Marin. 1980. Evidence from aphasia: Isolating the components of a production model. *Language Production I,* ed. B. Butterworth: 221.

Safir, K. 1979. Metrical structure in Capanahua. *Working Papers in Linguistics, Massachusetts Institute of Technology* 1:95.

Sakiyama, S. 1981. Phrasal pitch in the Japanese language. *The Study of Sounds* 19:187.

Saltarelli, M. 1983. The mora unit in Italian phonology. *Folia Linguistica* 17:7.

Salzmann, Z. 1956. Arapaho I: phonology. *International Journal of American Linguistics* 22:49.

Samuel, A.G. 1989. Insights from a failure of selective adaptation. *Perception and Psychophysics* 45:485.

Santangelo, S. 1905. Il vocalismo del dialetto d'Adernò. *Archivio glottologico italiano* 16:479.

Sapir, E. 1921. *Language: An Introduction to the Study of Speech*. New York.

Sasse, H.-J. 1977. A note on wh-movement. *Lingua* 41:343.

Sato, Y. 1993. The durations of syllable-final nasals and the mora hypothesis in Japanese. *Phonetica* 50:44.

Sauzet, P. 1989. L'accent du grec ancien et les relations entre structure métrique et représentation autosegmentale. *Langages* 95:81.

Sawashima, M., Y. Kakita and S. Hiki. 1973. Activity of the extrinsic laryngeal muscles in relation to Japanese word accent. *Annual Bulletin, Research Institute of Logopedics and Phoniatrics* 7:19.

Sawashima, M. and S. Niimi. 1974. Laryngeal conditions in articulations of Japanese voiceless consonants. *Annual Bulletin, Research Institute of Logopedics and Phoniatrics* 8:13.

Sawashima, M., J. Hirose, H. Yoshioka and S. Kiritani. 1982. Interaction between articulatory movements and vocal pitch control in Japanese word accent. *Annual Bulletin, Research Institute of Logopedics and Phoniatrics* 16:11.

Sawashima, M. and H. Hirose. 1983. Laryngeal gestures in speech production. *The Production of Speech*, ed. P.F. MacNeilage: 11. New York.

Schade, J. 1908. *De Correptione Attica*. Dissertation, Greifswald.

Schane, S.A. 1987. The resolution of hiatus. *Papers from the 23rd Annual Regional Meeting of the Chicago Linguistic Society II*: 279.

Scharf, B. 1978. Loudness. *Handbook of Perception IV*, ed. E.C. Carterette and M.P. Friedman: 187. New York.

Schauber, E. 1978. Focus and presupposition: A comparison of English intonation and Navajo particle placement. *Elements of Tone, Stress, and Intonation*, ed. D.J. Napoli: 144. Washington, D.C.

Scheindler, A. 1896. Metrische Studien zu Sophokles. *Serta Harteliana* 14. Vienna.

Scherer, K.R. 1971. Randomized splicing: A note on a simple technique for masking speech content. *Journal of Experimental Research of Personality* 5:155.

Scherer, K.R. 1981. Speech and emotional states. *Speech Evaluation in Psychiatry*, ed. J. Darby: 189. New York.

Scherer, K.R. 1982. Methods of research on vocal communication. *Handbook of Methods in Nonverbal Behavior Research*, ed. K.R. Scherer and P. Ekman: 136. Cambridge.

Scherer, K.R. and J.S. Oshinsky. 1977. Cue utilization in emotion attribution from auditory stimuli. *Motivation and Emotion* 1:331.

Scherer, K.R., D.R. Ladd and K.E.A. Silverman. 1984. Vocal cues to speaker affect: Testing two models. *Journal of the Acoustical Society of America* 76:1346.

Schiffman, H.R. and D.J. Bobko. 1974. Effects of stimulus complexity on the perception of brief temporal intervals. *Journal of Experimental Psychology* 103:156.

Schiffman, H.R. and D.J. Bobko. 1977. The role of number and familiarity of stimuli in the perception of brief temporal intervals. *American Journal of Psychology* 90:85.

Schindler, R.M. 1978. The effects of prose context on visual search for letters. *Memory and Cognition* 6:124.

Schmid, W. 1908. Aphorismen zur griechischen Metrik. *Württemberg Korrespondenzblätter* 1908:414.

Schmitt, A. 1924. *Untersuchungen zur allgemeinen Akzentlehre mit einer Anwendung auf den Akzent des Griechischen und Lateinischen*. Heidelberg.

Schmitt, A. 1935. Zum Verständnis der Positionslänge. *Glotta* 23:80.

Schmitt, A. 1953. *Musikalischer Akzent und antike Metrik*. Münster.

Schroeder, O. 1908. *Vorarbeitungen zur griechischen Versgeschichte*. Leipzig.

Schroeder, O. 1909. *Aristophanis Cantica*. Leipzig.

Schuh, R.G. 1978. Tone rules. *Tone: A Linguistic Survey*, ed. V.A. Fromkin: 221. New York.

Schulman, R. 1989. Articulatory dynamics of loud and normal speech. *Journal of the Acoustical Society of America* 85:295.

Schwartz, M. 1970. Duration of /s/ in /s/-plosive blends. *Journal of the Acoustical Society of America* 47:1143.

Schwartz, M.F. 1987. Patterns of speech production deficit within and across aphasia syndromes. *The Cognitive Neuropsychology of Language*, ed. M. Coltheart, G. Sartori and R. Job: 163. London.

Schwartz, M.F., M.C. Linebarger and E.M. Saffran. 1985. The status of the syntactic deficit theory of agrammatism. *Agrammatism*, ed. M.-L. Kean: 83. New York.

Schwyzer, E. 1923. *Dialectorum Graecorum Exempla Epigraphica Potiora*. Hildesheim.

Schwyzer, E. 1959. *Griechische Grammatik I*. Third edition. Munich.

Scott, D.R. 1982. Duration as a cue to the perception of a phrase boundary. *Journal of the Acoustical Society of America* 71:996.

Scott, D.R., S.D. Isard and B. de Boysson-Bardies. 1985. Perceptual isochrony in English and in French. *Journal of Phonetics* 13:155.

Scott, G. 1978. The Fore language of Papua. *Pacific Linguistics* 1978:B47.

Sealey, R. 1963. Stress as a factor in Classical Greek accentuation. *Greece and Rome* 10:11.

Sebastian-Gallès, N., E. Dupoux, J. Segui and J. Mehler. 1992. Contrasting syllabic effects in Catalan and Spanish. *Journal of Memory and Language* 31:18.

Sebeok, T.A. and D.J. Umiker-Sebeok. 1976. *Speech Surrogates: Drum and Whistle Systems.* The Hague.

Sedlacek, K. and A. Sychra. 1963. Die Melodie als Faktor des emotionellen Ausdrucks. *Folia Phoniatrica* 15:89.

Segui, J., J. Mehler, U. Frauenfelder and J. Morton. 1982. The word frequency effect and lexical access. *Neuropsychologia* 20:615.

Seidler, A. 1812. *De Versibus Dochmiacis Tragicorum Graecorum, Pars Posterior.* Leipzig.

Seiler, H.-J. 1965. Accent and morphophonemics in Cahuilla and Uto-Aztecan. *International Journal of American Linguistics* 31:50.

Selkirk, E.O. 1974. French liaison and the X̄-notation. *Linguistic Inquiry* 5:573.

Selkirk, E.O. 1980. Prosodic domains in phonology: Sanskrit revisited. *Juncture,* ed. M. Aronoff and M.-L. Kean: 107. Saratoga.

Selkirk, E.O. 1984. *Phonology and Syntax: The Relation between Sound and Structure.* Cambridge, Mass.

Selkirk, E.O. 1986. On derived domains in sentence phonology. *Phonology Yearbook* 3:371.

Selkirk, E.O. 1990. On the nature of prosodic constituency. *Papers in Laboratory Phonology I,* ed. J. Kingston and M.E. Beckman: 179. Cambridge.

Selkirk, E.O. and K. Tateishi. 1988. Constraints on minor phrase formation in Japanese. *Papers from the 24th Annual Regional Meeting of the Chicago Linguistic Society I*: 316.

Selkirk, E.O. and T. Shen. 1990. Prosodic domains in Shanghai Chinese. *The Phonology-Syntax Connection,* ed. S. Inkelas and D. Zec: 313. Chicago.

Selkirk, E.O. and K. Tateishi. 1991. Syntax and downstep in Japanese. *Interdisciplinary Approaches to Language: Essays in Honor of S.-Y. Kuroda,* ed. C. Georgopoulos and R. Ishihara: 519. Dordrecht.

Serruys, D. 1904. Les procédes toniques d'Himerius et les origines du "cursus" byzantine. *Philologie et linguistique. Mélanges offerts à Louis Havet*: 475. Paris.

Shadle, C. 1985. Intrinsic fundamental frequency of vowels in sentence context. *Journal of the Acoustical Society of America* 78:1562.

Shaffer, L.H. 1982. Rhythm and timing in skill. *Psychological Review* 89:109.

Shapiro, B.E. and M. Danly. 1985. The role of the right hemisphere in the control of speech prosody in propositional and affective contexts. *Brain and Language* 25:19.

Shallice, T. 1988. *From Neuropsychology to Mental Structure.* Cambridge.

Shattuck-Hufnagel, S. 1979. Speech errors as evidence for a serial-ordering mechanism in sentence production. *Sentence Processing,* ed. W.E. Cooper and E.C.T. Walker: 295. Hillsdale.

Shattuck-Hufnagel, S. 1983. Sublexical units and suprasegmental structure in speech production planning. *The Production of Speech,* ed. P. MacNeilage: 109. New York.

Shattuck-Hufnagel, S. 1987. The role of word-onset consonants in speech production planning. *Motor and Sensory Processes of Language,* ed. E. Keller and M. Gopnik: 17. Hillsdale.

Shattuck-Hufnagel, S. 1988. Acoustic-phonetic correlates of stress shift. *Journal of the Acoustical Society of America* 84:S98.

Shaw, P.A. 1985. Modularization and substantive constraints in Dakota lexical phonology. *Phonology Yearbook* 2:173.

Shen, X.S. 1990. Tonal coarticulation in Mandarin. *Journal of Phonetics* 18:281.

Sherzer, J. 1982. Play languages: With a note on ritual languages. *Exceptional Language and Linguistics,* ed. L.K. Obler and L. Menn: 175. New York.

Shewan, A. 1923. Hiatus in Homeric verse. *Classical Quarterly* 17:13.

Shibatani, M. 1990. Japanese. *The World's Major Languages,* ed. B. Comrie: 855. Oxford.

Shiffrin, R.M. and W. Schneider. 1977. Controlled and automatic human information processing. *Psychological Review* 84:127.

Shih, C. 1985. *The Prosodic Domain of Tone Sandhi in Chinese.* Ph.D. dissertation, University of California, San Diego.

Shih, C.-L. 1988. Tone and intonation in Mandarin. *Working papers, Cornell Phonetics Laboratory* 3:83.

Shimizu, K. and M. Dantsuji. 1981. A study on the perception of fundamental frequency declination. *Studia Phonologica* 15:18.

Shipley, W.F. 1964. *Maidu Grammar.* Berkeley.

Shipley-Brown, F., W.O. Dingwall, C.I. Berlin, G. Yeni-Komshian and S. Gordon-Salant. 1988. Hemispheric processing of affective and linguistic intonation contours in normal subjects. *Brain and Language* 33:16.

Shipp, T., T. Doherty and S. Haglund. 1988. Physiologic factors in vocal vibrato. *Journal of the Acoustical Society of America* 84:S83.

Shockey, L.R. 1973. *Phonetic and Phonological Properties of Connected Speech.* Ph.D. dissertation, Ohio State University.

Sidtis, J.J. and B.T. Volpe. 1988. Selective loss of complex pitch or speech discrimination after unilateral cerebral lesion. *Brain and Language* 34:235.

Sievers, E. 1893. *Grundzüge der Phonetik.* Leipzig.

Sievers, E. 1893b. *Altgermanische Metrik.* Halle.

Sigurd, B. 1973. Maximum rate and minimum duration of repeated syllables. *Language and Speech* 16:373.

Silva-Corvalán, C. 1983. On the interaction of word order and intonation: Some OV constructions in Spanish. *Discourse Perspectives on Syntax,* ed. F. Klein-Andreu: 117. New York.

Silverman, K. 1984. What causes vowels to have intrinsic fundamental frequency? *Cambridge Papers in Phonetics and Experimental Linguistics* 3.

Silverman, K. 1985. Vowel intrinsic pitch influences the perception of intonational prominence. *Journal of the Acoustical Society of America* 77:S38.

Silverman, K. 1986. F_0 segmental cues depend on intonation: The case of the rise after voiced stops. *Phonetica* 43:76.

Silverman, K. 1987. *Natural Prosody for Synthetic Speech.* Ph.D. dissertation, Cambridge University.

Silverman, K. 1990. The separation of prosodies. *Papers in Laboratory Phonology I,* ed. J. Kingston and M.E. Beckman: 139. Cambridge.

Silverman, K. and J.B. Pierrehumbert. 1990. The timing of prenuclear high accents in English. *Papers in Laboratory Phonology I,* ed. J. Kingston and M.E. Beckman: 72. Cambridge.

Silverstein, R.O. 1976. A strategy for utterance production in Hausa. *Studies in African Linguistics* Supplement 6:233.

Simada, Z. and H. Hirose. 1970. The function of the laryngeal muscles in respect to the word accent distinction. *Annual Bulletin, Research Institute of Logopedics and Phoniatrics* 4:27.

Simada, Z., S. Horiguchi, S. Niimi and H. Hirose. 1991. Devoicing of Japanese /u/: An electromyographic study. *Proceedings of the XIIth International Congress of Phonetic Sciences II*: 54. Aix-en-Provence.

Simmons, D.C. 1980. *Extralinguistic Usages of Tonality in Efik Folklore.* University, Al.

Simon, H.A. and R.K. Sumner. 1968. Pattern in music. *Formal Representation of Human Judgment,* ed. B. Kleinmuntz: 219. New York.

Simon, M.E. 1989. *An Analysis of the Postposing Construction in Japanese.* Ph.D. dissertation, University of Michigan.

Simpson, J. and M. Withgott. 1986. Pronominal clitic clusters and templates. *Syntax and Semantics* 19:149.

Sivertsen, E. 1956. Pitch problems in Kiowa. *International Journal of American Linguistics* 22:117.

Sjölund, R. 1938. *Metrische Kürzung im Griechischen.* Dissertation, Uppsala.

Slis, I.H. 1986. Assimilation of voice in Dutch as a function of stress, word boundaries, and sex of speaker and listener. *Journal of Phonetics* 14:311.

Slootweg, A. 1988. Metrical prominence and syllable duration. *Linguistics in the Netherlands,* ed. P. Coopmans and A. Hulk: 139. Dordrecht.

Smith, B.L. 1987. Effects of bite block speech on intrinsic segment duration. *Phonetica* 44:65.

Smith, C. 1991. Sentences in texts: A valediction for sentence topic. *Interdisciplinary Approaches to Language: Essays in Honor of S.-Y. Kuroda,* ed. C. Georgopoulos and R. Ishihara: 545. Dordrecht.

Smith, C.L. 1991. The timing of vowel and consonant gestures in Italian and Japanese. *Proceedings of the XIIth International Congress of Phonetic Sciences IV*: 234. Aix-en-Provence.

Snell, B. 1958. Muta cum liquida. *Glotta* 36:160.

Snell, B. 1962. *Griechische Metrik.* Second edition. Göttingen.

Snyders, J. 1969. Le langage par tambours à San Cristoval, British Solomon Islands. *Journal de la Société des Océanistes* 24:133.

Sobolevski, S.L. 1964. Ad locutionem graecam cognoscendam quid conferat versuum structura? *Eirene* 2:34.

Sokolowski, F. 1955. *Lois sacrées de l'Asie Mineure.* Paris.

Solomon, N.P., G.N. McCall, M.W. Trosset and W.C. Gray. 1989. Laryngeal configuration and constriction during two types of whispering. *Journal of Speech and Hearing Research* 32:161.

Sommer, F. 1907. Zum inschriftlichen νῦ εφελκυστικόν. *Festschrift der 49 Philologenversammlung*: 1. Basel.

Sommerstein, A.H. 1973. *The Sound Pattern of Ancient Greek.* Oxford.

Sonoda, Y. 1987. Effect of speaking rate on articulatory dynamics and motor event. *Journal of Phonetics* 15:145.

Sorensen, J.M., W.E. Cooper and J.M. Paccia. 1978. Speech timing of grammatical categories. *Cognition* 6:135.

Sportiche, D. 1988. A theory of floating quantifiers. *Proceedings of the 17th Annual Meeting of the North Eastern Linguistics Society*: 581.

Srebot-Rejec, T. 1988. *Word Accent and Vowel Duration in Standard Slovene.* Munich.

Stanford, W.B. 1939. *Ambiguity in Greek Literature.* Oxford.

Stark, J.A. 1988. Aspects of automatic versus controlled processing, monitoring, metalinguistic tasks, and related phenomena in aphasia. *Linguistic Analyses of Aphasic Language,* ed. W.U. Dressler and J.A. Stark: 179. New York.

Stark, J.A. and R. Wytek. 1988. Syntactic and semantic factors of auditory sentence comprehension in aphasia. *Linguistic Analyses of Aphasic Language,* ed. W.U. Dressler and J.A. Stark: 82. New York.

Starks, D. 1987. Word Ordering: More than ordering subjects, objects and verbs. *Native American Languages and Grammatical Typology,* ed. P.D. Kroeber and R.E. Moore: 215. Bloomington.

Steele, S. 1978. Word order variation: A typological study. *Universals of Human Language IV,* ed. J. Greenberg: 585. Stanford.

Steele, S.A. 1985. *Vowel Intrinsic Fundamental Frequency in Prosodic Context.* Ph.D. dissertation, University of Texas, Dallas.

Stemberger, J. 1983. *Speech Errors and Theoretical Phonology.* Bloomington.

Stemberger, J. 1985. An interactive model of language production. *Progress in the Psychology of Language I,* ed. W.A. Ellis: 143. Hillsdale.

Stephens, L.D. 1985. The lexical diffusion of vowel shortening in Classical Latin: Iambic verbs. *Helios* 12:39.

Stephens, L.D. 1985b. Trends in the prosodic evolution of the Greek choliamb. *Greek, Roman, and Byzantine Studies* 26:83.

Stephens, L.D. 1985c. On the restructuring of the ancient Greek system of word prosody. *La Parola del Passato* 224:367.

Stephens, L.D. 1988. Remarks on accentual prose rhythm. *Helios* 15:41.

Stephens, L.D. 1988b. Contiguous resolution and substitution in the Greek comic trimeter. *Quaderni Urbinati* 28:123.

Stephens, L.D. 1990. Initial *ῥ-* in Attic. *Illinois Classical Studies* 15:55.

Steriade, D. 1982. *Greek Prosodies and the Nature of Syllabification.* Ph.D. dissertation, Massachusetts Institute of Technology.

Steriade, D. 1988. Greek accent: A case for preserving structure. *Linguistic Inquiry* 19:271.

Steriade, D. 1988b. Review of G.N. Clements and S.J. Keyser. *CV Phonology: A Generative Theory of the Syllable. Language* 64:118.

Steriade, D. 1988c. Reduplication and syllable transfer in Sanskrit and elsewhere. *Phonology* 5:73.

Stern, T. 1957. Drum and whistle "languages": An analysis of speech surrogates. *American Anthropologist* 59:487.

Sternberg, S., S. Monsell, R.L. Knoll and C.E. Wright. 1978. The latency and duration of rapid movement sequences: Comparisons of speech and typewriting. *Information Processing in Motor Control and Learning,* ed. G.E. Stelmach: 117. New York.

Stetson, R.H. 1905. A motor theory of rhythm and discrete succession. *Psychological Review* 12:250, 292.

Stetson, R.H. 1931. Breathing movements in singing. *Archives Néerlandaises de Phonétique Expérimentale* 6:115.

Stetson, R.H. 1951. *Motor Phonetics.* Amsterdam. Retrospective edition, ed. J.A.S. Kelso and K.G. Munhall. 1988. Boston.

Stevens, A.M. 1968. *Madurese Phonology and Morphology.* New Haven.

Stinton, T.C.W. 1977. Interlinear hiatus in trimeters. *Classical Quarterly* 27:67.

Stoll, G. 1984. Pitch of vowels: Experimental and theoretical investigation of its dependence on vowel quality. *Speech Communication* 3:137.

Stone, M. 1981. Evidence for a rhythm pattern in speech production: Observations of jaw movement. *Journal of Phonetics* 9:109.

Story, G. 1989. A report on the nature of Carrier pitch phenomena. *Athapaskan Linguistics: Current Perspectives on a Language Family,* ed. E.D. Cook and K.D. Rice: 99. Berlin.

Stowell, T. 1979. Stress systems of the world, unite! *Working Papers in Linguistics, Massachusetts Institute of Technology* 1:51.

Strangert, E. 1978. Temporal aspects of rhythm in Swedish. *Nordic Prosody,* ed. E. Gårding, G. Bruce and R. Bannert: 103. Lund.

Strangert, E. 1984. Temporal characteristics of rhythmic units in Swedish. *Nordic Prosody III*, ed. C.-C. Elert, I. Johansson and E. Strangert: 201. Stockholm.

Strangert, E. 1985. *Swedish Speech Rhythm in a Cross-Language Perspective*. Umeå.

Strangert, E. 1991. Pausing in texts read aloud. *Proceedings of the XIIth International Congress of Phonetic Sciences IV*: 238. Aix-en-Provence.

Streeter, L.A. 1978. Acoustic determinants of phrase boundary perception. *Journal of the Acoustical Society of America* 64:1582.

Strik, H. and L. Boves. 1987. Regulation of intensity and pitch in chest voice. *Proceedings of the Eleventh International Congress of Phonetic Sciences VI:* 32. Tallinn.

Strik, H. and L. Boves. 1989. The fundamental frequency–subglottal pressure ratio. *Eurospeech 89 II*: 425. Paris.

Stucky, S. 1982. Free word order languages, free constituent order languages, and the gray area in between. *Proceedings of the 12th Annual Meeting of the North Eastern Linguistics Society*: 364.

Stucky, S. 1983. Verb phrase constituency and linear order in Makua. *Order, Concord and Constituency*, ed. G. Gazdar, E. Klein and G.K. Pullum: 75. Dordrecht.

Sturtevant, E.H. 1911. Notes on the character of Greek and Latin accent. *Transactions of the American Philological Association* 42:45.

Sturtevant, E.H. 1922. Syllabification and the syllabic quantity in Greek and Latin. *Transactions of the American Philological Association* 53:35.

Sturtevant, E.H. 1940. *The Pronunciation of Greek and Latin*, Second edition. Philadelphia.

Su, L.S., R. Daniloff and R. Hammarberg. 1975. Variation in lingual coarticulation at certain juncture boundaries. *Phonetica* 32:254.

Succo, F. 1906. *Rhythmischer Choral, Altarwesen und griechische Rhythmen*. Gütersloh.

Sugito, M. 1986. Acoustic characteristics of words with accent on "special moras" and accent differences between generations. *Kokugogaku* 147:92.

Sugito, M. and H. Hirose. 1978. An electromyographic study of the Kinki accent. *Annual Bulletin, Research Institute of Logopedics and Phoniatrics* 12:35.

Sugito, M. and H. Hirose. 1988. Production and perception of accentual devoiced vowels in Japanese. *Annual Bulletin, Research Institute of Logopedics and Phoniatrics* 22:21.

Summerfield, Q. 1981. Articulatory rate and perceptual constancy in phonetic perception. *Journal of Experimental Psychology: Human Perception and Performance* 7:1074.

Summers, W.V. 1987. Effects of stress and final-consonant voicing on vowel production: Articulatory and acoustic analyses. *Journal of the Acoustical Society of America* 82:847.

Sundberg, J. 1974. Articulatory interpretation of the "singing formant." *Journal of the Acoustical Society of America* 55:838.

Sundberg, J. 1975. Formant technique in a professional female singer. *Acustica* 32:89.

Sundberg, J. 1978. Synthesis of singing. *Swedish Journal of Musicology* 60:107.

Sundberg, J. 1979. Maximum speed of pitch changes in singers and untrained subjects. *Journal of Phonetics* 7:71.

Sundberg, J. 1982. Speech, song, and emotions. *Music, Mind, and Brain*, ed. M. Clynes: 137. New York.

Sundberg, J. 1987. *The Science of the Singing Voice*. DeKalb.

Svantesson, J.-O. 1988. Voiceless stops and F_0 in Kammu. *Working Papers in General Linguistics and Phonetics, Lund University* 34:116.

Svantesson, J.-O. 1989. Tonogenetic mechanisms in Northern Mon-Khmer. *Phonetica* 46:60.

Swinney, D.A., E.B. Zurif and A. Cutler. 1980. Effects of sentential stress and word class on comprehension in Broca's aphasics. *Brain and Language* 10:132.

Szabolcsi, A. 1981. The possessive construction in Hungarian: A configurational category in a nonconfigurational language. *Acta Linguistica Academiae Scientiarum Hungaricae* 31:261.

Szabolcsi, A. 1983. The possessor that ran away from home. *The Linguistic Review* 3:89.

Szemerenyi, O. 1964. *Syncope in Greek and Indo-European and the Nature of the Indo-European Accent.* Naples.

't Hart, J. 1981. Differential sensitivity to pitch distance, particularly in speech. *Journal of the Acoustical Society of America* 69:811.

't Hart, J. and A. Cohen. 1973. Intonation by rule: A perceptual quest. *Journal of Phonetics* 1:309.

't Hart, J., R. Collier and A. Cohen. 1990. *A Perceptual Study of Intonation.* Cambridge.

Takeda, K., Y. Sagisaka and H. Kuwabara. 1989. On sentence-level factors governing segmental duration in Japanese. *Journal of the Acoustical Society of America* 86:2081.

Tarlinskaja, M. 1989. General and particular aspects of meter: Literatures, epochs, poets. *Phonetics and Phonology* 1:121.

Tartter, V.C. 1989. What's in a whisper? *Journal of the Acoustical Society of America* 86:1678.

Tatsumi, M., O. Kunisaki and H. Fujisaki. 1976. Acoustic analysis and subjective evaluation of sung vowels. *Annual Bulletin, Research Institute of Logopedics and Phoniatrics* 10:191.

Taub, S.F. 1990. The effect of rate of speech on perception of syllabicity. *Journal of the Acoustical Society of America* 88:S128.

Taylor, A. 1988. The use of clitics as a diagnostic of phrase structure. *Proceedings of the Fifth Eastern States Conference on Linguistics*: 456. Columbus.

Taylor, A. 1990. *Clitics and Configurationality in Ancient Greek.* Ph.D. dissertation, University of Pennsylvania.

Taylor, D. 1955. Phonemes of the Hopkins dialect of Island Carib. *International Journal of American Linguistics* 21:233.

Tenenbaum, S. 1977. Left- and right-dislocations. *Haya Grammatical Structure.* Southern California Occasional Papers in Linguistics 6:161.

Teodorsson, S.T. 1974. *The Phonemic System of the Attic Dialect 450–340 B.C.* Lund.

Teodorsson, S.T. 1977. *The Phonology of the Ptolemaic Koine.* Lund.

Teodorsson, S.T. 1978. *The Phonology of Attic in the Hellenistic Period.* Uppsala.

Teranishi, R. 1980. Two-moras-cluster as a rhythm unit in spoken Japanese sentence or verse. Manuscript; cp. *Journal of the Acoustical Society of America* 67:S40.

Teranishi, R. 1990. A study on various prosody styles in Japanese speech synthesizable with the text-to-speech system. *Proceedings of the 1990 International Conference on Spoken Language Processing* 2:785. Kobe.

Teras, V. 1965. Eine Analogie zu Iktus und Akzent im lateinischen Sprechvers. *Estonian Poetry and Language*, eds. V. Kõressaar and A. Rannit (Estonian Learned Society in America): 84.

Terhardt, E. 1975. Influence of intensity on the pitch of complex tones. *Acustica* 33:345.

Terken, J. 1991. Fundamental frequency and perceived prominence of accented syllables. *Journal of the Acoustical Society of America* 89:1768.

Ternström, S., J. Sundberg and A. Colldén. 1988. Articulatory F_0 perturbations and auditory feedback. *Journal of Speech and Hearing Research* 31:187.

Tesak, J. and J. Dittmann. 1991. Telegraphic style in normals and aphasics. *Linguistics* 29:1111.

Thomas, E. and J. Brown Jr. 1974. Time perception and the filled-duration illusion. *Perception and Psychophysics* 16:449.

Thomas, K.D. 1990. Vowel length and pitch in Yavapai. *Journal of the Acoustical Society of America* 88:S53.

Thomassen, J.M. 1982. Melodic accent: Experiments and a tentative model. *Journal of the Acoustical Society of America* 71:1596.

Thorsen, N. 1980. A study of the perception of sentence intonation — Evidence from Danish. *Journal of the Acoustical Society of America* 67:1014.

Thorsen, N. 1980b. Intonation contours and stress group patterns of declarative sentences of varying length in ASC Danish. *Annual Report, Institute of Phonetics, University of Copenhagen* 14:1.

Thorsen, N. 1982. On the variability in F₀ patterning and the function of F₀ timing in languages where pitch cues stress. *Phonetica* 39:302.

Thorsen, N. 1985. Intonation and text in Standard Danish. *Journal of the Acoustical Society of America* 77:1205.

Thorsen, N. 1986. Sentence intonation in textual context: Supplementary data. *Journal of the Acoustical Society of America* 80:1041.

Thorsen, N. 1987. Intonation and text in Standard Danish. *Phonologica 1984*, ed. W.U. Dressler, H.G. Luschützky, O.E. Pfeiffer and J.R. Rennison: 301. Cambridge.

Thorsen, N. 1987b. Text and intonation — A case study. *Nordic Prosody IV*, ed. K. Gregersen and H. Basbøll: 71. Odense.

Threatte, L. 1977. Unmetrical spellings in Attic inscriptions. *California Studies in Classical Antiquity* 10:169.

Threatte, L. 1980. *The Grammar of Attic Inscriptions I: Phonology.* Berlin.

Thwing, R. and J. Watters. 1987. Focus in Vute. *Journal of African Languages and Linguistics* 9:95.

Tiedke, H. 1873. *Quaestionum Nonnianarum Specimen.* Berlin.

Tiedke, H. 1878. Quaestionum Nonnianarum specimen alterum. *Hermes* 13:59.

Tiedke, H. 1878b. Nonniana. *Hermes* 13:351.

Tiedke, H. 1879. De lege quadam, quam in versibus faciendis observavit Nonnus. *Hermes* 14:219.

Titze, I.R. 1989. On the relation between subglottal pressure and fundamental frequency in phonation. *Journal of the Acoustical Society of America* 85:901.

Titze, I.R. and J. Sundberg. 1992. Vocal intensity in speakers and singers. *Journal of the Acoustical Society of America* 91:2936.

Tod, M.N. 1933. *A Selection of Greek Historical Inscriptions.* Oxford.

Toman, J. 1986. Cliticization from NPs in Czech and comparable phenomena in French and Italian. *Syntax and Semantics* 19:123.

Tomlin, R. and R. Rhodes. 1979. An introduction to information distribution in Ojibwa. *Papers from the Fifteenth Regional Meeting, Chicago Linguistic Society*: 307.

Tompkins, C.A. and C.R. Flowers. 1985. Perception of emotional intonation by brain damaged adults. *Journal of Speech and Hearing Research* 28:527.

Topping, D.M. 1973. *Chamorro Reference Grammar.* Honolulu.

Torday, E. and T.A. Joyce. 1922. *Notes ethnographiques sur des populations habitant les bassins du Kasai et du Kwango oriental.* Brussels.

Tracey, H. 1958. Towards an assessment of African scales. *African Music* 2.1:15.

Tracey, H. 1963. The development of music. *African Music* 3.2:36.

Trager, F.H. 1971. The phonology of Picuris. *International Journal of American Linguistics* 37:29.

Tranel, B. 1981. *Concreteness in Generative Phonology: Evidence from French.* Berkeley.

Tranel, B. 1991. CVC light syllables, geminates and moraic theory. *Phonology* 8:291.

Trask, R. 1993. *A Dictionary of Grammatical Terms in Linguistics.* London.

Travis, L. and E. Williams. 1982. Externalization of arguments in Malayo-Polynesian languages. *The Linguistic Review* 2:57.

Treiman, R. 1983. The structure of spoken syllables: Evidence from novel word games. *Cognition* 15:49.

Treiman, R. 1992. Experimental studies of English syllabification. *Phonologica 1988,* ed. W. Dressler, H. Luschützky, O. Pfeiffer and J.R. Rennison: 273. Cambridge.

Treiman, R. and C. Danis. 1988. Syllabification of intervocalic consonants. *Journal of Memory and Language* 27:87.

Trubetzkoy, N.S. 1969. *Principles of Phonology.* Translated by C.A. Baltaxe. Berkeley.

Tryon, D.T. 1968. *Iai Grammar.* Canberra.

Tsukuma, Y. and J. Azuma. 1991. The acoustic characteristics of boundaries used in uttering telephone numbers in Mandarin Chinese, Japanese and English. *Proceedings of the XIIth International Congress of Phonetic Sciences II*: 258. Aix-en-Provence.

Tucker, A.N. 1962. The syllable in Luganda: A prosodic approach. *Journal of African Languages* 1:122.

Tucker, A.N. and J.T.O. Mpaayei. 1955. *A Maasai Grammar.* London.

Tucker, A.N. and M.A. Bryan. 1966. *Linguistic Analyses. The Non-Bantu Languages of North-Eastern Africa.* London.

Tucker, D.M., R.T. Watson and K.M. Heilman. 1977. Discrimination and evocation of affectively intoned speech in patients with right parietal disease. *Neurology* 27:947.

Tuller, B., K.S. Harris and J.A.S. Kelso. 1982. Stress and rate: Differential transformations of articulation. *Journal of the Acoustical Society of America* 71:1534.

Tuller, B. and J.A.S. Kelso. 1984. The timing of articulatory gestures: Evidence for relational invariants. *Journal of the Acoustical Society of America* 76:1030.

Tyler, L.K. 1985. Real-time comprehension processes in agrammatism. *Brain and Language* 26:259.

Ueda, M. 1978. Devoicing and elision of some vowels in Japanese and English. *Linguistic and Literary Studies in Honor of Archibald A. Hill,* ed. M.H. Jazavery, E. Polomé and W. Winter: 315. Lisse.

Uhlenbeck, E.M. 1965. Remarks on Javanese syntax. *Lingua* 15:53.

Uldall, E. 1960. Attitudinal meanings conveyed by intonation contours. *Language and Speech* 3:223.

Uldall, E. 1964. Dimensions of meaning in intonation. *In Honour of Daniel Jones,* ed. D. Abercrombie, D.B. Fry, P.A.D. MacCarthy, N.C. Scott and J.L.M. Trim: 271. London.

Ultan, R. 1969. Some general characteristics of interrogative systems. *Working Papers on Language Universals, Stanford University* 1:41.

Umeda, N. 1975. Vowel duration in American English. *Journal of the Acoustical Society of America* 58:434.

Umeda, N. 1981. Influence of segmental factors on fundamental frequency in fluent speech. *Journal of the Acoustical Society of America* 70:350.

Umeda, N. and C.H. Coker. 1975. Subphonemic details in American English. *Auditory Analysis and Speech Production,* ed. G. Fant and M.A.A. Tatham: 539. London.

Umeda, N. and A.M.S. Quinn. 1981. Word duration as an acoustic measure of boundary perception. *Journal of Phonetics* 9:19.

Umiker, D.J. 1974. Speech surrogates: Drum and whistle systems. *Current Trends in Lingusitics* 12:497. The Hague.

Usher, S. 1985. *Dionysius of Halicarnassus: The Critical Essays in Two Volumes.* Cambridge, Mass.

Uyeno, N.F. 1987. Functions of the theme marker *wa* from synchronic and diachronic perspectives. *Perspectives on Topicalization: The Case of Japanese wa,* ed. J. Hinds, S. Maynard and S. Iwasaki: 221. Amsterdam.

Uyeno, T., H. Hayashibe, K. Imai, H. Imagawa and S. Kiritani. 1981. Syntactic structures and prosody in Japanese: A study on pitch contours and the pauses at phrase boundaries. *Annual Bulletin, Research Institute of Logopedics and Phoniatrics* 15:91.

Vago, R.M. 1985. The treatment of long vowels in word games. *Phonology Yearbook* 2:329.

Vaissière, J. 1988. Prediction of velum movement from phonological specifications. *Phonetica* 45:122.

Välimaa-Blum, R. 1987. Phonemic quantity, stress, and the half-long vowel in Finnish. *Working Papers in Linguistics, Ohio State University* 36:101.

Vallduví, E. 1992. *The Informational Component.* New York.

van den Berg, J. 1968. Sound production in isolated human larynges. *Annals of the New York Academy of Sciences* 155.1:18.

van den Berg, R., C. Gussenhoven and T. Rietveld. 1992. Downstep in Dutch: Implications for a model. *Papers in Laboratory Phonology II*, ed. G.J. Docherty and D.R. Ladd: 335. Cambridge.

van Dommelen, W.A. 1991. F_0 and the perception of duration. *Proceedings of the XIIth International Congress of Phonetic Sciences II*: 282. Aix-en-Provence.

Van Lancker, D. 1980. Cerebral lateralization of pitch cues in the linguistic signal. *Papers in Linguistics* 13:201.

Van Lancker, D. and V.A. Fromkin. 1973. Hemispheric specialization for pitch and "tone." *Journal of Phonetics* 1:101.

Van Lancker, D. and J. Kreiman. 1986. Preservation of familiar speaker recognition but not unfamiliar speaker discrimination in aphasic patients. *Clinical Aphasiology* 16:234.

Van Lancker, D. and D. Kempler. 1986b. Comprehension of familiar phrases by left- but not by right-hemisphere damaged patients. *Working Papers in Phonetics, University of California, Los Angeles* 63:154.

van Petten, C. and K. Kutas. 1991. Influence of semantic and syntactic context on open- and closed-class words. *Memory and Cognition* 19:95.

van Raalte, M. 1986. *Rhythm and Metre.* Assen.

Vance, T.J. 1987. *An Introduction to Japanese Phonology.* Albany.

Vanier, M. and D. Caplan. 1990. CT-scan correlates of agrammatism. *Agrammatic Aphasia: A Cross-Language Narrative Sourcebook I,* ed. L. Menn and L.K. Obler: 37. Amsterdam.

Vayra, M. and C.A. Fowler. 1992. Declination of supralaryngeal gestures in spoken Italian. *Phonetica* 49:48.

Vende, K. 1972. Intrinsic pitch of Estonian vowels: Measurement and perception. *Estonian Papers in Phonetics* 1972:44.

Vendryes, J. 1945. *Traité d'accentuation grecque.* Paris.

Vennemann, T. 1987. Muta cum liquida: Worttrennung und Syllabierung im Gotischen. *Zeitschrift für deutsches Altertum und deutsche Literatur* 116:165.

Vennemann, T. 1988. The rule dependence of syllable structure. *On Language: Rhetorica, Phonologica, Syntactica,* ed. C. Duncan-Rose and T. Vennemann: 257. London.

Vennemann, T. 1988b. *Preference Laws for Syllable Structure.* Berlin.

Verbrugge, R.R. and D. Shankweiler. 1977. Prosodic information for vowel identity. *Journal of the Acoustical Society of America* 61:S39.

Vermeer, W. 1986. Some sandhi phenomena involving prosodic features (vowel length, stress, tone) in Proto-Slavic, Serbo-Croatian, and Slovenian. *Sandhi Phenomena in the Languages of Europe,* ed. H. Andersen: 577. Berlin.

Verner, K. 1877. Eine Ausnahme der ersten Lautverschiebung. *Zeitschrift für vergleichende Sprachforschung* 23:97.

Verrier, P. 1914. La quantité. *Revue de Phonétique* 4:134.

Vihman, E. 1974. Estonian quantity re-viewed. *Folia Linguistica* 11:415.

Vihman, M.M. 1982. Formulas in first and second language acquisition. *Exceptional Language and Linguistics,* ed. L.K. Obler and L. Menn: 261. New York.

Vilkman, E., O. Aaltonen, I. Raimo, J. Ignatius and P.V. Komi. 1987. On stress production in whispered Finnish. *Journal of Phonetics* 15:157.

Vilkman, E., O. Aaltonen, I. Raimo, P. Arajärvi and H. Oksanen. 1989. Articulatory hyoid-laryngeal changes *vs.* cricothyroid muscle activity in the control of intrinsic F_0 of vowels. *Journal of Phonetics* 17:193.

Viredaz, R. 1983. La graphie des groupes de consonnes en mycénien et en cypriote. *Minos* 18:125.

Vogel, F. 1923. Die Kürzenmeidung in der griechischen Prosa des IV. Jahrhunderts. *Hermes* 58:87.

Vogel, I. 1982. *La sillaba come unità fonologica.* Bologna.

Vogel, I. and I. Kenesei. 1987. The interface between phonology and other components of grammar: The case of Hungarian. *Phonology Yearbook* 4:243.

Vogelmann, A. 1877. *Über Taktgleichheit mit besonderer Berücksichtigung auf den Dochmius.* Stuttgart.

Vogt, H. 1938. Esquisse d'une grammaire du géorgien moderne. *Norsk Tidsskrift for Sprogvidenskap* 9:5.

von Leden, H. 1961. The mechanism of phonation. *Archives of Otolaryngology* 74:660.

von Mess, A. 1903. Zur Positionsdehnung vor muta cum liquida bei den attischen Dichtern. *Rheinisches Museum* 58:270.

Voorhis, P.H. 1971. Notes on Kickapoo whistle speech. *International Journal of American Linguistics* 37:238.

Voorhoeve, J. 1973. Safwa as a restricted tone system. *Studies in African Linguistics* 4:1.

Vos, P.G. 1977. Temporal duration factors in the perception of auditory rhythmic patterns. *Scientific Aesthetics* 1:183.

Voyles, J.B. 1974. Ancient Greek accentuation. *Glotta* 52:65.

Wachter, R. 1991. Abbreviated writing. *Kadmos* 30:49.

Wackernagel, J. 1889. *Das Dehnungsgesetz der griechischen Komposita.* Basel.

Wackernagel, J. 1914. *Akzentstudien II.* Nachrichten der göttingischen Gesellschaft der Wissenschaften 1914:20.

Wagner, R. 1921. Der Berliner Notenpapyrus. *Philologus* 77:289.

Wahlström, E. 1970. *Accentual responsion in Greek strophic poetry.* Commentationes Humanarum Litterarum 47. Helsinki

Walsh, T. and F. Parker. 1982. Consonant cluster abbreviation: An abstract analysis. *Journal of Phonetics* 10:423.

Ward, G.L. 1988. *The Semantics and Pragmatics of Preposing.* New York.

Warder, A.K. 1967. *Pali Metre.* London.

Watters, J.R. 1979. Focus in Aghem. *Southern California Occasional Papers in Linguistics* 7:137.

Weil, H. 1878. *The Order of Words in the Ancient Languages Compared to that of the Modern Languages.* Boston.

Weil, H. 1902. La valeur des syllabes longues et brèves dans les vers lyriques. *Etudes de littérature et de rythmique grecques*: 200. Paris.

Weismer, G. 1985. Speech breathing: Contemporary views and findings. *Speech Science: Recent Advances,* ed. R.G. Daniloff: 47. San Diego.

Weismer, G. and D. Ingrisano. 1979. Phrase level timing patterns in English. *Journal of Speech and Hearing Research* 22:516.

Weismer, G. and A.M. Fennell. 1985. Constancy of (acoustic) relative timing measures in phrase-level utterances. *Journal of the Acoustical Society of America* 78:49.

Welmers, W.E. 1952. Notes on the structure of Saho. *Word* 8:145.

Weniger, D. 1978. Dysprosody as part of the aphasic language disorder. *Advances in Neurology*, ed. F.C. Rose: 41. New York.

Wenk, B. and F. Wioland. 1982. Is French really syllable-timed? *Journal of Phonetics* 10:193.

West, M.L. 1969. Stesichorus redivivus. *Zeitschrift für Papyrologie und Epigraphik* 4:135.

West, M.L. 1970. A new approach to Greek prosody. *Glotta* 48:185.

West, M.L. 1982. *Greek Metre*. Oxford.

West, M.L. 1992. *Ancient Greek Music*. Oxford.

Westbury, J. and P. Keating. 1980. Central representation of vowel duration. *Journal of the Acoustical Society of America* 67:S37.

Westphal, R. 1867. *Griechische Rhythmik und Harmonik*. Leipzig.

Westphal, R. and H. Gleditsch. 1887. *Allgemeine Theorie der griechischen Metrik*. Third edition. Leipzig.

Whalen, D.H. 1991. Infrequent words are longer in duration than frequent words. *Journal of the Acoustical Society of America* 90:2311.

Whalen, D.H., A.S. Abramson, L. Lisker and M. Mody. 1990. Gradient effects of fundamental frequency on stop consonant voicing judgments. *Phonetica* 47:36.

Wheeler, B.I. 1885. *Der griechische Nominalaccent*. Dissertation, Strassburg.

Wheeler, M.W. 1986. Catalan sandhi phenomena. *Sandhi Phenomena in the Languages of Europe*, ed. H. Andersen: 475. Berlin.

White, J.W. 1912. *The Verse of Greek Comedy*. London.

Whiteley, W.H. 1958. *A Short Description of Item Categories in Iraqw*. Kampala.

Whitman, J. 1987. Configurationality parameters. *Issues in Japanese Linguistics*, ed. T. Imai and M. Saito: 351. Dordrecht.

Wickelgren, W.A. 1964. Size of rehearsal group and short-term memory. *Journal of Experimental Psychology* 68:413.

Wickelgren, W.A. 1967. Rehearsal grouping and hierarchical organization of serial position cues in short-term memory. *Quarterly Journal of Experimental Psychology* 19:97.

Wieman, L.A. 1976. Stress patterns of early child language. *Journal of Child Language* 3:283.

Wieneke, G., P. Janssen and H. Belderbos. 1987. The influence of speaking rate on the duration of jaw movements. *Journal of Phonetics* 15:111.

Wifstrand, A. 1933. *Von Kallimachos zu Nonnos*. Lund.

Wightman, C.W., S. Shattuck-Hufnagel, M. Ostendorf and P.J. Price. 1992. Segmental durations in the vicinity of prosodic phrase boundaries. *Journal of the Acoustical Society of America* 91:1707.

Wijnen, F. 1988. Spontaneous word fragmentations in children. *Journal of Phonetics* 16:187.

Wilamowitz-Moellendorff, U. von. 1895. *Commentariolum Metricum I*. Göttingen.

Wilamowitz-Moellendorff, U. von. 1896. *Aischylos' Orestie*. Berlin.

Wilamowitz-Moellendorff, U. von. 1909. *Euripides Herakles*. Third edition. Berlin.

Wilamowitz-Moellendorff, U. von. 1911. Über die Wespen des Aristophanes (II). *Sitzungsberichte der Königlich Preussischen Akademie der Wissenschaften* 23:504.

Willems, N. 1982. *English Intonation from a Dutch Point of View*. Dordrecht.

Willett, E. 1982. Reduplication and accent in Southeastern Tepehuan. *International Journal of American Linguistics* 48:168.

Williams, B. 1985. Pitch and duration in Welsh stress perception. *Journal of Phonetics* 13:381.

Williams, B. 1986. An acoustic study of some features of Welsh prosody. *Intonation in Discourse*, ed. C. Johns-Lewis: 35. San Diego.

Williams, C.E. and K.N. Stevens. 1969. On determining the emotional state of pilots during flight: An exploratory study. *Aerospace Medicine* 40:1369.

Williams, C.E. and K.N. Stevens. 1972. Emotions and speech: Some acoustical correlates. *Journal of the Acoustical Society of America* 52:1238.

Williams, C.E. and K.N. Stevens. 1981. Vocal correlates of emotional states. *Speech Evaluation in Psychiatry*, ed. J.K. Darby: 189. New York.

Williamson, K. 1979. Sentence tone in some Southern Nigerian languages. *Proceedings of the Ninth International Congress of Phonetic Sciences II*: 424. Copenhagen.

Wilson, W.A. 1963. Talking drums in Africa. In Sebeok et al. 1976:806.

Wiltshire, C.R. 1991. On syllable structure at two levels of analysis. *Papers from the 27th Regional Meeting of the Chicago Linguistic Society I*: 476.

Wingfield, A., L. Lombardi and S. Sokol. 1984. Prosodic features and intelligibility of accelerated speech. *Journal of Speech and Hearing Research* 27:128.

Winnington-Ingram, R.P. 1955. Fragments of unknown Greek tragic texts with musical notation. II. The Music. *Symbolae Osloenses* 31:29.

Winnington-Ingram, R.P. 1958. Ancient Greek music 1932–1957. *Lustrum* 3:42.

Witkowski, S. 1893. Observationes metricae ad Herodam. *Analecta Graeco-Latina Philologis Vindobonae Congregatis* 1. Krakow.

Wolff, H. 1962. Rárà: A Yoruba chant. *Journal of African Languages* 1:45.

Woo, N. 1972. *Prosody and Phonology*. Bloomington.

Woodbury, A.C. 1987. Meaningful phonological processes: A consideration of Central Alaskan Yupik Eskimo prosody. *Language* 63:685.

Woodrow, H.S. 1909. *A Quantitative Study of Rhythm*. Archives of Psychology 14. New York.

Woodrow, H.S. 1911. The role of pitch in rhythm. *Psychological Review* 18:54.

Woodrow, H.S. 1951. Time perception. *Handbook of Experimental Psychology*, ed. S.S. Stevens: 1224. New York.

Wright, S. and P. Kerswill. 1989. Electropalatography in the analysis of connected speech processes. *Clinical Linguistics and Phonetics* 3:49.

Wright, W. 1955. *A Grammar of the Arabic Language II*. Cambridge.

Wulfeck, B. 1988. Grammaticality judgments and sentence comprehension in agrammatic aphasia. *Journal of Speech and Hearing Research* 31:72.

Wunder, E. 1823. *Adversaria in Sophoclis Philoctetem*. Leipzig.

Wunderlich, E.C.F. 1810. *Demosthenis Oratio Pro Corona*. Göttingen.

Yip, M. 1982. Against a segmental analysis of Zahao and Thai: A laryngeal tier proposal. *Linguistic Analysis* 9:79.

Yip, M. 1984. The development of Chinese verse: A metrical analysis. *Language Sound Structure*, ed. M. Aronoff and R.T. Oehrle: 346. Cambridge, Mass.

Yokoyama, O.T. 1986. *Discourse and Word Order*. Amsterdam.

Yoshioka, H. 1981. Laryngeal adjustments in the production of the fricative consonants and devoiced vowels in Japanese. *Phonetica* 38:236.

Yoshioka, H. and H. Hirose. 1981. Laryngeal adjustments in Japanese word accent. *Annual Bulletin, Research Institute of Logopedics and Phoniatrics* 15:17.

Yoshioka, H., A. Löfqvist and H. Hirose. 1981b. Laryngeal adjustments in the production of consonant clusters and geminates in American English. *Journal of the Acoustical Society of America* 70:1615.

Yule, G.U. 1944. *The Statistical Study of Literary Vocabulary*. Cambridge.

Zaenen, A. 1980. *Extraction Rules in Icelandic*. Ph.D. dissertation, Harvard University.

Zawadzki, P.A. and H.R. Gilbert. 1989. Vowel fundamental frequency and articulator position. *Journal of Phonetics* 17:159.

Zec, D. 1988. *Sonority Constraints on Prosodic Structure.* Ph.D. dissertation, Stanford University.

Zec, D. and S. Inkelas. 1990. Prosodically constrained syntax. *The Phonology-Syntax Interface,* ed. S. Inkelas and D. Zec: 365. Chicago.

Zec, D. and S. Inkelas. 1991. The place of clitics in the prosodic hierarchy. *Proceedings of the Tenth West Coast Conference on Formal Linguistics*: 505.

Zee, E. 1978. Duration and intensity as correlates of F_0. *Journal of Phonetics* 6:213.

Zelkind, I. 1973. Factors in time estimation and a case for the internal clock. *Journal of General Psychology* 88:295.

Zide, N.H. 1966. Korku low tone and the Proto-Korku-Kherwarian vowel system. *Studies in Comparative Austroasiatic Linguistics,* ed. N.H. Zide: 214. The Hague.

Zieliński, T. 1925. *Tragodumenon Libri Tres.* Krakow.

Zingeser, L.B. and R.S. Berndt. 1990. Retrieval of nouns and verbs in agrammatism and anomia. *Brain and Language* 39:14.

Zinglé, H. 1978. Contribution expérimentale à l'étude du contour affectant le groupe accentuel allemand. *Travaux de l'Institut de Phonétique de Strasbourg* 10:1.

Zirin, R.A. 1970. *The Phonological Basis of Latin Prosody.* The Hague.

Zurif, E.B. and M. Mendelsohn. 1972. Hemispheric specialization for the perception of speech sounds: The influence of intonation and structure. *Perception and Psychophysics* 11:329.

Zwicky, A. 1970. Auxiliary reduction in English. *Linguistic Inquiry* 1:323.

Zwicky, A. 1972. On casual speech. *Papers from the Eighth Regional Meeting of the Chicago Linguistic Society*: 607. Chicago.

Zwicky, A. 1972b. Note on a phonological hierarchy in English. *Linguistic Change and Generative Theory,* ed. R. Stockwell and R. Macaulay: 275. Bloomington.

Zwicky, A. 1977. *On Clitics.* Indiana University Linguistics Club.

Zwicky, A. 1978. Arguing for constituents. *Papers from the Fourteenth Regional Meeting, Chicago Linguistic Society*: 503.

By the same authors

1975. Anceps. *Greek, Roman, and Byzantine Studies* 16:197.

1976. The Homeric hexameter and a basic principle of metrical theory. *Classical Philology* 71:141.

1977. *Two Studies in Latin Phonology.* Saratoga.

1977b. Preliminaries to an explicit theory of Greek metre. *Transactions of the American Philological Association* 107:103.

1978. The Greek appositives: Toward a linguistically adequate definition of caesura and bridge. *Classical Philology* 73:314.

1980. Rules for resolution: The Zielińskian canon. *Transactions of the American Philological Association* 110:63.

1980b. Latin prosody and meter: Brevis brevians. *Classical Philology* 75:142.

1981. Tribrach-shaped words in the tragic trimeter. *Phoenix* 35:22.

1981b. A new aspect of the evolution of the trimeter in Euripides. *Transactions of the American Philological Association* 111:43.

1982. Bridges in the Iambographers. *Greek, Roman, and Byzantine Studies* 22:305.

1982b. Towards a new theory of Greek prosody: The suprasyllabic rules. *Transactions of the American Philological Association* 112:33.

1983. Semantics, syntax and phonological organization in Greek: Aspects of the theory of metrical bridges. *Classical Philology* 78:1.

1984. *Language and Metre: Resolution, Porson's Bridge, and their Prosodic Basis.* Chico.

1985. Stress in Greek? *Transactions of the American Philological Association* 115:125.

1990. The Greek phonological phrase. *Greek, Roman, and Byzantine Studies* 31:421.

1991. Dionysius of Halicarnassus, *De Compositione Verborum* XI: Reconstructing the phonetics of the Greek accent. *Transactions of the American Philological Association* 121:229.

1993. Evidence from experimental psychology for the rhythm and metre of Greek verse. *Transactions of the American Philological Association* 123:379.

1994. The syntax and phonology of hyperbaton. *Classical Philology.*

| Index